AF879368

Pixologic ZBrush 2022

A Comprehensive Guide

(8th Edition)

CADCIM Technologies
525 St. Andrews Drive
Schererville, IN 46375, USA
(www.cadcim.com)

Contributing Authors

Sham Tickoo
Professor
Purdue University Northwest
Hammond, Indiana, USA

Mable Thomas
CADCIM Technologies
USA

CADCIM Technologies

Pixologic ZBrush 2022: A Comprehensive Guide
Sham Tickoo

CADCIM Technologies
525 St Andrews Drive
Schererville, Indiana 46375, USA
www.cadcim.com

Copyright ©2022 by CADCIM Technologies, USA. All rights reserved. Printed in the United States of America except as permitted under the United States Copyright Act of 1976.

No part of this publication may be reproduced or distributed in any form or by any means, or stored in the database or retrieval system without the prior permission of CADCIM Technologies.

ISBN 978-1-64057-149-5

Copy Editor
Anju Jethwani

Technical Editor
Arti Deshpande

NOTICE TO THE READER

Publisher does not warrant or guarantee any of the products described in the text or perform any independent analysis in connection with any of the product information contained in the text. Publisher does not assume, and expressly disclaims, any obligation to obtain and include information other than that provided to it by the manufacturer.

The reader is expressly warned to consider and adopt all safety precautions that might be indicated by the activities herein and to avoid all potential hazards. By following the instructions contained herein, the reader willingly assumes all risks in connection with such instructions.

The Publisher makes no representation or warranties of any kind, including but not limited to, the warranties of fitness for particular purpose or merchantability, nor are any such representations implied with respect to the material set forth herein, and the publisher takes no responsibility with respect to such material. The publisher shall not be liable for any special, consequential, or exemplary damages resulting, in whole or part, from the reader's use of, or reliance upon, this material.

DEDICATION

To teachers, who make it possible to disseminate knowledge
to enlighten the young and curious minds
of our future generations

To students, who are dedicated to learning new technologies
and making the world a better place to live in

THANKS

To employees of CADCIM Technologies and
Tickoo Institute of Emerging Technologies (TIET)
for their valuable help

Online Training Program Offered by CADCIM Tehnologies

CADCIM Technologies provides effective and affordable online and offsite training on various software packages including Computer Aided Design, Manufacturing and Engineering (CAD/CAM/CAE), computer programming languages, animation, architecture, and GIS. The training is delivered 'live' via Internet at any time, any place, and at any pace to individuals as well as the students of colleges, universities, and CAD/CAM/CAE training centers. The main features of this program are:

Training for Students and Companies in a Classroom Setting

Highly experienced instructors and qualified engineers at CADCIM Technologies conduct the classes under the guidance of Prof. Sham Tickoo of Purdue University Northwest, USA. This team has authored several textbooks that are rated "one of the best" in their categories and are used in various colleges, universities, and training centers in North America, Europe, and in other parts of the world.

Training for Individuals

CADCIM Technologies with its cost effective and time saving initiative strives to deliver the training in the comfort of your home or work place, thereby relieving you from the hassles of traveling to training centers.

Training Offered on Software Packages

CADCIM provides basic and advanced training on the following software packages:

***CAD/CAM/CAE**: CATIA, Pro/ENGINEER Wildfire, Creo Parametric, Creo Direct, SOLIDWORKS, Autodesk Inventor, Solid Edge, NX, AutoCAD, AutoCAD LT, AutoCAD Plant 3D, Customizing AutoCAD, EdgeCAM, and ANSYS*

***Architecture and GIS**: Autodesk Revit Architecture, AutoCAD Civil 3D, Autodesk Revit Structure, AutoCAD Map 3D, Revit MEP, Navisworks, Primavera, and Bentley STAAD Pro*

***Animation and Styling**: Autodesk 3ds Max, Autodesk 3ds Max Design, Autodesk Maya, Autodesk Alias, The Foundry NukeX, and MAXON CINEMA 4D*

***Computer Programming**: C++, VB.NET, Oracle, AJAX, and Java*

For more information, please visit the following link: ***https://www.cadcim.com***

> **Note**
> If you are a faculty member, you can register by clicking on the following link to access the teaching resources: ***https://www.cadcim.com/Registration.aspx***. The student resources are available at ***https://www.cadcim.com***. We also provide **Live Virtual Online Training** on various software packages. For more information, write us at ***sales@cadcim.com***.

Table of Contents

Chapter 4: SubTools and FiberMesh

Chapter 5: ZSpheres

Chapter 11: Lighting

Chapter 12: Rendering

Preface

Pixologic ZBrush 2022

Pixologic ZBrush 2022 is a powerful modeling and sculpting software developed by Pixologic Inc. This software is used for developing highly detailed characters for movies, games, and digital design projects.

Pixologic ZBrush 2022: A Comprehensive Guide textbook covers all features of ZBrush 2022 in a simple, lucid, and comprehensive manner. It gives in-depth details of the concepts and explains the usage and tools of ZBrush such as DynaMesh, NanoMesh, ZRemesher, ZModeler, NanoMesh, and KeyShot renderer. This textbook will unleash your creativity and transform your imagination into reality, thus helping you create realistic 3D models. This textbook caters to the needs of both the novice and advanced users of ZBrush 2022 and is ideally suited for learning at your convenience and at your pace.

This edition covers major enhancements in ZBrush 2022 such as Basrelief feature, bevelpro plugin, boolean operation, stager, and new brushes like knife brush, scribe brush, and so on. One new project is also added to make the readers understand and learn the major enhancements effectively.

The salient features of this textbook are as follows:

- **Tutorial Approach**
  The author has adopted the tutorial point-of-view and the learn-by-doing approach throughout the textbook. This approach will guide the users through the process of creating the models, adding textures to them, and animating them in the tutorials.

- **Real-World Models as Projects**
  The author has used about 24 real-world sculpting and modeling projects as tutorials in this textbook. This will enable the readers to relate the tutorials to the real-world models in the animation industry. In addition, there are about 20 exercises that are also based on the real-world modeling projects.

- **Tips and Notes**
  Additional information related to various topics is provided to the users in the form of tips and notes.

- **Learning Objectives**
  The first page of every chapter summarizes the topics that are covered in the chapter. This will help the users to easily refer to a topic.

- **Self-Evaluation Test, Review Questions, and Exercises**
  Every chapter ends with Self-Evaluation Test so that the users can assess their knowledge of the chapter. The answers to Self-Evaluation Test are given at the end of the chapter. Also, the Review Questions and Exercises are given at the end of each chapter and they can be used by the instructors as test questions and exercises.

- **Heavily Illustrated Text**
  The text in this book is heavily illustrated with about 550 diagrams and screen captures.

Symbols Used in the Text

Note
The author has provided additional information to the users about the topic being discussed in the form of notes.

Tip
Special information and techniques are provided in the form of tips that helps in increasing the efficiency of the users.

New: The author has provided this symbol next to the new topics and tutorials added in this edition of the textbook.

Enhanced: The author has provided this symbol next to the topics and tutorials enhanced in this edition of the textbook.

Formatting Conventions Used in the Text

Please refer to the following list for the formatting conventions used in this textbook.

• Names of palettes, subpalettes, buttons, sliders, and areas are written in boldface.	Example: The **Tool** palette, the **Geometry** subpalette, the **Load Tool** button, the **SDiv** slider, and the **DynaMesh** area.
• Names of dialog boxes and the check boxes are written in boldface.	Example: The **Projection Master** dialog box, the **Fade** check box.
• Names of the files are italicized.	Example: *c08tut3start.ZTL*

Naming Conventions Used in the Text

Flyout

A flyout is a menu that contains the tools having similar type of functions. Figure 1 shows the flyout displayed on choosing the Current Brush button.

Palettes

The palettes consist of tools and settings that are used to perform different tasks in ZBrush. Each palette is dedicated to a single set of related features. For instance, the **Color** palette consists of different buttons and sliders that are used to select solid and gradient colors for filling the canvas or an object. Figures 2 and 3 show the **Color** and **File** palettes, respectively.

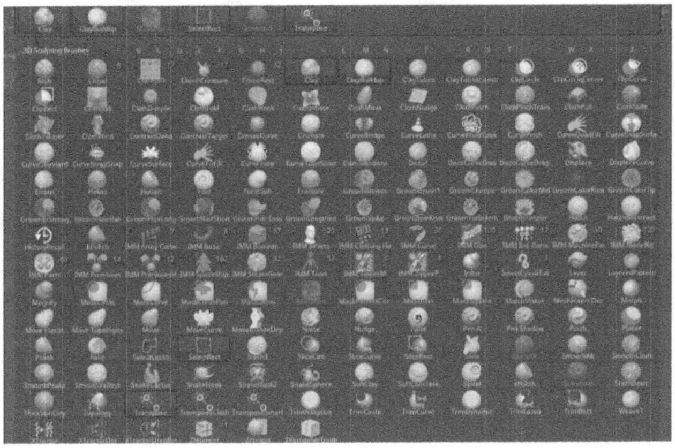

Figure 1 *The flyout displayed on choosing the Current Brush button*

Subpalettes

The subpalettes are the menus inside each palette containing different settings which are used for sculpting and modeling. Figure 4 shows the **Geometry** subpalette located in the **Tool** palette and Figure 5 shows the **UV Master** subpalette located in the **ZPlugin** palette.

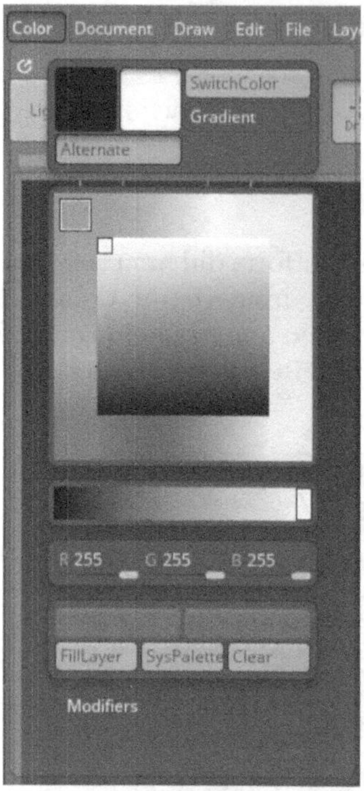

Figure 2 *The* ***Color*** *palette*

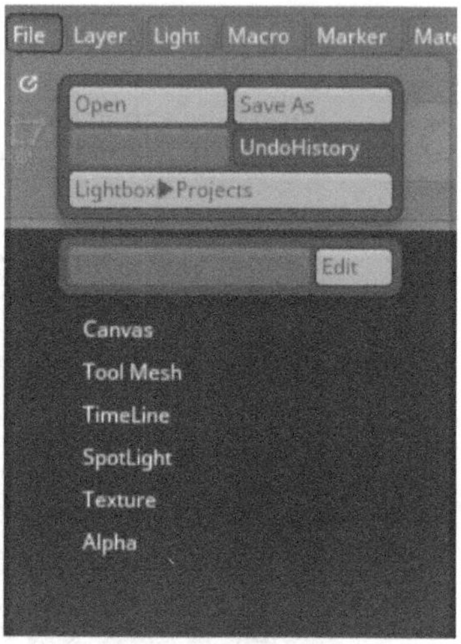

Figure 3 *The* ***File*** *palette*

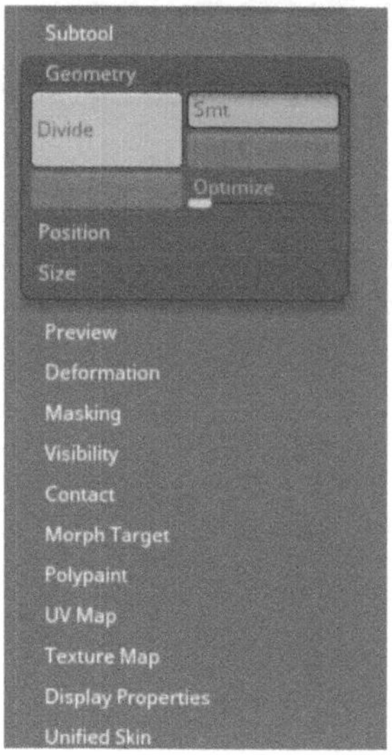

Figure 4 *The* ***Geometry*** *subpalette*

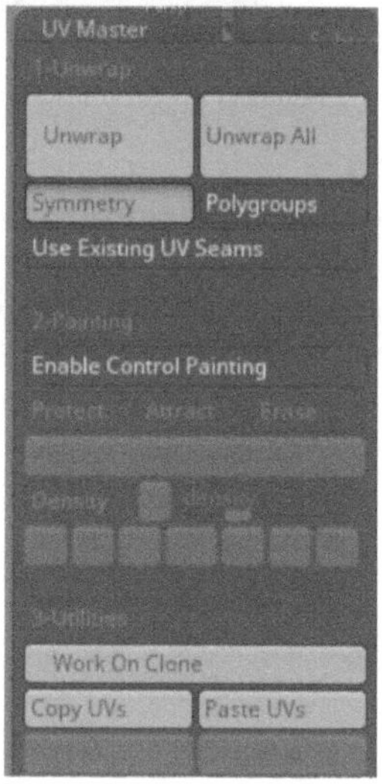

Figure 5 *The* ***UV Master*** *subpalette*

Free Companion Website

It has been our constant endeavor to provide you the best textbooks and services at affordable price. In this endeavor, we have come out with a Free Companion Website that will facilitate the process of teaching and learning of Pixologic ZBrush 2022. If you purchase this textbook, you will get access to the files on the Companion website.

The following resources are available for the faculty and students in this website:

Faculty Resources

- **Technical Support**
  You can get online technical support by contacting ***techsupport@cadcim.com***.

- **Instructor Guide**
  Solutions to all review questions and exercises in the textbook are provided in this guide to help the faculty members test the skills of the students.

- **ZBrush Files**
  The ZBrush files used in tutorials and exercises are available for free download.

- **Final Output**
  If you do an exercise or tutorial, you can compare your final output with the one provided in the CADCIM website.

- **Additional Resources**
  You can access additional learning resources by visiting *https://zbrushexperts.blogspot.com* and *https:/youtube.com/cadcimtech*.

- **Colored Images**
  You can download the PDF file containing color images of the screenshots used in this textbook from the CADCIM website.

Student Resources

- **Technical Support**
  You can get online technical support by contacting ***techsupport@cadcim.com***.

- **ZBrush Files**
  The ZBrush files used in tutorials and exercises are available for free download.

- **Final Output**
  If you do an exercise or tutorial, you can compare your final output with the one provided in the CADCIM website.

- **Additional Resources**
  You can access additional learning resources by visiting *https://zbrushexperts.blogspot.com* and *https://youtube.com/cadcimtech*.

- **Colored Images**
  You can download the PDF file containing color images of the screenshots used in this textbook from the CADCIM website.

If you face any problem in accessing these files, please contact the publisher at ***sales@cadcim.com*** or the author at ***stickoo@pnw.edu*** or ***tickoo525@gmail.com***.

Video Courses

CADCIM offers video courses in CAD, CAE Simulation, BIM, Civil/GIS, and Animation domains on various e-Learning/Video platforms. To enroll for the video courses, please visit the CADCIM website using the following link: *https://www.cadcim.com/video-courses*

eBooks

This textbook is also available in digital format with colored images. To access the eBook, please write to us at *sales@cadcim.com* or click on the following link: *https://ebooks.cadcim.com*

Stay Connected

You can now stay connected with us through Facebook and Twitter to get the latest information about our textbooks, videos, and teaching/learning resources. To get such updates, follow us on Facebook ***(www.facebook.com/cadcim)*** and Twitter (***@cadcimtech***). You can also subscribe to our YouTube channel ***(www.youtube.com/cadcimtech)*** to get the information about our latest video tutorials.

Chapter 1

Exploring ZBrush Interface

Learning Objectives

After completing this chapter, you will be able to:

- *Explore the ZBrush 2022 interface*
- *Work with various tools available in the ZBrush interface*
- *Open and save a ZTool and ZDocument*

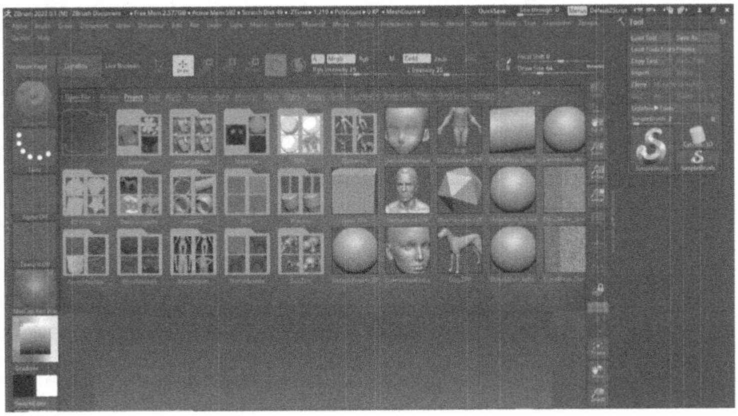

INTRODUCTION TO Pixologic ZBrush 2022

ZBrush is a modeling and sculpting software used to create realistic 3D models. It was developed by Pixologic Inc. in the year 1999. It has a unique blend of 2D, 2.5D, and 3D features. ZBrush consists of different tools that enable you to create or import 3D models, and then add high level details to them. This software enables you to sculpt on high resolution models that consist of millions of polygons. ZBrush is used by all the major animation studios worldwide. It has been used in the movies such as 300, Pirates of the Caribbean, Avatar, Hulk, and so on. ZBrush is compatible with different 3D software applications such as Maya, 3ds Max, CINEMA 4D, and Modo. Although ZBrush is a vast software to deal with, yet all the major tools available in ZBrush 2022 are discussed in this textbook. In this chapter, you will learn about the ZBrush interface.

STARTING ZBrush 2022

To start ZBrush 2022, double-click on the shortcut icon of ZBrush 2022 displayed on the desktop of your computer, as shown in Figure 1-1. This icon is automatically created on installing ZBrush 2022 on your computer. Double-click on the icon; the default ZBrush interface will be displayed along with its various components. Additionally, the **ZBrush : Home Page** window will be displayed, refer to Figure 1-2 and Figure 1-3.

Figure 1-1 *Starting ZBrush 2022 by choosing the icon from desktop*

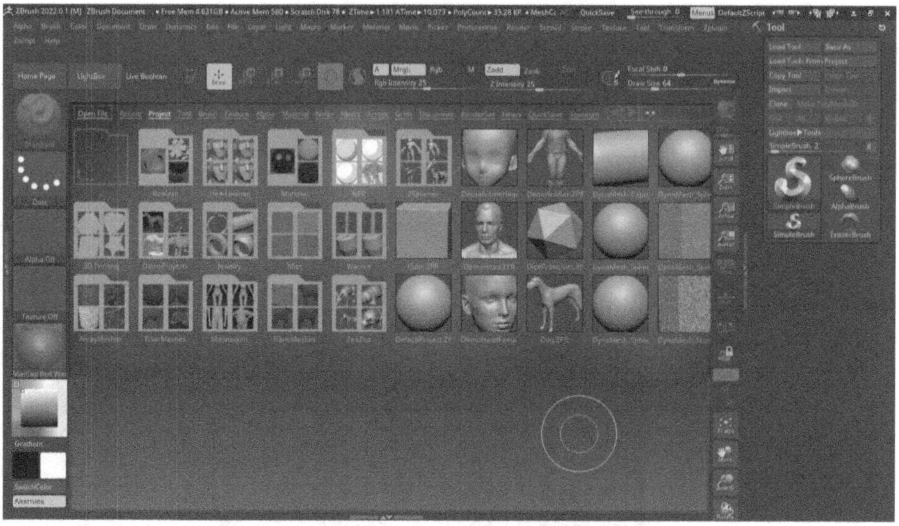

Figure 1-2 *The default ZBrush 2022 interface*

Figure 1-3 *The* ***ZBrush : Home Page*** *window*

EXPLORING THE ZBrush 2022 INTERFACE

ZBrush interface consists of components such as title bar, palettes, shelves, trays, and canvas. When you start ZBrush 2022 for the first time, the default interface will display various components of ZBrush 2022, refer to Figure 1-4. These components are discussed next.

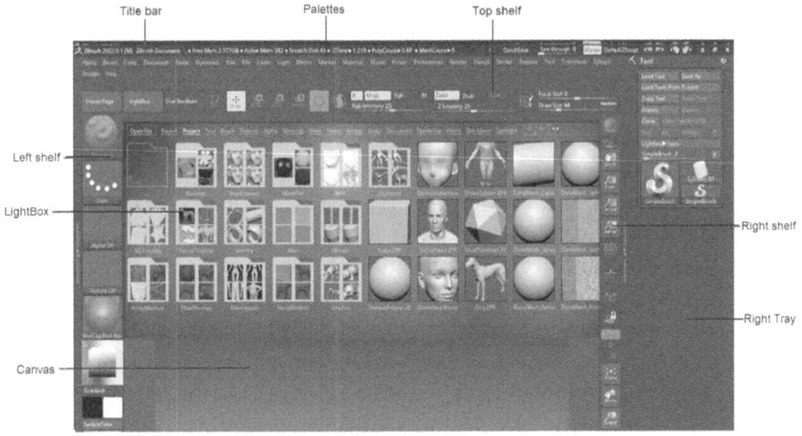

Figure 1-4 *Various components of the ZBrush 2022 interface displayed*

Title Bar

The title bar is located on the top of the ZBrush screen. In the title bar, various information such as version number, hardware ID, and memory usage is displayed on the left, refer to Figure 1-5. Besides this, the **QuickSave Project** button and the **See-through** slider are also present in the title bar. The **QuickSave Project** button is used to save the different stages of a file sequentially. These files can be accessed from the **QuickSave** tab of the **LightBox** browser. The **See-through** slider is used to increase or decrease the transparency in the ZBrush interface so that you can view the background screen. This slider makes it convenient for you to view the reference images in the background without importing a reference image or toggling back and forth between the image and interface. For example, if you are following the steps of a tutorial of ZBrush then you can view these steps in the background and follow the instructions with ease.

On the right side of the title bar, various buttons are displayed, as shown in Figure 1-6. The **Menus** button is used to toggle the display of the palettes. The **DefaultZScript** button is used to run the default scripting language present in ZBrush if it has been edited. The **Load Previous User Interface Colors**, **Load Next User Interface Colors**, **Load Previous User Interface Layout**, and **Load Next User Interface Layout** buttons are used to change the color and the layout of the screen, respectively. These presets enable you to customize the ZBrush screen.

Figure 1-5 Partial view of the Title bar

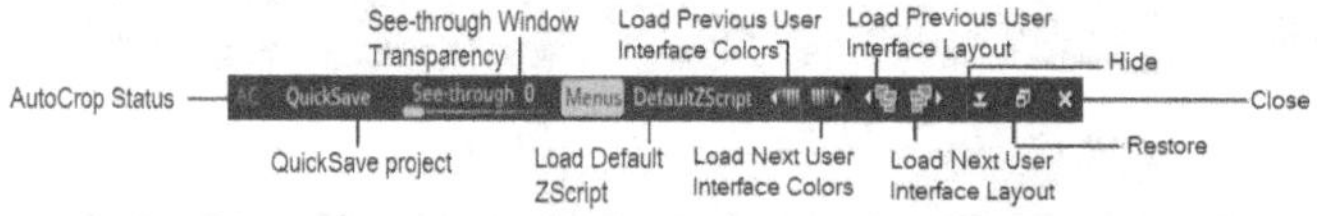

Figure 1-6 Partial view of the title bar (right side)

Canvas

The canvas is the drawing area where you can sculpt or create 3D models. It covers most of the area of the ZBrush interface, refer to Figure 1-4. The 3D models thus created can be saved as 2D illustrations. A 2D illustration is called ZBrush document and is saved in the ZBR format. The 3D models are called ZBrush tools and are saved in the ZTL format. By default, the Alpha icon is displayed at the left corner of the canvas. On choosing the **Edit** button, the CamView will be displayed at the right corner of the canvas, as shown in Figure 1-7. You can also access the CamView from the **Preferences** palette. To do so, choose the **Preferences** palette; the subpalettes will be displayed, refer to Figure 1-8. Next, choose the **CamView** subpalette; the **CamView** subpalette is expanded. Notice that in this subpalette, the **CamView On** button is chosen. The **CamView On** button allows the model to be oriented in different directions like front, back, left, right, top, and bottom. The **Size** slider is used to set the size of CamView. The **Next** button is used to change the existing default CamView icon. When you click on the **Next** button, you will notice that the CamView icon in the canvas area is replaced by the presets, refer to Figure 1-9. The **Make Camview** button is used to create custom preset for the Camview icon. When you choose this button, the selected model is converted as a custom preset that replaces the existing icon. Also, the model and the Camview icon are rotated by 360 degrees. Additionally, an image of model in different orientations is created in the **Texture** palette and displayed on the thumbnail of the **Current Texture** button. You can use this image as a texture for any model.

Note

While creating custom CamView presets, it is important to ensure that the model faces front side along the blue Z axis line.

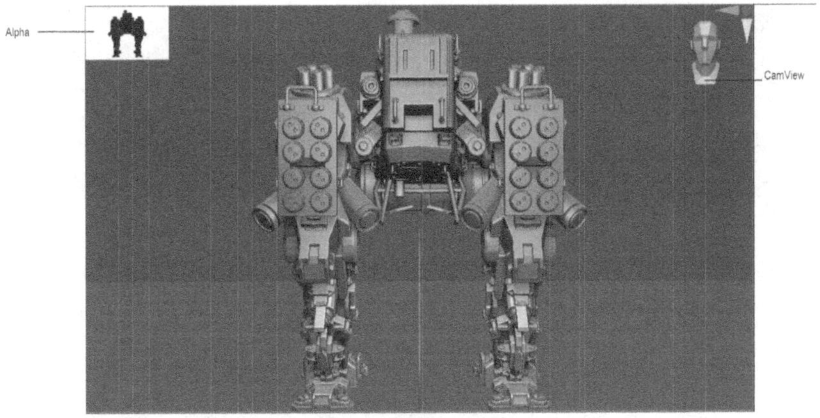

Figure 1-7 The Alpha and CamView in the canvas

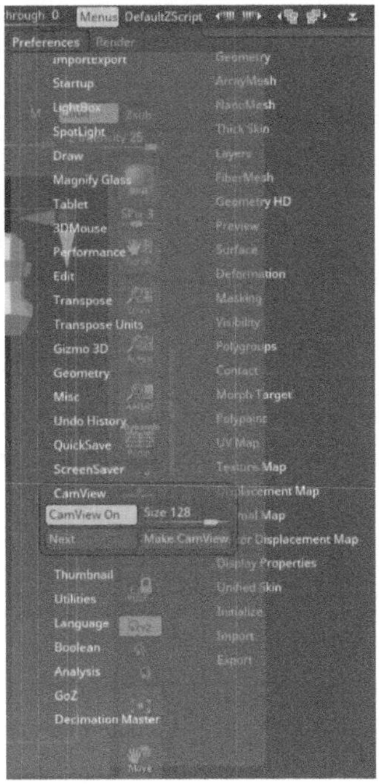

Figure 1-8 The ***CamView*** *subpalette in the* ***Preferences*** *palette*

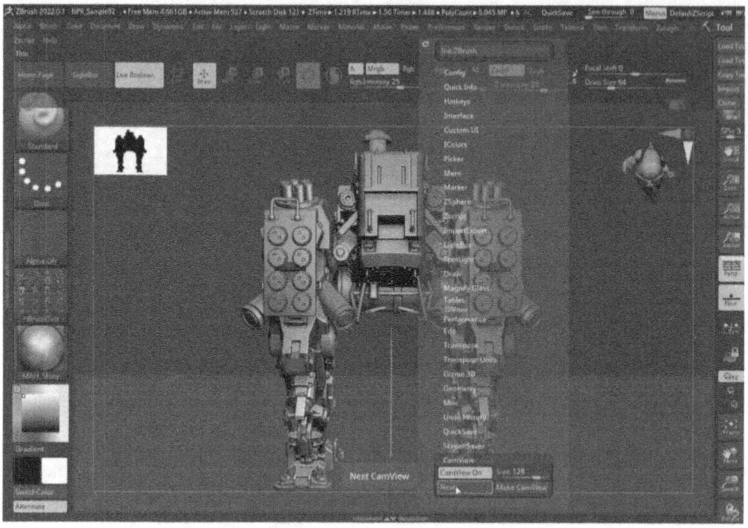

Figure 1-9 The CamView icon changed

Palettes

Palettes are located below the Title bar. They are organized alphabetically, starting from the **Alpha** palette and ending at the **Zscript** palette, refer to Figure 1-10. These palettes are discussed next.

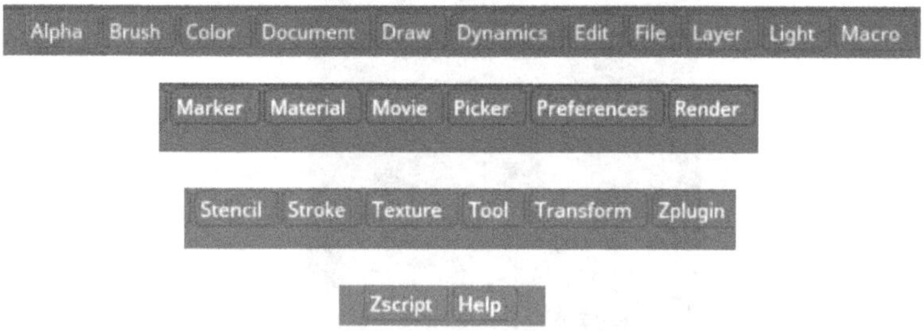

Figure 1-10 The palettes

Alpha

The **Alpha** palette consists of various gray scale images known as alphas. Alphas are available in different patterns. They determine the shape of the brush used in painting and sculpting. This palette also contains different subpalettes that are used to modify the alpha images as required.

Brush

The **Brush** palette consists of different types of 3D sculpting brushes. Besides this, it has different subpalettes that are used to modify the brush settings. The **Standard** brush is the default sculpting brush in ZBrush.

> **Tip**
> *You can change the size of the brush by using the [and] keys. The [key is used to reduce the size of the brush tip while the] key is used to increase the size of the brush tip.*

Color

The **Color** palette consists of different buttons and sliders that are used to select solid and gradient colors for filling the canvas or an object.

Document

The options in the **Document** palette are used to open, import, export, resize, and save a ZBrush document. A ZBrush document is a 2D illustration and is saved in the *ZBR* format. If you save a 3D object using the **Document** palette, it will be converted into a 2D illustration and cannot be edited further. You can also import a Photoshop file using the **Document** palette.

Draw

The **Draw** palette consists of different options that can be used to modify the settings of the 3D as well as 2D sculpting brushes. These options enable you to change the size, focal shift, and intensity of the brush stroke. In addition to this, these options help you to determine whether a sculpting brush will raise the surface of an object or push it in.

Dynamics

The newly introduced **Dynamics** palette in ZBrush 2022 consists of different options that can be used for simulation. The options in the **Dynamics** palette are primarily meant for creating cloth but are capable of performing a wide range of tasks. For example, you can set different parameters for collision. Also, it includes dynamic thickness as a supporting feature that provides thickness to a cloth.

Edit

The **Edit** palette consists of options that enable you to undo or redo the modifications made in ZBrush. Alternatively, you can press CTRL+Z to undo an operation and CTRL+SHIFT+Z to redo an operation.

File

The options in the **File** palette are used to open and save a ZBrush project. A ZBrush project is a combination of different files. If you save a 3D model using the **Save As** button in the **File** palette, its 2D illustration, Zscript, materials, alphas, and different textures will be saved along with the 3D model. You can also save multiple 3D models in a ZBrush project. The models are saved in the *.ZPR* format.

Note

*A ZBrush document is a still 2D image that can be used as an illustration. Therefore, if you save a 3D model as a document, you will not be able to edit it further in the 3D space. To avoid this, you should always save your 3D work using the options available in the **Tool** palette. In ZBrush, a 3D model is referred as ZTool. A ZBrush project contains a ZTool as well as its 2D illustration. A ZBrush project can save multiple ZTools simultaneously. However, it is not recommended to save multiple ZTools in a single ZBrush project as it results in a bigger file size which takes more system resources and slows down the system.*

Layer

The **Layer** palette enables you to work in 16 different layers. Each layer represents a separate canvas. You can merge different layers into a single ZBrush document.

Light

The **Light** palette consists of different types of lights that can be used to light up a scene. Besides this, the **Light** palette also contains different subpalettes that are used to modify light settings in a scene.

Macro

The different options in the **Macro** palette are used to record the series of actions performed in ZBrush. Instead of repeating the same actions again and again, you can save different actions in a macro. The recorded macro can be loaded whenever required.

Marker

The **Marker** palette stores information about the orientation, colors, brush strokes, and position of the ZTools modeled by you. You can redraw a model by using the properties stored in the **Marker** palette.

Material

The **Material** palette consists of a library of different materials that can be applied to an object to give it an appearance of different materials such as glass, silver, water, gold, chrome, and so on. This palette also enables you to modify the settings in the materials as required.

Movie

The options in the **Movie** palette are used to record small movies from the canvas. These movies can be used for illustrating your workflow to other users.

Picker

The options in the **Picker** palette are used to pick information such as color, orientation, depth, and so on from the canvas.

Preferences

The options in the **Preferences** palette are used to customize the ZBrush interface and its behavior. Using these options, you can restore the default interface of ZBrush after making any changes in the interface, load and save hot keys, change the color and layout of the ZBrush interface, and record the ZScript automatically.

Render

The **Render** palette consists of options that are used to render a scene. When you render a scene, the rendered output of the scene will be displayed in the canvas instead of a separate window.

Stencil

The options in the **Stencil** palette are used to create patterns with different shapes. A stencil is used to mark out the areas where strokes will be applied. An alpha can be converted into a stencil by choosing the **Make St** button in the **Transfer** subpalette of the **Alpha** palette, refer to Figure 1-11.

Stroke

The **Stroke** palette consists of options that determine the strength and behavior of brush strokes on the canvas.

Texture

The options in the **Texture** palette help in applying textures to an object. Textures are the 2D images and can be created in ZBrush or can be imported from other sources.

Tool

The **Tool** palette is one of the most important palettes in ZBrush. It consists of various buttons that are used to open, save, import, and export ZTools. In addition to this, it contains a library of inbuilt 3D primitives, ZTools, and 2.5D brushes. When you choose the Current Tool button from the **Tool** palette, a flyout will be displayed, as shown in Figure 1-12.

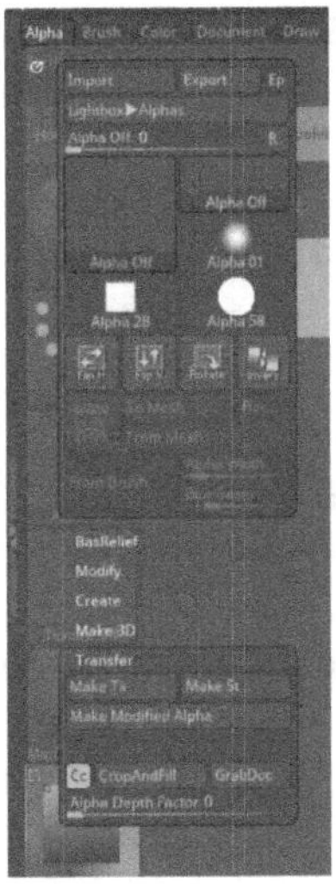

***Figure 1-11** The **Make St** button in the **Transfer** subpalette*

This flyout is divided into three areas namely, **Quick Pick**, **3D Meshes**, and **2.5D Brushes**. The **Quick Pick** area stores a library of 3D primitives and 2.5D brushes that were used recently. The **3D Meshes** area contains a library of default 3D models in ZBrush. It also contains primitive 3D objects such as sphere, cube, rectangle, cone, and so on. You can select any one of these 3D primitives and draw it in the canvas by pressing and holding the left mouse button and then dragging the cursor in the canvas area.

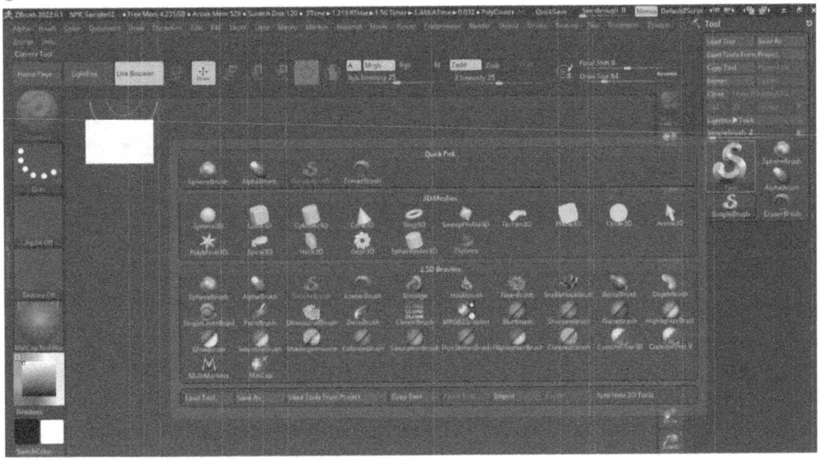

***Figure 1-12** The flyout displayed on choosing the Current Tool button from the **Tool** palette*

The third area of the **Tool** palette is **2.5D Brushes**. It consists of a library of brushes that are used to add detail to a 2D illustration. The options in the **Tool** palette will be discussed in depth in the later chapters.

Note

If you use a 2.5D brush on a 3D object, the object will be converted into a 2.5D illustration.

Transform
The **Transform** palette consists of different buttons and sliders that are used in modeling, positioning, scaling, rotating, and editing 3D objects.

Zplugin
The options in the **Zplugin** palette are used to access different ZBrush plug-ins that are installed on the computer.

Zscript
ZBrush has an in-built scripting language known as Zscript. ZScripts can be loaded by using the options in the **Zscript** palette.

Trays
Trays are the areas on the ZBrush interface in which you can store different palettes and buttons. The trays are located on the left, right, and bottom of the canvas. By default, the **Tool** palette is docked in the right tray. The left and right trays can be opened or closed by clicking on the arrows adjacent to the left and right shelves. The bottom tray can be opened and closed by double-clicking on the arrow keys below the canvas.

Shelves
Shelves are the areas that contain the most commonly used buttons and controls. The shelves can be classified into top, left, and right shelves. These shelves are discussed next.

Top Shelf
The top shelf is located below the palettes. It consists of different buttons and sliders, as shown in Figure 1-13. Most commonly used buttons and sliders in the top shelf are discussed next.

***Figure 1-13** The top shelf*

Home Page
On choosing the **HomePage** button, the **ZBrush: Home Page** window will be displayed. This button is located at the top shelf where the Projection Master used to be in the previous releases.

LightBox
On choosing the **LightBox** button, the **LightBox** browser that contains a library of ZBrush documents, ZTools, ZBrush projects, brushes, alphas, textures, materials, array, and so on will be displayed, refer to Figure 1-14. All ZBrush files can be easily accessed by using the **LightBox** browser, without navigating through different folders on your system. The browser also contains a library of default 3D models which can be modified, as required.

Live Boolean
The **Live Boolean** feature allows you to perform the boolean operations on two or more meshes. With the help of this feature, you can create a complex design with ease. To

understand the functioning of the boolean operation, choose the Current Tool button from the **Tool** palette; a flyout will be displayed. Choose the **Sphere3D** primitive from this flyout and then drag the cursor on the canvas; a sphere will be created in the canvas. Next, choose the **Edit** button from the top shelf and then choose the **Make PolyMesh3D** button from the **Tool** palette; the sphere will be converted into a polymesh. Now, add another object of your choice from the **Subtool** palette by choosing the **Append** button. Next, choose the **Live Boolean** button from the top shelf and click one of the icons located at the top of the appended primitive in the **Subtool** palette; the boolean operation will be displayed in the viewport. Figure 1-15 shows the boolean operation when the Subtraction icon is clicked.

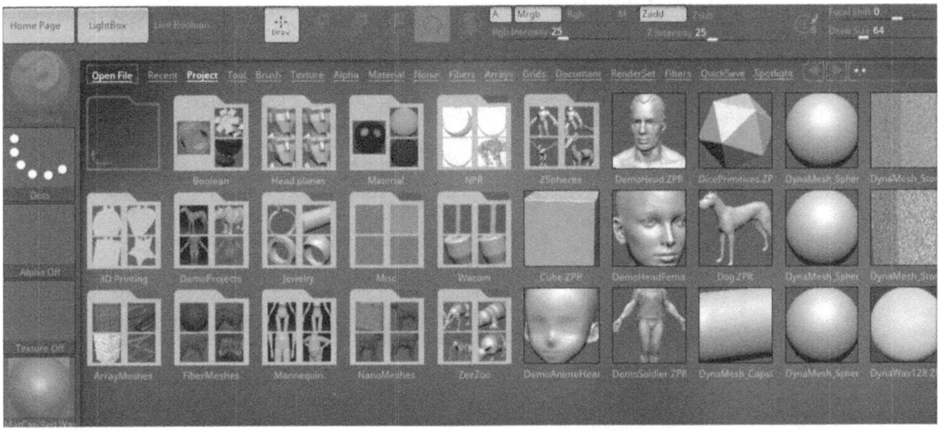

***Figure 1-14** The **LightBox** browser*

***Figure 1-15** The live boolean operation*

Note

There are four icons available for boolean operations: Addition, Subtraction, Union, and Intersection. 

Edit
The **Edit** button is used to enable the sculpting brushes so that you can add details to a 3D model. Whenever a 3D primitive is created in the canvas, you need to choose the **Edit** button from the top shelf. If this button is not chosen, ZBrush will remain in paint mode and dragging the cursor on the canvas will simply place copies of 3D objects in it, refer to Figure 1-16. To make changes in a 3D model, you need to make sure that the **Edit** button is chosen.

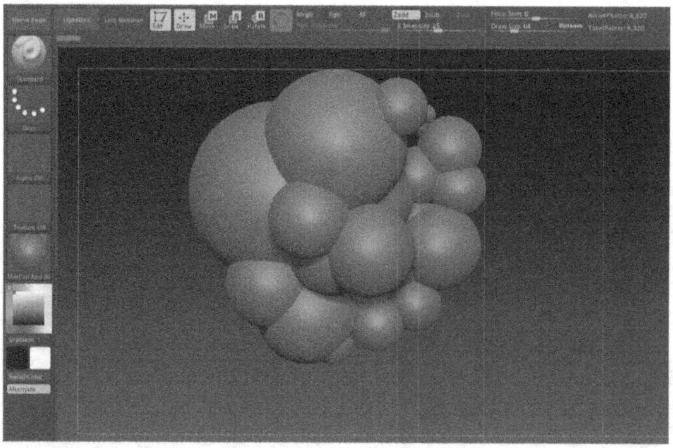

Figure 1-16 *Copies of the 3D objects placed in the canvas*

Draw
The **Draw** button allows you to draw a 3D object by first choosing a 3D model from the **Tool** palette and then dragging the cursor in the canvas. It allows you to sculpt 3D objects when the **Edit** button is chosen. However, if the **Edit** button is not chosen, dragging the cursor on the canvas will simply place copies of 3D objects in it.

Move, Scale, Rotate, and Gizmo 3D
The **Move**, **Scale**, and **Rotate** buttons are used to position, scale, and rotate the 3D object in the canvas, respectively. The **Move**, **Scale**, and **Rotate** buttons can also be invoked by pressing the W, E, and R, keys, respectively. When any of these buttons is chosen, and the **Edit** button is not chosen then a gizmo parallel to the canvas will appear, as shown in Figure 1-17. If you want to move the object around the canvas, choose the **Move** button and then drag the cursor on the area inside the gizmo.

For scaling the object uniformly, choose the **Scale** button, and then drag the cursor on the canvas. For scaling the object vertically, drag the cursor on the pink arc on the gyro vertically. For scaling the object horizontally, drag the cursor on the cyan arc horizontally, as shown in Figure 1-18. For rotating the object freely by using the **Rotate** button, drag the cursor on the area within the gizmo but not on the rings. On doing so, the orientation of gizmo will change, as shown in Figure 1-19.

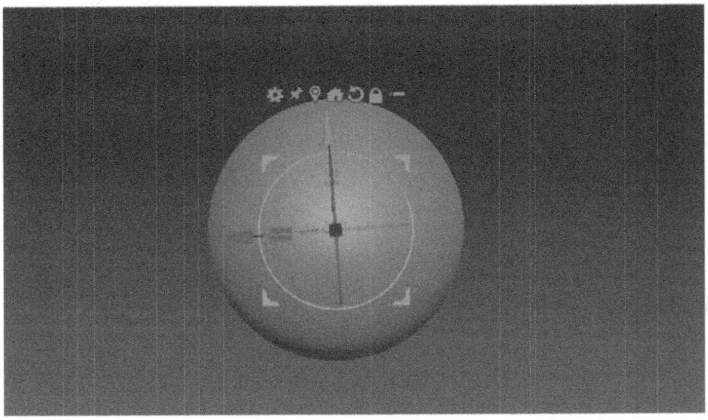

Figure 1-17 *Gizmo displayed on choosing the* ***Move*** *button*

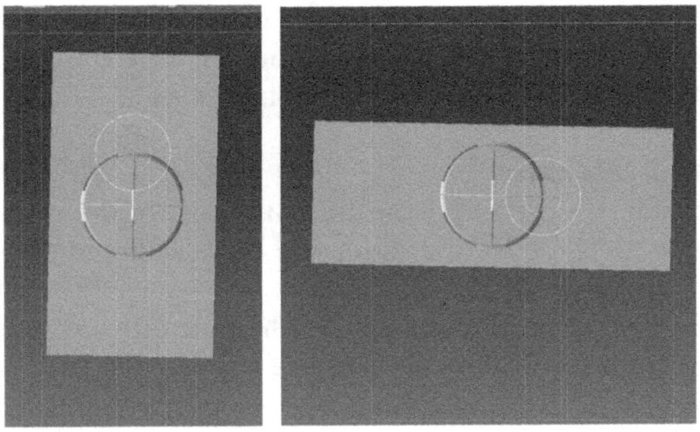

Figure 1-18 *The vertical and horizontal scaling using gyro*

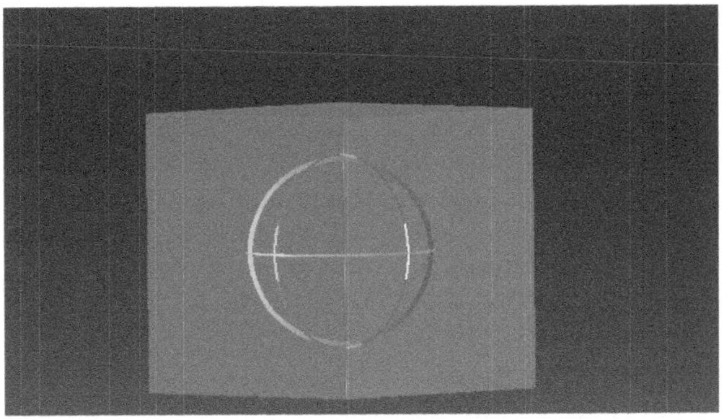

Figure 1-19 *Rotating the object using gyro*

If you choose the **Move** button when the **Edit** button is chosen, only the vertices of the object will move and not the entire object. If any of the manipulator buttons is chosen, the **Gizmo 3D Y** button will be automatically chosen and gizmo will appear in the model.

The Gizmo 3D manipulator will appear automatically to transpose the model in the scene. You can disable the gizmo by choosing the **Gizmo 3D Y** button.

When the **Gizmo 3D Y** button is active, you can work with some options in the **Preferences** palette. You can set the size, show/hide the information, and reset the gizmo in the scene.

Tip

You can move an object in the canvas in the edit mode by dragging the cursor on the canvas with the ALT key pressed. To scale an object, press and hold the left mouse button with the ALT key pressed, and then release the ALT key. To rotate an object, press and hold the left mouse button and drag the cursor.

Sculptris Pro Mode

The **Sculptris Pro Mode** button gives you the freedom to easily sculpt your model. When you activate this button and start sculpting, the model will be more smoother. The smoothness is determined by the brush size.

Mrgb, Rgb, and M

These buttons are used to fill colors and apply materials to an object. The **Mrgb** button is used to fill an object with both material and color. The **Rgb** button is used to fill an object only with color. The **M** button is used to fill an object with the material only.

Rgb Intensity and Z Intensity

The **Rgb Intensity** slider is used to control the intensity of the color applied to an object. The higher the value specified for the slider, the more will be the intensity of color.

The **Z Intensity** slider is used to control the depth of the brush stroke. The higher the value specified for slider, the more will be the depth of stroke.

Zadd, Zsub, and Zcut

The **Zadd** and **Zsub** buttons are used to determine whether a sculpting brush will raise the surface of an object or push it in. If you choose the **Zadd** button, the surface of the object will be elevated and if you choose the **Zsub** button, the surface will be pushed in. The **Zcut** button is used to create holes in a surface. It is activated when the **Edit** button is not chosen.

The ALT key toggles the alternate mode for the **Zadd** and **Zsub** buttons. If you sculpt a surface by choosing the **Zadd** button and holding the ALT key, it will be pushed in instead of being raised. Similarly, holding the ALT key with the **Zsub** button chosen will raise the surface of an object. The **Z Intensity** slider controls how much each stroke of the brush raises, lowers, or cuts into the surface of the 3D object.

Remember Draw Size Per Brush

The **Remember Draw Size Per Brush** button is used to remember the size of brush previously set. By default this button is deactivated. When you activate this button, it allows you to remember the size you set for each sculpting brush excluding the Smooth and Mask brush types.

Focal Shift and Draw Size

The **Focal Shift** slider is used to change the softness or fall off of the edge of the brush. The **Draw Size** slider is used to change the size of the brush. The higher the value of this slider, the bigger will be the size of the brush. The sculpting brush in ZBrush will be displayed as two concentric circles. The diameter of the outer circle determines the size of the brush and the diameter of the inner circle determines the focal shift. The **Dynamic** option located on the right of the **Draw Size** slider helps in sculpting. If this option is chosen then the brush size is adjusted automatically depending on the scale of the model.

Remember Dynamic Mode Per Brush

The **Remember Dynamic Mode Per Brush** button is used to control the dynamic size for each brush independently. When this button is deactivated and the **Dynamic** option located at the right of the **Draw Size** slider is off, the radius of brush changes with the zoom level in the canvas. When the **Remember Dynamic Mode Per Brush** button is activated, the radius of the brush remains same even if the zoom level is changed.

Left Shelf

The left shelf consists of different buttons that contain libraries for various brushes, strokes, alphas, textures, materials, and colors, as shown in Figure 1-20. All these libraries can also be accessed through the palettes. However, the left shelf enables easy access to these libraries. The brushes, strokes, alphas, textures, and materials will be discussed in later chapters. The different buttons in the left shelf are discussed next.

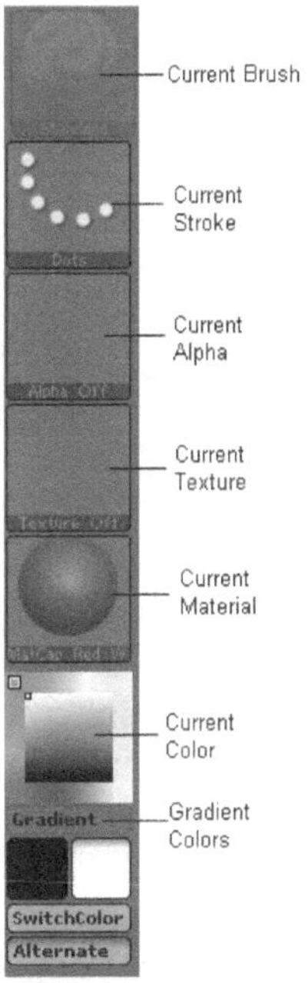

Figure 1-20 *The left shelf*

Current Brush

The Current Brush button is used to invoke a flyout that has different types of sculpting brushes, refer to Figure 1-22. Whenever you select a brush from the flyout, its icon will be displayed on the Current Brush button.

By default, the **Standard** brush icon is displayed on this button. This flyout consists of the **Quick Pick** and **3D Sculpting Brushes** areas. The **Quick Pick** area consists of the recently chosen brushes and the **3D Sculpting Brushes** area consists of all the brushes in ZBrush.

Current Stroke

The Current Stroke button is used to invoke a flyout that consists of different types of strokes, as shown in Figure 1-22. A stroke is a pattern which determines how the painting and sculpting will be done.

Figure 1-21 The flyout displayed on choosing the Current Brush button

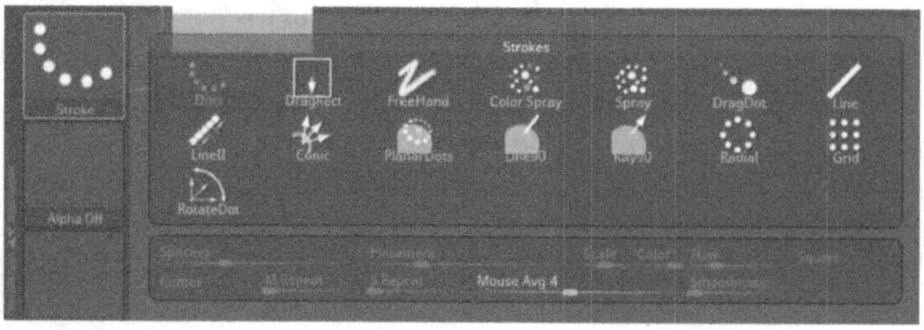

Figure 1-22 The flyout displayed on choosing the Current Stroke button

If you select a stroke from the flyout, its icon will be displayed on the Current Stroke button. By default, the **Dots** stroke icon is displayed on this button.

Current Alpha

The Current Alpha button is used to invoke a flyout that consists of different types of alpha images, as shown in Figure 1-23. The different gray scale images in this flyout are known as alphas.

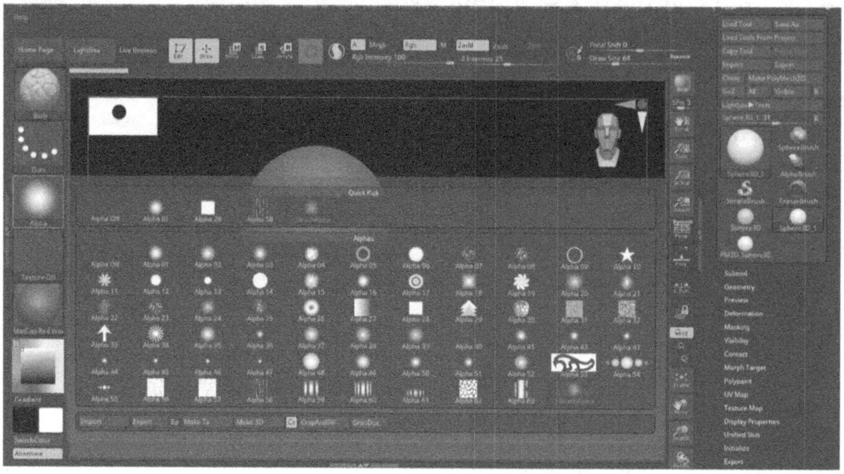

Figure 1-23 The flyout displayed on choosing the Current Alpha button

Alphas come in different shapes and determine the shape of brush that will be used in painting and sculpting.

Current Texture

The Current Texture button is used to invoke a flyout that consists of different types of texture images, as shown in Figure 1-24. Textures are the 2D images that can be created in ZBrush or can be imported from other sources.

Figure 1-24 The flyout displayed on choosing the Current Texture button

Current Material

The Current Material button is used to invoke a flyout that consists of different types of materials such as glass, silver, water, and gold, as shown in Figure 1-25. These materials can be applied to an object to give it the appearance of the specified material.

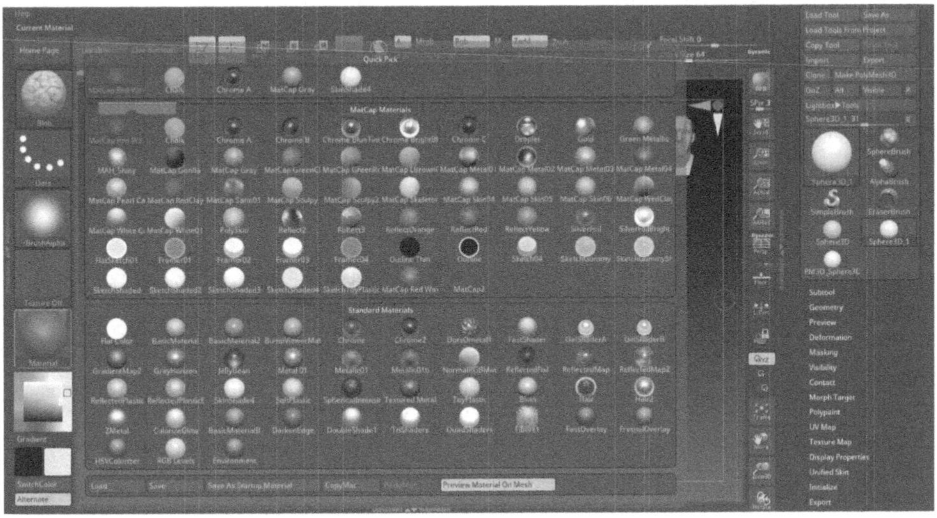

Figure 1-25 A flyout displayed on choosing the Current Material button

Current Color

The **Current Color** swatch is located just below the Current Material button. It is used to pick a color from the canvas and fill a 3D object with the selected color. If you hover the cursor on the color picker, the RGB value of the color is displayed beneath the cursor, as shown in Figure 1-26.

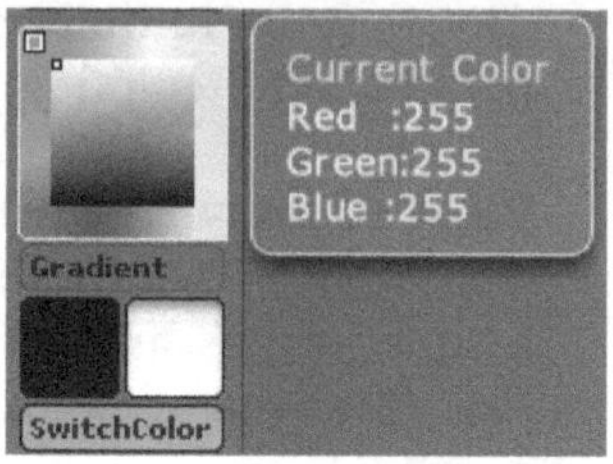

Figure 1-26 The RGB value of a color displayed

Gradient Colors

The **Gradient Colors** button is used to produce a gradient effect with the help of the **Secondary Color** and **Main Color** swatches available below it. The gradient will be produced from the main color to the secondary color. The color swatch below the **Gradient Colors** button represents the secondary and the main color used for gradient filling. The **SwitchColor** button located below this button is used to interchange the primary and secondary colors.

Right Shelf

The right shelf consists of different buttons and sliders that are used for rendering and navigating through canvas, refer to Figure 1-27. These buttons and sliders are explained next.

Figure 1-27 The right shelf

BPR

BPR stands for Best Preview Render. This button is used to produce high quality realistic renders on the canvas. It displays details including shadows, depth, transparency, and so on in the rendered scene. This button will render an object only when the **Edit** button is chosen.

SPix

SPix stands for Sub Pixel. This slider controls the quality of antialiasing in the render. Antialiasing is a technique used to smoothen the uneven projections on the edges of an image, thereby producing high quality images. These uneven projections occur because the screen does not have the required resolution to represent a smooth line. The value of the **SPix** slider varies between 0 and 7. If you set the value of the **SPix** slider to 7, the highest quality of antialiasing will be achieved.

Scroll

The **Scroll** button is used to move the canvas. Press and hold the left mouse button on the **Scroll** button and then drag the cursor to scroll the canvas.

Zoom

The **Zoom** button is used to zoom in and zoom out the canvas. To zoom in and zoom out the canvas, place the cursor on this button and drag the cursor upward or downward. Alternatively, you can zoom in and zoom out the canvas by using + (plus) and - (minus) keys, respectively.

Actual

The **Actual** button is used to display a document at its 100% size. If you have zoomed in or zoomed out the canvas, you can return to the actual canvas size by choosing this button. Alternatively, press the 0 key to return to the actual size of the canvas.

AAHalf

The **AAHalf** button is used to reduce the display of canvas to half of its original size. Alternatively, press CTRL+0 to reduce the canvas to half of its original size.

Persp

The **Persp** button is used to enable the perspective distortion in the canvas. This button gets activated when an object is created in the canvas.

Floor

The **Floor** button is used to display the floor grid in all the axes. This button gets activated when an object is created in the canvas. By default, the Y-axis is selected. If you select all the axes in the floor grid, the floor grid in all the selected axes will be activated, as shown in Figure 1-28.

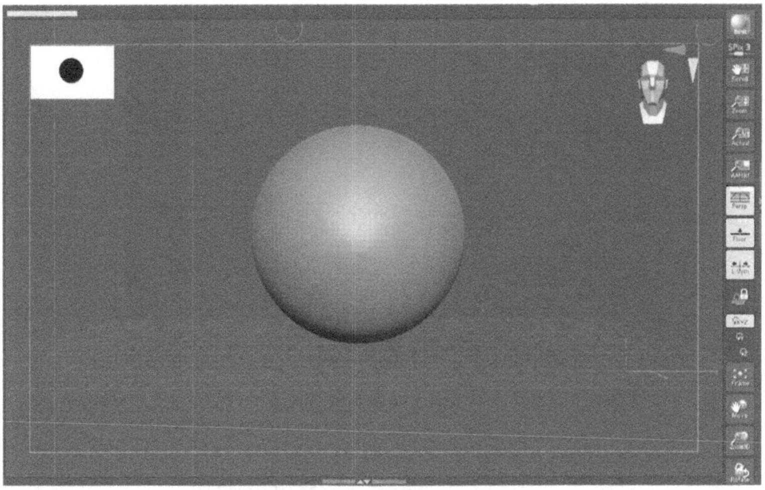

Figure 1-28 *Floor grid activated in all the axes*

Local

The **Local** button is used to transform the last edited area of a 3D object into the center point of rotation or scaling.

L. Sym

The **L. Sym** button is used with the subtools. In ZBrush, subtools are different 3D objects which combine to form a single 3D object. For instance, if you have modeled a character and its clothes separately, both of these will be referred to as subtools. The **L. Sym** button activates the mirroring of symmetry across the subtool axes.

Rotation Buttons

The three rotation buttons are located just below the **L. Sym** button. These buttons control the rotation of an object along different axes. The **XYZ** button rotates the object in all the axes. The **Y** and **Z** buttons rotate an object in Y and Z axes, respectively. For rotating an object along any of the axes, press and hold the left mouse button and drag the cursor over the canvas.

Frame

The **Frame** button is used to fit an object into the canvas, as shown in Figure 1-29. To choose this button, the **Edit** button should be already chosen. Alternatively, press F to fit an object into the canvas.

Move, Scale, and Rotate

The **Move**, **Scale**, and **Rotate** buttons are used to move, scale, and rotate a 3D object in the canvas, respectively. These buttons are used when a 3D object is in the **Edit** mode. These operations can be carried out by placing the cursor on these buttons and then dragging them.

Note

*All these buttons are also available in the **Transform** palette.*

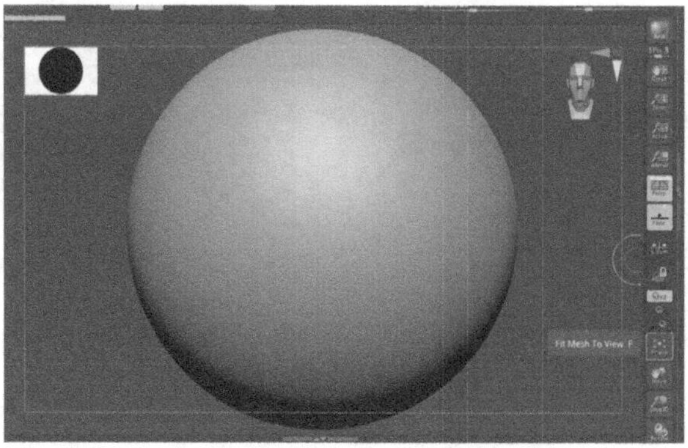

Figure 1-29 *The object fitted into the canvas*

PolyF

The **PolyF** button is used to display the polygon edges of a 3D object, as shown in Figure 1-30.

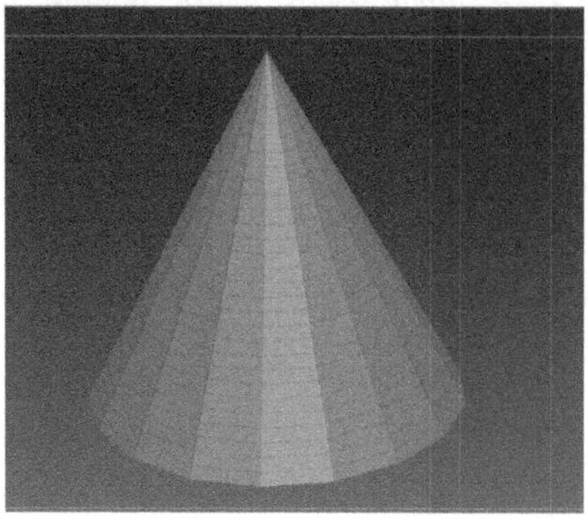

Figure 1-30 *The polygon edges of a 3D object*

Transp

The **Transp** button activates the transparency of different subtools that are not selected in the list of subtools present in the **SubTool** subpalette, refer to Figure 1-31. On choosing this button, different subtools such as clothes and accessories used in the 3D model become transparent, as they are not selected in the **SubTools** subpalette.

In Figure 1-31, the default 3D model present in the **LightBox** browser has been used. To load this model in the canvas, choose the **Tool** tab in the **LightBox** browser. Next, double-click on the **DemoSoldier.ZTL** file in the **LightBox** browser. Press and hold the left mouse button and drag the cursor in the canvas; the model will be created in the canvas. After loading the model, choose the **Edit** button from the top shelf to switch to the edit mode. Next, choose the **Transp** button.

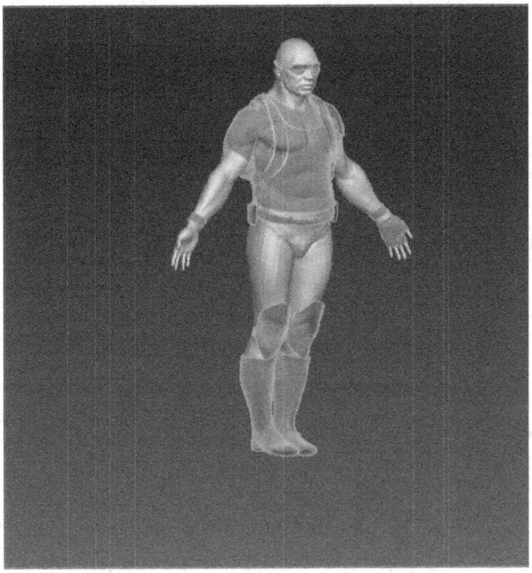

Figure 1-31 *Transparency created in the subtools*

Ghost

The **Ghost** button is used in combination with the **Transp** button. When you choose the **Transp** button, the **Ghost** button is automatically activated. However, if this button is not activated, the subtools will remain transparent but their color and texture will be displayed, as shown in Figure 1-32.

Solo

The **Solo** button is used to hide all the deselected subtools used in the model. On choosing this button, only the selected subtool will be displayed, as shown in Figure 1-33. In this figure, all the clothes and accessories of the 3D model have disappeared, as only the 3D model is selected. The subtools that have disappeared can be restored back by choosing this button again.

Xpose

The **Xpose** button is used to separate the subtools from the base model, as shown in Figure 1-34. On choosing this button, the subtools start moving and are separated from the base model.

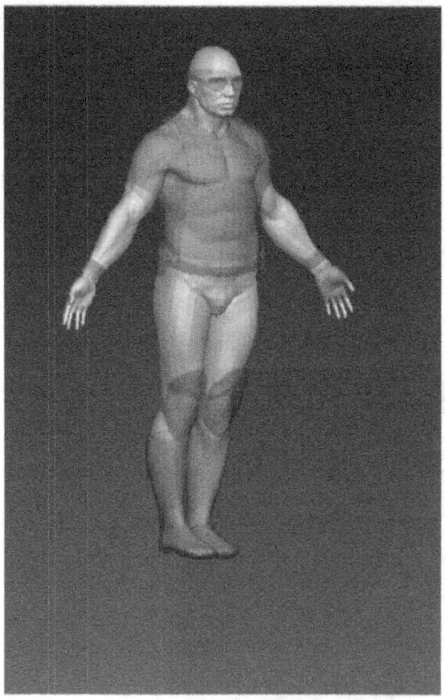

Figure 1-32 Color in transparent subtools displayed

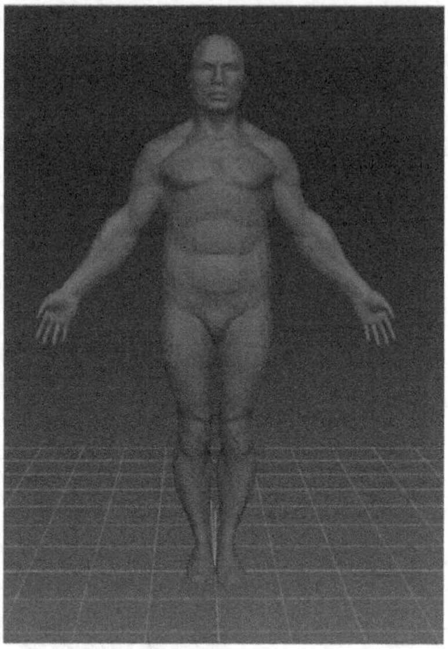

Figure 1-33 The selected subtool displayed

Figure 1-34 The subtools separated from the model

OPENING AND SAVING A ZTOOL AND ZBRUSH DOCUMENT

In ZBrush, a 3D model is known as ZTool. In order to save the ZTool, you need to save your 3D model using the **Tool** palette. The model will be saved in the *ZTL* format by choosing the **Save As** button in the **Tool** palette, refer to Figure 1-35. The saved ZTool can be opened later by using the **Load Tool** button in the **Tool** palette. You can load the project file by using the **Load Tools From Project** button in the **Tool** palette, refer to Figure 1-32. When you choose the **Load Tools From Project** button, the **Load Project** dialog box will be displayed, refer to Figure 1-36.

The ZBrush document only contains the 2D illustration and not the full 3D model. Therefore, if you save a 3D model as a document, only the 2D version of its current view will be saved. This document cannot be edited further in 3D space and can only be used as an illustration. If you want to save a 3D object as an illustration, you must save your 3D model using the **Document** palette by choosing the **Save As** button, refer to Figure 1-37. It will be saved in the *ZBR* format. Once saved, the ZBrush document can be opened by using the **Open** button from the **Document** palette.

You can also save all your ZTools as a project using the **File** palette. To save a project, choose the **File** palette to expand it. In this palette, choose the **Save As** button, refer to Figure 1-38; the **Save Project** dialog box will be displayed, refer to Figure 1-39. In this dialog box, enter the desired name in the **File Name** text box and then choose the **Save** button. It will be saved in the .ZPR format.

***Figure 1-35** The **Save As** button in the **Tool** palette*

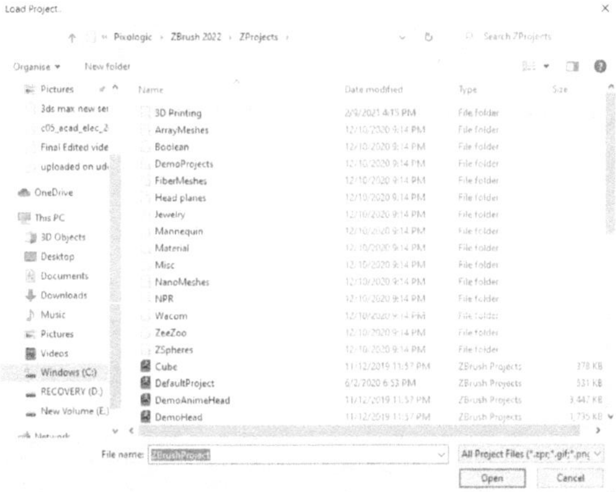

***Figure 1-36** The **Load Project** dialog box*

Tip

On hovering the mouse pointer on different buttons and sliders in ZBrush, the full names of these buttons and sliders will be displayed. If you press and hold the CTRL key while hovering the mouse pointer on the buttons and sliders, a brief description about them will also be displayed.

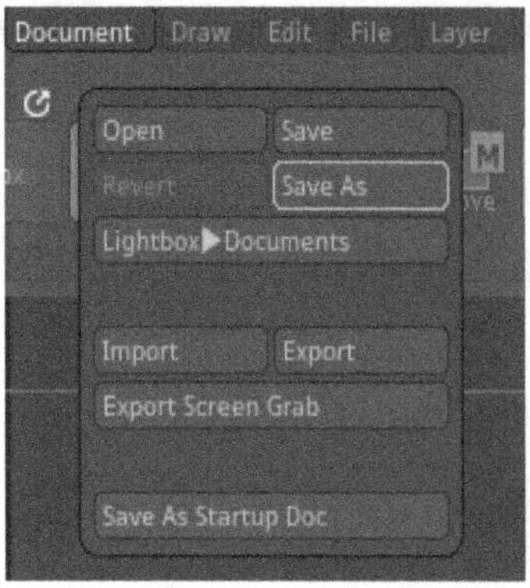

*Figure 1-37 The **Save As** button in the **Document** palette*

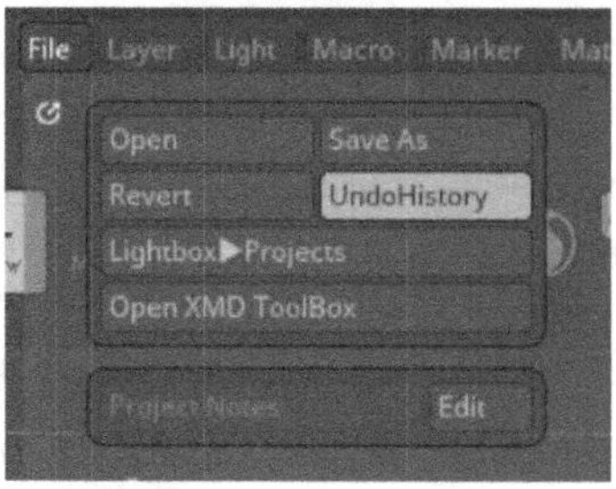

*Figure 1-38 The **Save As** button in the **File** palette*

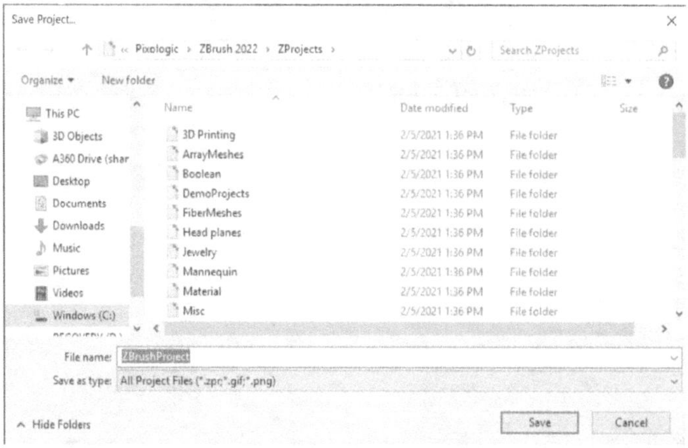

*Figure 1-39 The **Save Project** dialog box*

HOT KEYS

In ZBrush, you can use shortcut keys to invoke the commonly used features. These keys are also referred to as hot keys which help you work efficiently and faster. The most commonly used keys and their functions are listed in Table 1-1.

Table 1-1 Commonly used keys and their functions

Key	Function
CTRL+S	Saves a complete ZBrush Project
SHIFT+CTRL+T	Saves a 3D model
9	Quick Save
CTRL+Z	Undo
SHIFT+CTRL+Z	Redo
Tab	Show/hides floating palettes
, [comma key]	Show/hides Lightbox
G	Invokes the **Projection Master** tool
T	Activates the 3D edit mode
Q	Activates the Draw mode
W	Activates the **Move** tool
E	Activates the **Scale** tool
R	Activates the **Rotate** tool
I	Changes the Rgb Intensity
U	Changes the Z Intensity
O	Changes the Focal Shift
S	Adjusts the draw size of the brush
V	Switches colors in the color swatches
0	Displays the actual size of the canvas
P	Activates Perspective Distortion
F	Fits the mesh to view
SHIFT+R	Invokes BPR renderer
CTRL+R	Cursor Selective Render
CTRL+0	Displays the antialiased half size of the canvas
SHIFT+P	Displays Floor Grid
SHIFT+F	Draws Polyframe

Self-Evaluation Test

Answer the following questions and then compare them to those given at the end of this chapter:

1. In which of the following formats a ZBrush document is saved?

    (a) .ZBR (b) .ZTL
    (c) .ZBD (d) None of these

2. Which of the following palettes is used to change the focal shift and intensity of the brush stroke?

    (a) **Brush** (b) **File**
    (c) **Document** (d) **Draw**

3. The **HomePage** button is located at the __________ .

4. The __________ brush is the default sculpting brush in ZBrush.

5. The term BPR stands for __________ .

6. The value of the **SPix** slider varies from __________ to __________ .

7. The ZBrush canvas can be zoomed in and zoomed out with the help of the [and] keys. (T/F)

8. The **Transp** button is used to hide all the deselected subtools used in the model. (T/F)

9. The **Actual** button is used to display a document at its 100% size. (T/F)

Review Questions

Answer the following questions:

1. In which of the following shelves is the **QuickSave** button located?

   (a) Top shelf (b) Title bar
   (c) Left shelf (d) Right shelf

2. In which of the following shelves is the **Current Color** button located?

   (a) Top shelf (b) Left shelf
   (c) Right shelf (d) None of these

3. Which of the following buttons is used to control the quality of antialiasing in the render?

   (a) **Material** (b) **Texture**
   (c) **Local Symmetry** (d) **SPix**

4. Which of the following buttons is used to display the polygon edges of a 3D object?

   (a) **PolyF** (b) **Xpose**
   (c) **SPix** (d) **Frame**

5. The __________ button is used to enable the sculpting brushes.

6. The __________ key toggles the alternate mode for the **Z Add** and **Z Sub** buttons.

7. The palettes in ZBrush are organized alphabetically, starting from __________ to __________.

8. The **LightBox** browser is located on the right side of the canvas. (T/F)

9. In ZBrush, a 3D model is known as ZProject. (T/F)

10. The **Marker** palette stores information about the orientation, colors, brush strokes, and position of the 3D object. (T/F)

Answers to Self-Evaluation Test

1. a, **2.** d, **3.** top shelf, **4. Standard**, **5.** Best Preview Render, **6.** 0 to 7, **7.** F, **8.** F, **9.** T

Chapter 2

Sculpting Brushes

Learning Objectives

After completing this chapter, you will be able to:
- *Understand digital sculpting*
- *Work with different types of sculpting brushes*

INTRODUCTION

Digital sculpting in ZBrush offers a very efficient and artistic way to create models. It allows you to add subtle details to 3D models which help in achieving photorealistic and hyperrealistic outputs. Furthermore, in ZBrush, Dynamics system is used along with special cloth sculpting brushes. These brushes use the Dynamics engine to give unique capabilities for interacting with the cloth surface. In this chapter, you will learn about the use of different brushes in sculpting.

SCULPTING BRUSHES

Enhanced

The sculpting brushes are used to modify the shape of a 3D model. These brushes push, pull, smoothen, grab, and pinch a 3D model depending on the type of brush chosen. ZBrush contains an extensive library of brushes. Before using these brushes, you need to create a 3D primitive object or load a model from the **LightBox** browser. After creating a 3D primitive object or loading a model, you need to choose the **Edit** button in the top shelf. If this button is not chosen, then ZBrush will be in the paint mode and drawing on the canvas will simply create copies of the 3D model in the canvas.

The different brushes in ZBrush can be accessed either from the **Brush** palette located at the top of the interface or using the Current Brush button from the left shelf, refer to Figures 2-1 and 2-2. Before using any brush, you can change its settings in the **Brush** palette. In addition to this, you can also modify the brush size and depth by using the settings in the top shelf, refer to Figure 2-3.

Note

Some of the brushes are available in the ***Brush*** *tab of the* ***LightBox*** *browser such as* ***IMM Bricks.ZBP****,* ***InsertHCylinder.ZBP****,* ***InsertRing.ZBP****, and so on.*

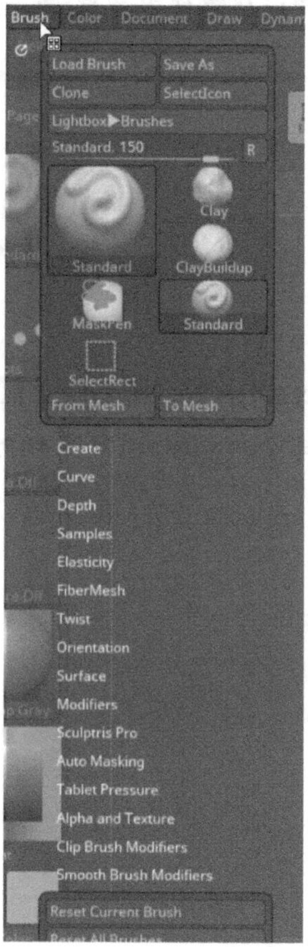

Figure 2-1 *Partial view of the* ***Brush*** *palette in the top shelf*

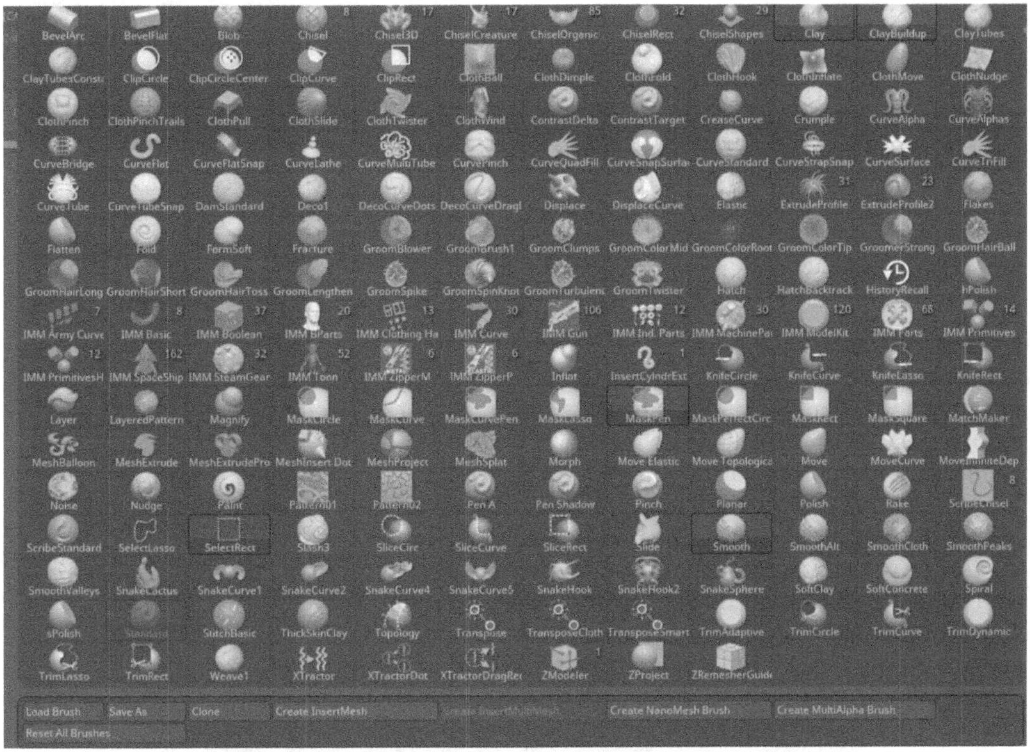

Figure 2-2 The brushes accessed from the left shelf on choosing the Current Brush button

Figure 2-3 The different brush settings in the top shelf

After creating a 3D primitive object in the canvas, it should be converted into a polymesh. Polymesh is a collection of polygons or faces that form the surface of a mesh. When you drag a brush on a 3D primitive object, a message box will be displayed, prompting you to convert the 3D primitive object into polymesh, refer to Figure 2-4. You can also import 3D models created in external software applications. These 3D models are imported as polymeshes. The sculpting, texturing, and mapping can only be done on the polymeshes. To convert a 3D primitive object into a polymesh, choose the **Make PolyMesh3D** button from the **Tool** palette, refer to Figure 2-5. After converting a 3D primitive object into polymesh, you can increase the number of polygons so that you can sculpt easily at different resolutions. Most commonly used sculpting brushes in ZBrush are discussed next.

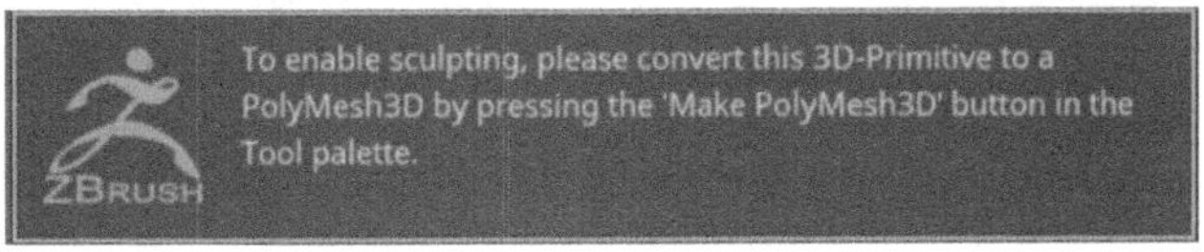

Figure 2-4 Message box displayed on using a brush on a 3D primitive object

Note

*Before using the brushes on a polymesh, it is recommended to increase the number of polygons in the object. For achieving a greater level of detail on the object, you need to have larger number of polygons. When you place an object on the canvas, it has lower number of polygons. If you start sculpting on low poly objects, the output will not carry a high level of detail. To increase the number of polygons in the object, expand the **Geometry** subpalette in the **Tool** palette, and then choose the **Divide** button.*

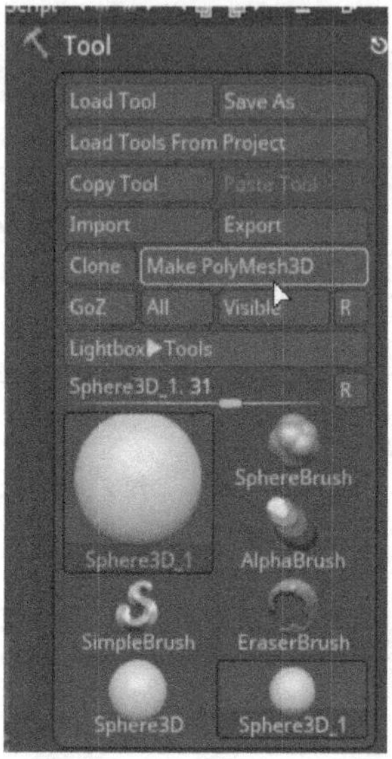

***Figure 2-5** The **Make PolyMesh3D** button in the **Tool** palette*

BevelArc Brush

The **BevelArc** brush is used to sculpt a round bevel shape along an edge. To sculpt using this brush, first create a 3D primitive object in the canvas. To do so, choose the Current Tool button from the **Tool** palette; a flyout will be displayed, refer to Figure 2-6. Choose the **Cube3D** primitive from this flyout. Next, press and hold the left mouse button and drag the cursor on the canvas to create a cube. After creating the cube, choose the **Edit** button from the top shelf and then choose the **Make PolyMesh3D** button from the **Tool** palette; the primitive object will be converted into a polymesh. Next, expand the **Geometry** subpalette in the **Tool** palette, and then choose the **Smt** button to deactivate it. Now, click thrice on the **Divide** button.

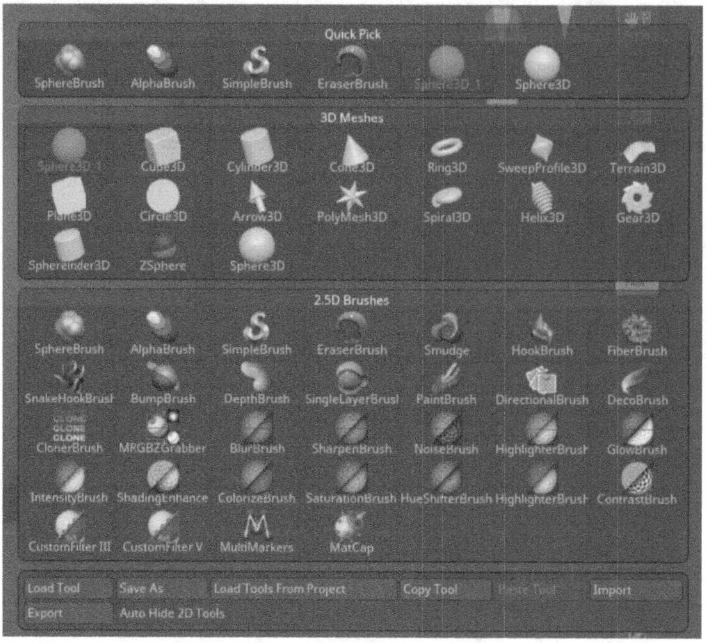

***Figure 2-6** Flyout displayed on choosing the Current Tool button*

Choose the Current Brush button from the left shelf; a flyout containing different sculpting brushes will be displayed. Choose the **BevelArc** brush from this flyout. If required, adjust the size of the brush using the '[' or ']' keys. Next, click on the cube at both sides of an edge which you want to bevel, refer to Figure 2-7. Next, move the brush back and forth all over across the edge to get the desired bevel shape, refer to Figure 2-8. Note that you also need to adjust the **Draw Size** slider in the top shelf to get the desired bevel shape.

You can also choose the **Activate Symmetry** button in the **Transform** Palette and then you can choose the **X**, **Y**, or **Z** button depending on the axis along which the symmetrical edges need to be beveled. You need to use the **R** button for activating the radial symmetry.

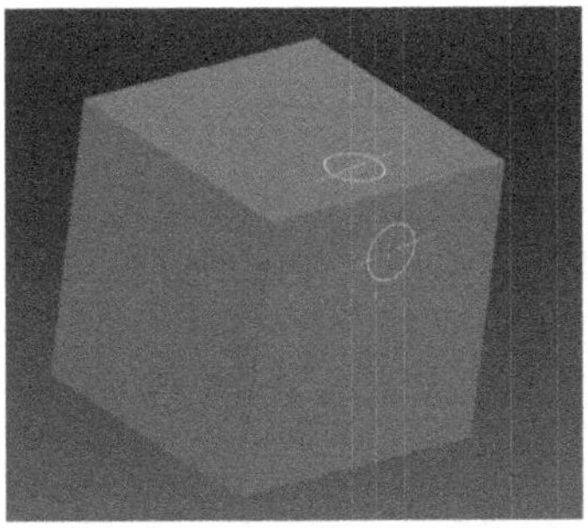

Figure 2-7 *Clicking on the mesh at both sides of the edge*

Figure 2-8 *Arc bevel shape created across the edge*

Note

You will know about the Symmetry feature in the ***Transform*** *palette in detail in Chapter 3.*

BevelFlat Brush

The **BevelFlat** brush is used to sculpt a flat bevel shape along an edge. To sculpt using this brush, first create a 3D primitive object in the canvas. To do so, choose the Current Tool button from the **Tool** palette; a flyout will be displayed, refer to Figure 2-6. Choose the **Cube3D** primitive from this flyout. Next, press and hold the left mouse button and drag the cursor on the canvas to create a cube. After creating the cube, choose the **Edit** button from the top shelf and then choose the **Make PolyMesh3D** button from the **Tool** palette; the primitive object will be converted into a polymesh. Next, expand the **Geometry** subpalette in the **Tool** palette, and then choose the **Smt** button to deactivate it. Now, click thrice on the **Divide** button.

Choose the Current Brush button from the left shelf; a flyout containing different sculpting brushes will be displayed. Choose the **BevelFlat** brush from this flyout. If required, adjust the size of the brush using the '[' or ']' keys. Next, click on the cube at both sides of the edge which you want to bevel, refer to Figure 2-7. Next, move the brush back and forth all over across the edge to get the desired flat bevel shape, refer to Figure 2-9. Note that you also need to adjust the value in the **Draw Size** slider in the top shelf to get the desired bevel shape.

You can also choose the **Activate Symmetry** button in the **Transform** Palette and then you can choose the **X**, **Y**, or **Z** button depending on the axis along which the symmetrical edges need to be beveled. You need to use the **R** button for activating the radial symmetry.

Figure 2-9 *Flat bevel shape created across the edge*

Blob Brush

The **Blob** brush is used to add organic details to an object. This brush is ideal for creating fungus on the surface of an object. To sculpt using this brush, first create a 3D primitive object in the canvas. To do so, choose the Current Tool button from the **Tool** palette; a flyout will be displayed, refer to Figure 2-6. Choose the **Sphere3D** primitive from this flyout. Next, press and hold the left mouse button and drag the cursor on the canvas to create a sphere. After creating the sphere, choose the **Edit** button from the top shelf and then choose the **Make PolyMesh3D** button from the **Tool** palette; the primitive object will be converted into a polymesh. Next, expand the **Geometry** subpalette in the **Tool** palette, and then click thrice on the **Divide** button; the sphere will become smoother as more polygons are added, refer to Figure 2-10.

Choose the Current Brush button from the left shelf; a flyout containing different sculpting brushes will be displayed. Choose the **Blob** brush from this flyout. If required, adjust the size of the brush using the [or] key (square bracket key). Next, press and hold the left mouse button, and drag the cursor on the surface of the sphere; the shape of the sphere will be modified and will become blobby, refer to Figure 2-11.

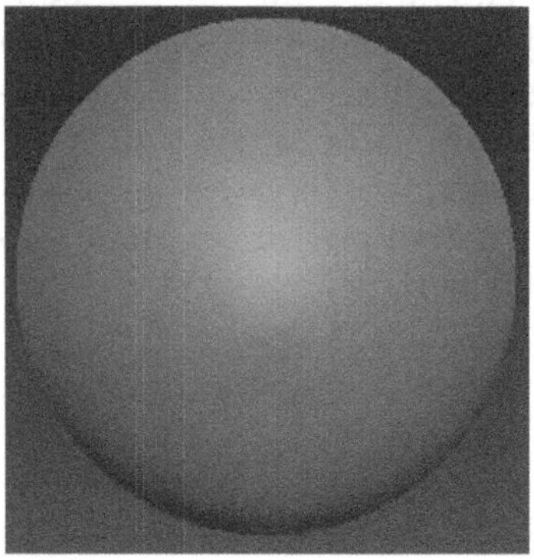

Figure 2-10 *The sphere smoothened*

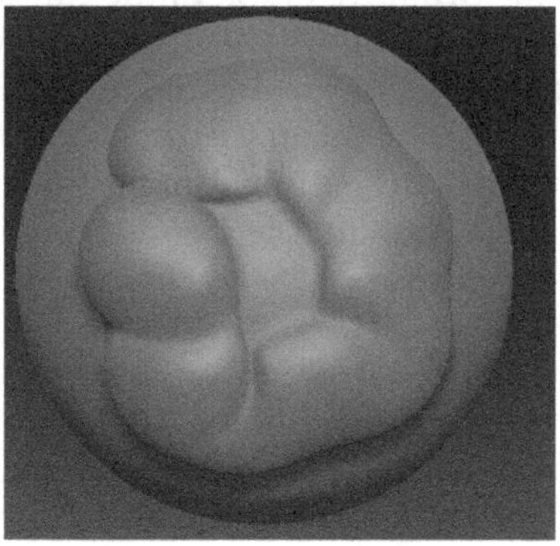

Figure 2-11 *Shape of the sphere modified using the **Blob** brush*

Clay Brushes

There are four types of Clay brushes, namely **Clay**, **ClayBuildup**, **ClayTubes**, and **ClayTubes Constant**, as shown in Figure 2-12. These brushes are discussed next.

Clay Brush

The **Clay** brush is used to add detail and depth to an object by using different alphas, refer to Figure 2-13. On choosing the **Zadd** button, the lump of clay will be created on a sculpture and an effect will be created as if the sculpture scooped on the clay has been taken off, choosing the **Zsub** button.

Figure 2-12 *The clay brushes*

Figure 2-13 *Patterns created using different alphas*

ClayBuildup Brush

The **ClayBuildup** brush is used to increase the volume of an object significantly. On choosing this brush, a rectangular alpha gets automatically assigned to it. You can also choose other alpha images from the flyout displayed on choosing the Current Alpha button from the left shelf. To increase the volume of an object using this brush, press and hold the left mouse button and drag the cursor continuously on the surface of the object, refer to Figure 2-14.

ClayTubes Brush

The **ClayTubes** brush is similar to the **ClayBuildup** brush with the only difference that it does not produce displacement in the surface of the object, refer to Figure 2-15. On choosing this brush, a rectangular alpha gets automatically assigned to it. It gives an effect similar to an effect produced when a wooden tool is used on the surface of a wet lump of clay.

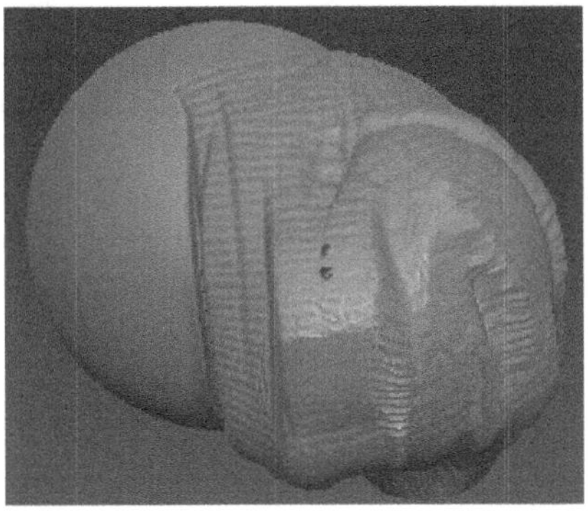

Figure 2-14 *Volume of the sphere increased using the* ***ClayBuildup*** *brush*

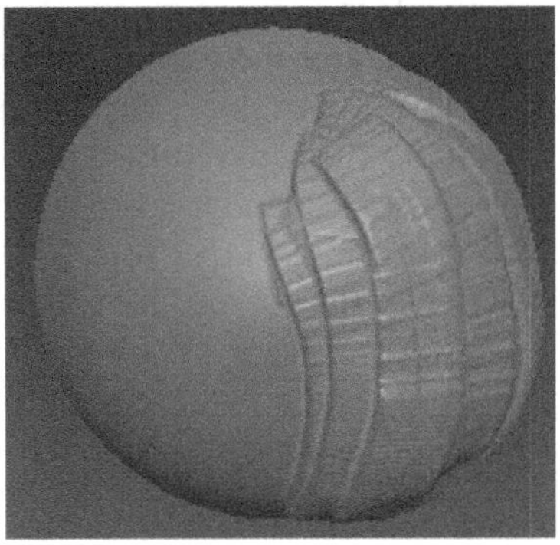

Figure 2-15 *Volume of the sphere increased using the* ***ClayTubes*** *brush*

ClayTubes Constant Brush

The **ClayTubes Constant** brush is similar to the **ClayTubes** brush with the only difference that it keeps the sample rate of radius at a constant rate.

Cloth Brushes

ZBrush has special cloth brushes to control cloth sculpting. These special brushes are used to work on dynamic cloth surface. By using these brushes, you can create the folds or can freely move into the geometry as per the requirements, refer to Figure 2-16. There are thirteen types of cloth brushes, namely **ClothBall, ClothDimple, ClothFold, ClothHook, ClothInflate, ClothMove, ClothNudge, ClothPinch**, **ClothPinchTrail**, **ClothPull**, **ClothSlide**, **ClothTwister**, and **ClothWind**, refer to Figure 2-17. These brushes are discussed next.

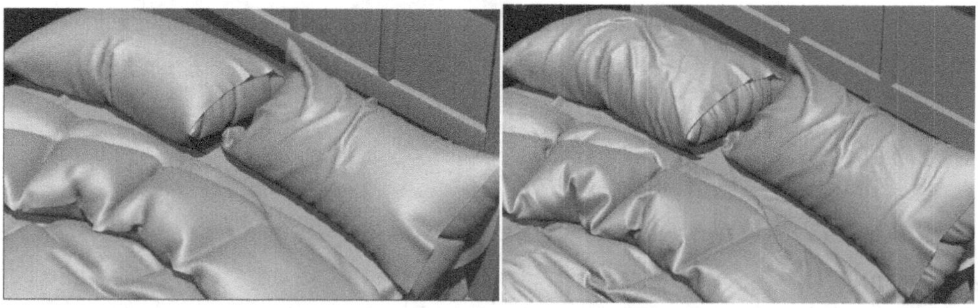

Figure 2-16 *Creating folds using cloth brushes in the scene*

Figure 2-17 *The **Cloth** brushes*

ClothBall Brush

The **ClothBall** brush is used to expand the surface of an object to a significant amount by pulling the polygons in a direction perpendicular to the surface. To sculpt using this brush, choose the **LightBox** button from the top shelf; the LightBox browser will be displayed. Next, choose the **Tool** tab in the LightBox browser. Next, double-click on the **DemoSoldier. ZTL** file in the LightBox browser; the model will be created in the canvas, as shown in Figure 2-18. Make sure the **Edit** button from the top shelf is chosen. Choose the **Geometry** subpalette in the **Tool** palette and choose the **Dynamic** button from the ***Dynamic Subdiv*** area. Next, choose the Current Brush button from the left shelf; a flyout containing different sculpting brushes will be displayed. Choose the **ClothBall** brush from this flyout. Expand the **SubTool** subpalette in the **Tool** palette. Now, choose **vest** from the list. Notice that the shirt is selected in the canvas area. Now, use the **ClothBall** brush to sculpt both hands of the shirt, as shown in Figure 2-19.

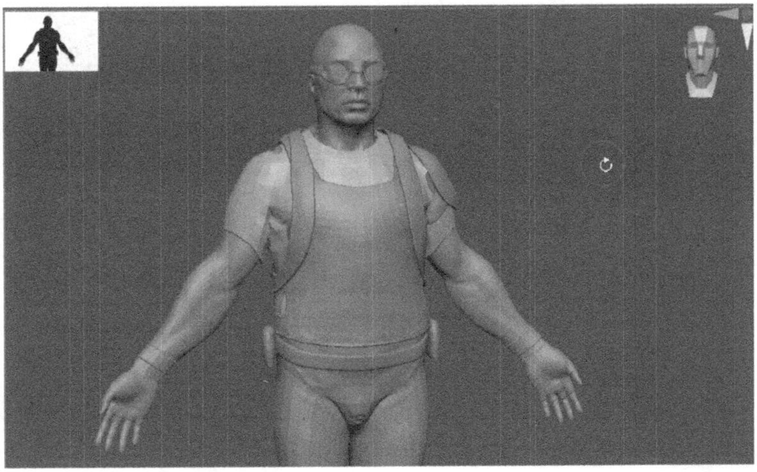

Figure 2-18 The ***DemoSoldier.ZTL*** *file*

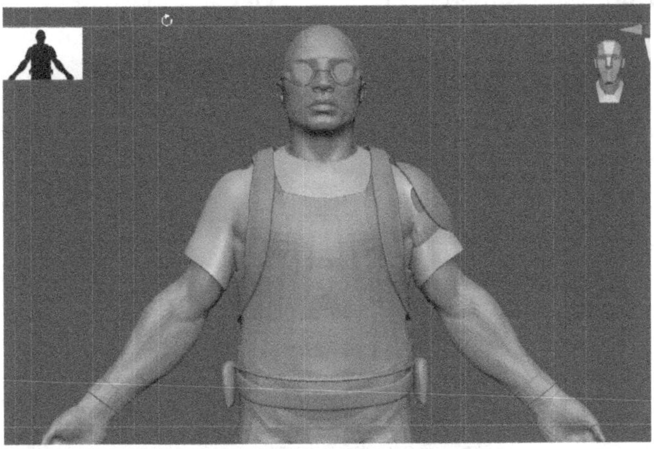

Figure 2-19 Sculpting both hands of the shirt by using the ***ClothBall*** *brush*

ClothDimple Brush

The **ClothDimple** brush is used to create a small hollow portion on the surface of an object. For example, by using this brush you can create button on a pillow. To sculpt using this brush, first create a 3D primitive object in the canvas. Choose the **Edit** button from the top shelf and then choose the **Make PolyMesh3D** button from the **Tool** palette; the primitive object will be converted into a polymesh. Next, expand the **Geometry** subpalette in the **Tool** palette, and then click on the **Dynamic** button in the **Dynamic Subdiv** area; the sphere will become smoother as more polygons are added. Choose the Current Brush button from the left shelf; a flyout containing different sculpting brushes will be displayed. Choose the **C** tab from the flyout; a list of brush starting with C will be displayed. Choose the **ClothDimple** brush from this flyout. If required, adjust the size of the brush using the [or] key (square bracket key). Next, press and hold the left mouse button, and drag the cursor on the surface of the sphere; the surface of the sphere will be modified and wrinkled, refer to Figure 2-20.

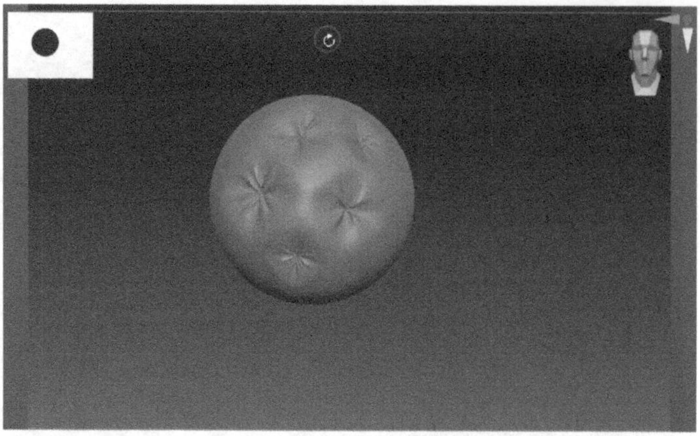

*Figure 2-20 The modified sphere using the **ClothDimple** brush*

ClothFold Brush

The **ClothFold** brush is used to create wrinkles and folds on the surface of an object. By using this brush, you can create wrinkles on a cloth, as shown in Figure 2-21.

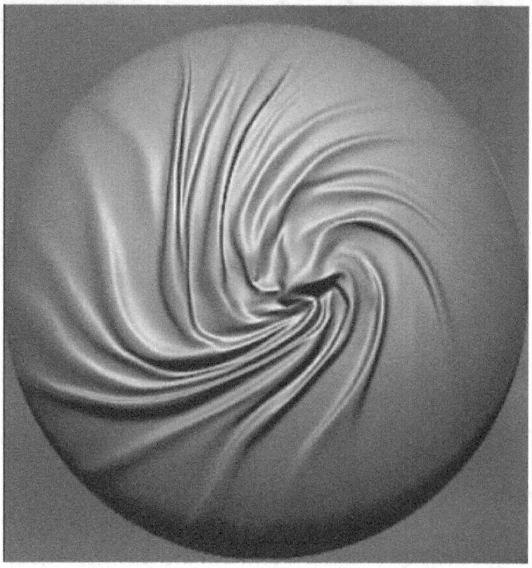

*Figure 2-21 The sculpted object using the **ClothFold** brush*

ClothHook Brush

To create an effect as if a cloth is grabbed, held, or dragged, choose the **ClothHook** brush. By using this brush, you can create the hanging cloth model, refer to Figure 2-22.

ClothInflate Brush

The **ClothInflate** brush is used to create an effect of covering an object by cloth. Figure 2-23 shows the sculpted object using the **ClothInflate** brush.

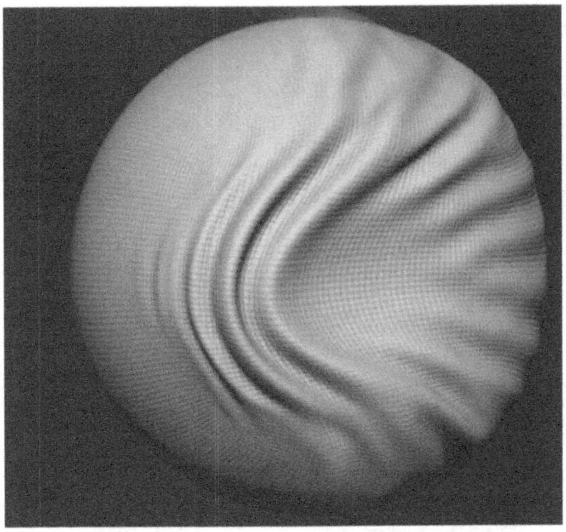

*Figure 2-22 The sculpted object using the **ClothHook** brush*

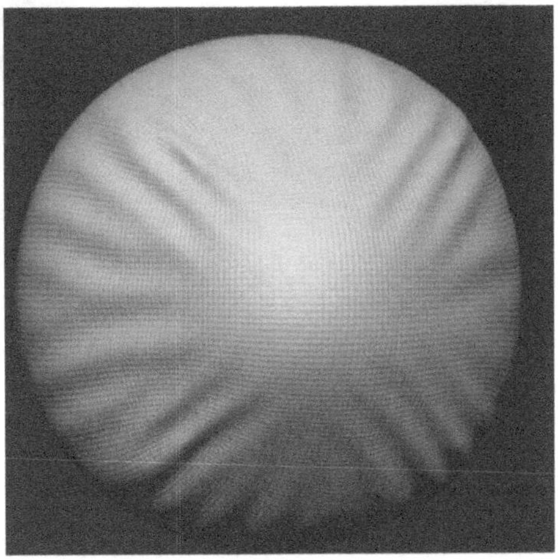

*Figure 2-23 The sculpted object using the **ClothInflate** brush*

ClothMove Brush

The **ClothMove** brush is used to control the stretching of cloth during the cloth simulation in Dynamic system, refer to Figure 2-24.

ClothNudge Brush

The **ClothNudge** brush is used to create ripples on the surface of an object. Figure 2-25 shows the sculpted object using the **ClothNudge** brush.

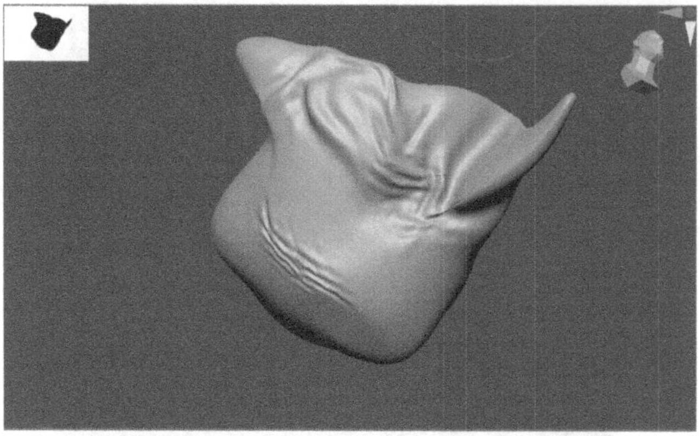

Figure 2-24 *The sculpted object using the **ClothMove** brush*

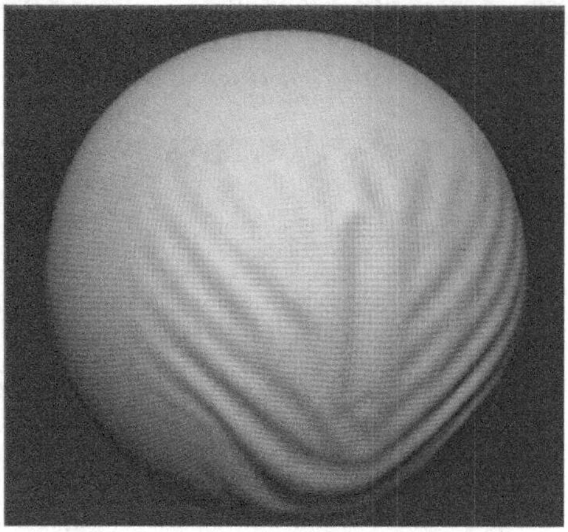

Figure 2-25 *The sculpted object using the **ClothNudge** brush*

ClothPinch Brush

The **ClothPinch** brush is used to create a crease on the surface of an object by pulling the surface. To sculpt using this brush, first create a 3D primitive object in the canvas. Next, make sure the **Edit** button is chosen from the top shelf. Choose the **Geometry** subpalette in the **Tool** Palette and choose the **Dynamic** button in the **Dynamic Subdiv** area. Next, choose the Current Brush button from the left shelf; a flyout containing different sculpting brushes will be displayed. Choose the **ClothPinch** brush from this flyout. Now, sculpt on an object using this brush, refer to Figure 2-26. Hold the ALT key to reverse the direction of the crease relative to the surface.

ClothPinchTrial Brush

The **ClothPinchTrial** brush is used to repeat the pinching along the path of the stroke on the object. By using this brush, you can create wrinkles in objects like pillows or wounds and scars in skin.

To sculpt using this brush, first create a 3D primitive object in the canvas. Next, make sure the **Edit** button is chosen from the top shelf. Choose the **Geometry** subpalette in the **Tool** Palette and choose the **Dynamic** button in the **Dynamic Subdiv** area. Next, choose the

Current Brush button from the left shelf; a flyout containing different sculpting brushes will be displayed. Choose the **ClothPinchTrial** brush from this flyout. Now, sculpt on an object using this brush, refer to Figure 2-27. Hold the ALT key to reverse the direction of the crease relative to the surface.

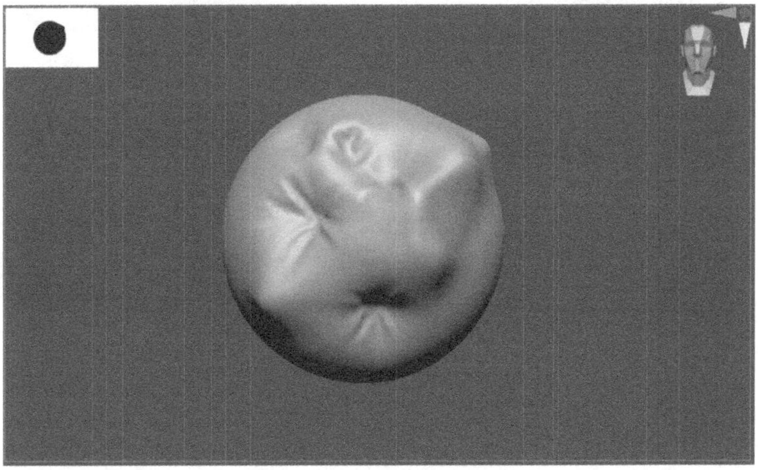

Figure 2-26 *The sculpted object using the **ClothPinch** brush*

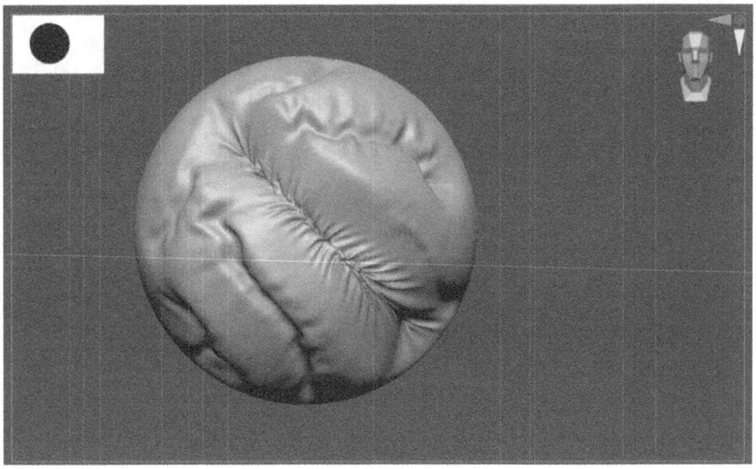

Figure 2-27 *The sculpted object using the **ClothPinchTrail** brush*

ClothPull Brush

The **ClothPull** brush is used to drag the surface of object to control the cloth drapes. To sculpt using this brush, first create a 3D primitive object in the canvas. Make sure the **Edit** button is chosen from the top shelf. Choose the **Geometry** subpalette in the **Tool** Palette and choose the **Dynamic** button. Next, choose the Current Brush button from the left shelf; a flyout containing different sculpting brushes will be displayed. Choose the **ClothPull** brush from this flyout. Now, sculpt on an object using this brush, refer to Figure 2-28.

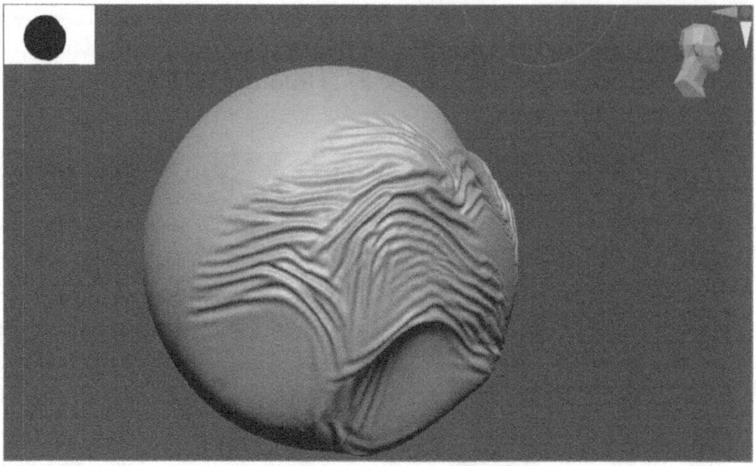

Figure 2-28 *The sculpted object using the* ***ClothPull*** *brush*

ClothSlide Brush

The **ClothSlide** brush is used to create multiple folds on the surface of the object. Hold the ALT key to indent the surface. Figure 2-29 shows the sculpted object using the **ClothSlide** brush.

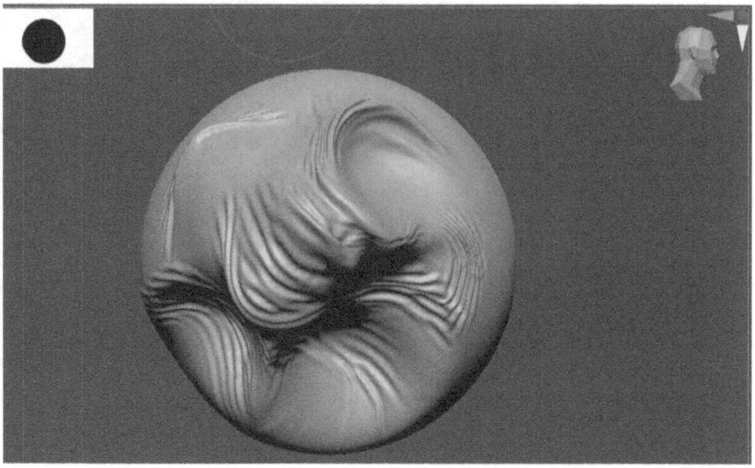

Figure 2-29 *The sculpted object using the* ***ClothSlide*** *brush*

ClothTwister Brush

The **ClothTwister** brush is used to twist the surface of an object in circular motion. Use negative value to twist in the opposite direction. To sculpt using this brush, first create a 3D primitive object in the canvas. Make sure the **Edit** button is chosen from the top shelf. Choose the **Geometry** subpalette in the **Tool** Palette and choose the **Dynamic** button. Next, choose the Current Brush button from the left shelf; a flyout containing different sculpting brushes will be displayed. Choose the **ClothTwister** brush from this flyout. Now, sculpt on an object using this brush, refer to Figure 2-30.

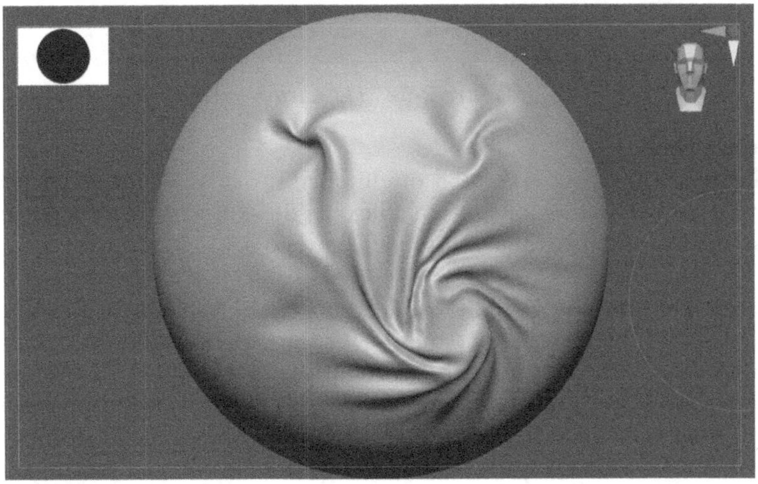

*Figure 2-30 The sculpted object using the **ClothTwister** brush*

ClothWind Brush

The **ClothWind** brush is used to create an effect as if the cloth is being blown on. By using this brush, you can create natural effects on loose fabrics. To sculpt using this brush, first create a 3D primitive object in the canvas. Next, make sure the **Edit** button is chosen from the top shelf. Choose the **Geometry** subpalette in the **Tool** Palette and choose the **Dynamic** button in the **Dynamic Subdiv** area. Next, choose the Current Brush button from the left shelf; a flyout containing different sculpting brushes will be displayed. Choose the **ClothWind** brush from this flyout. Now, sculpt on an object using this brush, refer to Figure 2-31.

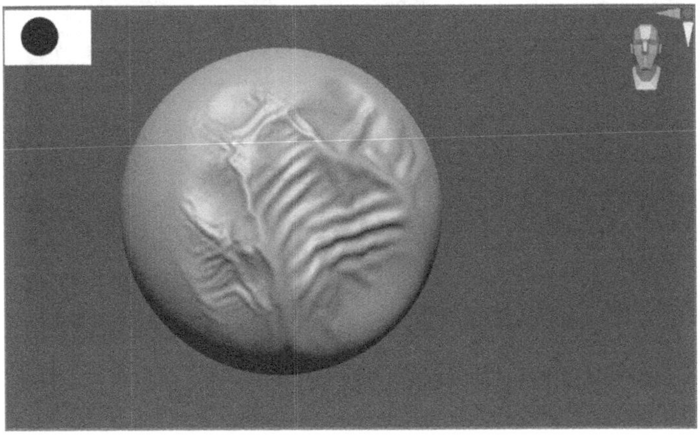

*Figure 2-31 The sculpted object using the **ClothWind** brush*

Clip Brushes

The **Clip** brushes are used to slice a particular area of a 3D model, without deleting the polygons in that model. Instead, these brushes squash and squeeze the polygons, without affecting the number of polygons in an object. There are four types of Clip brushes, namely **ClipCircle**, **ClipCircleCenter**, **ClipCurve**, and **ClipRect**, refer to Figure 2-32. These brushes are discussed next.

*Figure 2-32 The **Clip** brushes*

ClipCircle Brush

The **ClipCircle** brush uses a circular or elliptical stroke as a mask to squeeze the polygons. By using this brush, all the polygons that lie outside of the mask will be pushed to the border of the mask. The resulting object will have hard edges.

To squeeze the polygons of the 3D model, choose the Current Brush button from the left shelf; a flyout containing different sculpting brushes will be displayed. Choose the **ClipCircle** brush from this flyout; a message box prompting you to press CTRL+SHIFT to use this brush will be displayed, refer to Figure 2-33. Choose the **OK** button in this message box. Press and hold CTRL+SHIFT and then drag the cursor on the surface of the sphere; a marquee selection will be displayed, refer to Figure 2-34. Next, release the left mouse button; the shape of the sphere will be modified, as shown in Figure 2-35.

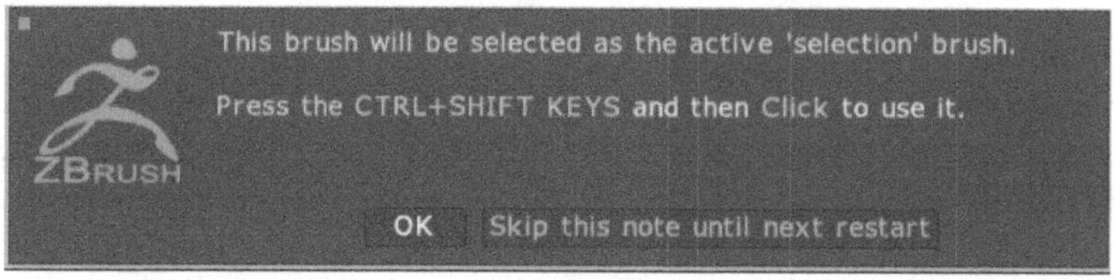

*Figure 2-33 The message box displayed on choosing the **ClipCircle** brush*

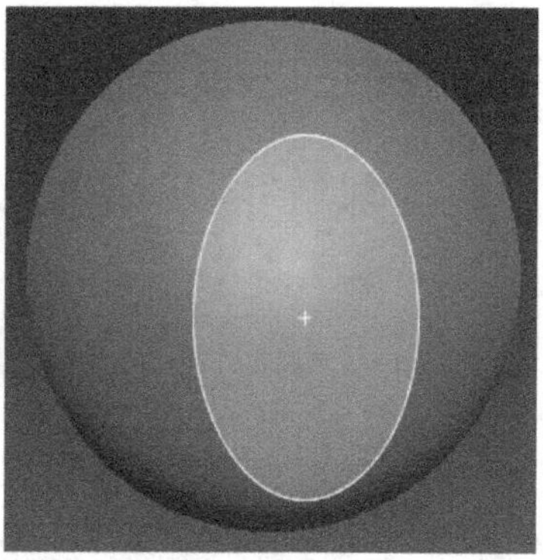

Figure 2-34 A elliptical marquee selection displayed

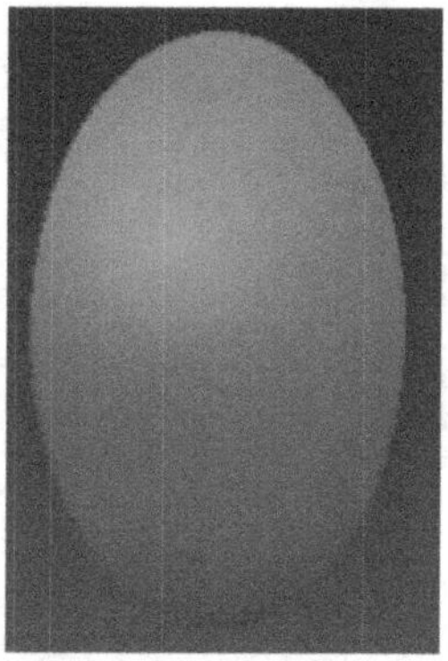

Figure 2-35 The shape of the sphere modified

ClipCircleCenter Brush

The **ClipCircleCenter** brush is similar to the **ClipCircle** brush, with the only difference that the brush stroke creates a perfect circular marquee selection as a mask, with its center point originating from the position where you first clicked and began dragging the cursor, refer to Figure 2-36. Figure 2-37 shows the shape of the sphere modified by using this brush.

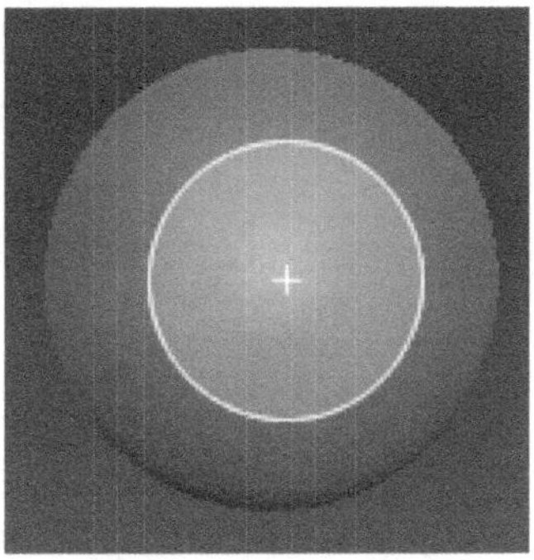

Figure 2-36 *A circular marquee selection displayed*

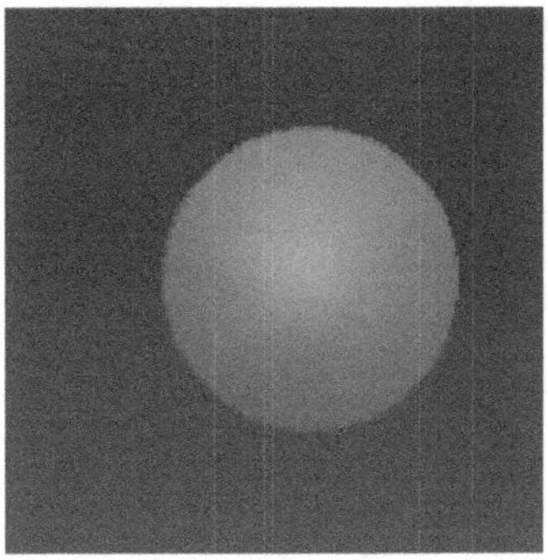

Figure 2-37 *The shape of the sphere modified*

ClipCurve Brush

The **ClipCurve** brush uses curves or straight lines to squeeze in the polygons. To invoke this brush, choose the Current Brush button from the left shelf; a flyout containing different sculpting brushes will be displayed. Choose the **ClipCurve** brush from this flyout; a message box prompting you to press CTRL+SHIFT to use this brush will be displayed. Choose the **OK** button in this message box. Press and hold CTRL+SHIFT and then drag the cursor on the surface of the sphere starting from top to bottom; a straight line with grey highlighted area around it will be displayed on the surface of the sphere, refer to Figure 2-38. Release the left mouse button; the shape of the sphere will be modified, as shown in Figure 2-39.

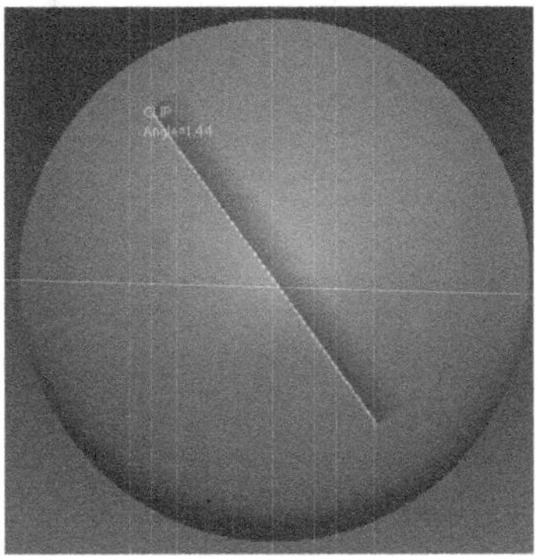

Figure 2-38 *A straight line displayed on the surface of the sphere*

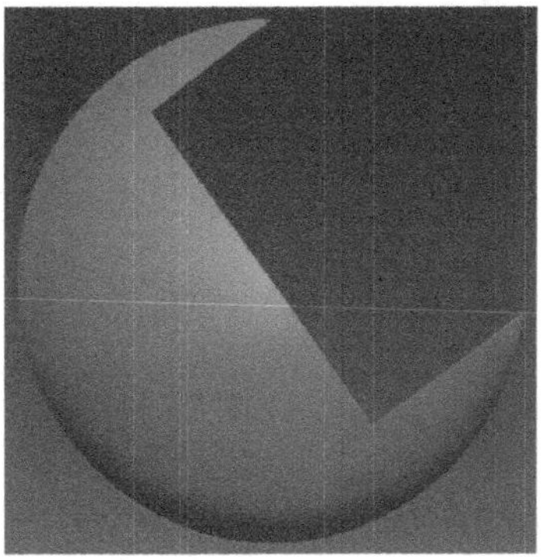

Figure 2-39 *Shape modified by using the **ClipCurve** brush*

You can change the position of the line by pressing SPACEBAR along with CTRL+SHIFT. In Figure 2-39, you will notice that the polygons in the direction of the grey highlighted area will be squeezed toward the line. On pressing the ALT key along with CTRL+SHIFT, a curved line will be created instead of the straight line, refer to Figure 2-40. On releasing the left mouse button, the polygons that are not in the direction of the grey highlighted area will be squeezed in, refer to Figure 2-41.

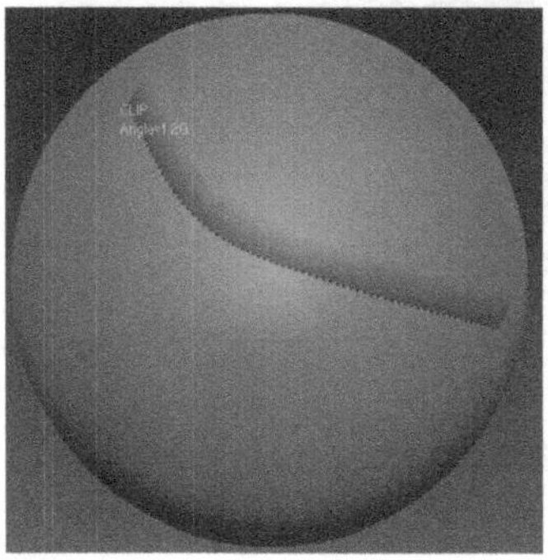

Figure 2-40 *A curved line displayed on the surface of the sphere*

Figure 2-41 *Shape modified by using the* ***ClipCurve*** *brush along with ALT*

ClipRect Brush

The **ClipRect** brush works similar to the **ClipCircle** brush with the only difference that it uses a rectangular marquee selection to squeeze in the polygons, refer to Figures 2-42 and 2-43.

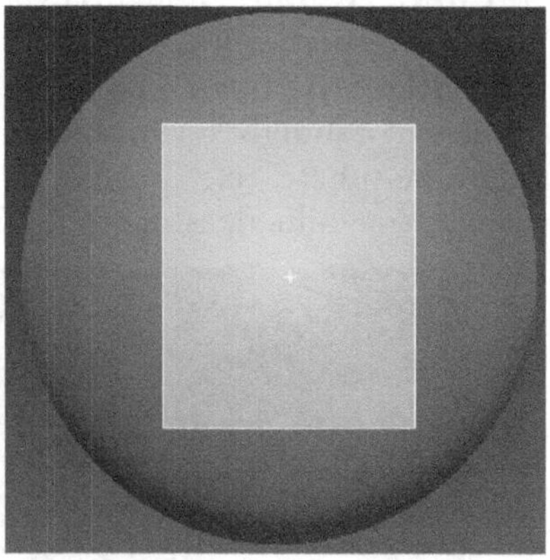

Figure 2-42 *A rectangular marquee selection displayed*

Figure 2-43 *The shape of the sphere modified*

CreaseCurve Brush

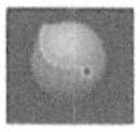

The **CreaseCurve** brush uses straight lines to create a creased edge on the surface of the 3D object. To invoke this brush, choose the Current Brush button from the left shelf; a flyout containing different sculpting brushes will be displayed. Choose the **CreaseCurve** brush from this flyout; a message box prompting you to press CTRL+SHIFT to use this brush will be displayed. Choose the **OK** button in this message box. Press and hold CTRL+SHIFT and then drag the cursor on the surface of the sphere starting from left to right; a straight line with grey highlighted area around it will be displayed on the surface of the sphere, refer to Figure 2-44. Release the left mouse button; the creased edge will be created, refer to Figure 2-45.

Crumple Brush

The **Crumple** brush is used to create creases on the surface of a 3D object, as shown in Figure 2-46. This brush can be used to create wrinkles on skin or clothes.

Figure 2-44 *A straight line with grey area*

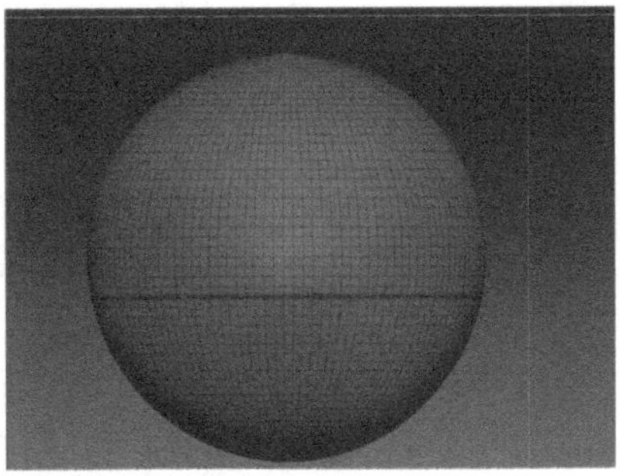

Figure 2-45 *The creased edge created on the sphere*

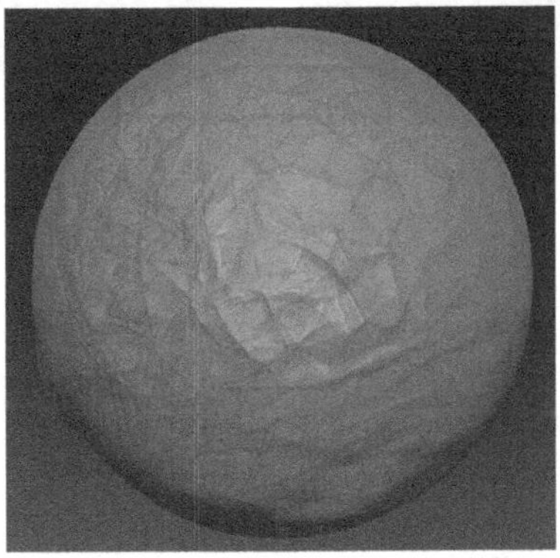

Figure 2-46 *A pattern created using the* ***Crumple*** *brush*

Curve Brushes

There are twenty one types of Curve brushes available in ZBrush, refer to Figure 2-47. Sixteen brushes are in the flyout that is displayed on choosing the Current Brush button and five brushes are placed in the **Brush** tab of the **LightBox** browser. The Curve brushes are used to create different curve patterns on a mesh. Most commonly used curve brushes are discussed next.

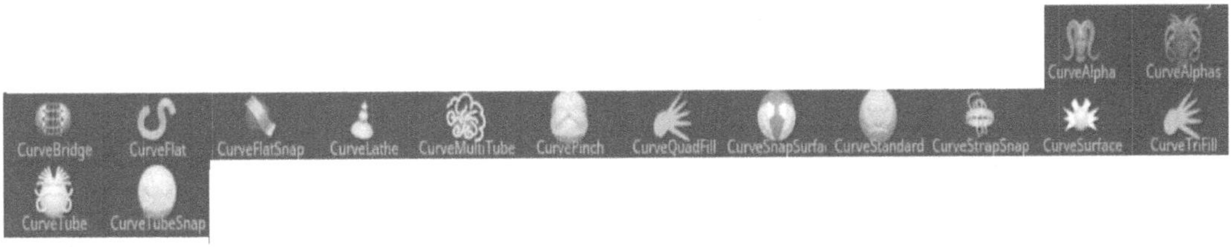

Figure 2-47 *The Curve brushes*

Note

Before using some of the curve brushes, you need to freeze the subdivision levels of the object. This can be done by choosing the ***Del Lower*** *button from the* ***Geometry*** *subpalette of the* ***Tool*** *palette.*

CurveBridge Brush

The **CurveBridge** brush is used to create a bridge geometry between two curves. To sculpt using this brush, choose the Current Brush button from the left shelf; a flyout containing different sculpting brushes will be displayed. Choose the **CurveBridge** brush from this flyout. Create a curve on the first sphere and then create another curve on the second sphere; the bridge geometry will be created between two curves on the surface of the spheres, as shown in Figure 2-48.

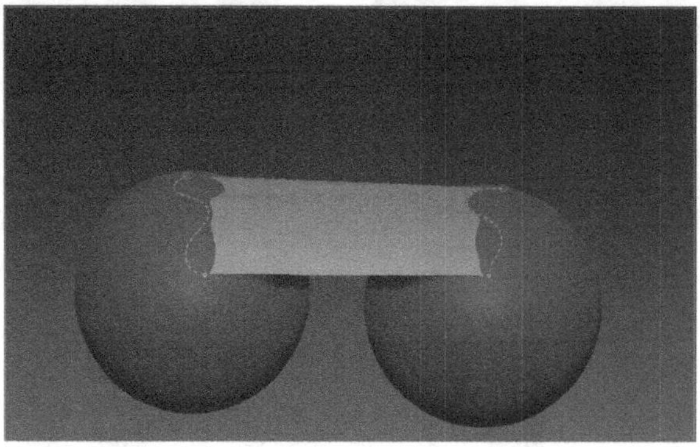

***Figure 2-48** The bridge geometry created between two curves*

CurveLathe Brush

The **CurveLathe** brush is used to create different shapes on the surface of the object. Before using this brush, make sure that the value in the **SDiv** slider is set to 1 or the geometry has not been subdivided. If you use this brush on a mesh which has been subdivided, a message box will be displayed, as shown in Figure 2-49.

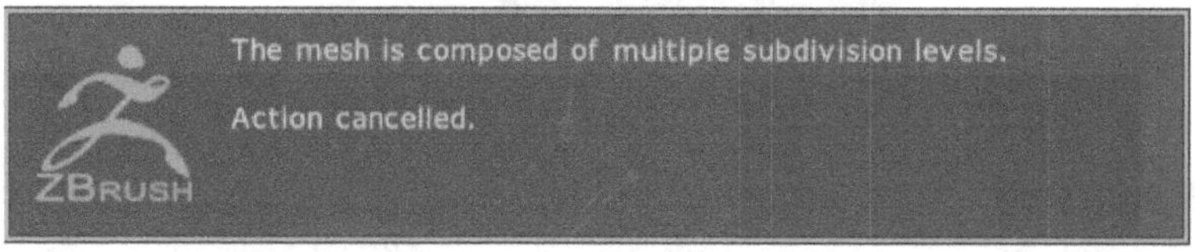

***Figure 2-49** The message box displayed on using the **CurveLathe** brush on a subdivided mesh*

To use this brush, create a plane in the canvas and convert it into polymesh. Choose the Current Brush button from the left shelf; a flyout containing different sculpting brushes will be displayed. Choose the **CurveLathe** brush from this flyout. Next, press and hold the left mouse button, and drag the cursor on the surface of the object to create the shape of your choice; a profile curve indicating the shape of the new mesh will be displayed, refer to Figure 2-50. Now, release the left mouse button; a new mesh will be created on the surface, as shown in Figure 2-51.

You can move, scale, and rotate the newly created mesh by choosing the **Move**, **Scale**, and **Rotate** buttons, respectively from the top shelf. You can also create a duplicate copy of the mesh. To do so, choose the **Move** button from the top shelf. Press and hold the left mouse button and drag the cursor on the surface of the mesh and then release the left mouse button; a line with three circles will be displayed, refer to Figure 2-52. Press and hold the CTRL key and the left mouse button and hover the cursor over the middle circle. Next, drag the cursor toward right; a duplicate copy of the mesh will be created, refer to Figure 2-53.

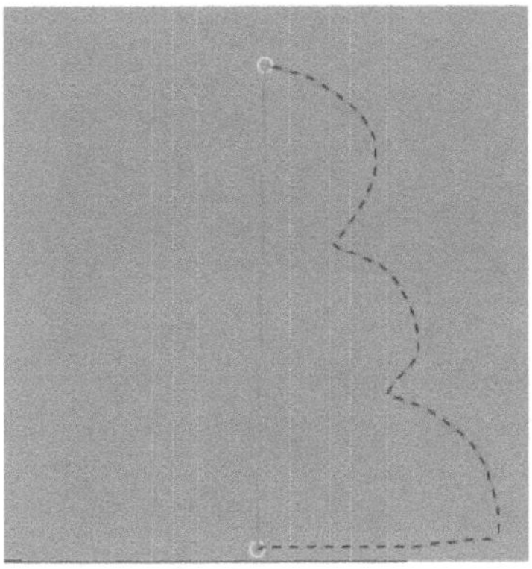

Figure 2-50 A profile curve created on the surface of plane

Figure 2-51 A new mesh created along the profile curve

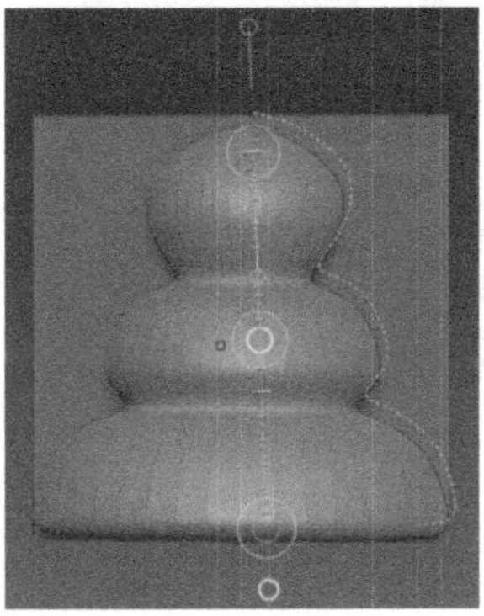

Figure 2-52 A line with three circles displayed

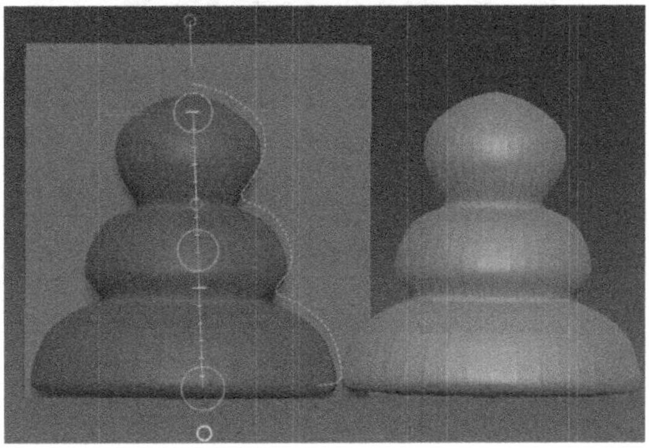

Figure 2-53 The duplicate copy of the mesh created

On creating a new mesh using this brush, you will notice that the color of the plane changes to grey and a mask is applied to it. To remove the mask, press and hold the CTRL key, and drag the cursor in the canvas area. After removing the mask, you cannot move, scale, or rotate the new mesh.

CurveLine Tube Brush

The **CurveLine Tube** brush is used to create a tube on the surface of an object along a straight line, refer to Figure 2-54. This brush does not work on the subdivided geometry. The **CurveLine Tube** brush is located in the **Brush** tab of the **LightBox** browser.

CurveMultiLathe Brush

The **CurveMultiLathe** brush is used to create multiple shapes on the surface of the object by drawing profile curves for different shapes, refer to Figure 2-55. Each of these shapes can be modified as required. This brush does not work on the subdivided geometry. The **CurveMultiLathe** brush is located in the **Brush** tab of **LightBox** browser.

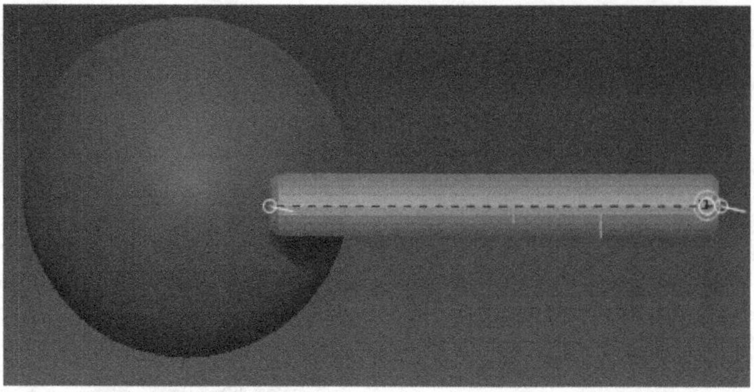

Figure 2-54 A tube created along the straight line

Figure 2-55 Multiple shapes created on the surface of a plane

CurveMultiTube Brush

The **CurveMultiTube** brush is similar to the **CurveTube** brush with the only difference that you can create multiple tubes on the surface of an object, refer to Figure 2-56. The shape of different tubes can be modified as required.

CurvePinch Brush

The **CurvePinch** brush is used to pinch the polygons of a mesh inward along the path defined by you. To sculpt using this brush, press and hold the left mouse button, and drag the cursor on the surface of the object to create the shape of your choice; a curve indicating the path will be displayed. After creating the path, hover the cursor on the surface of the path and click on it; the surface will be pinched along the path, as shown in Figure 2-57. You can modify the shape of the path either by moving the end points of the path created or by clicking on a point or by clicking on a point on the curve and then dragging the cursor.

CurveQuadFill Brush

The **CurveQuadFill** brush is used to create a planar mesh on the surface of an object. To use this brush, choose the Current Brush button from the left shelf; a flyout containing different sculpting brushes will be displayed. Choose the **CurveQuadFill** brush from this flyout. Next, press and hold the left mouse button and drag the cursor to draw an outline for the planar mesh that you want to create, refer to Figure 2-58. Next, release the left mouse button; the planar mesh will be created on the surface of the object, refer to Figure 2-59. The shape of the newly created mesh can be modified by moving different points of the path.

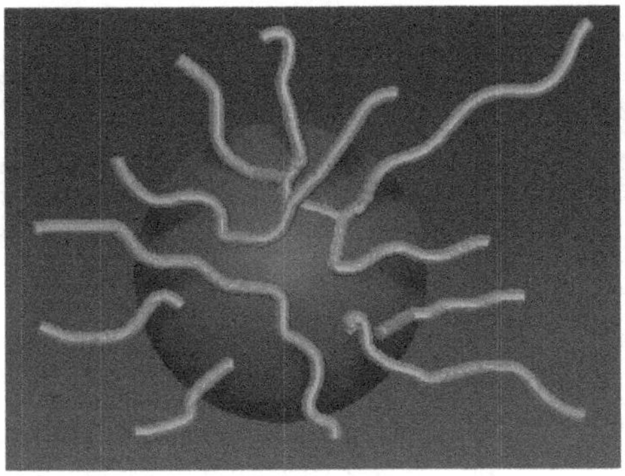

Figure 2-56 Multiple tubes created on the surface of a sphere

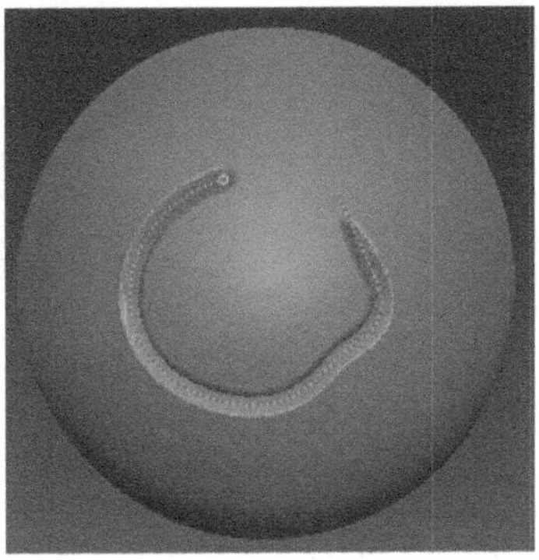

Figure 2-57 The polygons pinched along the path

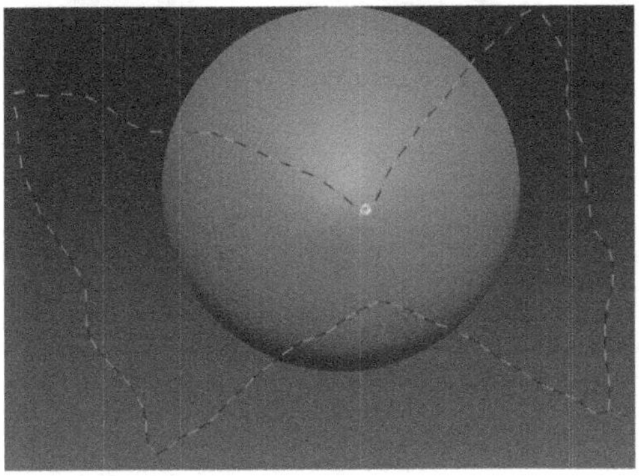

Figure 2-58 An outline drawn on the surface of the sphere

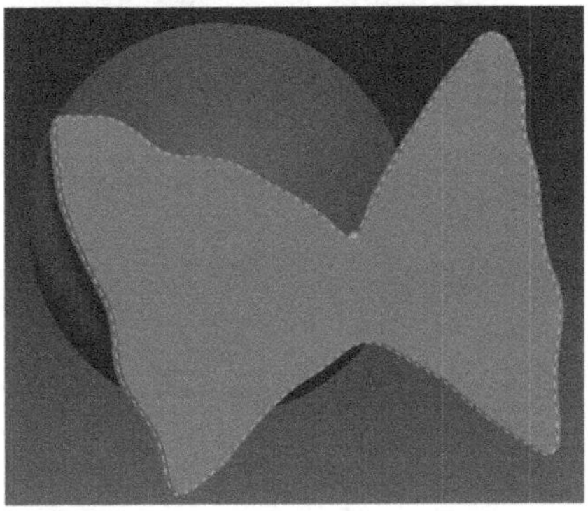

Figure 2-59 A planar mesh created on the surface of the sphere

CurveSnapSurface Brush

The **CurveSnapSurface** brush is used to create surfaces between multiple number of curves created on the surface of the object. To use this brush, choose the Current Brush button from the left shelf; a flyout containing different sculpting brushes will be displayed. Choose the **CurveSnapSurface** brush from this flyout. Next, press and hold the left mouse button and drag the cursor to draw a curve, refer to Figure 2-60. Draw another curve below the curve drawn previously, refer to Figure 2-61; a surface will be created between the two curves. Draw a third curve, refer to Figure 2-62; a surface will be created between the second and third curves. Continue drawing more curves to create the surface, as shown in Figure 2-63. The new surface can be moved by using the **Move** button at the top shelf.

CurveStandard Brush

The **CurveStandard** brush is used to pull out the geometry of an object in a specified path. To sculpt using this brush, press and hold the left mouse button, and drag the cursor on the surface of the object to create the desired shape, refer to Figure 2-64. After creating the path, click on it; a depth will be created along the path, as shown in Figure 2-65.

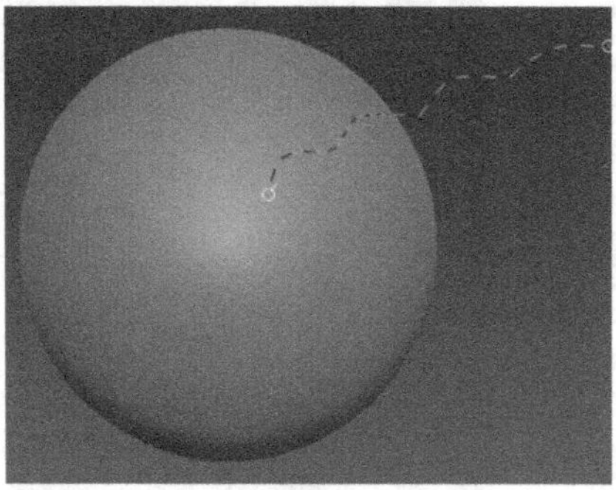

Figure 2-60 *A curve drawn on the surface of the sphere*

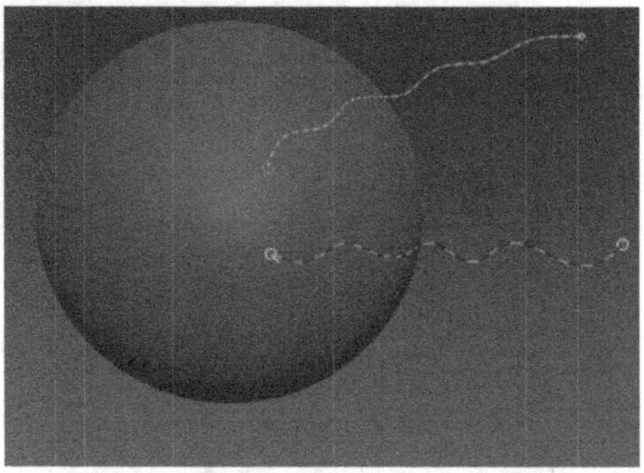

Figure 2-61 *Second curve drawn below the curve drawn previously*

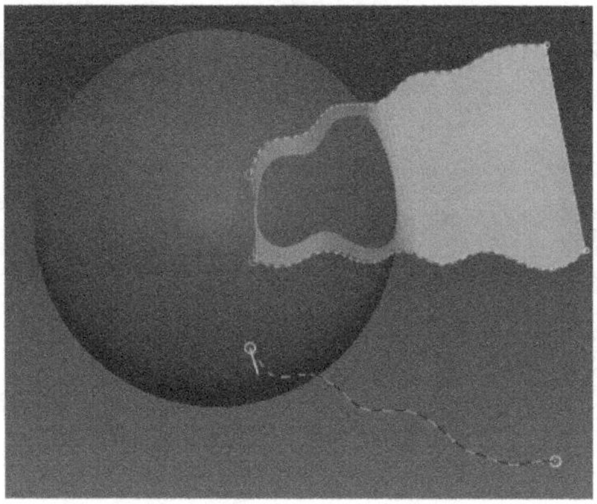

Figure 2-62 *Third curve drawn below the second curve*

Figure 2-63 *A surface created using the* ***CurveSnapSurface*** *brush*

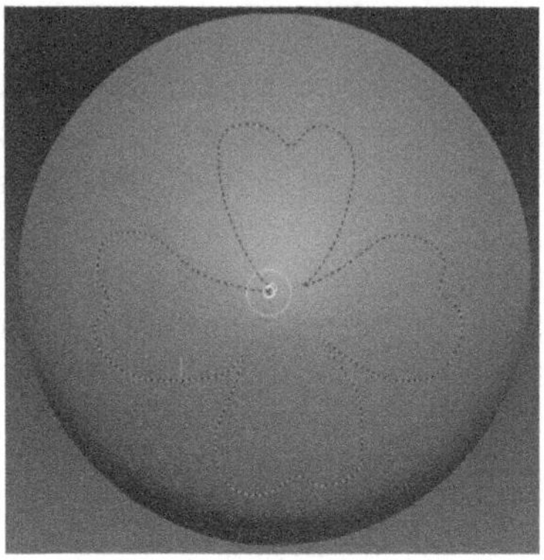

Figure 2-64 *A path created on the surface of the sphere*

Figure 2-65 *The depth created along the path*

CurveStrapSnap Brush

The **CurveStrapSnap** brush is used to create a ribbon like curved surface on an object. To use this brush, choose the Current Brush button from the left shelf; a flyout containing different sculpting brushes will be displayed. Choose the **CurveStrapSnap** brush from this flyout. Next, press and hold the left mouse button and drag the cursor to draw a curve, refer to Figure 2-66. Release the left mouse button; a surface resembling a ribbon will be created along the curve, refer to Figure 2-67.

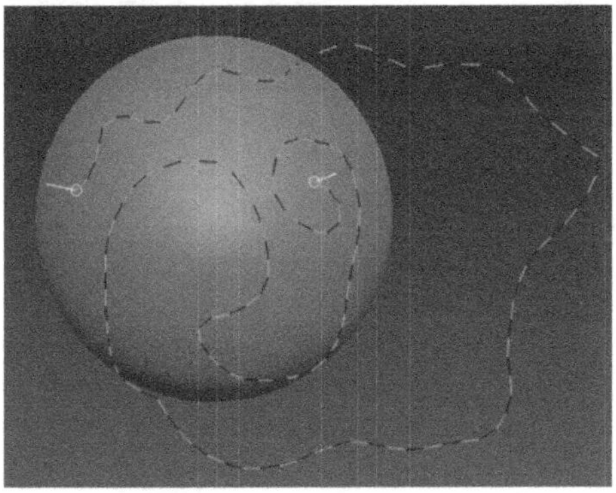

Figure 2-66 *A curve created on the surface of the sphere*

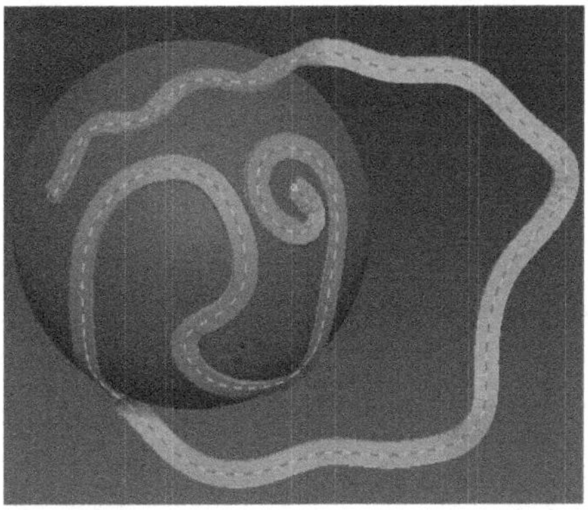

Figure 2-67 *A surface resembling a ribbon created along the curve*

CurveSurface Brush

The **CurveSurface** brush is used to create a new mesh on the surface of an object by drawing curves for the new mesh. This brush is ideal for creating a flowing cloth on the surface of an object or wings on a model. The thickness of the new mesh depends on the value of the **Draw Size** slider located in the top shelf. If the value of this slider is high, the mesh will be thicker. To use this brush on a cube converted into a polymesh, choose the Current Brush button from the left shelf; a flyout containing different sculpting brushes will be displayed. Choose the **CurveSurface** brush from this flyout. Next, press and hold the left mouse button and drag the cursor to draw a curve, refer to Figure 2-68. Draw another curve on the right side of the curve drawn previously, refer to Figure 2-69; the two curves will be snapped, refer to Figure 2-70. Similarly, draw more curves on the surface of the cube; the new mesh will be created on the surface of the cube, refer to Figure 2-71.

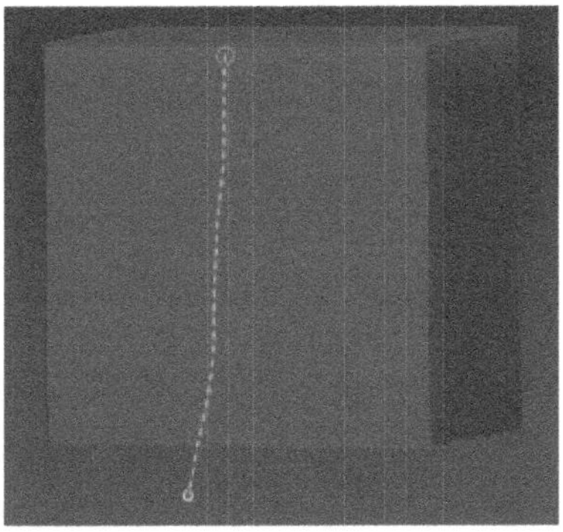

Figure 2-68 *A curve drawn on the surface of the cube*

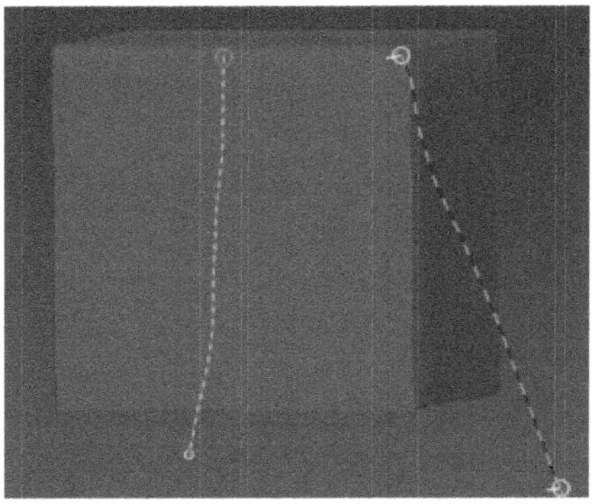

Figure 2-69 *Second curve drawn on the right side of the curve drawn previously*

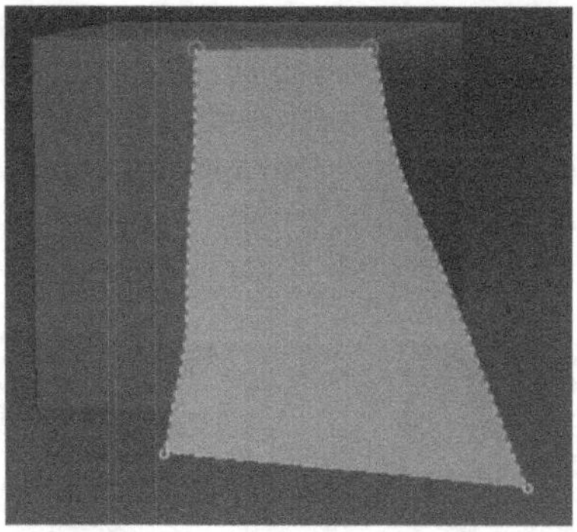

Figure 2-70 The two curves snapped

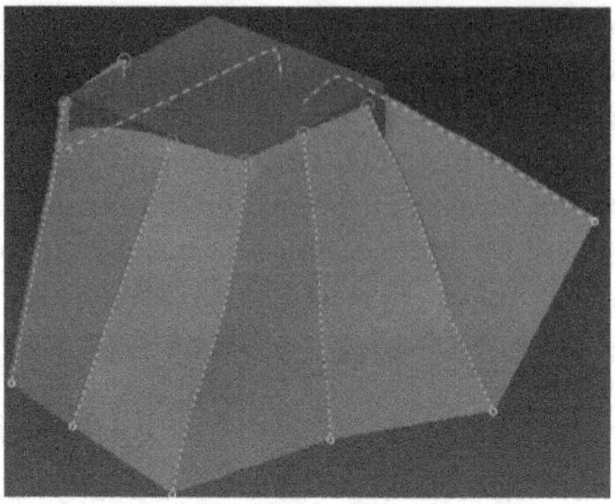

Figure 2-71 A new mesh created on the surface of the cube

CurveTriFill Brush

The **CurveTriFill** brush is used to create a planar surface by drawing an outline on the surface, refer to Figure 2-72.

CurveTube Brush

The **CurveTube** brush is used to create a curved tube on the surface of an object. The shape of the tube can be modified as required, refer to Figure 2-73.

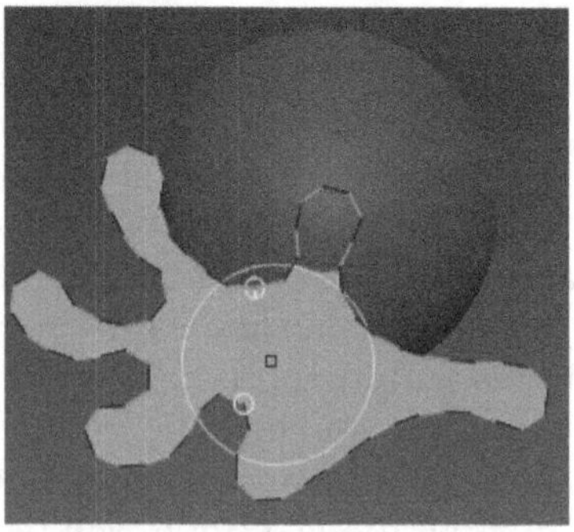

Figure 2-72 *A planar surface created using the **CurveTriFill** brush*

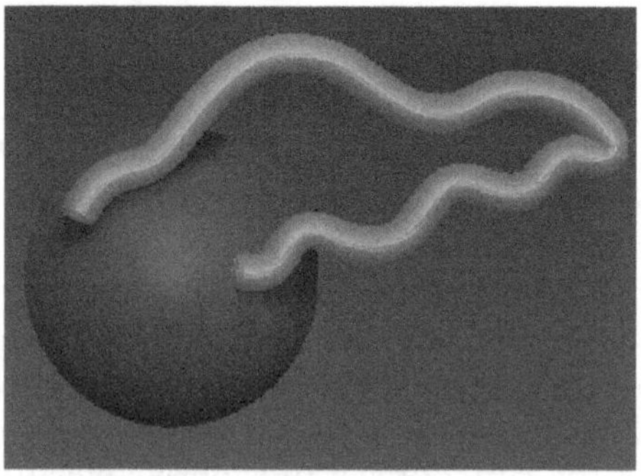

Figure 2-73 *A curved tube created using the **CurveTube** brush*

CurveTubeSnap Brush

The **CurveTubeSnap** brush is similar to the **CurveStrapSnap** brush with the only difference that instead of creating a ribbon like surface, it creates tubes.

Dam_Standard Brush

The **Dam_Standard** brush is used to create very subtle details like wrinkles, clothing seams, machined bevels, and so on. On choosing this brush, the **Zsub** button gets automatically chosen. To use this brush, press and hold the left mouse button, and drag the cursor on the surface of the object; a seam will be created on its surface, refer to Figure 2-74.

Deco1 Brush

The **Deco1** brush is used with different alphas to create detailed decorative designs on an object, refer to Figure 2-75. When this brush is chosen, an alpha gets automatically assigned to it. To sculpt using this brush on a smoothened plane, choose the Current Brush button from the left shelf; a flyout containing different sculpting brushes will be displayed. Choose the **Deco1** brush from this flyout. Adjust the value of the **Draw Size** slider in the top shelf as required. Next, press and hold the left mouse button and drag the cursor slightly at different places on the surface of the plane; a pattern will be created on the surface of the plane, refer to Figure 2-75.

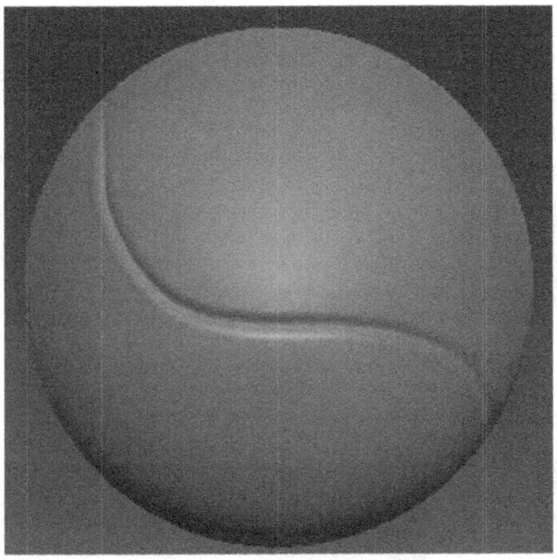

Figure 2-74 *A seam created in the sphere using the* ***Dam_Standard*** *brush*

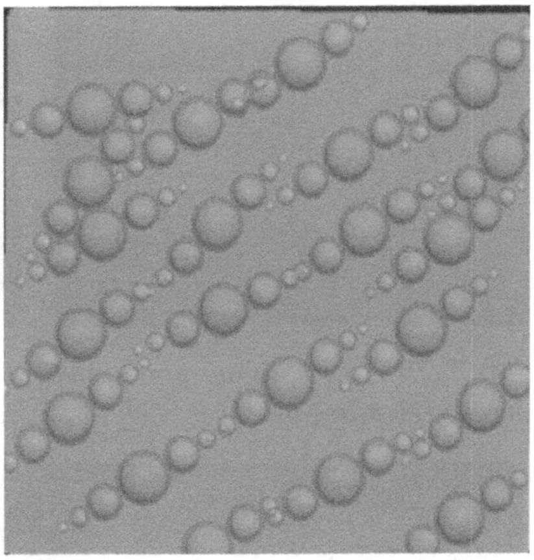

Figure 2-75 *A pattern created on the surface of a plane using the* ***Deco1*** *brush*

Displace Brush

The **Displace** brush is used to pull or push the polygons in a direction perpendicular to the surface of an object. To sculpt using this brush, choose the Current Brush button from the left shelf; a flyout containing different sculpting brushes will be displayed. Choose the **Displace** brush from this flyout. Adjust the value of the **Draw Size** slider as required, and set the value of **Z Intensity** slider to **100**. Next, press and hold the left mouse button, and drag the cursor slightly at different places on the surface of the sphere; the polygons will be pulled out perpendicularly, refer to Figure 2-76. To push the polygons in, you need to choose the **Zsub** button from the top shelf and then drag the cursor at different places, refer to Figure 2-77.

DisplaceCurve Brush

The **DisplaceCurve** brush is used to pull or push the polygons in a direction specified by creating a path curve. To sculpt using this brush, adjust the value of the **Draw Size** slider as required, and set the value of the **Z Intensity** slider to **60**. Next, press and hold the left mouse button and drag the cursor on the surface of the object to create the path curve, refer to Figure 2-78. After creating the path curve, hover the cursor on the surface of the path and click on it; the polygons will be pulled out along the path curve, as shown in Figure 2-79.

*Figure 2-76 The polygons pulled out using the **Displace** brush*

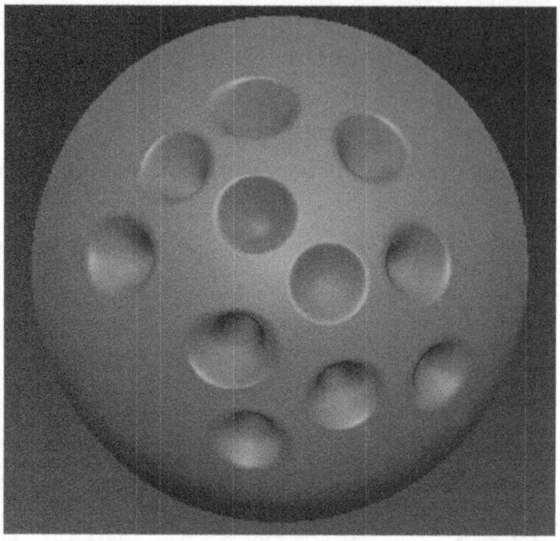

*Figure 2-77 The polygons pushed in using the **Displace** brush*

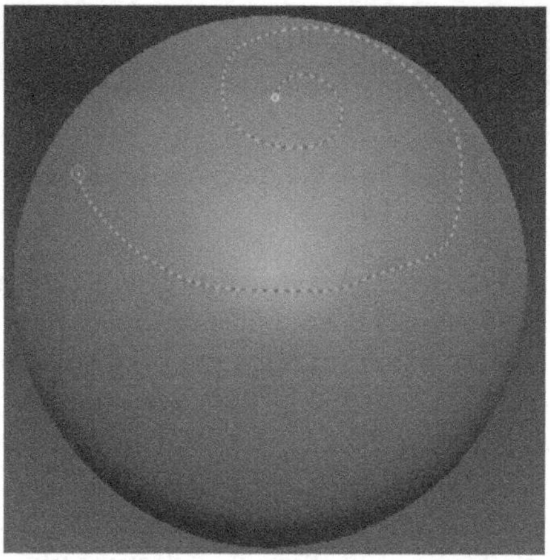

Figure 2-78 The path curve created on the surface of the sphere

Figure 2-79 The polygons pulled out along the path curve

DecoCurve Dots Brush

This brush is used to project the selected alpha along the curve path. This brush has the arrow alpha selected by default. While dragging the curve start and end points, the alpha will leave a trail of sculpted details along its path. You can continue dragging the curve along a new path for further additions or subtractions.

DecoCurveDragDot Brush

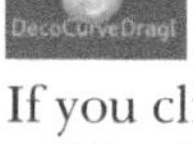

This brush is used to project the alpha along a curve line path. By default, the arrow alpha is selected in this brush also. It draws a curve line on the surface of the model. If you click and drag the ends of the curve line, the projection of a single instance of the alpha will begin along the curve line. It also moves along the mesh surface.

Elastic Brush

The **Elastic** brush is used to displace the polygons of the surface without changing the original shape of an object, refer to Figure 2-80. In Figure 2-80, you will notice that there is deformation in the surface but the original curves in the sphere are retained.

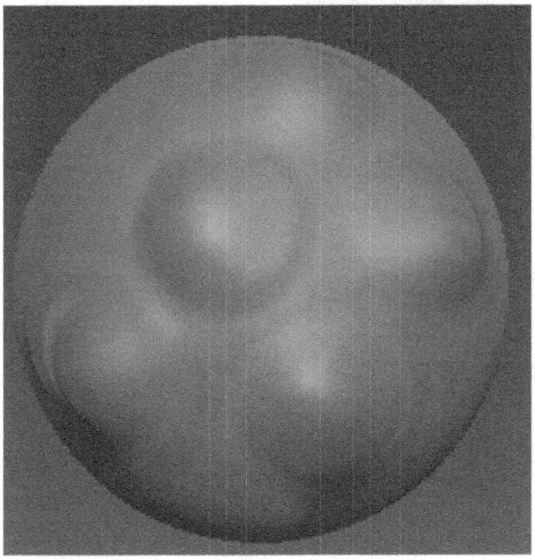

Figure 2-80 The original shape of the sphere maintained

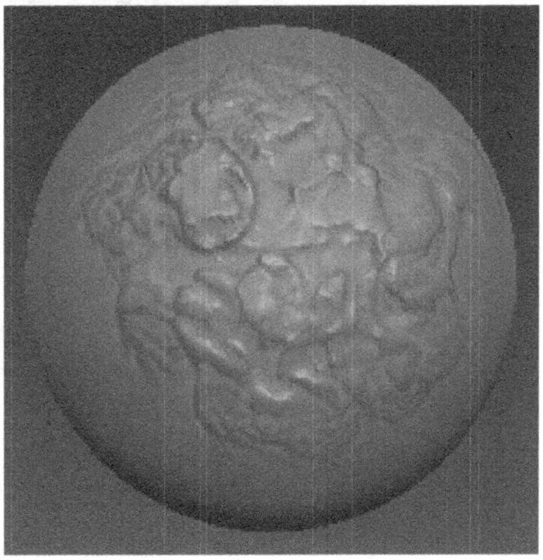

Figure 2-81 Flakes created on the surface of a sphere

Flakes Brush

The **Flakes** brush is used to create roughness on the surface of an object, refer to Figure 2-81. This brush can be used to create rust or flake like effect on a surface, refer to Figure 2-82.

Flatten Brush

The **Flatten** brush is used to flatten the displaced or extruded surface of an object. Figure 2-83 shows a surface on which the **Flakes** brush has been applied and the same surface using the **Flatten** brush on it.

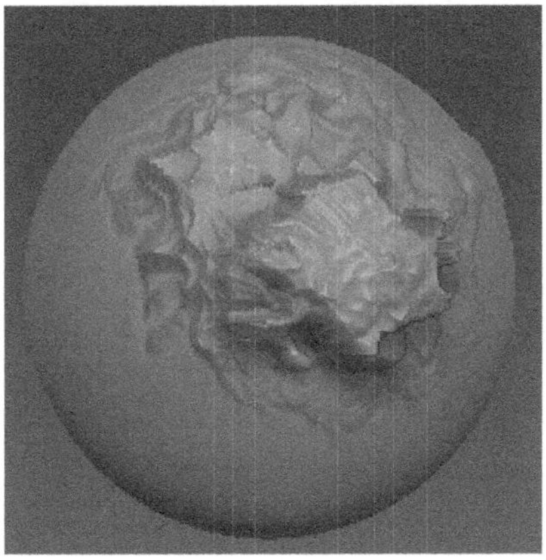

*Figure 2-82 Flakes created on the surface of a sphere using the **Flakes** brush*

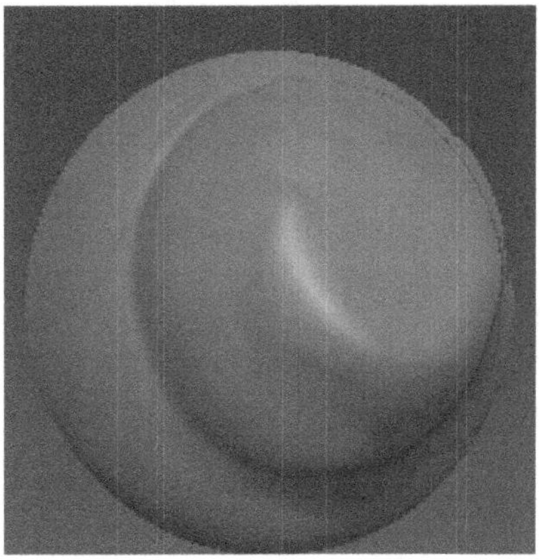

*Figure 2-83 The surface of the sphere flattened using the **Flatten** brush*

Fold Brush

The **Fold** brush is used to fold the polygons inward along the path on which you drag the cursor on the surface of an object, refer to Figure 2-84.

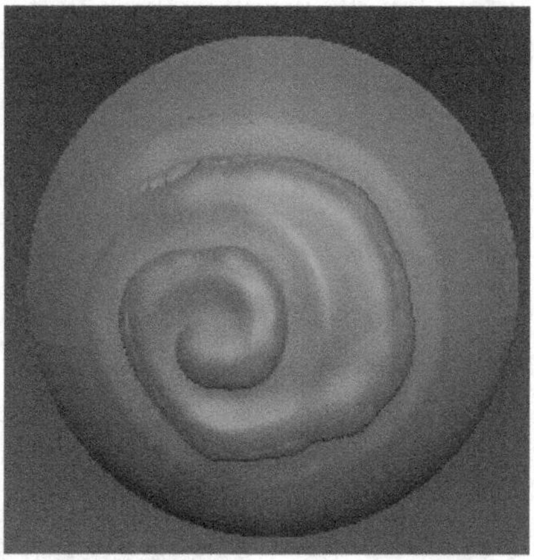

Figure 2-84 *Folds created on the surface of a sphere*

FormSoft Brush

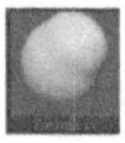

The **FormSoft** brush is used to create smooth displacement in the surface of an object.

Fracture Brush

The **Fracture** brush is used to make the surface of an object disordered and uneven. This brush is best suited for creating rocky surfaces or crystals.

Groom Brushes

The Groom brushes are used to sculpt the **FiberMesh** in ZBrush. The **FiberMesh** is mainly used to create hair on the surface of an object. It is also used to generate different types of fibers, fur, plants, flowers, and so on. The **FiberMesh** option can be accessed from the **Tool** palette.

The Groom brushes have been designed specifically for the **FiberMesh**. These brushes are used to edit fibers in the mesh to create different patterns and hairstyles. There are sixteen types of Groom Brushes, refer to Figure 2-85. These brushes will be discussed in detail in the Chapter 4.

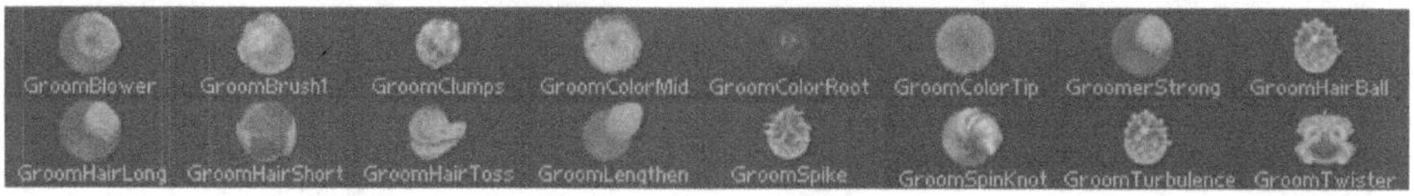

Figure 2-85 *The Groom brushes*

hPolish Brush

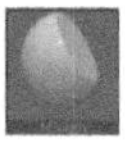

The term **hPolish** stands for hard polish. The **hPolish** brush is used to displace the surface of an object inward, so that the resulting surface has sharp and well defined edges, as shown in Figure 2-86.

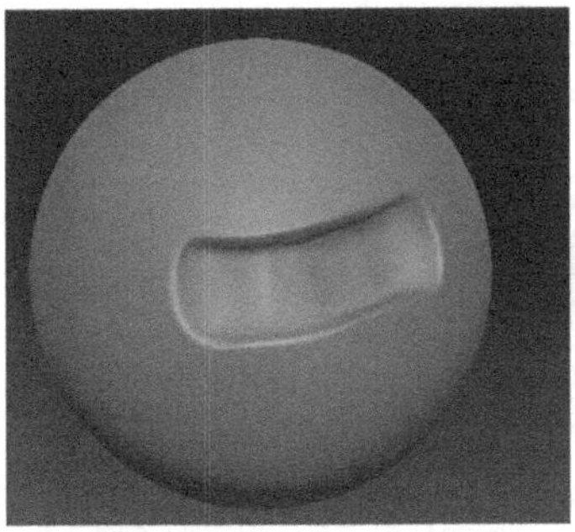

*Figure 2-86 Surface of the sphere modified by using the **hPolish** brush*

Hatch Brush

The **Hatch** brush is used to apply sculpting strokes on the object without picking up cursor. But this brush will add or subtract strokes in the forward direction. This functionality makes it easy to apply sculpting strokes in a sketch-like design, refer to Figure 2-87.

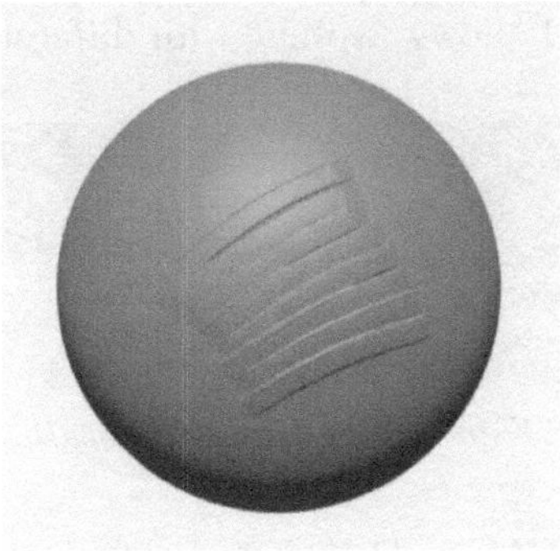

*Figure 2-87 Surface of the sphere modified by using the **Hatch** brush*

History Recall Brush

The **HistoryRecall** brush is used to capture the depth position of a model's sculpted details by using the Undo History timeline with history bar, refer to Figure 2-88. You can then project those details onto a completely different model by using the brush strokes.

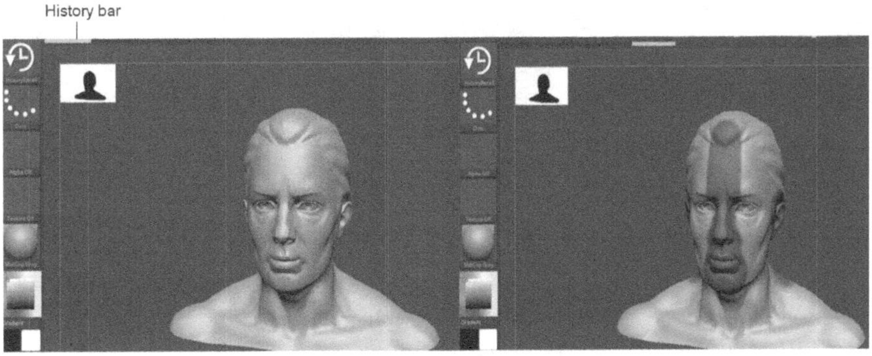

*Figure 2-88 Using the **HistoryRecall** brush*

HatchBacktrack Brush

The **HatchBacktrack** brush is used to create a ramp effect in the sculpted details, as shown in Figure 2-89.

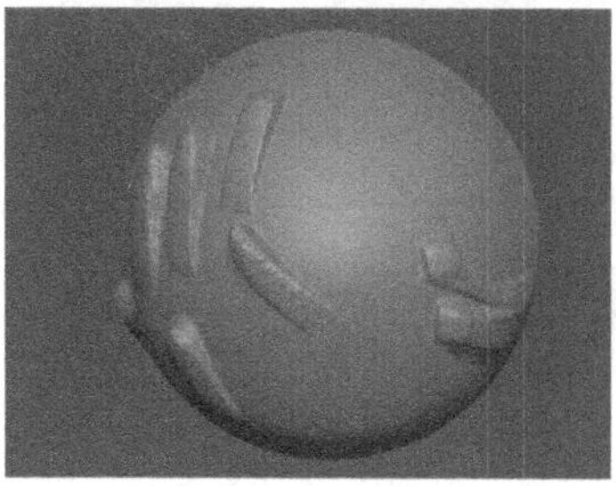

Figure 2-89 *Surface of the sphere modified by using the* ***HatchBacktrack*** *brush*

IMM Brushes

The term IMM stands for Insert Multi Mesh. The IMM brushes are used to insert different types of objects into an already existing geometry. There are eighteen types of IMM brushes, refer to Figure 2-90. Figure 2-91 shows a sphere with different types of objects inserted into it using IMM brushes.

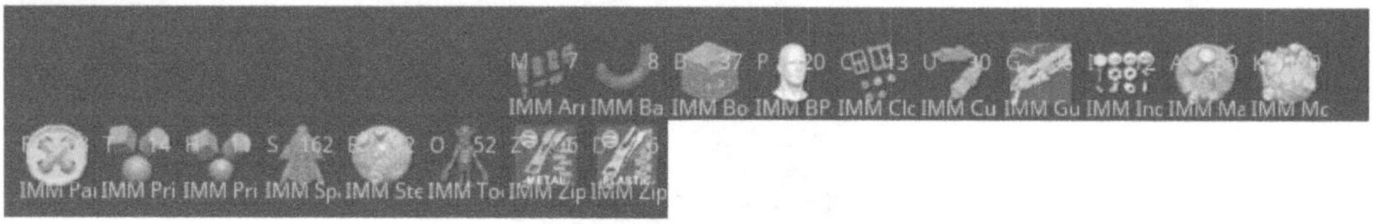

Figure 2-90 *The IMM brushes*

Before using some of the ***IMM*** *brushes, you need to freeze the subdivision levels of the object. This can be done by choosing the* ***Del Lower*** *button from the* ***Geometry*** *subpalette of the* ***Tool*** *palette.*

Inflat Brush

The **Inflat** brush is used to expand the surface of an object by a significant amount by pulling the polygons in a direction perpendicular to the surface, refer to Figure 2-92.

Figure 2-91 *Different objects inserted into a sphere using IMM brushes*

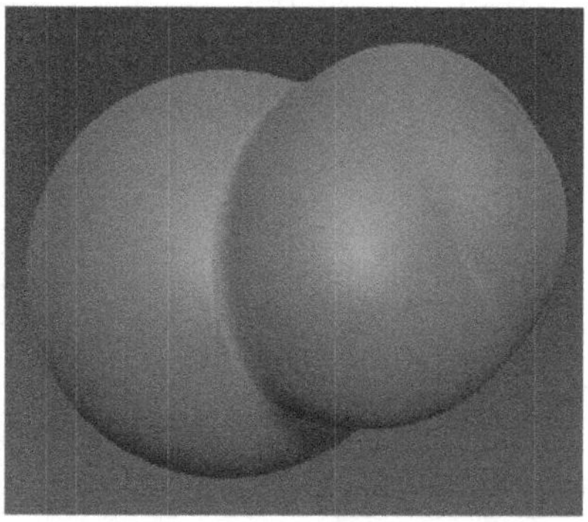

Figure 2-92 *Surface of the sphere expanded by using the* ***Inflat*** *brush*

Insert Brushes

The Insert brushes are used to insert different geometrical shapes like cube, sphere, cylinder, and so on, into an already existing geometry. There are ten types of Insert brushes. One Insert brush is available in the flyout displayed on choosing the Current Brush button and rest of the brushes are in the **Brush** tab of the **LightBox** browser, refer to Figures 2-93a and 2-93b. Figure 2-94 shows different shapes inserted into a sphere using these brushes. These brushes work only when the geometry has not been subdivided.

Figure 2-93 a *The Insert brushes*

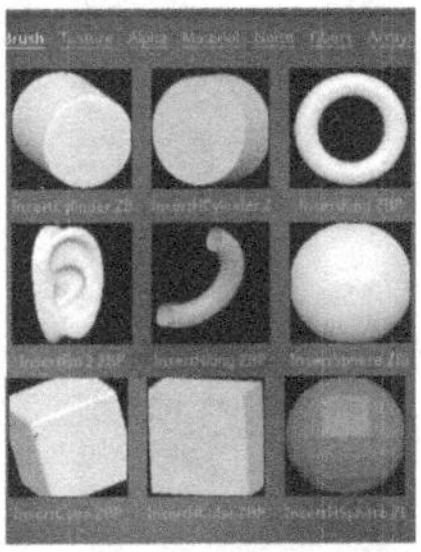

Figure 2-93 b *The Insert brushes in the* ***Brush*** *tab of the* ***LightBox*** *browser*

Figure 2-94 *Different shapes inserted into a sphere using the insert brushes*

Knife Brushes

In ZBrush 2022, four knife brushes are added namely: **KnifeCircle**, **KnifeCurve**, **KnifeLasso**, and **KnifeRect**. All these brushes are used to accurately create a cut along the mesh with a specific stroke. As the name of these brushes suggest, the **KnifeCircle** brush uses circular stroke, the **KnifeCurve** brush uses curve stroke, **KnifeLasso** brush uses lasso stroke, and the **KnifeRect** brush uses rectangular stroke.

You need to press CTRL+ SHIFT keys after selecting a specific knife brush and then apply the strokes. Also, in case of the **KnifeCurve** brush, you need to press ALT key as many times as you want to change the curvature of the curve drawn on the mesh.

Figures 2-95 through 2-98 show the cuts created on the sphere using these brushes. Note that the mesh created by using these brushes is a quad mesh so that it can be sculpted easily. Also, you can use the symmetry options in the **Transform** Palette to create symmetrical shapes using these brushes. It is important to note that knife brushes cannot cut holes through the center of mesh.

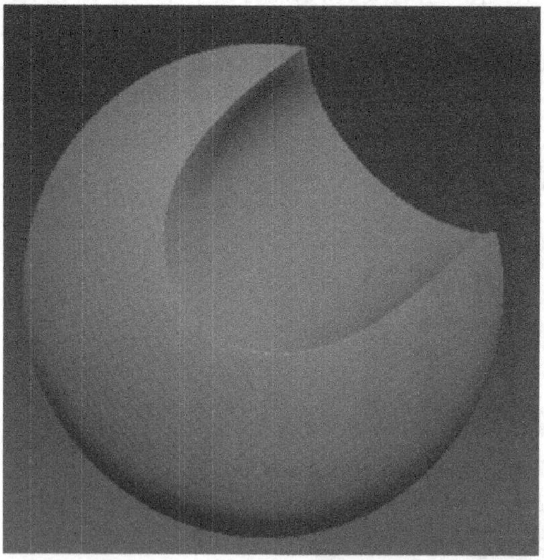

Figure 2-95 *Cut created using the **KnifeCircle** brush*

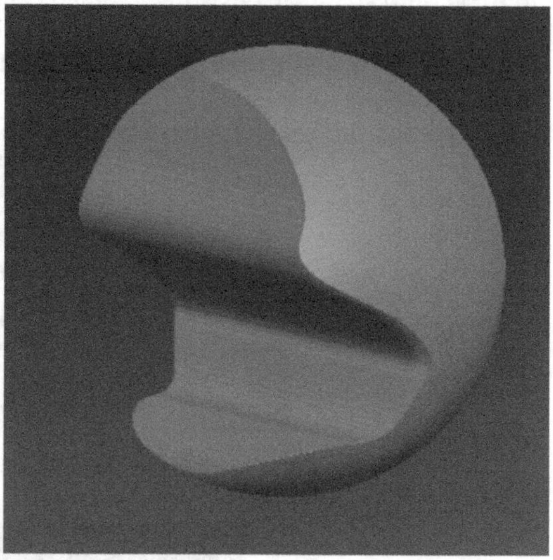

Figure 2-96 *Cut created using the **KnifeCurve** brush*

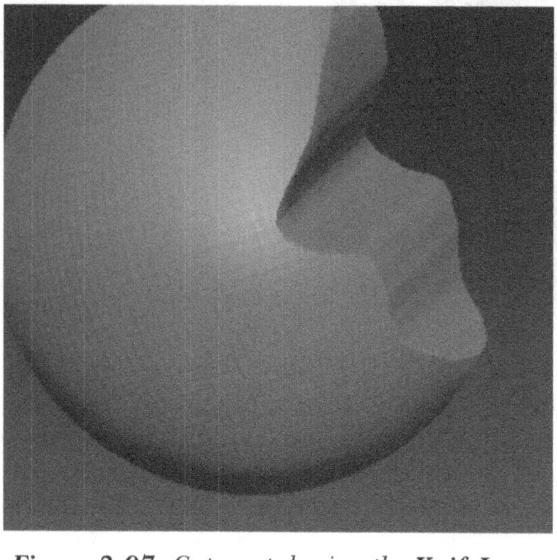

Figure 2-97 *Cut created using the **KnifeLasso** brush*

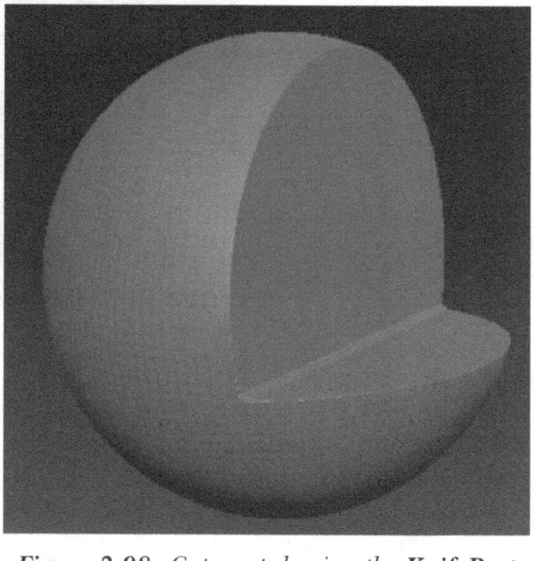

Figure 2-98 *Cut created using the **KnifeRect** brush*

Layer Brush

The **Layer** brush raises or lowers the surface of an object by a fixed amount depending on the value of **Z Intensity**. Using this brush, the depth of displacement remains constant throughout the surface of an object, without any overlapping strokes, refer to Figure 2-99.

Figure 2-99 *Constant displacement created using the* ***Layer*** *brush*

LayeredPattern Brush

The **LayeredPattern** brush is used to create different patterns on the surface of an object, refer to Figure 2-100. On choosing this brush, an alpha is automatically assigned to it. The depth of the pattern created on the surface remains constant throughout the surface.

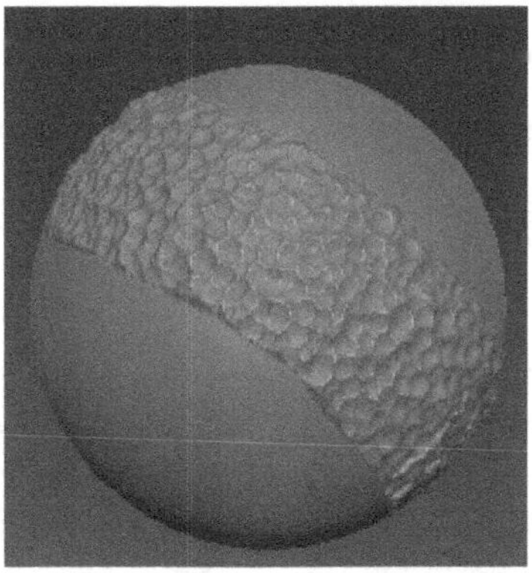

Figure 2-100 *A pattern created using the* ***LayeredPattern*** *brush*

Magnify Brush

The **Magnify** brush produces significant displacement on the surface of an object. The amount of magnification is determined by the value of the **Z Intensity** slider.

Mask Brushes

The Mask brushes are used to isolate a certain region of an object. If a particular area is masked on a surface, you cannot make any changes in that area. The unmasked area can be modified without affecting the masked area. There are eight types of Mask brushes, namely **MaskCircle**, **MaskCurve**, **MaskCurvePen**, **MaskLasso**, **MaskPen**, **MaskPerfectCirc**, **MaskSquare**, and **MaskRect**, refer to Figure 2-101.

Figure 2-101 *The mask brushes*

The **MaskCircle** brush uses a circular stroke to create a mask. The circular area that comes under the mask cannot be sculpted or modified. To use this brush, choose the Current Brush button from the left shelf; a flyout containing different sculpting brushes will be displayed. Choose the **MaskCircle** brush from the flyout; a message box will be displayed prompting you to press the CTRL key to use this brush, refer to Figure 2-102.

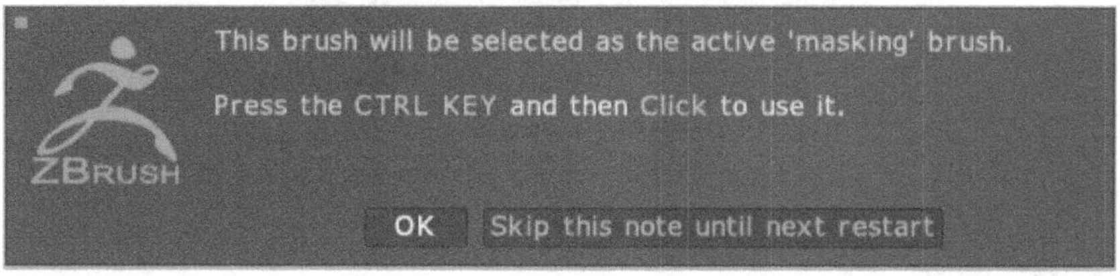

Figure 2-102 *The message box displayed on choosing the* ***MaskCircle*** *brush*

Choose the **OK** button to close this message box. Next, press and hold the CTRL key and drag the cursor on the surface of the sphere; a marquee selection will be displayed, refer to Figure 2-103. Next, release the left mouse button; a grey colored circular mask will be created on the surface of the sphere, as shown in Figure 2-104. You can also invert the mask by pressing CTRL+I.

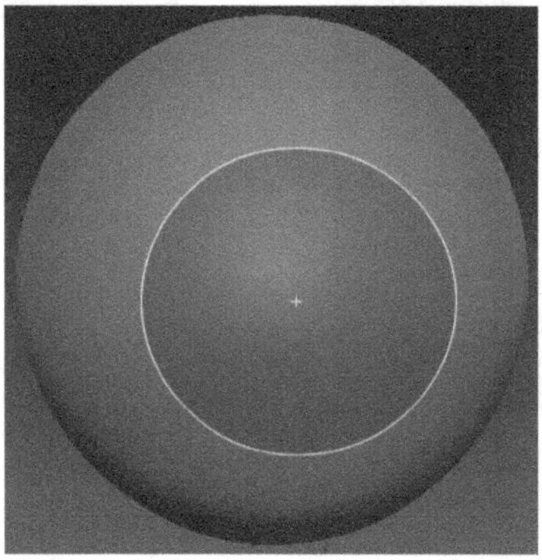

Figure 2-103 *A circular marquee selection displayed*

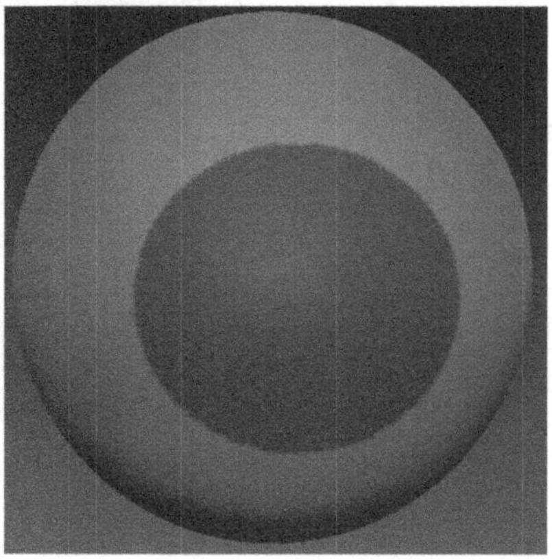

Figure 2-104 *A circular mask created on the surface of the sphere*

The **MaskCurve** brush uses curves or straight lines to create a mask on the surface of an object. To use this brush, choose the Current Brush button from the left shelf; a flyout containing different sculpting brushes will be displayed. Choose the **MaskCurve** brush from this flyout; a message box will be displayed prompting you to press the CTRL key to use this brush. Choose the **OK** button in this message box.

Next, press and hold the CTRL key and then drag the cursor on the surface of the sphere starting from top to bottom; a straight line with grey highlighted area will be displayed on the surface of the sphere, refer to Figure 2-105. Next, release the left mouse button; a mask will be created on the surface of the sphere, as shown in Figure 2-106.

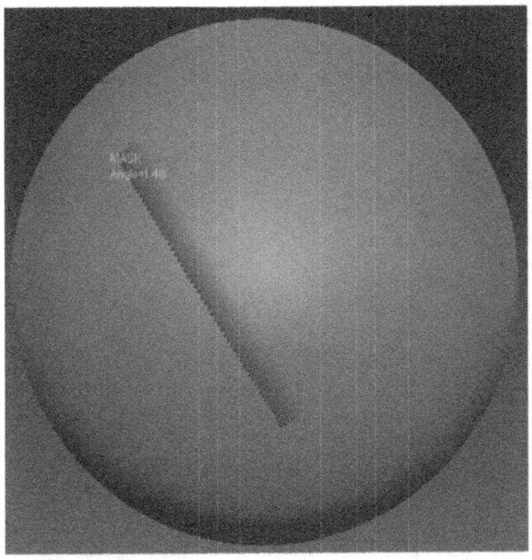

Figure 2-105 *A straight line displayed on the surface of the sphere*

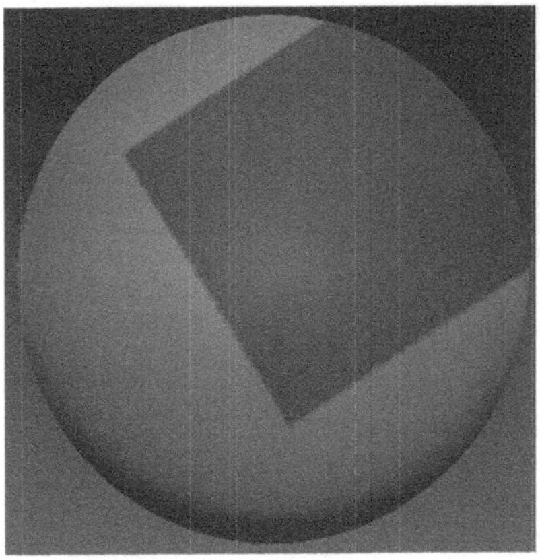

Figure 2-106 *A mask created on the surface of the sphere*

The **MaskCurvePen** brush is used to create a mask along the curve path. To sculpt using this brush, press and hold the CTRL key and drag the cursor on the surface of the sphere to create a curve path of your choice, refer to Figure 2-107. After creating the path, make sure the CTRL key is pressed, and then click on the path; a mask will be created along the path, as shown in Figure 2-108.

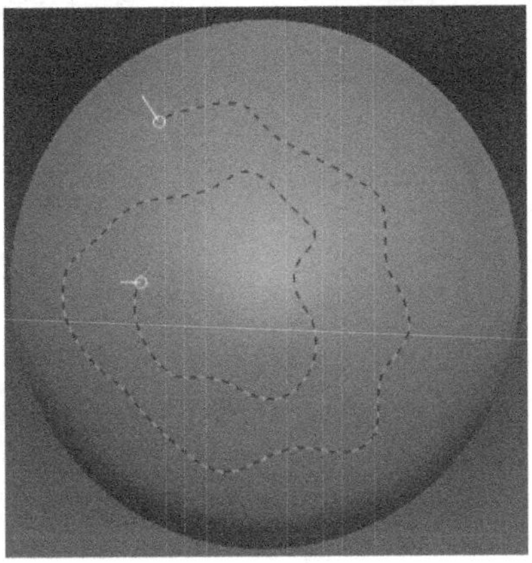

Figure 2-107 *A path curve created on the surface of the sphere*

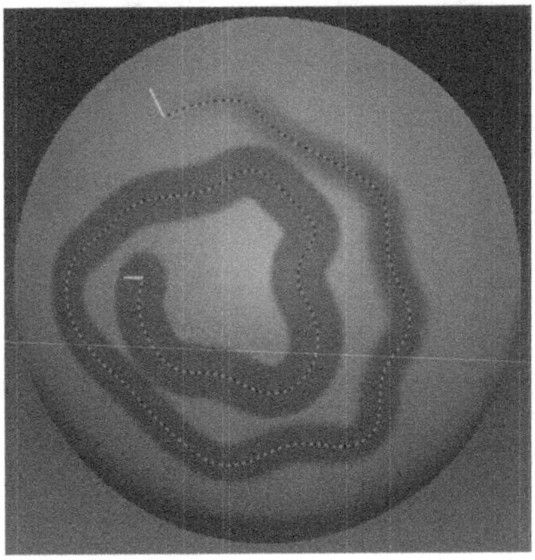

Figure 2-108 *A mask created along the path curve*

The **MaskLasso** brush is used to create freeform masks on the surface of an object using a mask overlay, refer to Figure 2-109. The **MaskPen** brush is used to draw a mask of any desired shape using a free hand, refer to Figure 2-110. It gives you the feel of working with a pen. The **MaskRect** brush is similar to **MaskCircle** brush with the only difference that it uses a rectangular stroke as a mask.

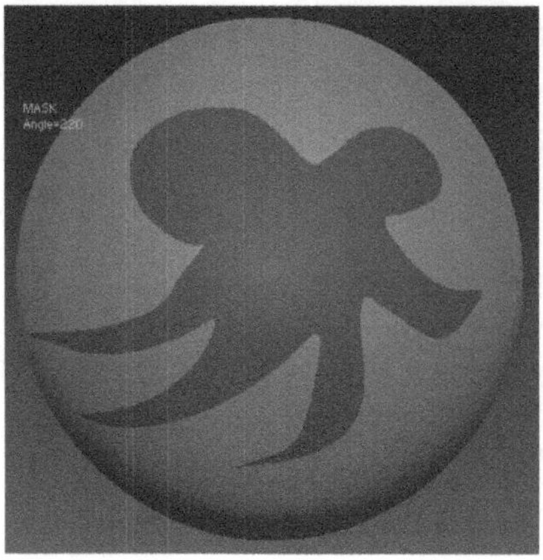

Figure 2-109 *A freeform mask created using the mask overlay*

Figure 2-110 *A mask drawn with freehand using the* ***MaskPen*** *brush*

You can remove a mask from a particular area of the mask by pressing CTRL+ALT and then by dragging the cursor on that particular area, refer to Figures 2-111 and 2-112. To remove the entire mask from a surface, press and hold the CTRL key and then drag the cursor on the canvas area. You can also use different alpha images to create masks on the surface of an object.

Figure 2-111 *A mask created using the* ***MaskPen*** *brush*

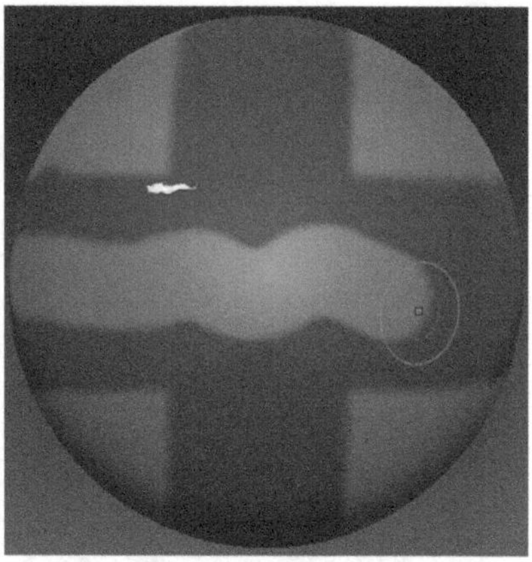

Figure 2-112 *An area of the mask removed*

MatchMaker Brush

The **MatchMaker** brush is used to fit one mesh into the contours of another mesh. For example, if you have modelled a human face and a mask separately, then you can fit the mask into the contours of a face by pressing and holding the left mouse button and by dragging the cursor on the surface of the mask.

MeshInsert Dot Brush

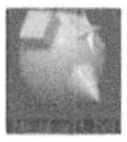

The **MeshInsert Dot** brush is used to insert one 3D object into another. To use this brush, choose the Current Brush button from the left shelf; a flyout containing different sculpting brushes will be displayed. Choose the **MeshInsert Dot** brush from the flyout. Next, choose the **Brush** palette to expand it. In this palette, choose the **Modifiers** subpalette, refer to

Figure 2-113. Next, choose the **MeshInsert Preview** button; a flyout will be displayed, refer to Figure 2-114. From the **3D Meshes** area of this flyout, choose the required primitive. Next, press and hold the left mouse button and drag the cursor on the surface of the sphere; the chosen primitive will be created on the surface of the sphere, refer to Figure 2-115. You can insert more primitives into the sphere by choosing the **MeshInsert Preview** button again, refer to Figure 2-116.

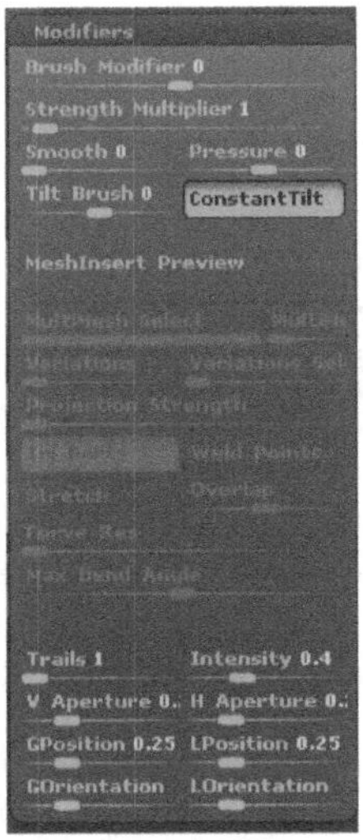

*Figure 2-113 The **Modifiers** subpalette in the **Brush** palette*

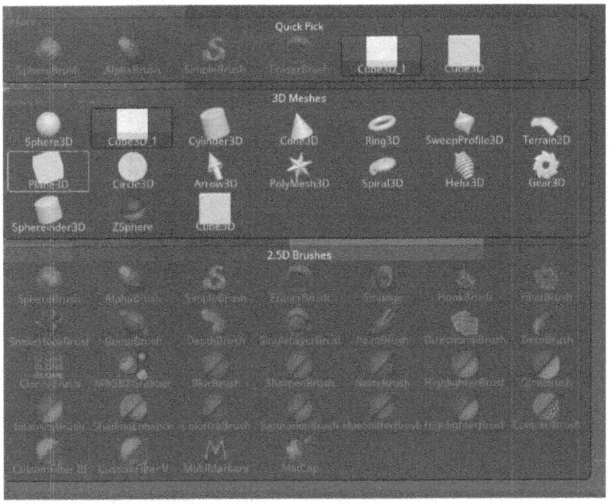

*Figure 2-114 The flyout displayed on choosing the **MeshInsert Preview** button*

Figure 2-115 A cube created on the surface of the sphere

Figure 2-116 Different types of primitives inserted on the surface of the sphere

Note

*Before using the **MeshInsert Dot** brush, make sure that the value of the **SDiv** slider is 1. This can be done by choosing the **Del Lower** button from the **Geometry** subpalette of the **Tool** palette.*

Morph Brush

The **Morph** brush is used to apply the saved modification to a 3D object. This modified state of the model is known as morph. To use this brush, choose the Current Brush button from the left shelf; a flyout containing different sculpting brushes will be displayed. Choose the **ClayBuildup** brush from this flyout. Press and hold the left mouse button and drag the cursor on the surface of the sphere to create a pattern of your choice, refer to Figure 2-117. Next, in the **Tool** palette, expand the **Morph Target** subpalette, refer to Figure 2-118. Now, choose the **StoreMT** button in this subpalette; the current state of the sphere will be stored.

***Figure 2-117** A pattern created using the **ClayBuildup** brush*

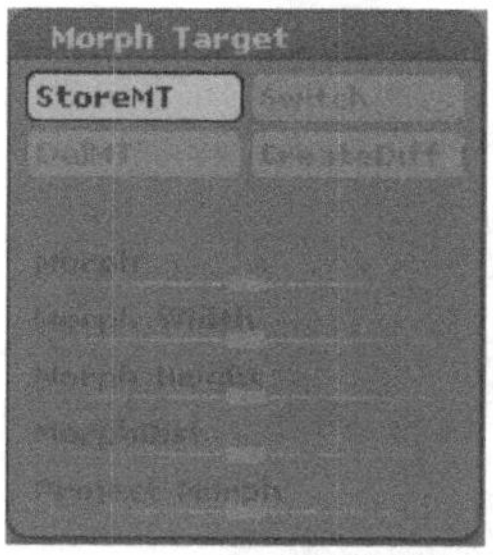

***Figure 2-118** The **Morph Target** subpalette in the **Tool** palette*

Choose the Current Brush button from the left shelf; a flyout containing different sculpting brushes will be displayed. Choose the **ClayTubes** brush from this flyout, and then press and hold the left mouse button and drag the cursor on the surface of the sphere to create another pattern on the existing pattern, refer to Figure 2-119. Next, choose the **Morph** brush and then press and hold the left mouse button, and drag the cursor on the surface of the sphere, refer to Figure 2-120; the pattern created earlier will be displayed again and the new pattern will disappear.

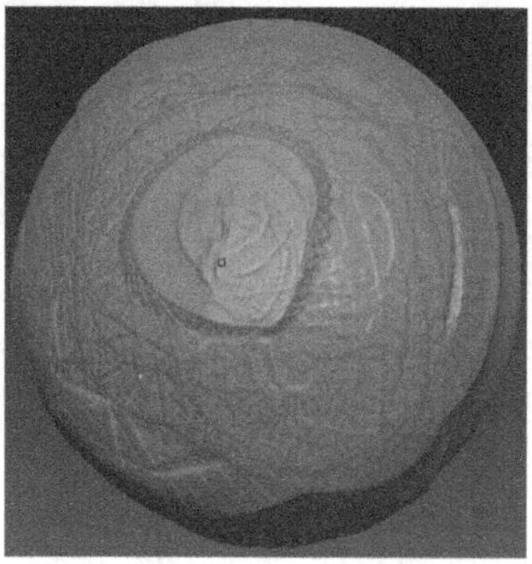

***Figure 2-119** A pattern created on the existing pattern*

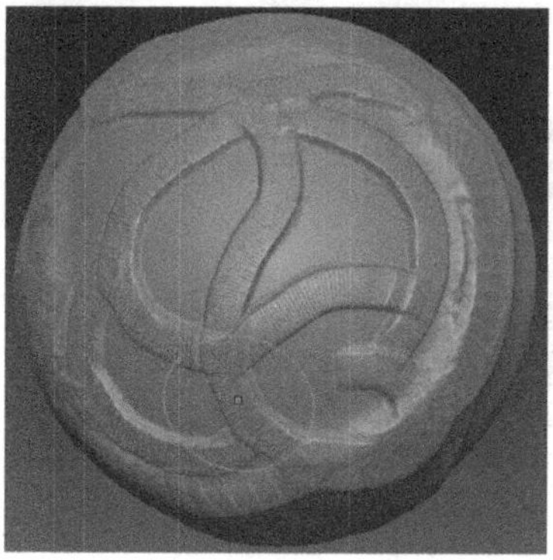

***Figure 2-120** Cursor dragged on the surface of the sphere*

Move Brushes

There are five types of Move brushes, namely **Move Elastic**, **Move Topological**, **Move**, **MoveCurve**, and **MoveInfinteDepth**, as shown in Figure 2-121.

The **Move Elastic** brush is used to deform a 3D object by moving its polygons but less amount of stretching is made in the polygons. The **Move Topological** brush is used to modify areas where the cursor is dragged, without affecting the surrounding geometry. This brush can be used to modify facial expressions. For instance with the help of this brush, you can move the eyelid of a character without affecting the other areas of the eye. The **Move** brush is the most commonly used brush in ZBrush. It is used to form the basic shape of your model, refer to Figure 2-122.

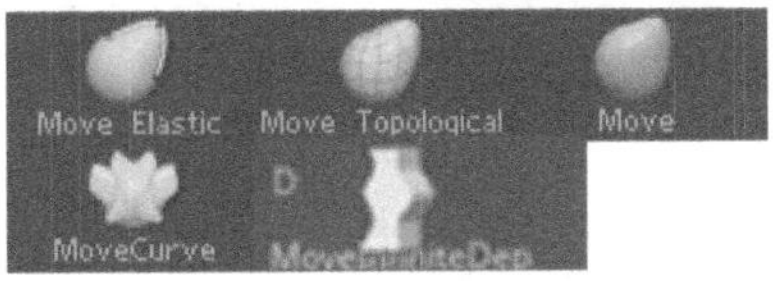

Figure 2-121 *The Move brushes*

The **MoveCurve** brush is used to move the polygons of an object along the path curve, refer to Figure 2-123. The working of this brush is similar to the **DisplaceCurve** brush.

Figure 2-122 *Shape of the sphere modified using the* ***Move*** *brush*

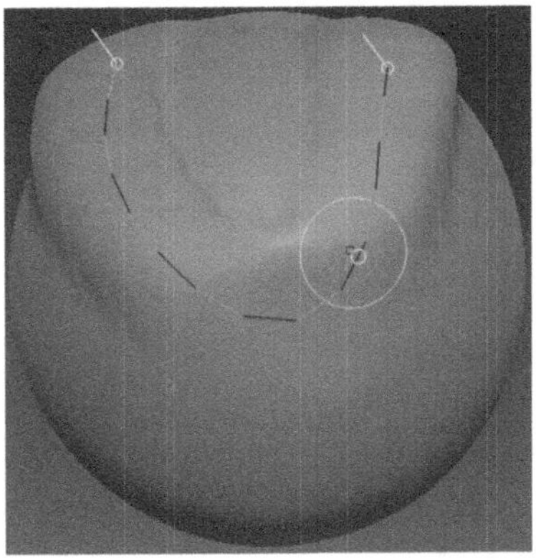

Figure 2-123 *The polygons moved along the path curve*

The **MoveInfiniteDepth** brush moves the surface of a model relative to the camera based on the orientation of the model. This brush evaluates the camera view irrespective of the local coordinates of the model. This in turn determines the depth direction of the brush stroke and you need not have to use masking or the **Gizmo 3D** tool.

Noise Brush

The **Noise** brush adds noise to a surface, thus making it rough. In Figure 2-124, the noise pattern has been created by dragging the cursor on the surface of the sphere continuously. This brush can be used to sculpt rocky surfaces. At very low value of the **Z Intensity** slider, this brush can also be used to add pores to the nose of a human face.

Nudge Brush

The **Nudge** brush moves the polygons in the direction of brush stroke. You can change the geometry of an object using this brush.

Pen Brushes

The Pen brushes are used in the **Quick Sketch** mode or painting on the polygons. There are two types of Pen brushes, namely **Pen A** and **Pen Shadow**, refer to Figure 2-125. Each of the pen brush creates different types of strokes. The **Pen A** brush creates a simple paint stroke, whereas the **Pen Shadow** brush creates an embossed stroke.

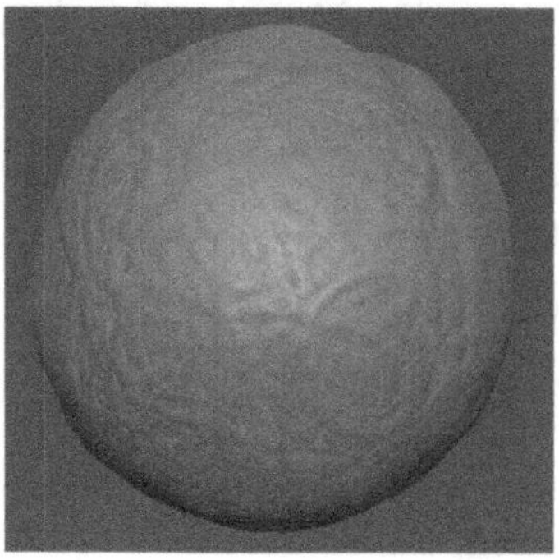

*Figure 2-124 Fractal noise added using the **Noise** brush*

Figure 2-125 The pen brushes

Pinch Brush

The **Pinch** brush is used to pinch the vertices of an object. This brush is useful in adding subtle details like dimples and cuts to a human face.

Planar Brush

The **Planar** brush is used to flatten the surface of an object, refer to Figure 2-126. This brush converts an elevated surface into a planar surface.

Polish Brush

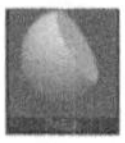

The **Polish** brush is used to flatten and smoothen the surface of an object to make it look like a metallic object.

Rake Brush

The **Rake** brush is used to produce scratch like effect on the surface of an object, refer to Figure 2-127.

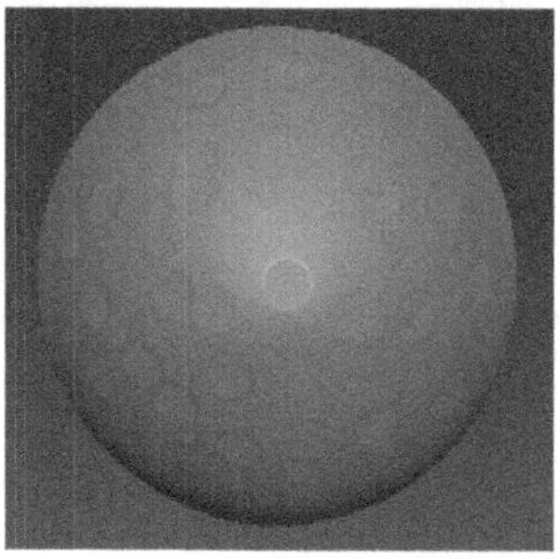

Figure 2-126 The surface of the sphere flattened

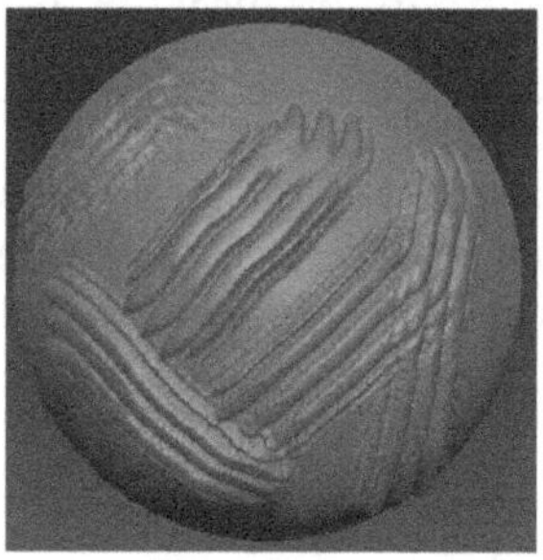

Figure 2-127 Scratches created on the surface of a sphere

Scribe Brushes

There are two types of Scribe brushes namely the **ScribeChisel** and **ScribeStandard**, as shown in Figure 2-128. These brushes are used to carve a shape into the surface of a mesh with falloff controls. Figure 2-129 shows the sphere on which strokes are created using the **ScribeChisel** and **ScribeStandard** brushes. You can also adjust the intensity of the stroke along its length. To do so, click on the **Stroke** palette and set **1** in the **SubSteps** spinner of the **Curve** area. Next, apply the strokes on the sphere. Notice the difference in the strokes by changing the value in the **SubSteps** spinner, refer to Figure 2-130. The shape of the stroke applied can also be changed by dragging red circles that are available at both the ends of the curve drawn, refer to Figure 2-131. You can also click in between the curve and drag to change the shape of the curve, refer to Figure 2-132.

Figure 2-128 *The Scribe brushes*

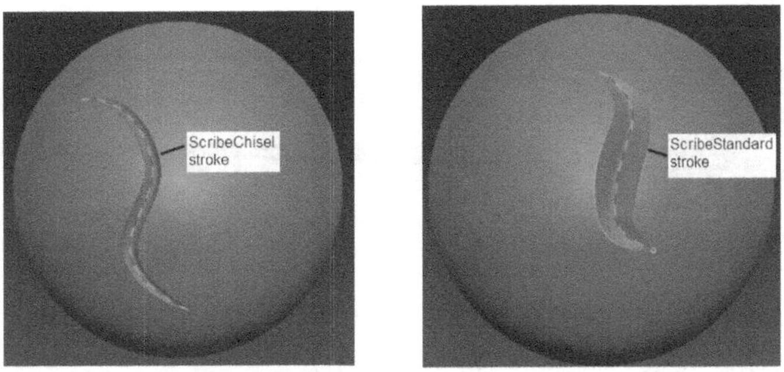

Figure 2-129 *Strokes created using the **ScribeChisel** and **ScribeStandard** brushes*

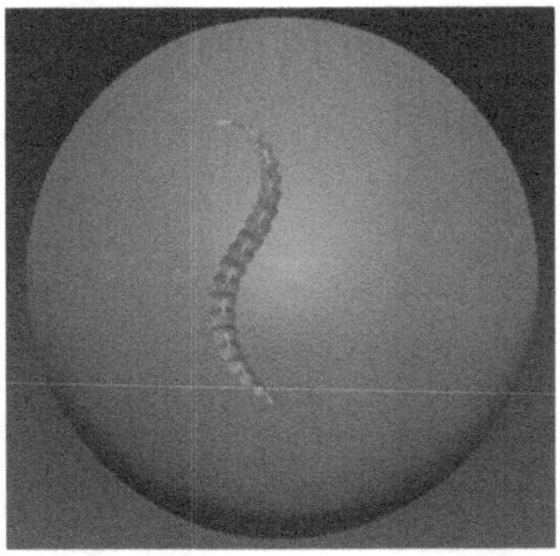

Figure 2-130 *Strokes changed by changing the value in the **SubSteps** spinner*

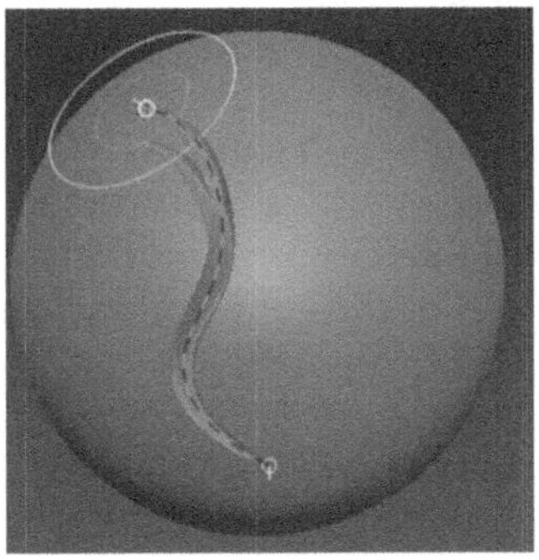

Figure 2-131 *Dragging the red circle*

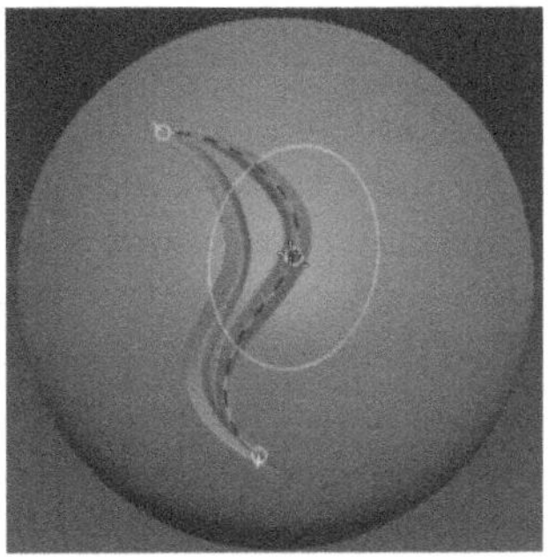

Figure 2-132 *Clicking in between the curve and dragging*

Select Brushes

There are two types of Select brushes namely the **SelectLasso** and **SelectRect**, as shown in Figure 2-133. These brushes are used to select and modify a particular area of an object. The **SelectLasso** brush enables you to draw the desired shape and the **SelectRect** brush uses rectangular stroke to select an area. To use this brush, choose the Current Brush button from the left shelf; a flyout containing different sculpting brushes will be displayed. Choose the **SelectLasso** brush from this flyout; a message box will be displayed prompting you to press CTRL+SHIFT to activate this brush, refer to Figure 2-134.

Figure 2-133 *The select brushes*

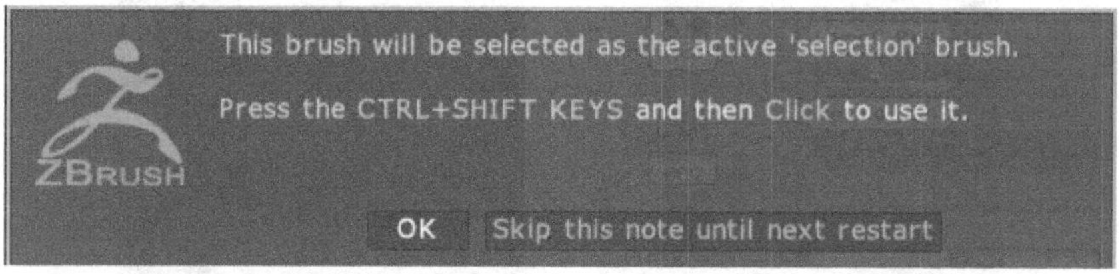

Figure 2-134 *The message box displayed on choosing the* ***SelectLasso*** *brush*

Press CTRL+SHIFT, and then press and hold the left mouse button. Next, drag the cursor on the surface of the sphere to create a selection area on the sphere; a green colored selection mask will be displayed, refer to Figure 2-135. Release the left mouse button; the selected area of the sphere will be displayed on the canvas, refer to Figure 2-136.

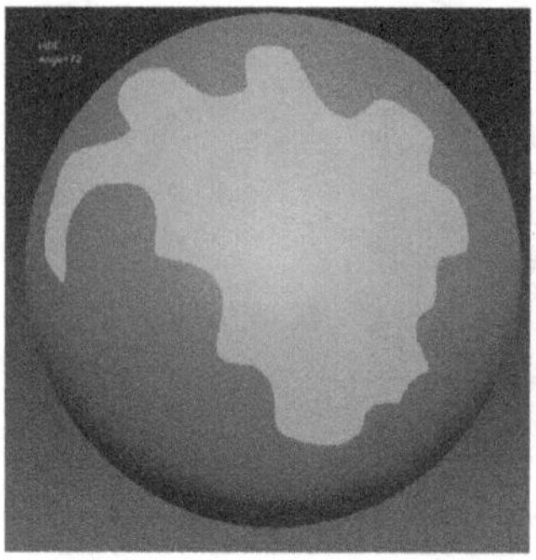

Figure 2-135 *Green selection mask displayed on the surface*

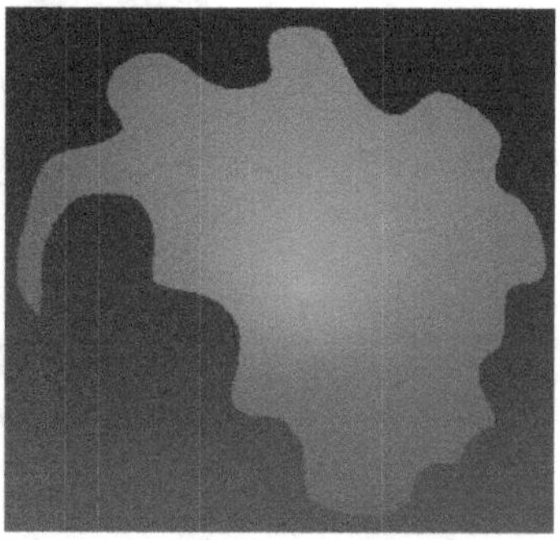

Figure 2-136 *The selected area displayed in the canvas*

Next, sculpt the selected area using different brushes, refer to Figure 2-137. In this figure, the **Standard** brush and the **ClayBuildup** brush have been used to sculpt the selected area. After sculpting the selected area, press and hold the CTRL+SHIFT key and the left mouse button, and then click on the canvas area; the complete model of the sphere along with the modified selection area will be displayed in the canvas area, refer to Figure 2-138.

The working of **SelectRect** brush is similar to **SelectLasso** brush with the only difference that a rectangular selection mask is created using this brush, refer to Figures 2-139 and 2-140.

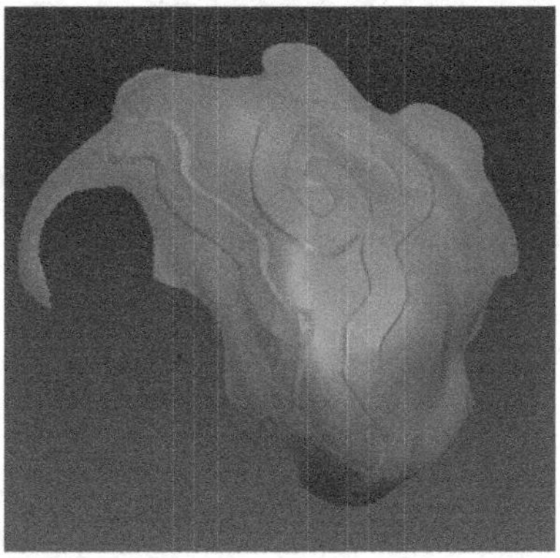

Figure 2-137 *The selected area sculpted using different brushes*

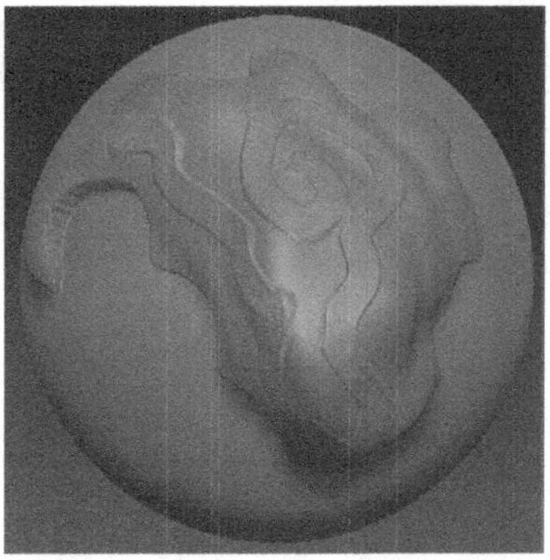

Figure 2-138 *The complete sphere displayed in the canvas*

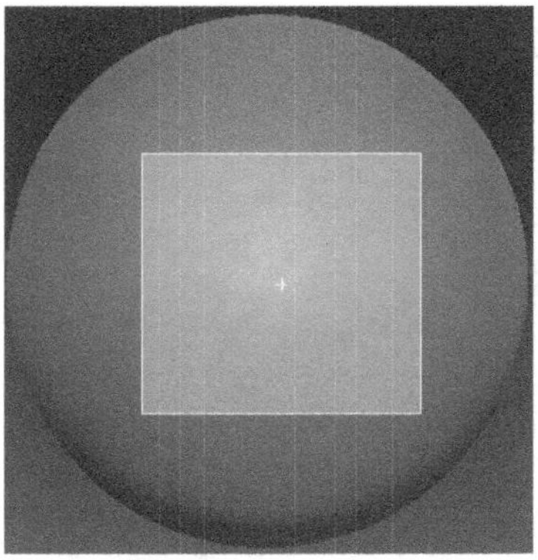

Figure 2-139 *The green colored rectangular selection displayed*

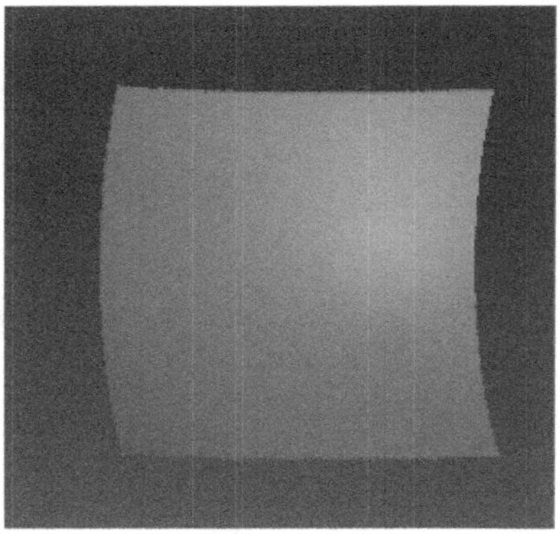

Figure 2-140 *The selected area of the sphere displayed in the canvas*

Slash3 Brush

The **Slash3** brush is used to produce an effect resembling a pattern produced if a soft surface is cut by a knife, refer to Figures 2-141 and 2-142.

Slice Brushes

There are three types of Slice brushes, namely the **SliceCirc**, **SliceCurve**, and **SliceRect**, as shown in Figure 2-143. Before using these brushes, you need to make sure that the geometry is not subdivided.

The **SliceCirc** brush is used to divide an object into a number of parts using a circular selection area, such that each part can be modified individually. To understand the working of this brush, create a sphere in the canvas and convert it into polymesh. Next, choose the **PolyF** button from the right shelf to view the polygon distribution of the sphere, refer to Figure 2-144.

Choose the Current Brush button from the left shelf; a flyout containing different sculpting brushes will be displayed. Choose the **SliceCirc** brush from this flyout; a message box will be displayed prompting you to press CTRL+SHIFT to activate this brush, refer to Figure 2-145.

*Figure 2-141 Pattern produced using the **Slash3** brush*

*Figure 2-142 Pattern produced using the **Slash3** brush*

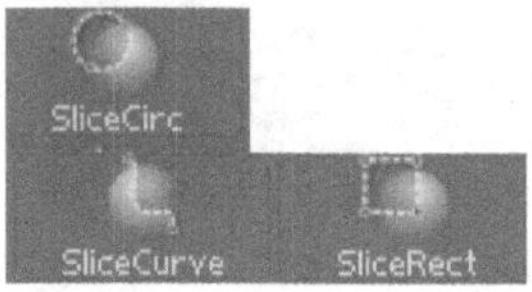

Figure 2-143 The slice brushes

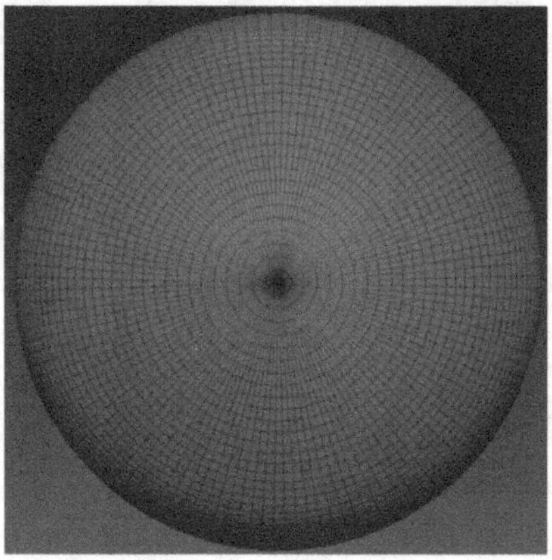

Figure 2-144 The polygons of the sphere displayed

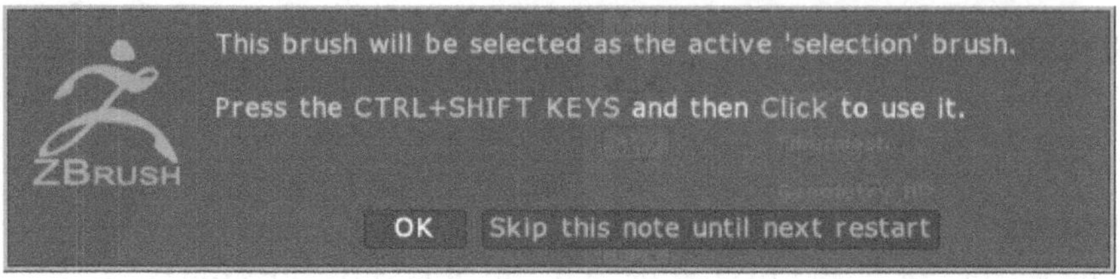

*Figure 2-145 The message box displayed on choosing the **SliceCirc** button*

Press CTRL+SHIFT and then drag the cursor on the surface of the sphere; a circular selection mask will be displayed, refer to Figure 2-146. Release the left mouse button; the color of the selected area will change and it will be split into a separate group, refer to Figure 2-147. Press the CTRL+SHIFT keys and then click on the split area; it will be displayed in the canvas and rest of the sphere will disappear, refer to Figure 2-148. Next, sculpt the selected area using the **Standard** brush, refer to Figure 2-149. After sculpting the selected area, press and hold the CTRL+SHIFT key and then click on the canvas area; the complete model of the sphere along with the modified selection area will be displayed in the canvas area, refer to Figure 2-150.

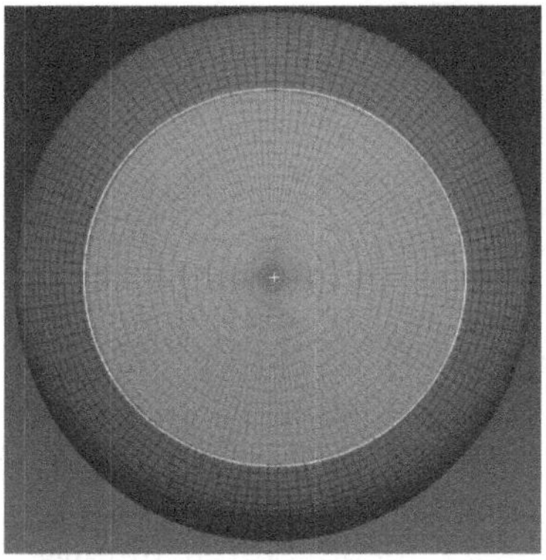

Figure 2-146 *A circular selection mask displayed on the sphere*

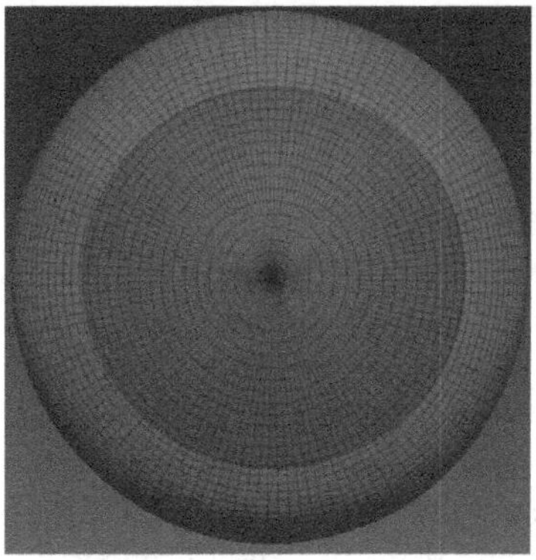

Figure 2-147 *The selected area of the mask separated from the sphere*

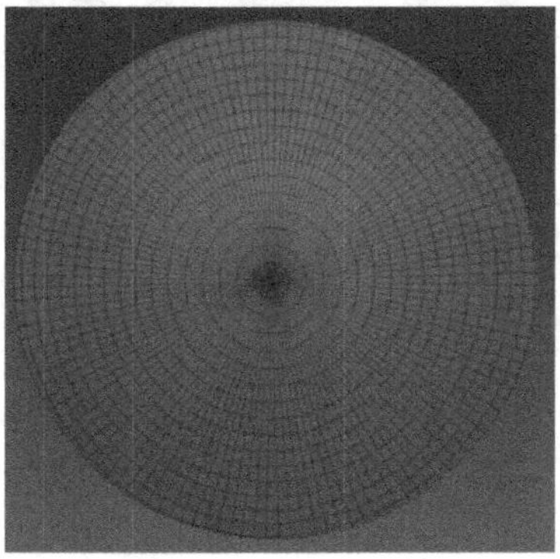

Figure 2-148 *The selected area displayed in the canvas*

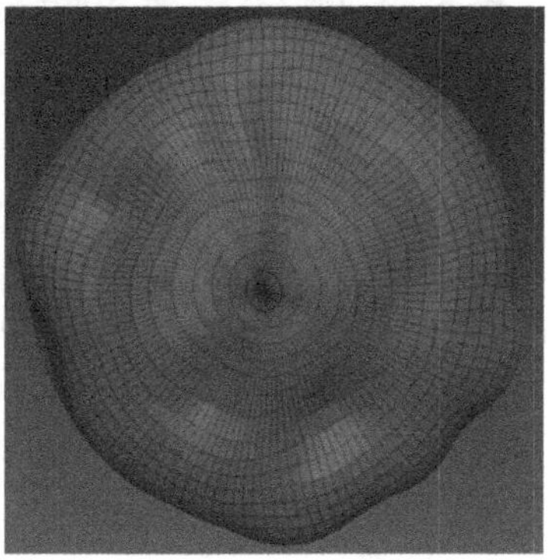

Figure 2-149 *The selected area sculpted using the **Standard** brush*

The **SliceCurve** brush uses curves or straight lines to split an object into separate groups, refer to Figure 2-151. The **SliceRect** brush works similar to the **SliceCirc** brush with the only difference that instead of creating a circular selection area, it creates a rectangular selection area, refer to Figure 2-152.

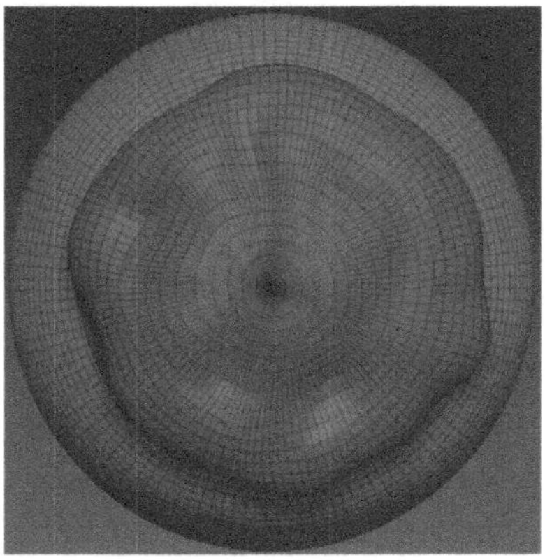

Figure 2-150 *The complete sphere displayed in the canvas*

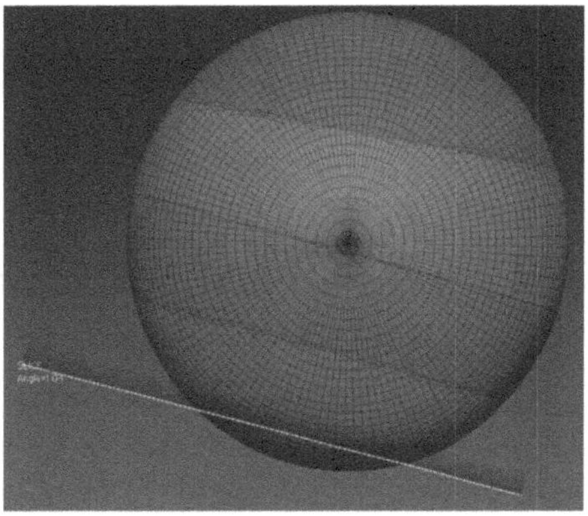

Figure 2-151 *The sphere divided into different parts using the **SliceCurve** brush*

Slide Brush

The **Slide** brush is used to slide out the polygons of an object in the outward direction, refer to Figure 2-153.

Smooth Brushes

There are five types of Smooth brushes, namely **Smooth, SmoothPeaks, SmoothAlt, SmoothCloth,** and **SmoothValleys**, as shown in Figure 2-154. The **Smooth** brush is used to even out the displaced surface in order to create a smoother appearance. To invoke this brush, choose the Current Brush button from the left shelf; a flyout containing different sculpting brushes will be displayed. Choose the **Standard** brush from this flyout. Next, choose the Current Alpha button from the left shelf; a flyout containing different alpha images will be displayed. Choose the **Alpha 05** alpha image from this flyout. Next, press and hold the left mouse button and drag the cursor on the surface of the sphere to create the pattern, as shown in Figure 2-155.

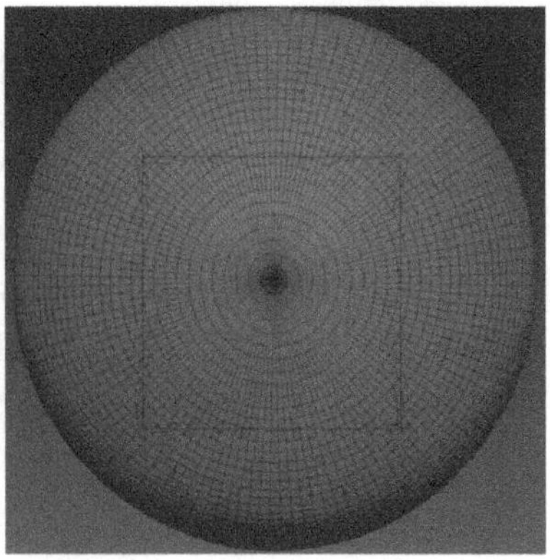

Figure 2-152 *A rectangular selection area created on the surface of sphere*

Figure 2-153 *The polygons slid outward using the **Slide** brush*

Figure 2-154 *The Smooth brushes*

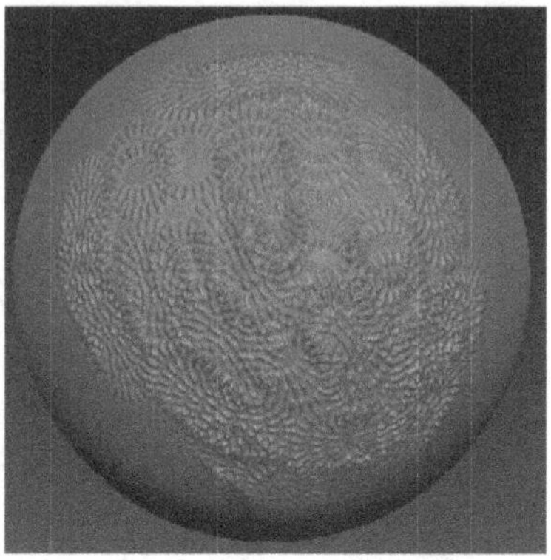

Figure 2-155 *Pattern created using the **Standard** brush*

Next, choose the **Smooth** brush; a message box prompting to press SHIFT to activate this brush will be displayed, refer to Figure 2-156. Choose the **OK** button from this message box. Press

SHIFT and then press and hold the left mouse button. Next, drag the cursor on the surface of the sphere; the sculpted area of the sphere will become smoother, refer to Figure 2-157.

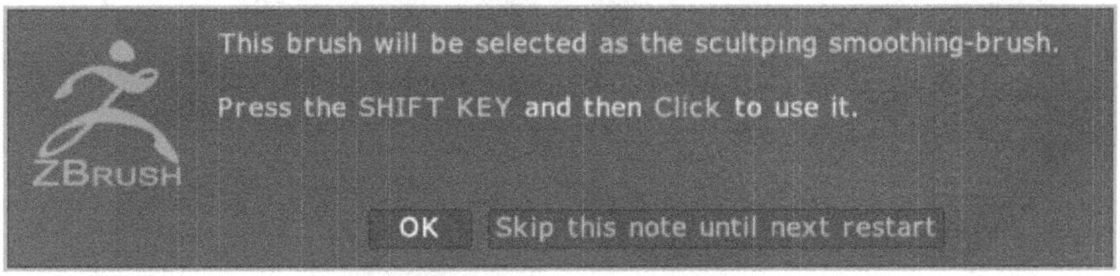

Figure 2-156 *The message box displayed on choosing the* ***Smooth*** *brush*

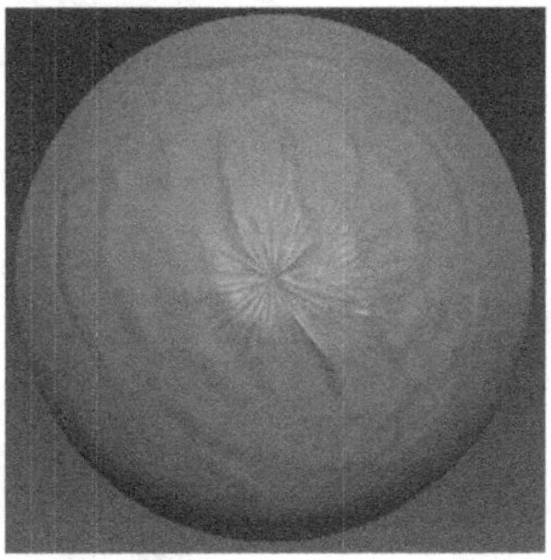

Figure 2-157 *The surface smoothened using the* ***Smooth*** *brush*

The **SmoothPeaks** brush is used to smoothen the surface of the peaks created on an object, refer to Figure 2-158. In Figure 2-159, the peak has been created using the **ClayBuildup** brush. The **SmoothValleys** brush is used to smoothen the surface of the cavities created on an object, refer to Figures 2-160 and 2-149. In Figure 2-161, the cavity has been created using the **ClayBuildup** brush and by choosing the **Zsub** button from the top shelf.

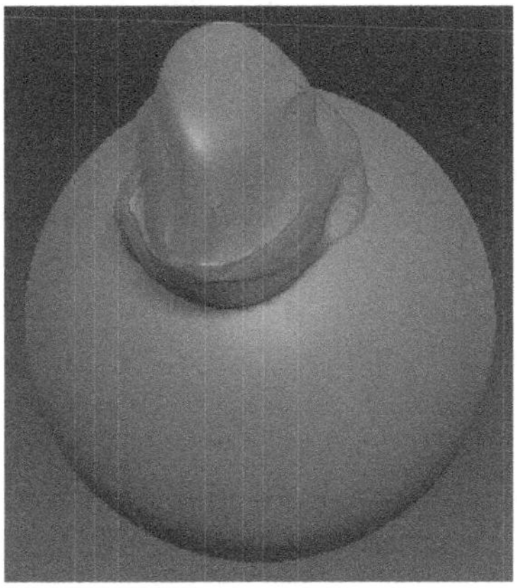

Figure 2-158 *Peak smoothened using the* ***SmoothPeaks*** *brush*

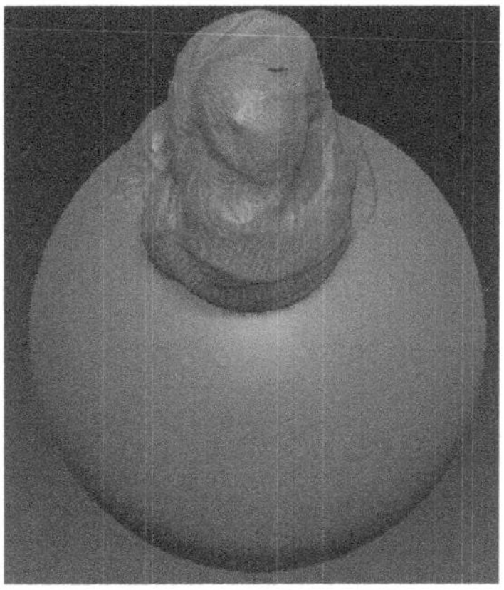

Figure 2-159 *Peak created using the* ***ClayBuildup*** *brush*

The **SmoothAlt** brush is used to smoothen a surface while retaining its volume. Figure 2-162 shows DemoTreeFrog model before using the **SmoothAlt** brush and Figure 2-163 shows the DemoTreeFrog model after using the **SmoothAlt** brush in the marked area.

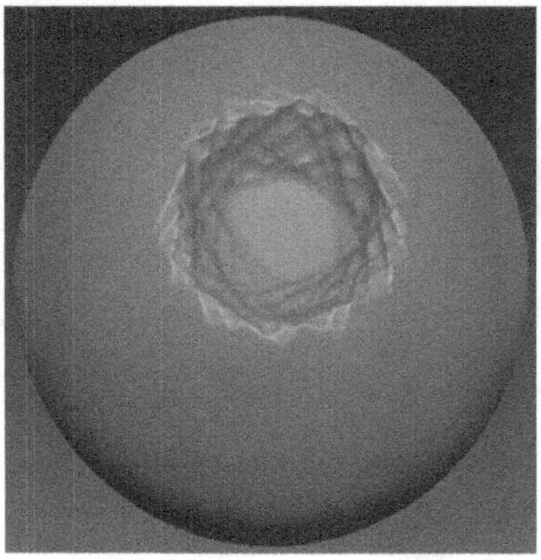

Figure 2-160 *Cavity created using the* ***ClayBuildup*** *brush*

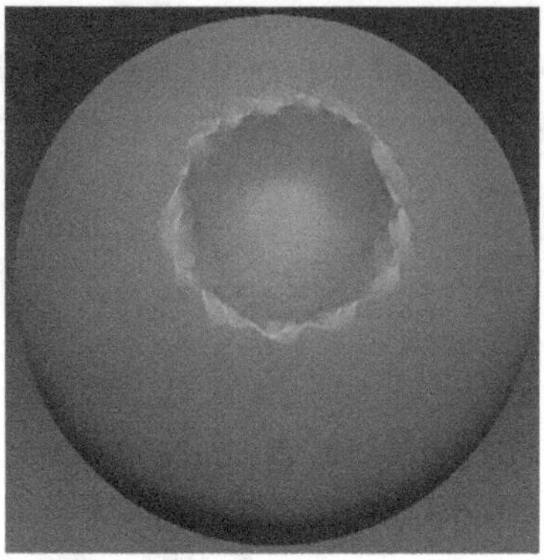

Figure 2-161 *Cavity smoothened using the* ***SmoothValleys*** *brush*

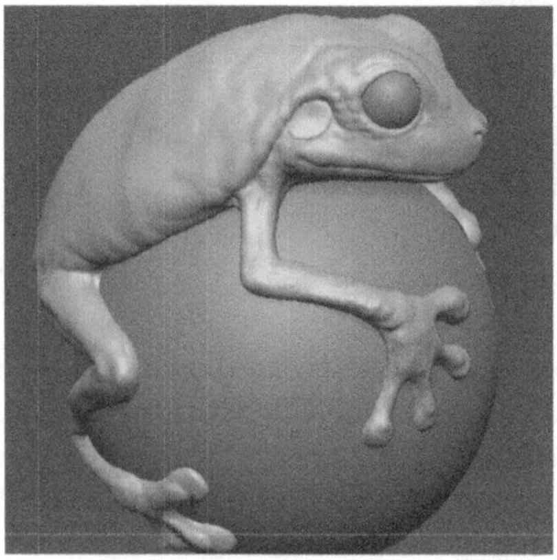

Figure 2-162 *The DemoTreeFrog model before using the* ***SmoothAlt*** *brush*

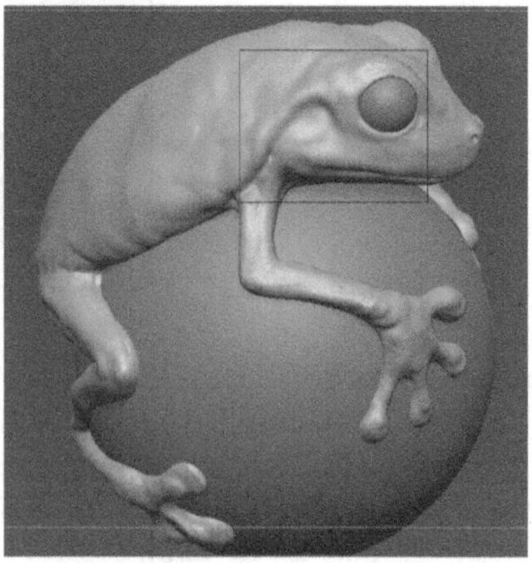

Figure 2-163 *The DemoTreeFrog model after using the* ***SmoothAlt*** *brush in the marked area*

The **SmoothCloth** brush is used to smoothen edges at the border of a surface. This brush is most suitable when you use any primitive as a cloth and you want to smoothen its border edges.

Note that you can adjust the parameters in the **Smooth Brush modifiers** area of the **Brush** Palette to modify the effect of all the brushes mentioned above.

Snake Brushes

There are eight types of Snake brushes, namely the **SnakeCactus, SnakeHook, SnakeHook2**, **SnakeSphere, SnakeCurve1, SnakeCurve2, SnakeCurve4,** and **SnakeCurve5**, as shown in Figure 2-164. Note that the snakecurve brushes have been introduced in ZBrush 2022. The Snake brushes are used to pull out the surface in order to create a different type of appearance such as cactus, horn etc. To invoke these brushes, choose the Current Brush button from the left shelf; a flyout containing different sculpting brushes will be displayed. Choose one of the snake brushes from this flyout. Next, choose the **Stroke** palette; the flyout will be displayed. Choose the **SculptPro** from the flyout. Next, press and hold the left mouse button and drag the cursor on the surface of the sphere to create different types of shapes.

In case of Snakecurve brushes, you first need to create a curve using the brush and then pull the created curve to get the desired shape. Figure 2-165 shows the curve drawn on a sphere using the **SnakeCurve1** brush and Figure 2-166 shows the shape created on the sphere after pulling the drawn curve. Note that symmetry feature in the **Transform** palette can also be used while using Snake brushes, refer to Figure 2-166.

Figure 2-164 *The snake brushes*

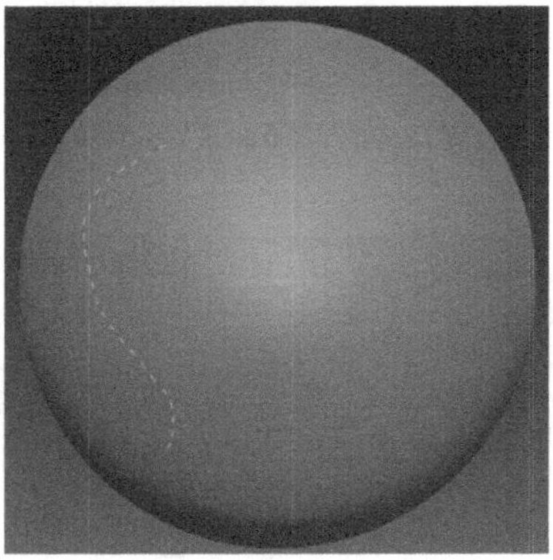

Figure 2-165 *Curve drawn using the **SnakeCurve1** brush*

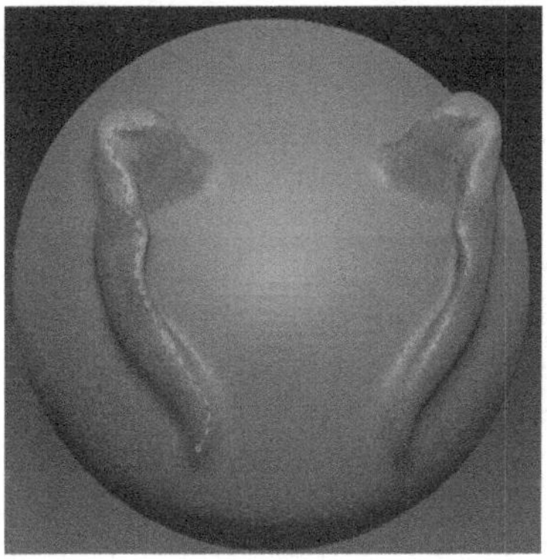

Figure 2-166 *Shape created after pulling the drawn curve*

SnakeHook Brush

The **SnakeHook** brush is used to pull out strands from a surface. These strands have narrow ends. This brush is ideal for making barks, horns, and so on, refer to Figure 2-167.

SnakeCactus Brush

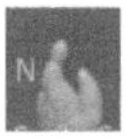

The **SnakeCactus** brush is used to pull out strands from a surface, refer to Figure 2-167. These strands have replicate the look of cactus. This brush is ideal for making cactus.

SnakeSphere Brush

The **SnakeSphere** brush is used to pull out strands from a surface, refer to Figure 2-168. These strands have the look of fingers. This brush is useful to create the fingers for characters.

Soft Brushes

There are two types of Soft brushes, namely the **SoftClay** and **SoftConcrete**, as shown in Figure 2-168. These brushes use alpha images to add detail to an object quickly. By default, the **SoftClay** brush uses a rectangular alpha to add depth and the **SoftConcrete** brush uses a stone like alpha to add depth to an object, refer to Figures 2-169 and 2-170. In the **SoftClay** brush, the edges of the alpha image are smooth. However, in the **SoftConcrete** brush, the edges of the alpha image are hard.

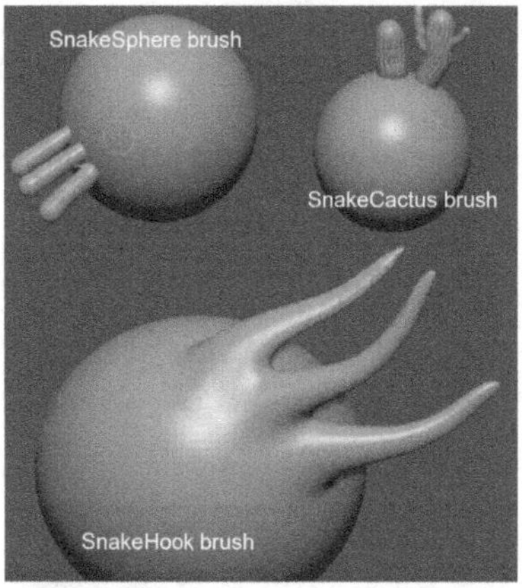

Figure 2-167 *Strands pulled out using the Snake brushes*

Figure 2-168 *The soft brushes*

Figure 2-169 *Rectangular alpha added using the* ***SoftClay*** *brush*

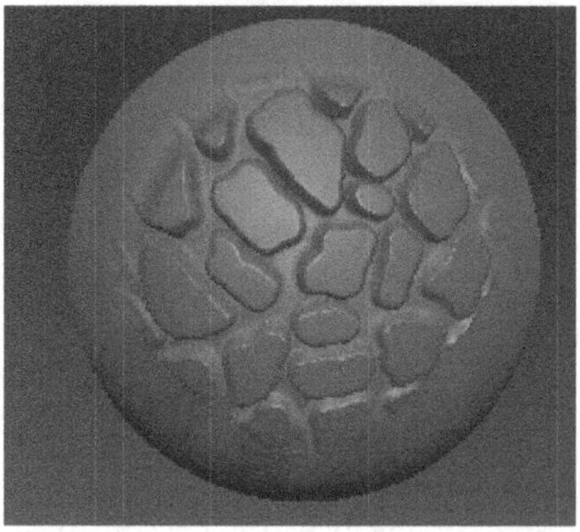

Figure 2-170 *A stone like alpha added using the* ***SoftConcrete*** *brush*

Spiral Brush

The **Spiral** brush is used to create twisted displacement in the surface of an object, refer to Figure 2-171.

sPolish Brush

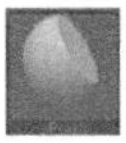

The **sPolish** brush stands for the soft polish brush. This brush is used to smoothen or polish the extruded surface of an object.

Standard Brush

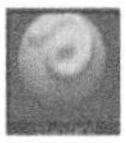

The **Standard** brush is the default brush in ZBrush. It raises the surface of a mesh or pushes it inward, depending on the settings made. If you choose the **Z Add** button, the surface of the mesh will be raised. In organic modeling, the **Standard** brush can be used to sculpt a nose on the face of a character. Similarly, if you choose the **Zsub** button, the surface of the mesh will be pushed inwards. While modeling human faces, it can be used to sculpt eye sockets on the face of a character.

The **Z Intensity** slider will determine the strength of the stroke. Higher the value of intensity, higher will be the degree of elevation. The **Draw Size** slider helps you in controlling the size of the brush and the **Focal Shift** slider controls the softness or fall off of the edge of the brush. If you sculpt with the **Zadd** button chosen and hold the ALT key, the surface will be pushed inward instead of being raised. Similarly, holding the ALT key with the **Zsub** button chosen will raise the surface of an object. Figure 2-172 shows a sphere sculpted by using the **Zadd** and **Zsub** settings of the **Standard** brush.

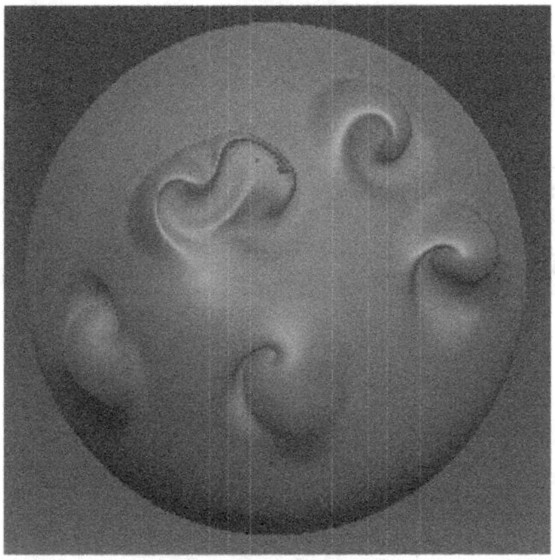

Figure 2-171 *Twisted displacement produced by using the* ***Spiral*** *brush*

Figure 2-172 *A sphere sculpted by the* ***Standard*** *brush*

StitchBasic Brush

The **StitchBasic** brush is used to create a pattern of stitches on the surface of an object. This brush is ideal for sculpting clothes and leather accessories.

Topology Brush

The **Topology** brush is used to create a new mesh on an existing object. This brush is ideal for creating accessories on a human model. This brush can be used if the geometry has not been subdivided. This brush will be discussed in detail in later chapters.

Transpose Brush

The **Transpose** brush is used to move, rotate, or scale an object. This brush can also be used to pose a character. To invoke this brush, choose the Current Brush button from the left shelf; a flyout containing different sculpting brushes will be displayed. Choose the **Transpose** brush from this flyout; an action line will be displayed on the surface of the spiral, refer to Figure 2-173.

Press and hold the left mouse button and drag the cursor on the surface of the spiral; the size of action line will be increased, refer to Figure 2-174.

On choosing the **Transform** brush, you will notice that the **Move** button in the top shelf gets automatically chosen. This button will enable you to move the spiral in the canvas. To move the spiral, hover the cursor over the center of the circle that is at the middle on the action line and then press and hold the left mouse button. Next, drag the cursor; the position of the spiral will change in the canvas accordingly.

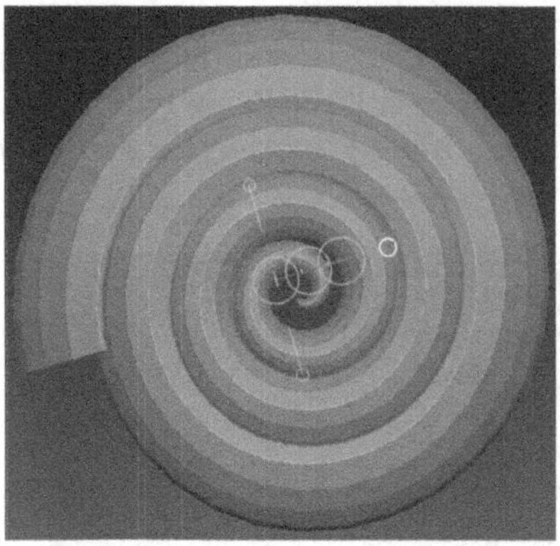

Figure 2-173 *Action line displayed on the spiral*

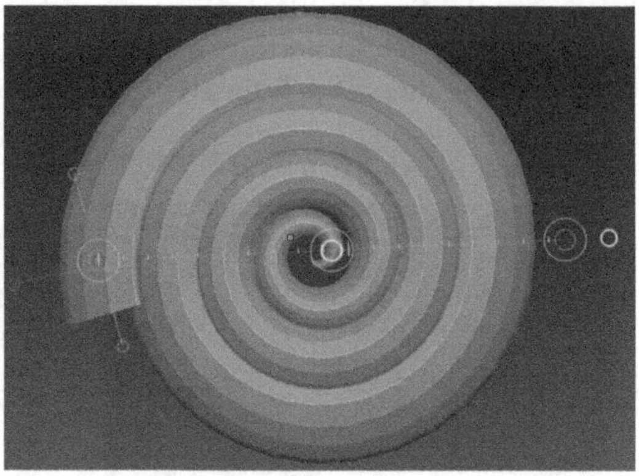

Figure 2-174 *Size of the action line increased*

To scale the spiral, choose the **Scale** button from the top shelf and hover the cursor over the center of the circle that is at the middle on the action line and then drag the cursor in the canvas; the spiral will be scaled, refer to Figures 2-175 and 2-176.

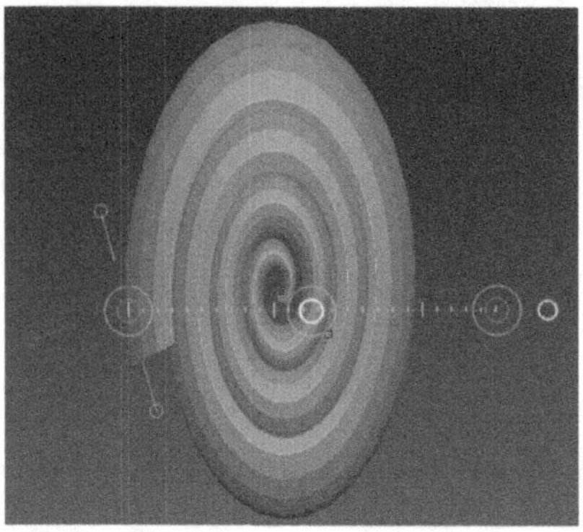

Figure 2-175 *Spiral scaled up vertically*

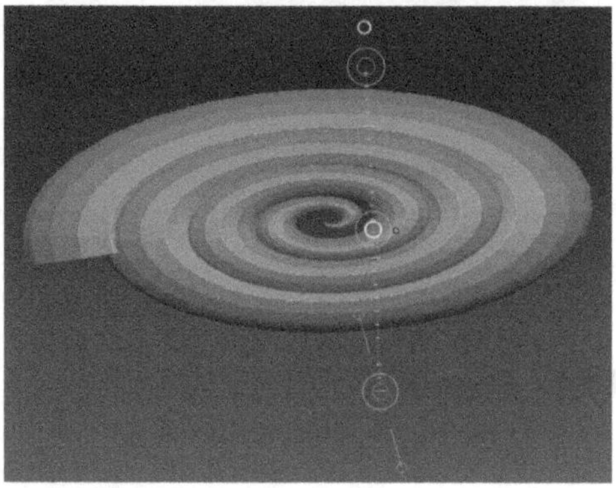

Figure 2-176 *Spiral scaled up horizontally*

To scale the spiral uniformly, hover the cursor at the centre of the end most circles of the action line and then press and hold the left mouse button. Next, drag the cursor in the canvas area; the spiral will be scaled uniformly. Similarly, you can rotate the spiral in the canvas by choosing the **Rotate** button from the top shelf.

Note

To change the position of the action line on the surface of an object, drag the cursor on the object at different positions; the action line will be displayed at those positions. To flip the direction of the action line, click on the green circle at the end of the action line.

You can also bend the surface of an object by using the **Transpose** brush. To do so, create an object in the canvas and convert it into polymesh. Next, choose the **Transpose** brush; a small action line will be created on the surface of the object. Press and hold the left mouse button and drag the cursor on the surface of the object; the size of the action line will be increased, refer to

Figure 2-177. Hover the cursor over the center of the circle that is at the middle on the action line. Press and hold the ALT key and the left mouse button and drag the cursor downward; the surface of the object will be bent, refer to Figure 2-178.

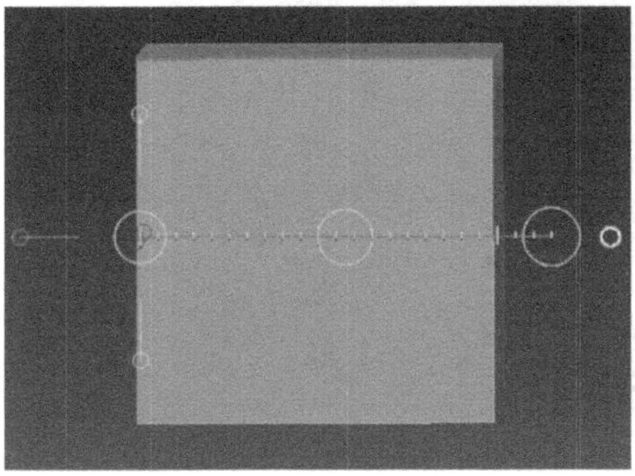

Figure 2-177 *Action line displayed on the spiral*

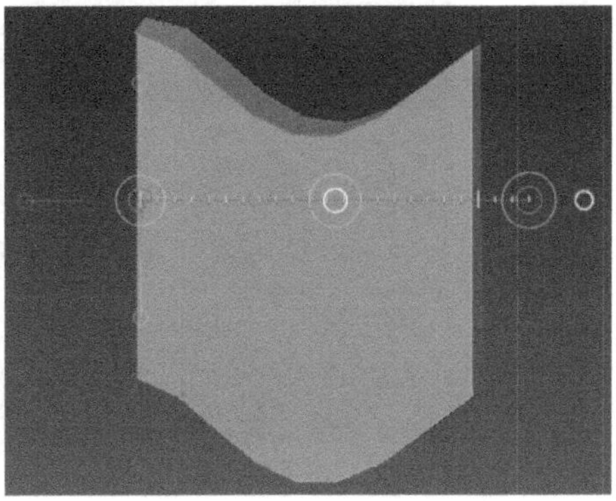

Figure 2-178 *Surface of the cube bent using the* ***Transpose*** *brush*

TransposeSmartMask Brush

The **TransposeSmartMask** brush is used to mask distinct areas of a surface. This brush detects the curved areas in the surface and creates a mask around them. To understand the working of this brush, choose the **LightBox** button from the top shelf; the **LightBox** browser will be displayed. In the **Tool** tab of this browser, double-click on the **Dog.ZTL** file. Press and hold the left mouse button and drag the cursor on the canvas; the model of the dog will be loaded in the canvas, refer to Figure 2-179.

After loading the model, choose the **Edit** button from the top shelf, and then choose the **TransposeSmartMask** brush. Press and hold the CTRL key and the left mouse button and drag the cursor on the surface of the model; the size of action line will increase and a mask will be created on the top area of the model, refer to Figure 2-180. To increase the area of the mask, drag the cursor on the surface of the model such that its size is increased significantly, refer to Figure 2-181.

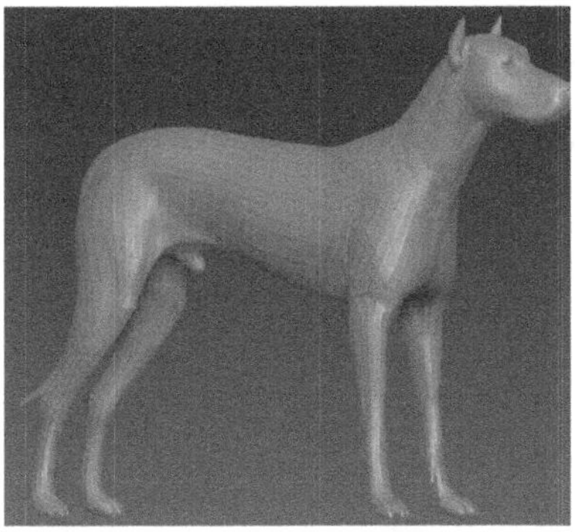

Figure 2-179 *Model of the dog created in the canvas*

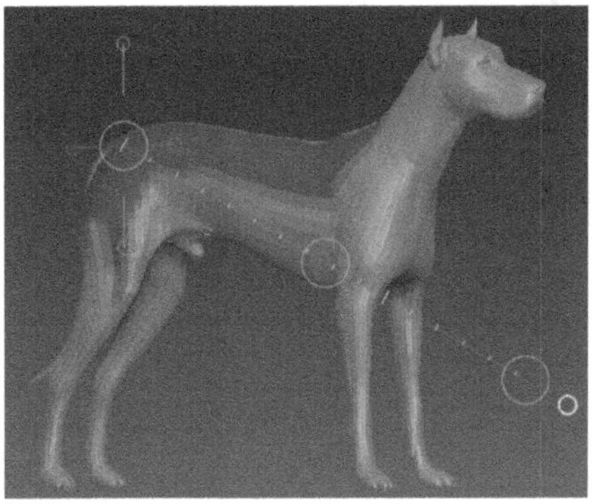

Figure 2-180 *Mask created on the top area of the model*

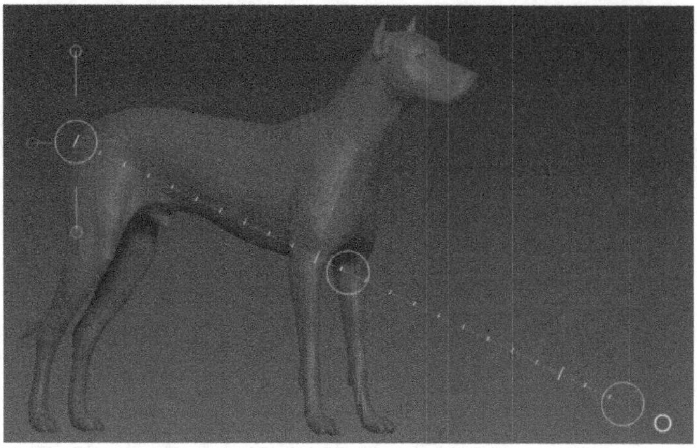

Figure 2-181 *Mask created on the entire surface of the model*

Trim Brushes

The Trim brushes are used to make the surface of an object flat. There are six types of Trim brushes namely: **TrimAdaptive**, **TrimCircle**, **TrimCurve**, **TrimDynamic**, **TrimLasso**, and **TrimRect**, refer to Figure 2-182. The **TrimAdaptive** brush is used to create planes on the curved surface by slicing the curve. The **TrimCircle** brush uses circular shape to slice the geometry and create new polygons. The **TrimCurve** brush uses curves or straight lines to slice the geometry and create new polygons. The **TrimDynamic** brush creates planes on the surface and maintains the curvature of the surface. The **TrimLasso** brush uses desired shape to slice the geometry and create new polygons. The **TrimRect** brush works similar to **TrimCircle** brush with the only difference that it uses a rectangular marquee selection to slice the geometry and create new polygons on the squeezed area.

Figure 2-182 *The Trim brushes*

Weave1 Brush

The **Weave1** brush is used with different alphas to create different patterns on an object, refer to Figure 2-183.

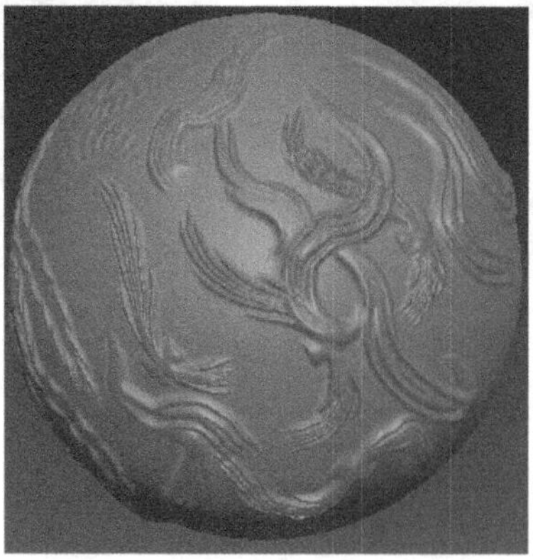

Figure 2-183 *Different patterns created using the* ***Weave1*** *brush*

XTractor Brush

This brush is used to copy the sculpting details from one area to the other area of the model. You can capture sculpted details by pressing the G key and then dragging a path along the detailed surface that you intend to capture into an alpha. Once those details are captured into an alpha, you can reapply the details to other areas along a stroke path. You can add fine details to the copied area by using the **Focal Shift** slider and the **Draw Size** slider.

XTractor DragDot Brush

The **Xtractor DragDot** brush is used capture the sculpt details by clicking once on any point of a sculpted surface. To capture the selected area as an alpha, press G. Once the alpha has been captured, you can reapply the alpha by clicking on the surface and dragging the detail in different position.

XTractor DragRect Brush

The **XTractor DragRect** brush is used to capture sculpted details by clicking and dragging over a sculpted surface. To capture a region as an alpha, press G. Once the alpha has been captured, you can reapply the details in the same way as discussed above.

ZProject Brush

The **ZProject** brush is mainly used in texturing. If you want to texture a human face, then you need to keep the reference image along with the 3D model in the canvas area. By using the **ZProject** brush, you can transfer the texture from the reference image into your 3D model. The **ZProject** brush uses the Z axis of the canvas to transfer sculpting and texturing details either from the canvas or from other subtools. This brush will be discussed in detail in later chapters.

ZRemesherGuides Brush

The **ZRemesherGuides** brush is used to control the flow of edges in geometry. This brush is used in combination with the **ZRemesher** feature. The **ZRemesher** is used to edit the existing topology of an object. The **ZRemesherGuides** brush facilitates this by enabling you to draw curves on the surface of an object. These curves decide the edge loop flow in the geometry. The **ZRemesher** features and the **ZRemesherGuides** brushes will be discussed in detail in the later chapters.

ZModeler

The **ZModeler** brush is used for modeling. This brush contains most of the common functions that can be applied in 3D modeling. The **ZModeler** brush functions in two parts: Actions and Targets. Both functions are correlated to each other. The action is the function itself and the target is the object to which the action will be applied. To understand the function of this brush, first create a 3D primitive object in the canvas. To do so, choose the Current Tool button from the **Tool** palette; a flyout will be displayed, refer to Figure 2-6. Choose the **Cube3D** primitive from this flyout. Next, press and hold the left mouse button and drag the cursor on the canvas to create a cube. After creating the cube, choose the **Edit** button from the top shelf and then choose the **PolyF** from the right shelf. Now, choose the **Initialize** subpalette and then adjust the values in the **Hdivide** and **Vdivide** edit boxes.

Now, choose the **Make PolyMesh3D** button from the **Tool** palette; the primitive object will be converted into a polymesh. Choose the **Current Brush** button from the left shelf; a flyout containing different sculpting brushes will be displayed. Choose the **ZModeler** brush from this flyout, as shown in Figure 2-184. If required, adjust the size of the brush using the [or] key. Now, when you hover the cursor over the polygon area of the primitive, the red squared highlighted area will be displayed, as shown in Figure 2-185. Right-click on the highlighted area; the **ZMODELER** window will be displayed, a shown in Figure 2-186. After that you can choose **Extrude** from the **Polygon Actions** area and **A Single Poly** from the **Target** area. Next, in the canvas area, you can drag the cursor to extrude the selected polygon.

***Figure 2-184** Choosing the **ZModeler** brush from the flyout*

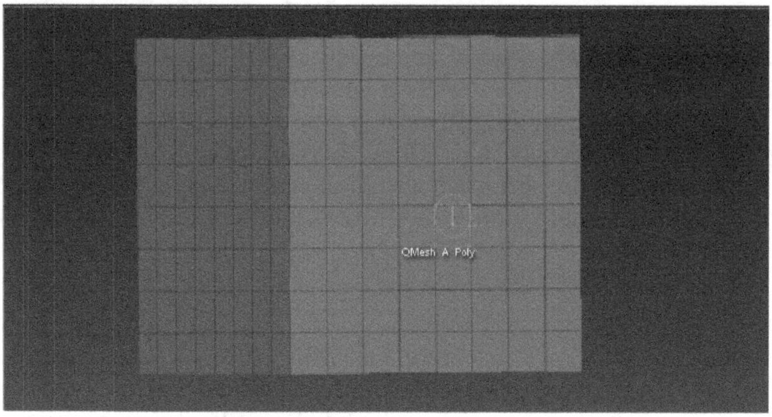

***Figure 2-185** The highlighted area of the primitive*

Next, hover the mouse on the edge/point of the primitive and then right-click; the **ZMODELER** window will be displayed with respective options for edge/point, as shown in Figures 2-187 and 2-188. You can use these options for quickly generating a wide variety of shapes.

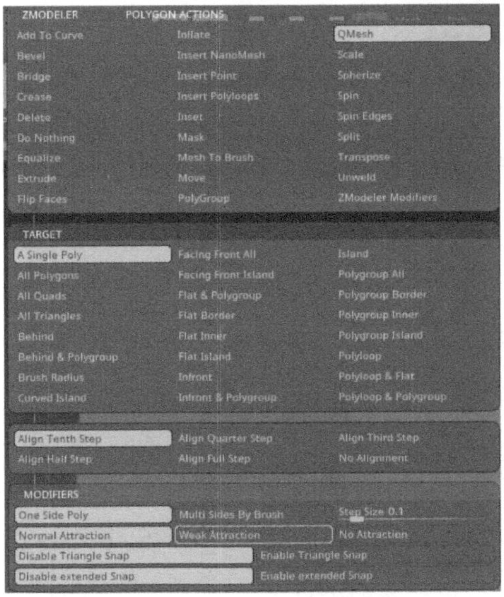

Figure 2-186 The ***ZMODELER*** *window*

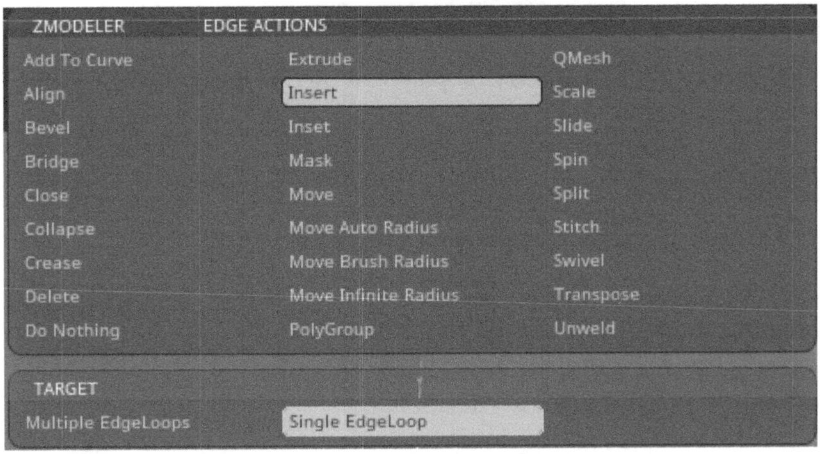

Figure 2-187 The ***ZMODELER*** *window with options corresponding to edge*

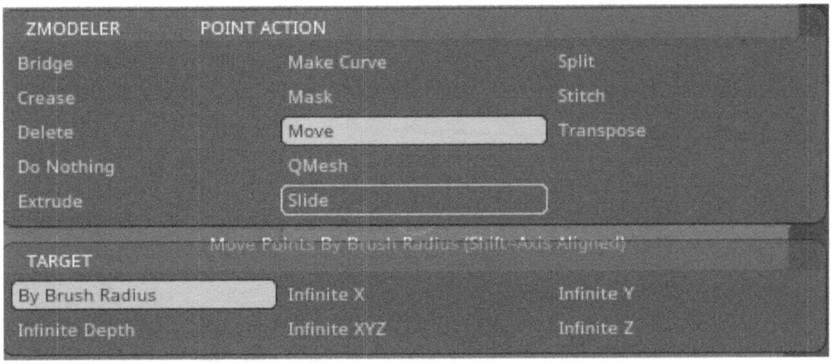

Figure 2-188 The ***ZMODELER*** *window with options corresponding to point*

Self-Evaluation Test

Answer the following questions and then compare them to those given at the end of this chapter:

1. Which of the following hot keys is used to activate the Clip brushes?

(a) CTRL+ALT	(b) CTRL+SHIFT
(c) CTRL	(d) None of these

2. The __________ brush is used to add wrinkles to an object.

3. The __________ brushes are used in the **Quick Sketch** mode or painting on the polygons.

4. The __________ brush is used mainly in texturing.

5. The __________ brush is used to create a pattern of stitches on the surface of an object.

6. The __________ brush is used to control the flow of edges in the geometry.

7. The __________ brush is used to control the cloth drape.

8. The **Divide** button in the **Geometry** subpalette is used to decrease the number of polygons in a mesh. (T/F)

9. The **MatchMaker** brush is used to fit one mesh into the contours of another mesh. (T/F)

10. The **Smooth** brush is activated by pressing the ALT key. (T/F)

11. Each time you subdivide a model with subdivision history using the **Divide** button, the **SDiv** slider should be at its highest setting. (T/F)

12. The **Hatch** brush is used to apply sculpting strokes on the object without picking up cursor. (T/F)

Review Questions

Answer the following questions:

1. Which of the following keys activates the alternate mode for the **Z Add** button and the **Z Sub** button?

(a) ALT	(b) SHIFT
(c) CTRL	(d) SPACEBAR

2. The term IMM stands for __________ .

3. The __________ brush is used to add organic details to an object.

4. The __________ brush is used to create a new mesh on the surface of an object by drawing curves for the new mesh.

5. The __________ brush uses a circular stroke to create a mask on the surface of an object.

6. The **Inflat** brush is used to expand the surface of an object by a significant amount. (T/F)

7. The **Rake** brush is used to isolate a certain region of an object. (T/F)

8. The **Transpose** brush is activated when the brush is in the **Draw** mode. (T/F)

9. The **CurveBridge** brush is used to create a bridge geometry between two curves. (T/F)

Answers to Self-Evaluation Test

1. b, **2. Crumple**, **3.** Pen, **4. ZProject**, **5.** Eight, **6. QRemesherGuide**, 7. **ClothPull** **8.** F, **9.** T, **10.** F, **11.** T 12. T

Chapter 3

Introduction to Digital Sculpting

Learning Objectives

After completing this chapter, you will be able to:

- *Understand digital sculpting*
- *Learn about different subpalettes in Tool palette*
- *Understand the usage of the Projection Master*

INTRODUCTION

In ZBrush, you can create organic as well as inorganic models using the primitive objects. Organic modeling refers to creation of living things such as humans, animals, plants, mythical characters, and insects. Inorganic modeling refers to creation of non-living things such as buildings, cars, and gadgets. ZBrush enables you to create models with complete details using the digital sculpting. In this chapter, you will learn about the process of digital sculpting using different tools and techniques.

DIGITAL SCULPTING

Digital sculpting is also known as sculpt modeling or 3D sculpting. In digital sculpting, brushes are used to modify a 3D object. Sculpting is primarily used in high poly modeling. The high poly models created in ZBrush are extensively used in movies, games, photorealistic illustrations, and so on. In ZBrush terminology, a 3D model is referred to as digital clay. Digital clay in ZBrush can be created in a number of different ways, such as by using one of the default models or primitives present in ZBrush or importing a polygon model that has been created in different modeling software applications such as Autodesk 3ds Max or Maya. The default models that come with ZBrush can be accessed through the **LightBox** browser which is located at the top of the canvas, refer to Figure 3-1. ZBrush also contains a library of primitives such as cube, sphere, cone, and so on. These primitives can be accessed from the flyout that is displayed on choosing the Current Tool button in the **Tool** palette, refer to Figure 3-2.

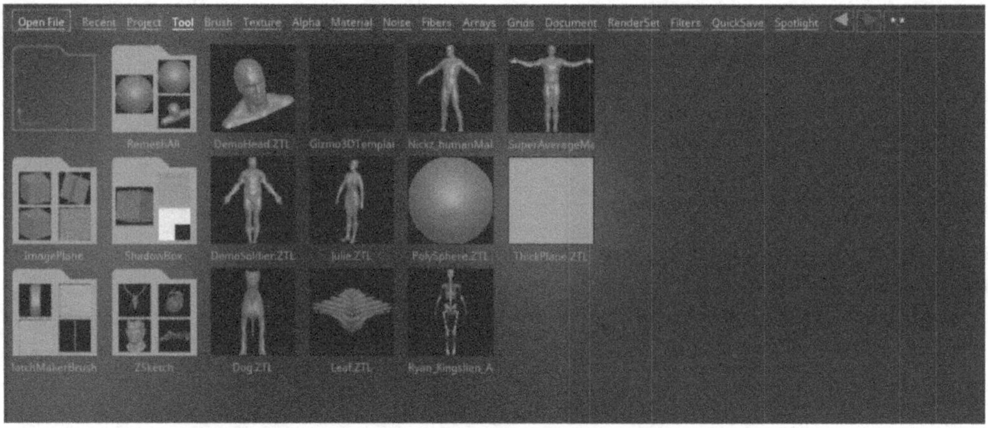

Figure 3-1 *The* ***LightBox*** *browser*

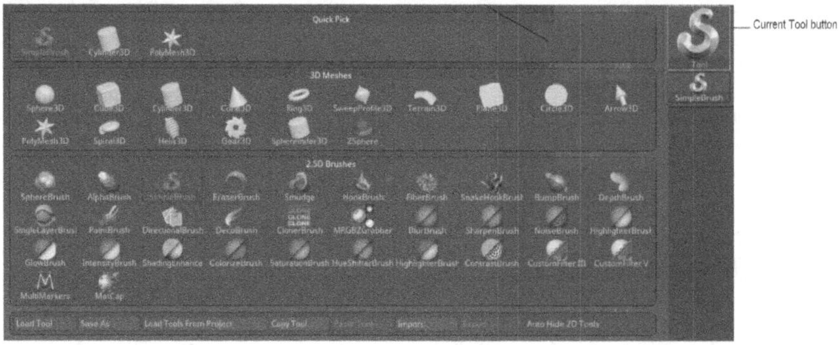

Figure 3-2 *The primitives accessed through the flyout*

Use of Symmetry in Digital Sculpting

The symmetry feature in ZBrush allows you to quickly sculpt symmetrical objects such as face. The symmetry can be activated by choosing the **Activate Symmetry** button located in the **Transform** palette, as shown in Figure 3-3.

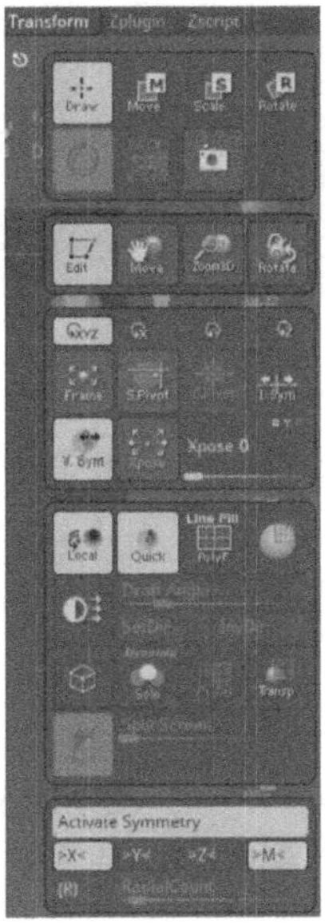

Figure 3-3 The ***Activate Symmetry*** *button in the* ***Transform*** *palette*

Symmetry can be activated along all the three axes. As the **>X<** button is chosen by default on choosing the **Activate Symmetry** button, the symmetry is activated along the X-axis. To deactivate symmetry along X-axis, you need to choose the **>X<** button. To activate symmetry along other axes, you need to choose the corresponding buttons such as **>Y<** and **>Z<** located below the **Activate Symmetry** button. When you activate symmetry, the modifications you make on one side will be reflected on the other side as well, depending on the axis chosen, refer to Figure 3-4. In Figure 3-4, the symmetry has been activated along X-axis and the pattern drawn on the plane is mirrored on the other side as well. ZBrush also has an option that enables you to create radial patterns on a circular surface. To activate radial symmetry, choose the **(R)** button located below the **Activate Symmetry** button, refer to Figure 3-3. The **RadialCount** slider located next to the **(R)** button enables you to decide the number of times a pattern will be mirrored across the selected axis. In Figure 3-5, the radial symmetry has been activated along the Z-axis and the value of **RadialCount** is equal to 8. The pattern in Figure 3-5 has been drawn by using the **Standard** brush.

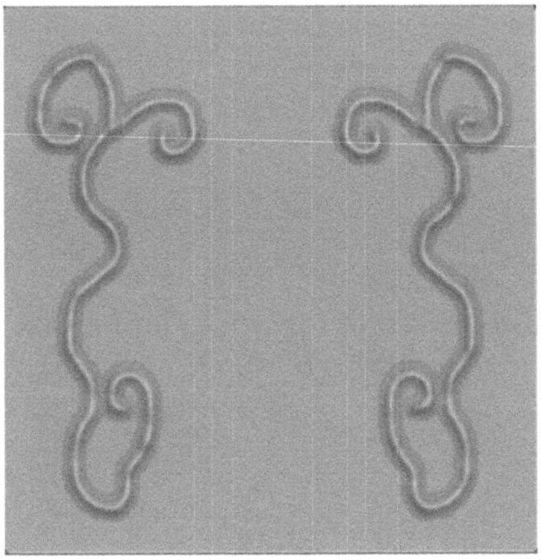

Figure 3-4 Pattern drawn with the symmetry activated along X axis

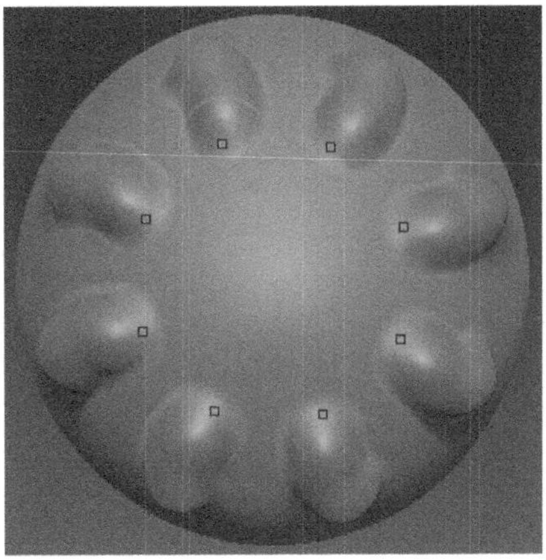

Figure 3-5 Radial pattern drawn with the symmetry activated along Z axis

Use of Alpha in Digital Sculpting

Alpha images are patterns that determine the shape of brush that will be used in painting and sculpting. ZBrush has a library of grey scale alpha images. These images can be accessed from the flyout displayed on choosing the Current Alpha button located in the left shelf, refer to Figure 3-6. Alpha images are most commonly used with clay brushes and the **Decol** brush.

***Figure 3-6** The alpha patterns*

The flyout displayed on choosing the Current Alpha button consists of two main areas: **Quick Pick** and **Alphas**. The **Quick Pick** area consists of the most commonly used alphas. The **Alphas** area consists of all the alpha images available in ZBrush.

There are some buttons available at the bottom of the flyout, namely **Import**, **Export**, **Ep**, **Make Tx**, **Make 3D**, **Cc**, **CropAndFill**, and **GrabDoc**, refer to Figure 3-6. These buttons are discussed next.

Import

The **Import** button is used to import images that can be used as alphas. These images can be the PSD or bitmap images.

Export

The **Export** button saves an alpha as an image file, and this file can be used in other software applications.

Ep

Ep stands for Export Processed Alpha. This button is used to export an alpha that has been modified by using different settings in the **Alpha** palette. If this button is not chosen, then the alpha would be exported unchanged.

Make Tx

The **Make Tx** button is used to convert an alpha image into a texture.

Make 3D

The **Make 3D** button is used to convert a selected alpha image into a 3D object. On choosing this button, the selected alpha will be displayed as a 3D object in the canvas.

Cc

Cc stands for clear color. If this button is chosen along with the **CropAndFill** button, then the color applied on the object will disappear. The **CropAndFill** button is discussed next.

CropAndFill

The **CropAndFill** button crops an object in the canvas according to the dimensions of the selected alpha and fills it with the alpha image. On choosing this button, a warning message will be displayed asking whether you want to continue with this operation or not, refer to Figure 3-7. If you choose the **Yes** button, the object will be cropped and filled with the alpha, refer to Figure 3-8. You can also modify the pattern of the alpha using different strokes. The library of different strokes can be accessed either through the **Stroke** palette located at the top of the interface or from the left shelf.

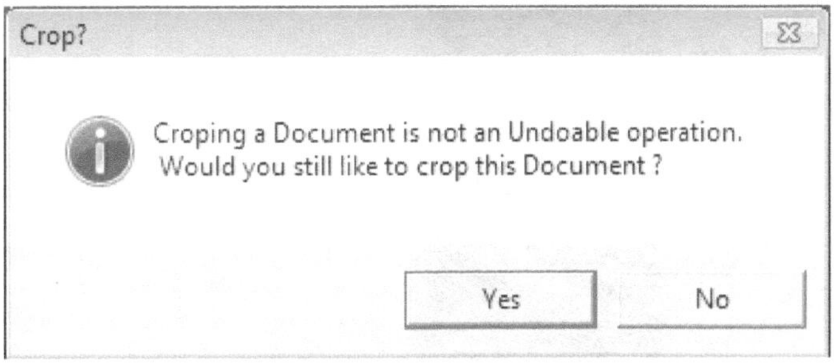

***Figure 3-7** The warning message displayed on choosing the **CropAndFill** button*

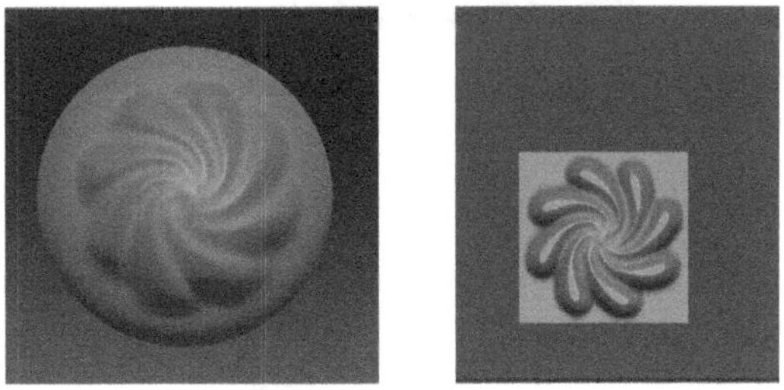

***Figure 3-8** Object cropped by using the **CropAndFill** button*

GrabDoc

The **GrabDoc** button is used to capture a screenshot of the canvas as an alpha. This button enables you to create your own alphas using different brushes and then take a capture of that alpha. The alpha created can be used later in sculpting.

Tool Palette

The **Tool** palette is one of the most important palettes in ZBrush. It consists of all the tools required for modeling and sculpting. The **Tool** palette is divided into a number of subpalettes. These subpalettes appear when you choose a primitive from the flyout displayed on choosing the Current Tool button, refer to Figure 3-9. These subpalettes are also displayed when you load a model from the **LightBox** browser into the canvas. On expanding a subpalette, various settings are displayed in it. The most commonly used subpalettes in the **Tool** palette are discussed next.

Note

*When you convert the primitive to polymesh 3D by using the **Make PolyMesh 3D** button from **Tool** pallete, some new subpalettes are added in the **Tool** palette*

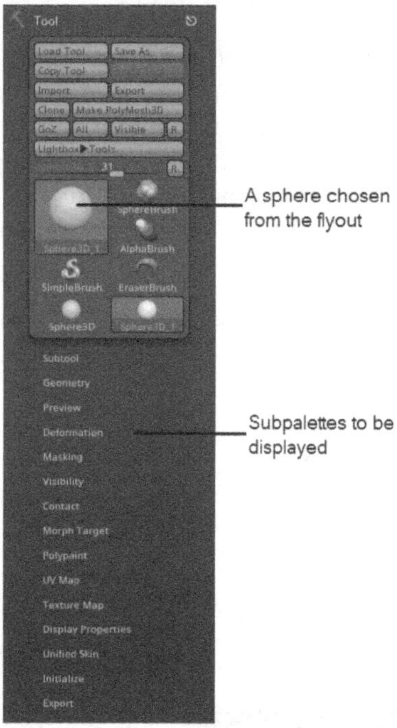

***Figure 3-9** Subpalettes displayed on choosing a primitive*

SubTool

In ZBrush, a 3D object is also known as a ZTool. A ZTool comprises of different 3D objects and it can be split into subtools. For instance, if a face and eyeballs are modeled separately, they will be displayed in the **SubTool** subpalettes as two different entities. You can select a subtool by pressing the ALT key and then clicking on that subtool in the canvas. Once a particular subtool is active, it can be edited without affecting the other subtools. The subtools will be discussed in detail in the later chapters.

Geometry

The **Geometry** subpalette comprises the option that are used to modify the polygons in a ZTool. Every ZTool in ZBrush consists of polygons which can be viewed by choosing the **PolyF** button located in the right shelf. In ZBrush, you can work on a ZTool that comprises of millions of polygons. To achieve a high level of detail on a ZTool, you need to have larger number of polygons. When you create a ZTool in the canvas, it has less number of polygons. You can change the number of polygons by using the **Geometry** subpalette. In addition to this, you can manage the flow of polygons in a ZTool using this subpalette.

The settings in the **Geometry** subpalette vary depending on the ZTool that has been created in the canvas. If you create a primitive 3D model, the settings in the **Geometry** subpalette will be displayed, as shown in Figure 3-10. When you convert a primitive model into a polymesh by choosing the **Make PolyMesh3D** button in the **Tool** palette, the settings will be displayed as shown in Figure 3-11. If you create a ZSphere in the canvas, the settings will be displayed as shown in Figure 3-12.

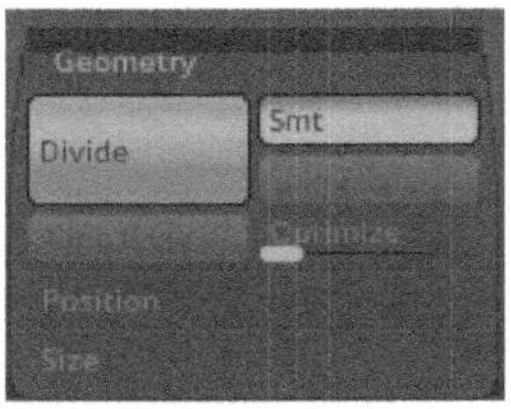

*Figure 3-10 The **Geometry** subpalette displayed on creating a primitive model*

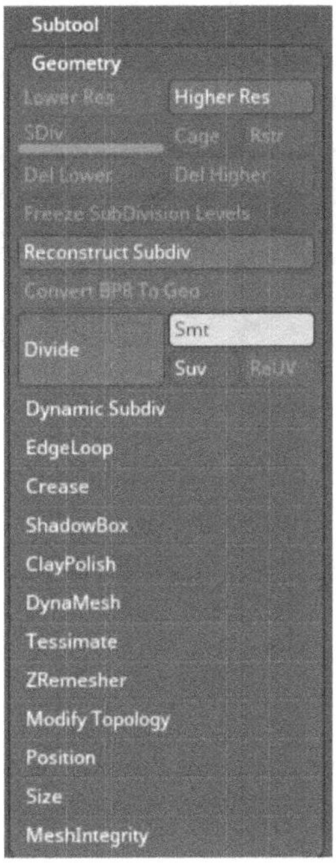

*Figure 3-11 The **Geometry** subpalette displayed on converting a primitive model into a polymesh*

The **Geometry** subpalette is mostly used when a primitive model has been converted into a polymesh. Some of the major tools in the **Geometry** subpalette corresponding to a polymesh are discussed next.

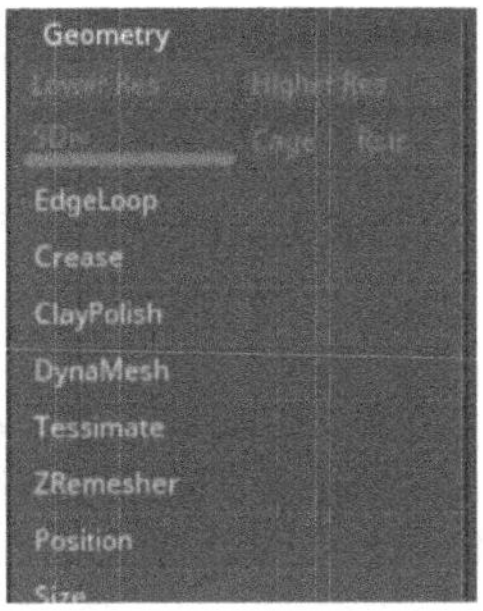

*Figure 3-12 The **Geometry** subpalette displayed on creating a ZSphere*

Lower Res

The **Lower Res** button is used to display the ZTool at its lower subdivision level so that you can move back and forth between the low poly and subdivided ZTools.

Higher Res

The **Higher Res** button is used to switch to the ZTool at higher subdivision levels so that you can move back and forth between the low poly ZTool and the subdivided ZTool. At lower subdivisions, you can sculpt major details in a ZTool and at higher subdivisions you can add subtle details. For example, if you are sculpting a face in ZBrush, you can add nose, eye sockets, and lip area at the lower subdivision levels. After adding the major details, you can move to the higher subdivision levels and add further details, such as pores, wrinkles, and face cuts.

SDiv

The **SDiv** slider is used to scroll through all the subdivision levels. You can press D to move to a higher subdivision level and press SHIFT+D to move to a lower subdivision level. Each time you subdivide the ZTool using the **Divide** button, the **SDiv** slider should be at its highest subdivision level. Alternatively, you can press CTRL+D to move to a higher subdivision level. If it is not at its highest subdivision level, a message box will be displayed, as shown in Figure 3-13.

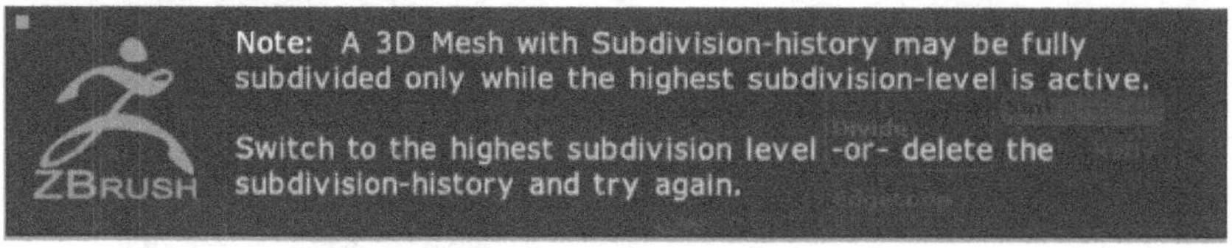

*Figure 3-13 A message box displayed when the **SDiv** slider is not at its highest subdivision level*

Cage

The **Cage** button is used to retain the shape and placement of the polygons even if the geometry is divided a number of times. If this button is not chosen and the geometry is divided, the shape and placement of the polygons at the lower subdivision levels changes. This button is deactivated when the object is at its highest subdivision level.

Rstr

The **Rstr** button is used to restore the geometry to higher subdivision levels by avoiding the changes that have been made at the lower subdivision levels.

Del Lower

The **Del Lower** button is used to delete all subdivision levels below the current **SDiv** value.

Del Higher

The **Del Higher** button is used to remove all subdivision levels above the current **SDiv** value.

Freeze SubDivision Levels

The **Freeze Subdivision Levels** button is used to store all subdivision levels and display the ZTool at the lowest subdivision level. This button enables you to make changes in the geometry of a ZTool at its lowest subdivision level.

Reconstruct Subdiv

The **Reconstruct Subdiv** button is used to decrease the subdivision levels in a ZTool. On choosing this button, a low resolution model having a low number of polygons will be displayed.

Convert BPR to Geo

The **Convert BPR to Geo** button is used to convert a **FiberMesh** into an editable geometry. The **FiberMesh** will be discussed in detail in the later chapters.

Divide

The **Divide** button is used to increase the number of polygons in the ZTool. ZBrush gives you an option to switch to the lower subdivision level model so that you can move back and forth between the low poly ZTool and the subdivided ZTool. At lower subdivisions, you can sculpt the major details in a model, and at higher subdivisions, you can add fine details.

Smt

The **Smt** button located next to the **Divide** button is activated by default. As a result, the ZTool is smoothened each time you click on the **Divide** button. If this button is not chosen, the hard edges of the model will be visible even if you subdivide the ZTool.

Suv

The **Suv** button is used to smoothen the UV coordinates of a ZTool when the geometry is subdivided. This button will be discussed in detail in the later chapters.

Dynamic Subdiv

The options in the **Dynamic Subdiv** area are used to apply dynamic smoothening to the models without dividing the polygons. This feature is mainly designed to work in association with the **ZModeler** brush and low polygonal models.

EdgeLoop

The **EdgeLoop** area comprises the options which can be used to select and modify the loop of edges.

Crease

The **Crease** area comprises of the options that are used to define one or both sides of the edge of an object, thus creating a crease which is partially round. When crease tags are assigned to the edges of an open mesh (such as a plane object), they protect the edges from shrinking inward when smoothening is performed. You can crease all the edges of the selected mesh. Also, you can set the crease edge tolerance and bevel the edges using the **Bevel** button.

ShadowBox

The **Shadow Box** buttonl establishes a three-sided box that will allow masking on all three planes. If more then one plane is masked, then ShadowBox will create a mesh at the point where the mask intersects. On choosing this button, a mesh will be created on the plane where there is a mask. The parameters in the **Shadowbox** area and their usage is discussed in detail in Chapter 9.

ClayPolish

ClayPolish is a post-process operation which can be used to modify the topological structure of a model and move its edges based on various settings. During this operation, the surface of the model can be polished while sharpening and cleaning the angles. This operation can also create special effects on the edges of the model.

Dynamesh

The **DynaMesh** area is displayed only when an object is created in the canvas and is converted into a polymesh.

Tessimate

The **Tessimate** area consists of two buttons: **Tessimate** and **Decimate**. The **Tessimate** button is used to increase the polygons in the model and the **Decimate** button is used to decrease the polygons in the model.

ZRemesher

ZRemesher is used for remeshing or retopologizing a mesh. Additionally, ZRemesher is used to create a new topology for the selected subtool that consists of millions of polygons. This enables you to control the flow of polygons in a mesh as per your requirement. Besides this, ZRemesher also enables you to convert a model with millions of polygons into a model with less number of polygons.

Modify Topology

The options in this area are used to easily modify topology for subdivision surfaces. Using these options, you can delete the hidden polygons from mesh, insert a new mesh into the selected mesh, close all open holes of the mesh, and so on.

Stager

The options in the **Stager** area are used to set the home and target position of the model. To do so, choose the **LightBox** button; the **LightBox** browser is displayed. Next, choose **DemoProjects** from the **Project** tab; various files are displayed. Double-click on **DemoTreeFrog.ZPR**; the model will be displayed in the canvas with a message box, as shown in Figure 3-14. Next, choose brush and expand the **SubTool** subpalette . Now, select the **Eyes** subtool from the subtool list and using the left mouse button, move the cursor upward below the **Demo_TreeFrog**. Next, select the **Demo_TreeFrog** subtool and expand the **Merge** area. Now, choose the **MergeDown** button; the **Demo_TreeFrog** and **Eyes** subtools in the **SubTool** subpalette are merged. Now, expand the **Stager** area, activate the **Move** tool and then move the **MapCap Sphere**, as shown in Figure 3-15. Next, choose the **Home Stage** button to set the home position. Next, using the **Move** tool, move **MatCap Sphere** to the target position and choose the **Target Stage** button from the **Stager** area, as shown in Figure 3-16. Now, choose the **Switch Stage** button to switch the **MatCap Sphere** from home position to target position.

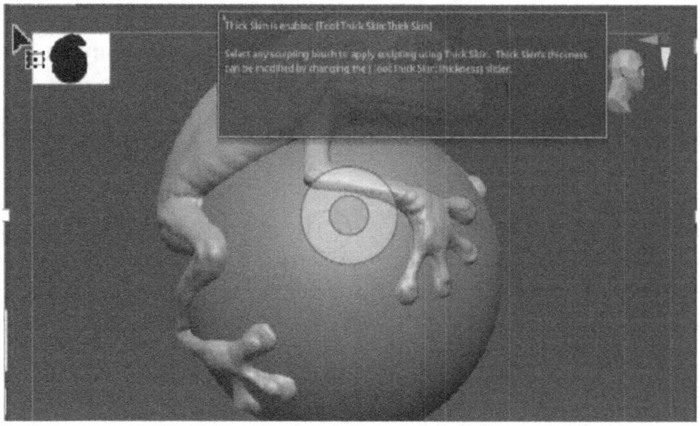

Figure 3-14 The DemoTreeFrog.ZPR model

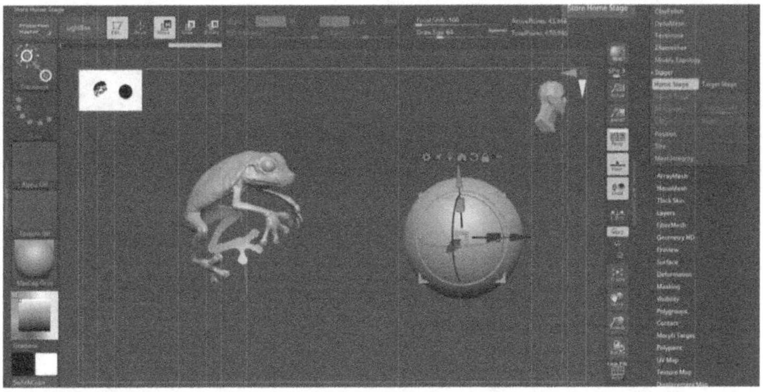

Figure 3-15 Setting the home position of the ***MatCap Sphere*** *model*

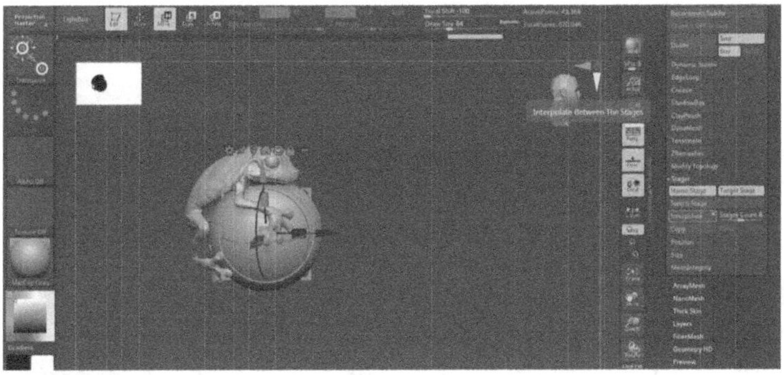

Figure 3-16 Setting the target position of the ***MatCap Sphere*** *model*

Position

The options in the **Position** area are used to move the selected subtool along the X, Y, and Z positions.

Size

The sliders in the **Size** area are used to adjust the size of the selected subtool. The value set in this slider is absolute so setting the value back to the previous value will restore the previous size.

MeshIntegrity

In the **MeshIntegrity** area, the **Check Mesh Integrity** button is used to check the integrity of the mesh and the **Fix Mesh** button is used to repair topology of your mesh.

Layers

The **Layers** subpalette, as shown in Figure 3-17, is used to manage a complex ZBrush scene in such a way that different stages of the scene development are saved in different layers, thus enabling you to modify different stages independently. You can add detail to each layer separately and the intensity of the depth created can be changed by moving the sliders below each layer. You can rename or delete any layer by choosing the **Delete** or **Rename Layer** button, respectively. In the **Layers** subpalette, you can create sixteen different layers. New layers can be created by choosing the **New** button in the **Layers** subpalette. The **Bake All** button is used to bake all layers and transfer the results of all those layers to the ZTool in the canvas.

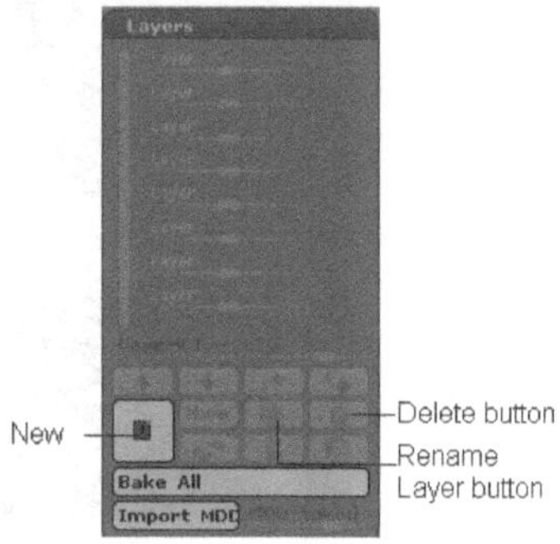

***Figure 3-17** The **Layers** subpalette*

FiberMesh

The **FiberMesh** subpalette is used to create hair or fiber on the surface of an existing object. This subpalette consists of different settings that are used to modify the geometry of the fibers. These settings enable you to create different hairstyles. The **FiberMesh** will be discussed in detail in the later chapters.

Geometry HD

The **Geometry HD** subpalette is used to add additional level of high definition subdivisions in a model. After adding subdivisions to the model, you cannot add or delete the standard subdivision levels. This subpalette enables you to add a higher level of detail to a model that cannot be achieved by subdividing the geometry in the **Geometry** subpalette.

Preview

The **Preview** subpalette enables you to view and change the orientation of the 3D object on the canvas. It consists of a small preview area in which the 3D object will be visible, refer to Figure 3-18. You can move the object inside the preview area. The changes made in the orientation of the object inside the preview area are reflected in the canvas as well.

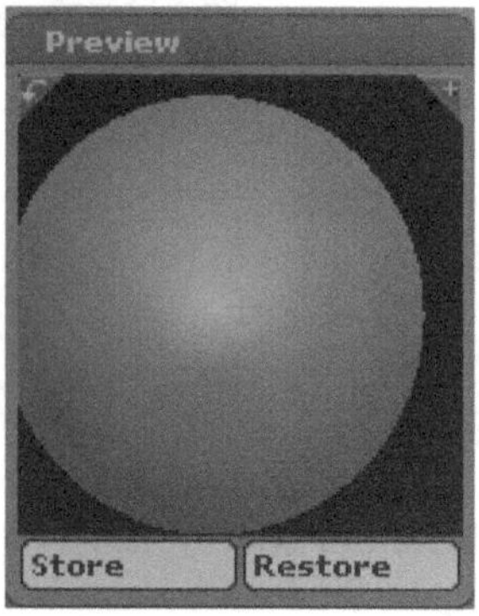

***Figure 3-18** The preview area in the **Preview** subpalette*

Surface

The **Surface** subpalette, as shown in Figure 3-19, is used to add noise to a ZTool. To add noise to a ZTool, choose the **Noise** button in the **Surface** subpalette; the **NoiseMaker** window containing the preview of the object will be displayed, refer to Figure 3-20. You can change the magnitude of the noise by dragging the **Scale** slider, refer to Figure 3-20. After adjusting the magnitude of the noise, choose the **OK** button; the noise will be applied to the ZTool in the canvas.

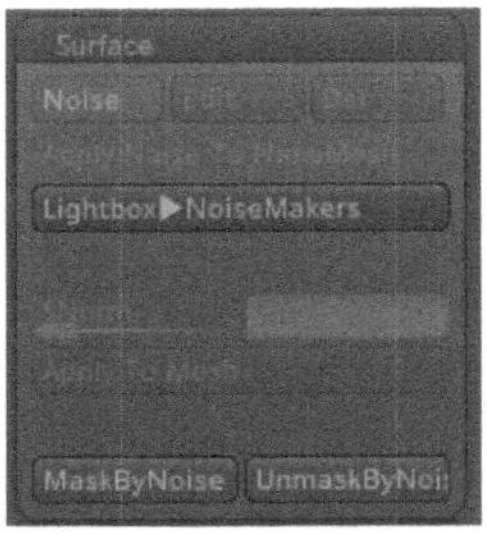

*Figure 3-19 The **Surface** subpalette*

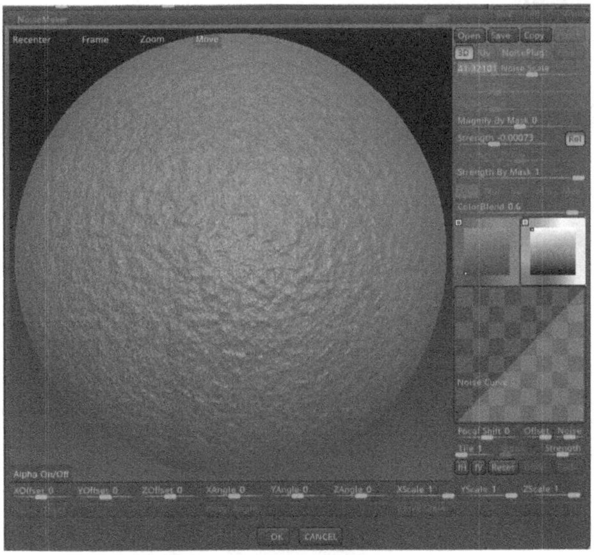

*Figure 3-20 The **NoiseMaker** window*

Deformation

The **Deformation** subpalette is used to change specifications such as orientation, angle of rotation, and size of a ZTool. It also contains various options such as **Bend**, **Skew**, **Flatten**, **Twist**, **Taper**, **Squeeze**, **Inflate**, and **Gravity**, refer to Figure 3-21. These options enable you to modify a ZTool as required.

Masking

The **Masking** subpalette is used with the mask brushes. The settings in this subpalette enable you to invert, blur, sharpen, clear, or clear a mask created on the surface of an object. You can also apply the mask on the surface of an object by color or alpha.

Visibility

The **Visibility** subpalette is used with the mask brushes. The settings in this subpalette enable you to grow, shrink, hide, and show a mask created on the surface of an object.

Contact

The **Contact** subpalette is used to establish points of contact between different subtools. These contact points will enable movement of a subtool with respect to another subtool. This palette is mainly used for the posing of the ZTools. For instance, if you model a face and eyeballs separately, then on moving the face, the eyeballs will remain stationary. Now, if you establish a point of contact between the face subtool and the eyeballs subtools, the eyeballs will move along with the face.

Morph Target

The **Morph Target** subpalette is used to save the current state of a ZTool before making any further changes so that you can switch back and forth between the saved geometry and the changed geometry.

Polypaint

The **Polypaint** subpalette is used to paint colors on a ZTool. The colors can be selected using the color picker. The subpalette consists of two buttons, namely **Colorize** and **Grd**, refer to Figure 3-22. The **Colorize** button is used to paint colors directly into the polygons of an object and the **Grad** button is used to add gradient to the ZTool.

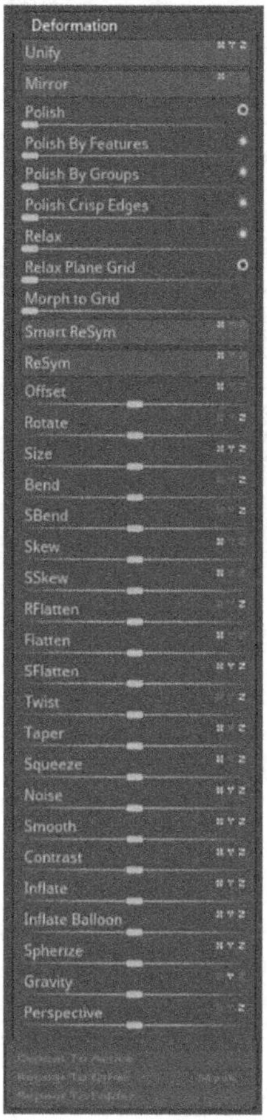

*Figure 3-21 The **Deformation** subpalette*

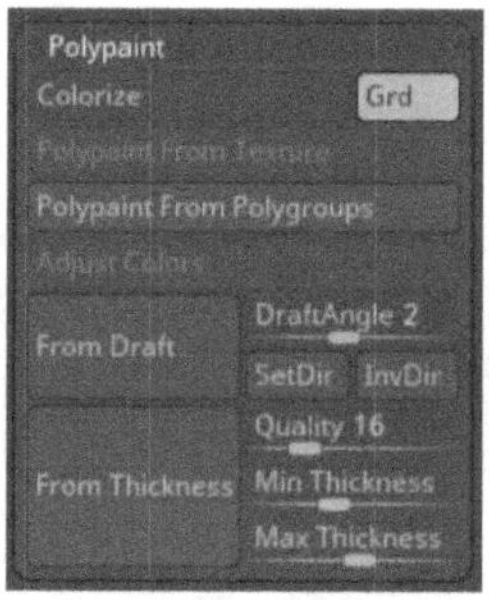

*Figure 3-22 The **Polypaint** subpalette*

UV Map

The **UV Map** subpalette is used to unwrap a ZTool. The ZTool can be unwrapped only when it is at its lowest subdivision level. This subpalette will be discussed in detail in the later chapters.

Texture Map

The **Texture Map** subpalette is used to select and assign texture to a ZTool. ZBrush has an inbuilt library of textures. This subpalette also gives you an option to import textures from other locations.

Unified Skin

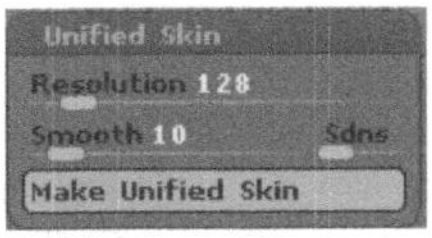

*Figure 3-23 The **Make Unified Skin** button in the **Unified Skin** subpalette*

The **Unified Skin** subpalette is used to create a new ZTool when it is applied to an existing ZTool. The new ZTool thus created will have smooth edges between different parts and the polygons in it will be distributed uniformly. To create a new ZTool, choose the **Make Unified Skin** button from this palette, as shown in Figure 3-23. The new ZTool will appear in the tool library with the term Skin prefixed before the name of the actual ZTool. If you choose the new ZTool from the library, it will appear on the canvas. The new ZTool will have a large number of polygons as compared to the actual ZTool, refer to Figure 3-24.

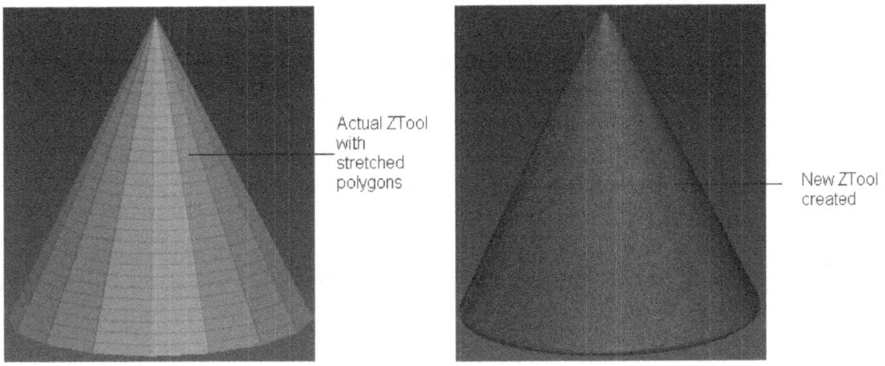

*Figure 3-24 The ZTool created after choosing the **Make Unified Skin** button*

The **Resolution** slider in this palette is used to change the number of polygons in the new ZTool. Its value ranges from 16 to 1024. By default, its value is 128. The **Smooth** slider is used to change the smoothness of the new ZTool. Its value ranges from 0 to 100.

Initialize

The **Initialize** subpalette is used to change the dimensions of the ZTool as required. Figure 3-25 shows the **Initialize** subpalette when the primitive is not converted to polymesh. After converting a primitive into polymesh, the options in the **Initialize** subpalette are changed.

Note

*When you convert a primitive model into a polymesh by choosing the **Make Polymesh 3D** button from the **Tool** palette, the options in the **Initialize** subpalette control the mesh primitives based on the **X**, **Y**, and **Z** resolution sliders.*

Export

The **Export** subpalette is used to export a ZTool to other locations. This subpalette consists of two buttons namely, **Qud** and **Tri**, refer to Figure 3-26. These buttons determine whether the polygons in the exported ZTool will be in the shape of quadrilaterals or triangles.

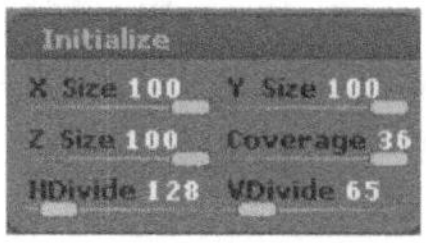

*Figure 3-25 The **Initialize** subpalette*

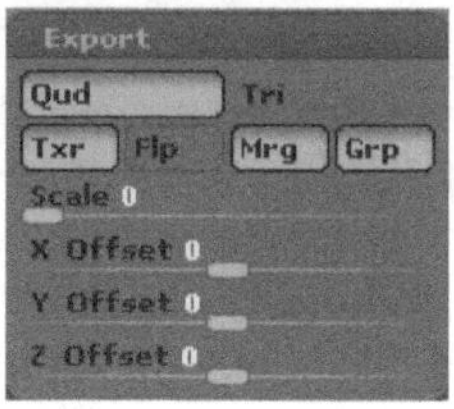

*Figure 3-26 The **Export** subpalette*

Projection Master

The **Projection Master** button is used to add details to a 3D model by temporarily converting it into a 2.5D image. The **Projection Master** button can be accessed either from the **Zplugin** palette or by pressing the G key. It enables you to sculpt and texture the visible portion of a ZTool. After choosing the **Projection Master** button, the visible portion of a 3D model is converted into a 2.5D illustration on the canvas. The 3D model is temporarily removed from the canvas and you can add detail to the 2.5D representation of the model.

To add details to a model using the **Projection Master**, you have to make sure that the model has been subdivided properly and is at its highest subdivision level. Next, choose the **Projection Master** button from the **Zplugin** palette, refer to Figure 3-27; the **Projection Master** dialog box will be displayed, as shown in Figure 3-28. The options in this dialog box are discussed next.

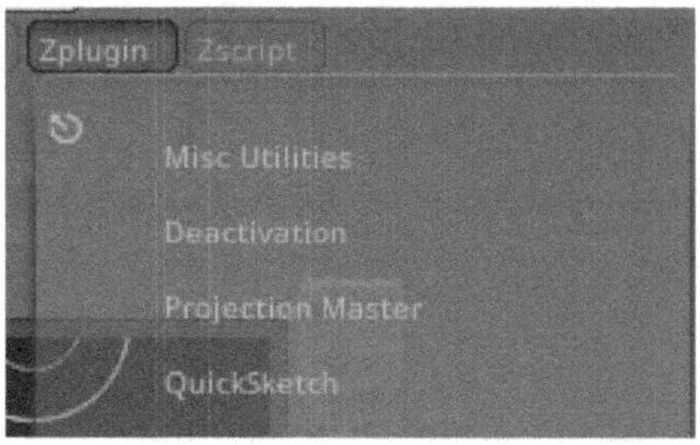

*Figure 3-27 The **Projection Master** button in the **Zplugin** palette*

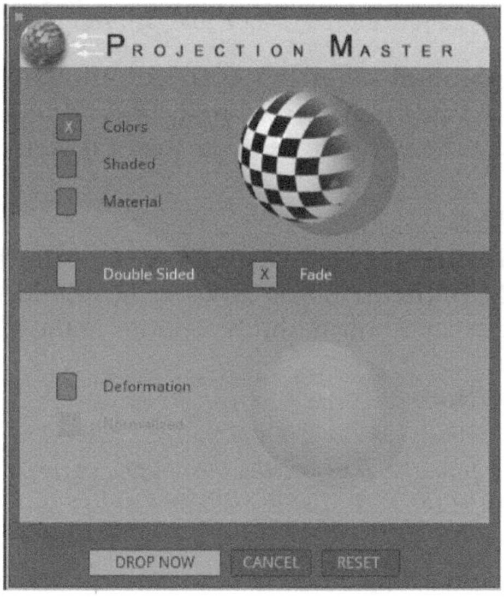

*Figure 3-28 The **Projection Master** dialog box*

Colors

This check box is used to paint color on a portion of the 3D model. By default, the **Color** check box is selected. As a result, when you choose the **DROP NOW** button, a message box will be displayed, refer to Figure 3-29. Choose the **Activate Polypainting** button from this message box; the 3D model will be converted into its 2.5D illustration and you can color only the portion that is visible in the canvas. Next, you need to select the colors from the color swatch and then paint the desired colors on the visible area of the 2.5D illustration, refer to Figure 3-30. After painting the model, choose the **Projection Master** button from the **Zplugin** palette; the **Projection Master** dialog box will be displayed again, refer to Figure 3-31. Choose the **PICKUP NOW** button from this dialog box; the illustration will be again converted into a 3D model, with the color applied on it.

Similar to applying colors, you can also apply depth to the model by using the **Z Add** button located in the top shelf.

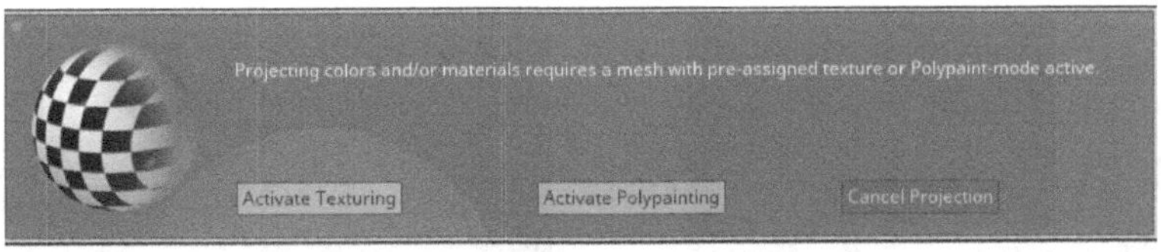

Figure 3-29 *Message box displayed on choosing the* ***DROP NOW*** *button*

Figure 3-30 *Colors painted on the 2D illustration*

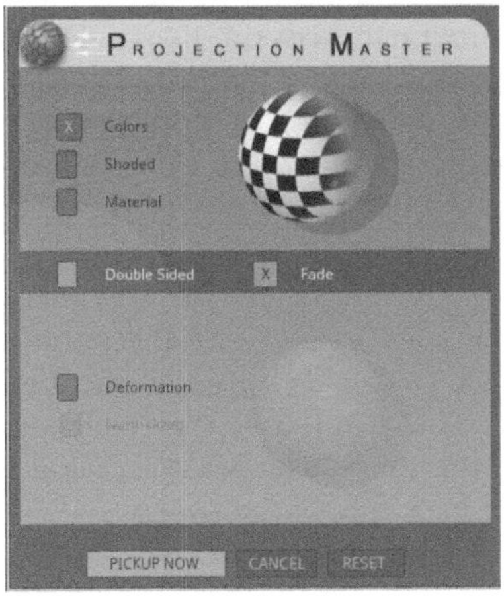

Figure 3-31 *The* ***PICKUP NOW*** *button in the* ***Projection Master*** *dialog box*

Shaded

The **Shaded** check box is used to add different attributes such as lights, shadows, and reflectivity to a ZTool. You need to select this check box along with the **Colors** check box. After selecting the **Colors** and **Shaded** check boxes from the **Projection Master** dialog box, choose the **DROP NOW** button. Next, start painting on the 2.5D illustration of the 3D model, refer to Figure 3-32. After painting on the visible surface, choose the **Projection Master** button again. Now, in the **Projection Master** dialog box, choose the **PICKUP NOW** button; the 2.5D illustration will be converted into a 3D model and shading will be applied to the surface that was visible while painting, refer to Figure 3-33.

Figure 3-32 *The 2.5D illustration of the model painted*

Figure 3-33 *Shading applied on the visible portion of the model*

Material

The **Material** check box enables you to paint materials on the surface of a ZTool. To do so, choose the **Material** check box from the **Projection Master** and then choose the **DROP NOW** button; a dialog box will be displayed. Choose the **Activate Polypainting** button from this dialog box; the 3D model will be converted into its 2.5D illustration. Now, you need to choose the materials from the flyout displayed on choosing the Current Material button from the left shelf, refer to Figure 3-34. Next, paint the desired materials on the visible area of the 2.5D illustration. After painting the materials on the model, choose the **Projection Master** button from the **Zplugin** palette; the **Projection Master** dialog box will be displayed again. Choose the **PICKUP NOW** button from this dialog box; the illustration will be again converted into a 3D model containing the materials applied on the 2.5D illustration, refer to Figure 3-35.

Double Sided

The **Double Sided** check box is used to replicate the painting on the opposite side of the ZTool. Before selecting this check box, make sure that the ZTool has not been converted into a polymesh. Figure 3-36 shows colors painted on the 2D illustration of a sphere as the **Double Sided** check box is selected in the **Projection Master** dialog box and Figure 3-37 shows the painted colors replicated on the back side of the sphere.

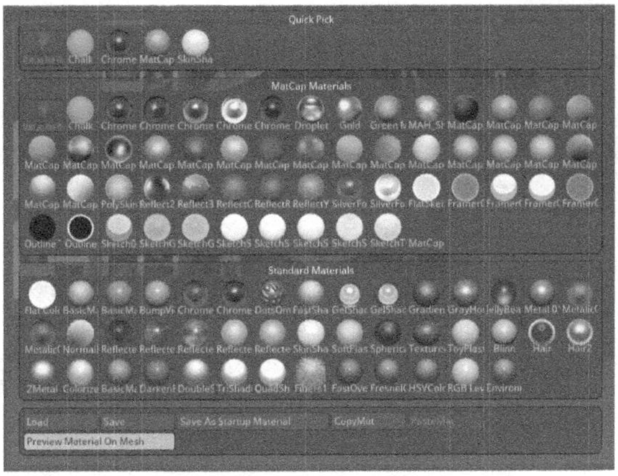

Figure 3-34 The flyout displayed

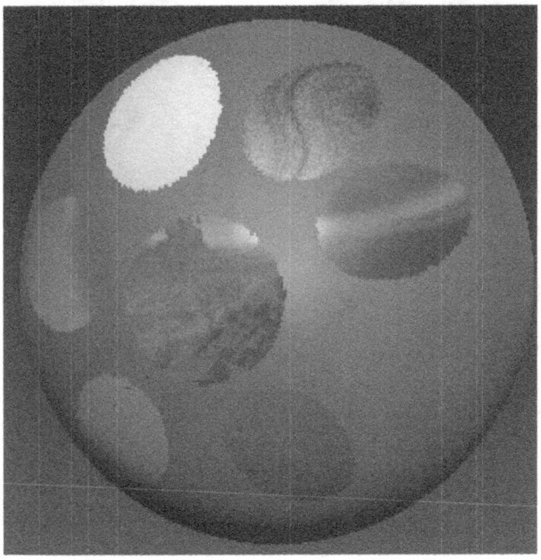

Figure 3-35 The 3D model with painted materials

Fade

The **Fade** check box is used to fade the color in those areas of the model that are not perpendicular to the screen. By default, the **Fade** check box is selected. The effect of the **Fade** option will be less at the areas perpendicular to the screen. Figure 3-38 shows the 2D illustration of a painted sphere with the **Fade** check box selected in the **Projection Master** dialog box and Figure 3-39 shows the fade effect on the sphere.

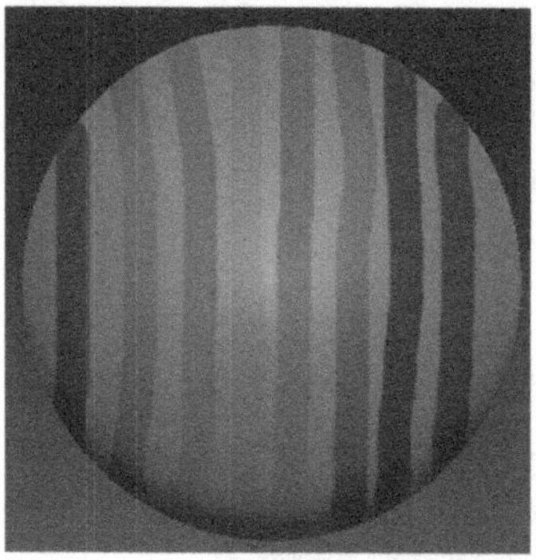

Figure 3-36 *Different colors painted on the 2D illustration*

Figure 3-37 *Painted colors replicated on the backside of the sphere*

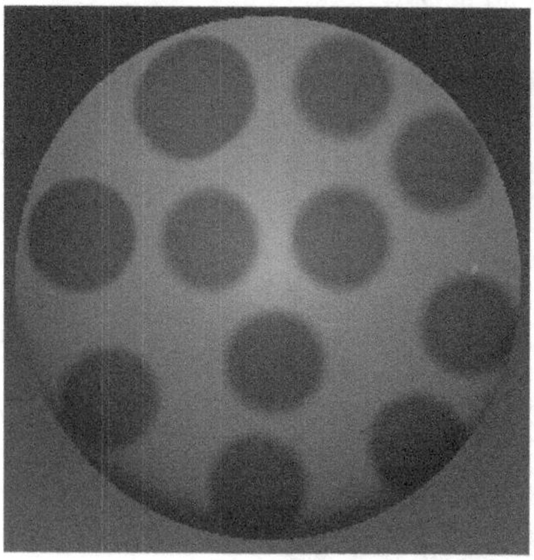

Figure 3-38 *The 2D illustration of a sphere painted with the* ***Fade*** *check box selected*

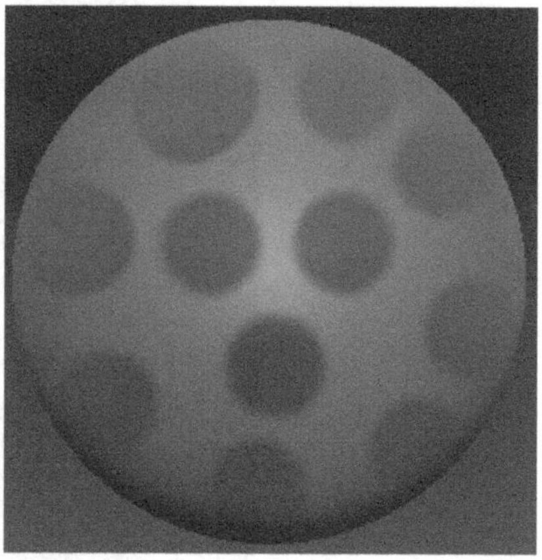

Figure 3-39 *Effect after selecting the* ***Fade*** *check box on the sphere*

Deformation

The **Deformation** check box is used to sculpt finer details on the surface of a model, which cannot be achieved in the normal 3D mode. When the **Projection Master** button is chosen, new stroke types are added to the flyout displayed on choosing the Current Stroke button, refer to Figure 3-40. These strokes along with the alphas enable you to sculpt different patterns on the surface of the model. But before selecting this check box, you have to make sure that the primitive object has been converted into a polymesh and is subdivided. If you use this option on a primitive object, a message box will be displayed, as shown in Figure 3-41.

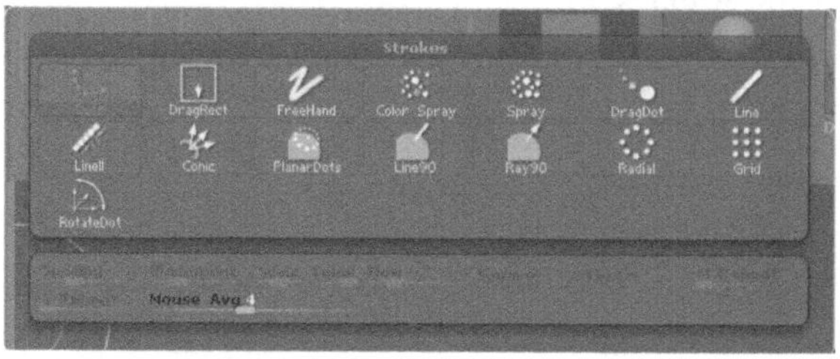

Figure 3-40 *New stroke types added in the Stroke flyout*

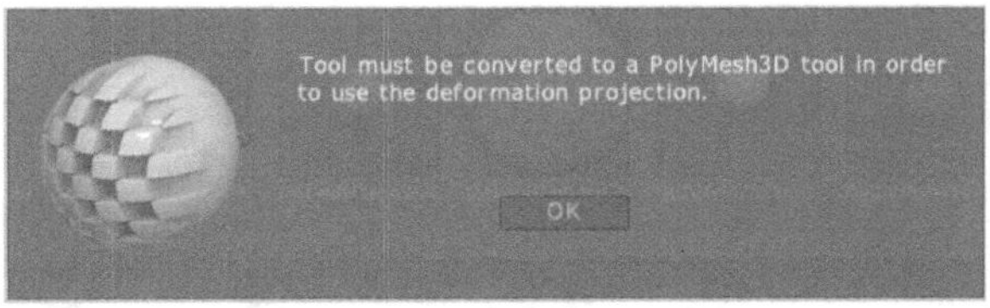

***Figure 3-41** The message displayed on selecting the **Deformation** check box for a primitive object*

The **Line** stroke enables you to sculpt straight lines on the surface of an object, which cannot be achieved in the normal 3D mode. The depth of the sculpting can be controlled by adjusting the value in the **Zadd** slider. On selecting the **Deformation** and **Color** check boxes together, you can add desired colors to the sculpted areas.

Figure 3-42 shows different patterns created on the surface of a sphere by using different strokes and alphas with the **Deformation** check box selected in the **Projection Master** dialog box.

The patterns created on the surface can be moved, scaled, or rotated by using the **Move**, **Scale**, and **Rotate** buttons, respectively. To move the last pattern created on the surface, choose the **Move** button; a gyro will be displayed. For moving the object upward, click on the pink arc and drag the cursor upward, and for moving the object toward left, click on the cyan arc and drag the cursor toward left, refer to Figure 3-43.

For sculpting using the **Deformation** check box, you can choose different types of 2.5D brushes available in the flyout that is displayed on choosing the Current Tool button located in the **Tool** palette, refer to Figure 3-44. This flyout contains about 32 different brushes. You can choose any of these brushes, depending on the sculpting to be done.

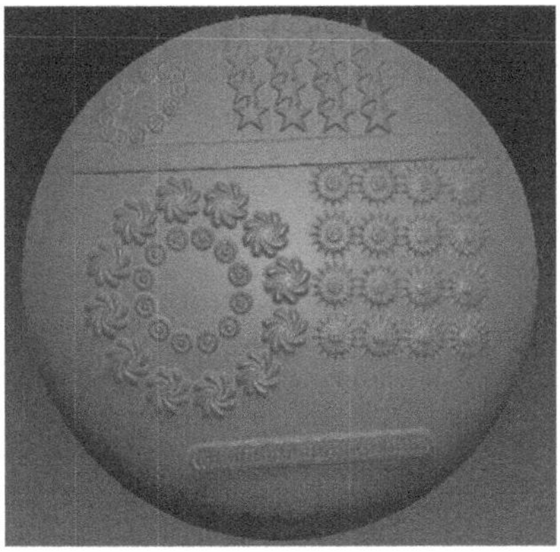

***Figure 3-42** Different patterns created using different strokes and alphas*

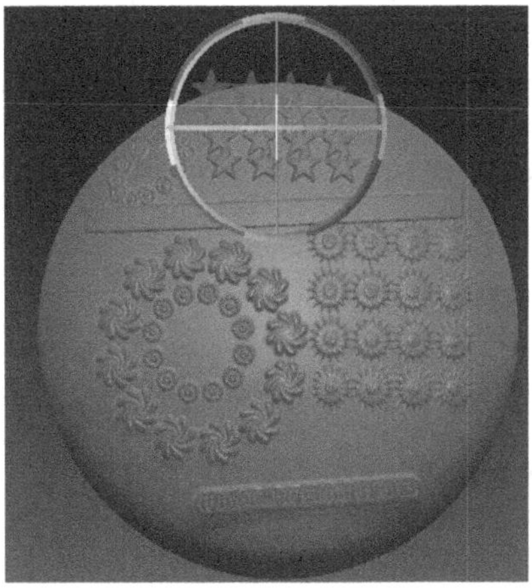

***Figure 3-43** Moving a pattern toward left*

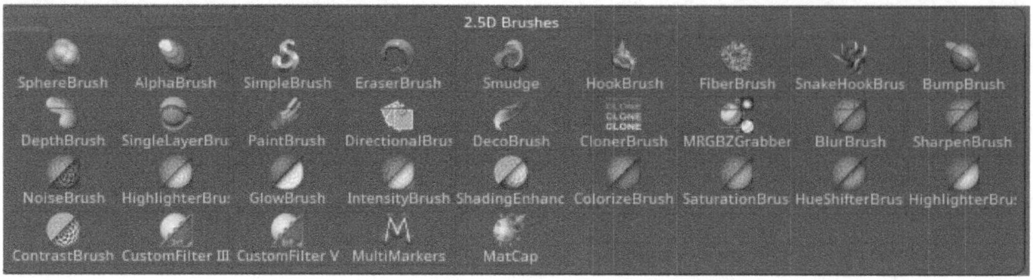

Figure 3-44 *The 2.5D brushes in the **Tool** flyout*

Figure 3-45 shows different types of sculpting done on the sphere by using different 2.5D brushes.

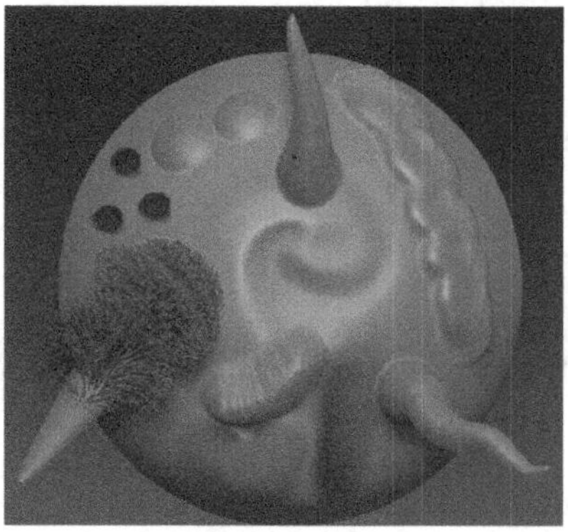

Figure 3-45 *Different types of sculpting done by using different 2.5D brushes*

Normalized

The **Normalized** check box is used along with the **Deformation** check box. On selecting this check box, the deformation occurred on the model will be projected at right angles to the surface of the ZTool. This check box is mostly used when the depth of deformation is significantly large. If this check box is not selected, the deformation will occur towards the screen facing the canvas.

DROP NOW

The **DROP NOW** button is used to convert a 3D model into a 2.5D illustration. After choosing this button, you cannot move, rotate, or scale the model.

PICKUP NOW

The **PICKUP NOW** button is used to pick up the sculpting and texturing pattern from the 2.5D illustration and transfer it to the 3D model. On choosing this button, the 2.5D illustration will be converted back to the 3D model.

ARRAY MESH

The **Arrays** tab in the **LightBox** browser is used to create duplicate instances of a geometry in various patterns and shapes. You can modify and control the duplication process using the attributes of the array. To do so, choose the **LightBox** button; the **LightBox** browser that contains a library of ZBrush documents, ZTools, ZBrush projects, brushes, alphas, textures, materials, array, and so on will be displayed, refer to Figure 3-46. Next, choose the **Arrays** tab; the array presets will be displayed, as shown in Figure 3-47. You can also access and control the attributes of the array by choosing the **Array Mesh** button from the **ArrayMesh** subpalette of the **Tool** palette, refer to Figure 3-48.

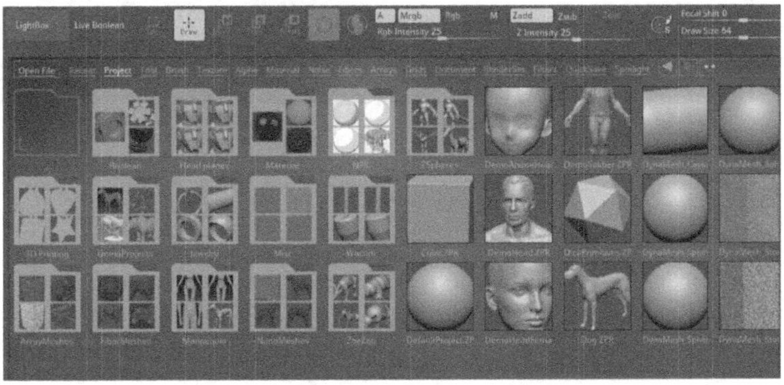

Figure 3-46 The **LightBox** browser displayed

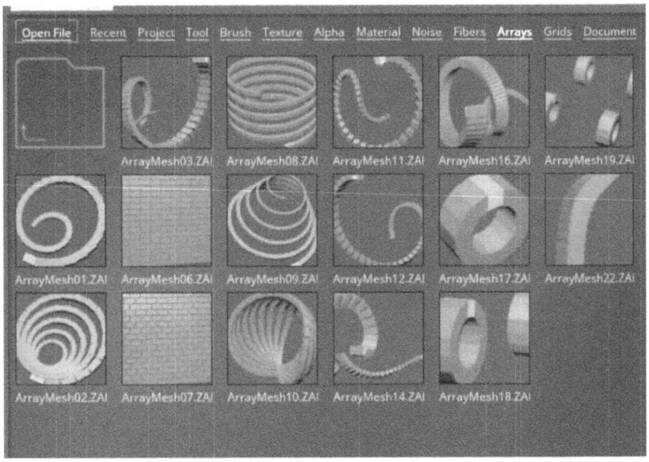

Figure 3-47 The array presets displayed

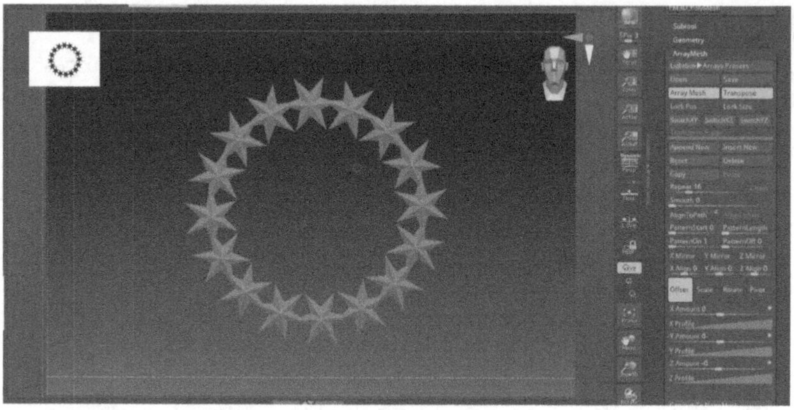

Figure 3-48 *Setting the attributes of array*

TUTORIALS

Before you start the tutorials of this chapter, you need to browse to the *Documents* folder and then create a new folder with the name *ZBrushprojects*. In the *ZBrushprojects* folder, create another folder with the name *c03*.

Tutorial 1

In this tutorial, you will create a turtle shell using a sphere and different sculpting brushes. The final output of the model is shown in Figure 3-49. **(Expected time: 20 min)**

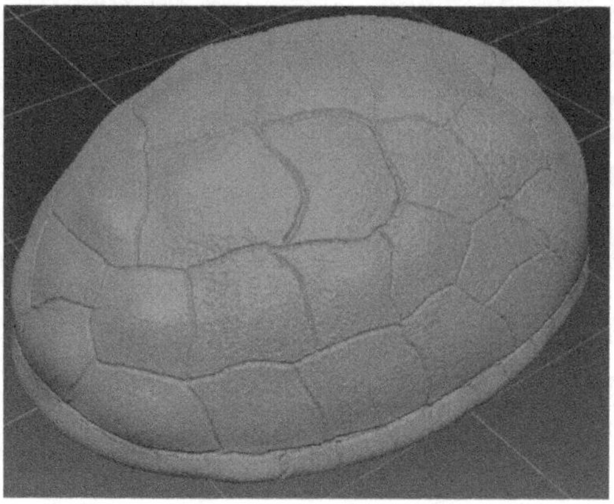

Figure 3-49 *The turtle shell*

The following steps are required to complete this tutorial:

a. Create the basic shape of the turtle shell.
b. Create divisions in the shell.
c. Add details to the shell.
d. Save the model.

Creating the Basic Shape of the Turtle Shell

In this section, you will create the basic shape of the turtle shell using the *DynaMesh_Sphere_32.ZPR* file located in the **LightBox** browser.

1. Before starting this tutorial, you have to initialize ZBrush to its default state. Choose the **Init ZBrush** button from the **Preferences** palette; ZBrush is initialized to its default state.

2. Double-click on **DynaMesh_Sphere_32.ZPR** in the **Project** tab of the **LightBox** browser, refer to Figure 3-50. The sphere is created on the canvas, as shown in Figure 3-51.

   In the **DynaMesh_Sphere_32.ZPR** file, the symmetry will be activated in the X-axis by default. As a result, the sculpting done will be mirrored along the X-axis.

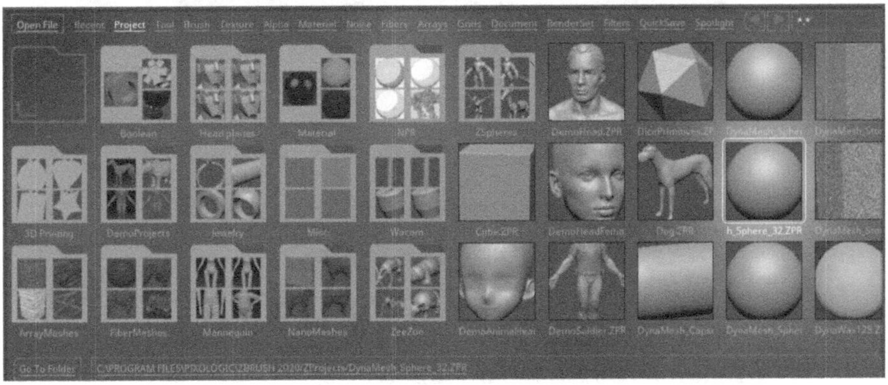

*Figure 3-50 The **DynaMesh_Sphere_32.ZPR** file chosen from the **LightBox** browser*

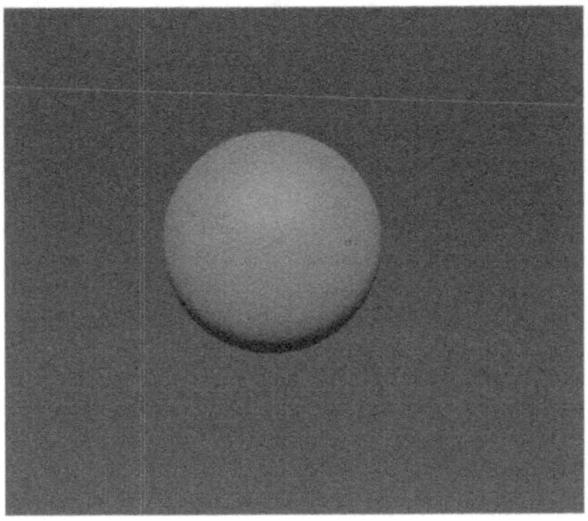

*Figure 3-51 The **DynaMesh_Sphere_32** model created on the canvas*

Note

*If the **LightBox** browser does not appear on opening the ZBrush window, it can be displayed by choosing the **LightBox** button located in the top shelf, refer to Figure 3-52.*

***Figure 3-52** The **LightBox** button in the top shelf*

3. Choose the Current Brush button from the left shelf; a flyout containing different sculpting brushes is displayed. Choose the **ClipRect** brush from this flyout, as shown in Figure 3-53; a message box is displayed prompting you to press CTRL+SHIFT keys to activate this brush, refer to Figure 3-54. Choose the **OK** button to close this message box.

***Figure 3-53** Choosing the **ClipRect** brush from the flyout*

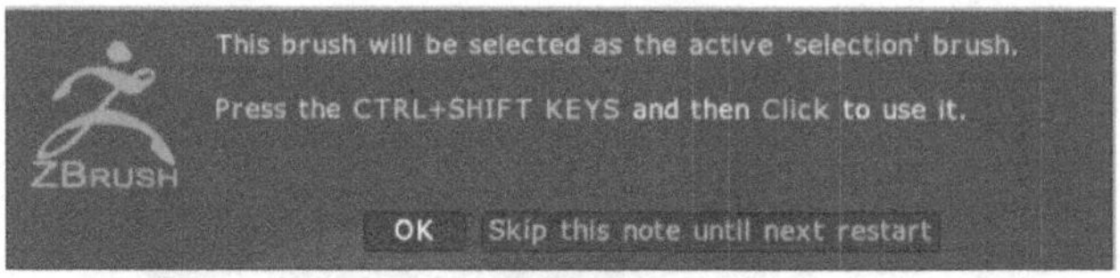

***Figure 3-54** Message box displayed on choosing the **ClipRect** brush*

4. Press CTRL+SHIFT keys and then press and hold the left mouse button. Next, drag the cursor over the sphere; a rectangular marquee selection appears. Select the upper half of the sphere, refer to Figure 3-55. Now, release the left mouse button; the lower half of the sphere is deleted, refer to Figure 3-56.

5. Expand the **Deformation** subpalette in the **Tool** palette, refer to Figure 3-57. You need to increase the size of the sphere along the Z-axis using the **Size** slider.

6. Deactivate the x and y options corresponding to the **Size** slider by choosing the **x** and **y** buttons located on the right side of the slider, refer to Figure 3-58.

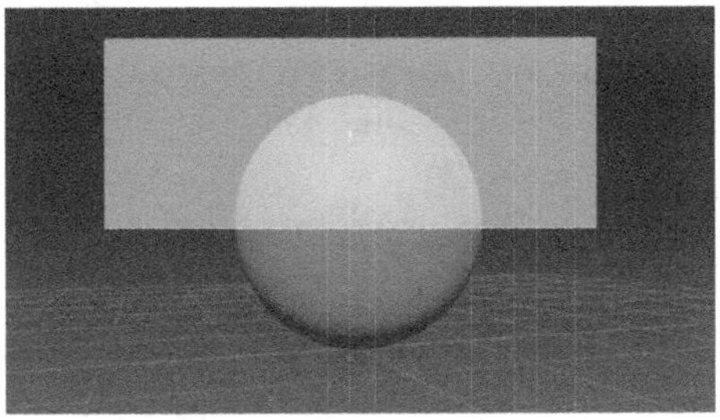

Figure 3-55 *Upper part of sphere selected using the marquee selection*

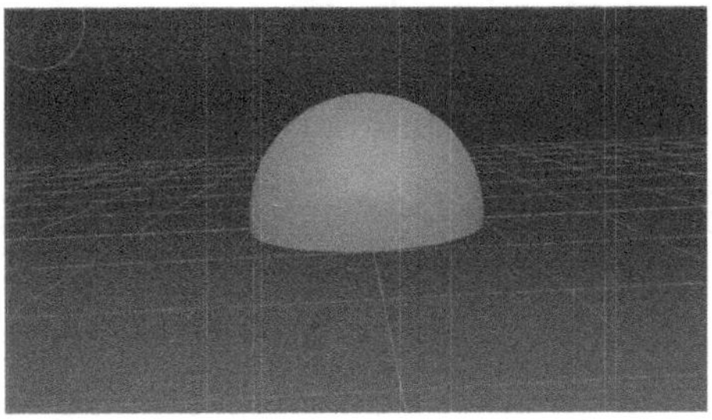

Figure 3-56 *Lower half of the sphere deleted*

7. Set the value of the **Size** slider to **20** by dragging the slider toward right; the sphere is elongated along the Z-axis. Alternatively, you can enter **20** in the edit box displayed on clicking on the slider, refer to Figure 3-59

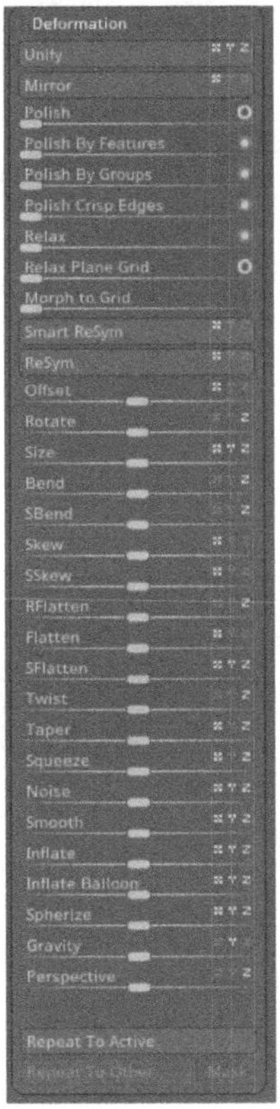

Figure 3-57 *The* ***Deformation*** *subpalette expanded*

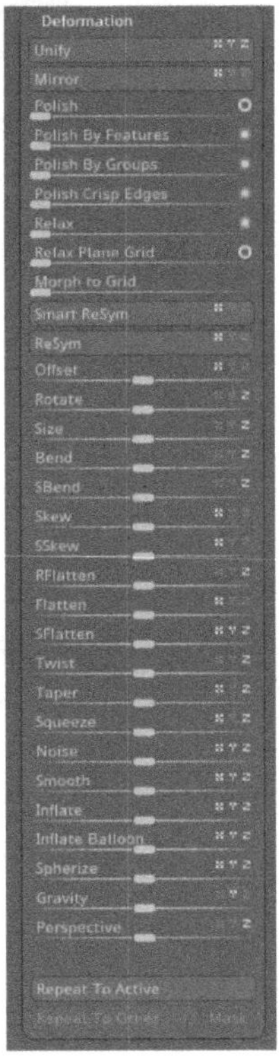

Figure 3-58 *The* **x** *and* **y** *options deactivated*

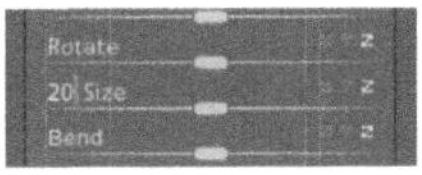

Figure 3-59 *Value entered in the edit box*

8. Expand the **SubTool** subpalette in the **Tool** palette. Next, in this subpalette, choose the **Rename** button; the **Please enter subtool title** window consisting of a text box is displayed. Enter **turtle shell** in this text box and press ENTER; the sphere primitive is renamed as *turtle shell*.

9. To view the elongated *turtle shell*, you need to switch to its top view. To do so, press and hold the left mouse button, and drag the cursor downward in the canvas area; the view is rotated and the top view of the *turtle shell* is displayed, refer to Figure 3-60.

10. Rotate the view of the canvas such that you can view the side view of *turtle shell*. Choose the Current Brush button from the left shelf; a flyout containing different sculpting brushes is displayed. Choose the **Standard** brush from this flyout if not already chosen, as shown in Figure 3-61. Make sure that the **Zadd** button is chosen in the top shelf. Set the value of the **Z Intensity** slider to **20** and of the **Draw Size** slider to **60**, as shown in Figure 3-62.

Figure 3-60 Top view of the turtle shell

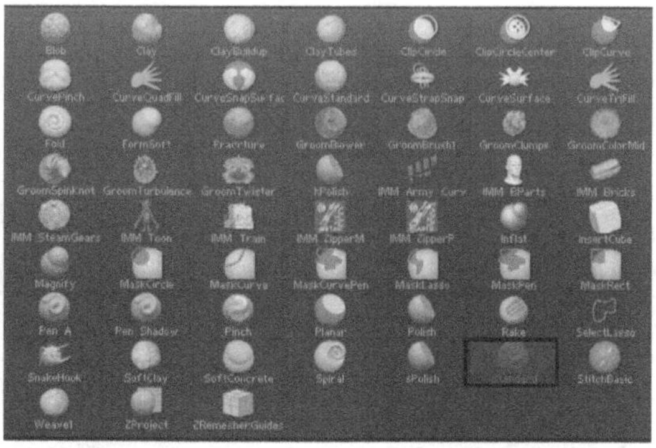

Figure 3-61 *The **Standard** brush chosen from the flyout*

11. Press and hold the left mouse button and drag the cursor on the lower part of the *turtle shell*; the depth is added to the lower part of the shell, as shown in Figure 3-63.

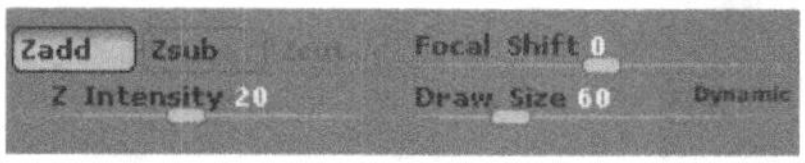

Figure 3-62 *Settings for the **Standard** brush for adding depth*

Figure 3-63 *Depth added to the lower part of the turtle shell using the **Standard** brush*

12. Expand the **Geometry** subpalette in the **Tool** palette. In this subpalette, click twice on the **Divide** button; the value of the **SDiv** slider becomes equal to **5**, refer to Figure 3-64, and the *turtle shell* becomes smoother.

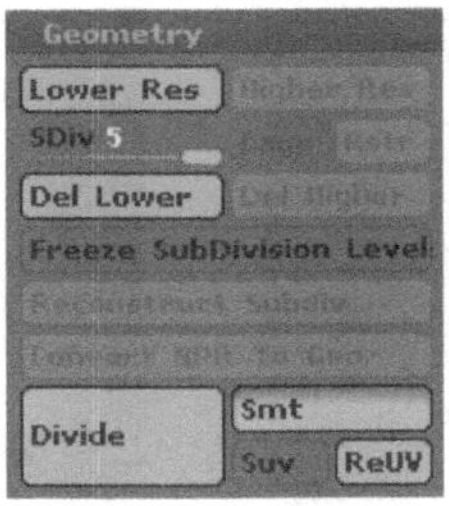

Figure 3-64 *Choosing the* ***Divide*** *button from the* ***Geometry*** *subpalette*

Creating Patterns on the Turtle Shell

In this section, you will create a pattern on the *turtle shell* using the **Standard** brush.

1. Make sure the **Standard** brush is chosen. Next, choose the **Zsub** button from the top shelf. Set the value of **Z Intensity** slider to **95** and the **Draw Size** slider to **8**, as shown in Figure 3-65.

2. In the **Transform** palette, press the X key to deactivate symmetry in the X-axis.

3. Choose the Current Stroke button from the left shelf; a flyout containing different types of strokes is displayed. Choose the **FreeHand** stroke from this flyout.

4. Press and hold the left mouse button and drag the cursor on the upper part of the *turtle shell* to create a pattern, as shown in Figure 3-66.

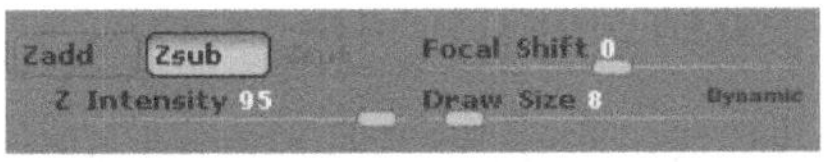

Figure 3-65 *Settings for the* ***Standard*** *brush for creating pattern*

Figure 3-66 *A pattern created on the upper part of the turtle shell using the* ***Standard*** *brush*

5. Continue creating the pattern on the entire upper part of the *turtle shell* using the same settings of the brush, refer to Figure 3-67.

6. Press and hold the left mouse button and drag the cursor to create another pattern on the lower part of the *turtle shell* using the brush settings mentioned above, refer to Figure 3-68.

Figure 3-67 *Pattern created on the entire upper part of the turtle shell*

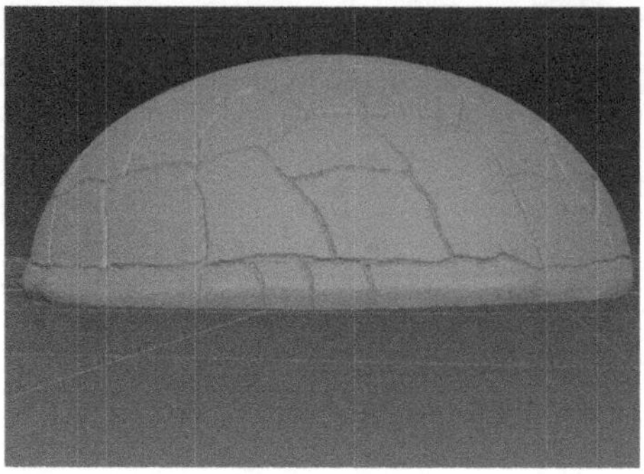

Figure 3-68 *Pattern created on the lower part of the turtle shell using the* ***Standard*** *brush*

7. Continue creating pattern on the lower part of the *turtle shell*, refer to Figure 3-69.

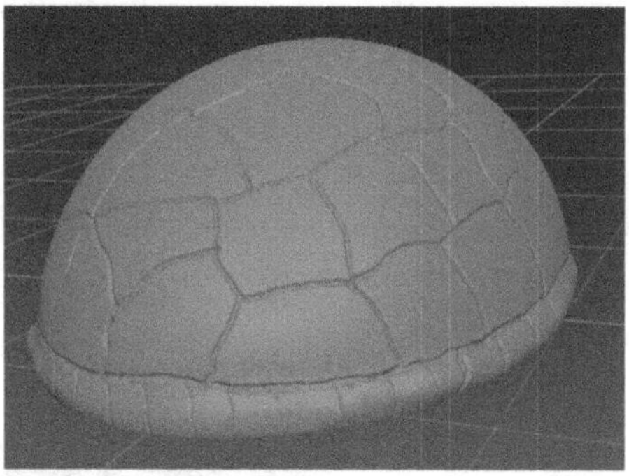

Figure 3-69 *Pattern created on the entire lower part of the turtle shell*

Adding Detail to the Turtle Shell

In this section, you will add detail to the *turtle shell* created in the previous section.

1. Make sure the **Standard** brush is chosen. Choose the **Zadd** button from the top shelf. Set the value of the **Z Intensity** slider to **8** and the **Draw Size** slider to **80**.

   Next, you will add depth to *turtle shell* to create a slightly uneven surface.

2. Press and hold the left mouse button and drag the cursor on the pattern created earlier; a depth is added to the pattern, refer to Figure 3-70.

3. Choose the Current Brush button from the left shelf; a flyout containing different sculpting brushes is displayed. Choose the **Fracture** brush from this flyout, as shown in Figure 3-71.

4. Set the value of the **Z Intensity** slider to **15** and the **Draw Size** slider to **80**.

5. Choose the Current Alpha button from the left shelf; a flyout containing different alpha images is displayed. Choose the **Alpha 07** alpha image from this flyout.

6. Press and hold the left mouse button and drag the cursor on the surface of the *turtle shell*; the final output is created, as shown in Figure 3-72.

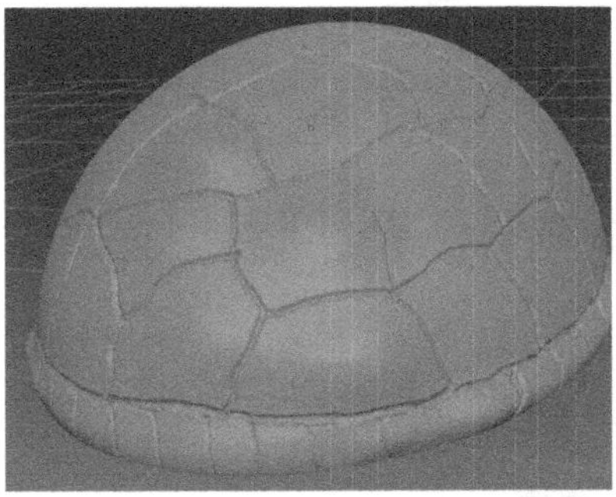

*Figure 3-70 Depth added to the pattern using the **Standard** brush*

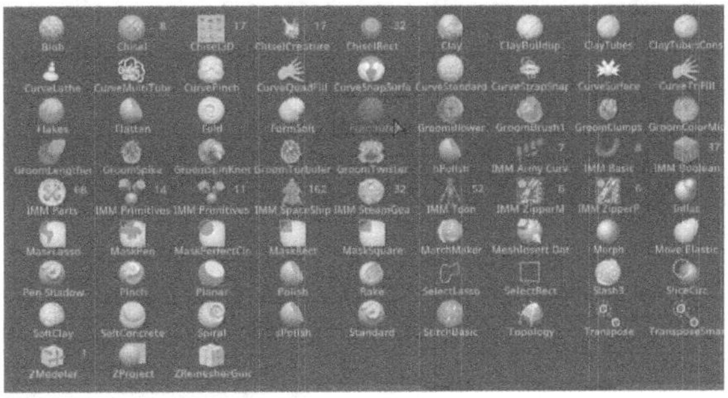

*Figure 3-71 The **Fracture** brush chosen*

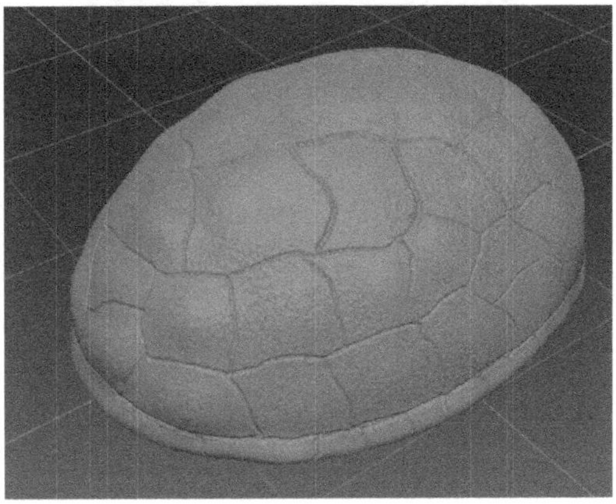

Figure 3-72 The final output

Saving the Model

In this section, you will save the file using the steps given next.

1. Choose the **Save As** button from the **Tool** palette; the **Save ZTool** dialog box is displayed. In this dialog box, browse to the location *\Documents\ZBrushprojects\c03*.

2. Enter **c03tut1** in the **File name** edit box and then choose the **Save** button.

Tutorial 2

In this tutorial, you will create a flower vase using radial symmetry. The final output of the flower vase is shown in Figure 3-73. **(Expected time: 20 min)**

The following steps are required to complete this tutorial:

a. Create the basic shape of flower vase.
b. Add decorative patterns to the flower vase.
c. Save the model.

Creating the Basic Shape of the Flower Vase

In this section, you will create the basic shape of a flower vase using the cylinder primitive and radial symmetry.

1. Choose the **Init ZBrush** button from the **Preferences** palette; ZBrush is initialized to its default state.

2. Choose the Current Tool button from the **Tool** palette; a flyout is displayed. Choose the **Cylinder3D** primitive from this flyout, refer to Figure 3-74.

***Figure 3-73** The flower vase*

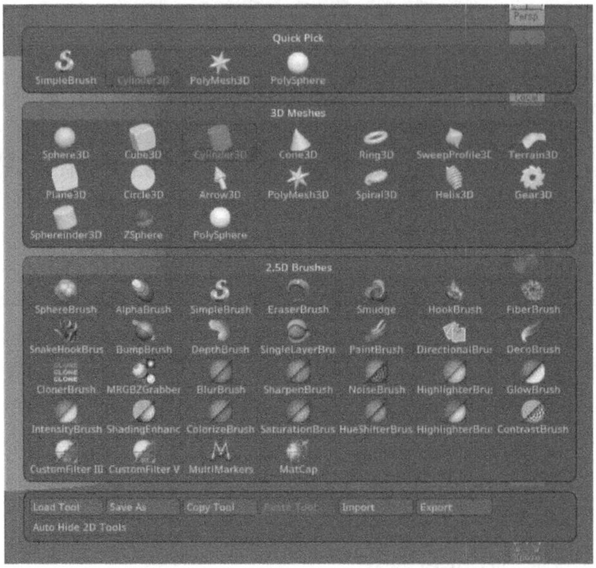

***Figure 3-74** **Cylinder3D** chosen from the flyout*

3. Press and hold the left mouse button and drag the cursor on the canvas; a cylinder is created in the canvas, as shown in Figure 3-75.

4. Choose the **Edit** button from the top shelf, as shown in Figure 3-76.

5. Press and hold the left mouse button and drag the cursor upward in such a way that the cylinder is rotated and stands vertical, as shown in Figure 3-77. While dragging the cursor, press the SHIFT key; the cylinder is snapped at a right angle to the canvas.

6. Choose the **Make PolyMesh3D** button from the **Tool** palette to convert the primitive cylinder into a polymesh, refer to Figure 3-78.

Figure 3-75 *The cylinder created in the canvas*

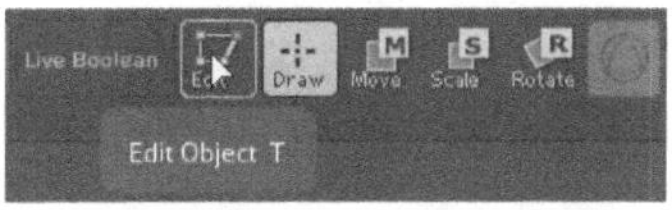

Figure 3-76 *The* ***Edit*** *button chosen from the top shelf*

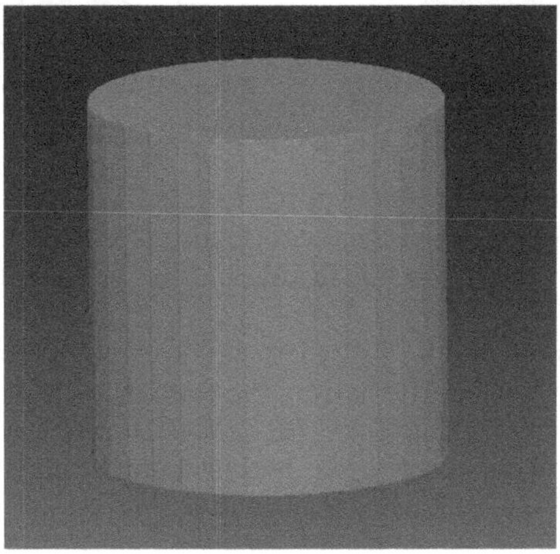

Figure 3-77 *The cylinder rotated*

After converting the cylinder into a polymesh, you need to subdivide the geometry such that the number of polygons in the cylinder increases making the cylinder smoother.

7. Expand the **Geometry** subpalette in the **Tool** palette. In this subpalette, click four times on the **Divide** button; the value of **SDiv** slider becomes equal to **5**, refer to Figure 3-79.

8. Expand the **SubTool** subpalette in the **Tool** palette. Next, in this subpalette, choose the **Rename** button; the **Please enter subtool title** window consisting of a text box is displayed.

Enter **flower vase** in this text box and press ENTER; the sphere primitive is renamed as *flower vase*.

9. Expand the **Deformation** subpalette in the **Tool** palette.

You need to increase the height of the sphere along the Y-axis using the **Size** slider.

10. Deactivate the x and z options corresponding to the **Size** slider by choosing the **x** and **z** buttons located on the right side of the slider.

*Figure 3-78 The **Make PolyMesh3D** button chosen from the **Tool** palette*

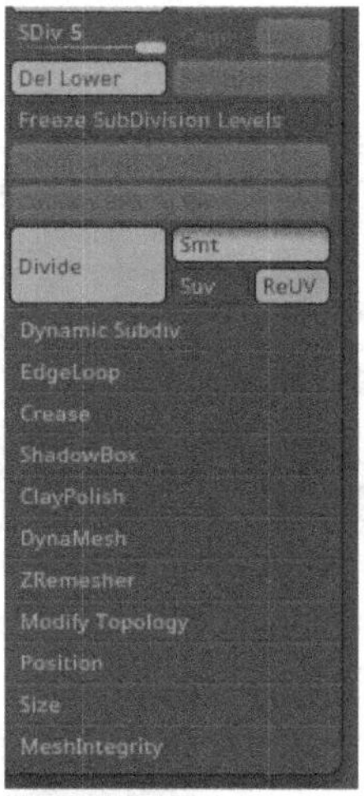

*Figure 3-79 Choosing the **Divide** button from the **Geometry** subpalette*

11. Set the value of the **Size** slider to **20** by dragging the slider toward right; the height of the cylinder increases along the Y-axis, refer to Figure 3-80. Alternatively, you can enter the value **20** in the edit box displayed on clicking on the slider.

12. Expand the **Transform** palette. In this palette, choose the **Activate Symmetry** button, refer to Figure 3-81. Next, choose the **(R)** button; the **RadialCount** slider is activated. By default, the **>X<** button is chosen. To deactivate this button, choose it again. Next, choose the **>Y<** button; the radial symmetry in the Y-axis is activated. In the **RadialCount** edit box, enter the value **40**; the radial symmetry is activated in the Y-axis in canvas, refer to Figure 3-82.

The **Radial Count** edit box is displayed when you click on the **RadialCount** slider.

Figure 3-80 Height of the cylinder increased

***Figure 3-81** The **Activate Symmetry** button chosen in the **Transform** palette*

***Figure 3-82** Radial symmetry activated in the Y-axis*

13. Choose the Current Brush button from the left shelf; a flyout containing different sculpting brushes is displayed. Choose the **Move** brush from this flyout, as shown in Figure 3-83.

14. Set the value of the **Draw Size** slider to **450** by entering the value in the edit box or by moving the **Draw Size** slider toward right, refer to Figure 3-84.

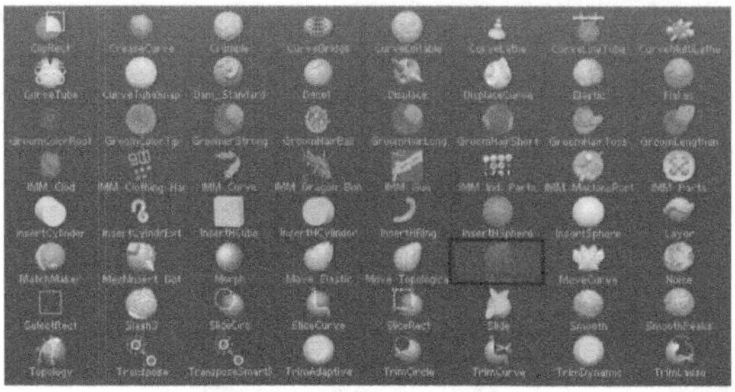

Figure 3-83 *The* ***Move*** *brush chosen*

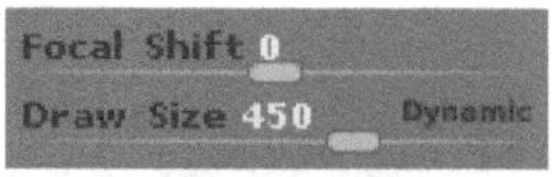

Figure 3-84 *The value of the* ***Draw Size*** *slider set to* ***450***

15. Press and hold the left mouse button, drag the cursor inward, and then drag it to the upward direction to form a new shape, as shown in Figure 3-85.

16. Set the value of the **Draw Size** slider to **550** so that the size of the **Move** brush increases. After increasing the size of the brush, move the upper part of the *flower vase* inward to create a neck for the *flower vase*, as shown in Figure 3-86.

17. Set the value of the **Draw Size** slider to **580** and then, using the **Move** brush, give a round shape to the *flower vase*, as shown in Figure 3-87.

Figure 3-85 *Top area of the cylinder dragged upward*

Figure 3-86 *Neck of the flower vase formed by using the* ***Move*** *brush*

Figure 3-87 *Round shape given to the flower vase*

18. Refine the shape of the *flower vase* using the **Move** brush, as shown in Figure 3-88.

Figure 3-88 *Shape of the flower vase refined by using the* ***Move*** *brush*

Adding Decorative Patterns to the Flower Vase

In this section, you will add decorative patterns to the *flower vase* using different alpha images.

1. Expand the **Geometry** subpalette in the **Tool** palette. In this subpalette, click twice on the **Divide** button; the value of the **SDiv** slider becomes equal to **7**.

2. In the **Transform** palette, enter the value **18** in the **RadialCount** edit box.

3. Set the value of the **Draw Size** slider in the top shelf to **75**.

4. Choose the Current Brush button from the left shelf; a flyout containing different sculpting brushes is displayed. Choose the **Layer** brush from this flyout.

5. Choose the Current Alpha button from the left shelf; a flyout containing different alpha images is displayed. Choose the **Alpha 28** alpha image from this flyout, refer to Figure 3-89.

Figure 3-89 *The* ***Alpha 28*** *alpha image chosen from the flyout*

6. Choose the Current Stroke button from the left shelf; a flyout containing different types of strokes is displayed. Choose the **FreeHand** stroke from this flyout, refer to Figure 3-90. Create a pattern on the top of the neck area of the *flower vase* using the **Layer** brush, as shown in Figure 3-91.

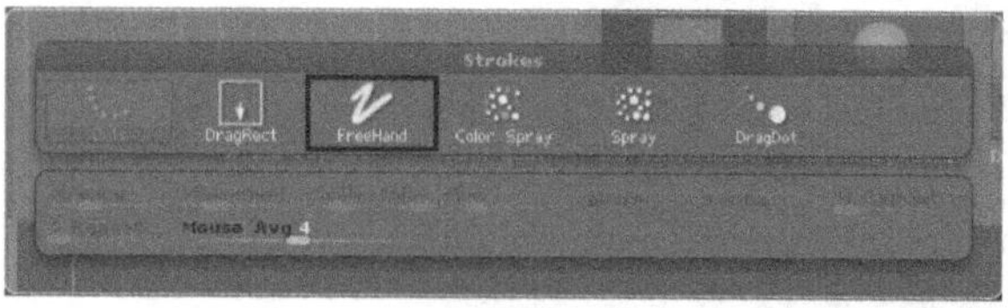

Figure 3-90 *The* ***FreeHand*** *stroke chosen from the flyout*

Figure 3-91 *Pattern created on the neck area*

7. Similarly, create the same pattern on the other parts of the *flower vase*, as shown in Figure 3-92.

8. Choose the Current Brush button from the left shelf; a flyout containing different sculpting brushes is displayed. Choose the **Standard** brush from this flyout.

9. Choose the Current Alpha button from the left shelf; a flyout containing different alpha images is displayed. Choose **Alpha 34** from this flyout, refer to Figure 3-93.

10. Choose the **Zsub** button from the top shelf and set the value of the **Z Intensity** slider to **20**.

Figure 3-92 Pattern created on the other parts of the flower vase

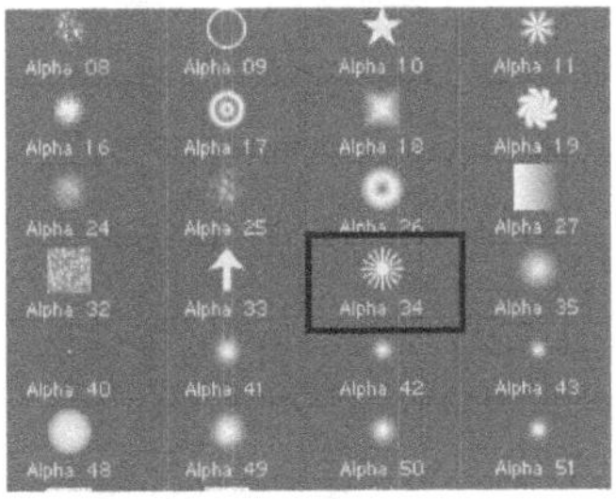

Figure 3-93 ***Alpha 34*** *chosen from the Alpha palette*

11. Choose the Current Stroke button from the left shelf; a flyout containing different types of strokes is displayed. Choose the **Dragrect** stroke from this flyout. Set the value in the **Draw Size** slider to 167 and create a pattern using **Alpha 34**, as shown in Figure 3-94.

12. Choose the Current Alpha button from the left shelf; a flyout containing different alpha images is displayed. Choose **Alpha 05** from this flyout, refer to Figure 3-95. Next, set the value of the **Draw Size** slider to **40**. Create a pattern on the previously applied pattern, refer to Figure 3-96.

Figure 3-94 The pattern created using ***Alpha 34***

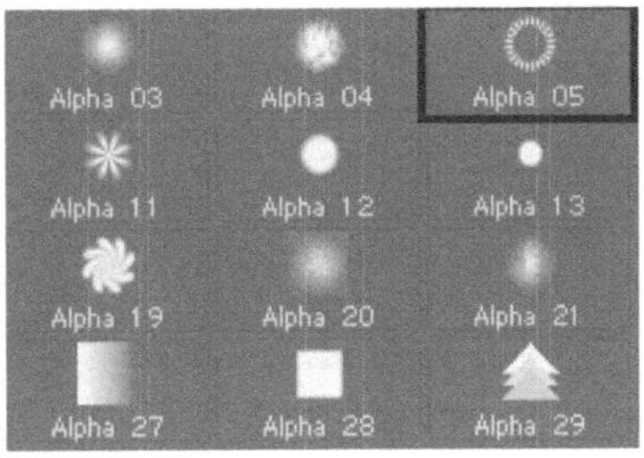

Figure 3-95 ***Alpha 05*** *chosen from the flyout*

13. Create different patterns on the *flower vase* using different alpha images so that the final model is created, as shown in Figure 3-97.

Figure 3-96 *The pattern created using* ***Alpha 05***

Figure 3-97 *The final model of the flower vase*

Saving the Model

In this section, you will save the file using the steps given next.

1. Choose the **Save As** button from the **Tool** palette; the **Save ZTool** dialog box is displayed. In this dialog box, browse to the location *\Documents\ZBrushprojects\c03*.

2. Enter **c03tut2** in the **File name** edit box and then choose the **Save** button.

Tutorial 3

In this tutorial, you will create an ornamental door using different types of alpha images and the **Projection Master** dialog box. The final output of the model is shown in Figure 3-98.

(Expected time: 30 min)

Figure 3-98 *Final model of the door*

The following steps are required to complete this tutorial:

a. Create the basic shape of door.
b. Add details to the door using the **Projection Master**.
c. Add details to the door outside.
d. Save the model.

Creating the Basic Shape of Door

In this section, you will create the basic shape of the door using a plane.

1. Choose the **Init ZBrush** button from the **Preferences** palette; the message box is displayed. Choose the **Yes** button from the message box; ZBrush is initialized to its default state.

2. Choose the Current Tool button from the **Tool** palette; a flyout is displayed. Choose the **Plane3D** primitive from this flyout. Press and hold the left mouse button and drag the cursor on the canvas; a plane is created in the canvas, refer to Figure 3-99. Next, choose the **Edit** button from the top shelf to switch to the edit mode.

Figure 3-99 *The* ***Plane3D*** *primitive created on the canvas*

3. Expand the **Initialize** subpalette in the **Tool** palette. In this subpalette, set the value of **H Radius** slider to **66**, refer to Figure 3-100; the shape of plane changes, as shown in Figure 3-101.

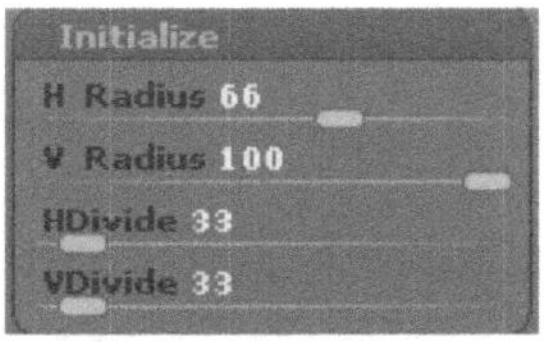

Figure 3-100 *The value of* ***H Radius*** *slider changed to* ***66***

Figure 3-101 *Shape of the plane changed*

4. Choose the **Make PolyMesh3D** button from the **Tool** palette to convert the primitive into a polymesh.

   After converting the plane into a polymesh, you need to subdivide the geometry so that the number of polygons in the plane increases thus making it smoother.

5. Set the value of the **SDiv** slider in the **Geometry** subpalette to **5** by clicking on the **Divide** button four times.

6. Expand the **SubTool** subpalette in the **Tool** palette. Next, in this subpalette, choose the **Rename** button; the **Please enter subtool title** window consisting of a text box is displayed. Enter **door** in this text box and press ENTER; the sphere primitive is renamed as *door*.

Adding Details to the Door Using the Projection Master

In this section, you will add details to *door* using the **Projection Master** dialog box.

1. Choose the **Projection Master** button from the **Zplugin** palette; the **Projection Master** dialog box is displayed.

> **Note**
> *When the **Projection Master** dialog box is displayed, choose the **Reset** button to initialize different settings in this dialog box. If this button is not chosen, **Projection Master** will retain the last used settings.*

2. Select the **Deformation** check box from the **Projection Master** dialog box and make sure other check boxes are not selected, refer to Figure 3-102. Next, choose the **DROP NOW** button from this dialog box; a message box is displayed. Choose the **Activate Polypainting** button from this message box; the 3D plane is converted into its 2.5D illustration.

3. Choose the Current Stroke button from the left shelf; a flyout containing different types of strokes is displayed. Choose the **Line** stroke from this flyout, refer to Figure 3-103.

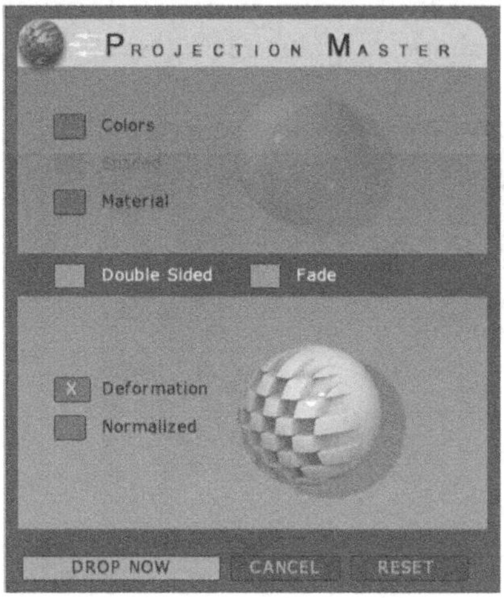

*Figure 3-102 The **Deformation** check box selected*

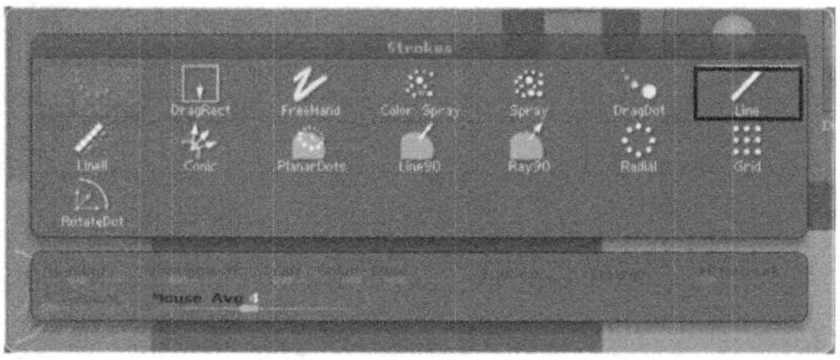

*Figure 3-103 The **Line** stroke chosen in the flyout*

4. Choose the Current Alpha button from the left shelf; a flyout containing different alpha images is displayed. Choose the **Alpha 28** alpha image from this flyout.

5. Make sure that the **Zadd** button is chosen in the top shelf. Next, set the value of the **Draw Size** slider to **10**. Press and hold the left mouse button and draw a line on the left side of the *door*, as shown in Figure 3-104. While drawing the line, press and hold the SHIFT key to create straight strokes.

6. Draw two more lines on the top and right side of the *door* to create the frame, as shown in Figure 3-105.

Figure 3-104 *Line drawn on the left side of the door*

Figure 3-105 *Frame created for the door*

7. Create another frame for the door, as shown in Figure 3-106.

8. Choose the Current Stroke button from the left shelf; a flyout containing different types of strokes is displayed. Choose the **LineII** stroke from this flyout.

9. Set the value of the **Draw Size** slider to **15** and the value of the **Z Intensity** slider to **10**. Press and hold the left mouse button and draw a vertical line in the middle of the *door* to create a vertical partition, as shown in Figure 3-107.

Figure 3-106 *Another frame created for the door*

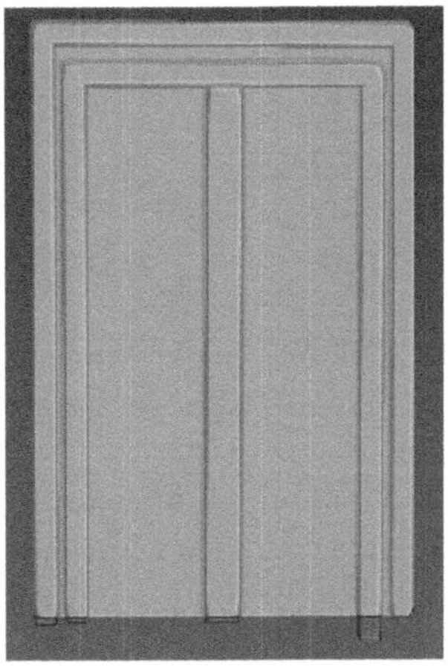

Figure 3-107 *A vertical partition created in the middle of the door*

10. Draw a horizontal line in the middle of the *door* to create a horizontal partition, as shown in Figure 3-1085.

11. Choose the **Zsub** button from the top shelf. Next, set the value of the **Draw Size** slider to **2**. Press and hold the left mouse button, and draw vertical and horizontal lines on the partitions, as shown in Figure 3-109.

Figure 3-108 *A horizontal partition created in the middle of the door*

Figure 3-109 *Vertical and horizontal lines created on the partitions*

12. Choose the **Projection Master** button from the **Zplugin** palette, the **Projection Master** dialog box is displayed. Choose the **PICKUP NOW** button from this dialog box; the 3D model is again displayed in the canvas.

Adding Details to the Door Outside

In this section, you will add decorative patterns to the door outside using different alpha images and the **Standard** brush.

1. Choose the Current Brush button from the left shelf; a flyout containing different sculpting brushes is displayed. Choose the **Standard** brush from this flyout, if not already chosen.

2. Make sure the **Zadd** button is chosen in the top shelf. Next, set the parameters in the top shelf as given below:

   Z Intensity: **100** Draw Size: **17**

3. Choose the Current Stroke button from the left shelf; a flyout containing different types of strokes is displayed. Choose the **DragRect** stroke from this flyout.

4. Choose the Current Alpha button from the left shelf; a flyout containing different alpha images is displayed. Choose the **Alpha 52** alpha image from this flyout, refer to Figure 3-110. This alpha will help you to create a knob for the door.

5. Press and hold the left mouse button and drag the cursor in the middle of the *door* to create a knob, as shown in Figure 3-111.

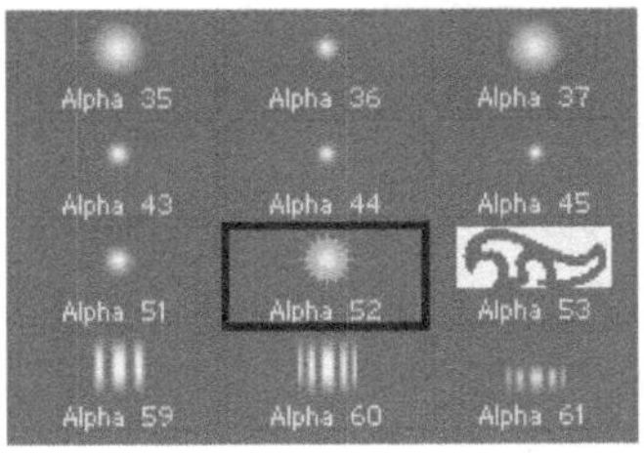

***Figure 3-110 Alpha 52** chosen in the flyout*

***Figure 3-111** Knob created for the door*

6. Expand the **Transform** palette. In this palette, choose the **Activate Symmetry** button; the **>X<** button is chosen by default. Next, choose the **>Y<** button, refer to Figure 3-112.

7. Choose the Current Alpha button from the left shelf; a flyout containing different alpha images is displayed. Choose the **Alpha 19** alpha image from this flyout.

8. Make sure the **Zadd** button is chosen in the top shelf. Next, set the parameters in the top shelf as given below:

   Z Intensity: **40** Draw Size: **35**

9. Press and hold the left mouse button and drag the cursor to create a pattern on any panel of the *door*; the pattern is replicated on the remaining panels, refer to Figure 3-113.

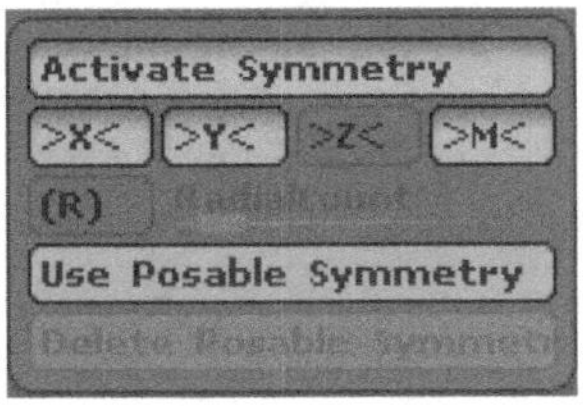

***Figure 3-112** Symmetry activated along X and Y axes*

***Figure 3-113 Alpha 19** applied to the door panels*

10. Choose the Current Alpha button from the left shelf; a flyout containing different alpha images is displayed. Choose the **Alpha 05** alpha image from this flyout. Next, press and hold the left mouse button and drag the cursor to create a border for the existing pattern; the final door model is created, as shown in Figure 3-114.

Figure 3-114 *Final model of the door*

Saving the Model

After completing the tutorial, you will save the file using the steps given next.

1. Choose the **Save As** button from the **Tool** palette; the **Save ZTool** dialog box is displayed. In this dialog box, browse to the location *\Documents\ZBrushprojects\c03*.

2. Enter **c03tut3** in the **File name** edit box and then choose the **Save** button.

Tutorial 4

In this tutorial, you will create a sailing boat using the **ZMODELER** brush. The final output of the model is shown in Figure 3-115. **(Expected time: 30 min)**

Figure 3-115 *The boat model*

The following steps are required to complete this tutorial:

a. Create the basic shape of the boat.
b. Add details to the boat using the ZModeler brush.
c. Create the sail cloth of the boat.
d. Design the boat.
e. Save the model.

Creating the Basic Shape of the Boat

In this section, you will create the basic shape of the boat using a sphere.

1. Choose the **Init ZBrush** button from the **Preferences** palette; the message box is displayed. Choose the **Yes** button from the message box; ZBrush is initialized to its default state.

2. Choose the Current Tool button from the **Tool** palette; a flyout is displayed. Choose the **Sphere3D** primitive from this flyout. Press and hold the left mouse button and drag the cursor on the canvas; a sphere is created in the canvas, refer to Figure 3-116. Next, choose the **Edit** button from the top shelf to switch to the edit mode.

Figure 3-116 *The* ***Sphere3D*** *primitive created in the canvas*

3. Expand the **Initialize** subpalette in the **Tool** palette. In this subpalette, set the value of the **HDivide** slider to **10** and the **VDivide** slider to **12**, refer to Figure 3-97; the shape of the sphere changes, as shown in Figure 3-117.

Figure 3-117 *Shape of the sphere changed*

4. In the **Initialize** subpalette of the **Tool** palette, set the value of the **X Size** slider to **66** and the **Coverage** slider to **180**. Figure 3-118 shows the changed shape of sphere.

Figure 3-118 *Shape of the sphere changed*

5. Choose the **PolyF** button from the right shelf; the segments of the sphere are displayed.

Adding Details to the Boat Using the ZModeler Brush

In this section, you will add detail to the boat using the **ZModeler** brush.

1. Choose the **Make PolyMesh3D** button from the **Tool** palette to convert the primitive into a polymesh.

2. Choose the Current Brush button from the left shelf; a flyout containing different sculpting brushes is displayed. Choose the **ZModeler** brush from this flyout.

3. Hover the cursor over the edge and click; the edge loop is created, as shown in Figure 3-119.

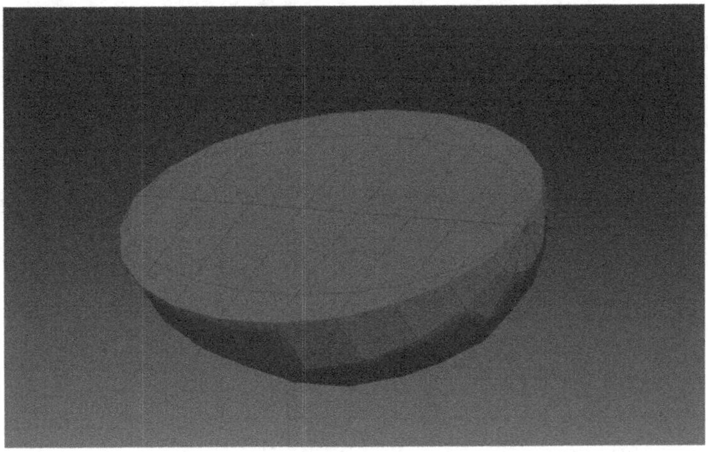

Figure 3-119 *The edge loop created*

4. Hover the cursor over the bottom-most point, hold the ALT key and click; the point is deleted and the shape of the sphere is changed, as shown in Figure 3-120.

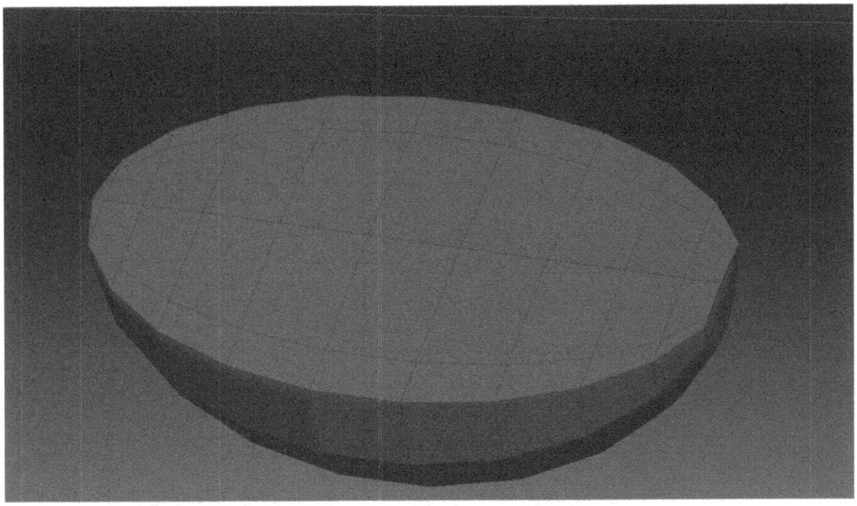

Figure 3-120 *The point deleted*

Next, you will extrude the polygon of sphere.

5. Click on the bottom center of the edge; an edge loop is created, as shown in Figure 3-121.

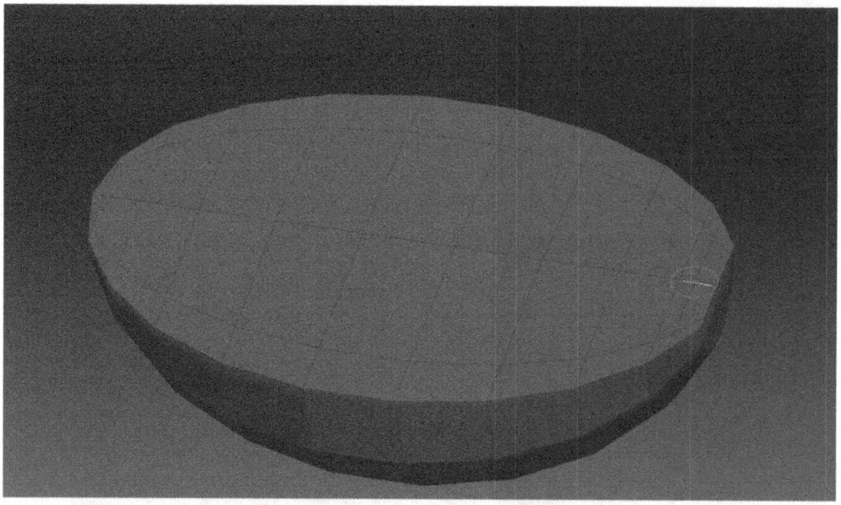

Figure 3-121 *The edge loop created*

6. Hover the cursor on the polygon of the sphere and then right-click; the **ZMODELER** window is displayed. Next, choose **Extrude** from the **Polygon Actions** area. Make sure the **A Single Poly** option is chosen in the **Target** area. Expand the **SubTool** subpalette of the **Tool** palette and choose the **Rename** button; the **Please enter subtool tile** text box is displayed. Now, enter **boat** in the text box.

7. Hold the ALT key, select the corners of the polygon of the boat, and move the corners upward, as shown in Figure 3-122.

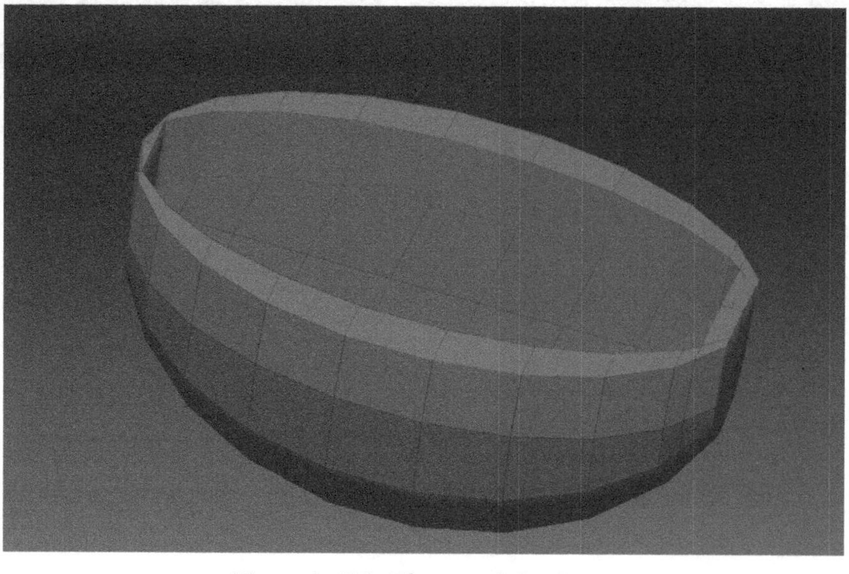

Figure 3-122 *The extruded polygon*

8. Select the polygons using the ALT key, as shown in Figure 3-123, and drag the cursor upward; the polygons are extruded, as shown in Figure 3-124 .

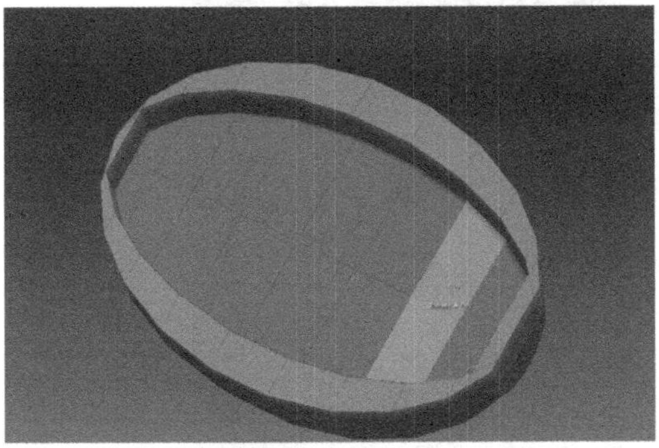

Figure 3-123 *The selected polygons*

Figure 3-124 *The polygons extruded*

9. Select the polygons of the *boat* and move them upward; the polygons are extruded, as shown in Figure 3-125.

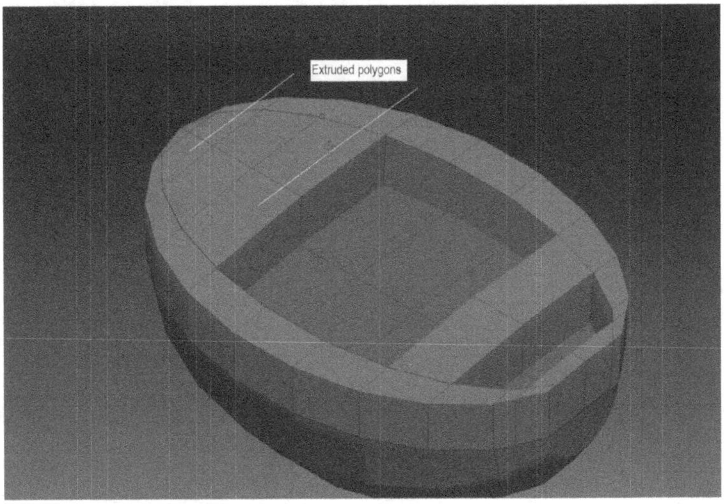

Figure 3-125 *The extruded polygons*

Next, to smoothen the mesh, add edges in the sphere.

10. Hover the cursor on the edge and click; the edge loop is added, as shown in Figure 3-126. Similarly, add more edges on the boat model, as shown in Figure 3-127.

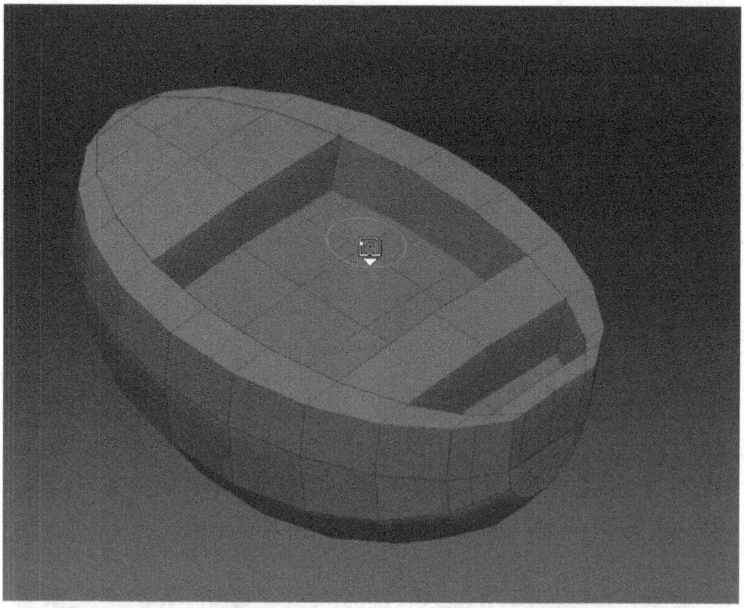

Figure 3-126 *The edge loop added*

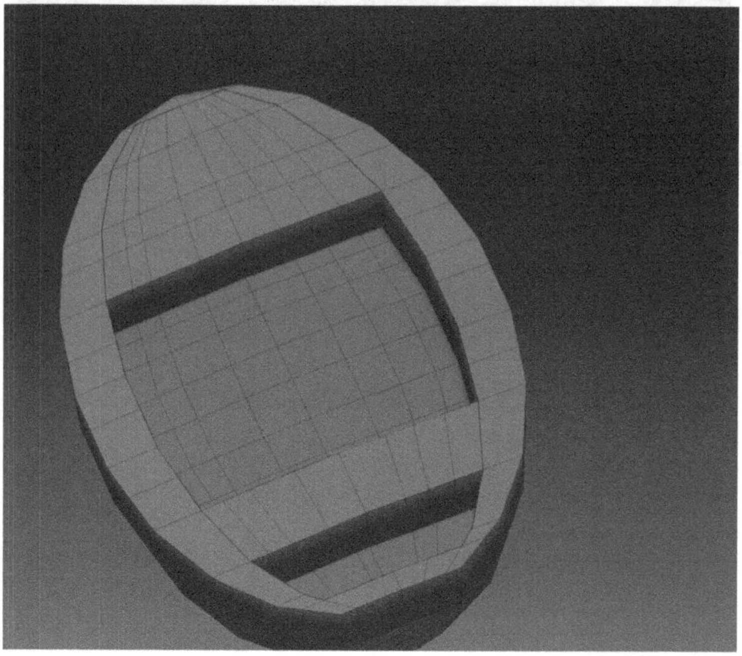

Figure 3-127 *The edge loops created*

11. Hover the cursor on any polygon of the *boat* and then right-click; the **ZMODELER** window is displayed. In this window, make sure the **Extrude** option in the **POLYGON ACTIONS** area and the **A Single Poly** option in the **Target** area is chosen.

12. Select the polygon of the sphere, as shown in Figure 3-128 and drag the cursor upward; the polygon is extruded, as shown in Figure 3-129.

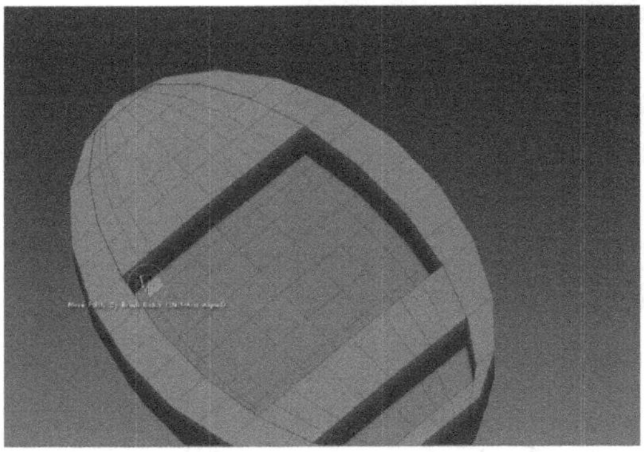

Figure 3-128 *Selected polygon*

Figure 3-129 *The extruded polygon*

Creating the Sail Cloth of the Boat

In this section, you will create the sail cloth of the boat.

1. Hover the cursor on the edge and click; the edge loop is added, as shown in Figure 3-130. Similarly, add more edges, as shown in Figure 3-131.

Figure 3-130 *The edge loop added*

Figure 3-131 Added edge loops

2. Hover the cursor on the polygon of the boat model and then right-click; the **ZMODELER** window is displayed. In this window, make sure the **Extrude** option in the **POLYGON ACTIONS** area and the **A Single Poly** option in the **Target** area is chosen.

3. Select the polygon of the *boat,* as shown in Figure 3-132, and extrude. Similarly, extrude the polygon on the opposite side, as shown in Figure 3-133.

Figure 3-132 Selected polygon

Figure 3-133 *Polygons extruded*

4. Hover the cursor on the point of the sailing cloth and right-click; the **ZMODELER** window is displayed. Next, choose the **Delete** option from the **POINT ACTION** area, as shown in Figure 3-134.

5. Hover the cursor on the point and click; the point is deleted and the shape of the sail cloth is changed. Similarly, delete the opposite point. Figure 3-135, shows the deleted points of the sail cloth.

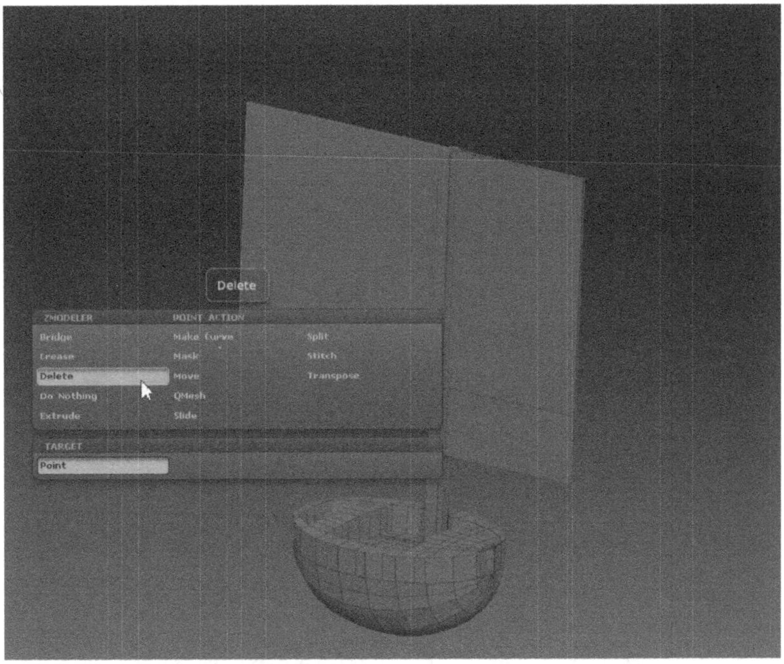

Figure 3-134 *Choosing the **Delete** option*

Figure 3-135 Deleted points

Designing the Boat

In this section, you will design the boat.

1. Hover the cursor over the boat edge and then right-click; the **ZMODELER** window is displayed. Next, make sure the **Insert** option in the **EDGE ACTIONS** area and the **Single EdgeLoop** option in the **TARGET** area is chosen. Now, click on the edge of the boat; the edge loop is created in the *boat*, as shown in Figure 3-136.

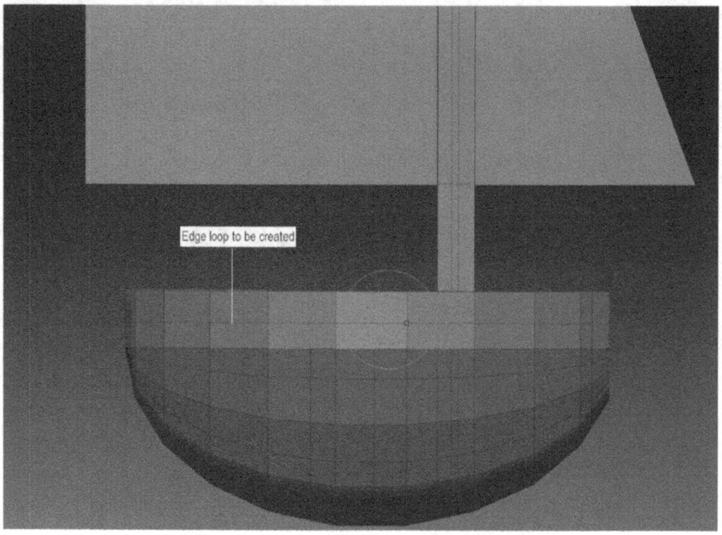

Figure 3-136 Edge loop created

2. Similarly, add more edges in the *boat*, as shown in Figure 3-137.

Figure 3-137 *The edge loops added*

3. Select polygons of the boat model using the ALT key, as shown in Figure 3-138. Right-click on the selected polygons; the **ZMODELER** window is displayed. Make sure the **Extrude** option in the **POLYGON ACTIONS** area and **A Single Poly** option in the **TARGET** area is chosen.

Figure 3-138 *The edges added*

4. Now, drag the cursor on the selected polygons; the polygons are extruded, as shown in Figure 3-139.

Figure 3-139 *The polygons extruded*

Saving the Model

In this section, you will save the file using the steps given next.

1. Choose the **Save As** button from the **Tool** palette; the **Save ZTool** dialog box is displayed. In this dialog box, browse to the location *\Documents\ZBrushprojects\c03*.

2. Enter **c03tut4** in the **File name** edit box and then choose the **Save** button.

Tutorial 5

In this tutorial, you will create a finger ring using Array Mesh. The final output of the model is shown in Figure 3-140. **(Expected time: 30 min)**

The following steps are required to complete this tutorial:

a. Create a flower.
b. Add details to the flower.
c. Create an array of flower.
d. Save the model.

Figure 3-140 The finger ring

Creating a Flower

In this section, you will create a flower using a sphere.

1. Choose the **Init ZBrush** button from the **Preferences** palette; the message box is displayed. Choose the **Yes** button from the message box; ZBrush is initialized to its default state.

2. Choose the Current Tool button from the **Tool** palette; a flyout is displayed. Choose the **Sphere3D** primitive from this flyout. Press and hold the left mouse button and drag the cursor on the canvas; a sphere is created in the canvas, refer to Figure 3-141. Next, choose the **Edit** button from the top shelf to switch to the edit mode.

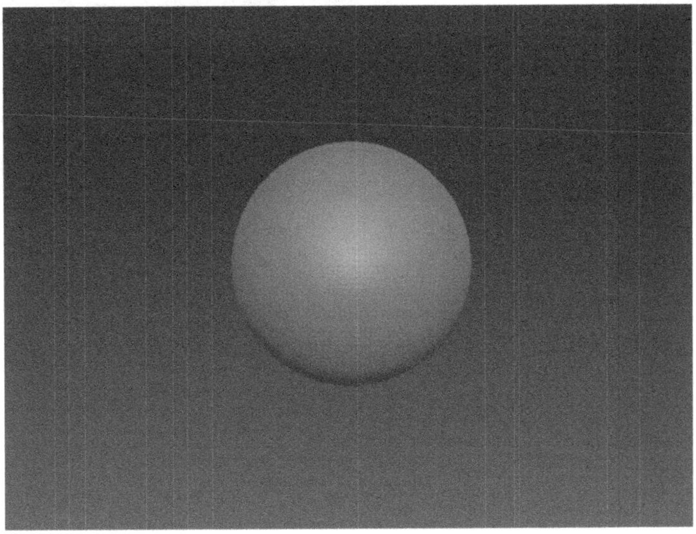

Figure 3-141 Sphere created in the canvas

3. Choose the **Make PolyMesh3D** button from the **Tool** palette to convert the primitive into a polymesh.

4. Expand the **Transform** palette. In this palette, choose the **Activate Symmetry** button,

refer to Figure 3-142. Next, choose the **(R)** button; the **RadialCount** slider is activated. By default, the **>X<** button is chosen in this palette. To deactivate this button, choose it again. Next, choose the **>Z<** button; the radial symmetry along the Z-axis is activated. In the **RadialCount** edit box, enter the value **13**; the radial symmetry is activated along the Z-axis in canvas, refer to Figure 3-143.

Note

*The **Radial Count** edit box is displayed when you click on the **Radial Count** slider.*

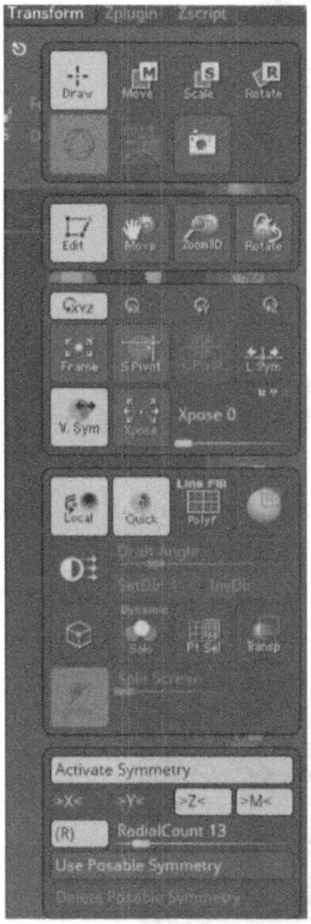

*Figure 3-142 The **Activate Symmetry** button chosen in the **Transform** palette*

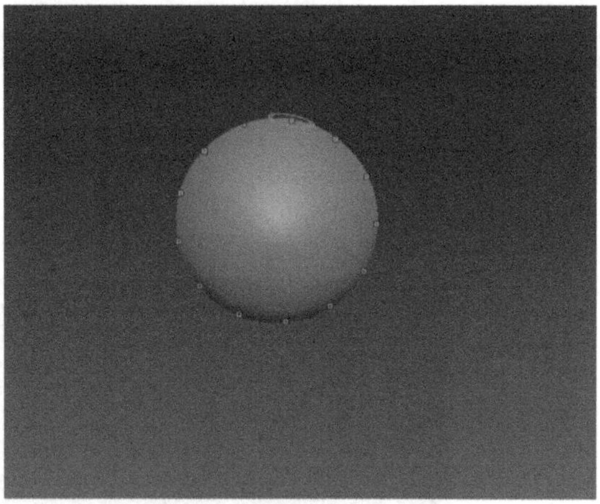

Figure 3-143 Radial symmetry activated along the Z-axis

5. Choose the Current Brush button from the left shelf; a flyout containing different sculpting brushes is displayed. Choose the **SnakeHook** brush from this flyout, as shown in Figure 3-144.

6. Set the value of the **Draw Size** slider to **160** by entering the value in the edit box or by moving the **Draw Size** slider toward right, refer to Figure 3-145.

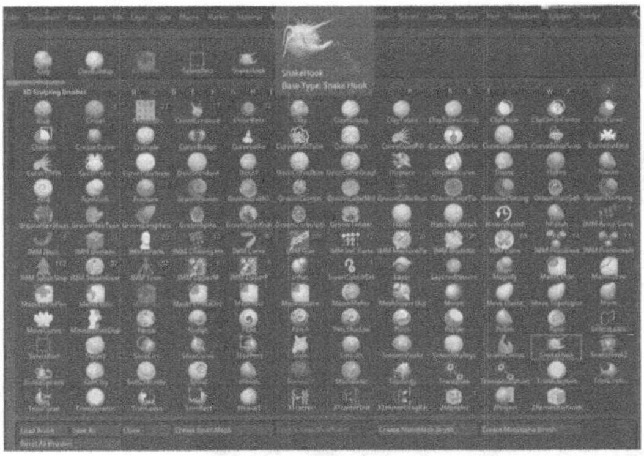

*Figure 3-144 The **Snakehook** brush chosen*

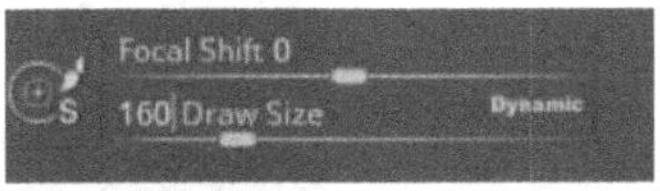

*Figure 3-145 The value of the **Draw Size** slider set to **160***

7. Press and hold the left mouse button and drag the cursor twice in the outward direction to form a thick petal of flower, as shown in Figure 3-146.

Figure 3-146 Dragging the cursor outward

Adding Detail to the Flower

In this section, you will add detail to the flower.

1. Expand the **Geometry** subpalette in the **Tool** palette. In this subpalette, click five times on the **Divide** button; the value of the **SDiv** slider becomes equal to 6; the flower is smoothened, as shown in Figure 3-147.

Figure 3-147 Shape of the flower smoothened

2. Choose the Current Brush button from the left shelf; a flyout containing different sculpting brushes is displayed. Choose the **Standard** brush from this flyout.

3. Choose the **Zsub** button from the top shelf. Next, set the value of the **Draw Size** slider in the top shelf to **70**.

4. Press and hold the left mouse button and then drag the cursor twice in the outward direction to form a shape shown in Figure 3-148. Next, press and hold the left mouse button and drag inward twice to form a shape, as shown in Figure 3-149.

Figure 3-148 Dragging the cursor twice in outward direction to form a shape

Figure 3-149 Dragging the cursor twice in inward direction to form a shape

6. Press and hold the left mouse button in the empty area of the canvas and drag the cursor upward in such a way that the flower is rotated and it stands vertical, as shown in Figure 3-150. While dragging the cursor, press the SHIFT key; the flower is snapped at a right angle to the canvas.

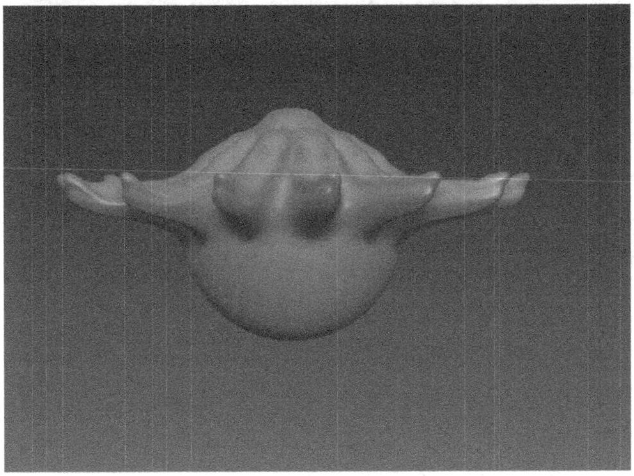

Figure 3-150 Flower rotated and standing vertical

7. Choose the **Move** button, as shown in Figure 3-151; a gyro is displayed, as shown in Figure 3-152. Next, hold the CTRL key and press and hold down the left mouse button on the green symbol and drag it in the upward direction, as shown in Figure 3-153. Notice that the unwanted area of the mesh is hidden, as shown in Figure 3-154.

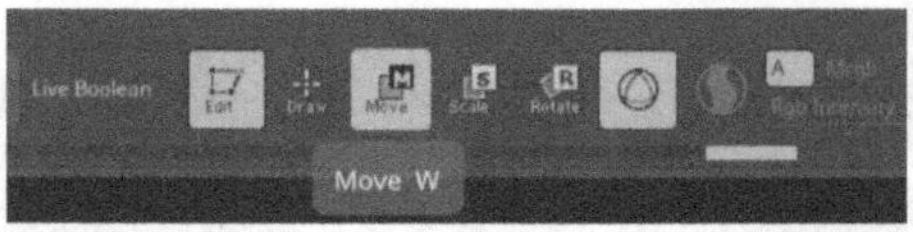

Figure 3-151 The **Move** button chosen

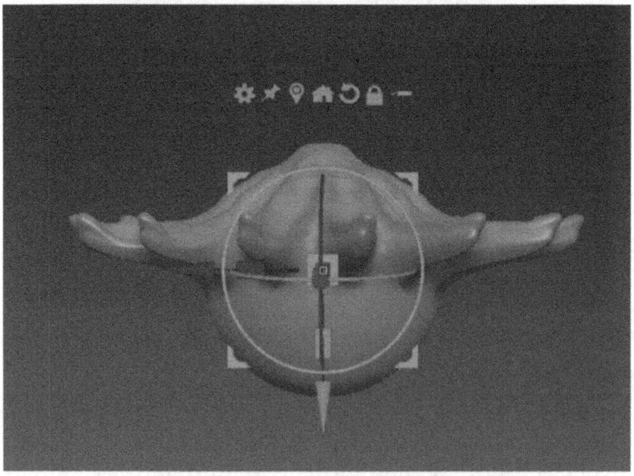

Figure 3-152 The gyro displayed

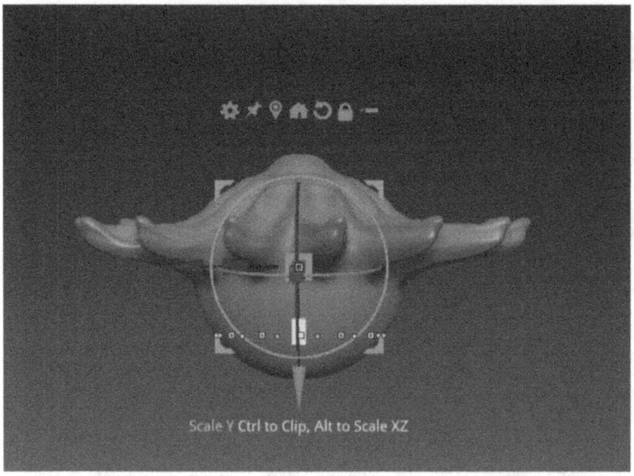

Figure 3-153 The green symbol of gyro highlighted

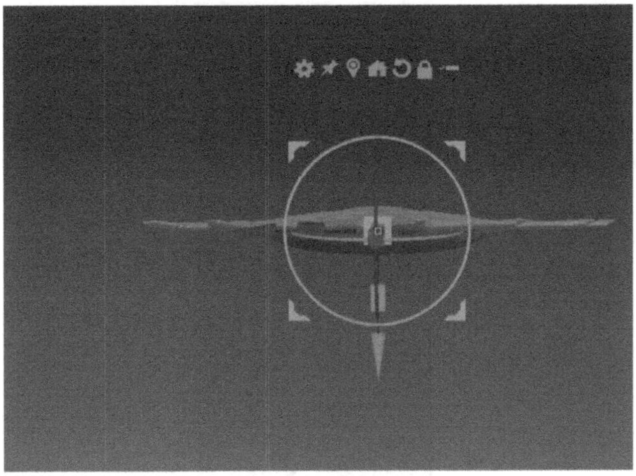

Figure 3-154 Unwanted area hidden

Creating an Array of Flowers

In this section, you will create an array of flower using the **Array Mesh** subpalette to create a ring like structure.

1. Make sure the **Draw** button is chosen. Expand the **Array Mesh** subpalette in the **Tool** palette, refer to Figure 3-155. Next, in this subpalette, choose the **Array Mesh** button and enter **7** in the **Repeat** slider. Next, drag the **X Amount** slider, as shown in Figure 3-156. Figure 3-157 shows the aligned array of flowers.

   The value in the **X amount** slider specifies the distance between the flowers in the array.

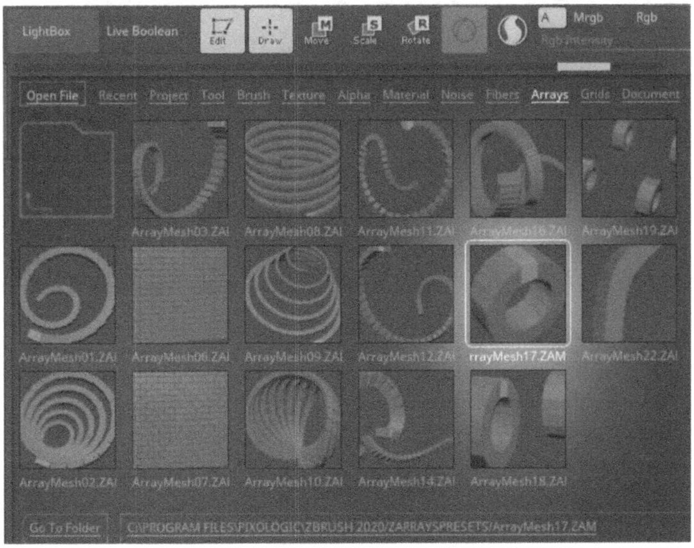

*Figure 3-155 The **Array Mesh** subpalette*

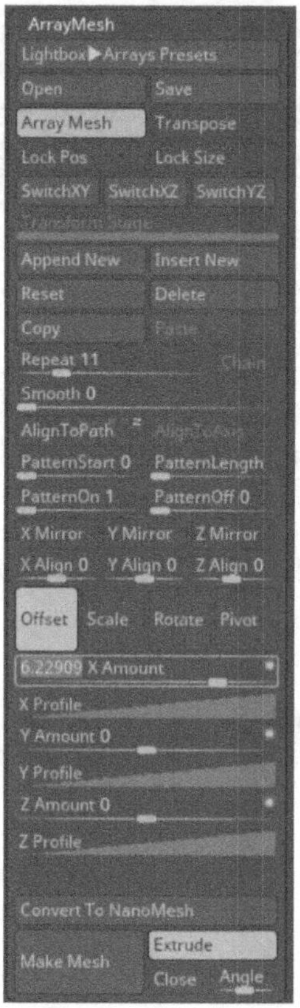

Figure 3-156 *The attributes in* ***Array Mesh***

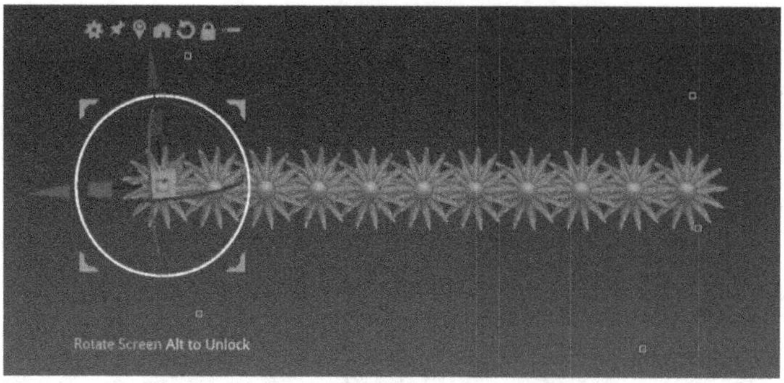

Figure 3-157 *Flowers aligned*

2. Choose the **LightBox** button; the **LightBox** browser is displayed. Next, choose the **Arrays** tab and then double-click on **ArrayMesh17.ZAM** in the **Arrays** presets of the **LightBox** browser, refer to Figure 3-158. The arrayed flower mesh is displayed as a ring. Next, in the **Array Mesh** subpalete, choose the **SwitchYZ** button; the ring like structure is created in the YZ direction.

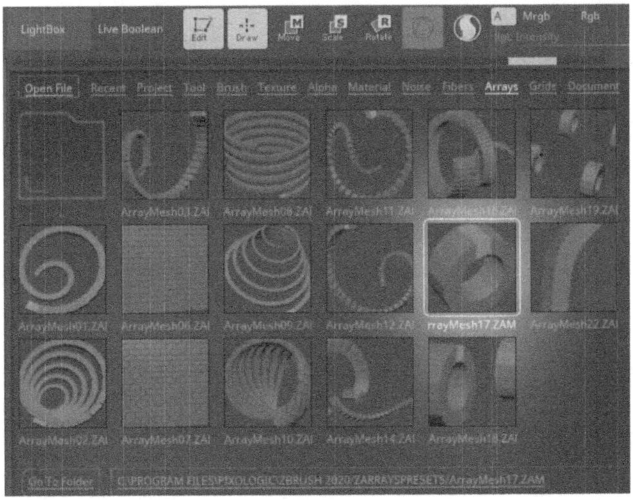

*Figure 3-158 The **ArrayMesh17.ZAM** file chosen from the **Arrays** browser*

3. Set **100** in the **Z Align** slider, as shown in Figure 3-159. The final output of ring is shown in Figure 3-160.

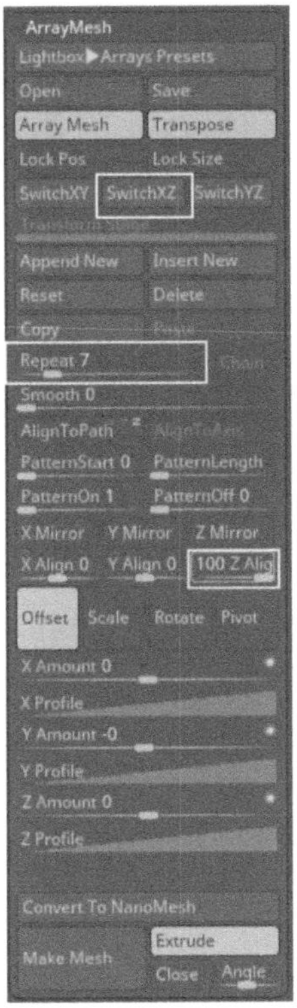

*Figure 3-159 Attributes set in the **Array Mesh** subpalette*

Figure 3-160 The finger ring

Saving the Model

In this section, you will save the file using the steps given next.

1. Choose the **Save As** button from the **Tool** palette; the **Save ZTool** dialog box is displayed. In this dialog box, browse to the location *\Documents\ZBrushprojects\c03*.

2. Enter **c03tut5** in the **File name** edit box and then choose the **Save** button.

Tutorial 6

In this tutorial, you will use Stager in the scene, as shown in Figure 3-161.

(Expected time: 30 min)

The following steps are required to complete this tutorial:

a. Create primitives.
b. Apply Stager.
c. Create design on stone.
d. Save the model.

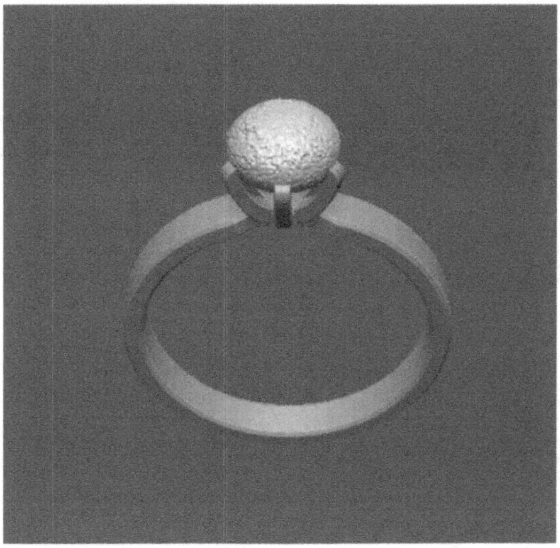

Figure 3-161 Using stager on ring

Creating Primitives

In this section, you will create the primitive for stager.

1. Choose the **LightBox** button; the **LightBox** browser is displayed. Next, choose the **Project** tab and then double-click on **Jewelry** in the **Project** tab of the **LightBox** browser. The jewelry presets are displayed, refer to Figure 3-162.

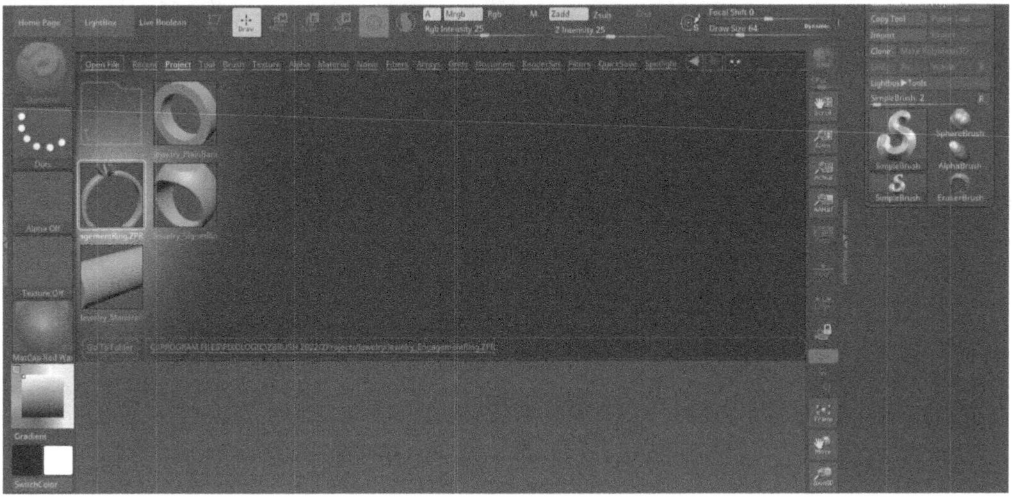

Figure 3-162 The jewelry presets

2. Double-click on **Jewelry_EngagementRing.ZPR** from the **Jewelry** presets; the model is displayed in the canvas, as shown in Figure 3-163. Expand the **Subtool** subpalette in the **Tool** palette; the thumbnail for **ThinRing** and **Prongs** is displayed in the subtool list.

Figure 3-163 The model displayed in the canvas

3. In the **Subtool** subpalette, choose the **Append** button; a flyout is displayed. Choose the **Sphere3D** primitive from this flyout, as shown in Figure 3-164; a sphere is created in the canvas and it overlaps ring, as shown in Figure 3- 165. Also, the thumbnail for the sphere is displayed in the subtool list. Select the thumbnail of the sphere in the list and then rename it to **Stone** using the **Rename** button. Activate the **Move** tool.

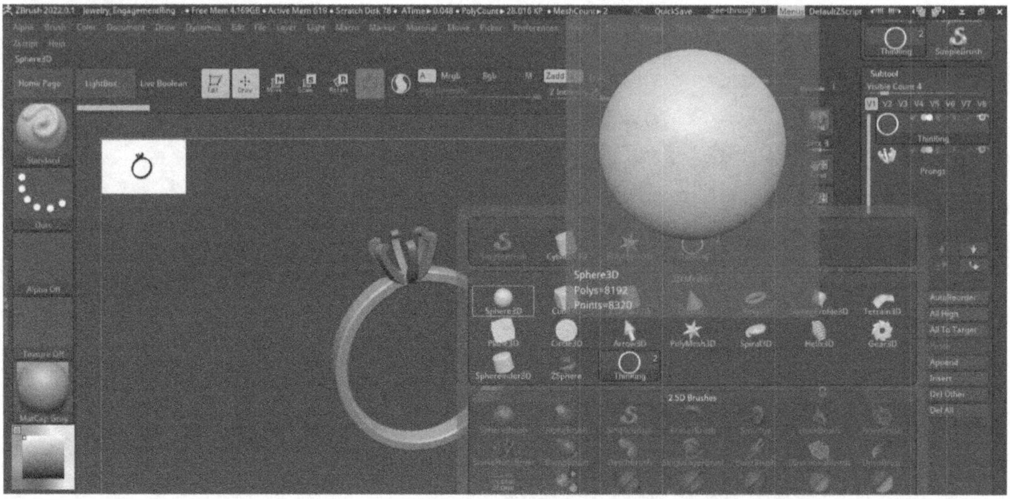

***Figure 3-164** Choosing the **Sphere3D** primitive*

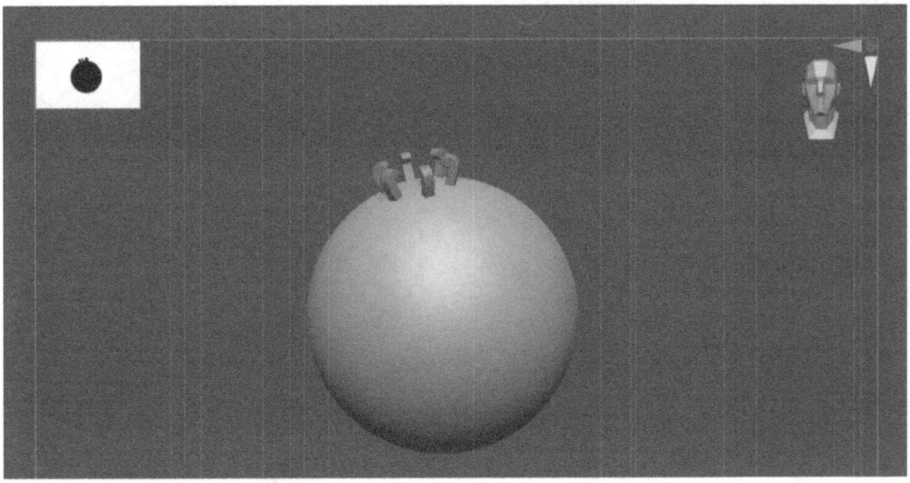

Figure 3-165 *Sphere created in the canvas*

Applying the Stager

In this section, you will apply the stager to model.

1. Expand the **Geometry** subpalette in the **Tool** palette. Next, expand the **Stager** area and choose the **Home Stage** button, as shown in Figure 3-166. Next, choose the **Scale** button from the top shelf; an action line is displayed. Next, press and hold the left mouse button and scale the *Stone*; the size of the *Stone* decreases, as shown in Figure 3-167.

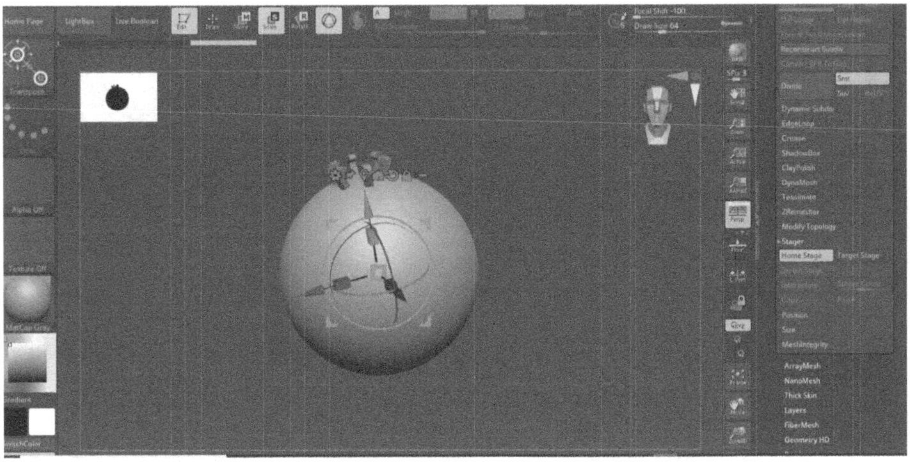

Figure 3-166 *The **Home Stage** button chosen from the **Stager** area*

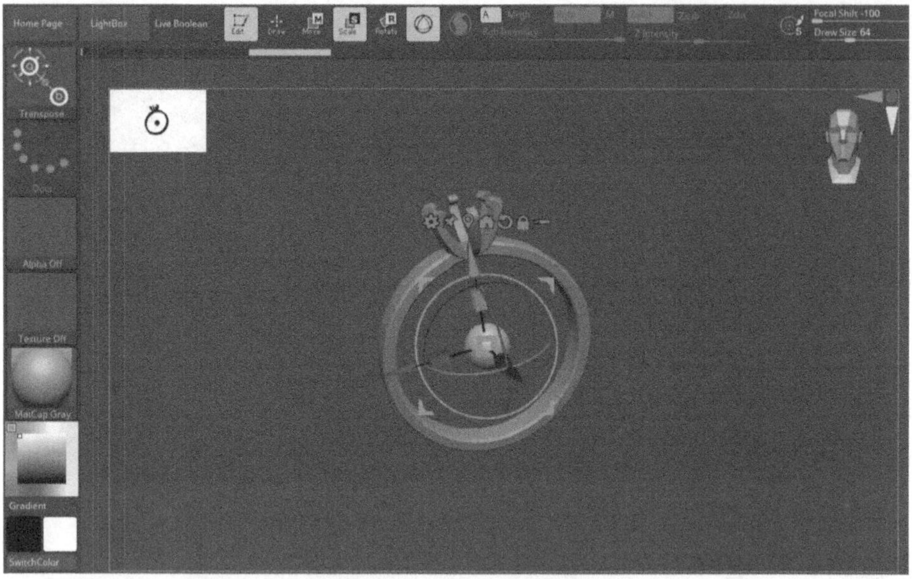

Figure 3-167 *Stone scaled*

2. Choose the **Move** button from the top shelf; an action line is displayed. Hover the cursor at the centre of the middle circle of the action line. Next, press and hold the left mouse button and drag the cursor upward to move the sphere at the top of *Prongs*. Scale and align the *stone*, refer to Figure 3-168 Choose the **Target Stage** button in the **Stager** area of the **Geometry** subpalette, as shown in Figure 3-169. Now, choose the **Switch Stage** button to switch the model from home stage to target stage.

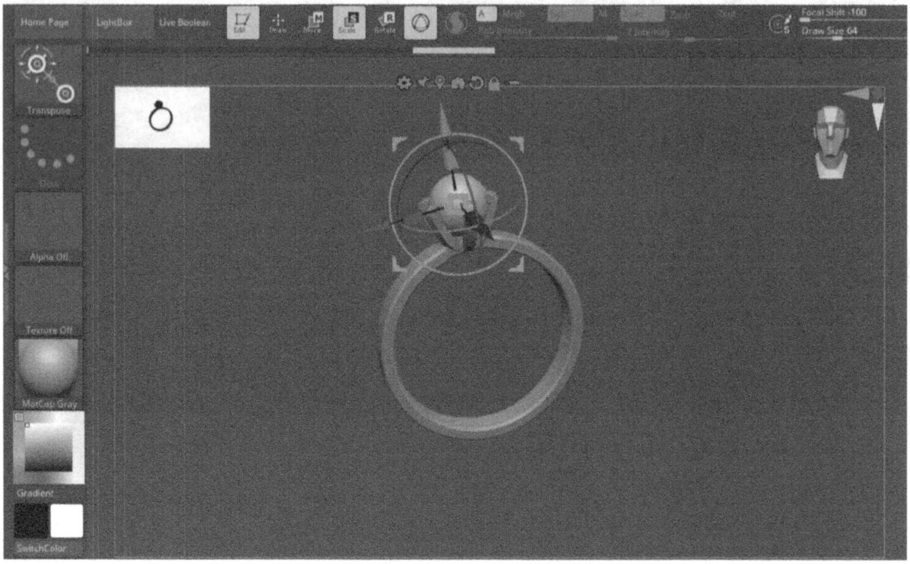

Figure 3-168 *The Stone set on the ring*

*Figure 3-169 **Choosing the Target Stage** button from **the Stager** area*

Creating Design on stone

In this section, you will design the stone using noise brush.

1. Choose the Current Brush button from the left shelf; a flyout containing different sculpting brushes is displayed. Choose the **Noise** brush from this flyout, as shown in Figure 3-170.

2. Set the value of the **Draw Size** slider to **140** by entering the value in the edit box or by moving the **Draw Size** slider toward right, refer to Figure 3-171.

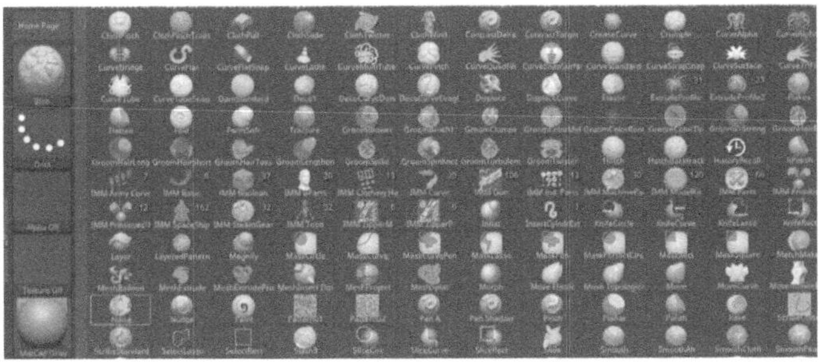

Figure 3-170 *The **Noise** brush chosen*

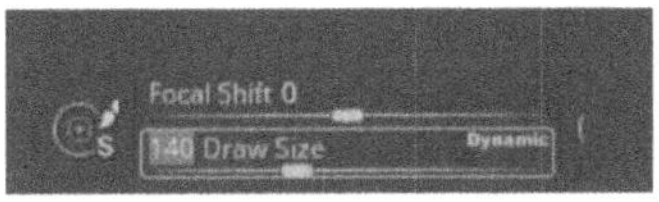

Figure 3-171 *The value of the **Draw Size** slider set to **140***

3. Press and hold the left mouse button and drag the cursor twice or thrice on the top of *stone*, as shown in Figure 3-172.

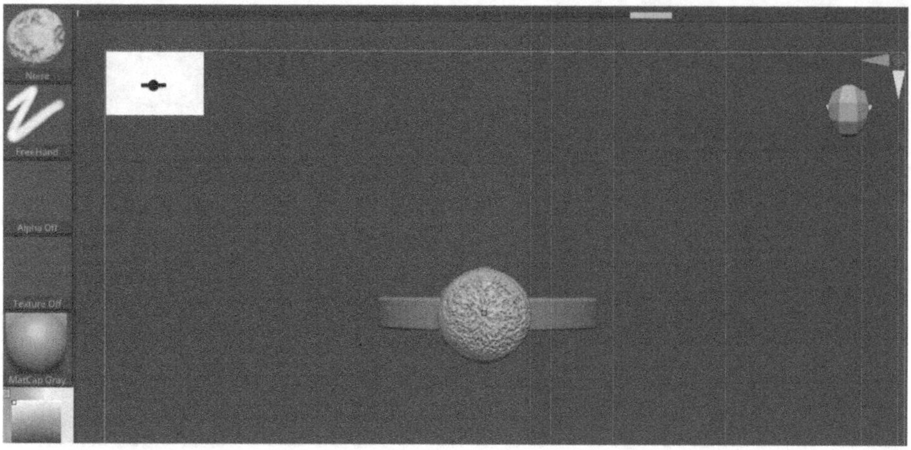

Figure 3-172 The noise brush dragged

Saving the Model

In this section, you will save the file using the steps given next.

1. Choose the **Save As** button from the **Tool** palette; the **Save ZTool** dialog box is displayed. In this dialog box, browse to the location *\Documents\ZBrushprojects\c03*.

2. Enter **c03tut6** in the **File name** edit box and then choose the **Save** button.

Self-Evaluation Test

Answer the following questions and then compare them to those given at the end of this chapter:

1. Which of the following buttons is used to capture a screenshot of the canvas as an alpha?

   (a) **Ep** (b) **GrabDoc**
   (c) **Make 3D** (d) **CropAndFill**

2. Which of the following buttons in the **Geometry** subpalette is used to retain the shape and placement of the polygons even if the geometry is divided a number of times?

   (a) **Rstr** (b) **Cage**
   (c) **Reconstruct Subdiv** (d) **Suv**

3. The **Deformation** subpalette is located in the __________ palette.

4. You can increase the number of polygons in the ZTool by choosing the ___________ button in the **Geometry** subpalette.

5. The __________ button is used to convert a primitive object into a polymesh.

6. The **Normalized** check box in the **Projection Master** dialog box is selected along with the __________ check box.

7. The **FreeHand** brush stroke is located in the **Brush** palette. (T/F)

8. The symmetry along X-axis can be activated by pressing the S key on your keyboard. (T/F)

9. The **DROP NOW** button in the **Projection Master** dialog box is used to convert a 2.5D illustration into a 3D model. (T/F)

10. The **Material** check box in the **Projection Master** dialog box is used to add different attributes such as lights, shadows, and reflectivity to a ZTool. (T/F)

Review Questions

Answer the following questions:

1. Which of the following combination of shortcut keys is used to activate the **ClipRect** brush?

   (a) CTRL+ALT (b) CTRL+SHIFT
   (c) CTRL (d) SHIFT

2. In which of the following subpalettes is the **Size** slider located?

   (a) **Deformation** (b) **Geometry**
   (c) **Surface** (d) **Initialize**

3. In which of the following palettes is the **Save As** button located?

   (a) **Draw** (b) **Picker**
   (c) **Render** (d) **Tool**

4. The __________ subpalette in the **Tool** palette is displayed only when the ZTool is in the primitive mode.

5. The **RadialCount** slider is located in the __________ palette.

6. The **SDiv** slider is located in the __________ subpalette of the **Tool** palette.

7. The **Deformation** check box in the **Projection Master** dialog box is used to sculpt finer details on the surface of a model which cannot be achieved in normal 3D mode. (T/F)

8. The **Morph Target** subpalette is used to establish points of contact between different subtools. (T/F)

9. The **Geometry HD** subpalette is used to create a new mesh on the surface of an already existing object. (T/F)

10. The **Surface** subpalette is used to add noise to a ZTool. (T/F)

EXERCISES

The output of the models used in the following exercises can be accessed by downloading the *c03_ZBrush_2022_exr.zip* file from *www.cadcim.com*. The path of the file is as follows: *Textbooks > Animation and Visual Effects > ZBrush > ZBrush 2022: A Comprehensive Guide*.

Exercise 1

Create the model of a table lamp using radial symmetry, as shown in Figure 3-173.

(Expected time: 15 min)

Figure 3-173 *Model of a table lamp*

Exercise 2

Create the model of a photo frame using the **Projection Master** dialog box, as shown in Figure 3-174. **(Expected time: 30 min)**

Figure 3-174 Model of a photo frame

Answers to Self-Evaluation Test

1. b, **2.** b, **3. Tool**, **4. Divide**, **5. Make PolyMesh3D**, **6. Deformation**, **7.** F, **8.** F, **9.** F, **10.** F

Chapter 4

SubTools and FiberMesh

Learning Objectives

After completing this chapter, you will be able to:

- *Work with the SubTool subpalette*
- *Work with the FiberMesh subpalette*
- *Understand different settings of FiberMesh*
- *Create scenes using different subtools and FiberMesh*

INTRODUCTION TO SUBTOOLS IN ZBrush

In ZBrush, subtools are sub components of an object. You can work individually on different components by selecting a subtool from the **SubTool** subpalette. For instance, to model a human head, you can model its face, eyes, and teeth separately. After modeling, you can work on each one of the subtools separately without disturbing the other subtools. Subtools play an important role in modeling complex objects.

SubTool SUBPALETTE

Enhanced

The **SubTool** subpalette is located in the **Tool** palette. This subpalette becomes visible only when an object is created in the canvas, refer to Figure 4-1. In this case, a sphere has been created in the canvas and a single thumbnail will be displayed in the **SubTool** subpalette. However, if an object is composed of multiple components, the **SubTool** subpalette displays the thumbnails of the list of objects that constitute it. For instance, the *DemoSoldier.ZPR* file in the **LightBox** browser is composed of different components, such as the main body, shirt, vest, backpack, and so on. These different elements can be termed as the subtools.

To load the *DemoSoldier.ZPR* model in the canvas, choose the **Project** tab in the **LightBox** browser. Next, double-click on the *DemoSoldier.ZPR* file in the **LightBox** browser and choose the **LightBox** browser again to close it. Press and hold the left mouse button and drag the cursor in the canvas; the model will be loaded in the canvas. After loading the model, choose the **Edit** button from the top shelf.

On loading the *DemoSoldier.ZPR* file in the canvas, the **SubTools** subpalette displays the thumbnails for all the objects that constitute it, refer to Figure 4-2.

The **SubTool** subpalette consists of various tools that enable you to manipulate each subtool in the list of thumbnails. You can toggle the visibility of each subtool by clicking on the eye icon corresponding to it. The tools and buttons in the **SubTool** subpalette are discussed next.

Visibility Sets

In ZBrush 2022, eight buttons are added to the **Subtool** subpalette for storing visibility of subtools. These buttons can also be termed as sets, refer to Figure 4-2. To understand how to store visibility of subtools using these sets, load the *DemoSoldier.ZPR* file from the **LightBox** browser. Next, make sure the **V1** button is chosen. Now, click on the eye icon corresponding to all the subtools except **DemoSoldier** to hide them. Next, choose the **V2** button. Now, click on the eye icon next to **DemoSoldier** to hide it and click on the eye icon of all the other subtools to make them visible. In this way, two visibility sets will be created, the V1 set that includes only the **DemoSoldier** subtool, and the V2 set that includes all the subtools except the **DemoSoldier** subtool. In this way, you can create upto eight visibility sets depending on your requirement.

Note

If any subtool is already selected when you create the visibility set, it will remain visible in that visibility set.

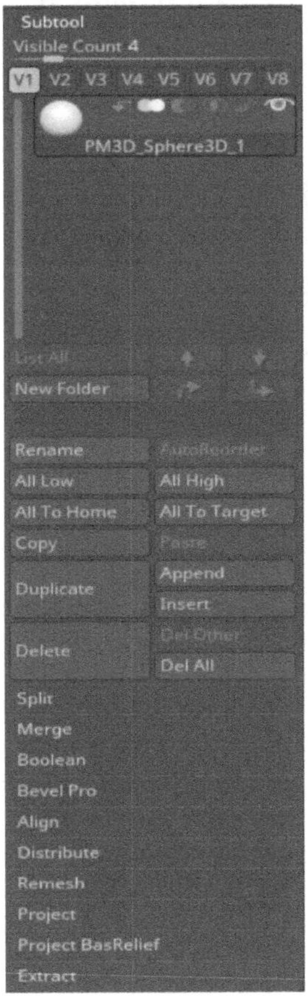

*Figure 4-1 The **SubTool** subpalette displayed on creating a sphere*

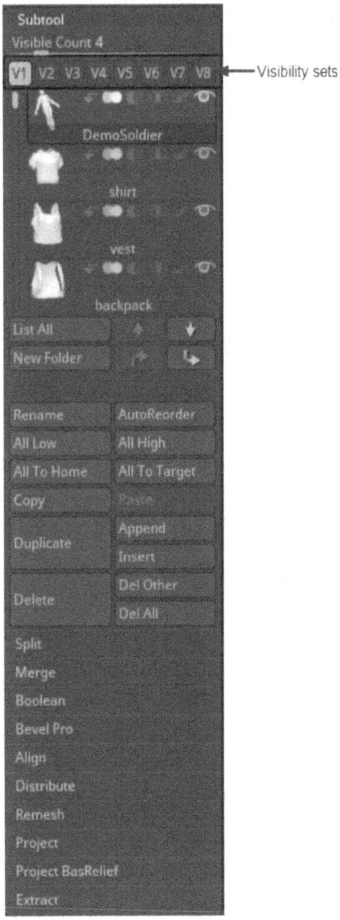

*Figure 4-2 The **SubTool** subpalette displayed on loading the **DemoSoldier***

List All

The **List All** button is used to display the list of all the subtools that constitute an object. This button is activated only when an object created in the canvas consists of more than one subtool. On choosing this button, a flyout containing thumbnails for all the subtools will be displayed, refer to Figure 4-3.

New Folder

To create a new folder in the **SubTool** subpalette, select a subtool that you want to put in the folder and then choose the **New Folder** button; the **Please Enter Folder Title** window will be displayed. Next, enter the name of the folder in this window. You will notice that the new folder with that name is created in the **Subtool** subpalette and the selected subtool will move to the folder. To add more subtools in this folder, select the subtool and drag it to the folder; the selected subtool will now be a part of that folder. Note that you cannot create a folder within the folder. Also, if you delete the last subtool from the folder, the folder will be automatically deleted.

Arrow Buttons

The arrow buttons, as shown in Figure 4-4, are used to select or move the subtools in the list. These buttons are activated only when an object contains more than one subtool.

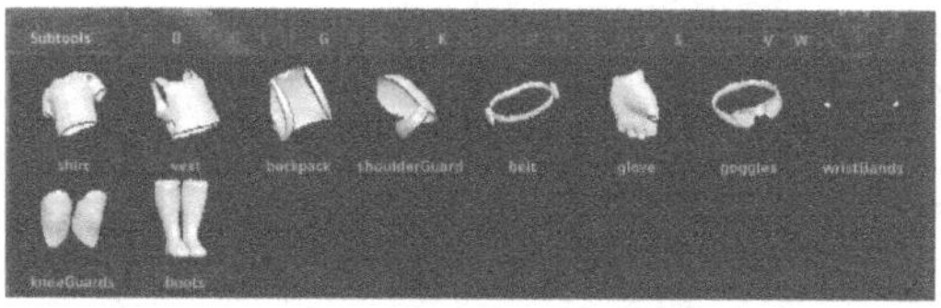

Figure 4-3 The flyout displayed on choosing the ***List All*** *button*

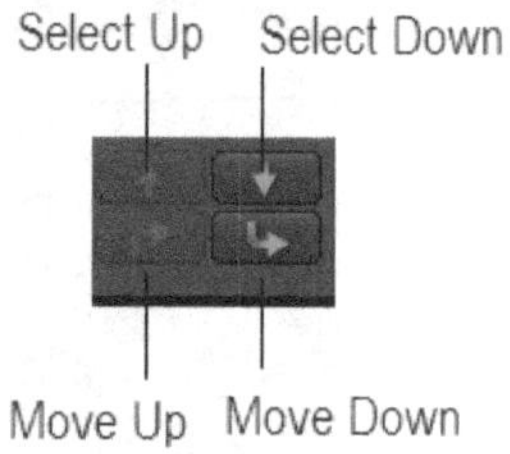

Figure 4-4 The arrow buttons

The **Select Up** button is used to select a subtool located above the currently selected subtool in the list and the **Select Down** button is used to select the subtool located below the currently selected subtool. The **Move Up** and **Move Down** buttons are used to move a subtool up or down in the list, respectively.

Rename

The **Rename** button is used to change the name of a particular subtool. To do so, select the required subtool in the list. Next, choose the **Rename** button from the palette; the **Please enter subtool title** window will be displayed, as shown in Figure 4-5. In this window, enter the desired new name for the subtool, and then press ENTER; the specified name will be displayed in the list.

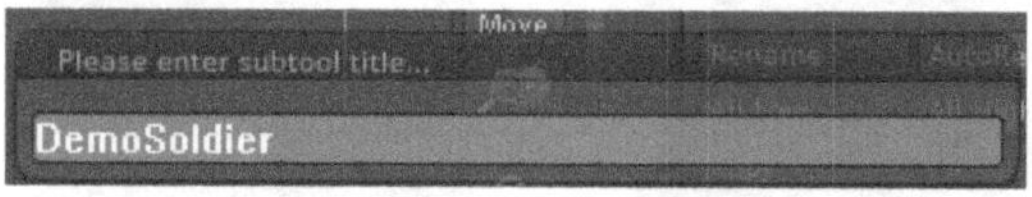

Figure 4-5 The ***Please enter subtool title*** *window*

AutoReorder

The **AutoReorder** button is used to arrange subtools in the list according to their polygon count.

All Low

The **All Low** button is used to display all the subtools in the canvas at their lowest subdivision levels, containing the least number of polygons. Figure 4-6 shows the model of the *DemoSoldier.ZTL* file before choosing the **All Low** button and Figure 4-7 shows the model after choosing the **All Low** button in the **SubTool** subpalette.

All High

The **All High** button is used to display all the subtools in the canvas at their highest subdivision levels, containing the maximum number of polygons. If you choose the **All Low** button to display a model at its lowest subdivision level, you can switch back to its highest subdivision level by choosing the **All High** button.

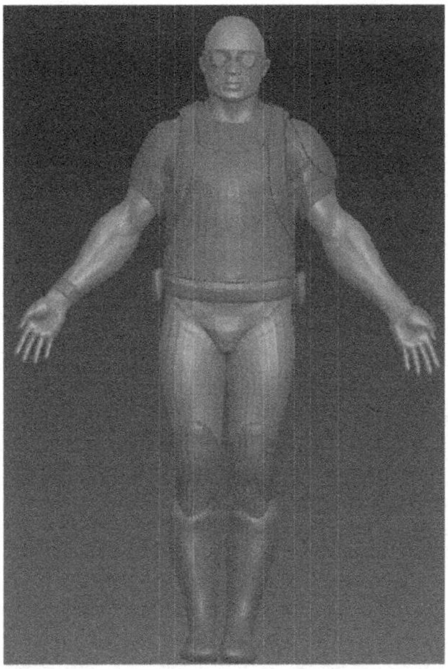

*Figure 4-6 The model of the DemoSoldier. ZTL before choosing the **All Low** button*

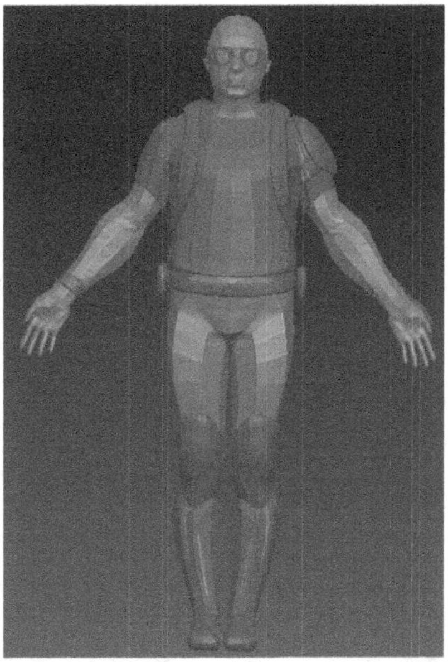

*Figure 4-7 The model of the DemoSoldier. ZTL after choosing the **All Low** button*

All To Home

The **All To Home** button is used to move all the subtools to the home stage but before using this button, you need to set the home stage for all the subtools.

All To Target

The **All To Target** button is used to move all the subtools to the target stage but before using this button, you need to set the target stage for all the subtools.

Note

*The process of setting the home stage and target stage and setting the parameters in the **Stager** area is discussed in detail in Chapter 3.*

Copy and Paste

These buttons are used to copy and paste the subtools from the **SubTool** palette. To do so, select the subtool in the subtool list. Next, choose the **Copy** button from the palette and then choose the **Paste** button; the copied subtool will be pasted in the **SubTool** palette.

Duplicate

The **Duplicate** button is used to create a copy of the selected subtool. To do so, select the subtool that you want to duplicate from the list of subtools and then choose the **Duplicate** button; a duplicate of the subtool will be displayed along with it in the list of subtools in the **SubTool** subpalette. When you create the duplicate of a subtool, it will overlap the existing subtool and will not be visible in the canvas. Choose the **Gizmo 3D** button to deactivate. To view the duplicate in the canvas, choose the **Move** button from the top shelf; the action line will be displayed. You can move the duplicate model using the action line, as discussed earlier.

Append

The **Append** button is used to add a new subtool to an object. On choosing this button, a flyout containing various primitive objects will be displayed, refer to Figure 4-8. Choose the required object from the flyout; the chosen object will be added to the model and will be visible in the canvas.

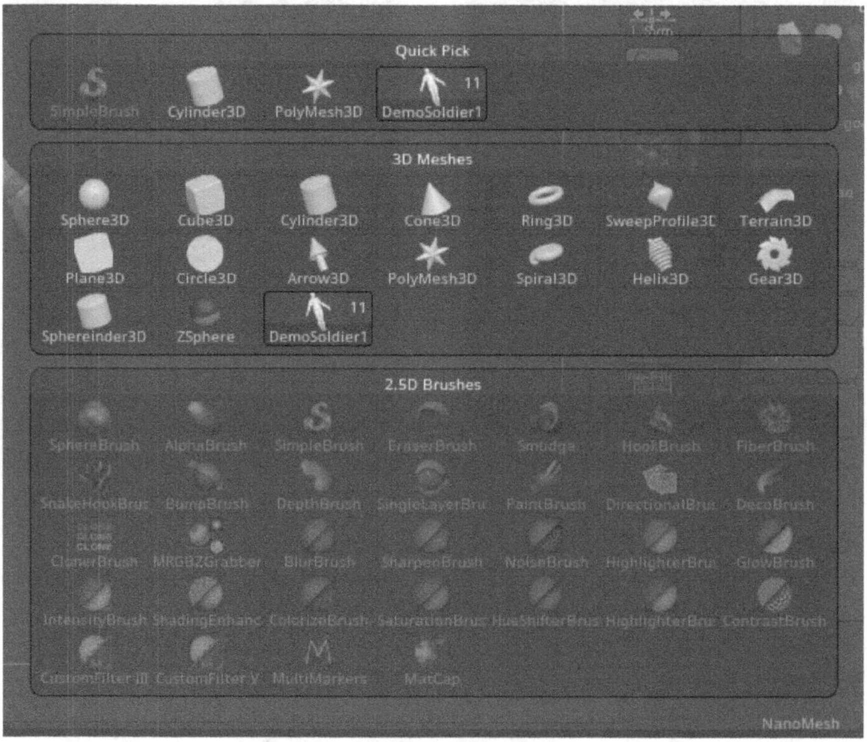

Figure 4-8 The flyout displayed on choosing the ***Append*** *button*

Insert

The **Insert** button is used to insert a Ztool below the currently selected subtool in the list. On choosing this button, a flyout will be displayed. Choose the required object from the flyout. Figure 4-9 shows a sphere that is inserted in the model by choosing the **Insert** button. In the list of subtools, the currently selected subtool is **vest**. On choosing the sphere from the flyout, a thumbnail for the sphere will be displayed just below the **boots** subtool, refer to Figure 4-10.

Delete

The **Delete** button is used to delete the currently selected subtool from the list. On choosing this button, a message box will be displayed, refer to Figure 4-11. In this message box, choose the **OK** button to delete the currently selected subtool.

Del Other

The **Del Other** button is used to delete all the subtools in the list except the currently selected subtool. On choosing this button, a message box will be displayed, asking you whether you want to continue the operation or not. Choose the **OK** button to delete the subtools.

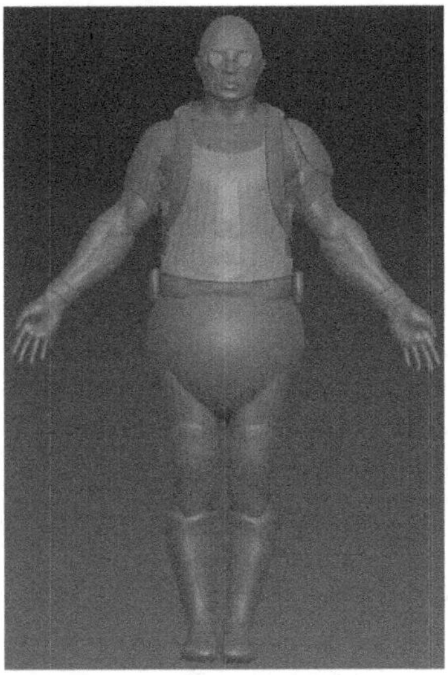

Figure 4-9 A sphere inserted inside the model

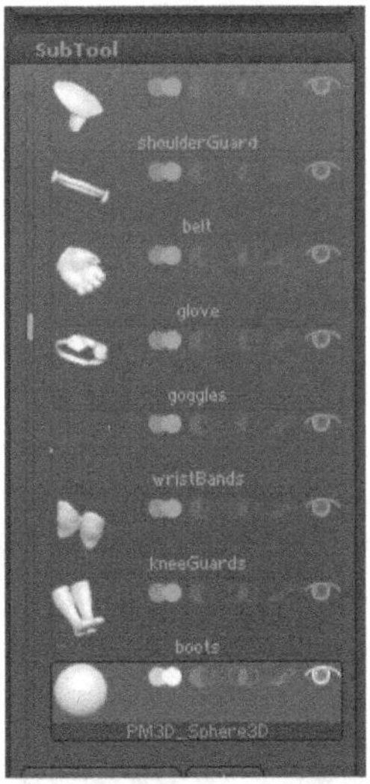

Figure 4-10 The thumbnail for the sphere displayed below the ***boots*** *subtool*

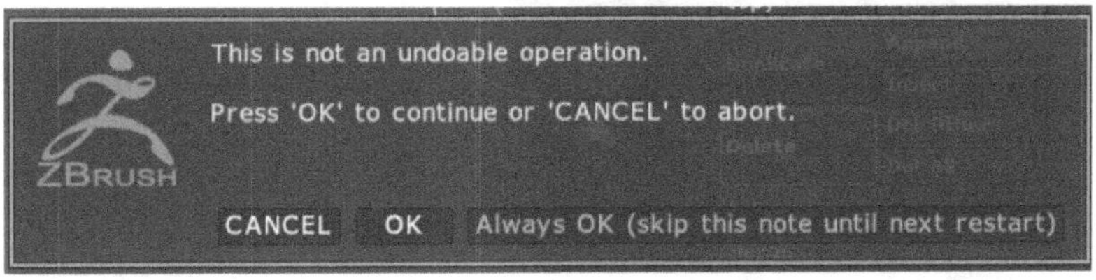

Figure 4-11 The message box displayed on choosing the ***Delete*** *button*

Del All

The **Del All** button is used to delete all the subtools in the list of subtools.

Split

The **Split** area, as shown in Figure 4-12, consists of various buttons that are used to split a partially visible ZTool into a number of subtools. The number of subtools depends on the parts of the mesh that have been hidden in the viewport. By default, this button is not activated. To split a ZTool, you need to select the required parts of the ZTool that need to be split by using the CTRL+SHIFT keys.

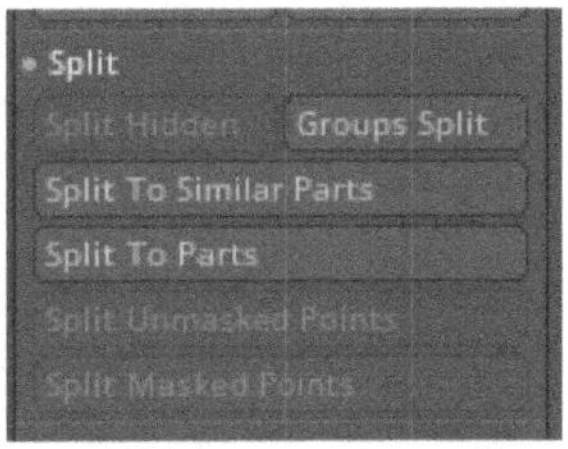

Figure 4-12 The ***Split*** *area*

Merge

The **Merge** area consists of various buttons that are used to combine different subtools together such that they form a single group.

Boolean

You can create complex models by performing boolean operations, namely addition, subtraction, or intersection on two or more subtools. To initiate the boolean process, first you need to choose the **Live Boolean** button available in the top shelf. On doing so, buttons in the **Boolean** area are activated. Now, based on the intended boolean operation, you need to arrange the subtools in the interface, refer to Figure 4-13. Next, first you need to select the subtool on which boolean operation is going to be performed and then choose the arrow button located next to it, refer to Figure 4-14. Now, select the other subtool and then choose the desired boolean operator button located next to the subtool, refer to Figure 4-14. Next, choose the **Make Boolean Mesh** button from the **Boolean** area in the **Subtool** subpalette. On doing so, boolean mesh will be created and displayed in the **Tool** palette with the name **UMesh_PM3D_Cube3D_1**. If you click on **UMesh_PM3D_Cube3D_1** in the **Tool** palette, it will be displayed as a subtool in the **Subtool** subpalette and the subtools that were used for performing boolean operation will be removed. Figure 4-15 shows the subtraction boolean operation carried out on cube and sphere. Figure 4-16 shows intersection operation carried out on cube and sphere.

Note

Before carring out boolean operation, you need to increase the subdivision levels of the subtools for better results.

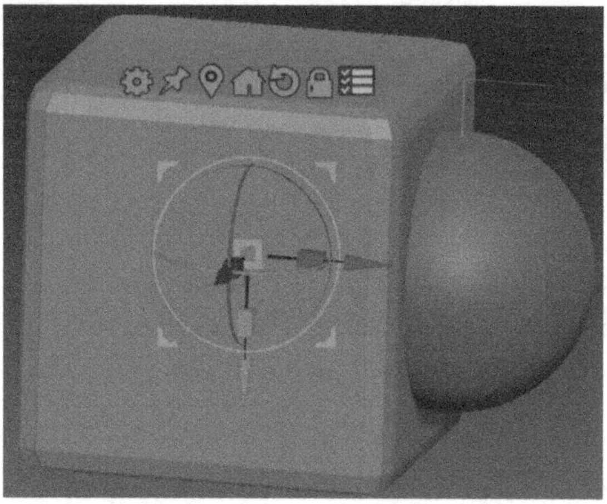

Figure 4-13 Subtools arranged for boolean operation

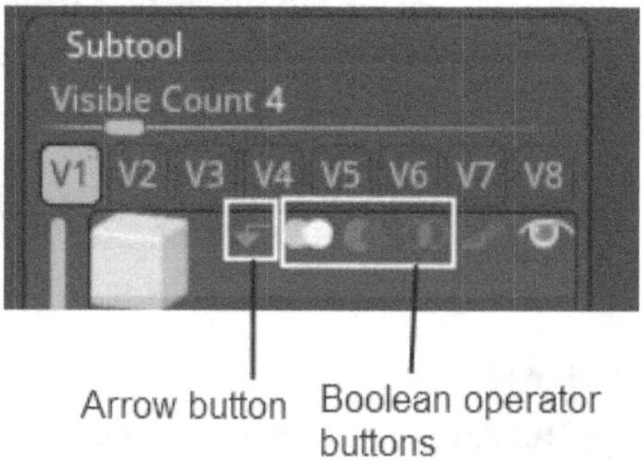

Figure 4-14 Various buttons used in the boolean operation

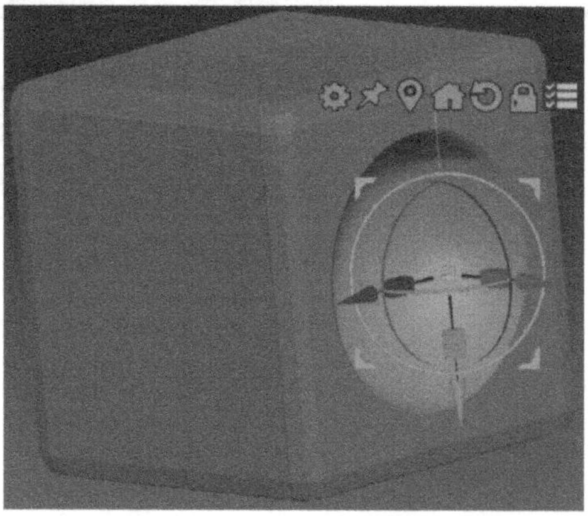

Figure 4-15 Subtraction boolean operation carried on cube and sphere

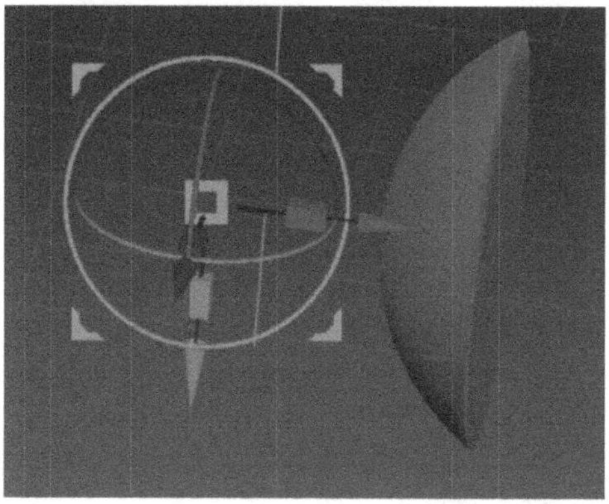

Figure 4-16 Intersection boolean operation on cube and sphere

BevelPro

In ZBrush 2022, new **BevelPro** plugin is introduced. With this plugin, you can create complex bevels for a mesh. You need to use polygroups and can also use masking to determine exactly which edges to be beveled. Beveling is done along the borders of polygroup. Note that beveling cannot be done for partially hidden meshes. To understand the process of bevelpro, choose the Current Tool button from the **Tool** palette and then choose the **Sphereinder** primitive from the flyout displayed. Next, press and hold the left mouse button and drag the cursor on the canvas to create a sphereinder. Now, choose the **Edit** button from the top shelf and then expand the **Initialize** subpalette. In this subpalette, enter **250** in the **Coverage** slider; the Spherinder object will be modified, refer to Figure 4-17. Next, open the **Transform** palette and choose the **PolyF** button from it.

Choose the **Make PolyMesh3D** button from the **Tool** palette; the Spherinder3D object will be converted into a polymesh. Next, expand the **Polygroups** subpalette in the **Tool** palette, and then choose the **Group By Normals** button from it. Notice that polygroups for Spherinder 3D object will be modified, refer to Figure 4-18. Now, choose the **BevelPro** button from the **BevelPro** area in the **Subtool** subpalette. On doing so, the **BevelPro** plugin will be launched, refer to Figure 4-19. In this plugin, a number of parameters are available at the left for modifying the bevel shape and a preview window is available at the right to preview the bevel shape. After setting the desired parameters, choose the **OK** button; you will return to ZBrush and a beveled Spherinder3D object will be displayed, refer to Figure 4-20.

Figure 4-17 *Modified Sphereinder3D object*

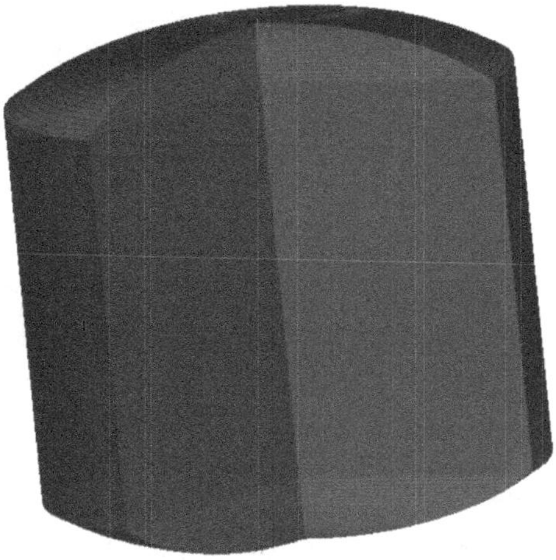

Figure 4-18 *Modified polygroups of Sphereinder3D object*

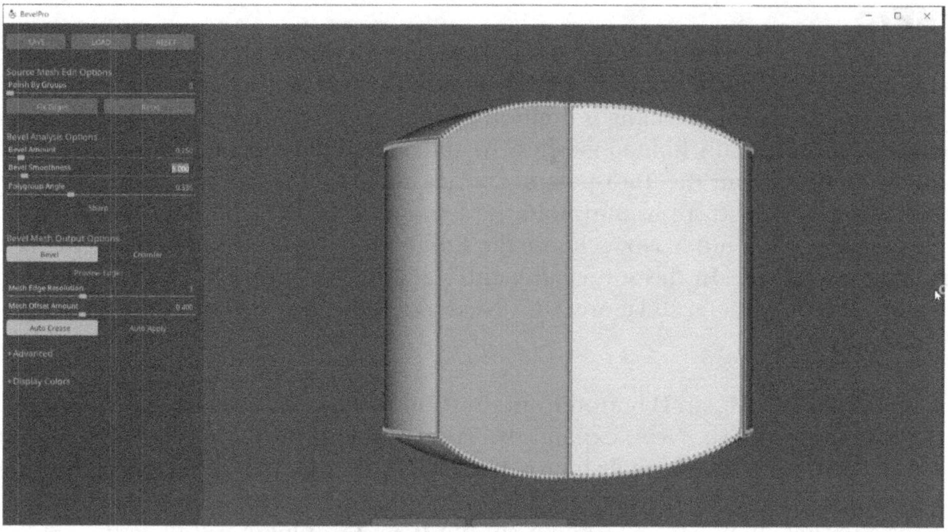

Figure 4-19 The ***BevelPro*** *plugin launched*

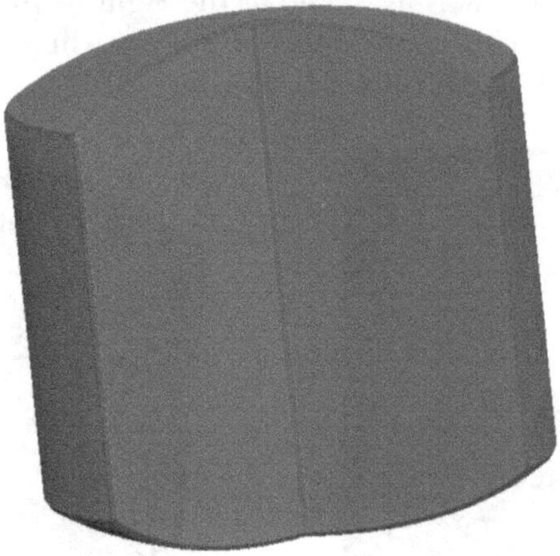

Figure 4-20 The ***Spherinder3D*** *object beveled*

Align

The **Align** area, as shown in Figure 4-21, consists of six buttons that are used to align all the subtools with respect to the selected subtool. Figure 4-22 shows the alignment of **DemoSoldier** and other subtools when the **Align Top Edges** button is chosen from the **Align** area. You will notice that top edges of all the subtools are aligned with respect to the top edge of the **DemoSoldier** subtool. Figure 4-23 shows the alignment of **DemoSoldier** and other subtools when the **Align Vertical Centers** button is chosen from the **Align** area. You will notice that vertical centers of all the subtools are aligned with respect to the vertical center of the **DemoSoldier** subtool.

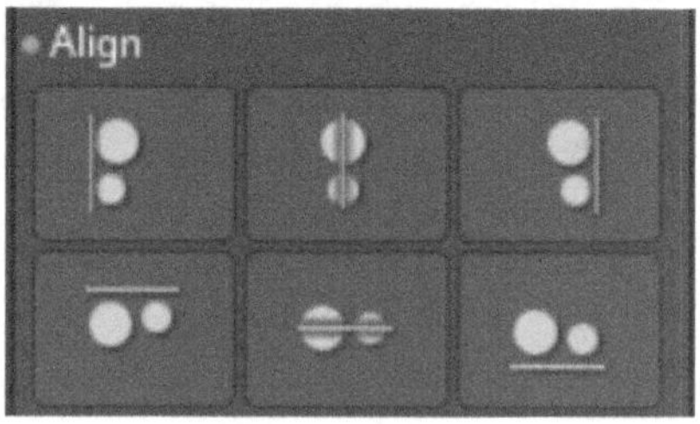

Figure 4-21 The ***Align*** *area*

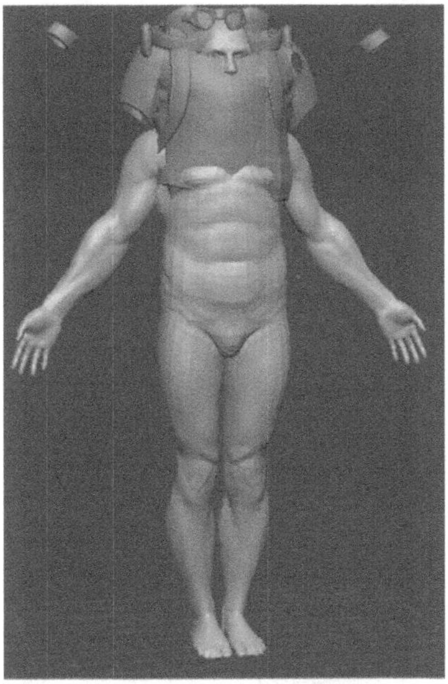

Figure 4-22 *Subtools aligned with respect to the top edges of the DemoSoldier subtool*

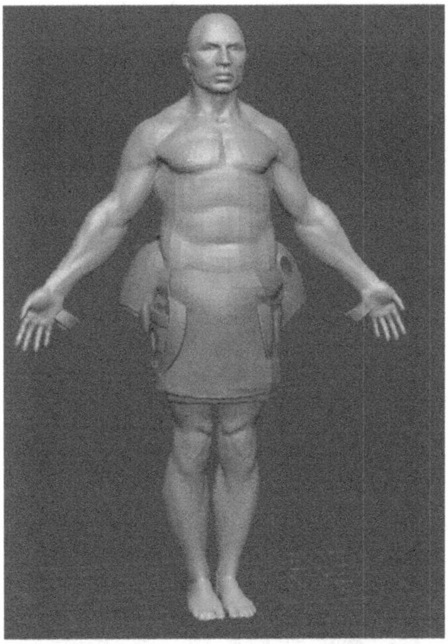

Figure 4-23 *Subtools aligned with respect to the vertical center of the DemoSoldier subtool*

Distribute

The **Distribute** area, as shown in Figure 4-24, consists of six buttons that are used to distribute all the subtools with respect to the selected subtool. Figure 4-25 shows the distribution of **DemoSoldier** and other subtools when the **Distribute Vertical Centers** button is chosen from the **Distribute** area. You will notice that the vertical centers of the subtools are distributed with respect to the vertical center of the **DemoSoldier** subtool. Figure 4-26 shows the distribution of **DemoSoldier** and other subtools when the **Distribute Top Edges** button is chosen. You will notice that top edges of the subtools are distributed with respect to the top edge of the **DemoSoldier** subtool.

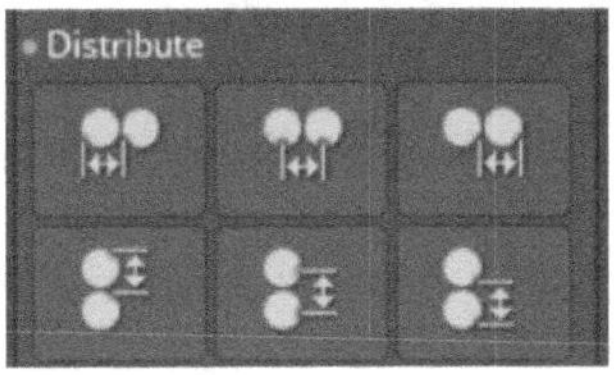

Figure 4-24 *The* ***Distribute*** *area*

Remesh

The **Remesh** area consists of different buttons and sliders that are used to create a new mesh on the existing ZTool. The new mesh created will be composed of quad polygons and is displayed in the list of subtools.

Project

The **Project** area consists of different buttons and sliders that are used to project the sculpting details from the visible subtool to the selected subtool.

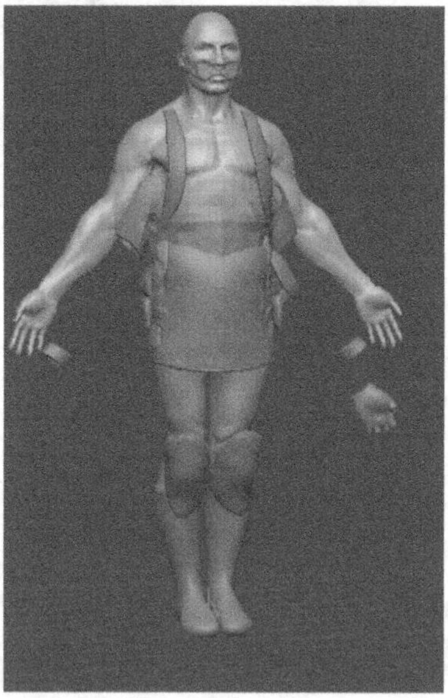

*Figure 4-25 Subtools distributed with respect to the vertical center of the **DemoSoldier** subtool*

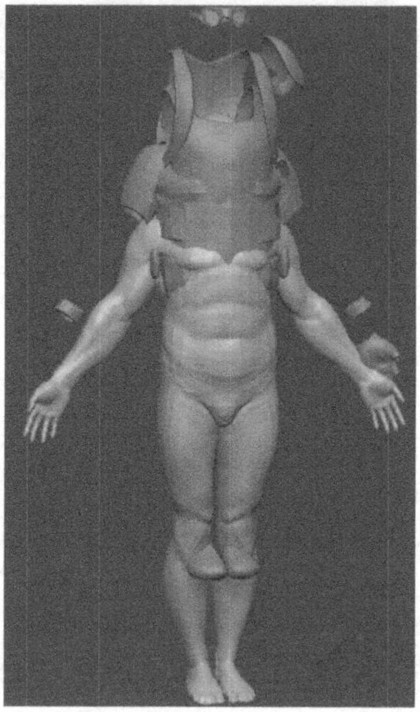

*Figure 4-26 Subtools distributed with respect to the top edges of the **DemoSoldier** subtool*

ProjectBasRelief

In Zbrush 2022, a new feature, BasRelief, has been added in the **ProjectBasRelief** area, refer to Figure 4-27. It consists of a number of parameters to create embossed surfaces with stunning details that resemble the traditional relief sculpture. To understand this feature, load **DemoDog.ZPR** model from the **Project** tab in the **LightBox** browser. Next, choose the **Append** button from the **Subtool** subpalette and choose **Cylinder3D** from the flyout displayed; the **PM3D_Cylinder3D1** subtool will be added to the scene. Next, align **PM3D_Cylinder3D1** and **Dog**, as shown in Figure 4-28.

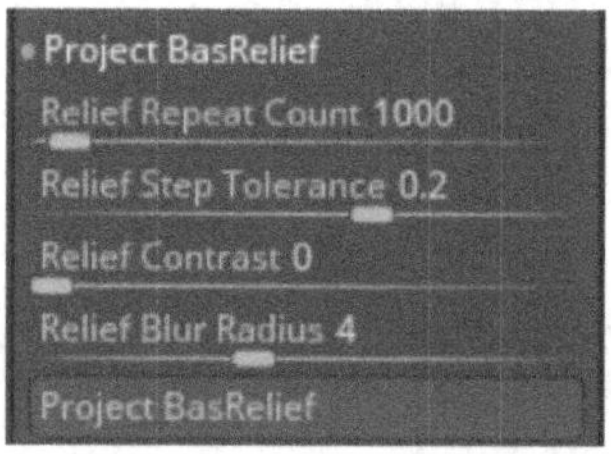

*Figure 4-27 The **ProjectBasRelief** area*

Make sure the **PM3D_Cylinder3D1** subtool is selected and then choose the **DynaMesh** button from the **DynaMesh** area in the **Geometry** subpalette. Next, set the parameters in the **ProjectBasRelief** area in the **Subtool** subpalette and then choose the **ProjectBasRelief** button; the embossed dog surface will be displayed on the cylinder, refer to Figure 4-29. The parameters in the **ProjectBasRelief** area are discussed next.

Relief Repeat Count

The **Relief Repeat Count** slider specifies the number of times the Bas Relief algorithm will run. Normally, the default value 1000 will work but in some cases, you may need to modify the value to get the desired result.

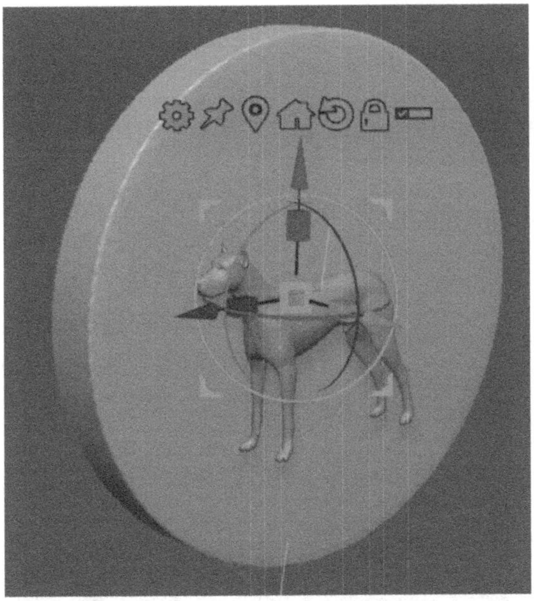

Figure 4-28 PM3D_Cylinder3D1 and Dog aligned

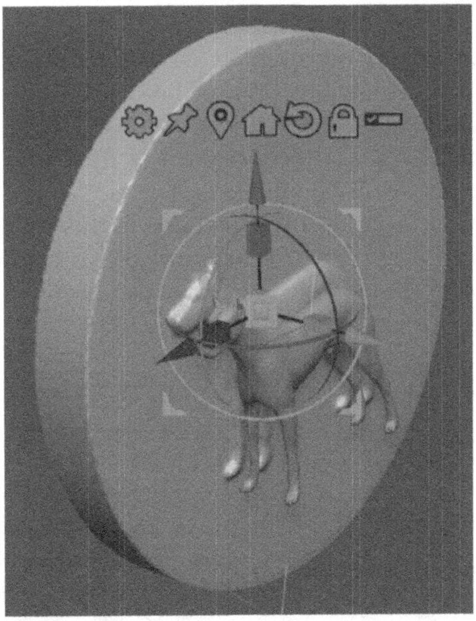

Figure 4-29 Embossed dog surface displayed

Relief Step Tolerance

The **Relief Step Tolerance** slider is used to control the effect of basrelief between the areas of the selected surface where the embossed surface is not available. Note that the lower value in the slider will result in a softer surface.

Relief Contrast

The **Relief Contrast** slider is used to control the contrast value added to the embossed surface. You can enhance the detailing of the embossed surface using this slider.

Relief Blur Radius

The **Relief Blur Radius** slider is used to control the amount of smoothening at the edges of the embossed surface.

ProjectBasRelief

After setting the values in the sliders mentioned above, you can choose the **ProjectBasRelief** button to get the basrelief result.

Extract

The **Extract** area consists of different buttons and sliders that are used to extract a new mesh from the selected subtool. These buttons and sliders are used in combination with the Mask brushes. The Mask brushes enable you to draw any desired shape and then extract it from the base model. To do so, choose the **Extract** button first and then the **Accept** button located below it; the new mesh extracted from the subtool will be displayed in the list of subtools. The **Extract** button is ideal for creating clothes on a human body.

FiberMesh IN ZBrush

The **FiberMesh** subpalette is used to create a fiber mesh on the surface of an object. The **FiberMesh** subpalette is located in the **Tool** palette, refer to Figure 4-30. This subpalette is displayed only when an object created in the canvas is converted into a polymesh. You can create hair, fur, grass, and so on, from the object using different settings in this subpalette. The different types of groom brushes available in the **Brush** palette enable you to modify the shape of the fibrous mesh created on the surface of an object.

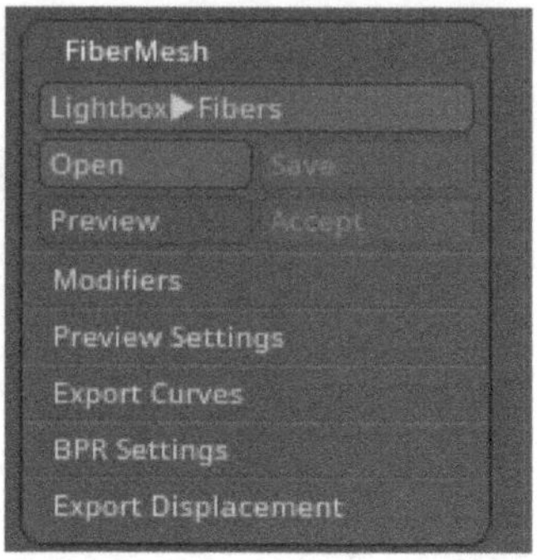

***Figure 4-30** The **FiberMesh** subpalette*

For creating fibers, you need to have a surface on which the fibers will be generated. So before creating fibers, select the area on the surface where you want the mesh to be generated. The area can be selected by using the mask brush. To understand the working of the **FiberMesh** subpalette, load the *DemoHead.ZTL* file from the **LightBox** browser, refer to Figure 4-31.

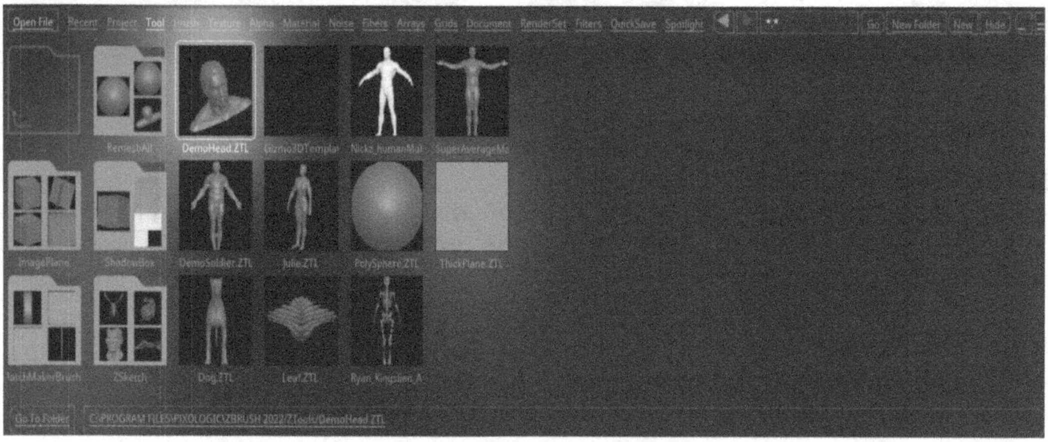

***Figure 4-31** The DemoHead.ZTL file chosen from the **LightBox** browser*

After loading the model in the canvas, choose the **Edit** button from the top shelf and then click twice on the **Divide** button in the **Geometry** subpalette such that the value of the **SDiv** slider becomes **5**. Next, press and hold the CTRL key and then draw a mask on the head of the model, as shown in Figure 4-32. After drawing the mask on the head, choose the **Preview** button in the **FiberMesh** subpalette, as shown in Figure 4-33; a fiber mesh will be created on the masked area, as shown in Figure 4-34.

In the **Preview** mode, you can modify the mesh using different tools and settings in the **Modifiers** area, refer to Figure 4-35. Once you get the desired mesh, you can expand the **Modifiers** area and adjust the settings as required. Next, choose the **Accept** button from the **FiberMesh** subpalette; a message box will be displayed, prompting you to activate the fast preview rendering mode of the mesh, as shown in Figure 4-36.

In this message box, choose the **Yes** button; the rendered preview of the mesh will be displayed, as shown in Figure 4-37. Also, the new mesh will be displayed as a subtool in the **SubTool** subpalette.

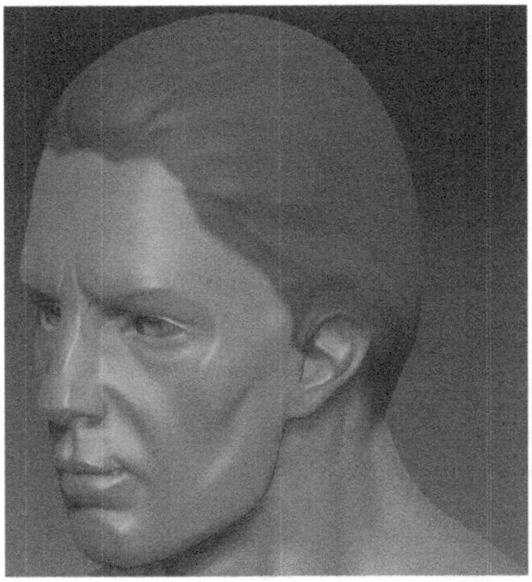

Figure 4-32 *A mask drawn on the head of the model*

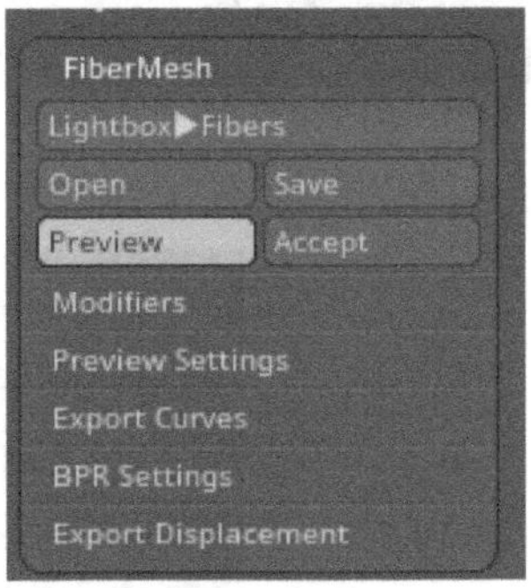

Figure 4-33 *The* ***Preview*** *button chosen from the* ***FiberMesh*** *subpalette*

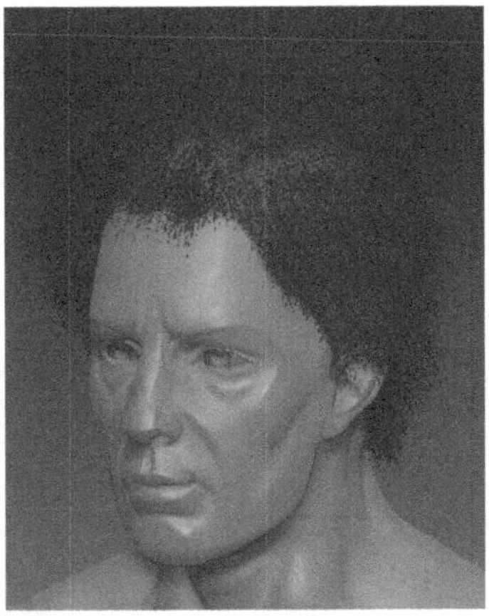

Figure 4-34 *The fiber mesh created on the masked area of the head*

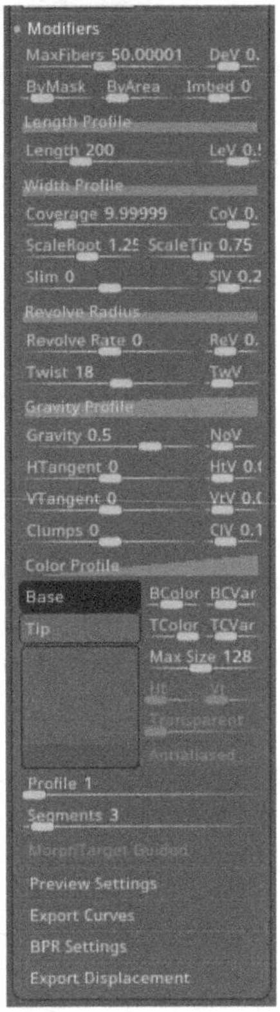

Figure 4-35 *The* ***Modifiers*** *area*

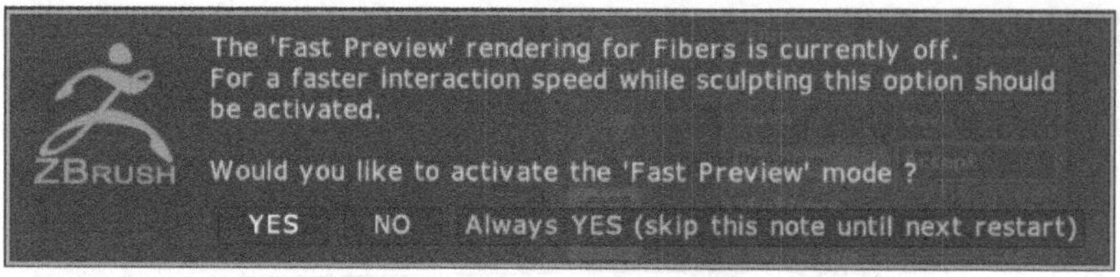

Figure 4-36 *Message box displayed on choosing the **Accept** button*

Figure 4-37 *The final rendered preview of the fiber mesh*

FiberMesh Settings

The different buttons and sliders in the **FiberMesh** subpalette in the **Tool** palette help to create different types of fibers and hairstyles. These buttons and sliders are discussed next.

LightBox Fibers

The **LightBox Fibers** button is used to display the Lightbox containing different types of inbuilt fiber meshes present in ZBrush, refer to Figure 4-38. To apply any inbuilt fiber to an object, double-click on it in the **LightBox** browser; the fibre mesh will be displayed on the surface of the object.

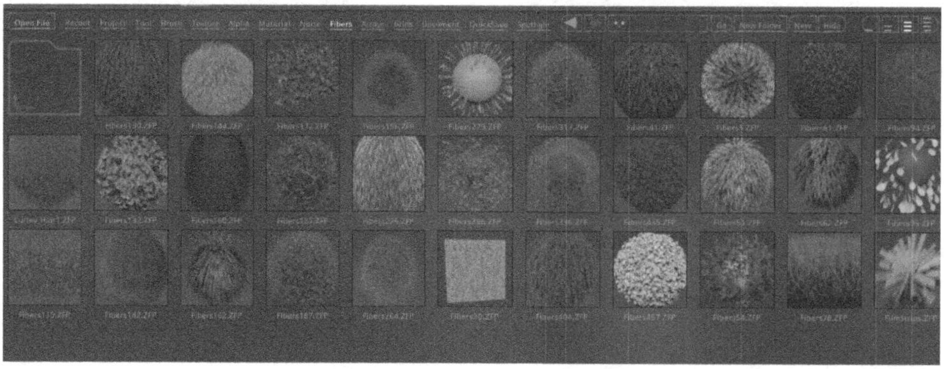

Figure 4-38 *The inbuilt fibres in the **LightBox** browser*

Open

The **Open** button is used to open the saved fiber meshes and then apply them to the surface of an object. On choosing this button, the **Load Fibers Preset** dialog box will be displayed, as shown in Figure 4-39. Choose the desired fiber mesh from this dialog box. Next, choose the **Open** button; the fiber mesh will be applied to the object.

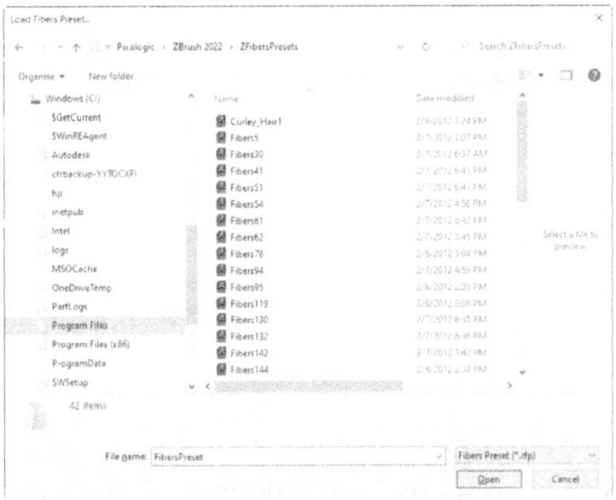

*Figure 4-39 The **Load Fibers Preset** dialog box*

Save

The **Save** button is used to save the current settings of a fiber mesh as a preset which can later be applied to any fiber mesh. On choosing this button, the **Save Fibers Preset** dialog box will be displayed. This dialog box enables you to save the fiber mesh preset with the required name.

Preview

The **Preview** button is used to view the fiber mesh on the surface of an object in the canvas. In the **Preview** mode, you can change the length, color, and other attributes of the fiber mesh using different attributes in the **Modifiers** area. If you rotate the object in this mode, the fiber mesh will disappear temporarily.

Accept

The **Accept** button is used to convert the fiber mesh into a subtool that can be sculpted and painted using different types of brushes. On choosing this button, the different attributes in the **Modifiers** area are deactivated and the mesh cannot be modified.

Modifiers

The **Modifiers** area consists of different attributes that enable you to modify the appearance of a fiber mesh. These attributes are active only when the **Preview** button is chosen. Some of these attributes are discussed next.

MaxFibers

The **MaxFibers** slider is used to generate the required number of fibers on the fiber mesh. Figure 4-40 shows a mesh containing 2000 fibers and Figure 4-41 shows a mesh containing 10,000 fibers. To create 2000 and 10,000 fibers, set the value in the **MaxFibers** slider to **2** and **10**, respectively.

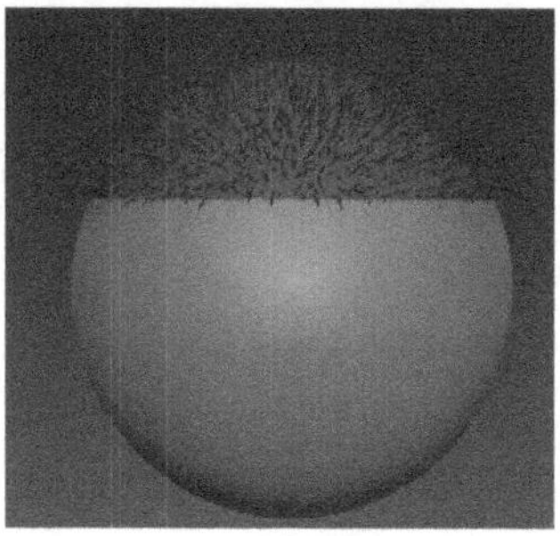

Figure 4-40 The mesh containing 2000 fibers

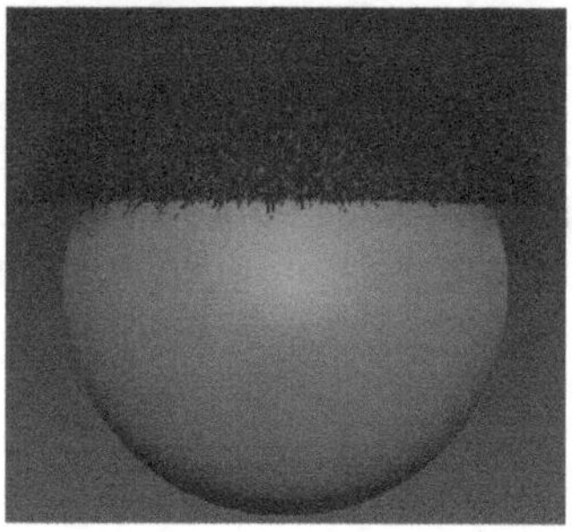

Figure 4-41 The mesh containing 10,000 fibers

DeV

The term DeV stands for Density Variations. The **DeV** slider is used to change the variation in the density of fibers in a fiber mesh.

ByMask

The **ByMask** slider is used to adjust the influence of the mask on the fibers created. A stronger intensity of mask will create longer fibers.

ByArea

The **ByArea** slider is used to adjust the influence of the polygons on the fibers. If the polygons on a surface are bigger in size, the fibers created on that surface will be longer and thicker.

Imbed

The **Imbed** slider is used to adjust the orientation of the roots of the fibers. It is used to specify whether the root of the fibers will be lying on the surface of the object or will be imbedded deep into it.

Length

The **Length** slider is used to adjust the length of the fibers. If the value of this slider is higher, the fibers will be longer. Figure 4-42 shows the fiber mesh with the value of the **Length** slider set to **50** and Figure 4-43 shows the fiber mesh with the value of the **Length** slider set to **1000**.

Coverage

The **Coverage** slider is used to change the width of the fibers. If the value of this slider is higher, the fibers will be thicker.

ScaleRoot

The **ScaleRoot** slider is used to increase or decrease the size of the roots of an individual fiber in the fiber mesh.

ScaleTip

The **ScaleTip** slider is used to increase or decrease the size of the tip of an individual fiber in the fiber mesh.

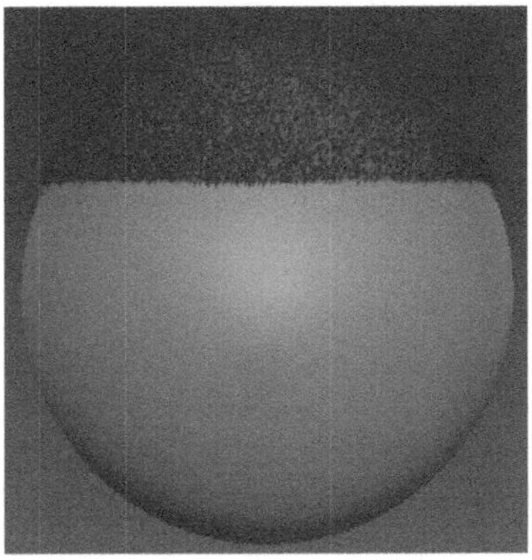

*Figure 4-42 Fiber mesh with the value of the **Length** slider set to **50***

*Figure 4-43 Fiber mesh with the value of the **Length** slider set to **1000***

Slim

The **Slim** slider is used to decrease the depth of the fibers in the fiber mesh.

Revolve Rate

The **Revolve Rate** slider is used to curl the fibers in the fiber mesh. It is ideal for creating curly and wavy hair.

Twist

The **Twist** slider is used to create twists in the fiber strands to give them a realistic appearance.

Gravity

The **Gravity** slider is used to make the ends of the fibers drop downward. Figure 4-44 shows the fiber mesh with the value of the **Gravity** slider set to **1**.

*Figure 4-44 The fiber mesh with the value of **Gravity** slider set to **1***

HTangent

The **HTangent** slider is used to change the direction of fibers horizontally. The setting of this slider can be useful for creating a feather-like mesh.

VTangent

The **VTangent** slider is used to change the direction of fibers vertically. The setting of this slider can be useful for creating a feather-like mesh.

Clumps

The **Clumps** slider is used to attract the tips of the fibers. To separate the tips of the fibers, the value of these fibers is set to negative.

Base Color

The **Base Color** button is used to choose the color for the base of the fibers. On choosing this button, a color picker window will be displayed. You can choose the required color from this window.

Tip Color

The **Tip Color** button is used to choose the color for the tip of the fibers.

Groom Brushes

The Groom brushes are used to sculpt the fiber mesh. ZBrush comes with different types of Groom brushes. To access these brushes, choose the Current Brush button; a flyout containing different brushes including the Groom brushes will be displayed. These brushes enable you to create different hairstyles by selecting the required brush and then dragging the cursor on the surface of the fiber mesh. Some of the Groom brushes are discussed next.

GroomBlower

The **GroomBlower** brush is used to simulate the effect of a blow dryer on wet hair. It separates the hair strands from each other. Figure 4-45 shows the effect produced by the **GroomBlower** brush.

GroomBrush1

The **GroomBrush1** brush is used to comb the hair and is similar to a real life hair brush.

GroomClumps

The **GroomClumps** brush is used to join the hair strands together to form clumps of hair, refer to Figure 4-46.

GroomColorMild

The **GroomColorMild** brush is used to paint the hair with the desired color, refer to Figure 4-47. To use this brush, select a color from the color palette located in the left shelf; the color of the mesh on which the hair is created will change. Start painting on the surface of the hair with the desired colors. You can restore the default color of the hair by choosing the white color from the color palette.

GroomHairBall

The **GroomHairBall** brush is used to roll the tips of hair into round clumps, refer to Figure 4-48.

GroomHairToss

The **GroomHairToss** brush is used to move the hair strands in different directions to create the hairstyles as required, refer to Figure 4-49.

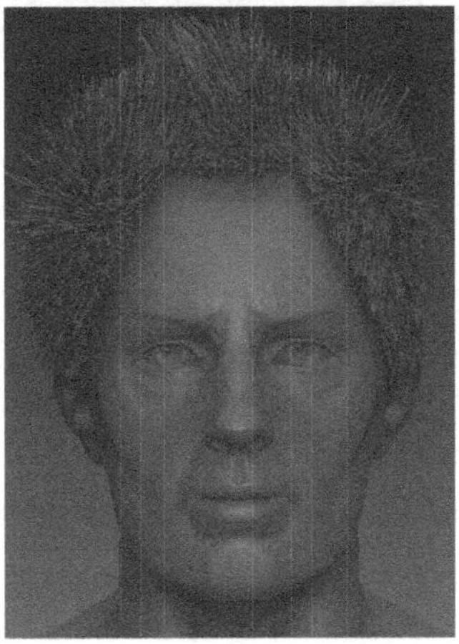

Figure 4-45 Effect produced by the ***GroomBlower*** *brush*

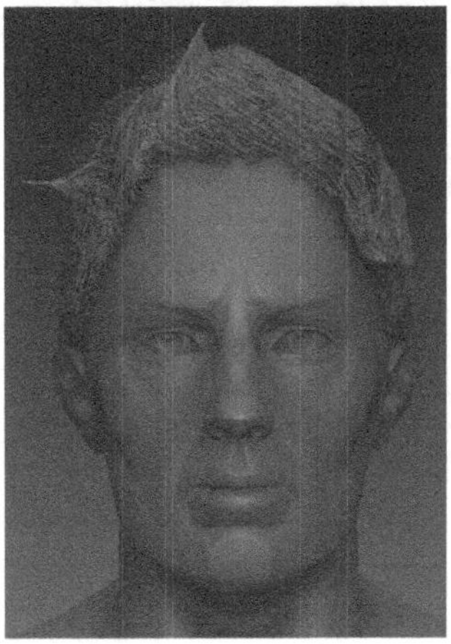

Figure 4-46 Effect produced by the ***GroomClumps*** *brush*

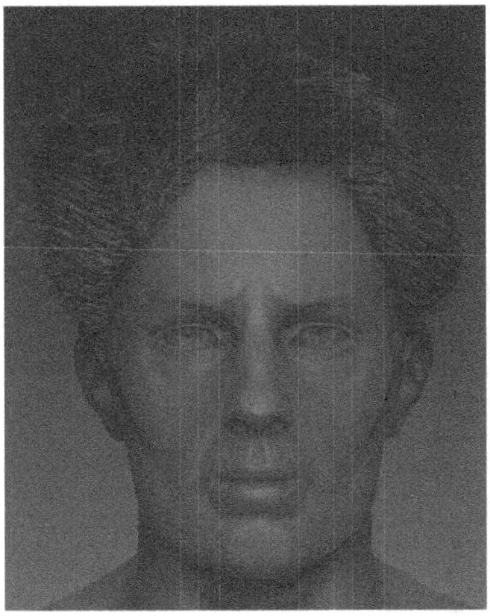

Figure 4-47 Effect produced by the ***GroomColorMild*** *brush*

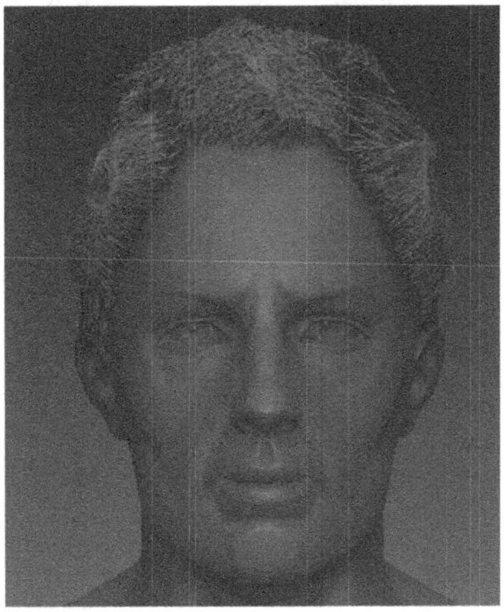

Figure 4-48 Effect produced by the ***GroomHairBall*** *brush*

GroomSpike

The **GroomSpike** brush is used to create spikes in the hair, refer to Figure 4-50.

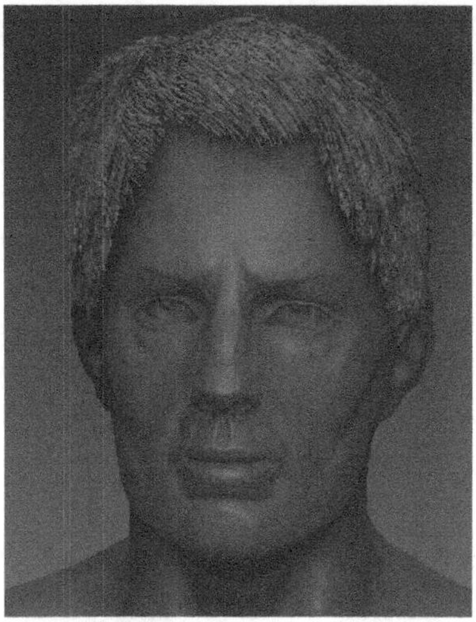

Figure 4-49 *Effect produced by the* ***GroomHairToss*** *brush*

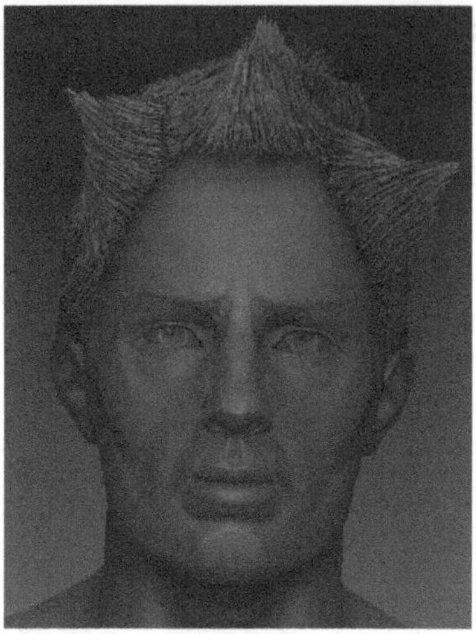

Figure 4-50 *Effect produced by the* ***GroomSpike*** *brush*

TUTORIALS

Before you start the tutorials of this chapter, navigate to *\Documents\ZBrushprojects* and then create a new folder with the name *c04*.

Tutorial 1

In this tutorial, you will create an ice cream cone and sculpt it using different brushes. The final output of the ice cream model is shown in Figure 4-51. **(Expected time: 20 min)**

Figure 4-51 *The ice cream cone*

The following steps are required to complete this tutorial:

a. Create the cone.
b. Create the ice cream scoop.
c. Save the model.

Creating the Cone

In this section, you will create an ice cream cone using the **Cone 3D** primitive and sculpt it using different brushes.

1. Choose the **Init ZBrush** button from the **Preferences** palette; the message box is displayed . Choose the **Yes** button from the message box; ZBrush is initialized to its default state. To close the **LightBox** browser, choose the **LightBox** button.

2. Choose the Current Tool button from the **Tool** palette; a flyout is displayed. Choose the **Cone3D** primitive from this flyout.

3. Press and hold the left mouse button, and then drag the cursor in the canvas; a cone is created in the canvas, as shown in Figure 4-52.

4. Choose the **Edit** button from the top shelf.

5. Press and hold the left mouse button and drag the cursor downward in such a way that the cone rotates and stands vertically. While dragging the cursor, press the SHIFT key; the cone is snapped at right angle to the canvas, refer to Figure 4-53.

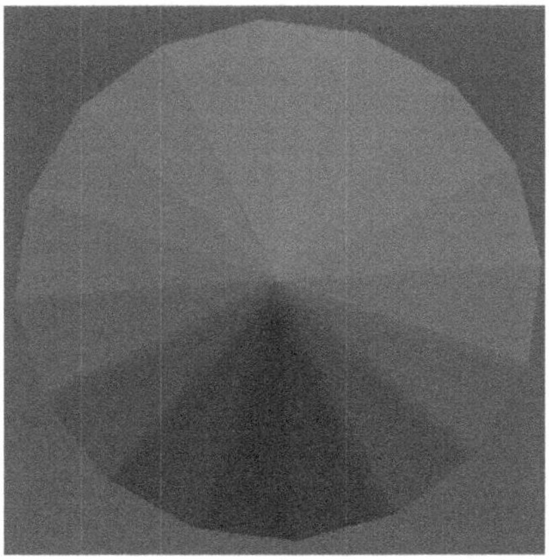

Figure 4-52 *The cone created in the canvas*

Figure 4-53 *The cone snapped to the canvas*

6. Expand the **Initialize** subpalette in the **Tool** palette. In this subpalette, set the values of both the **X Size** and **Y Size** sliders to **50**, refer to Figure 4-54; the radius of the cone decreases.

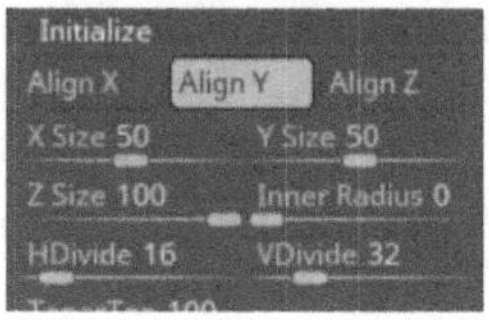

***Figure 4-54** The values set in the **X Size** and **Y Size** sliders*

7. Choose the **Make PolyMesh3D** button from the **Tool** palette; the cone is converted into a polymesh.

   After converting the cone into a polymesh, you need to subdivide the geometry so that the number of polygons in the cone increase to make it smoother.

8. Set the value of the **SDiv** slider in the **Geometry** subpalette to **5** by clicking on the **Divide** button four times; the cone becomes smoother, refer to Figure 4-55.

9. In the **SubTool** subpalette, choose the **Rename** button; the **Please enter subtool title** window consisting of a text box is displayed. Enter **ice cream cone** in this text box and press ENTER; the **Cone3D** primitive is renamed as *ice cream cone*.

10. In the **Transform** palette, choose the **Activate Symmetry** button. Next, choose the **(R)** button; the **RadialCount** slider is activated. By default, the **>X<** button is chosen. To deactivate this button, choose it again. Next, choose the **>Z<** button; the radial symmetry in the Z-axis is activated. Click on the **RadialCount** slider to display the **RadialCount** edit box. Next, enter the value **60** in the **RadialCount** edit box, refer to Figure 4-56.

11. Choose the Current Brush button from the left shelf; a flyout containing different sculpting brushes is displayed. Choose the **Standard** brush from this flyout.

12. Set the value of the **Draw Size** slider to **30**. Next, press and hold the left mouse button, and create the patterns at the top of the *ice cream cone*, as shown in Figure 4-57.

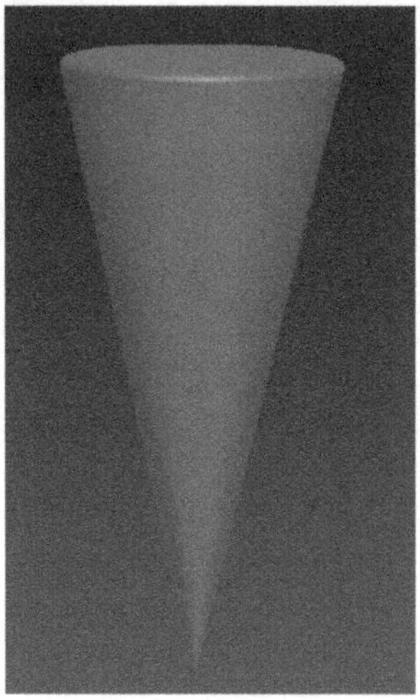

***Figure 4-55** The ice cream cone smoothened*

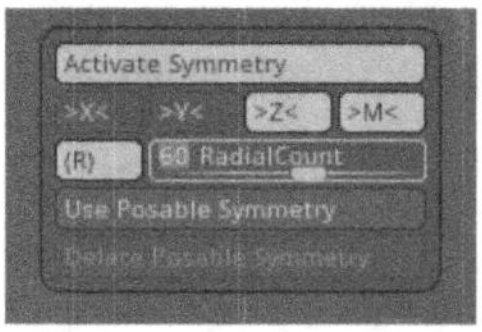

Figure 4-56** The value of the **RadialCount** slider set to **60

13. Choose the Current Brush button from the left shelf; a flyout containing different sculpting brushes is displayed. Choose the **Layer** brush from this flyout. In the **Transform** palette, choose the **(R)** and **>Z<** buttons; the radial symmetry in the Z-axis is deactivated.

14. Expand the Stroke palette. In this palette, expand the **Lazy Mouse** area. Next, choose the **LazyMouse** button in this area, if not already chosen, as shown in Figure 4-58.

Figure 4-57 *Patterns created at the top of the ice cream cone*

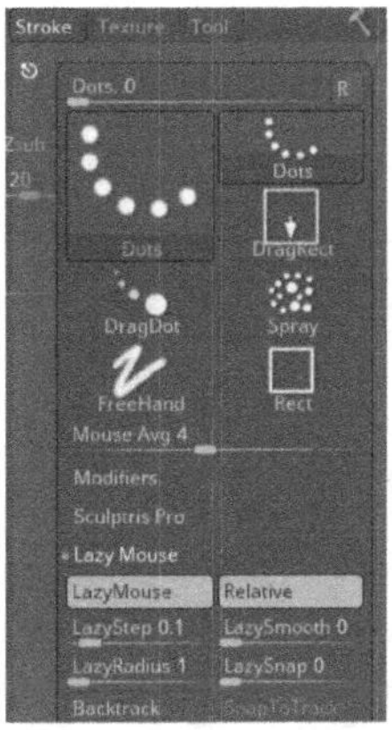

Figure 4-58 *The **LazyMouse** button chosen from the **Stroke** palette*

The **LazyMouse** button will enable you to draw the patterns very conveniently by dragging the red colored line that appears on choosing the **LazyMouse** button.

15. Set the value of the **Z Intensity** and **Draw Size** sliders to **40** and **12**, respectively. Next, press and hold the left mouse button and drag the cursor to create a criss-cross pattern on the entire surface of *ice cream cone*, refer to Figure 4-59.

Tip

*In order to get straight strokes using the **LazyMouse** button, you need to press the SHIFT key while dragging the red colored line on the surface of an object.*

Creating the Ice Cream Scoop

In this section, you will create the ice cream scoop using sphere and different sculpting brushes.

1. Expand the **SubTool** subpalette in the **Tool** palette. In this subpalette, choose the **Append** button, as shown in Figure 4-60; a flyout is displayed. Choose the **Sphere3D** primitive from this flyout; a sphere is created in the canvas and it overlaps *ice cream cone*, as shown in Figure 4-61. The thumbnail for the sphere is displayed in the subtool list. Select the thumbnail of the sphere in the list and then rename it to **scoop** using the **Rename** button.

2. Choose the **Gizmo 3D Y** button from the top shelf to deactivate it. Next, choose the **Move** button from the top shelf; an action line is displayed. Next, press and hold the left mouse button and drag the cursor on the surface of the sphere; the size of the action line increases.

Figure 4-59 *The crisscross pattern created on ice cream cone*

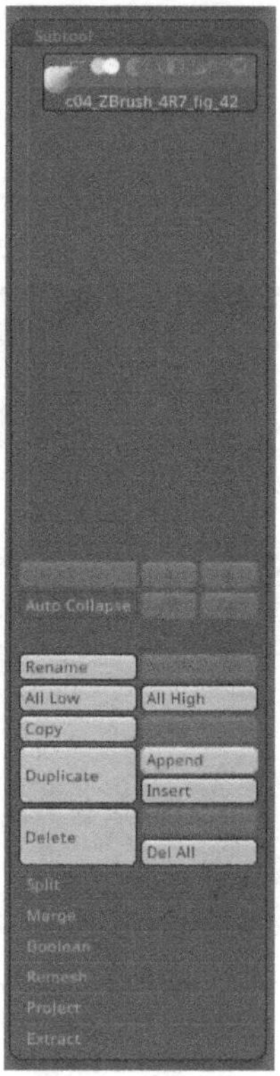

Figure 4-60 *The **Append** button chosen in the **SubTool** subpalette*

3. Hover the cursor at the centre of the middle circle of the action line, refer to Figure 4-62. Next, press and hold the left mouse button and drag the cursor upward to move the sphere at the top of *ice cream cone*.

Figure 4-61 *The sphere overlapping the ice cream cone*

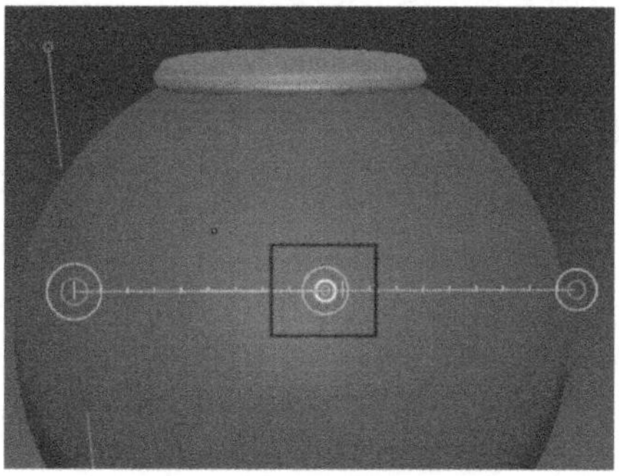

Figure 4-62 *The action line*

4. In the **Geometry** subpalette of the **Tool** palette, set the value of the **SDiv** slider to **5** by clicking on the **Divide** button four times; the sphere becomes smoother.

5. Expand the **Deformation** subpalette in the **Tool** palette. In this subpalette, move the **Size** slider toward left so that the size of *scoop* decreases and fits into the radius of the cone, as shown in Figure 4-63.

6. Choose the **Draw** button from the top shelf and then choose the Current Brush button from the left shelf; a flyout containing different sculpting brushes is displayed. Choose the **Move** brush from this flyout.

7. Set the value of the **Draw Size** slider in the top shelf to **250**. Next, press and hold the left mouse button and move the top portion of *scoop* upward, as shown in Figure 4-64.

8. Choose the Current Brush button from the left shelf; a flyout containing different sculpting brushes is displayed. Choose the **Standard** brush from this flyout.

9. Set the value of the **Draw Size** and the **Z Intensity** sliders to **80** and **25**, respectively. Next, press and hold the left mouse button and drag the cursor on the surface of *scoop* to create bumps in the *scoop*, as shown in Figure 4-65.

10. Again, choose the Current Brush button from the left shelf; a flyout containing different sculpting brushes is displayed. Choose the **Spiral** brush from this flyout.

11. Set the value of the **Draw Size** and the **Z Intensity** sliders to **200** and **100**, respectively. Next, press and hold the left mouse button and drag the cursor on the top of *scoop* to create its tip, refer to Figure 4-66.

Figure 4-63 *The scoop fitting inside the cone*

Figure 4-64 *The top portion of the scoop moved up using the **Move** brush*

Figure 4-65 *Bumps created in the scoop using the **Standard** brush*

Figure 4-66 *Shape of the scoop modified using the **Spiral** brush*

Saving the Model

In this section, you will save the file by following the steps given next.

1. Choose the **Save As** button from the **Tool** palette; the **Save ZTool** dialog box is displayed. In this dialog box, browse to the location *\Documents\ZBrushprojects\c04*.

2. Enter **c04tut1** in the **File name** edit box and then choose the **Save** button.

Tutorial 2

In this tutorial, you will create a monument using different subtools. The final output of the model is shown in Figure 4-67. **(Expected time: 45 min)**

The following steps are required to complete this tutorial:

a. Create the dome of the monument.
b. Create walls and roof of the monument.
c. Create the door of the monument.
d. Create different patterns on the walls of the monument.
e. Save the model.

Figure 4-67 The final model of the monument

Creating the Dome of the Monument

In this section, you will create the dome of the monument using a sphere and different sculpting brushes.

1. Choose the **Init ZBrush** button from the **Preferences** palette; the message box is displayed . Choose the **Yes** button from the message box; ZBrush is initialized to its default state.

2. Choose the Current Tool button from the **Tool** palette; a flyout is displayed. Choose the **Sphere3D** primitive from this flyout.

3. Press and hold the left mouse button, and drag the cursor on the canvas; a sphere is created in the canvas.

4. Choose the **Edit** button from the top shelf.

5. Choose the **PolyF** button from the right shelf; the polygon edges of the sphere are displayed.

6. Press and hold the left mouse button, and drag the cursor upward in such a way that the sphere is rotated. While dragging the cursor, keep the SHIFT key pressed; the sphere is snapped at right angle to the canvas, as shown in Figure 4-68. Choose the **PolyF** button again; the polygon edges on the sphere disappear.

7. Choose the **Make PolyMesh3D** button from the **Tool** palette to convert the primitive sphere into a polymesh.

8. In the **Geometry** subpalette of the **Tool** palette, set the value of the **SDiv** slider to **5** by clicking on the **Divide** button four times.

9. Rename the sphere to **dome** using the **Rename** button in the **SubTool** subpalette.

10. Choose the Current Brush button from the left shelf; a flyout containing different sculpting brushes is displayed. Choose the **ClipRect** brush from this flyout; a message box is displayed,

asking you to press CTRL+SHIFT keys to activate this brush. Choose the **OK** button to close this message box.

11. Press CTRL+SHIFT keys to activate the **ClipRect** brush and then press and hold the left mouse button. Next, drag the cursor over *dome*; a rectangular marquee selection appears. Select the upper half of *dome*. Now, release the left mouse button; the lower half of *dome* is deleted, refer to Figure 4-69.

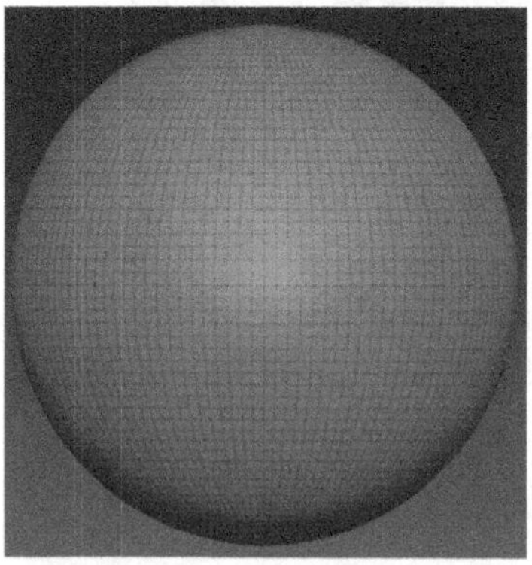

Figure 4-68 *The sphere snapped to the canvas*

Figure 4-69 *The lower half of the dome deleted*

12. Expand the **Transform** palette and then choose the **Activate Symmetry** button. Next, choose the **(R)** button; the **RadialCount** slider is activated. By default, the **>X<** button is chosen. To deactivate this button, choose it again. Next, choose the **>Y<** button; the radial symmetry in the Y-axis is activated. Set the value of the **RadialCount** slider to **60**, refer to Figure 4-70.

13. Choose the Current Brush button from the left shelf; a flyout containing different sculpting brushes is displayed. Choose the **ClayBuildup** brush from this flyout.

14. Choose the Current Stroke button from the left shelf; a flyout containing different types of strokes is displayed. Choose the **DragRect** stroke from this flyout.

15. Choose the Current Alpha button from the left shelf; a flyout containing different alpha images is displayed. Choose the **Alpha 28** alpha image from this flyout.

16. In the top shelf, set the parameters, as shown in Figure 4-71.

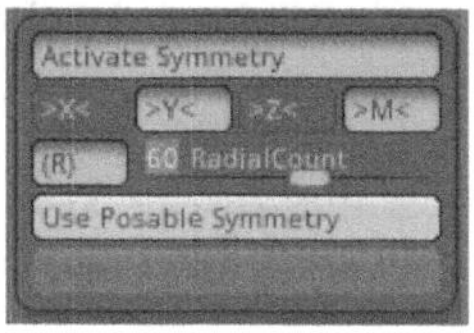

Figure 4-70 *Radial symmetry activated in Z-axis*

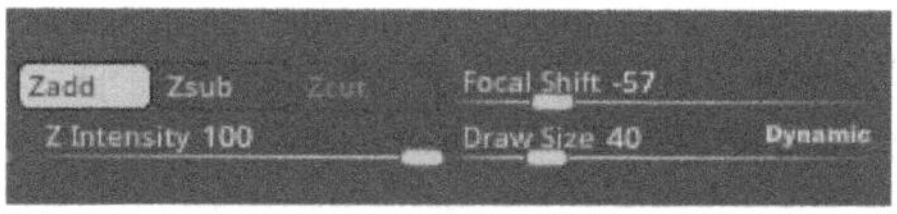

Figure 4-71 *Settings in the top shelf*

17. Press and hold the left mouse button and drag the cursor on the lower part of *dome* to create a pattern, as shown in Figure 4-72.

18. Choose the Current Brush button from the left shelf; a flyout containing different sculpting brushes is displayed. Choose the **Standard** brush from this flyout.

19. In the **Transform** palette, set the value of the **RadialCount** slider to **30**, as shown in Figure 4-73. Next, set the parameters in the top shelf, as shown in Figure 4-74.

Figure 4-72 *Pattern created on the lower part of the dome*

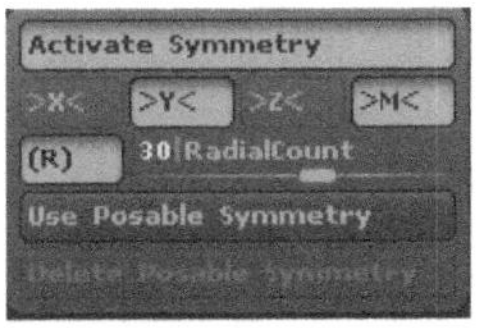

Figure 4-73 *The value of the* ***RadialCount*** *slider set to* ***30***

20. Choose the Current Stroke button from the left shelf; a flyout containing different types of strokes is displayed. Choose the **FreeHand** stroke from this flyout.

21. Press and hold the left mouse button and hover the cursor at the top of *dome*. Next, drag the cursor downward to create vertical lines on *dome*, as shown in Figure 4-75. While dragging the cursor, press and hold the SHIFT key to get straight strokes.

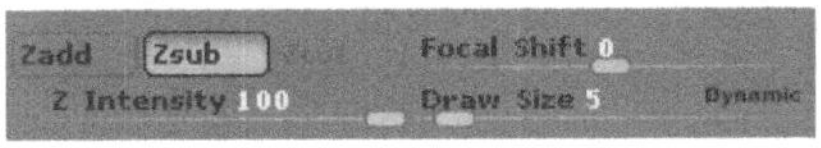

Figure 4-74 *Settings in the top shelf*

Figure 4-75 *Vertical lines created on the dome*

22. Similarly, create horizontal lines on *dome* by dragging the cursor from left to right; the tiles will be created, as shown in Figure 4-76.

23. Choose the Current Stroke button from the left shelf; a flyout containing different types of strokes is displayed. Choose the **DragRect** stroke from this flyout.

24. Choose the Current Alpha button from the left shelf; a flyout containing different alpha images is displayed. Choose the **Alpha 17** alpha image from this flyout.

25. Choose the **Zadd** button from the top shelf. Next, set the value of the **Z Intensity** slider to **30** and the **Draw Size** slider to **38**. Press and hold the left mouse button and drag the cursor at the bottom tiles of the dome to create the pattern on *dome*, refer to Figure 4-77. Next, deactivate the symmetry.

26. In the **SubTool** subpalette, choose the **Append** button; a flyout is displayed. Choose **Sphere3D_1** from this flyout; a new sphere is created in the canvas and it overlaps the existing sphere. Make sure that you select the thumbnail for the newly created sphere from the subtool list and rename it as **dome top**.

27. Make sure the **Gizmo 3D Y** button is deactivated. Choose the **Move** button from the top shelf and move **dome top** upward in such a way that it touches the top of **dome**. Next, in the **Geometry** subpalette of the **Tool** palette, set the value of the **SDiv** slider to **5** by clicking on the **Divide** button four times.

28. Expand the **Deformation** subpalette in the **Tool** palette. In this subpalette, move the **Size** slider toward the left so that the size of *dome top* decreases and it fits into the top of *dome*. Next, move *dome top* in such a way that its lower half portion is inserted into *dome*, refer to Figure 4-77.

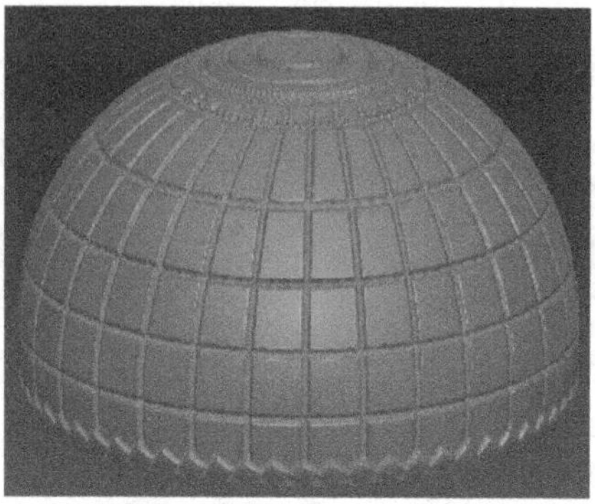

Figure 4-76 *Tiles created on the dome*

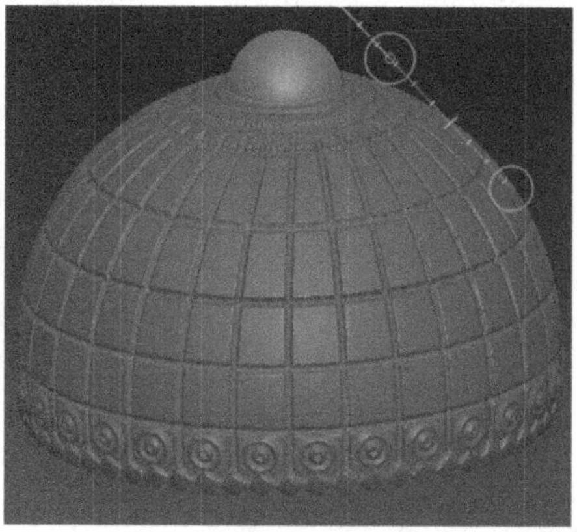

Figure 4-77 *The dome top scaled and moved to the top*

29. Make sure the **Draw** button is chosen. Choose the Current Stroke button from the left shelf; a flyout containing different types of strokes is displayed. Choose the **Dot** stroke from this flyout.

30. Choose the Current Alpha button from the left shelf; a flyout containing different alpha images is displayed. Choose **Alpha off** from this flyout.

31. Choose the **Draw** button from the top shelf. Next, choose the **Activate Symmetry** button from the **Transform** palette. Next, choose the **(R)** button; the **RadialCount** slider is activated. By default, the **>X<** button is chosen. To deactivate this button, choose it again. Next,

choose the **>Y<** button; the radial symmetry in the Y-axis is activated. Set the value **40** in the **RadialCount** slider .

32. Set the value of the **Z Intensity** slider to **40** and the **Draw Size** slider to **32**. Next, press and hold the left mouse button and drag the cursor on the surface of *dome top* to create a radial pattern, as shown in Figure 4--78.

    Next, you will create the finial for the monument using the **CurveLathe** brush.

33. Before using the **CurveLathe** brush on *dome top*, you have to make sure all lower division levels are deleted. To do so, choose the **Del Lower** button from the **Geometry** subpalette of the **Tool** palette, as shown in Figure 4-79.

Figure 4-78 *Pattern created on the dome top using radial symmetry*

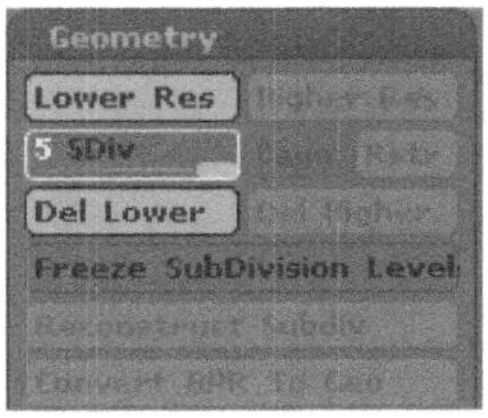

Figure 4-79 *The **Del Lower** button chosen in the **Geometry** subpalette*

34. Choose the **(R)** and **>Y<** buttons in the **Transform** palette; the radial symmetry in the Y-axis is deactivated.

35. Choose the Current Brush button from the left shelf; a flyout containing different sculpting brushes is displayed. Choose the **CurveLathe** brush from this flyout. Next, press and hold the left mouse button and draw a profile curve at the top of *dome top*, refer to Figure 4-80. Release the left mouse button; a finial is created on the surface of *dome top*, as shown in Figure 4-80.

Creating Walls and the Roof of the Monument

In this section, you will create the walls, roof, and pillars of the monument using the cylinder primitive and different sculpting brushes.

1. Choose the **Append** button in the **SubTool** subpalette; a flyout is displayed. Choose the **Cylinder3D** primitive from this flyout; a cylinder is created in the canvas and it overlaps the *dome*, as shown in Figure 4-81. The thumbnail for the cylinder is displayed in the subtool list. Make sure that you select the thumbnail for the cylinder in the list. Next, rename it to **walls**.

Figure 4-80 *Finial created on the dome top using the **CurveLathe** brush*

Figure 4-81 *Cylinder overlapping the dome*

2. Expand the **Geometry** subpalette. In this subpalette, click on the **Reconstruct Subdiv** button twice, as shown in Figure 4-82; a low resolution model of *walls* having less number of segments is displayed.

3. Make sure the **Gizmo 3D Y** button is deactivated. Choose the **Move** button from the top shelf; an action line is displayed. Move *walls* using the action line in such a way that *walls* lie below *dome*, as shown in Figure 4-83.

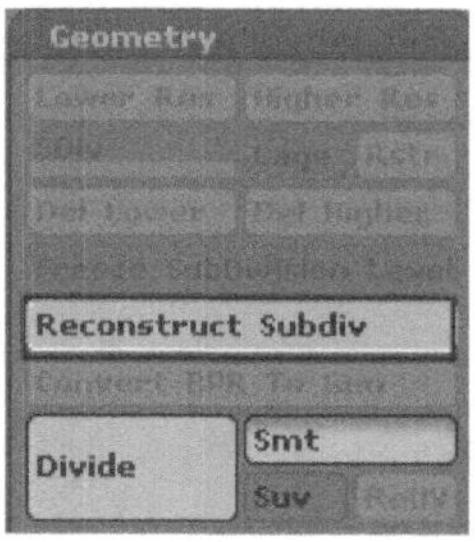

Figure 4-82 *The **Reconstruct Subdiv** button chosen from the **Geometry** subpalette*

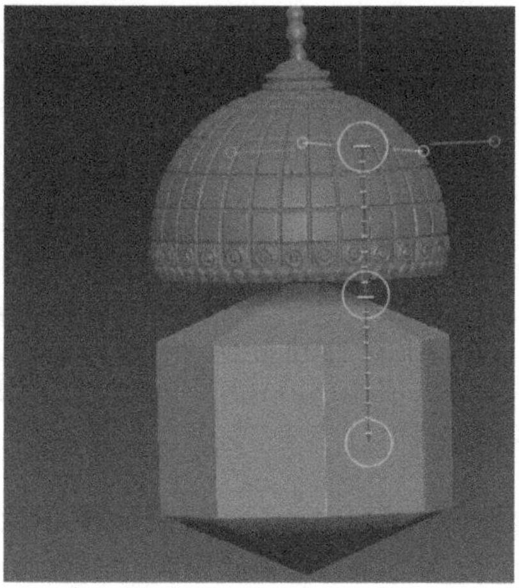

Figure 4-83 *The walls moved below the dome*

4. Expand the **Deformation** subpalette in the **Tool** palette.

You need to increase the height of *walls* along the Z-axis using the **Size** slider.

5. Deactivate the x and y options corresponding to the **Size** slider by choosing the **x** and **y** buttons located on the right side of the slider.

6. Set the value of the **Size** slider to **55** by dragging the slider toward right; the height of the cylinder increases along the Z-axis. Alternatively, you can enter the value **55** in the edit box displayed on clicking on the slider.

7. Choose the **Draw** button from the top shelf. Choose the Current Brush button from the left shelf; a flyout containing different sculpting brushes is displayed. Choose the **ClipRect** brush from this flyout; a dialog box is displayed, asking you to press CTRL+SHIFT keys to activate this brush. Choose the **OK** button to close this dialog box.

8. Press CTRL+SHIFT keys to activate the **ClipRect** brush and then press and hold the left mouse button. Next, drag the cursor over the cylinder; a rectangular marquee selection appears. Make a marquee selection on *walls*, as shown in Figure 4-84. Now, release the left mouse button; the lower and upper parts are deleted.

9. Make sure the **Gizmo 3D Y** button is deactivated. Choose the **Move** button from the top shelf and move *walls* using the action line, as shown in Figure 4-85.

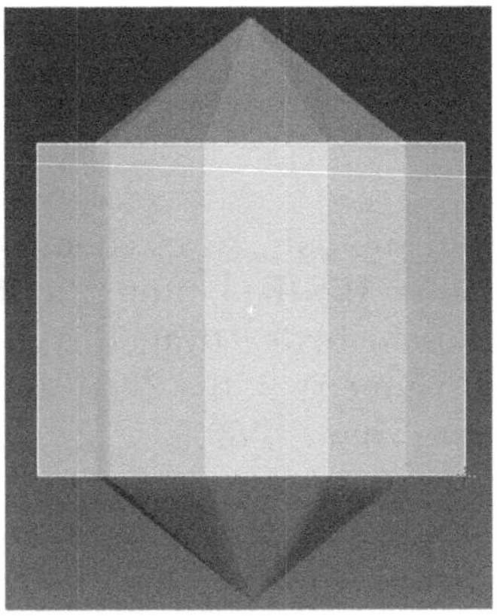

Figure 4-84 *Marquee selection on the walls*

Figure 4-85 *The walls moved under the dome*

10. Choose the **Append** button in the **SubTool** subpalette; a flyout is displayed. Choose **Cylinder3D** from this flyout; a cylinder is created in the canvas. Select the thumbnail for the newly created cylinder from the subtool list. Rename it to **roof**.

11. Expand the **Deformations** subpalette in the **Tool** palette. Decrease the size of *roof* along the Z-axis by choosing the **z** button and moving the **Size** slider toward left. Similarly, increase the size of *roof* along the X and Y axes. Make sure the **Move** button is chosen from the top shelf. Now, using the action line, move *roof* below *dome,* refer to Figure 4-86.

12. Choose *walls* from the subtool list. Expand the **Deformation** subpalette, and increase the size of *walls* along the X and Y axes, as shown in Figure 4-87. Make sure the **Move** button is chosen and the **Gizmo 3D Y** button is deactivated from the top shelf. Now, using the action line, move *walls* below *roof*.

Figure 4-86 *The roof scaled and moved below the dome*

Figure 4-87 *The size of the walls increased along X and Y axes*

13. In the **SubTool** subpalette, select *roof* from the list of subtools. In this subpalette, choose the **Duplicate** button; a copy of *roof* is created and displayed in the subtool list. Select the duplicate *roof* from the list. Make sure the **Move** button is chosen and the **Gizmo 3D Y** button is deactivated from the top shelf. Now, using the action line, move the duplicate *roof* below *walls*.

14. Expand the **Deformation** subpalette and increase the size of the duplicate *roof* along the X and Y axes, refer to Figure 4-88.

15. In the **SubTool** subpalette, select *roof* from the list of subtools. Next, choose the **Activate Symmetry** button from the **Transform** palette. Choose the **(R)** button; the **RadialCount** slider is activated. By default, the **>X<** button is chosen. To deactivate this button, choose it again. Next, choose the **>Z<** button; the radial symmetry in the Z-axis is activated. In the **RadialCount** edit box, enter the value **46**, refer to Figure 4-89.

16. Choose the **Draw** button from the top shelf, if not already chosen and then choose the **InsertHRing brush** from the **Brush** tab of the **LightBox** browser.

17. Choose the Current Stroke button from the left shelf; a flyout containing different types of strokes is displayed. Choose the **Dots** stroke from this flyout, if not already chosen.

18. In the top view, press and hold the left mouse button and drag the cursor at the corners of the *roof* to create the railings, refer to Figure 4-90.

    Next, you will create pillars for the monument using the **CurveLathe** brush.

19. Choose the **(R)** and **>Z<** buttons in the **Transform** palette; the radial symmetry in the Z-axis is deactivated.

Figure 4-88 Duplicate roof scaled along the X and Y axes

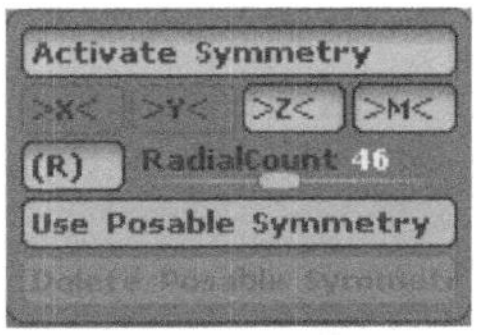

*Figure 4-89 The value of **RadialCount** slider set to **46***

20. Choose the Current Brush button from the left shelf; a flyout containing different sculpting brushes is displayed. Choose the **CurveLathe** brush from this flyout. Next, press and hold the left mouse button and draw a profile curve below *roof*. Release the left mouse button; a pillar is created, refer to Figure 4-91.

*Figure 4-90 Railing created using the **InsertHRing** brush*

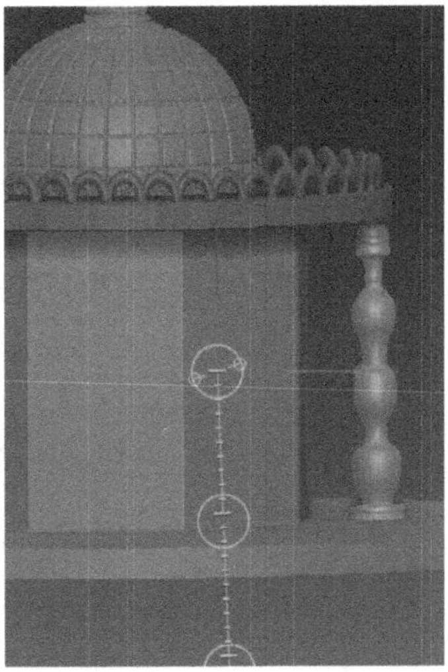

*Figure 4-91 Pillar created using the **CurveLathe** brush*

21. Make sure the **Gizmo 3D Y** button is deactivated. Choose the **Move** button from the top shelf; an action line is displayed. Press and hold the left mouse button and drag the cursor vertically to increase the size of the action line. Next, press the CTRL key and move the pillar on the left side using the action line; a duplicate copy of the pillar is displayed. Next, move the duplicate pillar to the other side of *walls* using the action line, refer to Figure 4-92.

Creating the Door of the Monument

In this section, you will create the door of the monument using a plane and the **Projection Master** dialog box.

1. Choose the **Append** button in the **SubTool** subpalette; a flyout is displayed. Choose **Plane3D** from this flyout; a plane is created in the canvas. The thumbnail for the plane is displayed in the subtool list. Make sure that you select the thumbnail for the plane in the list. Next, rename it to **door**.

2. Expand the **Deformations** subpalette in the **Tool** palette. You need to rotate *door* along the Y-axis using the **Rotate** slider.

3. Deactivate the x and z options corresponding to the **Rotate** slider by choosing the **x** and **z** buttons located on the right side of the slider. Next, activate the y option by choosing the **y** button.

4. Set the value of the **Rotate** slider by entering the value **-90** in the edit box displayed on clicking on the slider; *door* is rotated along the Y-axis.

5. Press and hold the left mouse button and drag the cursor in the canvas toward the left; the side view is displayed. Make sure the **Gizmo 3D Y** button is deactivated. Choose the **Move** button from the top shelf. Next, move the *door* to the front of *walls* using the action line. Next, switch back to the front view by dragging the cursor toward right.

6. In the **Deformation** subpalette of the **Tool** palette, deactivate the x option corresponding to the **Size** slider by choosing the **x** button located on the right side of the slider. Make sure the **y** and **z** buttons are chosen. Decrease the height and width of *door* by dragging the **Size** slider toward left. Next, choose the **Move** button from the top shelf and move *door*, as shown in Figure 4-93.

Figure 4-92 *Copy of the pillar created and moved toward left*

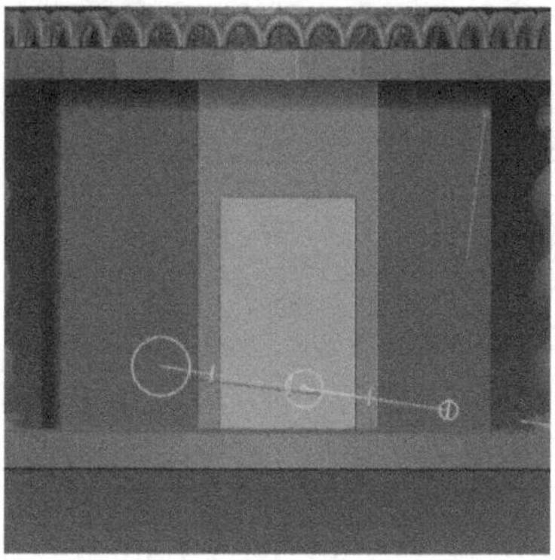

Figure 4-93 *The door moved using the action line*

7. Expand the **Geometry** subpalette in the **Tool** palette. In this subpalette, click on the **Divide** button four times; the value of the **SDiv** slider becomes **5**.

8. Choose the **ZPlugin** palette; a flyout is displayed. Expand **Projection Master** from the flyout and then choose the **Projection Master** button from the top shelf; the **Projection Master** dialog box is displayed.

9. Select the **Deformation** check box from the **Projection Master** dialog box and make sure that the other check boxes are not selected, refer to Figure 4-94. Next, choose the **DROP NOW** button from this dialog box; the 3D plane is converted into its 2.5D illustration.

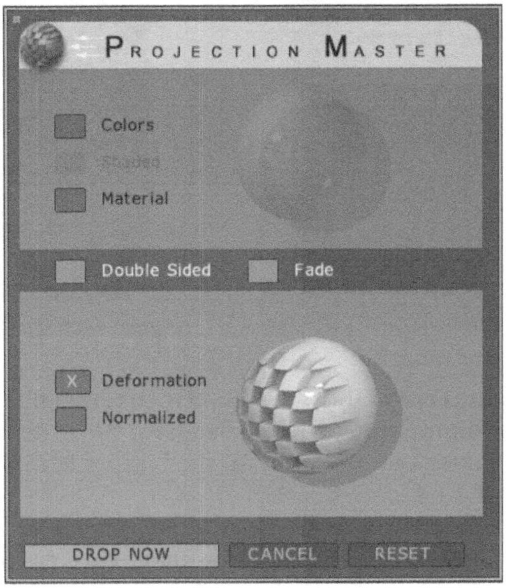

Figure 4-94 *The* ***Deformation*** *check box selected*

10. Choose the Current Stroke button from the left shelf; a flyout containing different types of strokes is displayed. Choose the **LineII** stroke from this flyout.

11. Choose the Current Alpha button from the left shelf; a flyout containing different alpha images is displayed. Choose the **Alpha 28** alpha image from this flyout.

12. Choose the **Zsub** button from the top shelf and set the value of the **Draw Size** slider to **2**. Next, press and hold the left mouse button and drag it to create the horizontal and vertical partitions of the *door*, as shown in Figure 4-95.

13. Choose the Current Stroke button from the left shelf; a flyout containing different types of strokes is displayed. Choose the **DragRect** stroke from this flyout. Next, press and hold the left mouse button and drag the cursor to create a pattern on top left panel of the door.

14. Choose the **Scale** button from the top shelf; a gyro is displayed. Hover the cursor on the pink ring of the gyro. Next, drag the cursor upward and release the left mouse button; the pattern is scaled up, refer to Figure 4-96.

15. Make sure the **Gizmo 3D Y** button is deactivated. Choose the **Move** button from the top shelf; a gyro is displayed. Press and hold the left mouse button, and then hover the cursor on the pink ring of the gyro. If required, drag the cursor upward to move the pattern to the centre of the panel.

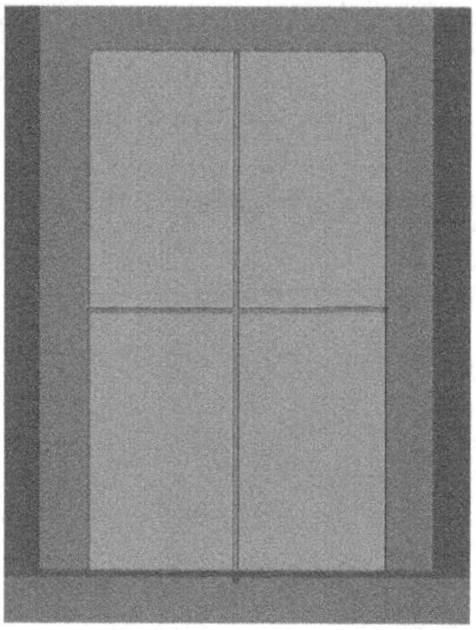

Figure 4-95 Horizontal and vertical partitions created on the door

Figure 4-96 The pattern scaled up

16. Press SHIFT+S to create a copy of the pattern and then press and hold the left mouse button. Now, hover the cursor on the pink ring of the gyro. Next, drag the cursor downward to move the copy of the pattern to the centre of the bottom left panel. Next, release the left mouse button and SHIFT+S.

17. Make sure the **Move** button is chosen in the top shelf. Press SHIFT+S and then press and hold the left mouse button. Now, hover the cursor on the blue ring of the gyro. Next, drag the cursor toward the right to move the copy of the pattern to the centre of the bottom right panel. Next, release the left mouse button.

18. Press SHIFT+S and then press and hold the left mouse button. Now, hover the cursor on the pink ring of the gyro. Next, drag the cursor upward to move the copy of the pattern to the centre of the top right panel. Next, release the left mouse button and SHIFT+S; the pattern is created on all the panels, refer to Figure 4-97.

19. Choose the **Draw** button and then choose the **Zadd** button from the top shelf. Next, press and hold the left mouse button and drag the cursor on any of the existing patterns; another pattern is created on the existing pattern. Scale and move the pattern such that it fits into the existing pattern. Copy the newly created pattern on all the panels, refer to Figure 4-98.

20. After copying the patterns, choose the **Draw** button from the top shelf. Next, choose the Current Alpha button from the left shelf; a flyout containing different alpha images is displayed. Choose the **Alpha 28** alpha image from this flyout.

21. Set the value of the **Draw Size** and the **Z Intensity** sliders to **25** and **40**, respectively. Next, press and hold the left mouse button and drag the cursor at the centre of any of the panels; a pattern is created. Copy the newly created pattern to all the panels, as shown in Figure 4-99.

22. Choose the Current Alpha button from the left shelf; a flyout containing different alpha images is displayed. Choose the **Alpha 54** alpha image from this flyout.

Figure 4-97 Pattern created on all the panels

Figure 4-98 Newly created pattern copied on all the panels

23. Set the value of the **Draw Size** and the **Z Intensity** sliders to **17** and **100**, respectively. Next, press and hold the left mouse button and drag the cursor at the centre of *door*; a knob is created, refer to Figure 4-100.

Figure 4-99 Pattern created on all the panels

Figure 4-100 Knob of the door created

24. Choose the **Projection Master** button from the top shelf; the **Projection Master** dialog box is displayed. Next, choose the **PICKUP NOW** button from this dialog box; the 2.5D illustration is converted back into a 3D model.

Creating Different Patterns on Walls of the Monument

In this section, you will create different patterns on the walls of the monument using the **Projection Master**.

1. Choose *walls* from the subtool list. Next, expand the **Geometry** subpalette. In this subpalette, choose the **Del Higher** button; all subdivision levels above the current **SDiv** value are deleted.

2. Choose the **Smt** button in the **Geometry** subpalette; it will be deactivated. If the **Smt** button is deactivated, the hard edges of the model will be visible even if you subdivide the geometry. Next, click on the **Divide** button seven times; the value of the **SDiv** slider is set to **8**.

3. Choose the **Projection Master** button from the top shelf; the **Projection Master** dialog box is displayed. Select the **Deformation** check box from this dialog box, and make sure that the other check boxes are cleared. Next, choose the **DROP NOW** button from this dialog box.

4. Choose the Current Stroke button from the left shelf; a flyout containing different types of strokes is displayed. Choose the **Grid** stroke from this flyout.

5. Choose the Current Alpha button from the left shelf; a flyout containing different alpha images is displayed. Choose the **Alpha 28** alpha image from this flyout.

6. Choose the **Zsub** button from the top shelf. Next, press and hold the left mouse button, and drag the cursor on the top of *door*; a grid pattern is created on *walls*, as shown in Figure 4-101.

7. Similarly, create different patterns on *walls* using different strokes and alpha images, refer to Figure 4-102.

Figure 4-101 *Grid pattern created on the walls*

Figure 4-102 *The final model of the monument*

8. Choose the **Projection Master** button from the top shelf again; the **Projection Master** dialog box is displayed. Next, choose the **PICKUP NOW** button from this dialog box; the 2.5D illustration is converted back into a 3D model, refer to Figure 4-102.

Saving the Model

In this section, you will save the file using the steps given next.

1. Choose the **Save As** button from the **Tool** palette; the **Save ZTool** dialog box is displayed. In this dialog box, browse to the location *\Documents\ZBrushprojects\c04*.

2. Enter **c04tut2** in the **File name** edit box and then choose the **Save** button.

Tutorial 3

In this tutorial, you will create a tennis ball using a sphere and the **FiberMesh**. The final output of the model is shown in Figure 4-103. **(Expected time: 20 min)**

Figure 4-103 *The final model of the tennis ball*

The following steps are required to complete this tutorial:

a. Create the basic model of a tennis ball.
b. Add FiberMesh to the ball.
c. Save the model.

Creating the Basic Model of the Tennis Ball

In this section, you will create the basic model of the ball using a sphere.

1. Choose the **Init ZBrush** button from the **Preferences** palette; the message box is displayed . Choose the **Yes** button from the message box; ZBrush is initialized to its default state.

2. Choose the **DynaWax128.ZPR** file from the **Project** tab of the **LightBox** browser, located at the top of the canvas by double-clicking on it, refer to Figure 4-104. The sphere is created on the canvas, as shown in Figure 4-105.

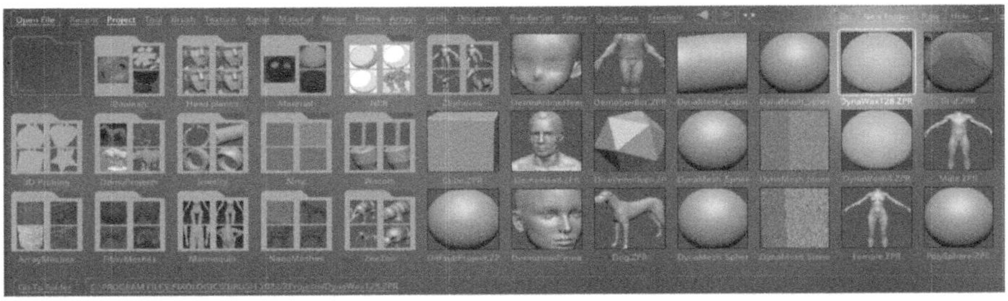

Figure 4-104 *The* ***DynaWax128.ZPR*** *file chosen from the* ***LightBox*** *browser*

3. Expand the **Geometry** subpalette. In this subpalette, click four times on the **Divide** button; the value of the **SDiv** slider becomes **5**, refer to Figure 4-106.

Figure 4-105 The ***DynaWax128.ZPR*** *created in the canvas*

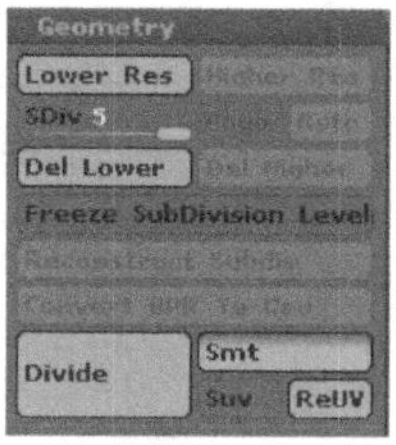

Figure 4-106 *Choosing the* ***Divide*** *button from the* ***Geometry*** *subpalette*

4. Expand the **SubTool** subpalette in the **Tool** palette. Next, in this subpalette, choose the **Rename** button; the **Please enter subtool title** window with a text box is displayed. Enter **tennis ball** in this text box; the sphere is renamed as *tennis ball*.

5. Choose the **Activate Symmetry** button from the **Transform** palette. By default, the **>X<** button is chosen. To deactivate this button, choose it again. Next, choose the **>Y<** button; the symmetry in the Y-axis is activated.

6. Choose the Current Brush button from the left shelf; a flyout containing different sculpting brushes is displayed. Choose the **MaskRect** brush from this flyout; a message box is displayed, asking you to press CTRL to activate this brush, as shown in Figure 4-107. Choose the **OK** button to close this message box.

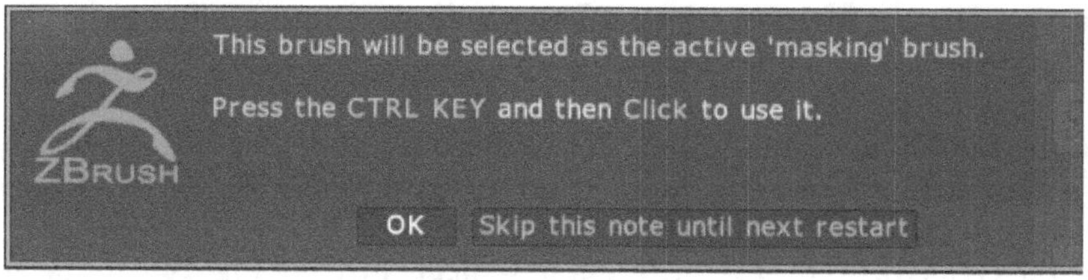

Figure 4-107 *Message box displayed on choosing the* ***MaskRect*** *brush*

7. Press CTRL and then press and hold the left mouse button. Next, drag the cursor over the sphere; a rectangular marquee selection appears. Select the upper part of the sphere, refer to Figure 4-108. Now, release the left mouse button. As the symmetry in the Y-axis is activated, a mask is created on the upper and lower parts of *tennis ball*, refer to Figure 4-109.

8. Press CTRL+I to invert the mask, refer to Figure 4-110.

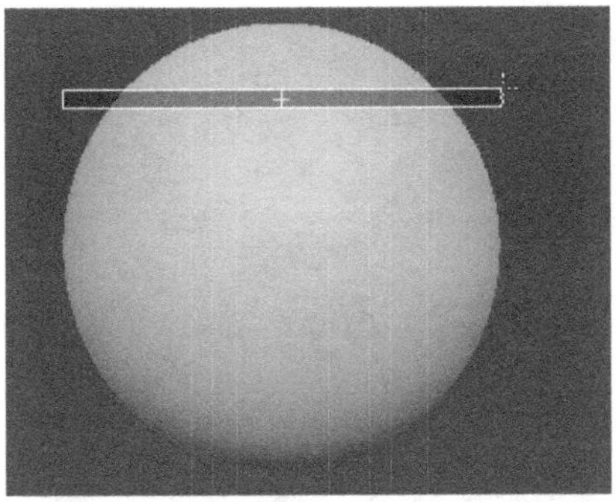

Figure 4-108 Upper part of the tennis ball selected

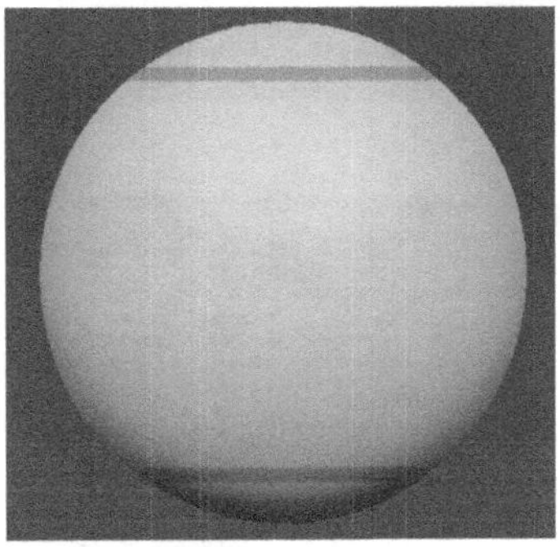

Figure 4-109 Mask created on lower and upper parts of the tennis ball

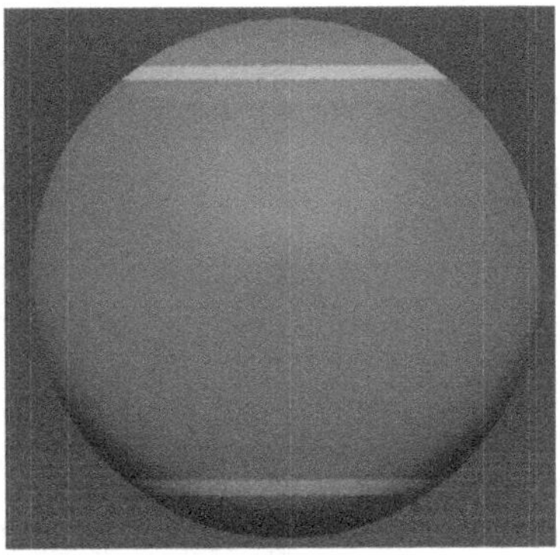

Figure 4-110 Mask on the tennis ball inverted

Adding FiberMesh to the Tennis Ball

In this section, you will add FiberMesh to *tennis ball.*

1. Expand the **FiberMesh** subpalette in the **Tool** palette. In this subpalette, choose the **Preview** button, refer to Figure 4-111. On choosing this button, a fibrous mesh is displayed on the *tennis ball,* refer to Figure 4-112.

2. Expand the **Modifiers** area in the **FiberMesh** subpalette. Click on the **MaxFibers** slider to display the **MaxFibers** edit box. Next, enter the value **200** in the **MaxFibers** edit box.

3. Enter the value **20** in the **Length** edit box, as shown in Figure 4-113; the length of the fibers decreases, refer to Figure 4-114.

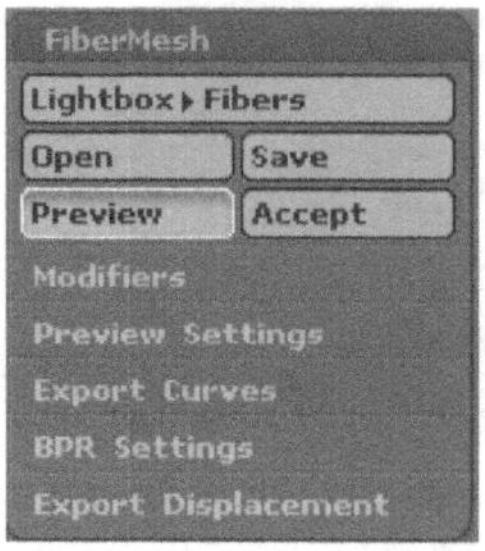

Figure 4-111 *Choosing the* ***Preview*** *button from the* ***FiberMesh*** *subpalette*

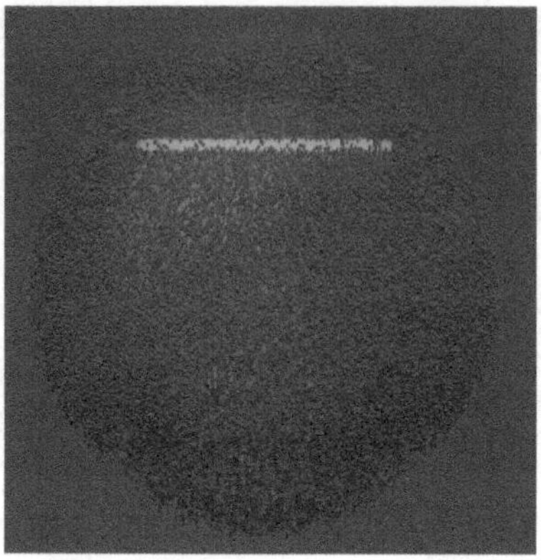

Figure 4-112 *Fibrous mesh displayed on the tennis ball*

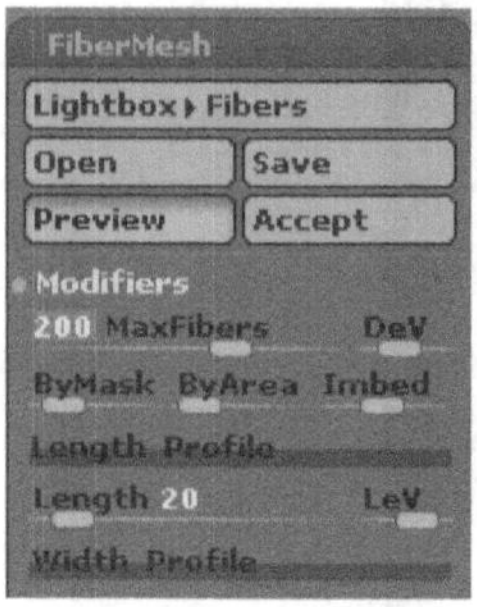

Figure 4-113 *The value in the* ***Length*** *edit box set to* ***20***

Figure 4-114 *Length of the fibers decreased*

4. Choose the **Base** swatch in the **Modifiers** area; a color picker window is displayed. Choose the light green color from this window, refer to Figure 4-115; the color of the roots of the fibers changes to light green.

5. Choose the **Tip** swatch in the **Modifiers** area; a color picker window is displayed. Again, choose the light green color from this window; the color of all the fibers changes to light green, refer to Figure 4-116.

6. Choose the **Accept** button from the **FiberMesh** subpalette; a message box prompting you to activate the fast preview rendering mode of the mesh will be displayed. In this message box, choose the **Yes** button; the rendered preview of the mesh will be displayed and the fiber mesh is displayed as a subtool in the **SubTool** subpalette.

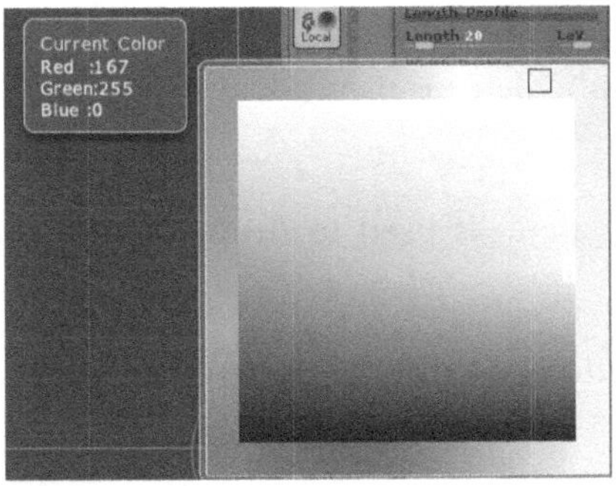

Figure 4-115 Color chosen from the color picker window

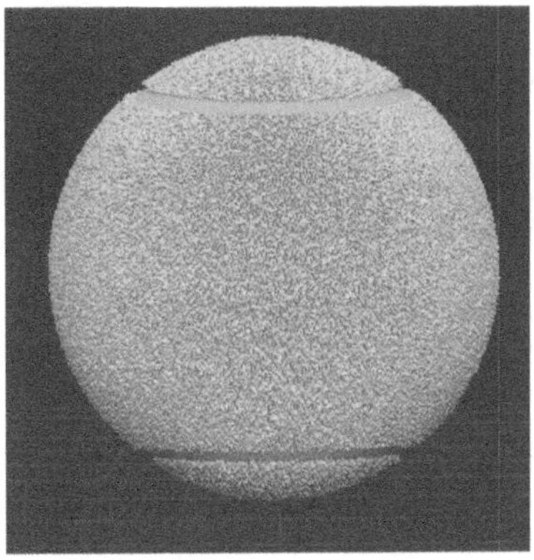

Figure 4-116 The color of the fibers changed to green

Saving the Model

In this section, you will save the file using the steps given next.

1. Choose the **Save As** button from the **Tool** palette; the **Save ZTool** dialog box is displayed. In this dialog box, browse to the location *\Documents\ZBrushprojects\c04*.

2. Enter **c04tut3** in the **File name** edit box and then choose the **Save** button.

Self-Evaluation Test

Answer the following questions and then compare them to those given at the end of this chapter:

1. Which of the following buttons is used to arrange the subtools in the list according to their polygon count?

   (a) **AutoReorder** (b) **All High**
   (c) **List All** (d) **Append**

2. Which of the following buttons converts the fiber mesh into a subtool?

   (a) **Preview** (b) **Extract**
   (c) **Append** (d) **Accept**

3. Which of the following brushes is used to roll the tips of hair into round clumps?

   (a) **GroomSpike** (b) **GroomHairToss**
   (c) **GroomHairBall** (d) **GroomClumps**

4. The __________ slider in the **FiberMesh** subpalette is used to change the width of the fibers.

5. The __________ button in the **SubTool** subpalette is used to display all the subtools in the canvas at their lowest subdivision levels.

6. The __________ slider in the **FiberMesh** subpalette is used to curl the fibers in the fiber mesh.

7. The **Length** slider in the **FiberMesh** subpalette is used to drop the ends of the fibers downward. (T/F)

8. The **Insert** button in the **SubTool** subpalette is used to insert another subtool below the currently selected subtool in the list. (T/F)

9. The **Delete Other** button in the **SubTool** subpalette is used to delete the currently selected subtool from the list. (T/F)

10. The **Open** button in the **FiberMesh** subpalette is used to view the fiber mesh on the surface of an object. (T/F)

Review Questions

Answer the following questions:

1. Which of the following sliders is used to adjust the orientation of roots of fibers?

   (a) **DeV** (b) **Imbed**
   (c) **MaxFibers** (d) **ByArea**

2. Which of the following sliders in the **FiberMesh** subpalette is used to adjust the influence of polygons on fibers?

   (a) **ByArea** (b) **Coverage**
   (c) **Slim** (d) **Imbed**

3. Which of the following sliders in the **FiberMesh** subpalette is used to decrease the depth of fibers in the fiber mesh?

   (a) **ScaleRoot** (b) **ScaleTip**
   (c) **Slim** (d) **Coverage**

4. The __________ button in the **SubTool** subpalette is used to select a subtool located above the currently selected subtool in the list.

5. The term **DeV** stands for __________ .

6. The __________ brush is used to create spikes in the fiber mesh.

7. The __________ button is used to change the name of a particular subtool.

8. The **DeV** slider in the **FiberMesh** subpalette is used to adjust the influence of the mask on the fibers created. (T/F)

9. In the **Preview** mode, you cannot change the length, color, and other attributes of the fiber mesh. (T/F)

EXERCISES

The output of the models used in the following exercises can be accessed by downloading the *c04_ZBrush_2022_exr.zip* file from *www.cadcim.com*. The path of the file is as follows: *Textbooks > Animation and Visual Effects > ZBrush > ZBrush 2022: A Comprehensive Guide*.

Exercise 1

Create the model of a house using different subtools, as shown in Figure 4-117.

(Expected time: 45 min)

Figure 4-117 *Model of a house*

Exercise 2

Create the scene using different subtools, refer to Figure 4-118. **(Expected time: 20 min)**

Figure 4-118 *Scene to be created for Exercise 2*

Answers to Self-Evaluation Test

1. a, **2.** d, **3.** c, **4. Coverage**, **5. All Low**, **6. Revolve Rate**, **7.** F, **8.** T, **9.** F, **10.** F

Chapter 5

ZSpheres

Learning Objectives

After completing this chapter, you will be able to:

- *Work with ZSpheres*
- *Understand ZSketching*
- *Understand rigging using ZSpheres*
- *Create basic models using ZSpheres*

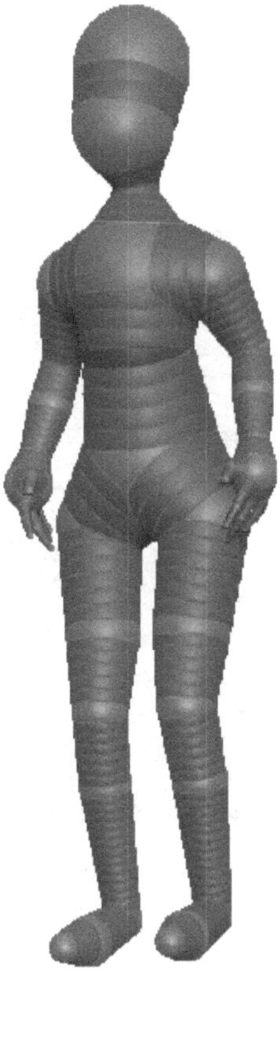

INTRODUCTION

ZSpheres are the modeling tools that can be connected to a network to create a basic structure of a model. You can access ZSpheres from the **Tool** palette. These tools are commonly used in organic modeling. In this chapter, you will learn about the process of creating an armature using ZSpheres.

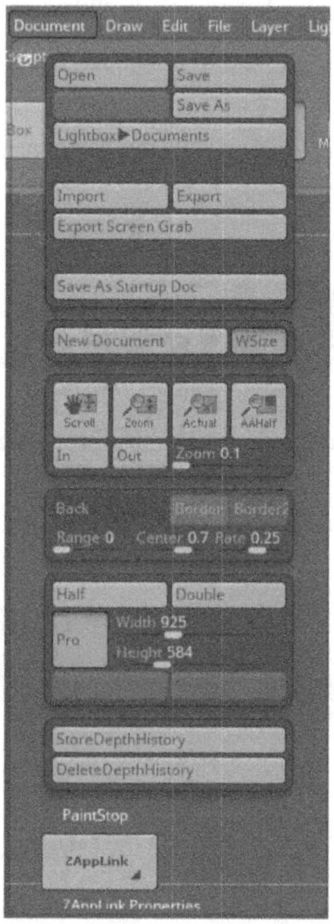

Figure 5-1 The value of the ***Range*** *slider set to* ***0***

Note

In this chapter, the background color of the canvas has been changed to white to help you to view the images better. To change the background color of the canvas, set the color in both the ***Secondary Color*** *and* ***Main Color*** *swatches in the left shelf to white. Next, choose the* ***Document*** *palette. In this palette, set the value of the* ***Range*** *slider to* ***0****, refer to Figure 5-1. The* ***Range*** *slider is used to add the gradient effect. If its value is set to* ***0****, no gradient will be displayed. Choose the* ***Back*** *button in this palette; the color of the canvas will change to white.*

CREATING ARMATURES USING ZSPHERES

To create a ZSphere in the canvas, choose the Current Tool button in the **Tool** palette; a flyout will be displayed. In this flyout, choose **ZSphere** from the **3D Meshes** area, refer to Figure 5-2. Next, press and hold the left mouse button and drag the cursor in the canvas area; a double colored ZSphere will be created, as shown in Figure 5-3. After creating the ZSphere, choose the **Edit** button from the top shelf.

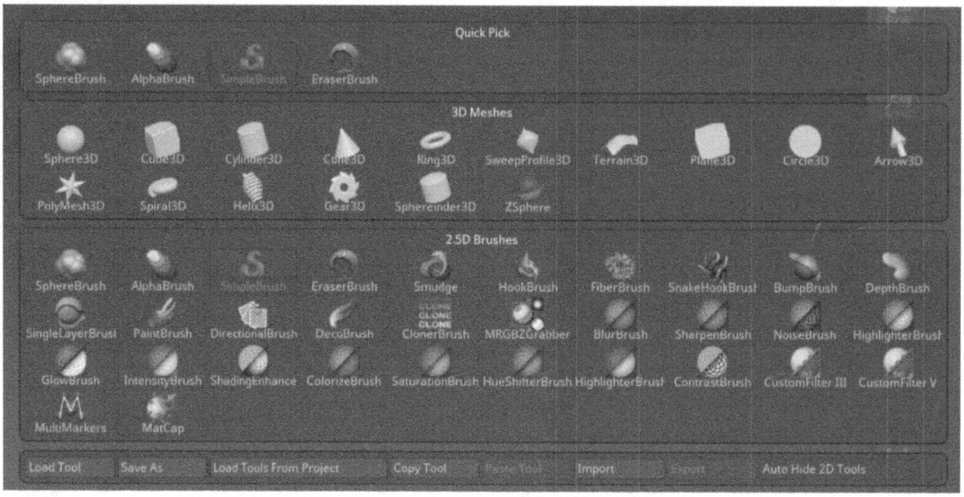

Figure 5-2 ***ZSphere*** *chosen from the* ***3D Meshes*** *area of the flyout*

Figure 5-3 *A double colored sphere created in the canvas*

Note

After creating a ZSphere in the canvas, make sure you choose the ***Edit*** *button in the top shelf.*

Hover the cursor over the ZSphere; three concentric circles connected with a line will be displayed on the surface of the ZSphere, refer to Figure 5-4. On moving the cursor over the surface of ZSphere, you will notice that the color of the innermost circle switches between red and green. The innermost circle will turn green as you hover the cursor over specific parts of the ZSphere. The green circle indicates the best place to add a new ZSphere. When you press and hold the left mouse button and drag the cursor; a new ZSphere will be created on the existing ZSphere, refer to Figure 5-5.

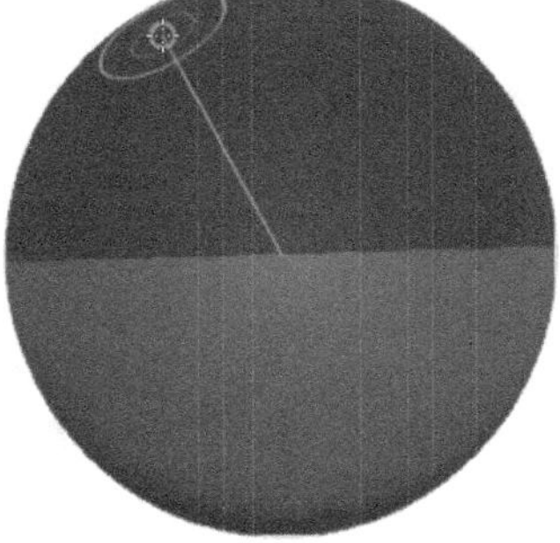

Figure 5-4 *Concentric circles displayed on the surface of ZSphere*

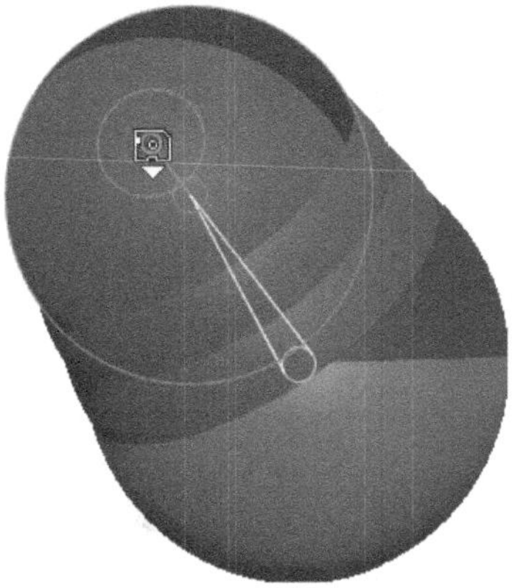

Figure 5-5 *New ZSphere created*

The new ZSphere will be connected to the previous ZSphere through a network of linked spheres. The white colored triangular icon displayed between two ZSpheres resembles the way bones are drawn.

You can move, rotate, or scale the ZSpheres as required. For moving a ZSphere, choose the **Move** button from the top shelf. On doing so, the **Draw** button will be deactivated. Next, select the newly created ZSphere by clicking on it, if not already selected, and move it away from the previous ZSphere. You will notice that the number of linked spheres between the two ZSpheres has increased and the size of the triangular icon has also increased, refer to Figure 5-6.

Similarly, you can scale and rotate the ZSpheres using the **Scale** and **Rotate** buttons, respectively. The linked spheres between the two ZSpheres can neither be moved, scaled, or rotated. However, if you want to move, scale, or rotate any of these linked spheres, you need to convert them into editable ZSpheres. To do so, choose the **Move** button from the top shelf, and click on the ZSphere which you want to move or rotate. On doing so, the sphere will be converted into an editable ZSphere, refer to Figure 5-7. After converting the linked sphere into an editable ZSphere, you can move or scale it as required, refer to Figures 5-8 and 5-9.

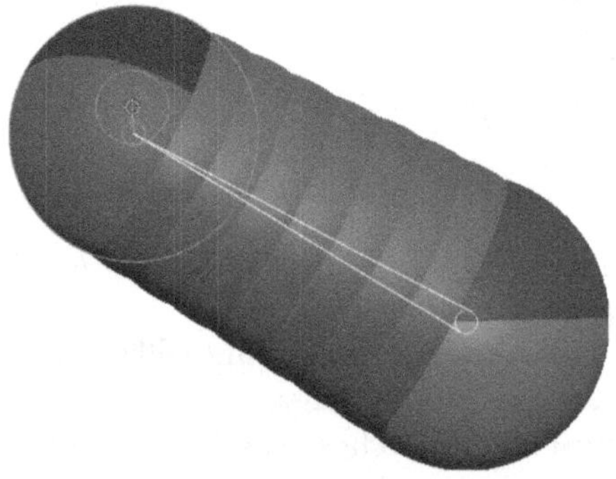

Figure 5-6 *Newly created ZSphere moved away from the previous ZSphere*

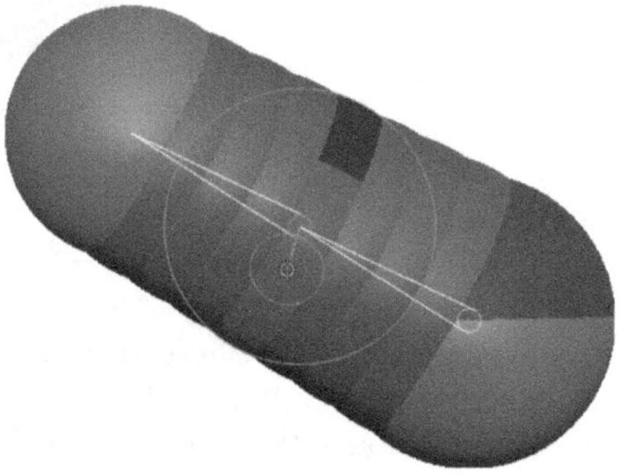

Figure 5-7 *Linked sphere converted into an editable ZSphere*

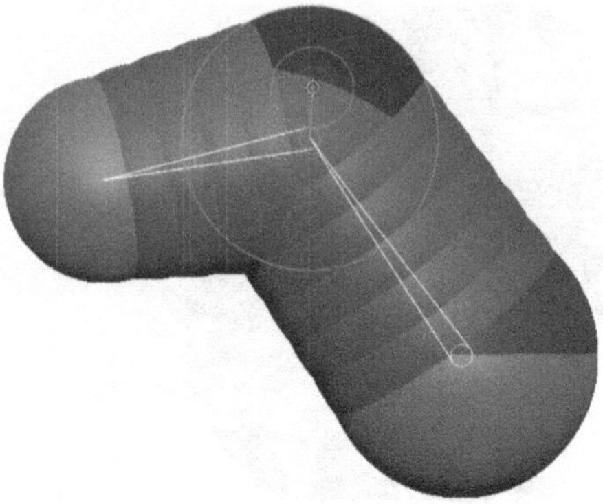

Figure 5-8 *The ZSphere moved using the* ***Move*** *button*

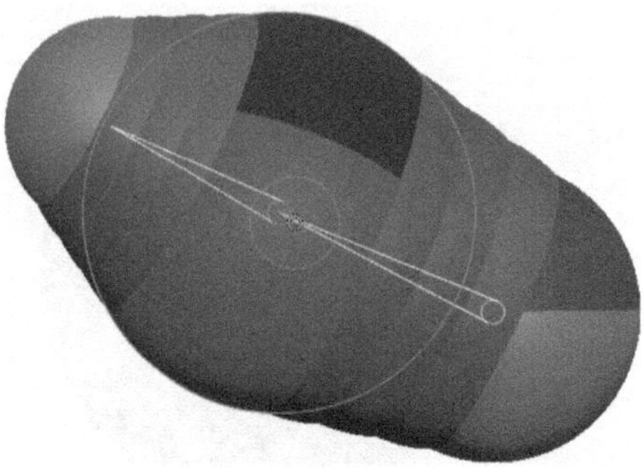

Figure 5-9 *The ZSphere scaled using the* ***Scale*** *button*

By converting the linked spheres into the editable ZSpheres, you can create different types of structures by moving, rotating, or scaling the ZSpheres. In addition to this, you can create different structures by creating new ZSpheres on existing ZSpheres, refer to Figure 5-10.

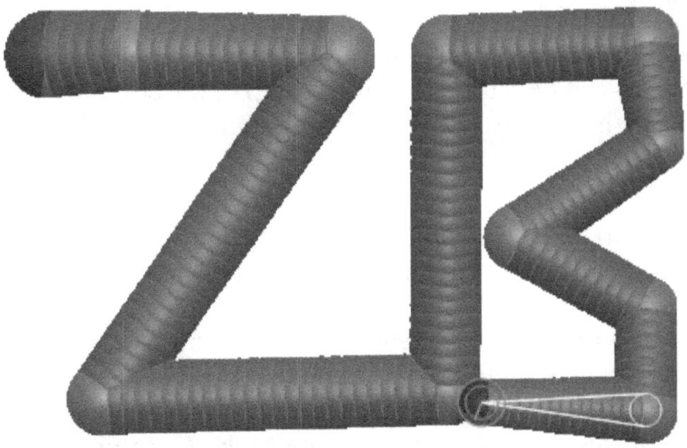

Figure 5-10 *Structure created using ZSpheres*

If you want to delete a ZSphere, choose the **Draw** button from the top shelf. Next, press and hold the ALT key and then click on the ZSphere that you want to delete.

To create two similar ZSpheres in a structure, you need to activate symmetry in any of the axes depending on where you want to position them. For instance, in Figure 5-11, similar ZSpheres have been created by activating the symmetry in the X-axis. Similarly, you can create a number of similar ZSpheres by activating the radial symmetry, refer to Figure 5-12. In this figure, the radial symmetry has been activated along the Z-axis.

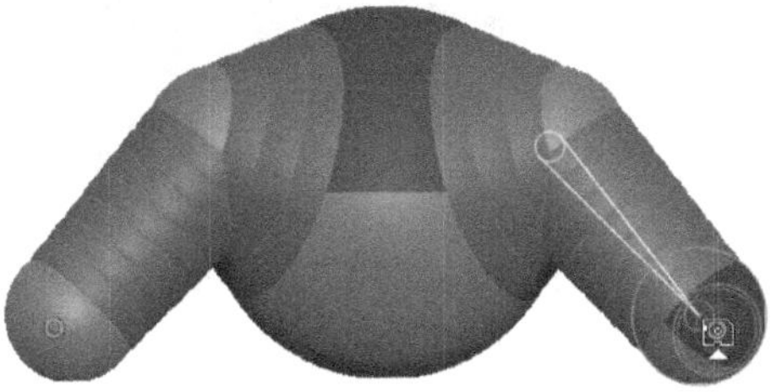

Figure 5-11 *Similar ZSpheres created by activating the symmetry in the X axis*

Figure 5-12 *Similar ZSpheres created by activating the radial symmetry*

Skinning in ZSpheres

Skinning is a process of converting the ZSphere structure into a polygon mesh. The polymesh created from the ZSpheres can be sculpted with the help of different 3D brushes. There are two types of skinning in ZBrush, namely unified skinning and adaptive skinning.

Unified Skinning

Unified skinning is used to convert a ZSphere structure into a polygon mesh with high poly resolution and equal sized polygons. The mesh produced from unified skinning is very smooth.

To convert a ZSphere into unified skin, create a structure using a network of ZSpheres, refer to Figure 5-13. The thumbnail with the name **ZSphere_1** will be displayed in the **Tool** palette, as shown in Figure 5-14. Next, expand the **Unified Skin** subpalette from the **Tool** palette, as shown in Figure 5-15. In this subpalette, choose the **Make Unified Skin** button; a thumbnail for the new skinned mesh with the name **Skin_ZSphere_1** will be displayed in the **Tool** palette. Next, double-click on this thumbnail; the skinned mesh will be displayed in the canvas. Choose the **PolyF** button in the right shelf to view the distribution of polygons in the skinned mesh. Alternatively, press SHIFT + F, refer to Figure 5-16.

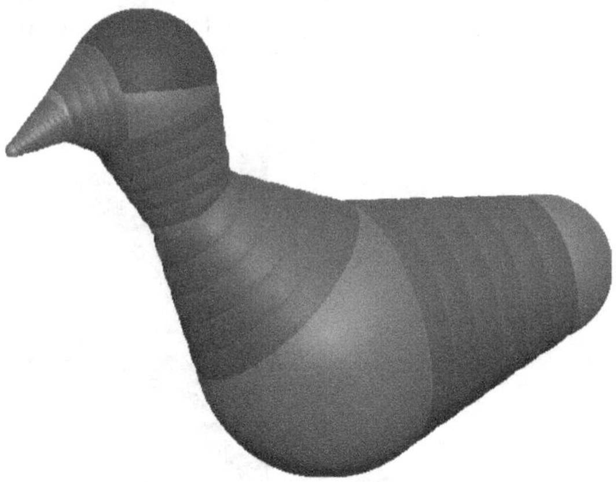

Figure 5-13 ZSphere structure created in the canvas

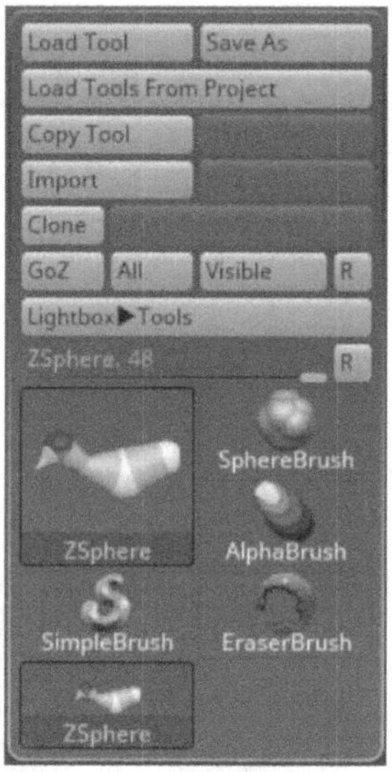

Figure 5-14 The thumbnail for the ZSphere displayed

You can sculpt the skinned mesh using different 3D brushes. Before converting Zsphere framework into a polygon mesh, you can specify the polygon resolution and smoothness of the polygon mesh using the **Resolution** and **Smooth** sliders in the **Unified Skin** subpalette.

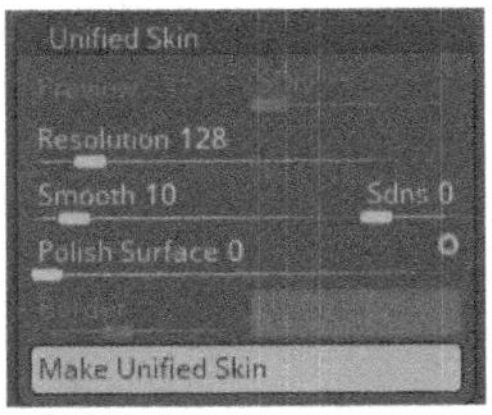

Figure 5-15 *The* ***Unified Skin*** *subpalette expanded*

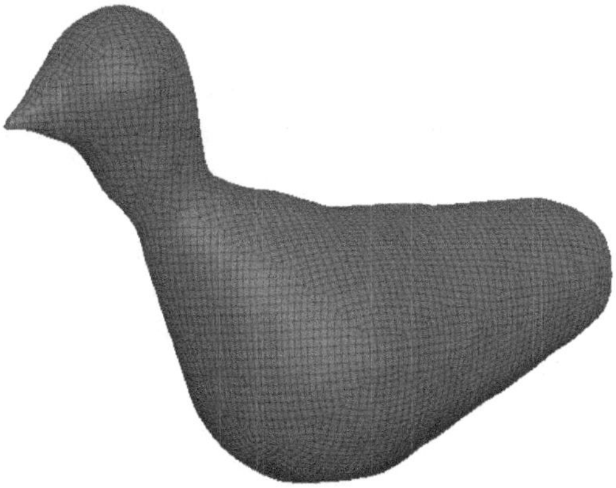

Figure 5-16 *The skinned mesh after choosing the* ***PolyF*** *button*

Adaptive Skinning

Adaptive skinning is the most commonly used skinning technique for the ZSpheres. This technique creates a low polygon mesh from the ZSphere structure. The size of polygons in this mesh is large.

To convert a ZSphere into an adaptive skin, create a structure using a network of ZSpheres, refer to Figure 5-13. Next, expand the **Adaptive Skin** subpalette from the **Tool** palette, as shown in Figure 5-17. In this subpalette, choose the **Make Adaptive Skin** button; a thumbnail for the new skinned mesh with the name **Skin_ZSphere_1** will be displayed in the **Tool** palette. Next, double-click on this thumbnail; the skinned mesh will be displayed in the canvas. Choose the **PolyF** button in the right shelf to view the distribution of polygons in the skinned mesh, refer to Figure 5-18.

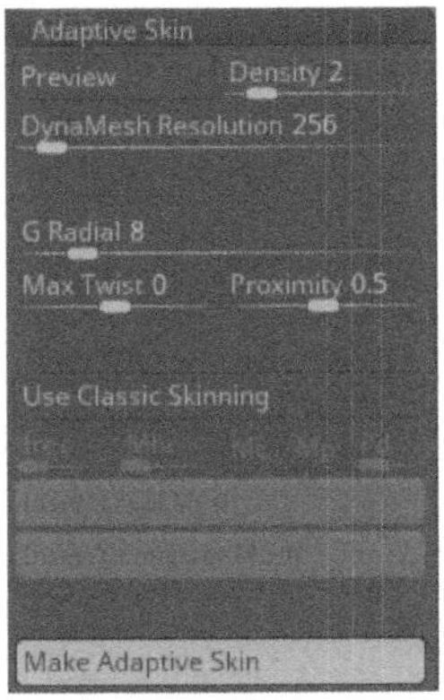

Figure 5-17 *The* ***Adaptive Skin*** *subpalette chosen*

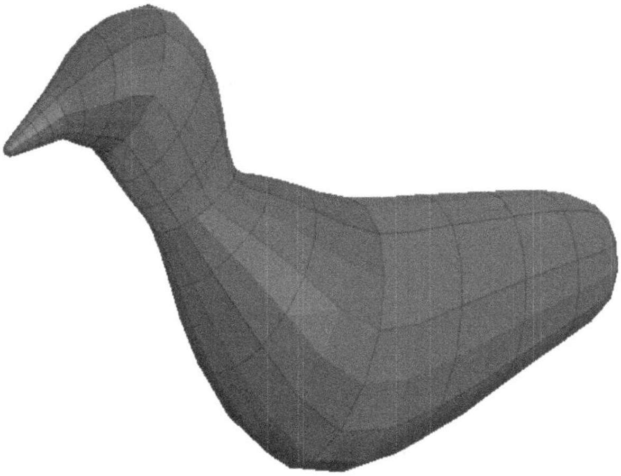

Figure 5-18 *The skinned mesh after choosing the* ***PolyF*** *button*

Before converting a Zsphere structure into a polygon mesh, you can specify the settings for the skinned mesh using the buttons and sliders in the **Adaptive Skin** subpalette. The **Adaptive Skin** subpalette is not displayed in the **Tool** palette, if the **Make Adaptive Skin** button is chosen. The different buttons and sliders in the **Adaptive Skin** subpalette are discussed next.

Preview

The **Preview** button is used to view the skinned mesh in canvas before the ZSphere structure is converted into adaptive skin. You can also view the skinned mesh in the canvas by pressing the A key. After previewing the skinned mesh, choose the **Preview** button again to switch back to the ZSphere mode or press the A key. Figures 5-19 and 5-20 show a ZSphere structure and its preview, respectively.

Figure 5-19 *The ZSphere structure*

Figure 5-20 *The preview of the ZSphere structure*

Density

The **Density** slider is used to increase or decrease the number of polygons in the skinned mesh. If the value in this slider is higher, the skinned mesh will contain more number of polygons and will be smoother. After setting the value of the **Density** slider, choose the **Preview** button to view the results. Figures 5-21 and 5-22 show the preview of the skinned mesh when the value of the **Density** slider is set to **1** and **7**, respectively.

G Radial

The **G Radial** slider is used to increase or decrease the number of spans in the skinned mesh. To increase or decrease the number of spans, choose the **PolyF** button from the right shelf. After setting the value of the **G Radial** slider, choose the **Preview** button; the preview of the skinned mesh will be displayed. Figures 5-23 and 5-24 show the preview of the skinned mesh with the **G Radial** slider value set to **4** and **20**, respectively and also the value of the **Density** slider is set to **1**.

*Figure 5-21 Preview of the mesh with the value of the **Density** slider set to **1***

*Figure 5-22 Preview of the mesh with the value of the **Density** slider set to **7***

*Figure 5-23 Preview of the mesh with the value of the **G Radial** slider set to **4***

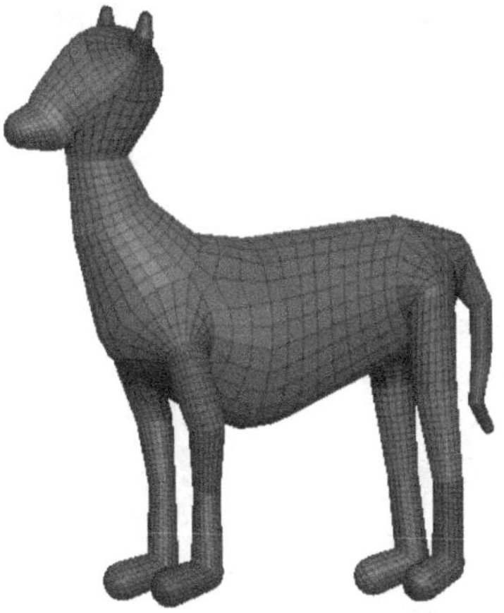

*Figure 5-24 Preview of the mesh with the value of the **G Radial** slider set to **20***

Max Twist

The **Max Twist** slider is used to twist the selected ZSphere in the structure. After setting the value of the **Max Twist** slider, choose the **Preview** button; the twisted ZSphere will be displayed.

Proximity

The **Proximity** slider is used to maintain the flow of geometry between the parent ZSphere and the intersecting ZSpheres that are created on its surface.

Use Classic Skinning

The **Use Classic Skinning** button is used to switch to the skinning technique that was available in the ZBrush 3 version. On choosing this button, the skinning technique in ZBrush gets deactivated and different settings for classic skinning get activated.

ZSketching

ZSketching is a technique that enables you to add a strip of linked spheres to the existing structure of ZSpheres. This technique also enables you to add more depth and detail to a model. After the creation of a ZSphere in the canvas, the **ZSketch** subpalette is displayed in the **Tool** palette, refer to Figure 5-25. The **ZSketch** subpalette consists of different buttons and sliders that help in adding depth to the ZSpheres using freehand sketching. These buttons and sliders are discussed next.

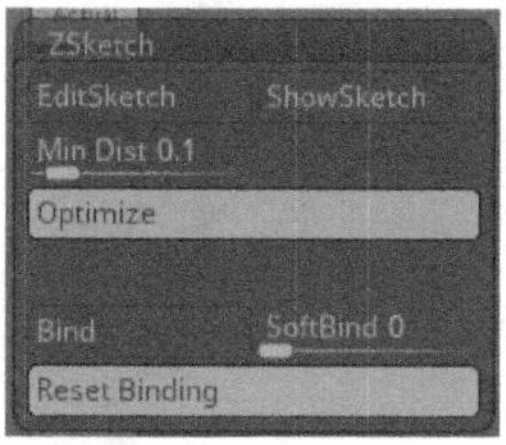

***Figure 5-25** The **ZSketch** subpalette in the **Tool** palette*

EditSketch

The **EditSketch** button is used to switch from normal draw mode to ZSketch mode. This button can be chosen by pressing SHIFT+A keys. To switch from normal draw mode to ZSketch mode, create a ZSphere in the canvas and then choose the **Edit** button. Next, expand the **ZSketch** subpalette. In this subpalette, choose the **EditSketch** button; the color of the ZSphere changes, refer to Figure 5-26. Next, press and hold the left mouse button and hover the cursor on the surface of the ZSphere and then drag the cursor to sketch different shapes using the strips of linked spheres, refer to Figure 5-27.

***Figure 5-26** The color of the ZSphere changed*

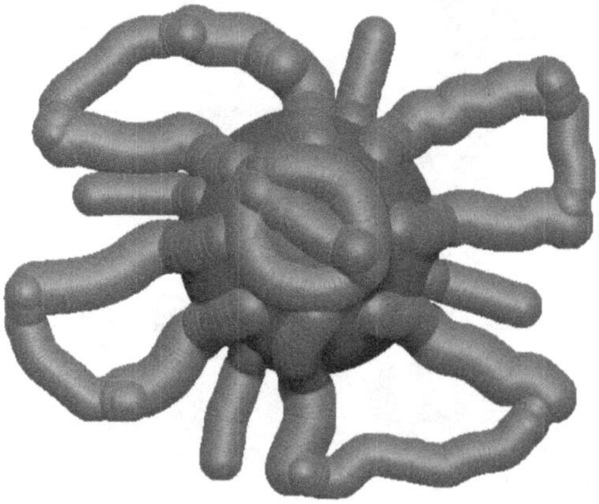

***Figure 5-27** Different shapes created using the strips of ZSpheres*

You can view the polymesh preview of the ZSketch by pressing the A key. In the preview of the ZSketch, you will notice that the parent ZSphere on which the sketching was done is not displayed, refer to Figure 5-28. To switch back to the ZSketching mode, press the A key again.

ShowSketch

The **ShowSketch** button is used to make the sketched strips of linked spheres transparent. This button enables you to adjust the underlying ZSphere structure as required. To make the sketched strips of linked spheres transparent, consider ZSpheres, refer to Figure 5-29, in which the symmetry has been activated in the X-axis. Expand the **ZSketch** subpalette. In this subpalette, choose the **EditSketch** button; the color of the ZSphere structure changes. Adjust the brush size as required. Press and hold the left mouse button and drag the cursor to create a sketch on the surface of the structure, refer to Figure 5-30. Choose the **EditSketch** button again to deactivate it. Next, choose the **ShowSketch** button; the sketched strips will be displayed with transparency, refer to Figure 5-31. The transparency in the strips enables you to adjust the underlying ZSphere structure.

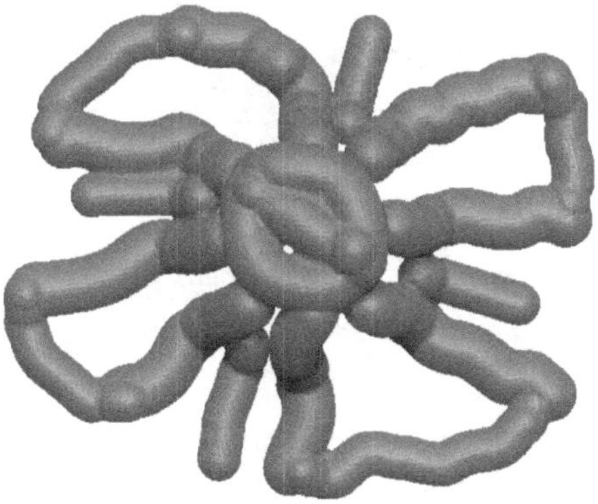

Figure 5-28 *Polymesh preview of the ZSketch*

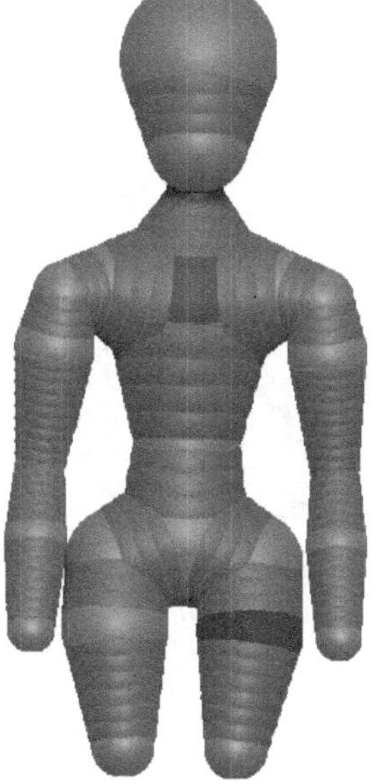

Figure 5-29 *A structure created using ZSpheres*

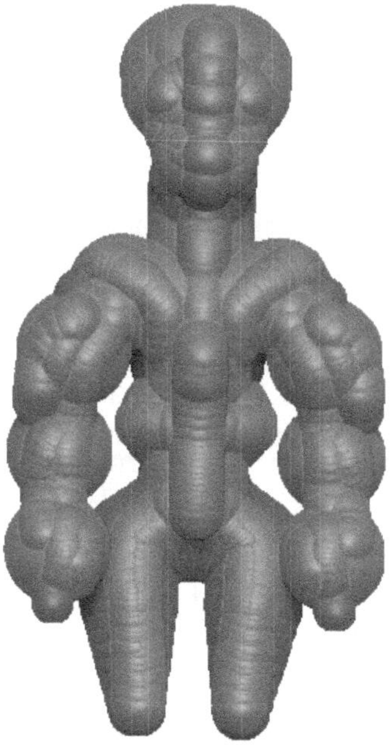

Figure 5-30 *ZSketching done on the surface of the structure*

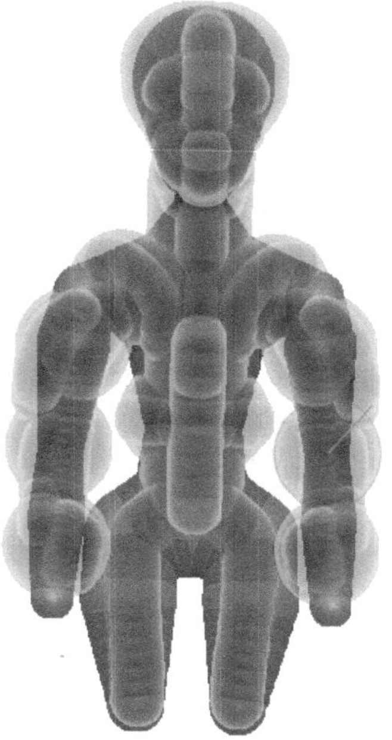

Figure 5-31 *Transparency in the sketched strips*

Min Dist

The term Min Dist stands for minimum ZSpheres distance. The **Min Dist** slider is used to specify the distance between the linked spheres in the strips that are sketched. Figures 5-32 and 5-33 show the strips with the value of the **Min Dist** slider set to **0.1** and **1**, respectively.

Figure 5-32** Strips with the value of the **Min Dist** slider set to **0.1

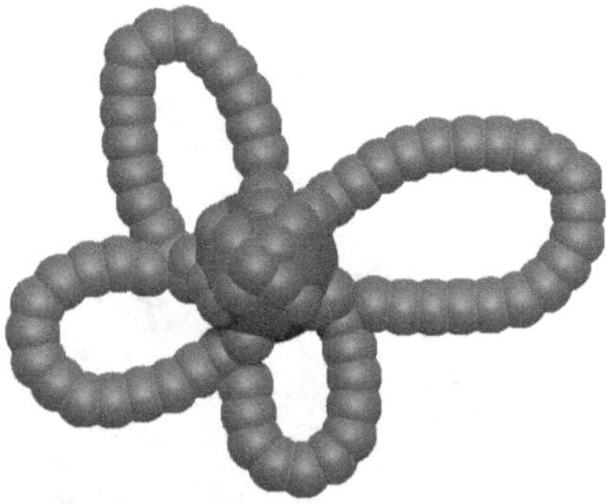

Figure 5-33** Strips with the value of the **Min Dist** slider set to **1

Optimize

The **Optimize** button is used to delete the unnecessarily linked spheres present in the strips of sketched spheres. The linked spheres that will be deleted will not be visible in the canvas.

Bind

The **Bind** button is used to bind the strip of linked spheres with the underlying ZSphere structure. After binding, you will notice that on moving the structure, the sketched strip will also move with it. This button is very useful in posing of the characters that have been created by using the ZSketching technique.

SoftBind

The **SoftBind** slider is used to specify the level of binding between the underlying structure and sketched strips. The higher value of the **SoftBind** slider produces more realistic results, while posing the characters.

Reset Binding

The **Reset Binding** button is used to rebind the sketched strips of the linked spheres to the ZSphere structure, if new ZSpheres are added to the existing ZSphere structure.

Brushes Used in ZSketching

There are about eight types of sculpting brushes that get activated from the Left shelf when you create a ZSphere in the canvas. To access these brushes, choose the Current Brush button; a flyout containing different brushes will be displayed, refer to Figure 5-34. These brushes are used in ZSketching and are discussed next.

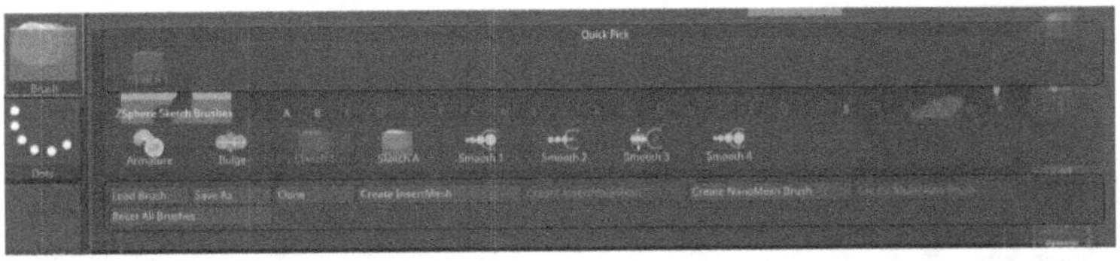

Figure 5-34 Flyout displayed on choosing the Current Brush button

Armature Brush

The **Armature** brush is used to sketch the strips of linked spheres in the canvas area. This brush is used for creating arms, legs, and fingers of a character. To sketch the strips of linked spheres, create a ZSphere in the canvas and then choose the **Edit** button. Next, expand the **ZSketch** subpalette. In this subpalette, choose the **EditSketch** button; the color of the ZSphere changes. Activate the symmetry in X-axis by pressing the X key. Next, press and hold the left mouse button and hover the cursor on the surface of the ZSphere, and then drag the cursor outward to create floating strips in the canvas area, refer to Figure 5-35.

After creating the strips using this brush, you will notice that on pressing the A key, only the skinned preview of the strips is displayed and the underlying ZSphere is not displayed, refer to Figure 5-36.

Figure 5-35 *Strips created using the* ***Armature*** *brush*

Figure 5-36 *The skinned preview of the strips*

Bulge Brush

The **Bulge** brush is used to bulge out the surface of the strips of linked spheres. If the **Z Intensity** slider is set to its maximum value, the surface of the object will be bulged out by a significant amount, refer to Figure 5-37.

Sketch Brushes

The sketch brushes are used to sketch the strips of ZSpheres on the surface of an underlying ZSphere. On creating a ZSphere, the **Sketch 1** brush is displayed by default.

Smooth Brushes

The smooth brushes are used to smoothen the surface of the strips. The level of smoothening depends upon the value of the **Z Intensity** slider. On choosing any of these brushes, a dialog box will be displayed, asking you to press SHIFT key to activate the selected brush. Press SHIFT and then press and hold the left mouse button. Next, drag the cursor on the surface of the strips; the strips will be smoothened, refer to Figure 5-38.

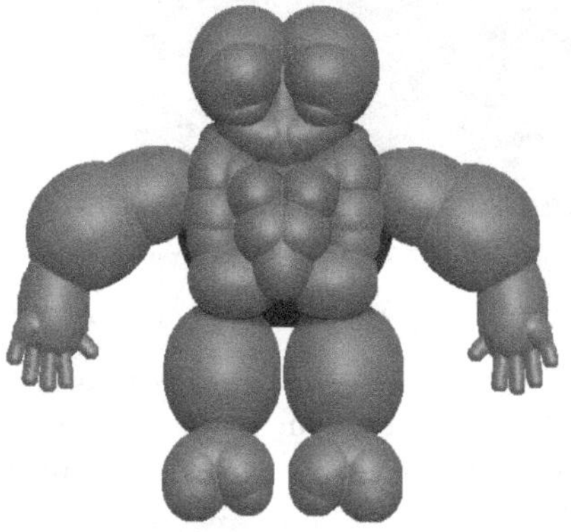

*Figure 5-37 Strips bulged out using the **Bulge** brush*

*Figure 5-38 Strips smoothened using the **Smooth 1** brush*

Rigging Using ZSpheres

Rigging is the process of adding bones and joints to an object. Rigging in ZBrush enables you to pose a character. Rigging in ZBrush is very basic. You can rig a character with the help of the **Rigging** subpalette in the **Tool** palette. The **Rigging** subpalette becomes visible only when a ZSphere is created in the canvas, refer to Figure 5-39.

Before rigging a character in ZBrush, you need to make sure that the character is at its lowest subdivision level. This enables you to pose a character conveniently and produce realistic results as the less number of polygons are easily manageable. To add bones and joints to an object, choose the **DemoSoldier.ZTL** file from the **Tool** tab of the **LightBox** browser, and create it in the canvas, refer to Figure 5-40. After creating the file, make sure that you choose the **Edit** button from the top shelf. Next, expand the **SubTool** subpalette. In this subpalette, choose the **DemoSoldier_1** subtool from the list of subtools, as shown in Figure 5-41.

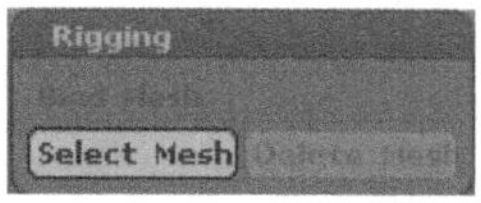

*Figure 5-39 The **Rigging** subpalette*

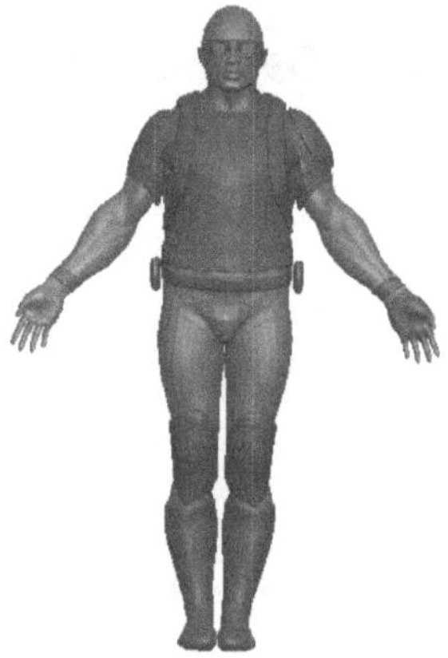

Figure 5-40 The DemoSoldier.ZTL file created in the canvas

Expand the **Geometry** subpalette and set the value of **SDiv** slider to **1**. Next, choose the **Del Higher** button in the **Geometry** subpalette, as shown in Figure 5-42; the character will be displayed at its lowest subdivision level.

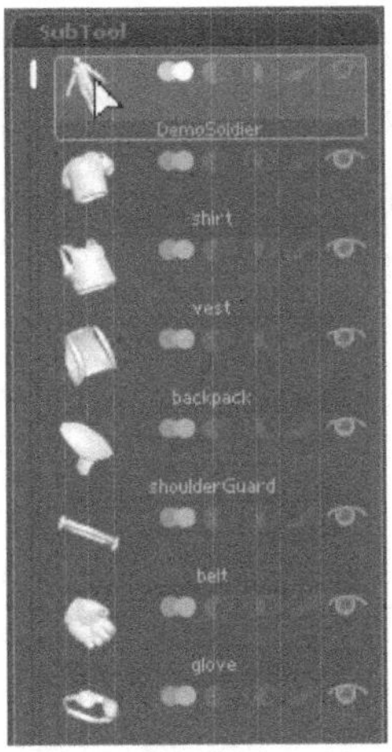

***Figure 5-41** The **DemoSoldier_1** subtool chosen from the **SubTool** subpalette*

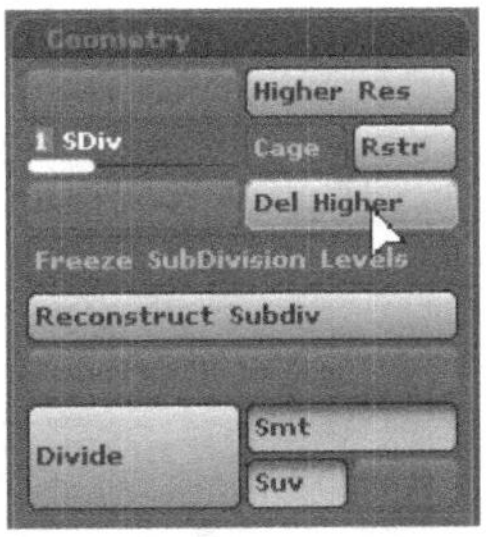

***Figure 5-42** The **Del Higher** button chosen from the **Geometry** subpalette*

After setting the *DemoSoldier* file to its lowest subdivision level, choose the Current Tool button in the **Tool** palette; a flyout will be displayed. Choose the **ZSphere** primitive from the **3D Meshes** area of this flyout, refer to Figure 5-43; the *DemoSoldier* file will disappear from the canvas and only a ZSphere will be visible in the canvas.

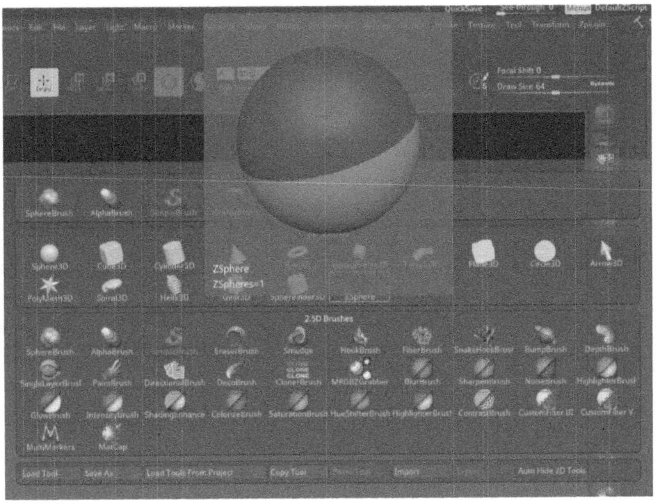

***Figure 5-43** **ZSphere** primitive chosen from the **3D Meshes** area of the flyout*

You will notice that after creating the ZSphere, the **Rigging** subpalette will be displayed in the **Tool** palette. From this subpalette, choose the **Select Mesh** button; a flyout consisting of 3D models will be displayed. The **Select Mesh** button enables you to choose the model that you want to rig. Choose the **DemoSoldier_1** model from this flyout, refer to Figure 5-44; the transparent model of the file will be displayed in the canvas, refer to Figure 5-45. Next, use the ZSphere visible at the middle of the model as the reference and activate the symmetry in the X axis. Using the ZSpheres, create the structure, as shown in Figure 5-46.

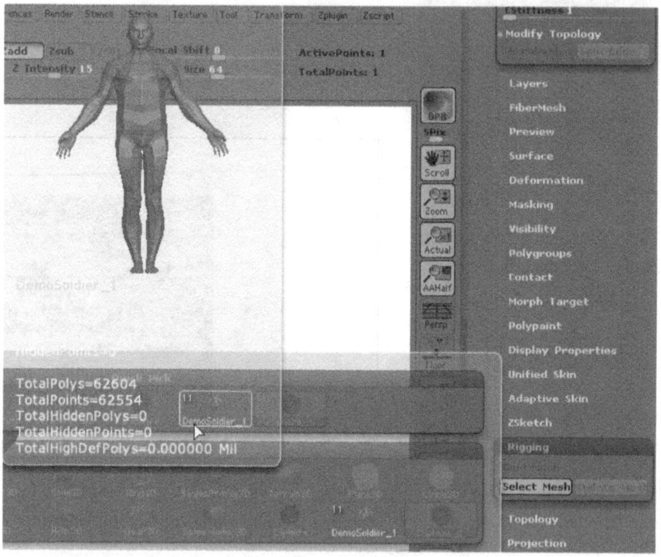

***Figure 5-44 DemoSoldier_1** chosen from the flyout*

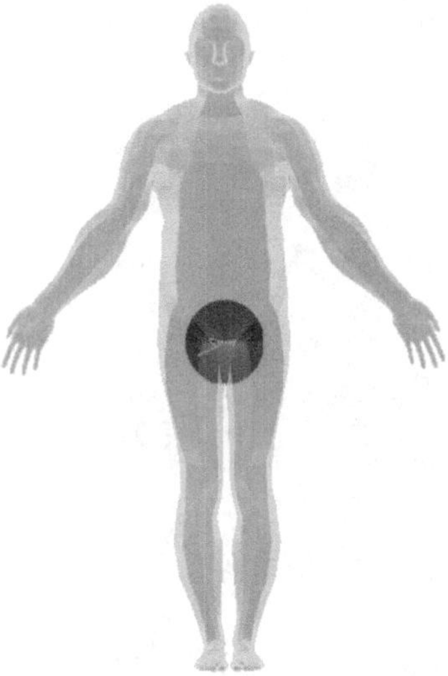

***Figure 5-45** The transparent model displayed in the canvas*

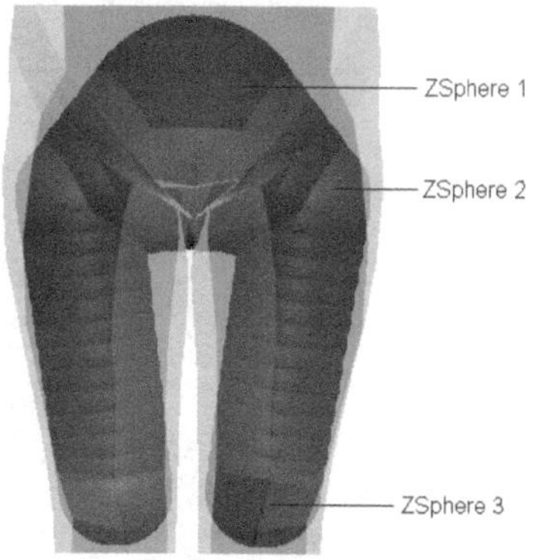

***Figure 5-46** Structure created using the ZSpheres*

Create a structure of a body inside the transparent model. While creating the structure, make sure you create new ZSpheres at the shoulders, elbows, and knees. If required, move and scale the ZSpheres such that the structure fits into the model, refer to Figure 5-47. In this figure, the editable ZSpheres have been highlighted. After creating the structure, choose the **Bind Mesh** button from the **Rigging** subpalette; the transparent model will bind with the ZSphere structure created. On moving the ZSpheres in the structure, the model will also move. Select the ZSphere from the elbow area and then move it upward; the elbow of the model will also move upward. Thus, creating a bend in the arm of the model, refer to Figure 5-48. Similarly, you can create bend in the knees of the model.

After posing the model, you need to skin it. To skin the model, expand the **Adaptive Skin** subpalette. In this subpalette, choose the **Make Adaptive Skin** button. Next, choose the thumbnail for the skinned model from the **Tool** palette; the posed model will be displayed in the canvas, refer to Figure 5-49. The posed model will not be smooth. To make it smooth, set the value of the **SDiv** slider in the **Geometry** subpalette to **5** by using the **Divide** button, refer to Figure 5-50.

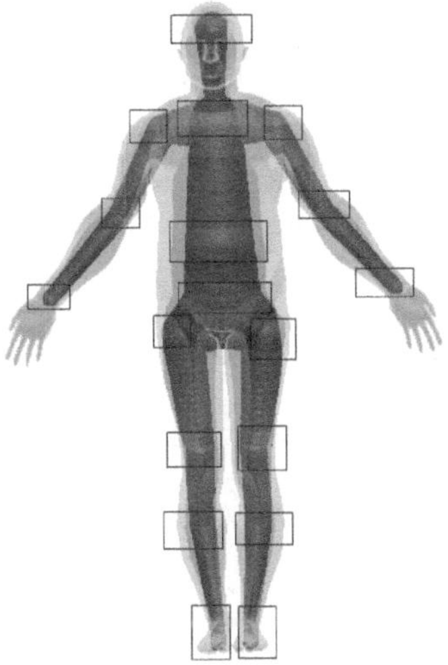

Figure 5-47 *Structure created inside the transparent model*

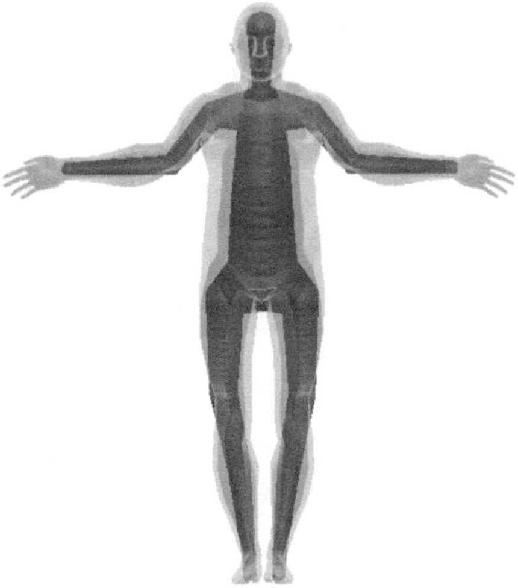

Figure 5-48 *Bend created in the elbow of the model*

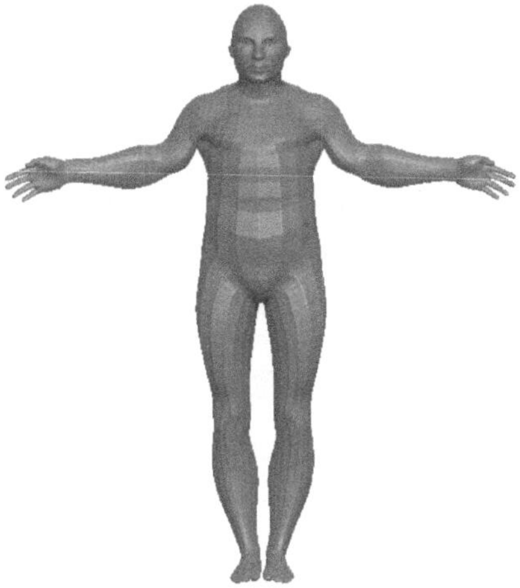

Figure 5-49 *The skinned model displayed in the canvas*

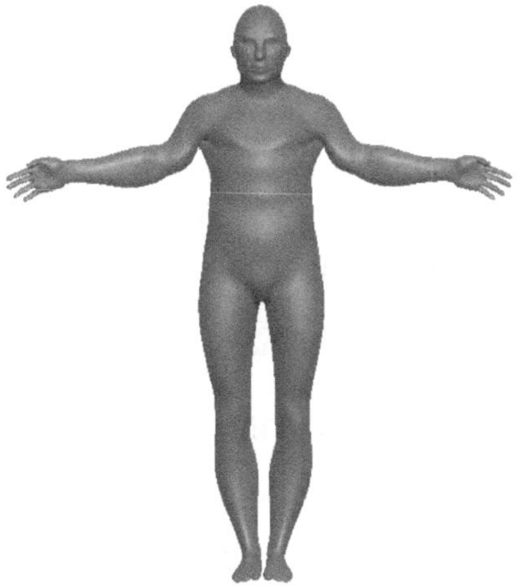

Figure 5-50 *The model smoothened by setting the value of the **SDiv** slider to **5***

TUTORIALS

Before you start the tutorials of this chapter, navigate to *\Documents\ZBrushprojects* and then create a new folder with the name *c05*.

Tutorial 1

In this tutorial, you will create the basic shape of a human body using ZSpheres. The final output of the model is shown in Figure 5-51. **(Expected time: 30 min)**

Figure 5-51 *Basic shape of the human body*

The following steps are required to complete this tutorial:

a. Create the torso of the human body.
b. Create the limbs.
c. Create the neck and the head.
d. Save the model.

Creating the Torso of the Human Body

In this section, you will create the torso of the human body using a framework of ZSpheres.

1. Choose the Current Tool button from the **Tool** palette; a flyout is displayed. In this flyout, choose the **ZSphere** primitive and create it on the canvas, as shown in Figure 5-52. Next, choose the **Edit** button from the top shelf.

2. Activate the symmetry in the X-axis by pressing the X key. Hover the cursor at the centre of the bottom portion of the ZSphere; a green circle is displayed, as shown in Figure 5-53.

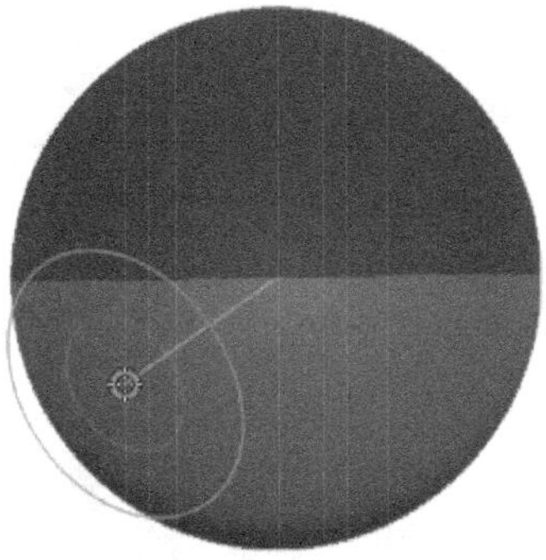

Figure 5-52 ZSphere created in the canvas

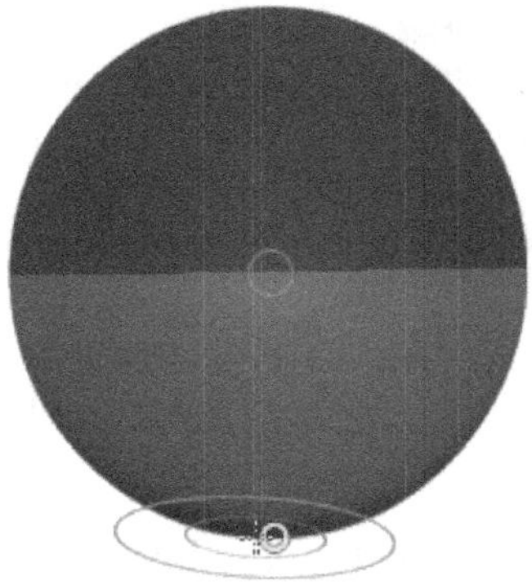

Figure 5-53 Green circle displayed

3. Create a second ZSphere at the position where the green circle is displayed, as shown in Figure 5-54.

4. Similarly, create a third ZSphere at the centre of the top portion of the ZSphere, refer to Figure 5-55. If required, choose the **Move** button from the top shelf and position the ZSpheres such that they lie in a straight line.

5. Choose the **Scale** button from the top shelf. Next, select the middle ZSphere by clicking on it. Press and hold the left mouse button and drag the cursor inward to scale down the ZSphere, as shown in Figure 5-56.

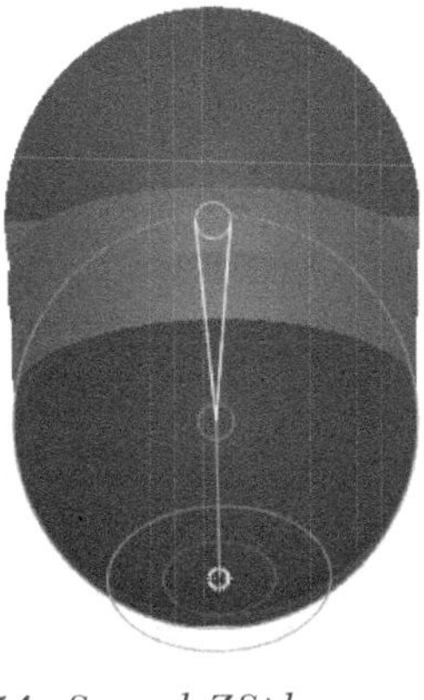

Figure 5-54 Second ZSphere created below the existing ZSphere

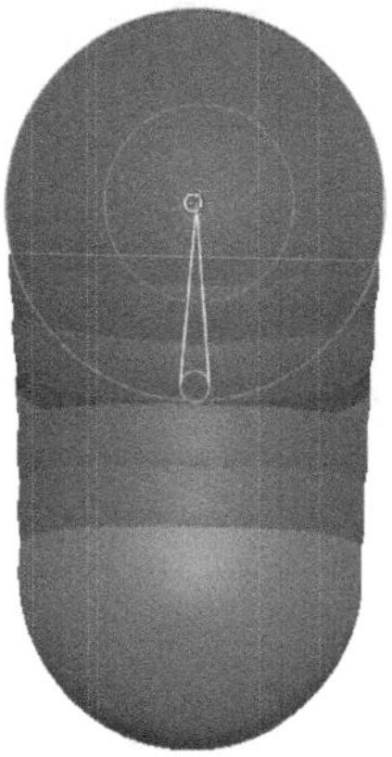

Figure 5-55 Third ZSphere created above the existing ZSphere

Creating the Limbs

In this section, you will create the hands and legs of the human body by creating new ZSpheres on the existing structure.

1. Choose the **Draw** button from the top shelf. Next, hover the cursor on the right side of the bottom ZSphere and create a ZSphere for the hips. As the symmetry is activated in the X-axis, a ZSphere is also created on the left side, refer to Figure 5-57.

2. Press and hold the left mouse button and drag the cursor in the canvas area toward the right till the side view of the structure is displayed. Next, move the newly created ZSpheres slightly backwards and position them, as shown in Figure 5-58. Again, switch back to the front view by dragging the cursor in the canvas area toward the left.

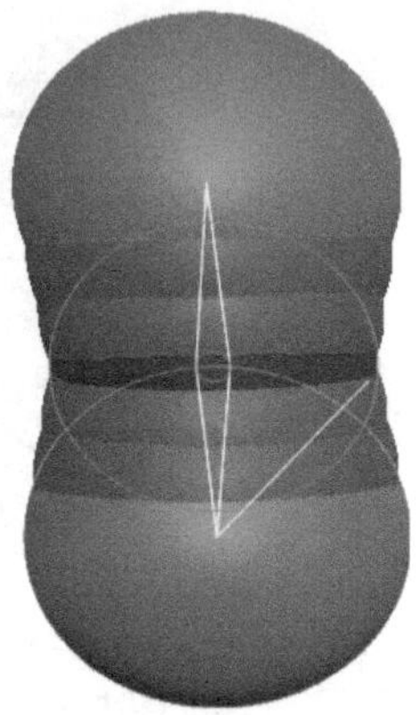

***Figure 5-56** Middle most ZSphere scaled using the **Scale** button*

***Figure 5-57** ZSphere created for the hips*

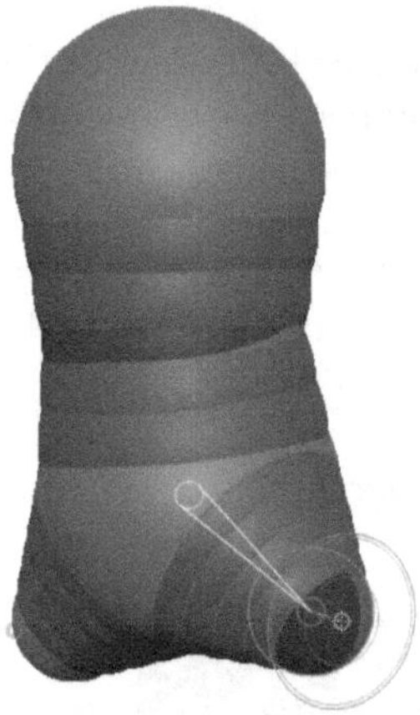

***Figure 5-58** Positioning ZSphere in the side view*

3. Create the ZSpheres for the shoulders of the body, refer to Figure 5-59. Position the shoulders in the side view, as discussed in Step 2.

4. Hover the cursor on the ZSphere created for the hips of the body. Next, create a new ZSphere on it and move it downward, as shown in Figure 5-60.

5. Create new ZSpheres for the arms and legs of the body and move them downward, refer to Figure 5-61.

6. Make sure the **Draw** button is chosen in the top shelf. Next, insert two editable ZSpheres on the legs by clicking on two linked ZSpheres, refer to Figure 5-62. Choose the **Scale** button from the top shelf and scale up the inserted ZSpheres, as shown in Figure 5-62.

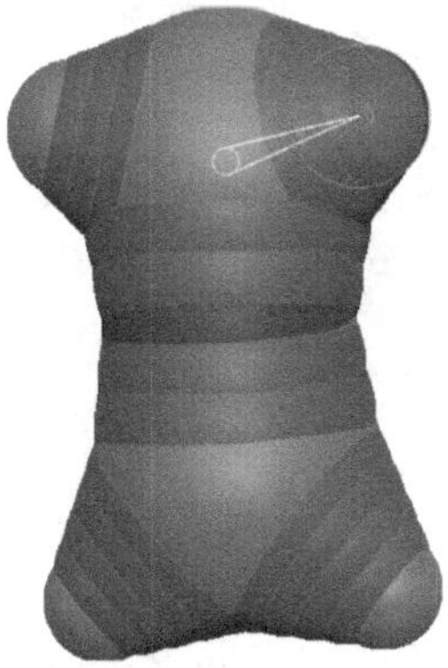

Figure 5-59 *ZSphere created for the shoulders*

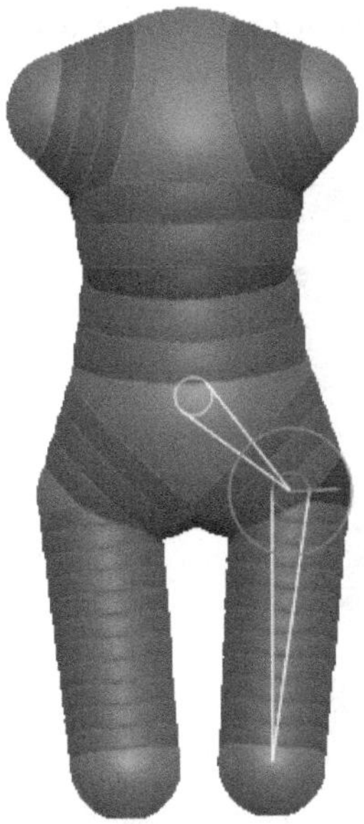

Figure 5-60 *ZSphere created and moved downward*

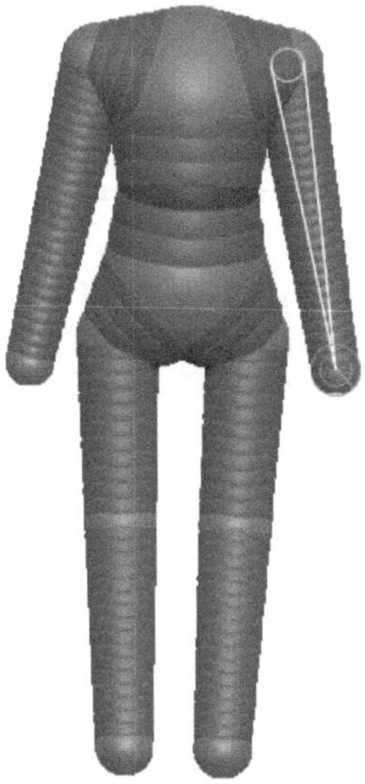

Figure 5-61 *ZSpheres created for the legs and the arms*

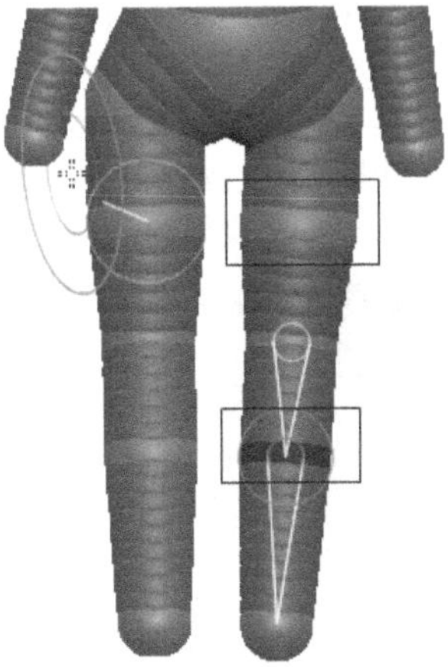

Figure 5-62 *Two new ZSpheres inserted and scaled*

7. Press and hold the left mouse button and drag the cursor in the canvas area toward the right till the side view of the structure is displayed. Next, choose the **Move** button from the top shelf and move the ZSpheres on the legs to position them, as shown in Figure 5-63. Switch back to the front view by dragging the cursor toward the left.

8. Choose the **Draw** button from the top shelf and create two new ZSpheres for the feet of the body. Next, choose the **Move** button and move the newly created ZSpheres toward the front. Choose the **Scale** button and scale up the middle ZSphere, as shown in Figure 5-64.

Figure 5-63 *The ZSpheres adjusted in the side view*

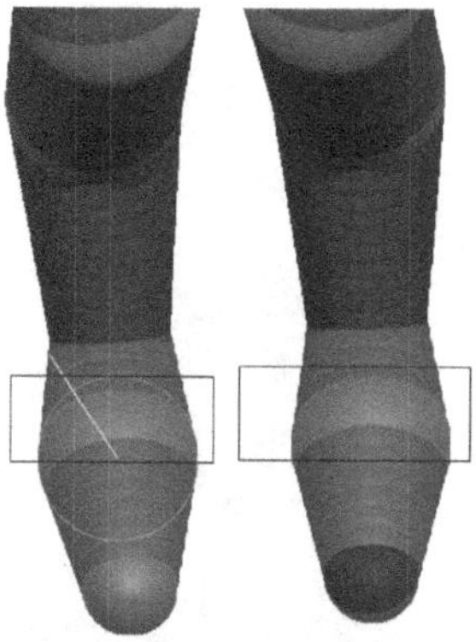

Figure 5-64 *Middle ZSphere scaled up*

9. Insert two editable ZSpheres on the arms by clicking on the two linked ZSpheres, refer to Figure 5-65.

10. Press and hold the left mouse button and drag the cursor in the canvas area toward the right till the side view of the structure is displayed. Next, move the inserted ZSpheres slightly backward in the side view to create a bend in the elbow, refer to Figure 5-65.

11. Create a new ZSphere for the palm of the hand, and move it downward, as shown in Figure 5-66.

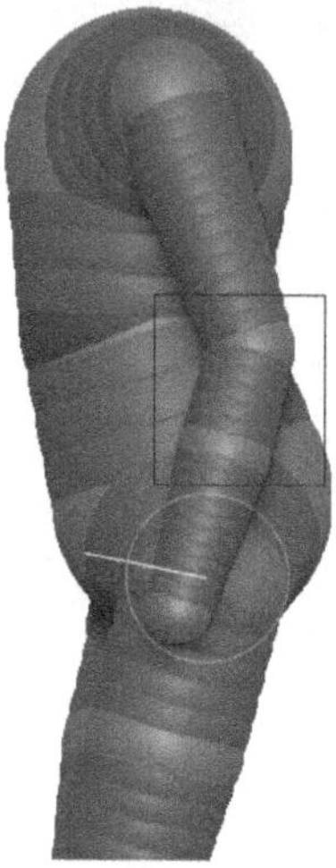

Figure 5-65 *Two new ZSpheres inserted and positioned in the side view*

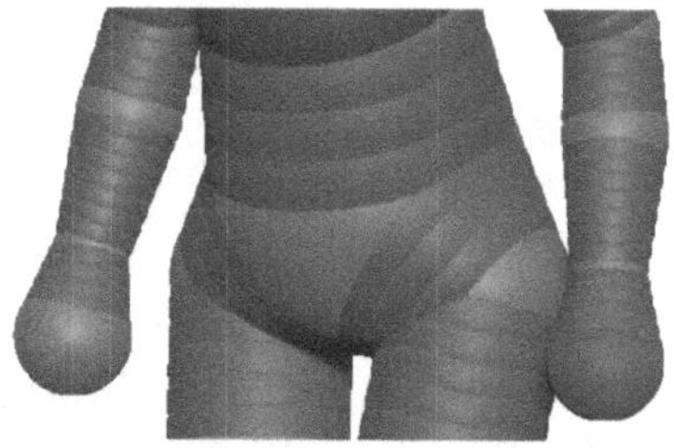

Figure 5-66 *New ZSphere created for the palm and moved downward*

12. Choose the **Move** button from the top shelf and select the ZSphere created for the palm. You will notice that its color changes. Hover the cursor at the area that divides the red and maroon tones of the ZSphere, as shown in Figure 5-67. Next, choose the **Draw** button and create a ZSphere for the knuckle of thumb and move it outward, as shown in Figure 5-68.

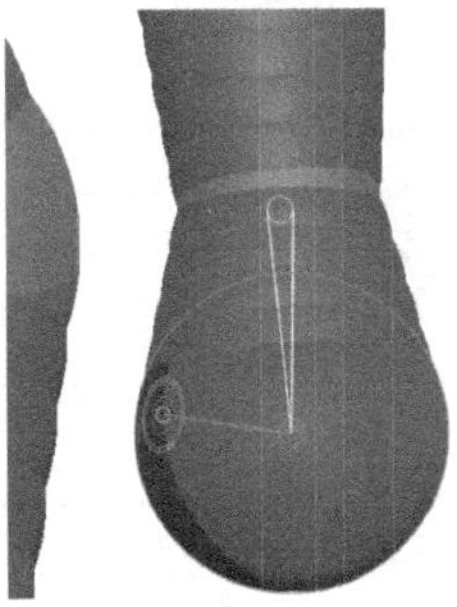

Figure 5-67 *Cursor hovered at the area dividing the red and maroon tones of the ZSphere*

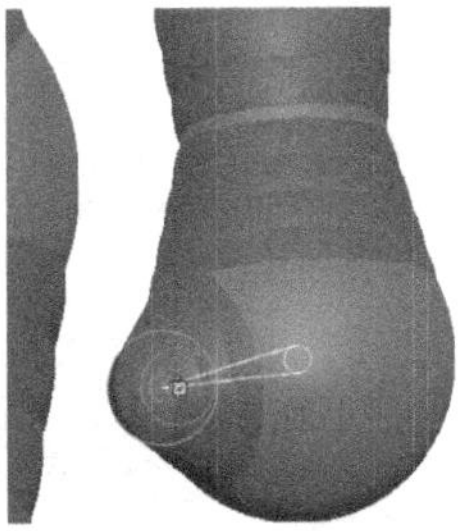

Figure 5-68 *ZSphere created and moved outward*

13. Create four more ZSpheres for the knuckles of the rest of the fingers and move them outward, as shown in Figure 5-69.

14. Create new ZSpheres for the thumb and the index finger and then move them outward, as shown in Figure 5-70.

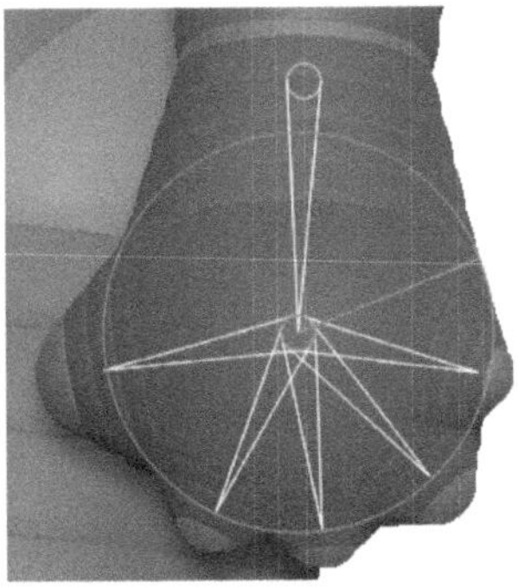

Figure 5-69 *Knuckles created for all the fingers of the hand*

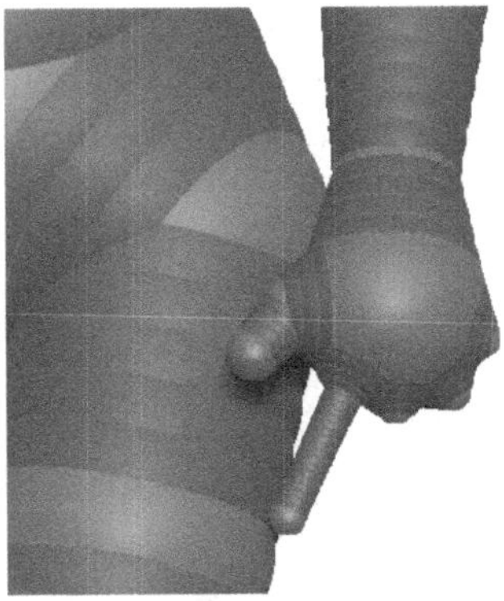

Figure 5-70 *Thumb and index finger created by creating ZSpheres and moving them outward*

15. Create the middle finger by creating a ZSphere at the knuckle and then moving it outward. Next, insert a ZSphere at the middle of the index finger and the middle finger by clicking on the linked spheres, as shown in Figure 5-71.

16. Similarly, create the ring finger and little finger and adjust them by scaling and moving the ZSpheres in them, refer to Figure 5-72.

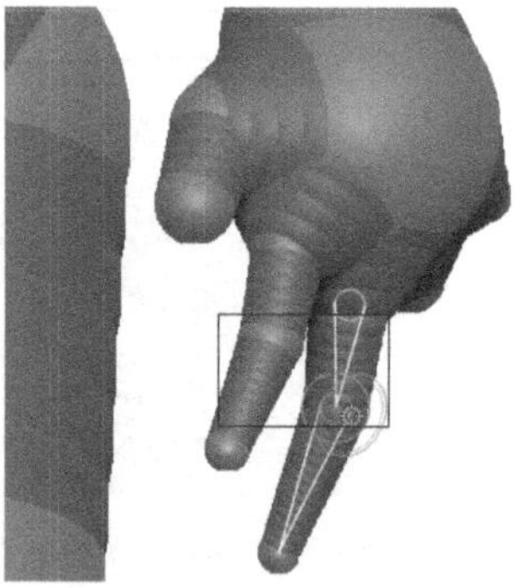

Figure 5-71 Two new ZSpheres inserted in the index finger and the middle finger

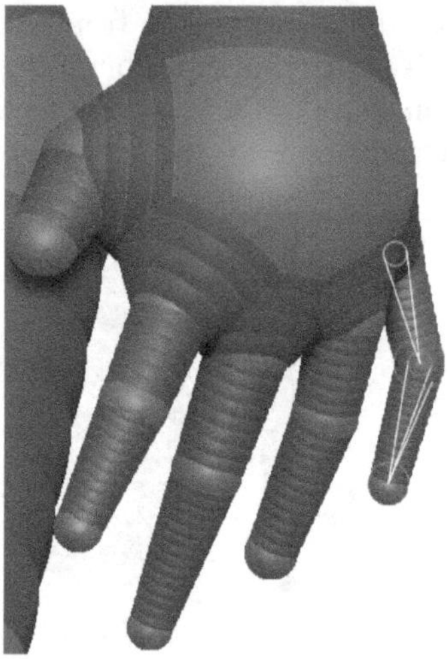

Figure 5-72 Ring finger and the little finger created using ZSpheres

Creating the Neck and the Head

In this section, you will create the neck and head of the human body by creating new ZSpheres on the existing structure.

1. Choose the **Move** button from the top shelf. Hover the cursor on the top-most ZSphere of the framework and place it at the middle of the area that divides the red and maroon tones of the ZSphere. Next, choose the **Draw** button, and create a ZSphere for the lower part of the neck, refer to Figure 5-73.

2. Create another ZSphere for the upper part of the neck, refer to Figure 5-74.

3. Create a ZSphere on the top of the neck for the lower part of the head, refer to Figure 5-75.

4. Similarly, create another ZSphere for the upper part of the head, refer to Figure 5-76.

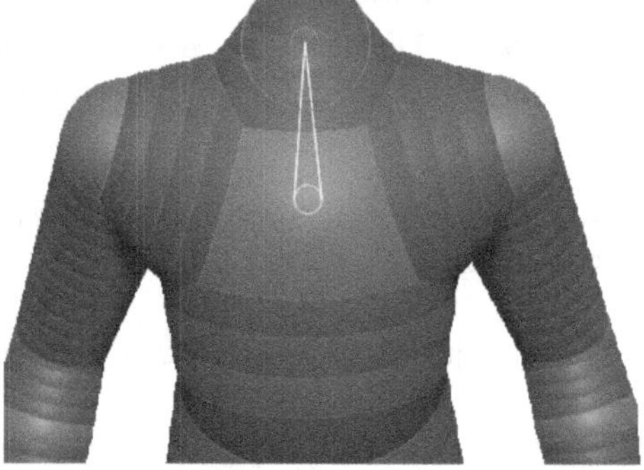

Figure 5-73 ZSphere created for the lower part of the neck

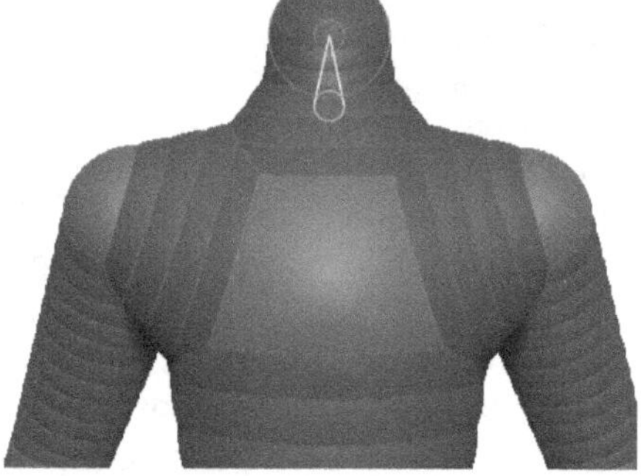

Figure 5-74 Second ZSphere created for the upper part of the neck

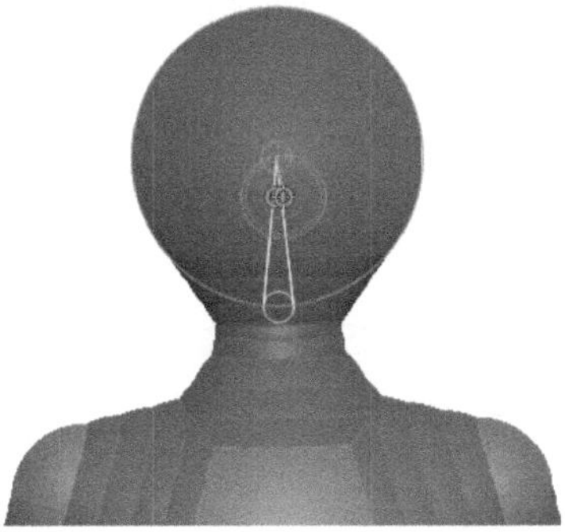

Figure 5-75 ZSphere created for the lower part of the head

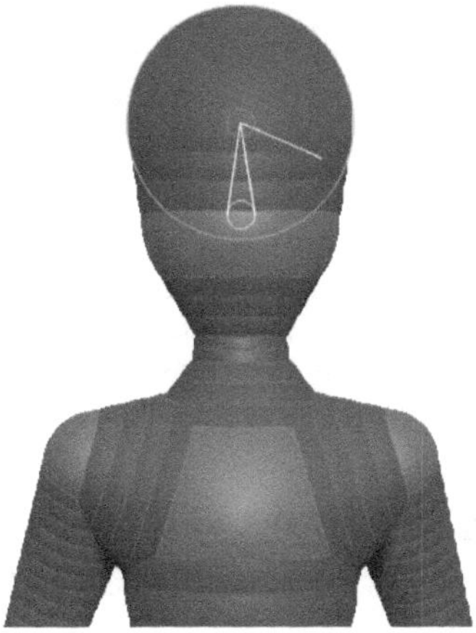

Figure 5-76 ZSphere created for the upper part of the head

If required, scale and move the ZSpheres in the structure to adjust the anatomy of the model, refer to Figure 5-77. You can view the skinned preview of the model by pressing the A key, refer to Figure 5-78.

Saving the Model

In this section, you will save the file using the steps given next.

1. Choose the **Save As** button from the **Tool** palette; the **Save ZTool** dialog box is displayed. In this dialog box, browse to the location *\Documents\ZBrushprojects\c05*.

2. Enter **c05tut1** in the **File name** edit box and then choose the **Save** button.

Figure 5-77 Final model of the body

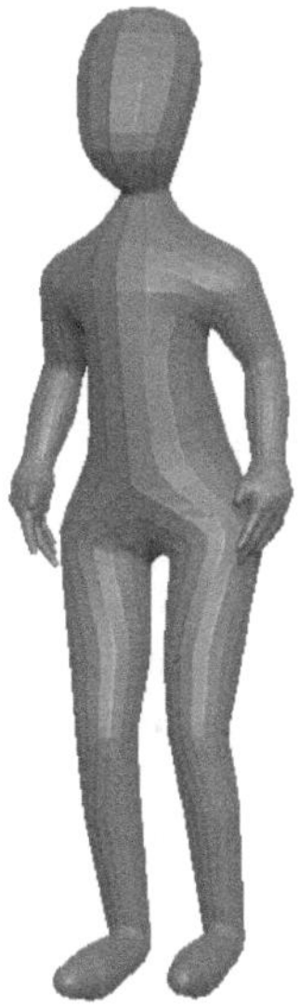

Figure 5-78 Skinned preview of the body

Tutorial 2

In this tutorial, you will create the basic shape of the head of stag deer using ZSpheres. The final output of the model is shown in Figure 5-79. **(Expected time: 30 min)**

The following steps are required to complete this tutorial:

a. Create the head and neck of the stag deer.
b. Create the antlers of the stag deer.
c. Save the model.

Creating the Head and Neck of the Stag Deer

In this section, you will create the head and neck of the stag deer using a framework of ZSpheres.

1. Choose the Current Tool button from the **Tool** palette; a flyout is displayed. In this flyout, choose the **ZSphere** primitive and create it on the canvas, as shown in Figure 5-80. Next, choose the **Edit** button from the top shelf. Activate the symmetry in the X-axis by pressing the X key.

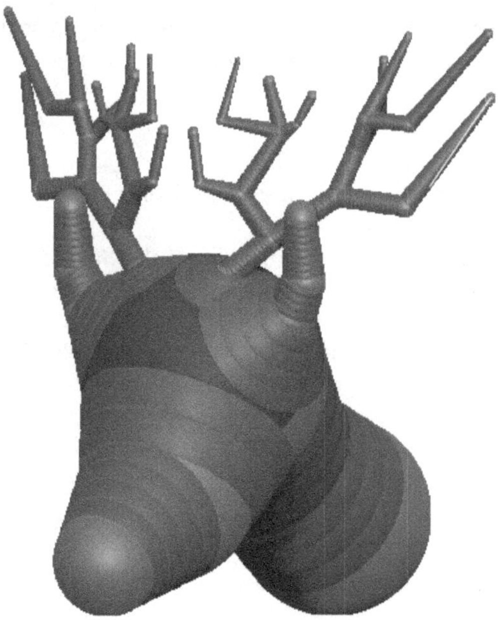

Figure 5-79 *Basic shape of the head of stag deer*

2. Hover the cursor at the area that divides the red and maroon tones of the ZSphere and create a ZSphere at the center, as shown in Figure 5-81.

Figure 5-80 *ZSphere created in the canvas*

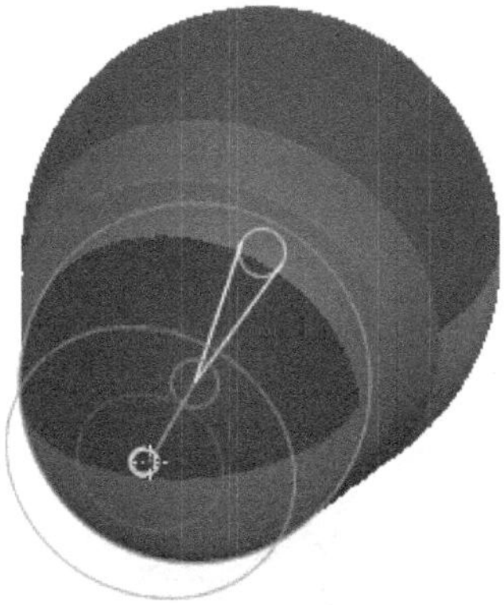

Figure 5-81 *ZSphere created at the center*

3. Create another ZSphere at the center of ZSphere created in Step 2, refer to Figure 5-82.

4. Choose the **Scale** button from the top shelf. Next, select the newly created ZSphere by clicking on it. Press and hold the left mouse button and drag the cursor inward to scale down the ZSphere. Now, choose the **Move** button from the top shelf and move the ZSphere slightly upward, refer to Figure 5-83.

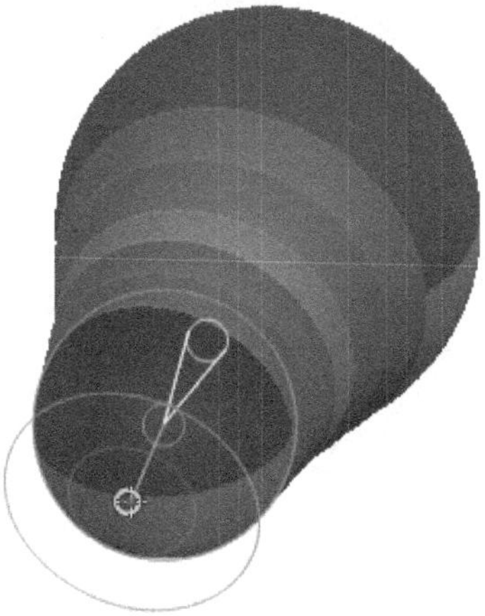

Figure 5-82 *Third Zsphere created*

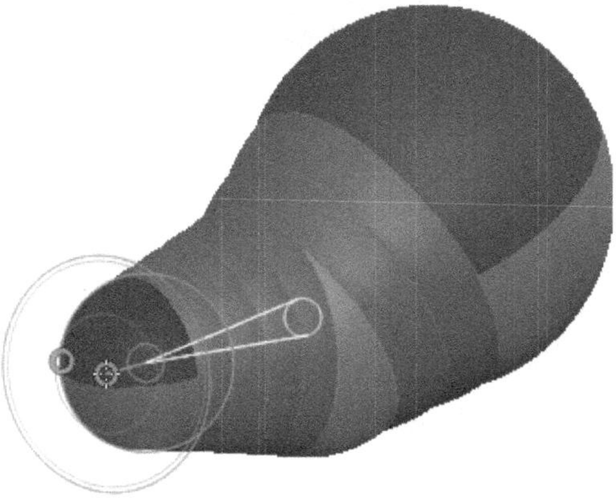

Figure 5-83 *ZSphere moved upward*

5. Create a new ZSphere on the topmost ZSphere to create an ear, refer to Figure 5-84. As the symmetry is activated in the X axis, a ZSphere is created on the opposite side also.

6. Create another ZSphere on the ZSphere created in Step 5, and move it upward using the **Move** button, refer to Figure 5-85.

7. Choose the **Draw** button from the top shelf and insert an editable ZSphere at the center of the ear by clicking on the linked ZSphere, refer to Figure 5-86. Next, choose the **Move** button from the top shelf, and move the newly inserted ZSphere slightly outward, as shown in Figure 5-87.

Figure 5-84 *ZSphere drawn for the ear*

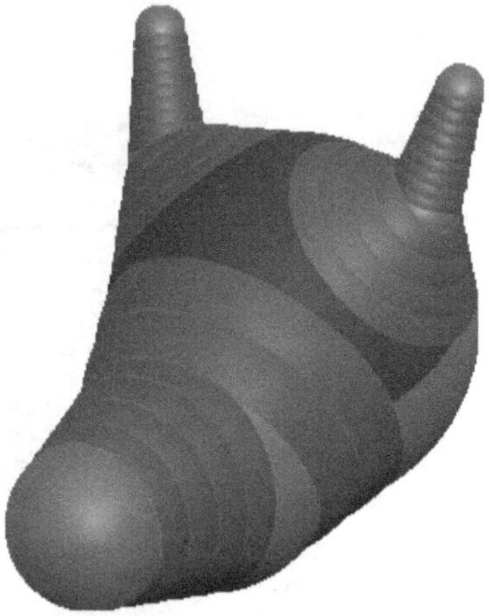

Figure 5-85 *ZSphere drawn and moved up*

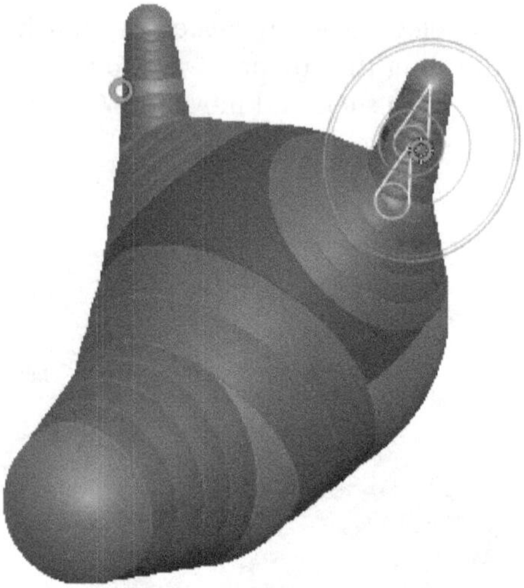

Figure 5-86 *ZSphere inserted at the centre*

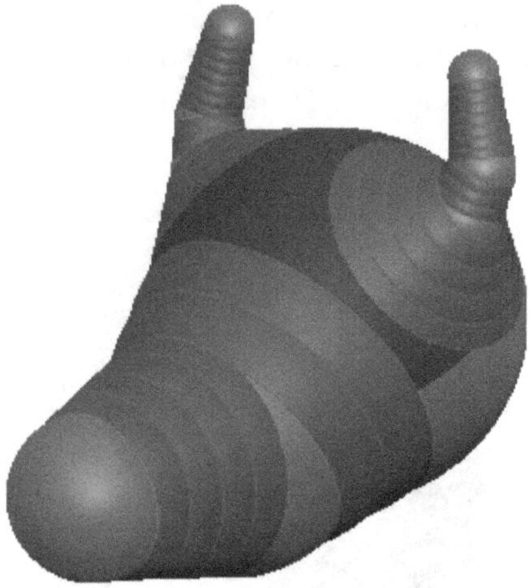

Figure 5-87 *ZSphere moved outward*

8. Choose the **Draw** button from the top shelf and create a new ZSphere for the neck of the deer, refer to Figure 5-88. Next, choose the **Move** button from the top shelf and move the newly created ZSphere outward, as shown in Figure 5-89.

9. Choose the **Draw** button from the top shelf and insert an editable ZSphere in the neck by clicking on the linked ZSphere, refer to Figure 5-90. Next, choose the **Scale** button from the top shelf, and scale down the inserted ZSphere, as shown in Figure 5-90.

10. Select the bottom ZSphere of the neck and scale it up to form the shape of the neck, refer to Figure 5-91.

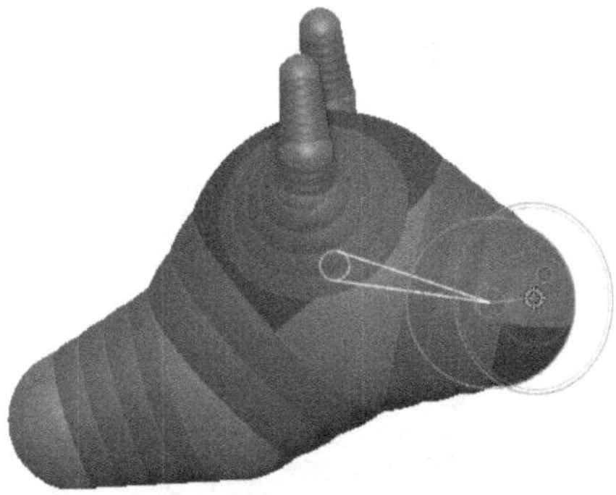

Figure 5-88 *ZSphere created for the neck*

Figure 5-89 *ZSphere moved outward*

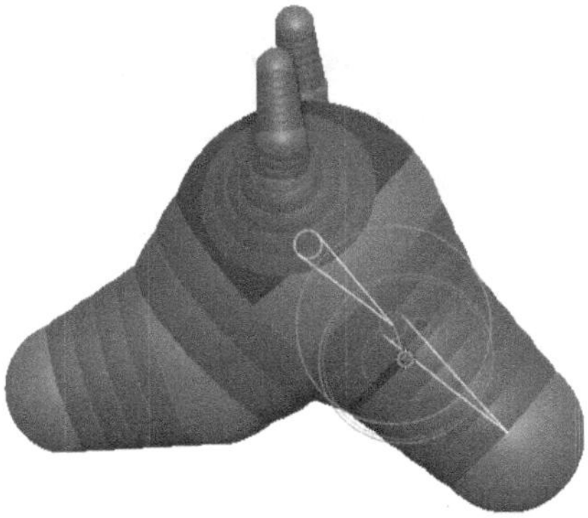

Figure 5-90 *ZSphere inserted in the neck and scaled down*

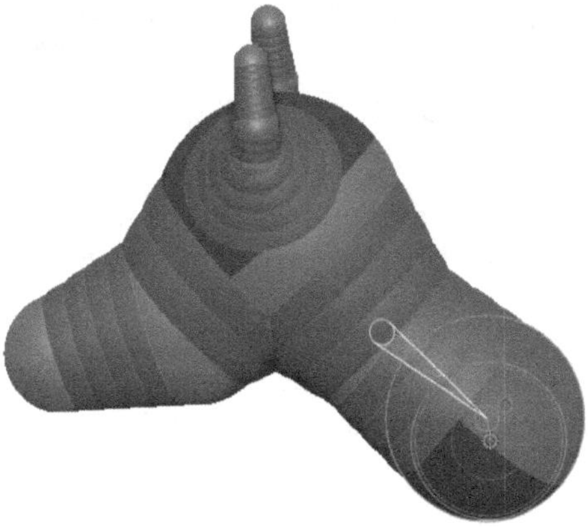

Figure 5-91 *ZSphere scaled up*

Creating the Antlers of the Stag Deer

In this section, you will create the antlers of the stag deer using ZSpheres.

1. Choose the **Draw** button from the top shelf and create a ZSphere on the head to form the base for the antler, refer to Figure 5-92.

2. Create a new ZSphere on the ZSphere created in Step 1. Next, choose the **Move** button and then move the newly created ZSphere up, refer to Figure 5-93.

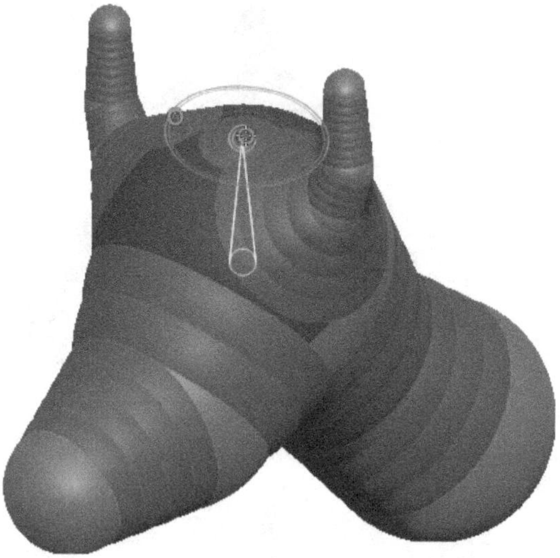

Figure 5-92 *ZSphere created for the antler*

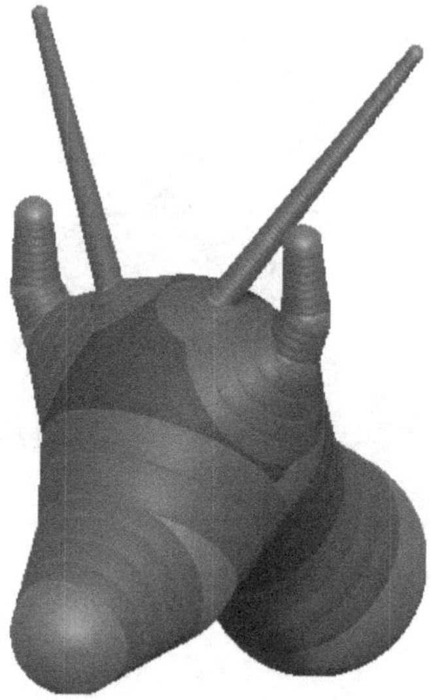

Figure 5-93 *ZSphere created and moved up*

3. Choose the **Draw** button from the top shelf and insert new ZSpheres on the linked sphere. Choose the **Move** button and move the inserted ZSpheres to form the structure, as shown in Figure 5-94.

4. Continue inserting more ZSpheres. Move and scale the inserted ZSpheres to create the structure of the antlers, as shown in Figure 5-95.

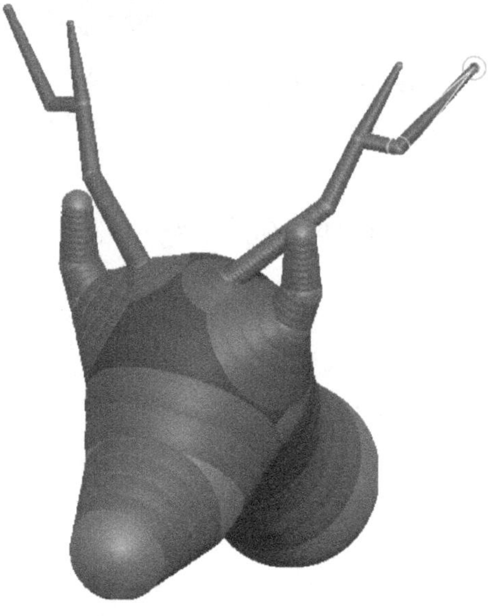

Figure 5-94 *New ZSpheres created and moved*

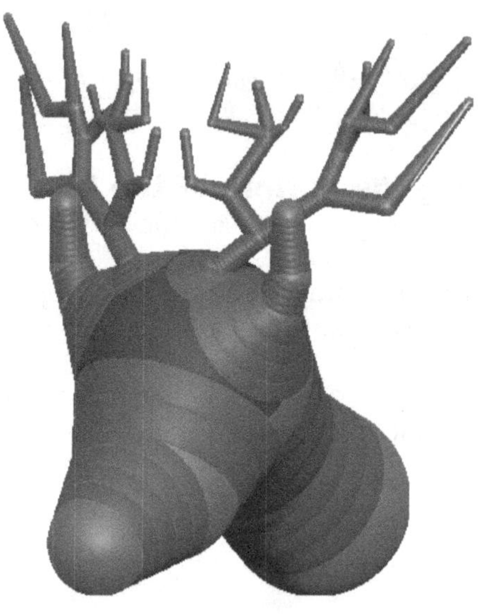

Figure 5-95 *Antlers of the deer created*

Saving the Model

In this section, you will save the file using the steps given next.

1. Choose the **Save As** button from the **Tool** palette; the **Save ZTool** dialog box is displayed. In this dialog box, browse to the location: *\Documents\ZBrushprojects\c05*.

2. Enter **c05tut2** in the **File name** edit box and then choose the **Save** button.

Self-Evaluation Test

Answer the following questions and then compare them to those given at the end of this chapter:

1. Which of the following sliders is used to increase or decrease the number of spans in the skinned mesh?

   (a) **Density** (b) **Proximity**
   (c) **G Radial** (d) **Max Twist**

2. Which of the following buttons is used to switch from the normal draw mode to the ZSketch mode?

   (a) **EditSketch** (b) **ShowSketch**
   (c) **Preview** (d) **Make Unified Skin**

3. The __________ brush is used to bulge out the surface of the strips of the linked spheres.

4. __________ is the process of adding bones and joints to an object.

5. The __________ brush is used to sketch the strips of ZSpheres on the canvas area.

6. The **Max Twist** slider is used to maintain the flow of geometry between the parent ZSphere and the intersecting ZSpheres that are created on its surface. (T/F)

7. On creating a ZSphere, the **Smooth 1** brush is displayed by default. (T/F)

8. The **SoftBind** slider is used to specify the level of binding between the underlying framework and sketched ZSpheres. (T/F)

9. The **Optimize** button is used to delete the unnecessary ZSpheres in the strips of ZSpheres that are not visible in the canvas. (T/F)

Review Questions

Answer the following questions:

1. Which of the following keys is used to view the skinned mesh in the canvas?

   (a) S (b) M
   (c) A (d) V

2. Which of the following hotkeys is used to switch from the normal draw mode to the ZSketch mode?

   (a) SHIFT+Z (b) SHIFT+D
   (c) CTRL+SHIFT+Z (d) SHIFT+A

3. In which of the following subpalettes is the **Bind Mesh** button located?

   (a) **ZSketch** (b) **Rigging**
   (c) **Adaptive Skin** (d) **Unified Skin**

4. ZSpheres are most commonly used in __________ modeling.

5. __________ skinning is used to convert a ZSphere framework into a polygon mesh in such a way that the polymesh consists of a large number of polygons that are equal in size.

6. The __________ button is used to switch to the classic skinning technique that was available in the ZBrush 3 version.

7. The term **Min Dist** stands for __________.

8. If you want to delete a ZSphere, press and hold the SHIFT key and then click on the ZSphere that you want to delete. (T/F)

9. If the value set in the **Density** slider is higher, the skinned mesh will contain more number of polygons and will be smoother. (T/F)

EXERCISES

The output of the models used in the following exercises can be accessed by downloading the *c05_ZBrush_2022_exr.zip* file from *www.cadcim.com*. The path of the file is as follows: *Textbooks > Animation and Visual Effects > ZBrush > ZBrush 2022: A Comprehensive Guide*.

Exercise 1

Create the model of a tree using ZSpheres, as shown in Figure 5-96.

(Expected time: 30 min)

Figure 5-96 *Model of a tree*

Exercise 2

Create the scene shown in Figure 5-97 using ZSpheres and different subtools.

(Expected time: 30 min)

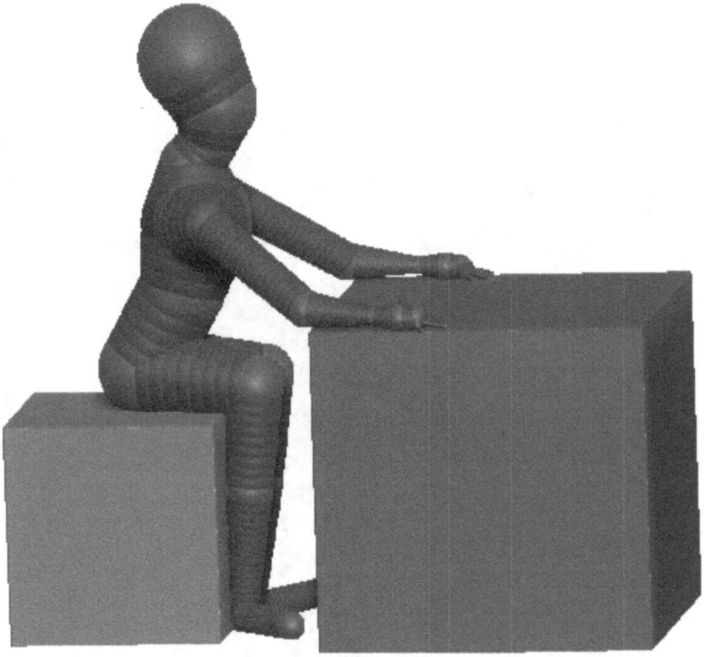

Figure 5-97 *Scene to be created for Exercise 2*

Answers to Self-Evaluation Test

1. c, **2.** a, **3. Bulge**, **4.** Rigging, **5. Armature**, **6.** F, **7.** F, **8.** T, **9.** T

Chapter 6

DynaMesh, NanoMesh, and ZRemesher

Learning Objectives

After completing this chapter, you will be able to:

- *Work with DynaMesh*
- *Work with ZRemesher*
- *Create different models using the DynaMesh tool*

INTRODUCTION

In ZBrush, you can create various types of models using different techniques. The models created in ZBrush have extremely high level of details that cannot be achieved in other modeling software applications. ZBrush uses brush based approach to add details to a model. Different studios such as Luma Pictures, Id Software, and Meteor Studio have used ZBrush for character creation. For instance, the characters Davy Jones in the movie Pirates of the Caribbean and Na'vi in the movie Avatar were created with ZBrush. In this chapter, you will learn about Dynamesh and ZRemesher that will help you in creating high detail models.

DynaMesh

DynaMesh modeling is similar to clay modeling. In clay modeling, you can expand the existing lump of clay by either stretching it or by adding new lumps to it. After stretching the clay, the actual consistency of the clay remains the same. DynaMesh uses the same approach for modeling. After converting any mesh into DynaMesh, the uniform polygon distribution of the mesh is maintained, irrespective of the stretching and deformation done in the mesh. You can convert any of the ZBrush primitives into DynaMesh. Besides this, you can also convert any existing geometry into DynaMesh. However, it is recommended to convert a mesh into DynaMesh during the initial stage of sculpting. DynaMesh is used to create a base mesh in ZBrush. It enables you to freely pull or push the polygons in the mesh without creating distortions in the geometry. It is very useful for creating the base mesh before adding details to it. On converting a distorted mesh into DynaMesh, you will notice that the polygons are distributed uniformly.

DynaMesh AREA

The **DynaMesh** area is displayed only when an object is created in the canvas and is converted into a polymesh. The different buttons and sliders of the **DynaMesh** tool can be accessed by expanding the **DynaMesh** area in the **Geometry** subpalette of the **Tool** palette, refer to Figure 6-1. The different buttons and sliders in this area are discussed next.

DynaMesh

The **DynaMesh** button is used to make the distribution of polygons in a mesh uniform. To distribute polygons uniformly in a mesh, create a sphere in the canvas and then choose the **Edit** button from the top shelf. Also, convert the sphere into polymesh by choosing the **Make PolyMesh 3D** button from the **Tool** palette. Next, choose the **PolyF** button in the **Transform** palette to view the distribution of polygons. Choose the Current Brush button from the left shelf; a flyout will be displayed. In this flyout, choose the **Move** brush and then by using this brush, deform the sphere, as shown in Figure 6-2. On doing this, you will notice that the polygons in the sphere have stretched. Next, choose the **DynaMesh** button from the **Geometry** subpalette; the stretched polygons will be uniformly distributed in the sphere, refer to Figure 6-3.

***Figure 6-1** The **DynaMesh** area in the **Geometry** subpalette*

After converting a mesh into DynaMesh, you can sculpt it using different brushes. The sculpting will again make the polygons stretched. To eliminate the stretching of the polygons and restore the uniform geometry distribution, press and hold the CTRL key and then drag the cursor on the open area of the canvas; the uniform distribution of polygons will be restored. You can remove any level of stretching by using the **DynaMesh** button.

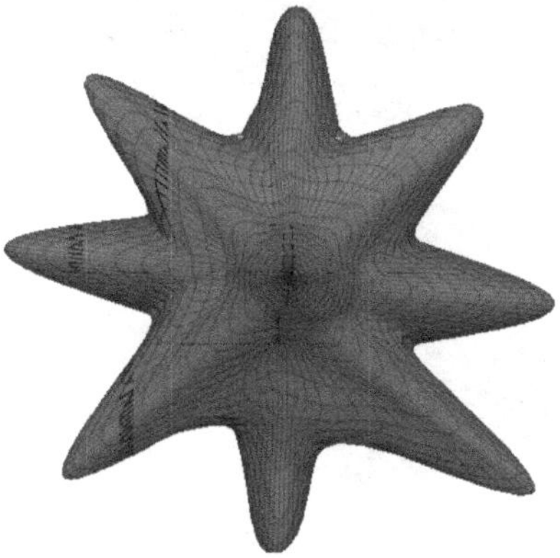

*Figure 6-2 The sphere deformed using the **Move** brush*

Figure 6-3 The stretched polygons distributed uniformly

Groups

The **Groups** button is used to split a mesh into separate pieces depending upon the number of poly groups in the mesh. If this button is not chosen, the mesh will not split into groups. To split the mesh into separate pieces, consider a sphere in the canvas and then choose the **Edit** button from the top shelf. Next, convert the sphere into a polymesh by choosing the **Make PolyMesh3D** button from the **Tool** palette. Also, make sure that the **PolyF** button is chosen in the **Transform** palette. Next, expand the **DynaMesh** area in the **Geometry** subpalette of the **Tool** palette and then choose the **DynaMesh** button; the sphere will become smoother. Next, choose **Insert-IMM** from the **Brush** tab of the **LightBox** browser located at the top of the canvas by double-clicking on it; the list of brushes is displayed. Now, choose the **InsertSphere** brush from the list. Next, press and hold the left mouse button and drag the cursor on the sphere; a new sphere is inserted in the existing sphere, refer to Figure 6-4. You will notice that the newly created sphere will be of different color. Next, press and hold the CTRL key and then drag the cursor on the empty area of the canvas twice; the new sphere will merge with the existing sphere and the color of both of them will become same, refer to Figure 6-5.

You can also merge the meshes by using the **Groups** button, but at the same time it will consider each mesh as a separate group that can be modified individually. To understand the working of this button, choose the **Groups** button from the **DynaMesh** area. Next, insert a cylinder into the existing geometry by using the **InsertCylinder** brush, refer to Figure 6-6. Next, press and hold the CTRL key and drag the cursor on the empty area of the canvas twice; the cylinder will merge with the existing sphere but its color will be different than that of the existing geometry, refer to Figure 6-7. The different color shows that the cylinder created is in a separate group and can be manipulated separately.

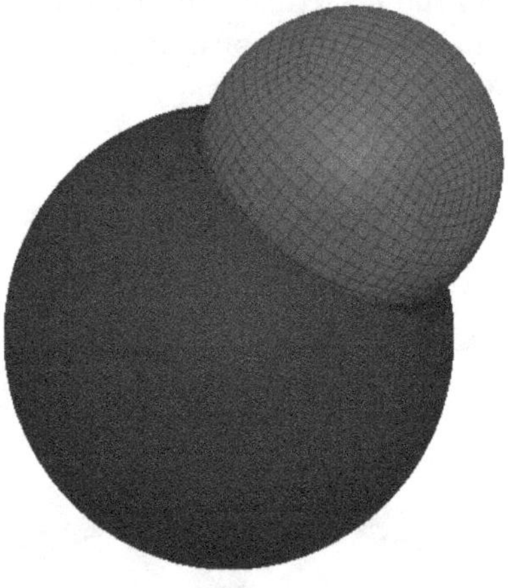

Figure 6-4 *A sphere inserted using the* ***InsertSphere*** *brush*

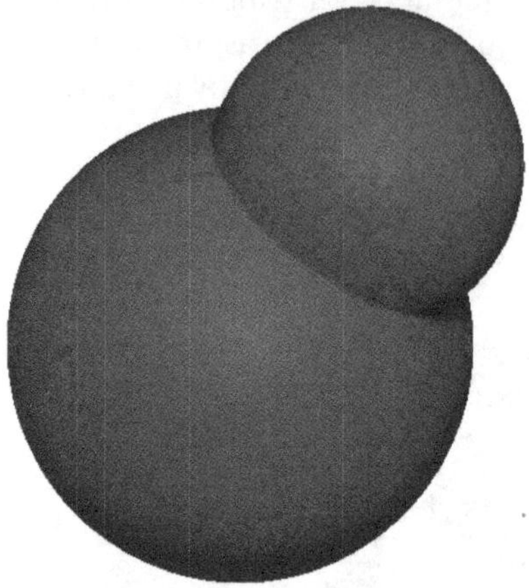

Figure 6-5 *Inserted sphere merged with the existing sphere*

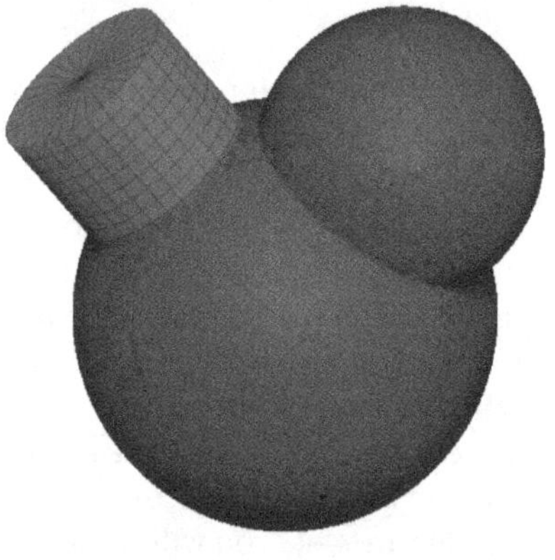

Figure 6-6 *Cylinder inserted using the* ***InsertCylinder*** *brush*

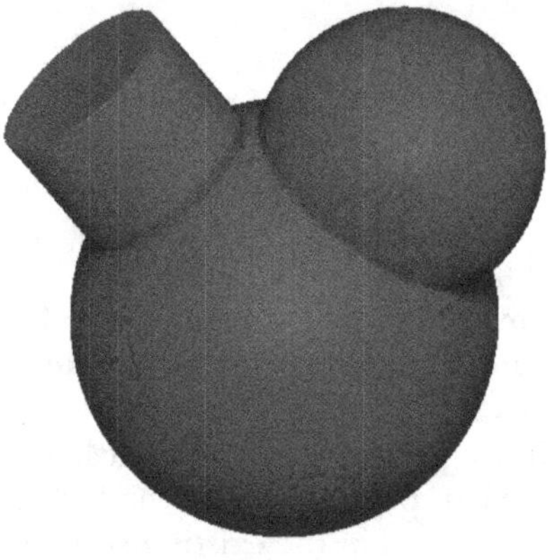

Figure 6-7 *New group created for the inserted cylinder*

To manipulate the newly created cylinder separately, press and hold the CTRL+SHIFT keys and click on the cylinder; only the cylinder will be displayed in the canvas and rest of the geometry becomes invisible. To display the entire geometry, again press and hold the CTRL+SHIFT keys and click anywhere in the canvas area. You can use different insert brushes to merge any mesh with an existing mesh. The **Groups** button will ensure that the inserted geometry will be in a separate group and can be manipulated separately.

You can also use the slice brushes to create groups in a mesh. To create groups in a mesh, consider the sphere in the canvas. Next, convert it into a polymesh. Make sure you choose the **PolyF** button in the **Transforms** palette.

Choose the Current Brush button from the left shelf; a flyout will be displayed. In this flyout, choose the **SliceCurve** brush; a message box will be displayed prompting you to press

CTRL+SHIFT to activate this brush. Press and hold CTRL+SHIFT and then drag the cursor on the surface of the sphere to create different groups, refer to Figure 6-8. Release the left mouse button; the color of the selected area will change and it will split into a separate group.

Choose the **Groups** button in the **DynaMesh** area. Next, choose the **DynaMesh** button; the DynaMesh model of the sphere containing different groups will be displayed. Next, press and hold the CTRL key and then drag the cursor on the open area of the canvas twice; the sphere will split and each group will be clearly visible. Choose the **PolyF** button from the **Transform** palette; the groups will be displayed, as shown in Figure 6-9. These different groups can be manipulated separately by pressing and holding the CTRL+SHIFT keys and clicking on the group that you want to manipulate.

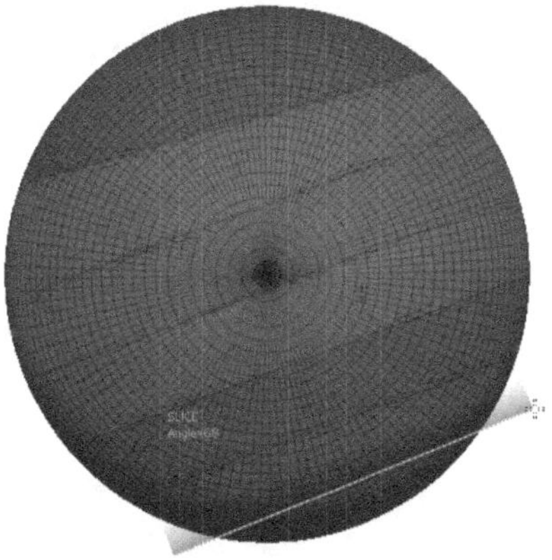

Figure 6-8 *Groups created using the* ***SliceCurve*** *brush*

Figure 6-9 *Split groups visible in the sphere*

Polish

The **Polish** button is used to polish the surface consisting of sharp edges. If this button is not chosen while converting a model into a DynaMesh, the resulting DynaMesh model will be smoothened and the edges present in it will not be sharpened. However, if this button is chosen, the resulting DynaMesh model will be smoothened, but its edges will be sharpened.

To understand the working of this button, choose the Current Tool button in the **Tool** palette; a flyout will be displayed. In this flyout, choose the **PolyMesh3D** primitive and create it in the canvas, refer to Figure 6-10. Choose the **Edit** button from the top shelf and convert the primitive into a polymesh. Next, choose the **DynaMesh** button in the **DynaMesh** area of the **Geometry** subpalette; the primitive will be converted into a DynaMesh, refer to Figure 6-11. You will notice that the edges in the DynaMesh will not be sharpened. Next, press CTRL+Z to undo the changes. Now, choose the **Polish** button and then choose the **DynaMesh** button from the **DynaMesh** area of the **Geometry** subpalette, refer to Figure 6-12; the primitive will be converted into DynaMesh, and this time the edges will be sharpened and the corners will be smoothened, refer to Figure 6-13.

*Figure 6-10 The **PolyMesh3D** primitive created in the canvas*

*Figure 6-11 The **PolyMesh3D** primitive converted into DynaMesh*

*Figure 6-12 The **DynaMesh** and **Polish** buttons chosen*

Figure 6-13 The primitive converted into DynaMesh

Blur

The **Blur** slider is used to control the level of smoothness and blurring in the edges of a primitive when it is converted into DynaMesh. Higher the value of the **Blur** parameter, more blurred the edges of the resulting DynaMesh will be. To understand how to set the smoothness and blurriness of a primitive using this slider, consider a **PolyMesh3D** primitive in the canvas. Choose the **Edit** button from the top shelf to convert the primitive into polymesh. Next, in the **DynaMesh** area of the **Geometry** subpalette, set the value of the **Blur** slider to **4**. Now, choose the **DynaMesh** button; the DynaMesh will be displayed, refer to Figure 6-14. Press CTRL+Z to undo the changes done previously. Set the value of the **Blur** slider to **100**; the object will be displayed, as shown in Figure 6-15.

Figure 6-14 *The **DynaMesh** with the value of **Blur** slider set to **4***

Figure 6-15 *The **DynaMesh** with the value of **Blur** slider set to **100***

Project

The **Project** button is used to retain the existing details in the model when it is converted into DynaMesh. By default, this button is chosen. To retain the existing details in the model, make sure the desired model is displayed in the canvas. For example, load the **DemoHead.ZTL** file from the **Tool** tab of the **LightBox** browser, and create it in the canvas, refer to Figure 6-16. Next, choose the **Project** button from the **DynaMesh** area to deactivate it and then choose the **DynaMesh** button from the **DynaMesh** area of the **Geometry** subpalette; a message box asking you to freeze the subdivision levels will be displayed, as shown in Figure 6-17. Choose the **YES** button from this message box; the *DemoHead.ZTL* file will be displayed at its lowest subdivision level. Next, choose the **DynaMesh** button; the DynaMesh model of the *DemoHead.ZTL* file will be displayed. In this model, the detail in the facial features will be lost, refer to Figure 6-18. Next, press CTRL+Z to undo the changes. Now, choose the **Project** button and then choose the **DynaMesh** button from the **DynaMesh** area of the **Geometry** subpalette; the *DemoHead.ZTL* file will be converted into DynaMesh, but this time the level of details in the facial features will be retained, refer to Figure 6-19.

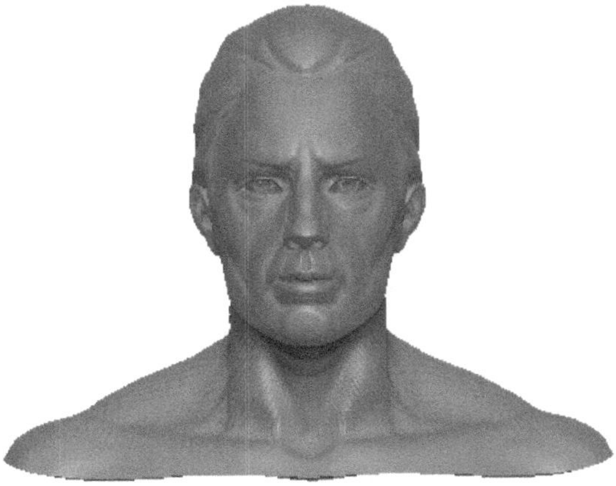

Figure 6-16 *The DemoHead.ZTL file created in the canvas*

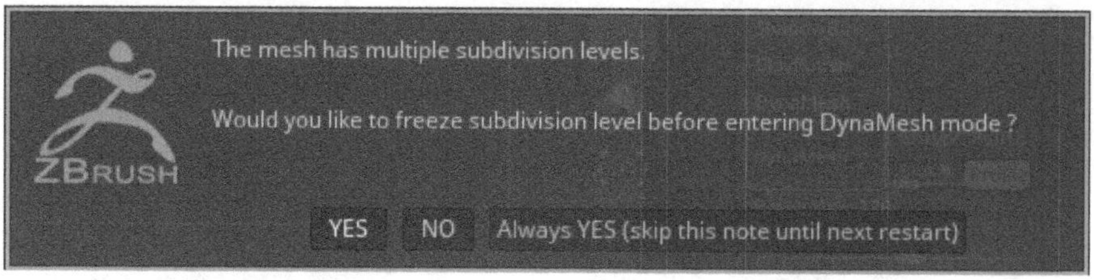

***Figure 6-17** The message box displayed on choosing the **DynaMesh** button*

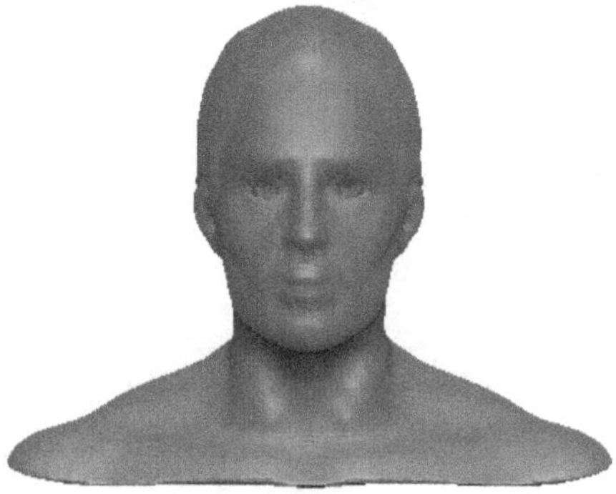

***Figure 6-18** The details lost on choosing the **DynaMesh** button*

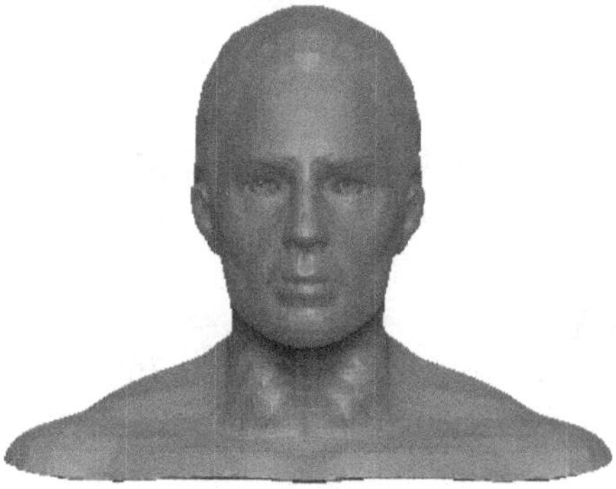

***Figure 6-19** The details retained on choosing the **DynaMesh** button with the **Project** button*

Resolution

The **Resolution** slider is used to control the number of polygons in DynaMesh. If the value of this slider is low, the DynaMesh will contain less number of polygons. To control the number of polygons, make sure the model is displayed in the canvas. For example, load the *Dog.ZTL* file from the **LightBox** browser, and create it in the canvas. Next, choose the **DynaMesh** button from the **DynaMesh** area of the **Geometry** subpalette; the DynaMesh will be displayed with the default value of the **Resolution** slider.

Choose the **PolyF** button from the **Transform** palette to view the polygons in the DynaMesh, refer to Figure 6-20. Next, press CTRL+Z to undo the changes. Now, set the value of the **Resolution** slider to **1000** and then choose the **DynaMesh** button; the number of polygons in the DynaMesh will increase, refer to Figure 6-21. Note that with the help of this slider, you can retain the detail in a model while converting it into DynaMesh. For example, if you refer to Figure 6-22, you can notice that, as the value of the **Resolution** slider has been set to **8** before choosing the **DynaMesh** button, all the detail in the *Dog.ZTL* model are lost. However, in Figure 6-23, as the value of the **Resolution** slider has been set to **1024**, all the details in the *Dog.ZTL* file are retained.

*Figure 6-20 Dynamesh created with the default value of **Resolution** slider*

*Figure 6-21 Dynamesh created with the value of **Resolution** slider set to **1000***

*Figure 6-22 The detail lost on setting the value of **Resolution** slider to **8***

*Figure 6-23 The detail retained on setting the value of **Resolution** slider to **1024***

Picker

The **Picker** button is used to select the density from the specific area. To choose the number of polygons, make sure the model is displayed in the canvas. For example, load the *Dog.ZTL* file from the **LightBox** browser, and create it in the canvas. Next, choose the **DynaMesh** area; parameters will be displayed in the**Dynamesh** area.

Choose the **PolyF** button from the **Transform** palette to view the polygons in the DynaMesh. Now, make sure the default value of the **Resolution** slider is set to **128**, refer to Figure 6-25 and then choose and drag the **Picker** button to model in the viewport. Notice that the value in the **Resolution** slider changes as you drag the button, refer to Figure 6-25. With the help of this slider, you can retain the detail in a model while converting it into DynaMesh. In Figure 6-25, the value of the **Resolution** slider is set to **48** and then choose the **Dynamesh** button; all the details in the *Dog.ZTL* model are lost, as the **Resolution** slider value is decreased, refer to Figure 6-26. More the value in the **Resolution** slider, more will be the details on the model after choosing the **Dynamesh** button.

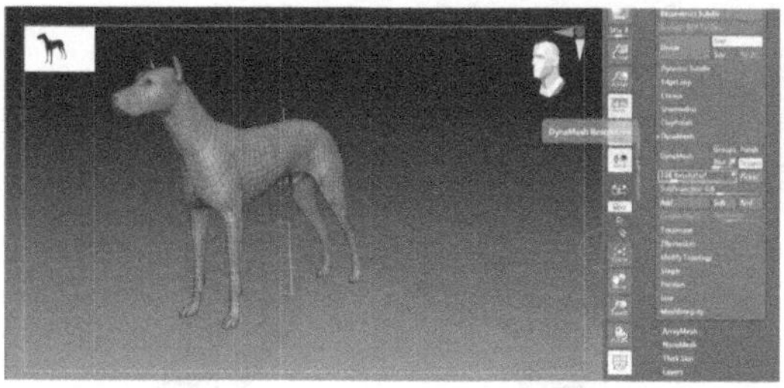

Figure 6-24 *The default value of the* ***Resolution*** *slider set to* ***128***

Figure 6-25 *Dragging* ***Picker*** *on model to set the value of the* ***Resolution*** *slider to* ***48***

Figure 6-26 *The details lost on setting the value of the* ***Resolution*** *slider to* ***48***

Sub Projection

The **Sub Projection** slider will control the placement of geometry when the **Project** button in **DynaMesh** subpalette is chosen. A higher value in the **Sub Projection** slider will apply more geometry to the edges of the mesh.

Add

The **Add** button is used to merge the intersecting meshes into an existing DynaMesh. The merged mesh could either be a new inserted mesh or the expanded geometry that intersects the surface of the mesh. To merge the intersecting meshes into an existing DynaMesh, consider a sphere in the canvas. Convert a sphere into polymesh and choose the **DynaMesh** button. Next, choose the Current Brush button in the left shelf; a flyout will be displayed. In this flyout, choose the **InsertHRing** brush. Next, drag the cursor on the surface of the sphere, a ring will be created on the surface of the sphere, as shown in Figure 6-27. Make sure the ring intersects the surface of the sphere.

You will notice that the color of the sphere will change and a mask will be applied on it. To remove the mask from its surface, press and hold the CTRL key and drag the cursor on the empty area of the canvas. Next, choose the **Add** button; the ring will be merged with the sphere, refer to Figure 6-28.

Sub

The **Sub** button is used to subtract an intersecting mesh from the existing DynaMesh to create holes in the surface. To understand the working of this button, consider a sphere in the canvas. After converting the sphere into a polymesh, choose the **DynaMesh** button. Next, choose **Insert-IMM** from the **Brush** tab of the **LightBox** browser located at the top of the canvas by double-clicking on it; the list of brushes is displayed. Now, choose the **InsertCylinder** brush from the list. Press and hold the ALT key and drag the cursor on the surface of the sphere; a cylinder will be created on its surface, as shown in Figure 6-29. Instead of pressing the ALT key, you can also choose the **Zsub** button from the top shelf.

Figure 6-27 *The ring created on the surface of the sphere*

Figure 6-28 *The ring merged with the sphere*

You will notice that the inserted cylinder will not be properly visible in the canvas. To make it visible, expand the **Display Properties** subpalette in the **Tool** palette. Choose the **Double** button from this subpalette, as shown in Figure 6-30; the complete cylinder will be displayed in the canvas, refer to Figure 6-31. If required, move the cylinder at the place where you want to create the hole. You will notice that the color of the sphere will change and a mask will be applied on it. To remove the mask from its surface, press and hold the CTRL key and drag the cursor on the open area of the canvas. Next, choose the **Sub** button; a hole will be created on the surface of the sphere, refer to Figure 6-32.

Figure 6-29 *The cylinder created on the surface of the sphere with the ALT key pressed*

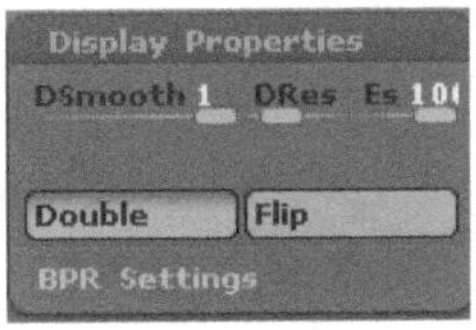

Figure 6-30 *The **Double** button chosen from the **Display Properties** subpalette*

Figure 6-31 The complete cylinder displayed

Figure 6-32 A hole created on the sphere

And

The **And** button is used to retain the intersecting geometry between two meshes and delete the remaining geometry. To understand the working of this button, consider a sphere in the canvas. After converting the sphere into a polymesh, choose the **DynaMesh** button. Next, choose **Insert-IMM** from the **Brush** tab of the **LightBox** browser located at the top of the canvas by double-clicking on it; the list of brushes are displayed. Now, choose the **InsertSphere** brush from the list.

Press and hold the ALT key and drag the cursor on the surface of the sphere; a new sphere will be created. You will notice that the inserted sphere is not properly visible in the canvas. To make it visible, expand the **Display Properties** subpalette in the **Tool** palette. Choose the **Double** button from this subpalette; the complete sphere will be displayed in the canvas, refer to Figure 6-33. You will notice that the color of the sphere will change and a mask will be applied on it. To remove the mask from its surface, press and hold the CTRL key and drag the cursor on the open area of the canvas. Next, choose the **And** button; the intersecting geometry will be retained and the remaining geometry will be deleted, refer to Figure 6-34.

Figure 6-33 The complete sphere displayed

Figure 6-34 Intersecting geometry retained

Create Shell

The **Create Shell** button is used to create a hole in the surface of a DynaMesh by inserting a mesh in it. To understand the working of this button, consider a sphere in the canvas. After converting the sphere into a polymesh, choose the **DynaMesh** button. Next, choose **Insert-IMM** from the **Brush** tab of the **LightBox** browser located at the top of the canvas by double-clicking on it; the list of brushes is displayed. Now, choose the **InsertCube** brush from the list. Press the ALT key and create the cube on the surface of the sphere. You will notice that the inserted cube is not properly visible in the canvas. To make it visible, expand the **Display Properties** subpalette in the **Tool** palette. Choose the **Double** button from this subpalette; the complete cube will be displayed in the canvas, refer to Figure 6-35.

Press and hold the CTRL key and drag the cursor on the open area of the canvas to remove the mask from the sphere. Next, choose the **Create Shell** button; a hole will be created, refer to Figure 6-36.

Figure 6-35 *The cube created on the surface of the sphere*

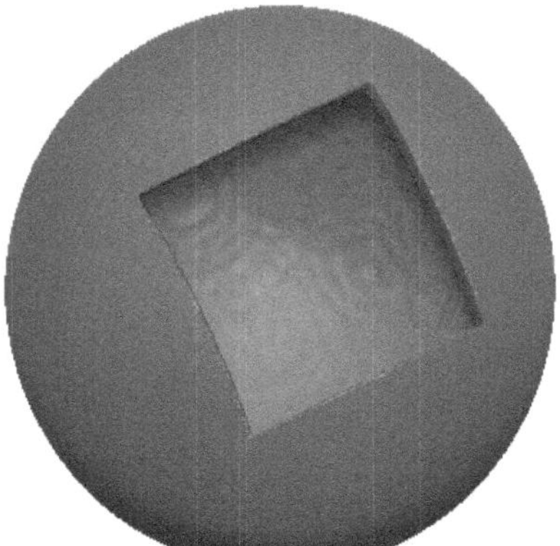

Figure 6-36 *The hole created on the surface of the sphere*

Thickness

The **Thickness** slider is used to control the depth of the hole created on the surface of the DynaMesh using the **Create Shell** button. The higher the value of the slider, the lower will be the depth of the hole.

ZRemesher

ZRemesher is used for remeshing or retopologizing the mesh. ZRemesher is used to create a new topology for the selected subtool that consists of millions of polygons. This enables you to control the flow of polygons in a mesh as per your requirement. Besides this, ZRemesher also enables you to convert a model with millions of polygons into a model with less number of polygons. You can project all the details from the high polygon mesh into a newly created mesh. You can use ZRemesher on polymesh models, DynaMesh, or ZSphere adaptive skin. If you want to use it on a primitive model, you need to convert it into a polymesh. The different buttons and sliders of ZRemesher can be accessed by expanding the **ZRemesher** area in the **Geometry** subpalette of the **Tool** palette, refer to Figure 6-37. These buttons and sliders are discussed next.

ZRemesher Button

The **ZRemesher** button is used to create a new polygon mesh and control the flow of edge with specific polycount. The change in topology is also referred to as retopologizing. If a 3D object consists of stretched polygons, the polygons become equal sized on choosing this button. To understand the working of this button, consider a *Gear3D* primitive in the canvas, refer to Figure 6-38. Next, choose the **Edit** button from the top shelf and then choose the **Make PolyMesh3D** button from the **Tool** palette; the primitive object will be converted into a polymesh.

Choose the **PolyF** button from the **Transform** palette to view the distribution of polygons, refer to Figure 6-35. In this figure, you will notice that the polygons are stretched. Next, expand the **Geometry** subpalette. In this subpalette, expand the **ZRemesher** area and then choose the **ZRemesher** button to change the distribution of polygons. This process will take some time and an orange colored bar showing the status of this process will be displayed below the palettes, refer to Figure 6-39. This status line disappears after some time and the stretched polygons become equal sized, refer to Figure 6-40.

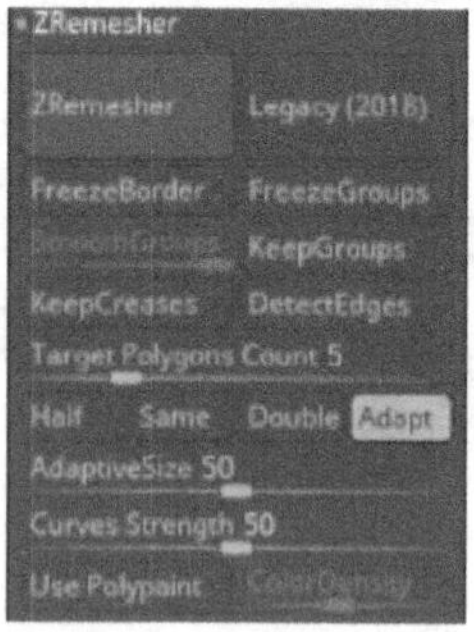

***Figure 6-37** Different buttons and sliders in the **ZRemesher** area*

***Figure 6-38** The Gear3D primitive created in the canvas*

***Figure 6-39** The orange colored bar showing the status*

ZRemesher can be used with the **ZRemesherGuides** brush to create a topology of your choice. This brush enables you to draw curves on the surface of an object to guide the flow of polygons according to the curves. To understand the working of the **ZRemesherGuides** brush, make sure the model is displayed in the canvas. For example, load the *DemoHead.ZTL* file from the **Tool** tab of the **LightBox** browser and create it in the canvas. Choose the **Edit** button from the top shelf. Next, choose the **PolyF** button from the **Transform** palette to view the distribution of polygons, refer to Figure 6-41.

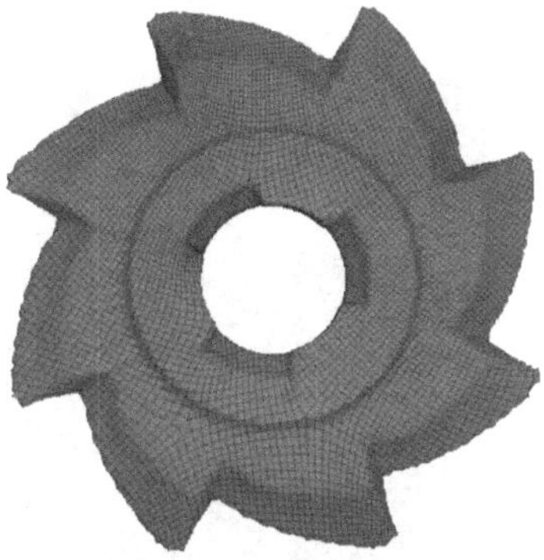

*Figure 6-40 Flow of polygons changed on choosing the **ZRemesher** button*

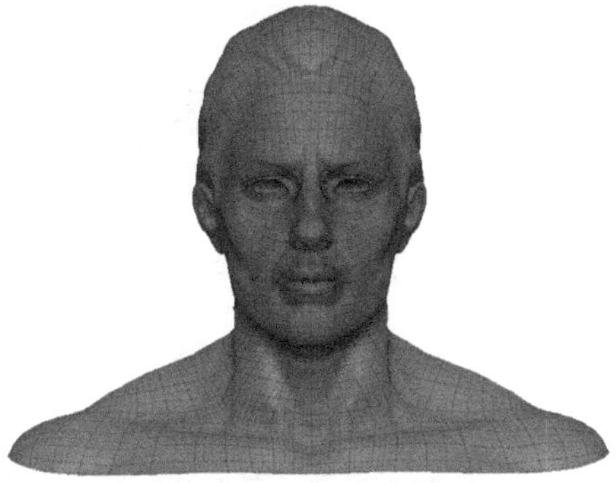

Figure 6-41 The DemoHead.ZTL model created in the canvas

Choose the Current Brush button from the left shelf; a flyout containing different types of brushes will be displayed. In this flyout, choose the **ZRemesherGuides** brush. Next, drag the cursor on the surface of the model to create curves on the surface of the model, refer to Figure 6-42. Continue creating more curves on the face of the model to create a path for the flow of polygons, refer to Figure 6-43. Next, choose the **ZRemesher** button from the **Geometry** subpalette; the flow of polygons will change after some time, refer to Figure 6-44.

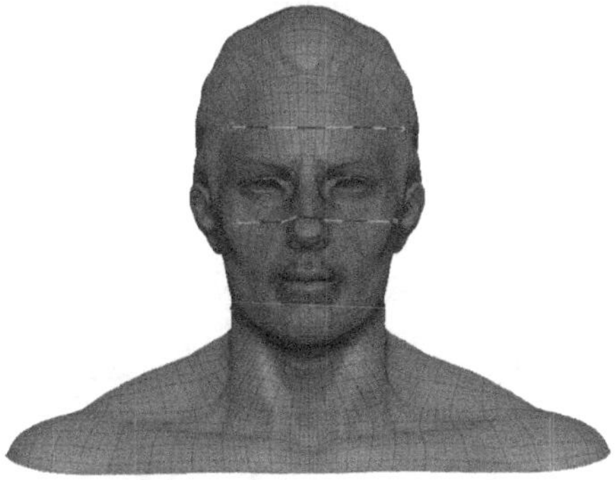

*Figure 6-42 Guide curves created using the **ZRemesherGuides** brush*

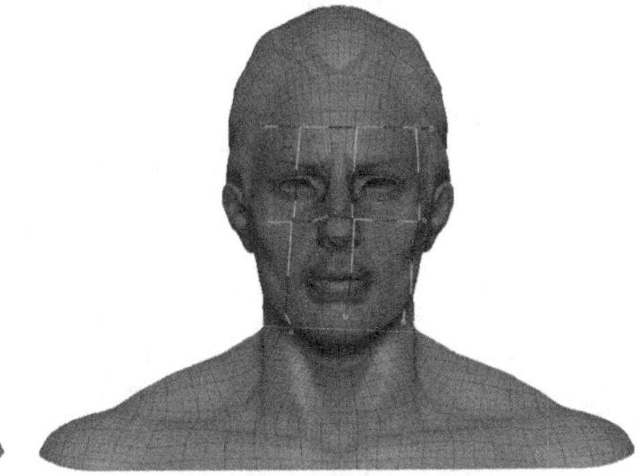

Figure 6-43 Guide curves created for the flow of polygons

FreezeBorder

The **FreezeBorder** button is used to maintain the same vertex numbers and their positions along the openings of the mesh while using the **ZRemesher** button. To maintain the same vertex numbers and their positions, make sure the desired model is displayed in the canvas. For example, load the *Dog.ZTL* file from the **Tool** tab of the **LightBox** browser and create it in the canvas. Next, choose the **Edit** button from the top shelf. Zoom in the canvas such that you can view the head of the model. Next, choose the **PolyF** button from the **Transform** palette to view the distribution of polygons, as shown in Figure 6-45.

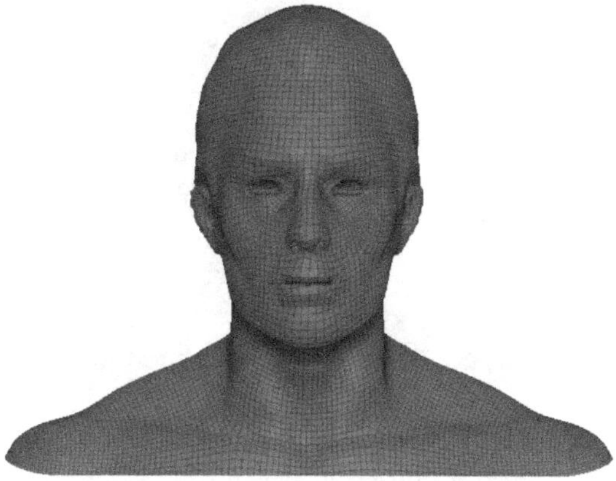

Figure 6-44 Flow of the polygons changed according to the guide curves

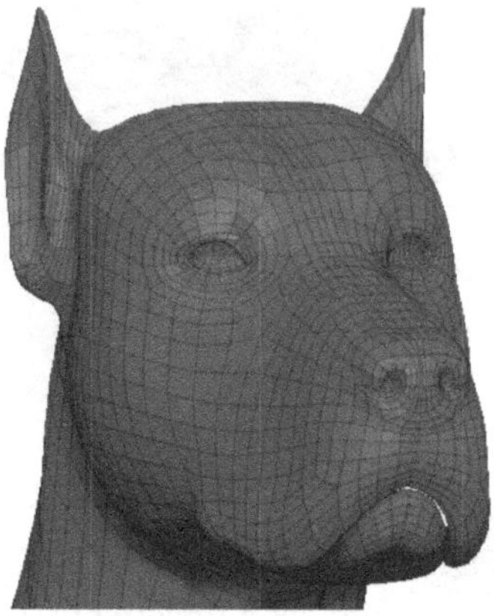

Figure 6-45 Polygons in the Dog.ZTL

Choose the **ZRemesher** button in the **Geometry** subpalette; the model will be retopologized after some time and the details around the nose and mouth will be lost, refer to Figure 6-46. Next, press CTRL+Z to undo the changes made previously. Choose the **FreezeBorde**r button and then choose the **ZRemesher** button; the model will be retopologized after some time. Note that the vertex numbers and their positions along the mesh's openings are maintained, refer to Figure 6-47.

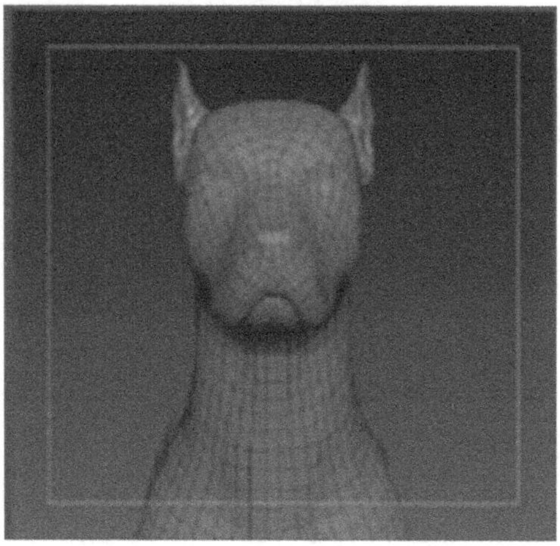

*Figure 6-46 Details lost on choosing the **ZRemesher** button*

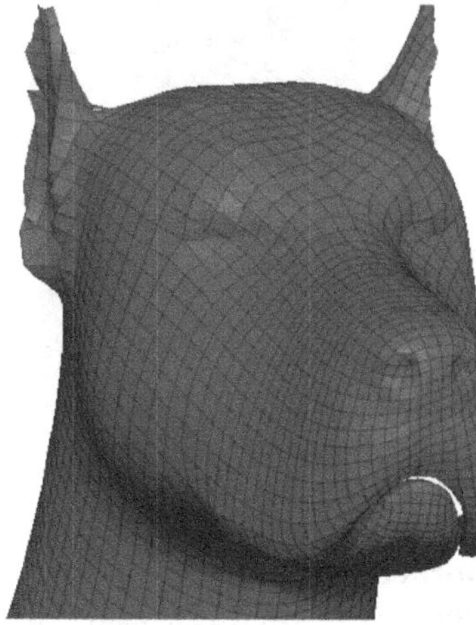

*Figure 6-47 Details around nose and mouth retained on choosing the **AutoMask** button*

FreezeGroup

The **FreezeGroup** button is used to retopolize each polygroup independently and keep their borders frozen.

KeepGroups

The **KeepGroups** button is used to retain the existing boundaries of each of the model's PolyGroups to reproduce those groups in the retopologized models. This option alters the topology while keeping the shape of the boundary. This results in a better topology flow. The **SmoothGroups Border** slider is active when the **KeepGroups** buttton is chosen.

Target Polygons Count

The **Target Polygons Count** slider is used to define the number of the polygons that will be present in the retopologized model. This slider enables you to increase or decrease the number of polygons in a model. If the value of this slider is set to **1**, the polygon count in the retopologized model will be equal to 1000. Figures 6-48 and 6-49 show the retopologized models of the *Dog.ZTL* file with the values in the **Target Polygons Count** slider set to **1** and **30**, respectively.

Figure 6-48 *Retopologized model with the* ***Target Polygons Count*** *slider set to* ***1***

Figure 6-49 *Retopologized model with the* ***Target Polygons Count*** *slider set to* ***30***

Half

The **Half** button is used to reduce the polygon count in a retopologized model to half of its original value. For instance, if a model contains 5000 polygons, its retopologized model will contain approximately 2500 polygons. The polygon count in a model can be viewed by hovering the cursor on its thumbnail in the **Tool** palette, refer to Figure 6-50. In this figure, you will notice that the number of polygons in the model of *Dog.ZTL* file is equal to 7984. Deactivate the **Adapt** button. On choosing the **Half** button before choosing the **ZRemesher** button, the polygon count in the retopologized model will become equal to 4419, refer to Figure 6-51.

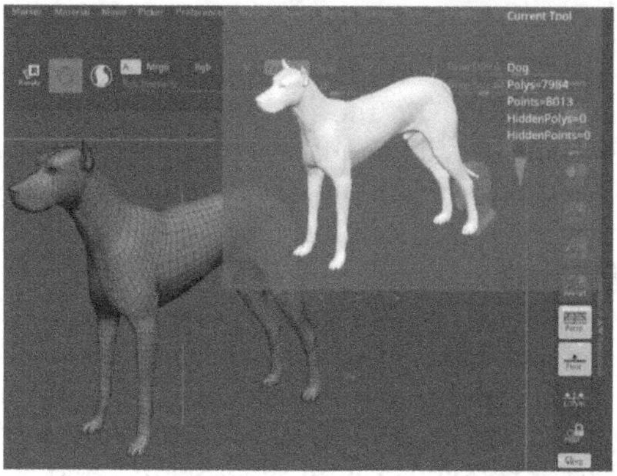

Figure 6-50 *The number of polygons equal to* ***7984***

Same

The **Same** button is used to keep the number of polygons in the retopologized model same as that of the original model. On choosing this button along with the **ZRemesher** button, the topology of the model will change but the polygon count in the retopologized model will remain the same.

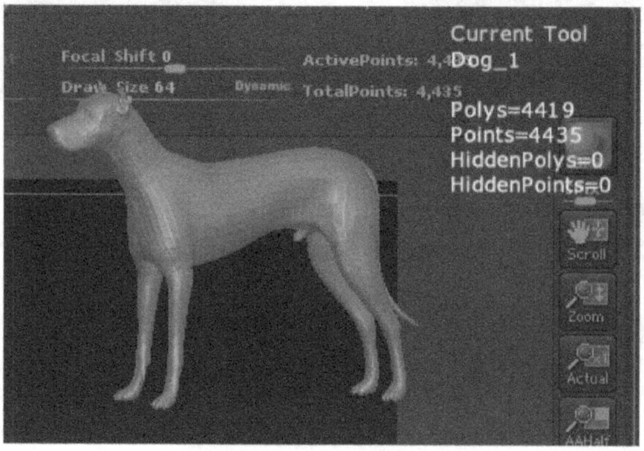

Figure 6-51 *The number of polygons reduced to 4419 after choosing the* ***Half*** *button*

Double

The **Double** button is used to increase the polygon count in a retopologized model to double of its original value. For instance, if a model contains 5000 polygons, its retopologized model will contain approximately 10,000 polygons.

Adapt

The **Adapt** button is used to change the size of the polygon to improve the flow of topology. It will give a clean topology.

Adaptive Size

The **AdaptiveSize** slider is used to create non-square polygons. It also factors the size of the polygons based upon the model's curvature.

Curve Strength

The **Curve Strength** slider is used to adjust the strength of the edge created by ZRemesher.

Use Polypaint

When you choose the **Use PolyPaint** button, the **Use PolyPaint** mode gets activated. This mode tells ZRemesher to pay attention to PolyPaint color while determining local polygon density as it creates the new topology. To paint in the **PolyPaint** mode, use the Standard brush in the RGB mode. The higher value of the **Polygon Density** slider specifies the red color within the painted area. The lower value of the **Polygon Density** slider specifies the blue color within the painted area.

Color Density

The **Color Density** slider specifies the factor that the ZRemesher will use to adjust polygon density while using polypaint. The **Color Density** slider will be activated when the **Use PolyPaint** button is chosen.

NanoMesh

NanoMesh is a feature of the **ZModeler** brush. This is a particle system in ZBrush. NanoMesh allows you to populate areas of a model with multiple instances of any geometry and then adjust it in a matter of seconds. **NanoMesh** area is displayed only when an instance of the primitive is created on the object in the canvas. The different buttons and sliders of the **NanoMesh** tool can be accessed by expanding the **NanoMesh** subpalette in the **Tool** palette, refer to Figure 6-52. The different buttons and sliders in this area are discussed next.

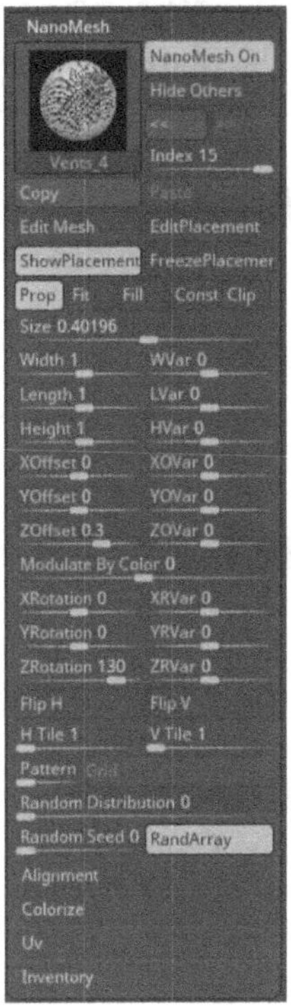

*Figure 6-52 The **NanoMesh** subpalette*

Preview Selected Nanomesh

The small preview of the selected NanoMesh is displayed in this area.

NanoMesh On

The **NanoMesh On** button is enabled when the NanoMeshes are applied to the model.

Hide Others

The **Hide Others** button is used to hide all the NanoMeshes applied on the model except for the currently selected one.

<< and >>

The **<<** and **>>** buttons are used to cycle through various existing NanoMesh indexes. These buttons are activated only when one NanoMesh is applied to the model.

Index

The **Index** slider is used to select a specific NanoMesh index from the current model. The **>>** and **<<** buttons are activated only when one NanoMesh applied to the model.

Copy and Paste

The **Copy** and **Paste** buttons are used to copy the settings from one NanoMesh index and paste it to another.

Edit Mesh

The **Edit Mesh** button is a toggle button that you can use to switch between the normal mode and the edit mesh mode.

While in the **Edit Mesh** mode, you can edit the NanoMesh with the various ZBrush sculpting and modeling tools. To return to the normal mode, choose the **Edit Mesh** button again.

Edit Placement

The **Edit Placement** button is used to edit the geometry on which NanoMesh will be placed. It is the reverse of the Edit Mesh. While in this mode, NanoMesh will be hidden and you can edit the geometry using various ZBrush sculpting and modeling tools. This will also work in solo mode.

ShowPlacement

The **ShowPlacement** button is used to display the placement of NanoMesh on the geometry. This button is chosen by default.

FreezePlacement

The **FreezePlacement** button is used to freeze the placement of NanoMesh on the geometry.

Fit

This button is used to keep the size of the inserted NanoMesh proportional. The shape of the NanoMesh will not be changed and distorted.

Fill

The **Fill** button is used to resize the inserted NanoMesh in such a way that it completely fills the placement polygons of the geometry. This results in non-uniform scaling and distorts the shape of the NanoMesh.

Constant

The **Constant** mode, when enabled, keeps a constant height for the NanoMesh, regardless of the size of the placement polygons.

Clip

The **Clip** button is used to prevent the topology of the insert mesh from the placement polygons. It does this by trimming off any part that would extend pass the edges.

Size

The **Size** slider is used to change the size of the NanoMesh. The original value is set by drag motion when inserting the NanoMesh on the placement polygons of the geometry through the **ZModeler** brush.

Width, Length, and Height

The **Width**, **Length**, and **Height** sliders are used to change the proportions of the NanoMesh. These slider values are affected by the **WVar**, **LVar**, and **HVar** variation sliders.

XOffset, YOffset, and ZOffset

The **XOffset**, **YOffset**, and **ZOffset** sliders are used to change the default positions of the NanoMesh. The default value for the **XOffsets** and **YOffsets** is **0**, and for the **ZOffset** is **1**. These slider values are affected by the **XOVar**, **YOVar**, and **ZOVar** sliders.

XRotation, YRotation, and ZRotation

The **XRotation**, **YRotation**, and **ZRotation** sliders are used to change the rotation of the NanoMesh.

These slider values are affected by the **XRVar**, **YRVar**, and **ZRVar** variation sliders.

Flip H and Flip V

The **Flip H** and **Flip V** (Flip Horizontal and Flip Vertical) buttons are used to mirror the inserted NanoMesh either horizontally or vertically.

H Tile and V Tile

The **H Tile** and **V Tile** (horizontal tile and vertical tile) sliders duplicate the inserted NanoMesh within the boundaries of each placement polygon.

Pattern

The **Pattern** slider is used to the distribute the NanoMesh inside the placement polygons in the geometry. The pattern of NanoMesh is created by the **H Tile** and **V Tile** sliders. The default pattern is a grid. To change the pattern of NanoMesh, you can change the **Pattern** slider value. Depending on the value of the **H Tile** and **V Tile** sliders, you can design a beautiful pattern, refer to Figure 6-53.

Random Distribution

The **Random Distribution** slider is used to distribute the NanoMesh randomly. Depending upon the value of the **H Tile** and **V Tile** sliders, you can distribute the pattern and create clusters of random meshes.

Random Seed

The **Random Seed** slider is used to modify the result of the **Random Distribution** slider without affecting the distribution of the NanoMesh. It changes the base randomization variables, resulting in different randomization values.

Figure 6-53 *The distribution of pattern of NanoMesh*

TUTORIALS

Before you start the tutorials of this chapter, navigate to *\Documents\ZBrushprojects* and then create a new folder with the name *c06*.

Tutorial 1

In this tutorial, you will create a coffee mug using a cylinder and the **DynaMesh** tool. The final output of the model is shown in Figure 6-54. **(Expected time: 20 min)**

Figure 6-54 *A coffee mug*

The following steps are required to complete this tutorial:

a. Create the body of the mug.
b. Create the handle of the mug.
c. Save the model.

Creating the Body of the Mug

In this section, you will create the body of the mug using a cylinder and the **DynaMesh** tool.

1. Choose the **Init ZBrush** button from the **Preferences** palette; the message box is displayed. Choose the **Yes** button from the message box; ZBrush is initialized to its default state.

2. Choose the Current Tool button from the **Tool** palette; a flyout is displayed. Choose the **Cylinder3D** primitive from this flyout and create it in the canvas.

3. Choose the **Edit** button from the top shelf.

4. Press and hold the left mouse button and drag the cursor downward in the canvas area such that the cylinder is rotated and stands vertically. While dragging the cursor, press the SHIFT key; the cylinder is snapped at right angle to the canvas.

5. Choose the **Make PolyMesh3D** button from the **Tool** palette to convert the primitive cylinder into a polymesh. Next, choose the **PolyF** button in the right shelf; the polygon edges are displayed in the cylinder, refer to Figure 6-55.

6. Expand the **Geometry** subpalette in the **Tool** palette. In this subpalette, expand the **DynaMesh** option and then choose the **DynaMesh** button; the polygon distribution in the cylinder will be modified, refer to Figure 6-56.

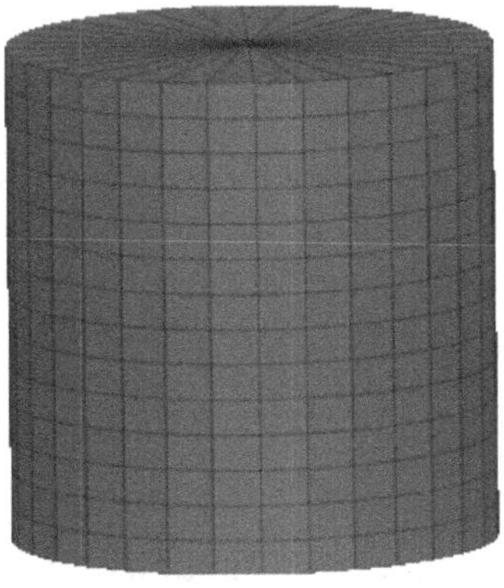

Figure 6-55 *The polygon edges displayed on choosing the **PolyF** button*

Figure 6-56 *The polygon distribution modified*

7. Press and hold the left mouse button and drag the cursor downward in such a way that the cylinder is rotated and its top is displayed. While dragging the cursor, press the SHIFT key; the cylinder is snapped to the canvas.

8. Expand the **SubTool** subpalette in the **Tool** palette. Next, in this subpalette, choose the **Rename** button; the **Please enter subtool title** window consisting of a text box is displayed. Enter **coffee mug** in this text box; the cylinder primitive is renamed as *coffee mug*.

9. Choose the Current Brush button from the left shelf; a flyout containing different sculpting brushes is displayed. Choose the **MaskCircle** brush from this flyout; a message box asking

you to press CTRL to use this brush will be displayed. Choose the **OK** button to close this message box.

10. Press and hold the CTRL key and choose the Current Stroke button; a flyout is displayed. In this flyout, choose the **Square** button. Similarly, choose the **Center** button located at the bottom of the flyout, refer to Figure 6-57. Next, release the CTRL key.

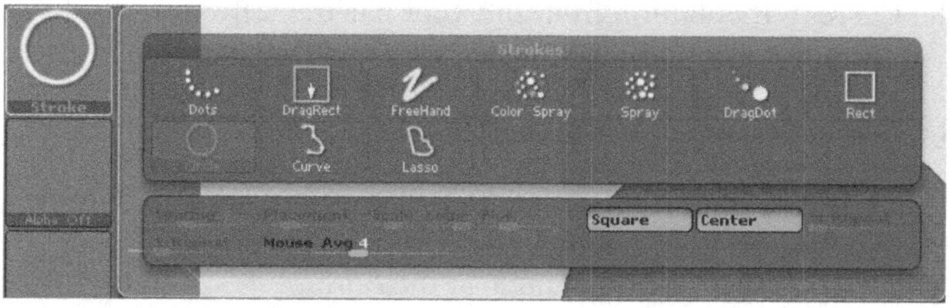

***Figure 6-57** The **Square** and **Center** buttons chosen from the flyout*

The **Square** and **Center** buttons will enable you to start the brush stroke from the centre of the *coffee mug* and create a perfect circle.

11. Activate the symmetry in the X-axis by pressing the X key.

12. Press and hold the CTRL key and place the cursor at the position where two red dots representing the symmetry overlap. Next, drag the cursor on the surface of *coffee mug* to create a circular stroke on the surface of the *coffee mug*, refer to Figure 6-58; a circular mask is applied on the top of the *coffee mug*.

    On rotating the view of the *coffee mug*, you will notice that the circular mask is applied on the bottom of the *coffee mug* also.

13. Choose the Current Brush button from the left shelf; a flyout containing different sculpting brushes is displayed. Choose the **MaskRect** brush from this flyout; a message box asking you to press CTRL to use this brush will be displayed. Choose the **OK** button to close this message box.

14. Press and hold the CTRL+ALT keys and drag the cursor at the bottom of the *coffee mug* to create a rectangular stroke, refer to Figure 6-59; the mask is removed from the bottom area.

    You can remove a mask from a particular area by pressing CTRL+ALT, and then dragging the cursor on that particular area.

15. Choose the **PolyF** button from the **Transform** palette; the polygon edges disappear from the surface of the *coffee mug*, refer to Figure 6-60.

16. Press CTRL+I; the mask is inverted, refer to Figure 6-61.

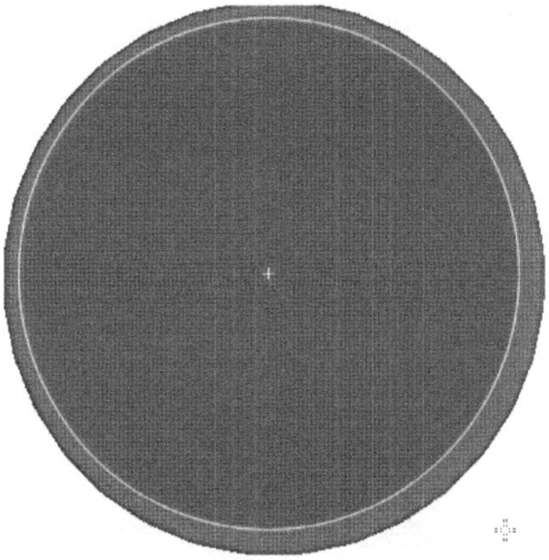

Figure 6-58 *A circular stroke created on the top of the coffee mug*

Figure 6-59 *A rectangular stroke created at the bottom of the coffee mug*

Figure 6-60 *Polygon edges disappeared from the surface*

Figure 6-61 *The mask inverted on the surface*

17. Expand the **Deformation** subpalette in the **Tool** palette.

    You need to change the offset of the unmasked area of the *coffee mug* along the Z-axis using the **Offset** slider.

18. Deactivate the x option corresponding to the **Offset** slider by choosing the **x** button located on the right side of the slider. Next, choose the **z** button to activate the z option.

19. Drag the **Offset** slider toward left; the unmasked area moves downward, refer to Figure 6-62 Continue dragging the slider till the unmasked area reaches the bottom of the *coffee mug*.

20. Press and hold the CTRL key and drag the cursor on the canvas area; the mask is removed from the surface of the *coffee mug*. You will notice that the geometry is distorted, refer to Figure 6-63.

Figure 6-62 *The unmasked area moved downward*

Figure 6-63 *The distorted geometry of the coffee mug*

22. Press and hold the CTRL key and drag the cursor on the canvas area again; some distortions are removed from the surface of the *coffee mug*. To remove the distortions completely, press and hold the SHIFT key; the **Smooth** brush is activated. Next, drag the cursor on the surface of the *coffee mug*; the surface of the *coffee mug* is smoothened, refer to Figure 6-64.

23. Make sure the **Activate Symmetry** button in the **Transform** palette is chosen. Next, choose the **(R)** button; the **RadialCount** slider is activated. By default, the **>X<** button is chosen. To deactivate this button, choose it again. Next, choose the **>Z<** button; the radial symmetry in the Z-axis is activated. In the **RadialCount** edit box, enter the value **73**, refer to Figure 6-65. This edit box is displayed when you click on the **RadialCount** slider.

24. Choose the Current Brush button from the left shelf; a flyout containing different sculpting brushes is displayed. Choose the **Move** brush from this flyout. Set the value of the **Draw Size** slider to **120**.

25. Press and hold the left mouse button, and drag the lower part of the *coffee mug* inward using the **Move** brush, as shown in Figure 6-66.

26. Choose the Current Brush button from the left shelf; a flyout containing different sculpting brushes is displayed. Choose the **Standard** brush from this flyout.

Figure 6-64 *The surface of the coffee mug smoothened*

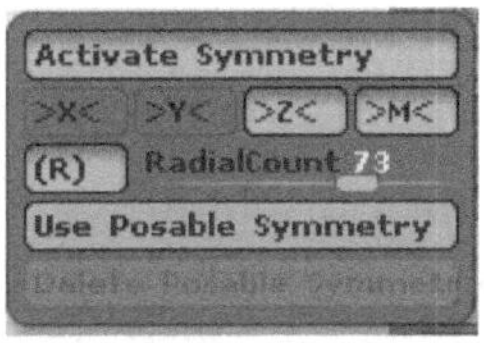

Figure 6-65 *The value of the* ***RadialCount*** *slider set to* ***73***

27. Choose the **Zsub** button from the top shelf and set the value of the **Z Intensity** slider to **30**.

28. Set the value of the **Draw Size** slider to **10**, and create a pattern, as shown in Figure 6-67.

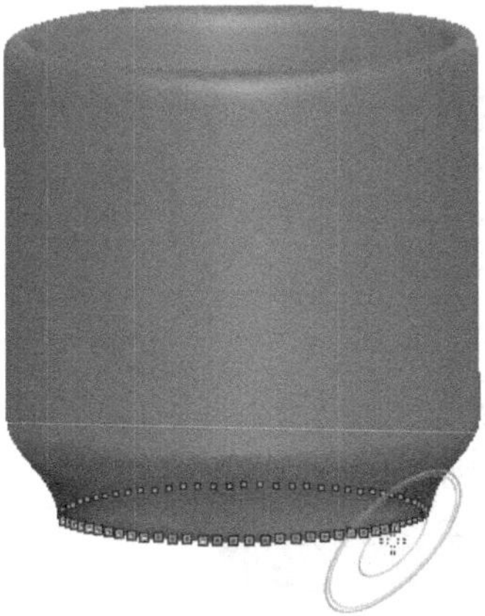

Figure 6-66 *The lower part of the coffee mug moved inward*

Figure 6-67 *A pattern created on the coffee mug*

29. Create the same pattern below the pattern created in Step 27, refer to Figure 6-68. Next, deactivate the symmetry by choosing the **Activate Symmetry** button in the **Transform** palette.

Creating the Handle of the Mug

In this section, you will create the handle of the mug using the **InsertHRing** brush.

1. Choose **Insert-IMM** from the **Brush** tab of the **LightBox** browser located at the top of the canvas by double-clicking on it; the list of brushes is displayed. Now, choose the **InsertHRing** brush from the list and drag the cursor on the right side of the *coffee mug* to create the handle of the *coffee mug*; a handle is created and a mask is applied on the *coffee mug*, refer to Figure 6-69.

2. Choose the Current Brush button from the left shelf; a flyout containing different sculpting brushes is displayed. Choose the **Move** brush from this flyout and refine the shape of the handle using the **Move** brush, refer to Figure 6-70.

3. Press and hold the CTRL key and drag the cursor on the canvas area; the mask is removed from the surface of the *coffee mug*.

4. Press and hold the CTRL key and drag the cursor on the canvas area again; the handle is merged with the *coffee mug* and the final model is created, refer to Figure 6-71.

Figure 6-68 *The same pattern created on the coffee mug*

Figure 6-69 *A handle created using the* ***InsertHRing*** *brush*

Figure 6-70 *The shape of the handle modified using the* ***Move*** *brush*

Figure 6-71 *The final model of the coffee mug*

Saving the Model

In this section, you will save the file using the steps given next.

1. Choose the **Save As** button from the **Tool** palette; the **Save ZTool** dialog box is displayed. In this dialog box, browse to the location: *\Documents\ZBrushprojects\c06*.

2. Enter **c06tut1** in the **File name** edit box and then choose the **Save** button.

Tutorial 2

In this tutorial, you will create a cartoon octopus using a sphere and the **DynaMesh** tool. The final output of the model is shown in Figure 6-72. **(Expected time: 20 min)**

Figure 6-72 *The final model of the cartoon octopus*

The following steps are required to complete this tutorial:

a. Create the body of the octopus.
b. Create the tentacles of the octopus.
c. Create the eyes of the octopus.
d. Add detail to the octopus.
e. Save the model.

Creating the Body of the Octopus

In this section, you will create the body of the octopus using a sphere and the **DynaMesh** tool.

1. Choose the **Init ZBrush** button from the **Preferences** palette; the message box is displayed. Choose the **Yes** button from the message box; ZBrush is initialized to its default state.

2. Choose the Current Tool button from the **Tool** palette; a flyout is displayed. Choose the **Sphere3D** primitive from this flyout and create it in the canvas, refer to Figure 6-73.

3. Choose the **Edit** button from the top shelf. Next, choose the **PolyF** button from the **Transform** palette; the polygon edges on the sphere are displayed.

4. Press and hold the left mouse button and drag the cursor downward in the canvas area such that the sphere is rotated. While dragging the cursor, press the SHIFT key; the sphere is snapped at right angle to the canvas, as shown in Figure 6-74.

Figure 6-73 *The sphere created in the canvas*

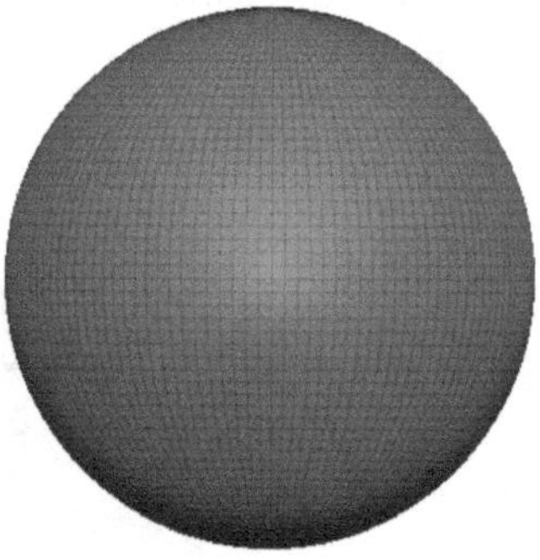

Figure 6-74 *The sphere rotated in the canvas*

5. Choose the Current Brush button from the left shelf; a flyout containing different sculpting brushes is displayed. Choose the **ClipRect** brush from this flyout; a message box is displayed, asking you to press CTRL+SHIFT keys to activate this brush. Choose the **OK** button to close this message box.

6. Press CTRL+SHIFT keys and then press and hold the left mouse button. Next, hover the cursor over the upper part of the sphere; a rectangular marquee selection appears. Select the upper part of the sphere, refer to Figure 6-75. Now, release the left mouse button and CTRL+SHIFT keys; the lower part of the sphere is deleted, refer to Figure 6-76.

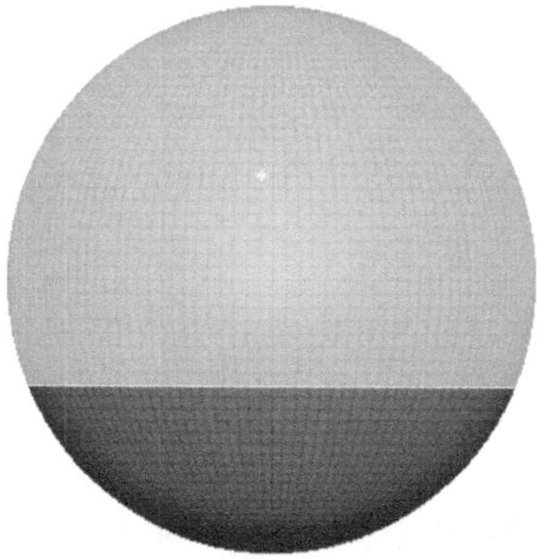

Figure 6-75 *The rectangular marquee selection created on the surface of sphere*

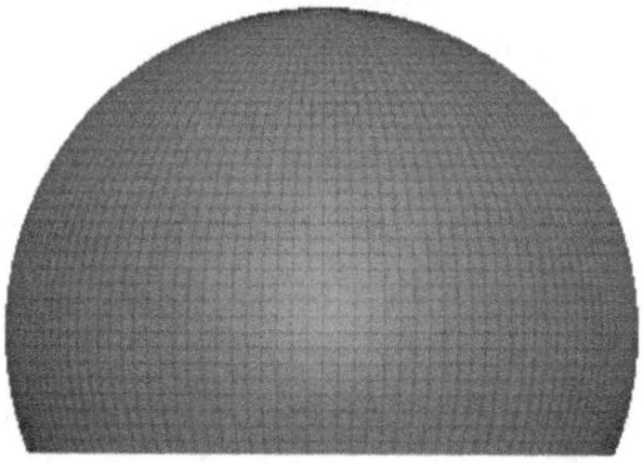

Figure 6-76 *The lower part of the sphere deleted*

7. Choose the **Make PolyMesh3D** button from the **Tool** palette to convert the primitive sphere into polymesh. Next, choose the **PolyF** button from the right shelf; the polygon edges on the sphere disappear.

8. Expand the **Geometry** subpalette in the **Tool** palette. In this subpalette, choose the **DynaMesh** button in the **DynaMesh** area; the sphere becomes smoother.

9. Expand the **SubTool** subpalette in the **Tool** palette. Next, in this subpalette, choose the **Rename** button; the **Please enter subtool title** window consisting of a text box is displayed. Enter **octopus** in this text box; the sphere primitive is renamed as *octopus*.

10. Choose the **Activate Symmetry** button from the **Transform** palette. Next, choose the **(R)** button; the **RadialCount** slider is activated. By default, the **>X<** button is chosen. To deactivate this button, choose it again. Next, choose the **>Z<** button; the radial symmetry in the Z-axis is activated. Set the value of the **RadialCount** slider to **50**, refer to Figure 6-77.

11. Choose the Current Brush button from the left shelf; a flyout containing different sculpting brushes is displayed. Choose the **Move** brush from this flyout and create the shape of the body using the radial symmetry and the **Move** brush, refer to Figure 6-78. If required, increase the brush size to create the shape of the body.

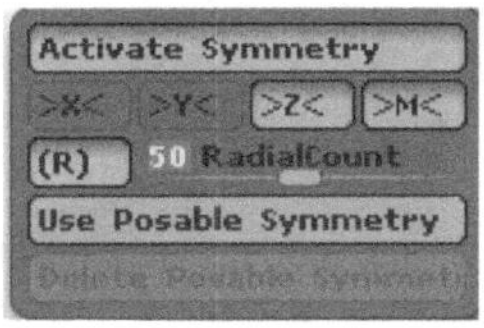

Figure 6-77 *The value of the* ***RadialCount*** *slider set to* ***50***

Figure 6-78 *The shape modified using the* ***Move*** *brush*

Creating the Tentacles of the Octopus

In this section, you will create the tentacles of the octopus using the **Inflat** and **Move** brushes.

1. Choose the **Transform** palette. In this palette, set the value of the **RadialCount** slider to **8**, refer to Figure 6-79.

2. Choose the Current Brush button from the left shelf; a flyout containing different sculpting brushes is displayed. Choose the **Inflat** brush from this flyout.

3. Decrease the brush size and drag the cursor on the lower part of the *octopus* to create base for the tentacles, refer to Figure 6-80. In this figure, you will notice that the geometry is stretched. To remove the stretching, press and hold the CTRL key and drag the cursor on the canvas area; the *octopus* is smoothened, refer to Figure 6-81.

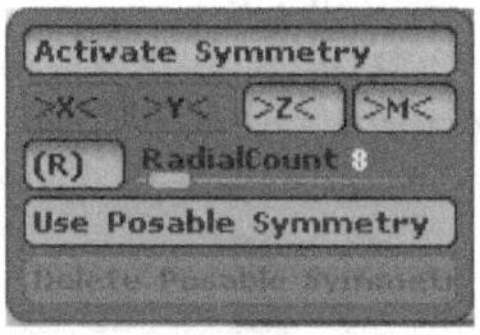

Figure 6-79 *The value of the* ***RadialCount*** *slider set to* ***8***

Figure 6-80 *Base for the tentacles created using the* ***Inflat*** *brush*

4. Choose the Current Brush button from the left shelf; a flyout containing different sculpting brushes is displayed. Choose the **Move** brush from this flyout and drag out the tentacles using this brush, refer to Figure 6-82.

Figure 6-81 *The surface of the octopus smoothened*

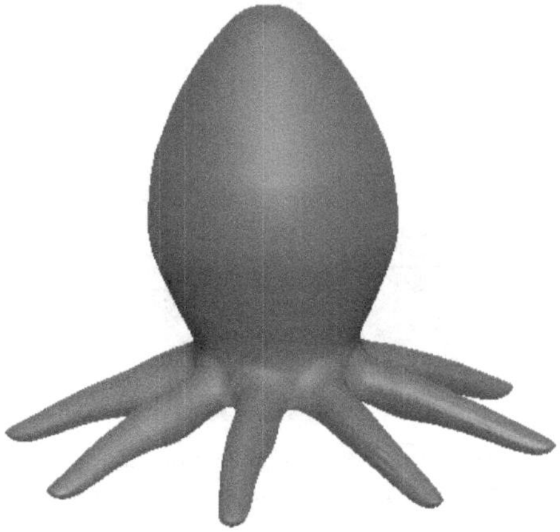

Figure 6-82 *The tentacles dragged out using the* ***Move*** *brush*

5. Drag the ends of the tentacles toward left using the **Move** brush, refer to Figure 6-83. The geometry is stretched again. To remove the stretching, press and hold the CTRL key and drag the cursor on the canvas area.

6. Press and hold the SHIFT key; the **Smooth** brush is activated. Next, with the SHIFT key pressed, drag the cursor at the ends of the tentacles to make them pointed and smooth, refer to Figure 6-84.

Figure 6-83 *Ends of the tentacles moved toward left*

Figure 6-84 *Ends of the tentacles smoothened using the* ***Smooth*** *brush*

7. Choose the Current Brush button from the left shelf; a flyout containing different sculpting brushes is displayed. Choose the **SnakeHook** brush from this flyout and drag out the tentacles toward left using this brush, refer to Figure 6-85.

8. Choose the Current Brush button from the left shelf; a flyout containing different sculpting brushes is displayed. Choose the **Inflat** brush from this flyout and drag the cursor on the surface of the tentacles to add depth to the tentacles, refer to Figure 6-86 If required, use the **Smooth** brush on the ends of the tentacles to make them pointed.

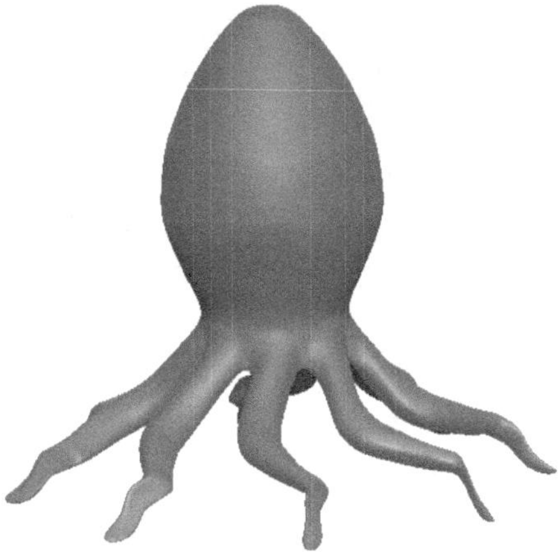

Figure 6-85 *Ends of the tentacles moved toward left using the* ***SnakeHook*** *brush*

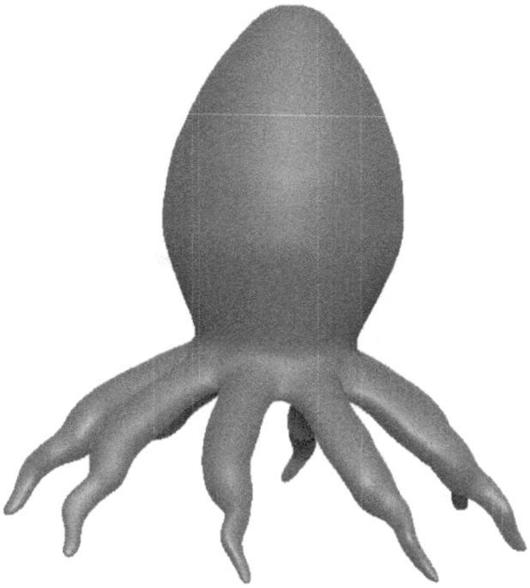

Figure 6-86 *Depth added to the tentacles using the* ***Inflat*** *brush*

Creating the Eyes of the Octopus

In this section, you will create the eyes of the octopus using the **InsertSphere** brush.

1. Choose the **(R)** and **>Z<** buttons in the **Transform** palette; the radial symmetry in the Z-axis is deactivated.

2. Press the X key to activate symmetry in the X-axis.

3. Choose the Current Brush button from the left shelf; a flyout containing different sculpting brushes is displayed. Choose the **Standard** brush from this flyout and then choose the **Zsub** button from the top shelf.

4. Decrease the brush size, if required. Next, drag the cursor on the surface of the *octopus* to create an eye socket, refer to Figure 6-87.

5. Choose the Current Brush button from the left shelf; a flyout containing different sculpting brushes is displayed. Choose the **Zadd** button and then choose the **InsertSphere** brush from this flyout and drag on the surface of eye sockets to create eyeball; a mask is applied on the surface of *octopus*, refer to Figure 6-88.

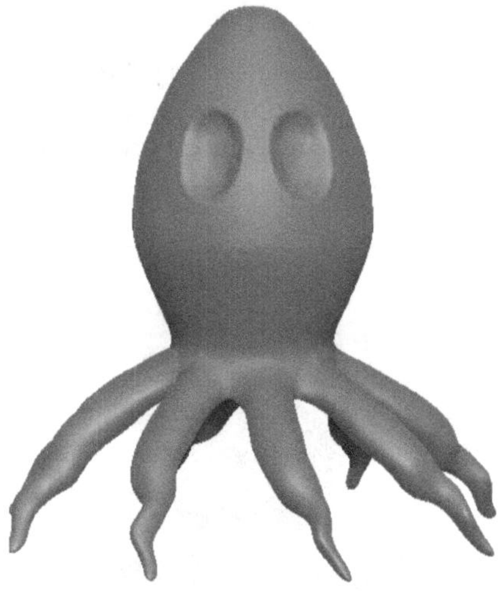

Figure 6-87 *Eye socket created using the* ***Standard*** *brush*

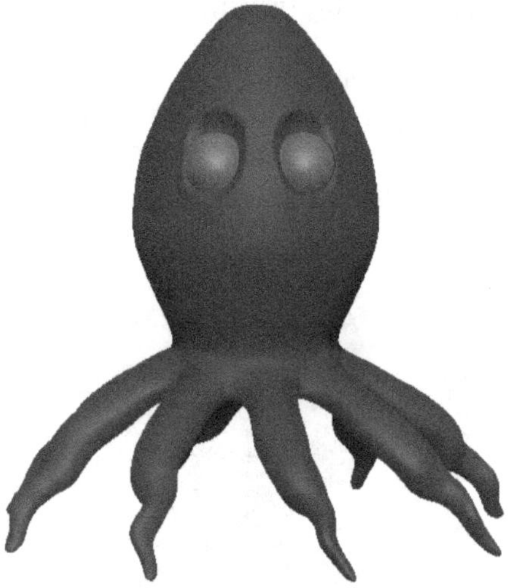

Figure 6-88 *Eye ball created using the* ***InsertSphere*** *brush*

6. Press and hold the CTRL key and drag the cursor on the canvas area twice; the mask is removed from the surface of *octopus* and the eyeball is merged with the socket, refer to Figure 6-89.

7. Make sure the **InsertSphere** brush is chosen. Press the ALT key and create another sphere on the eyeball, as shown in Figure 6-90. You will notice that a mask is applied on the surface of *octopus*. To remove the mask from its surface, press and hold the CTRL key and drag the cursor on the open area of the canvas. Next, choose the **Sub** button; a hole is created on the surface of the eye ball.

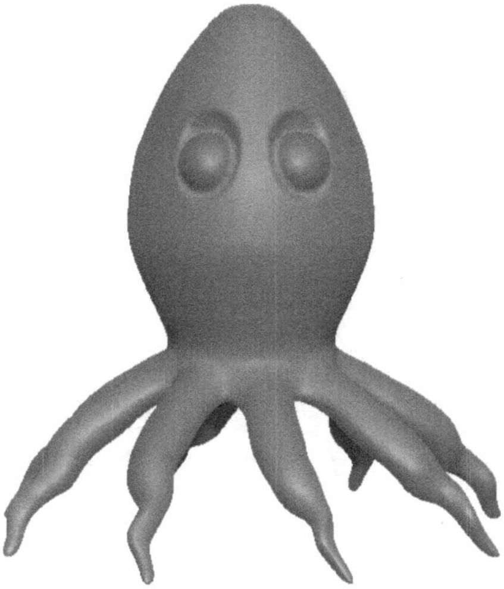

Figure 6-89 *Eyeball merged with the socket*

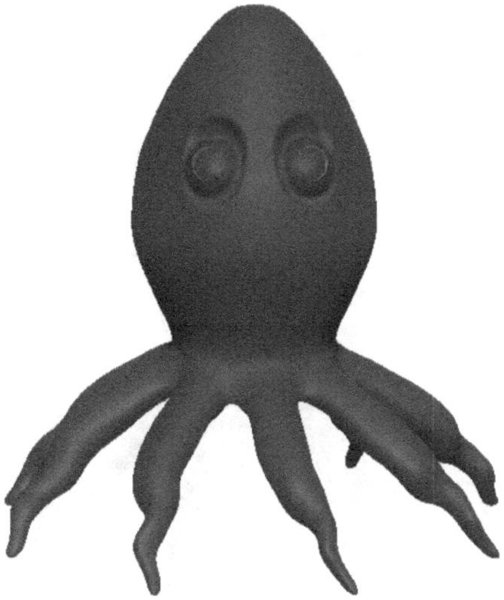

Figure 6-90 *A sphere created on eyeball with the ALT key pressed*

8. Create another smaller sphere on the hole created in Step 7 using the **InsertSphere** brush, refer to Figure 6-91. Press and hold the CTRL key and drag the cursor on the canvas area twice; the mask is removed from the surface of *octopus* and the newly created sphere is merged with the socket.

Adding Detail to the Octopus

In this section, you will add detail to the octopus using different alpha images.

1. Deactivate the symmetry in the X-axis by pressing the X key. Choose the Current Brush button from the left shelf; a flyout containing different sculpting brushes is displayed. Choose the **Standard** brush from this flyout.

2. Choose the Current Stroke button from the left shelf; a flyout containing different types of strokes is displayed. Choose the **DragRect** stroke from this flyout.

3. Choose the Current Alpha button from the left shelf; a flyout containing different alpha images is displayed. Choose the **Alpha 17** alpha image from this flyout and create a pattern on one of the tentacles of the *octopus*, refer to Figure 6-92. Continue creating the same pattern on all the tentacles, refer to Figure 6-93.

4. Choose the Current Stroke button from the left shelf; a flyout containing different types of strokes is displayed. Choose the **FreeHand** stroke from this flyout.

5. Choose the Current Alpha button from the left shelf; a flyout containing different alpha images is displayed. Choose the **Alpha 24** alpha image from this flyout. Next, increase the brush size and set the value of the **Z Intensity** slider in the top shelf to **4**. Press and hold the left mouse button and drag the cursor on the body of the *octopus* to create a noise pattern, as shown in Figure 6-94.

Figure 6-91 *Sphere created on the surface of the hole*

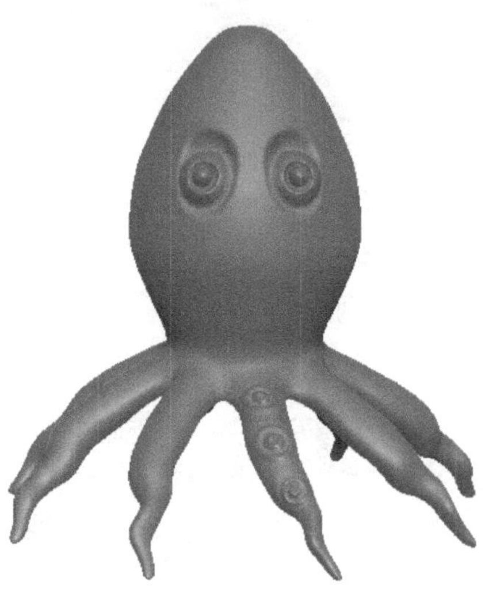

Figure 6-92 *Pattern created on a tentacle*

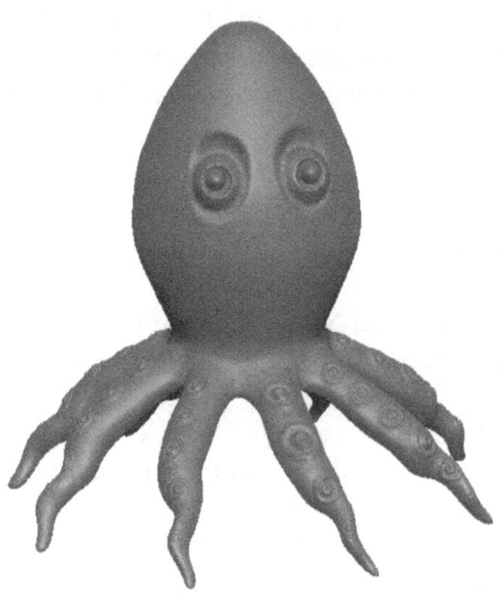

Figure 6-93 *Pattern created on all the tentacles*

Figure 6-94 *Noise pattern created on the body of the octopus*

Saving the Model

In this section, you will save the file using the steps given next.

1. Choose the **Save As** button from the **Tool** palette; the **Save ZTool** dialog box is displayed. In this dialog box, browse to the location: *\Documents\ZBrushprojects\c06*.

2. Enter **c06tut2** in the **File name** edit box and then choose the **Save** button.

Tutorial 3

In this tutorial, you will create a mannequin using the *DynaWax128.ZPR* file present in the **LightBox** browser and the **DynaMesh** tool. The final output of the model is shown in Figure 6-95. **(Expected time: 40 min)**

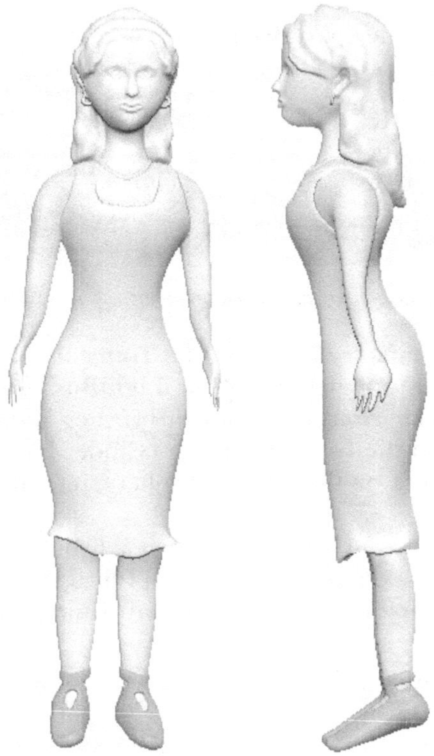

Figure 6-95 *The final model of the mannequin*

The following steps are required to complete this tutorial:

a. Create the body of the mannequin.
b. Create the outfit of the mannequin.
c. Create the hair of the mannequin.
d. Refine the face and hair of the mannequin.
e. Create the accessories for the mannequin.
f. Save the model.

Creating the Body of the Mannequin

In this section, you will create the body of the mannequin using the *DynaWax128.ZPR* file and the **DynaMesh** tool.

1. Choose the **Init ZBrush** button from the **Preferences** palette; ZBrush is initialized to its default state.

2. Choose the **DynaWax128.ZPR** file from the **Project** tab of the **LightBox** browser by double-clicking on it; a sphere is created in the canvas.

3. Expand the **Geometry** subpalette in the **Tool** palette. In this subpalette, choose the **DynaMesh** button; a message box is displayed asking you to freeze the subdivision levels, refer to Figure 6-96. Choose the **YES** button to freeze the subdivision levels. Now, choose the **DynaMesh** button from the **DynaMesh** area.

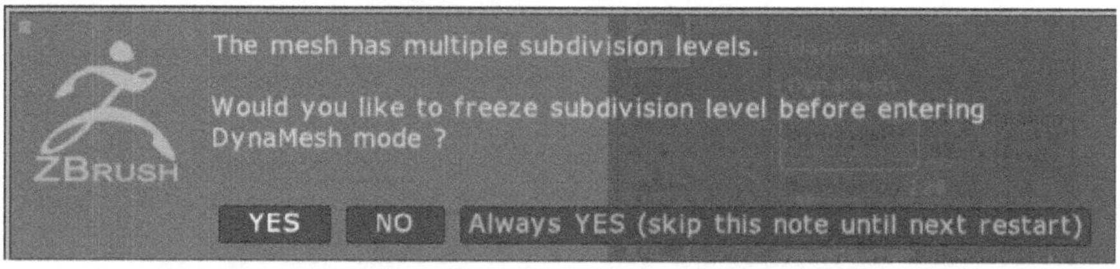

Figure 6-96 *The dialog box displayed on choosing the **DynaMesh** button*

4. Make sure the **Activate Symmetry** button in the **Transform** palette is deactivated. Next, choose **Insert-IMM** from the **Brush** tab of the **LightBox** browser located at the top of the canvas by double-clicking on it; the list of brushes is displayed. Now, choose the **InsertCylinder** brush from the list and create a cylinder below the sphere; a cylinder is created and a mask is applied on the surface of sphere, refer to Figure 6-97.

5. Choose the Current Brush button from the left shelf; a flyout containing different sculpting brushes is displayed. Choose the **Move** brush from this flyout and create the shape of the neck, refer to Figure 6-98. You need to adjust the brush size as required.

Figure 6-97 *A cylinder inserted using the **InsertCylinder** brush*

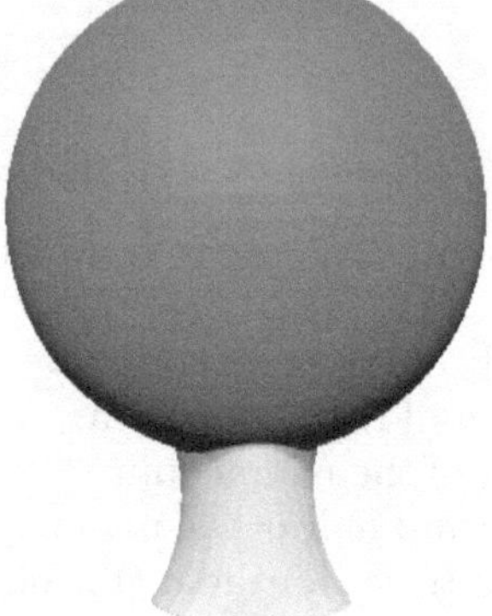

Figure 6-98 *Shape of the cylinder modified to create neck*

6. Modify the shape of the neck in the side view using the **Move** brush, as shown in Figure 6-99. Next, press CTRL+I; the mask is inverted, refer to Figure 6-100.

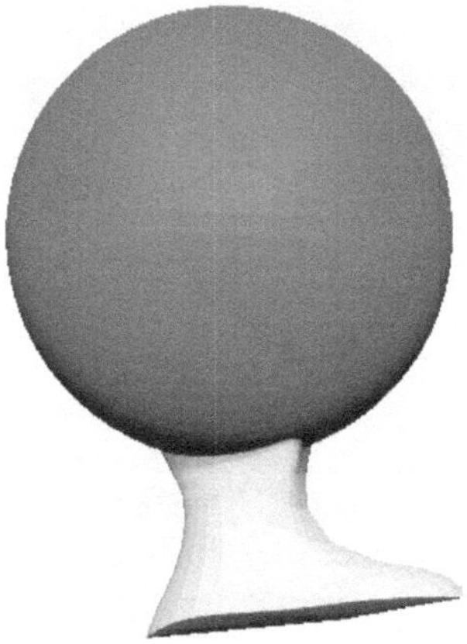

Figure 6-99 Shape of the neck modified in side view

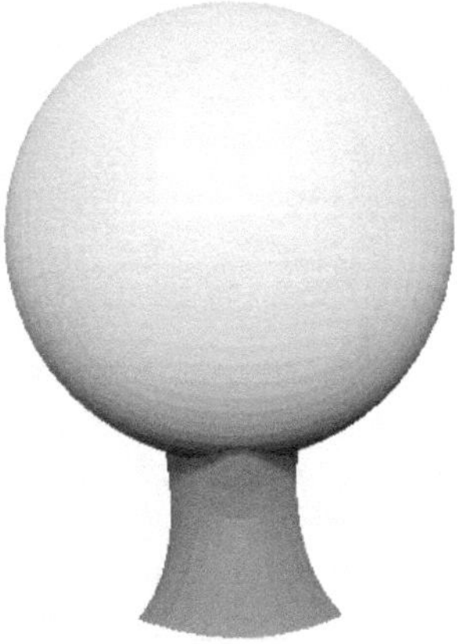

Figure 6-100 The mask inverted

7. Make sure the **Move** brush is chosen. Next, modify the shape of the sphere in the front and side views to create a head, refer to Figures 6-101 and 6-102.

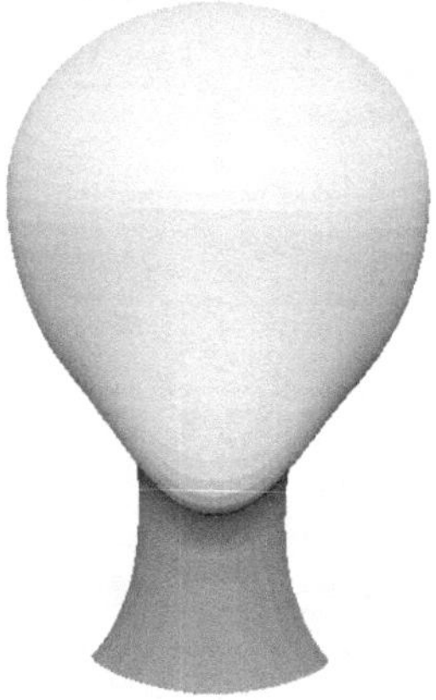

Figure 6-101 Shape of the sphere modified in front view

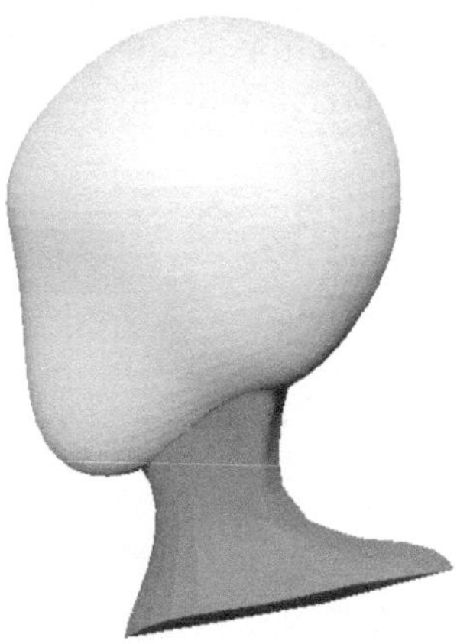

Figure 6-102 Shape of the sphere modified in side view

8. Press and hold the CTRL key and drag the cursor in the canvas area twice; the mask is removed and the neck is merged with the head, refer to Figure 6-103.

9. Choose the Current Brush button from the left shelf; a flyout containing different sculpting brushes is displayed. Choose the **InsertSphere** brush from this flyout and create a sphere below the neck; a mask is applied on the head and neck, refer to Figure 6-104.

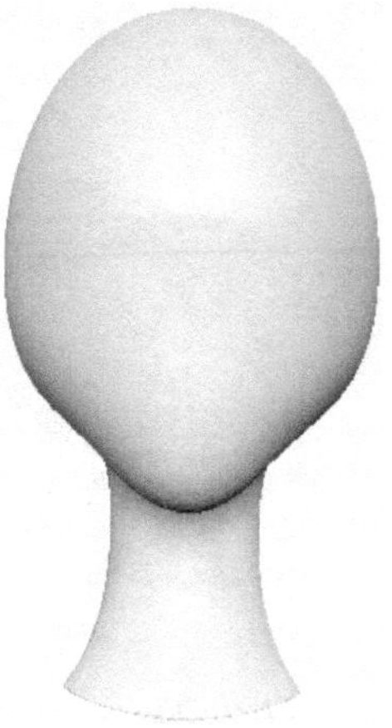

Figure 6-103 *The neck merged with the head*

Figure 6-104 *A sphere created using the* ***InsertSphere*** *brush*

10. Choose the Current Brush button from the left shelf; a flyout containing different sculpting brushes is displayed. Choose the **Move** brush from this flyout and using the **Move** brush create the shape of the torso, refer to Figure 6-105. Create a curve in the torso using the **Move** brush, refer to Figure 6-106.

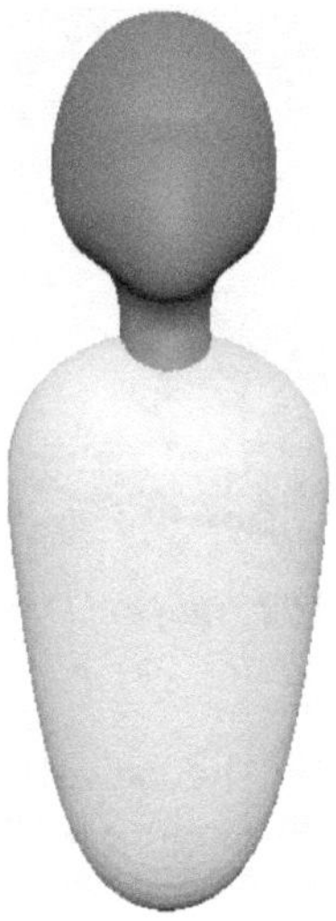

Figure 6-105 *Shape of the sphere modified to create a torso*

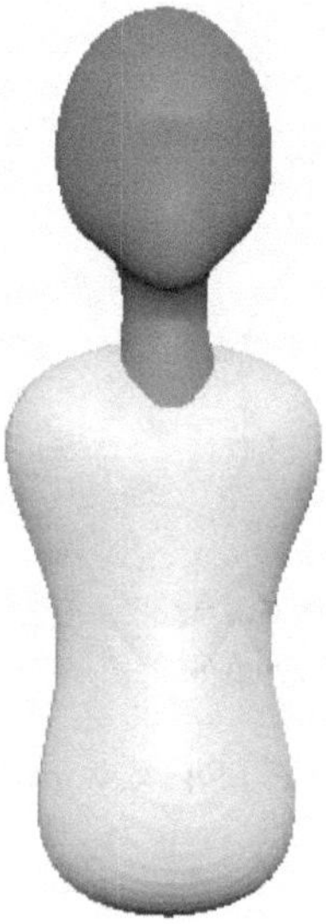

Figure 6-106 *A curve created using the* ***Move*** *brush*

11. Refine the shape of the torso in the side view using the **Move** brush, as shown in Figure 6-107. Next, press and hold the CTRL key and drag the cursor on the canvas area twice; the mask is removed and the torso is merged with the head. You will notice that a seam is created at the bottom of the neck. Press and hold the SHIFT key; the **Smooth** brush gets activated. Next, drag the cursor on the seam; the seam below the neck is removed, refer to Figure 6-108.

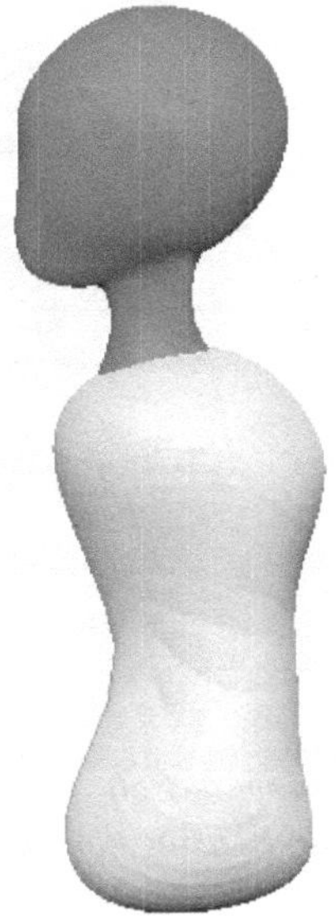

Figure 6-107 *The shape modified in the side view*

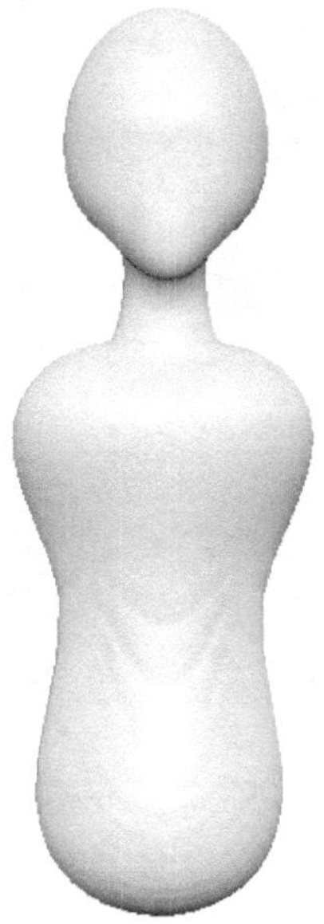

Figure 6-108 *The seam below the neck removed*

12. Choose the Current Brush button from the left shelf; a flyout containing different sculpting brushes is displayed. Choose the **InsertSphere** brush from this flyout and create a sphere on the bottom right side of the torso; a mask is applied on the head. Also, a torso and a sphere are inserted on the left side as the symmetry is activated in the X-axis by default.

13. Make sure the **Gizmo 3D Y** button is deactivated from the top shelf. Choose the **Move** button from the top shelf; an action line is displayed. Move the sphere using the action line to the position, as shown in Figure 6-109.

14. Choose the **Draw** button from the top shelf. Next, choose the Current Brush button from the left shelf; a flyout containing different sculpting brushes is displayed. Choose the **Move** brush from this flyout and using the **Move** brush, modify the shape of the newly created sphere, refer to Figure 6-110.

15. Make sure the **Move** brush is chosen. Modify the shape of the sphere to create legs, as shown in Figure 6-111.

16. Press and hold the CTRL key and drag the cursor in the canvas area; the mask is removed from the head and torso, refer to Figure 6-112.

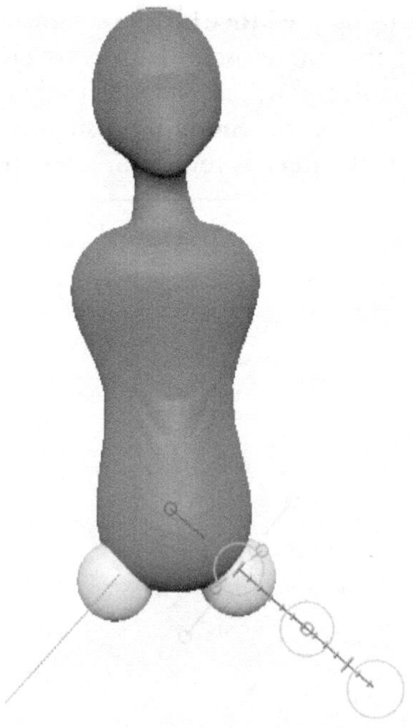

Figure 6-109 *Sphere moved using the action line*

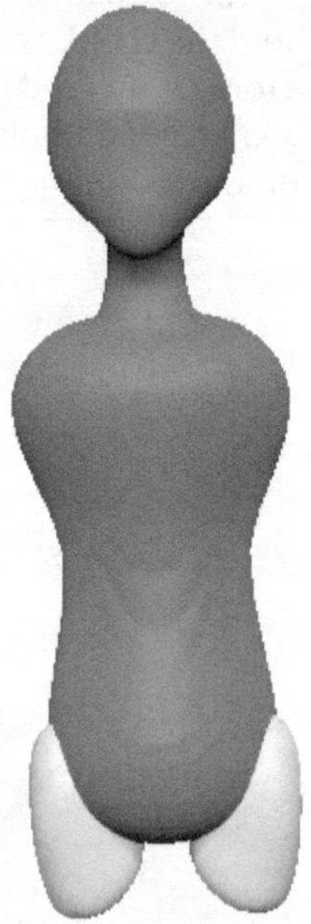

Figure 6-110 *The shape modified using the* ***Move*** *brush*

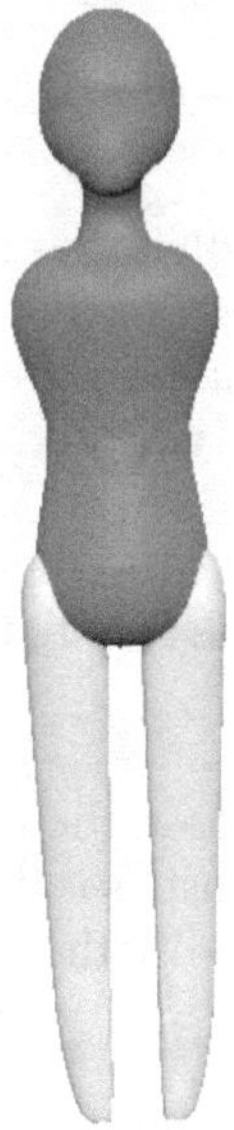

Figure 6-111 *The shape modified to create legs*

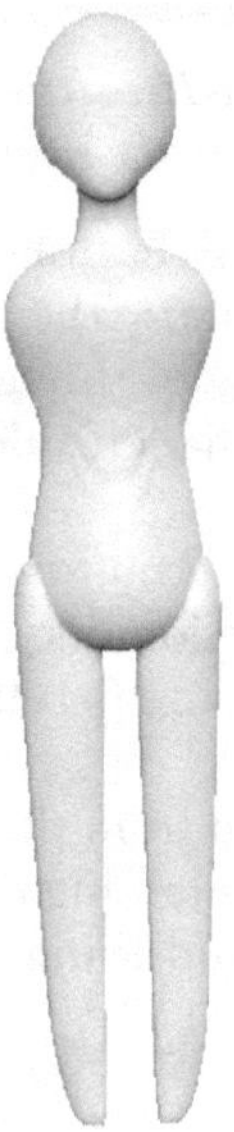

Figure 6-112 *The mask removed from the head and torso*

17. Press and hold the CTRL key and drag the cursor in the canvas area; the legs are merged with the torso. You will notice that a seam is created at the bottom of the torso. Press and hold the SHIFT key; the **Smooth** brush gets activated. Next, drag the cursor on the seam; the seam below the torso is removed, refer to Figure 6-113.

18. Make sure the **Move** brush is chosen. Modify the shape of the body in the side view, using the **Move** brush, refer to Figure 6-114.

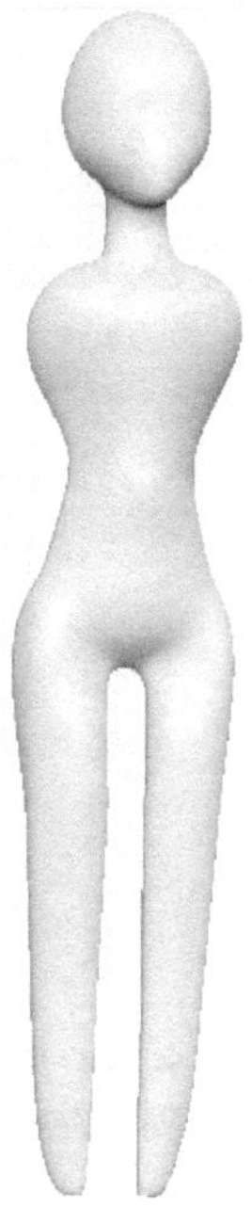

Figure 6-113 *The seam below the torso removed*

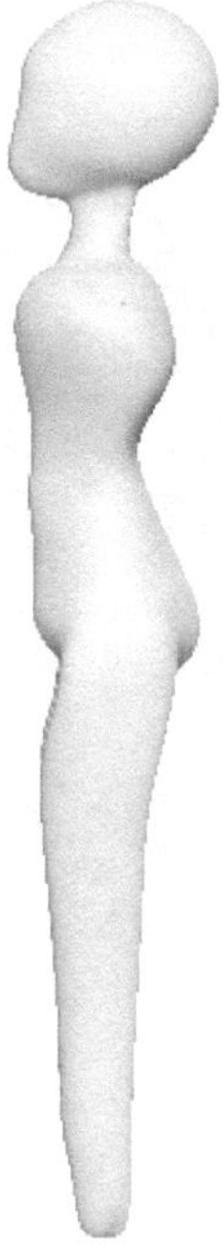

Figure 6-114 *The body adjusted in the side view*

19. Choose the Current Brush button from the left shelf; a flyout containing different sculpting brushes is displayed. Choose the **Inflat** brush from this flyout and add depth to the thighs and knees using this brush, refer to Figure 6-115.

20. Choose the Current Brush button from the left shelf; a flyout containing different sculpting brushes is displayed. Choose the **InsertSphere** brush from this flyout and create a sphere for shoulders on the top right side of the torso; a mask is applied on the body. Also, a sphere is inserted on the left side as the symmetry is activated in the X-axis by default, refer to Figure 6-116.

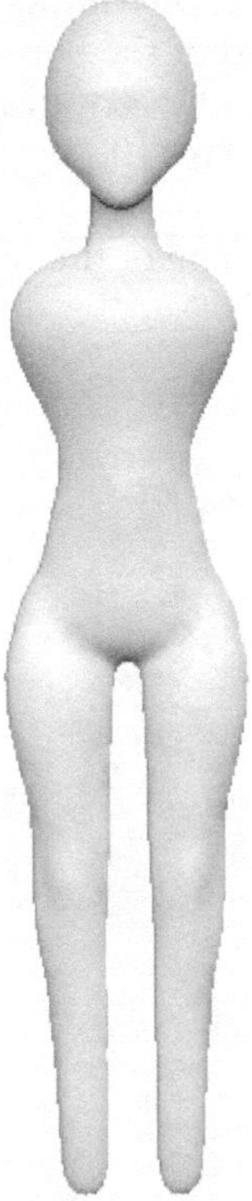

Figure 6-115 *Depth added to thighs and knees*

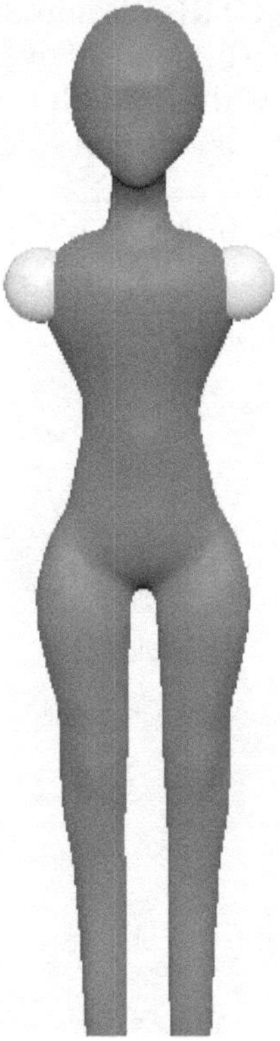

Figure 6-116 *Sphere created for the shoulders*

22. Choose the Current Brush button from the left shelf; a flyout containing different sculpting brushes is displayed. Choose the **Move** brush from this flyout and modify the newly created sphere in the front and side view to create the arms, refer to Figures 6-117 and 6-118.

22. Press and hold the CTRL key and drag the cursor in the canvas area twice; the mask is removed from the body and the arms are merged with the body. If a seam is created, you need to remove it using the **Smooth** brush, as discussed earlier.

23. Choose the Current Brush button from the left shelf; a flyout containing different sculpting brushes is displayed. Choose the **InsertSphere** brush from this flyout and create a sphere for the hand below the arms; a mask is applied on the body. Also, a sphere is inserted on the left side as the symmetry is activated in the X-axis by default, refer to Figure 6-119.

24. Choose the Current Brush button from the left shelf; a flyout containing different sculpting brushes is displayed. Choose the **Move** brush from this flyout and modify the shape of the sphere to create a palm, refer to Figure 6-120.

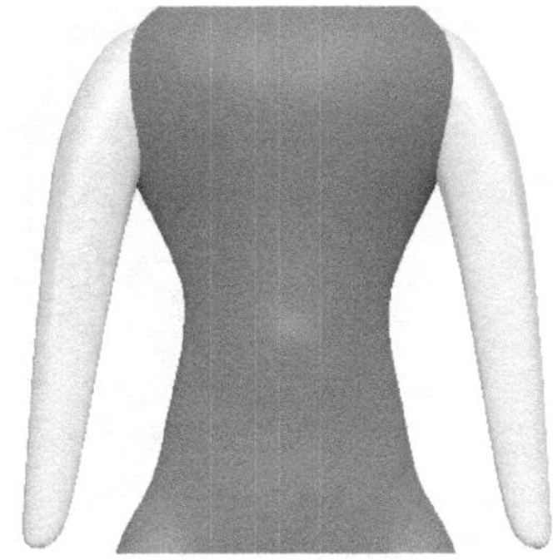

Figure 6-117 Shape modified to create arms

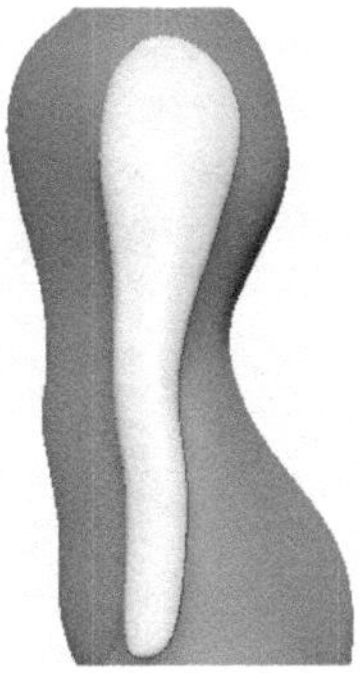

Figure 6-118 Shape modified in side view

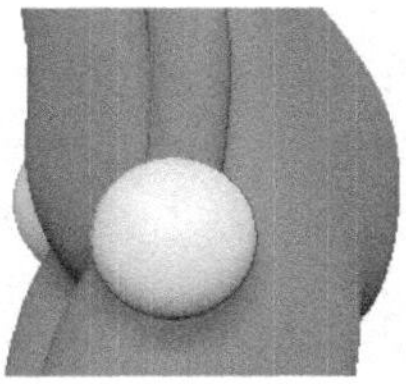

Figure 6-119 Sphere created for hand

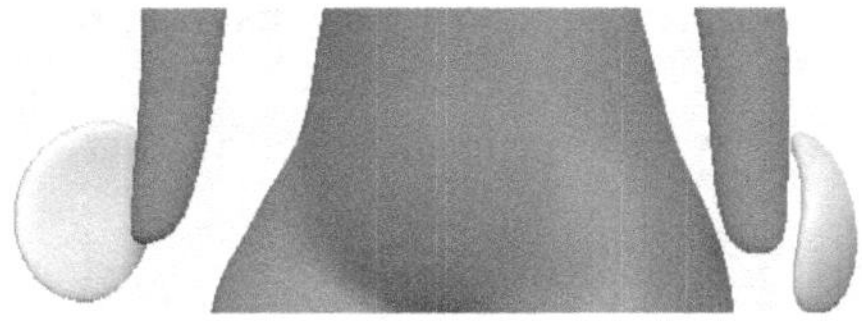

Figure 6-120 Shape of the sphere modified to create palm

25. Press CTRL+I; the mask is inverted and is applied on the palm. Modify the shape of the arm using the **Move** brush such that it fits into the palm, refer to Figure 6-121.

26. Choose the Current Brush button from the left shelf; a flyout containing different sculpting brushes is displayed. Choose the **InsertSphere** brush from this flyout and create a sphere on the palm to create the thumb, refer to Figure 6-122; a mask is applied on the body.

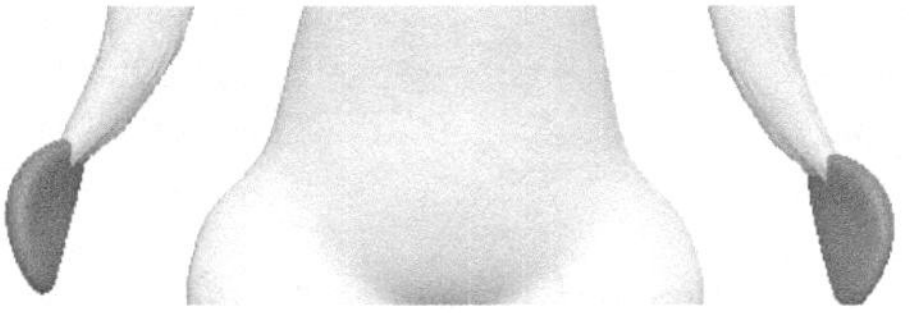

Figure 6-121 Shape of the arm adjusted according to the palm

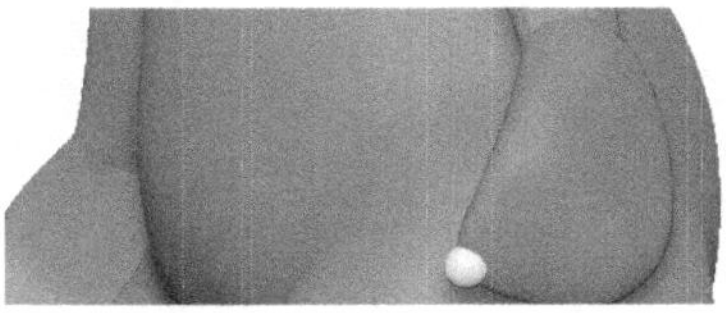

Figure 6-122 Sphere created for the thumb

27. Choose the Current Brush button from the left shelf; a flyout containing different sculpting brushes is displayed. Choose the **Move** brush from this flyout and modify the shape of the newly created sphere to create a thumb, refer to Figure 6-123.

28. Similarly create all the fingers of the hand, as shown in Figure 6-124. If required, position the fingers using the action line. Press and hold the CTRL key and drag the cursor in the canvas area twice; the fingers are merged with the palm. If a seam is created, you need to remove it using the **Smooth** brush.

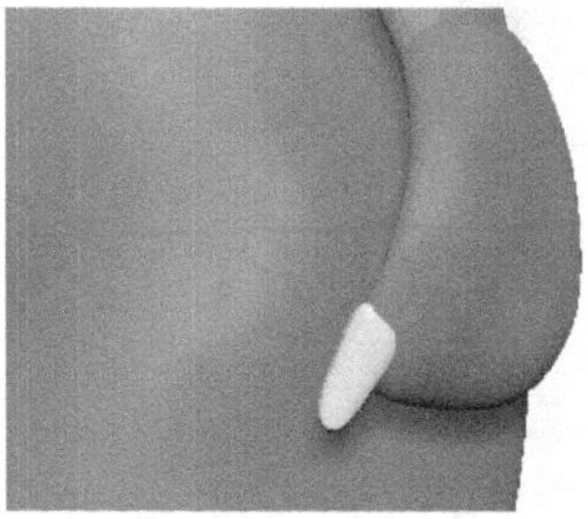

Figure 6-123 *Shape modified using the* ***Move*** *brush to create a thumb*

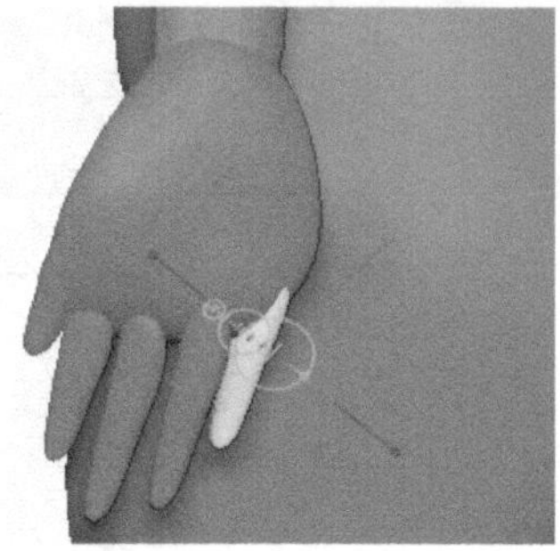

Figure 6-124 *Fingers created using the spheres*

29. Choose the Current Brush button from the left shelf; a flyout containing different sculpting brushes is displayed. Choose the **InsertSphere** brush from this flyout and create a sphere for the feet below the legs; a mask is applied on the body. Also, a sphere is inserted on the left side as the symmetry is activated in the X-axis by default, refer to Figure 6-125.

30. Choose the Current Brush button from the left shelf; a flyout containing different sculpting brushes is displayed. Choose the **Move** brush from this flyout and modify the shape of the newly created sphere to create the feet, refer to Figure 6-126. Next, press and hold the CTRL key and drag the cursor in the canvas area twice; the feet are merged with the legs.

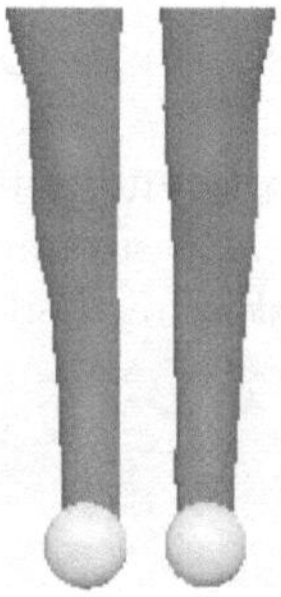

Figure 6-125 *Sphere created for the feet*

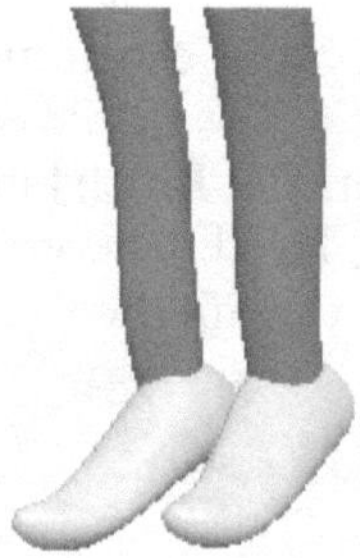

Figure 6-126 *Shape modified using the* ***Move*** *brush*

31. Choose the Current Brush button from the left shelf; a flyout containing different sculpting brushes is displayed. Choose the **Standard** brush from this flyout. Next, choose the **Zsub** button from the top shelf. Press and hold the left mouse button and drag the cursor to create eye sockets, refer to Figure 6-127.

32. Choose the **Zadd** button from the top shelf. Next, choose the Current Brush button from the left shelf; a flyout containing different sculpting brushes is displayed. Choose the **InsertSphere** brush from this flyout and create a sphere for the eyes inside the sockets; a mask is applied on the body. Also, a sphere is inserted on the left side as the symmetry is activated in the X-axis by default, refer to Figure 6-128.

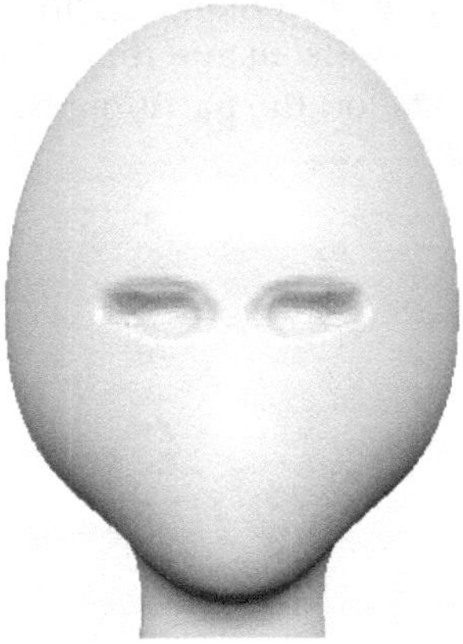

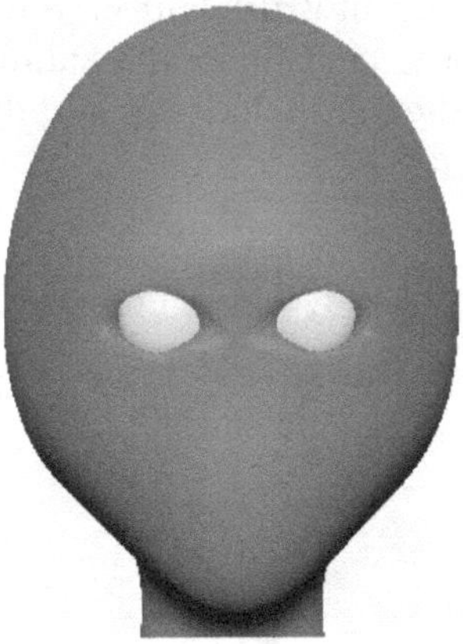

Figure 6-127 *Eye sockets created using the **Standard** brush*

Figure 6-128 *Sphere inserted for the eyes*

33. Press and hold the CTRL key and drag the cursor in the canvas area twice; the eyes are merged with the socket.

34. Choose the Current Brush button from the left shelf; a flyout containing different sculpting brushes is displayed. Choose the **Standard** brush from this flyout. Next, choose the **Zsub** button from the top shelf. Decrease the brush size and drag the cursor along the curve of eyes to create depth below the eyes. Choose the **Zadd** button from the top shelf and create depth above the eyes to create eyelids, refer to Figure 6-129.

35. Make sure the **Zadd** button is chosen in the top shelf. Next, drag the cursor between the eyes to create a nose, refer to Figure 6-129.

36. Choose the Current Brush button from the left shelf; a flyout containing different sculpting brushes is displayed. Choose the **Move** brush from this flyout and using this brush, create the shape of nose in the side view, refer to Figure 6-130.

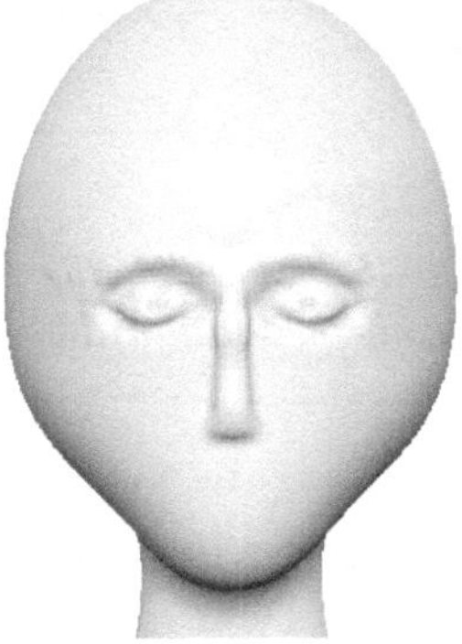

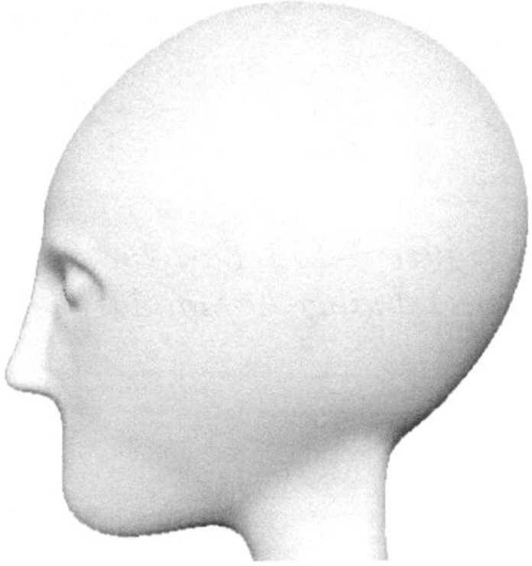

Figure 6-129 *Eyes and nose created using the **Standard** brush*

Figure 6-130 *Shape of the nose created in side view*

37. Choose the Current Brush button from the left shelf; a flyout containing different sculpting brushes is displayed. Choose the **Dam_Standard** brush from this flyout and using this brush, create partition for the lips, refer to Figure 6-131.

38. Choose the Current Brush button from the left shelf; a flyout containing different sculpting brushes is displayed. Choose the **Standard** brush from this flyout and then choose the **Zadd** button from the top shelf. Next, add depth above and below the partition using this brush, refer to Figure 6-132.

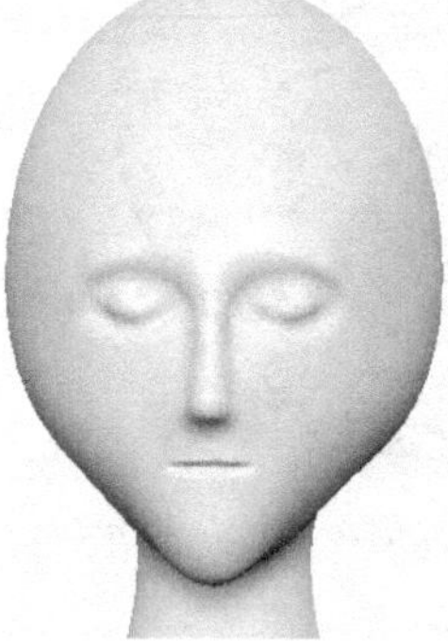

Figure 6-131 Partition created for the lips using the ***Dam_Standard*** *brush*

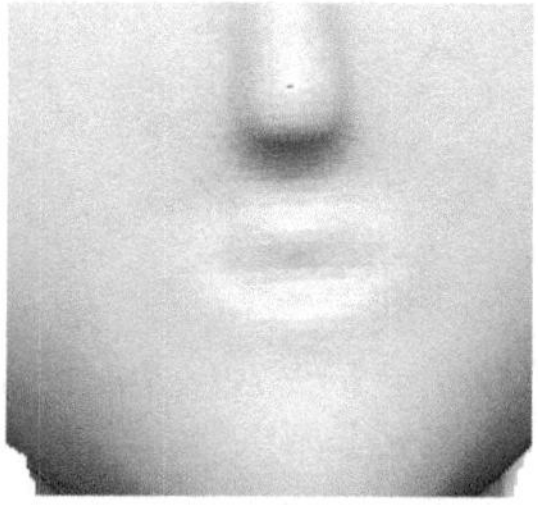

Figure 6-132 Depth created for the lips using the ***Standard*** *brush*

39. Make sure the **Standard** brush is chosen. Next, create a base for the ear in the side view, refer to Figure 6-133.

40. Choose the **Zsub** button from the top shelf. Next, create the shape of the ear in the side view using this brush, refer to Figure 6-134. If required, use the **Move** brush to refine the shape of the ear.

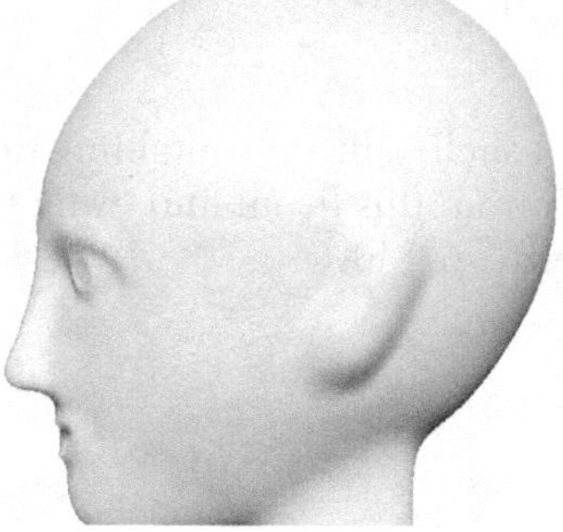

Figure 6-133 Base for the ear created using the ***Standard*** *brush*

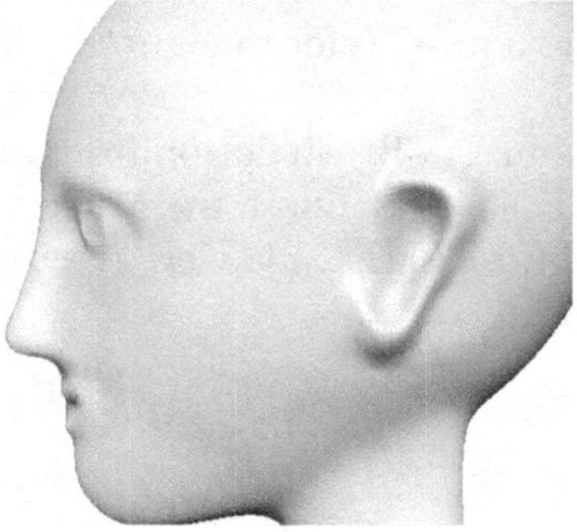

Figure 6-134 Shape of the ear created using the ***Standard*** *brush*

Creating the Outfit of the Mannequin

In this section, you will create the outfit of the mannequin.

1. Press and hold the CTRL key; the **MaskPen** brush is activated. Next, with the CTRL key pressed, create a mask on the upper part of the body to form the shape of the outfit, refer to Figure 6-135. Make sure you create a mask on the back side of the body.

2. Expand the **SubTool** subpalette in the **Tool** palette. In this subpalette, expand the **Extract** area, refer to Figure 6-136. Next, in this area, choose the **Extract** button. After some time, the shape of the mask is extracted from the surface of the body.

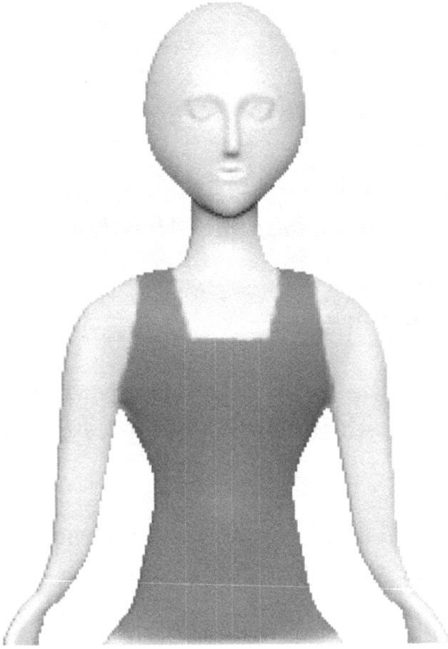

Figure 6-135 *Mask created for the outfit*

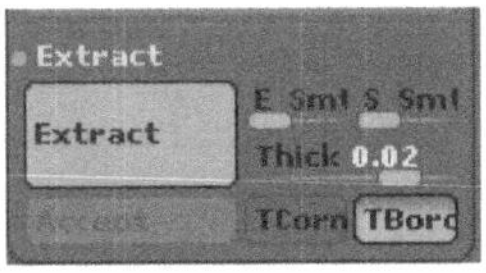

Figure 6-136 *The* ***Extract*** *area expanded*

3. Choose the **Accept** button; the extracted shape is displayed in the Subtool list as a separate entity. You will notice that the extracted shape cannot be edited. Choose the extracted shape in the Subtool list in the **SubTool** subpalette; its color changes. However, a mask is displayed on its surface. Next, press and hold the CTRL key and drag the cursor in the canvas area; the mask is removed, refer to Figure 6-137.

4. Choose the Current Brush button from the left shelf; a flyout containing different sculpting brushes is displayed. Choose the **Move** brush from this flyout and move the extracted shape downward to create an outfit, refer to Figure 6-138. You need to adjust the brush size as per your requirement.

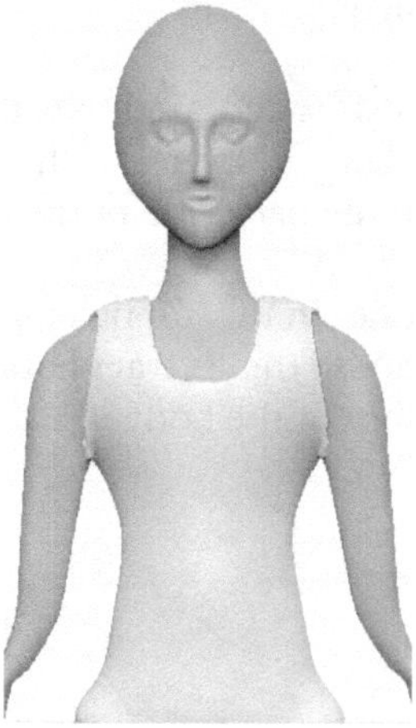

Figure 6-137 The mask removed from the surface

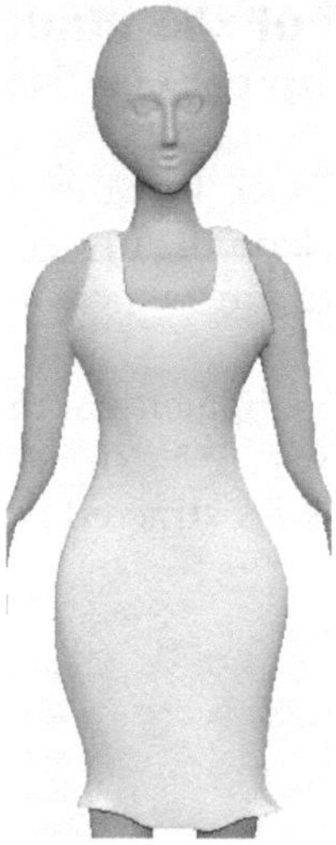

*Figure 6-138 The dress created using the **Move** brush*

Creating the Hair of the Mannequin

In this section, you will create the hair of the mannequin.

1. Select the thumbnail for the mannequin in the list of subtools. Press and hold the CTRL key; the **MaskPen** brush is activated. Next, with the CTRL key pressed, create a mask on the head, refer to Figure 6-139.

2. Expand the **SubTool** subpalette. In this subpalette, expand the **Extract** area. Next, in this area, choose the **Extract** button. After some time, the shape of the mask is extracted from the surface of the head.

3. Choose the **Accept** button; the extracted shape is displayed in the SubTool list as a separate entity. You will notice that the extracted shape cannot be edited. Choose the extracted shape in the SubTool list; its color changes. However, a mask is displayed on its surface, refer to Figure 6-140. Press and hold the CTRL key and drag the cursor in the canvas area; the mask is removed.

4. Choose the Current Brush button from the left shelf; a flyout containing different sculpting brushes is displayed. Choose the **Move** brush from this flyout and move the extracted shape downward to create a shape, as shown Figure 6-141. You need to adjust the brush size as per your requirement.

5. Choose the Current Brush button from the left shelf; a flyout containing different sculpting brushes is displayed. Choose the **Inflat** brush from this flyout and add depth to the hair, as shown Figure 6-142. If required, use the **Smooth** brush to remove any distortions in the geometry.

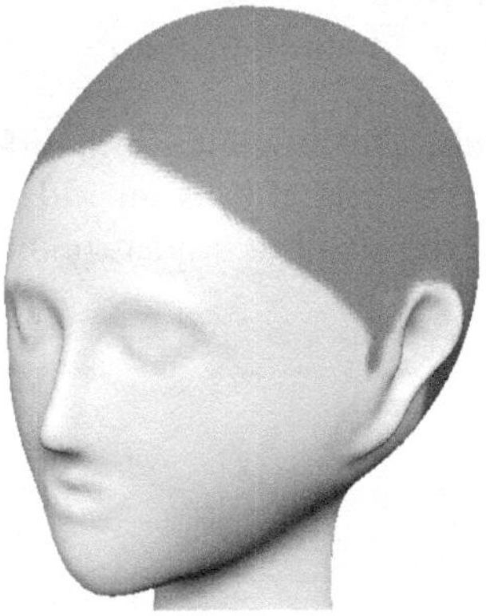

Figure 6-139 *Mask created for the hair*

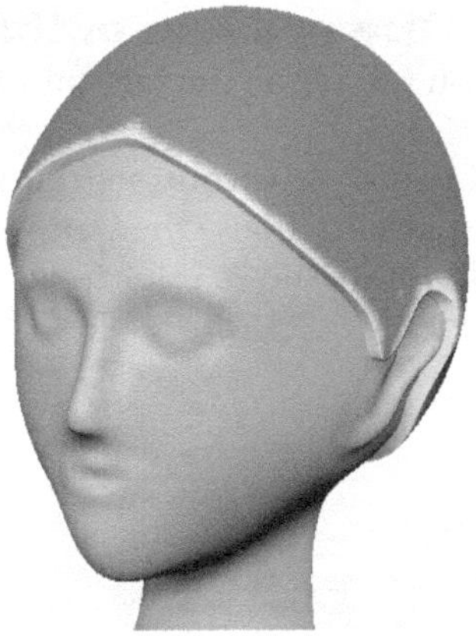

Figure 6-140 *Mask displayed on the surface*

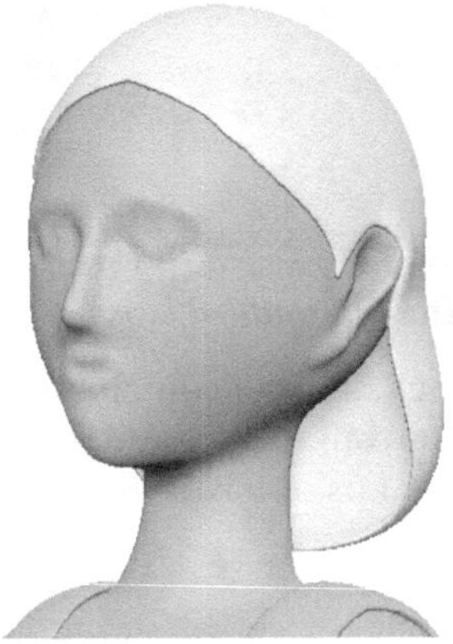

Figure 6-141 *Shape of the hair created using the **Move** brush*

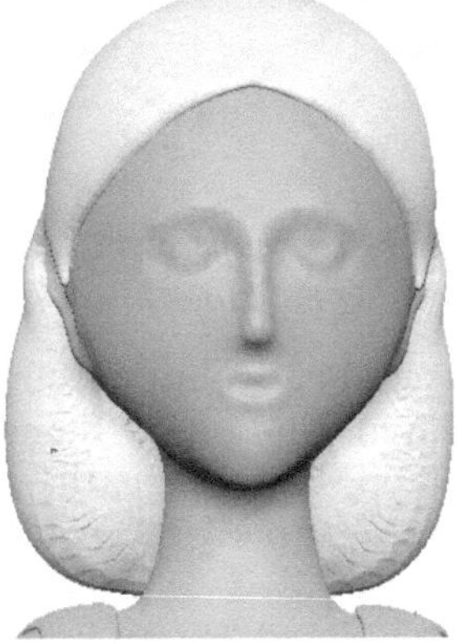

Figure 6-142 *Depth added using the **Inflat** brush*

6. Choose the Current Brush button from the left shelf; a flyout containing different sculpting brushes is displayed. Choose the **Move** brush from this flyout and modify the shape of the hair using this brush, refer to Figure 6-143.

7. In the **SubTool** subpalette, select the first subtool in the list. Next, choose the **MergeDown** button; a message box is displayed. Choose the **OK** button; the body and the outfit are merged.

8. Select the merged subtool, and again choose the **MergeDown** button; a message box is displayed. Choose the **OK** button; the body and the hair are merged. Next, press and hold the CTRL key and drag the cursor in the canvas area; the entire body is converted into DynaMesh.

Refining the Face and Hair of the Mannequin

In this section, you will refine the face and hair of the mannequin using different brushes.

1. Choose the Current Brush button from the left shelf; a flyout containing different sculpting brushes is displayed. Choose the **Dam_Standard** brush from this flyout and using this brush, create nostrils on the nose, refer to Figure 6-144. You need to adjust the brush size as per your requirement.

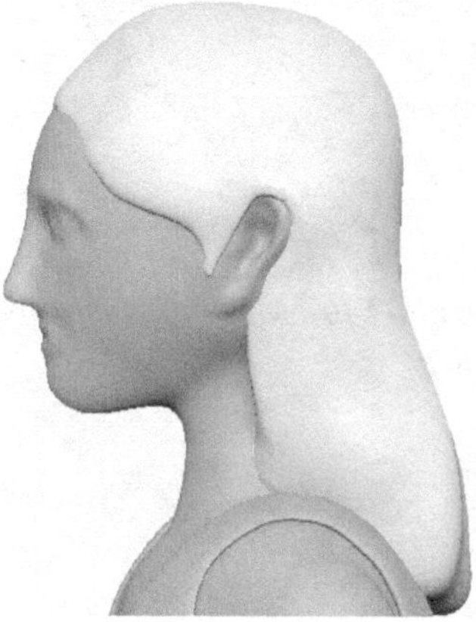

Figure 6-143 *Shape of the hair modified using the* ***Move*** *brush*

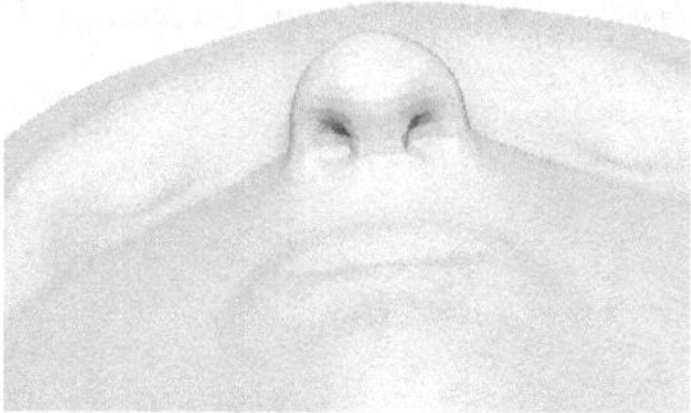

Figure 6-144 *Nostrils created using the* ***Dam_Standard*** *brush*

2. Choose the Current Brush button from the left shelf; a flyout containing different sculpting brushes is displayed. Choose the **Standard** brush from this flyout. Next, choose the **Zadd** button from the top shelf. Create the shape of the lips, refer to Figure 6-145. You need to adjust the brush size as per your requirement.

3. Choose the Current Brush button from the left shelf; a flyout containing different sculpting brushes is displayed. Choose the **Pinch** brush from this flyout. Drag the cursor at the ends of the lips to refine their shape, refer to Figure 6-146. Similarly, add depth to the eyes and hair using the **Standard** brush, refer to Figures 6-147 and 6-148.

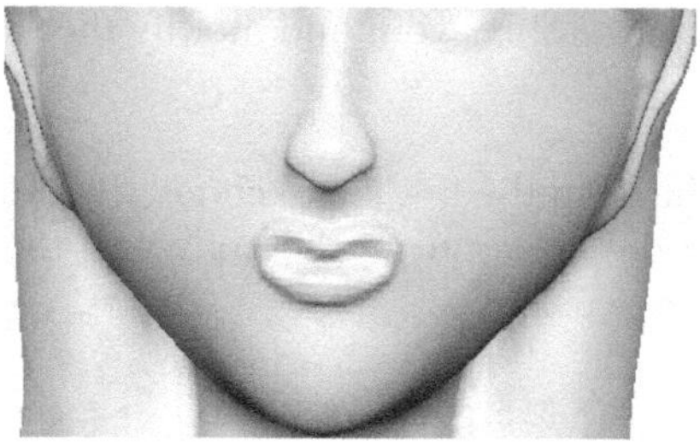

Figure 6-145 *Lips created using the* ***Standard*** *brush*

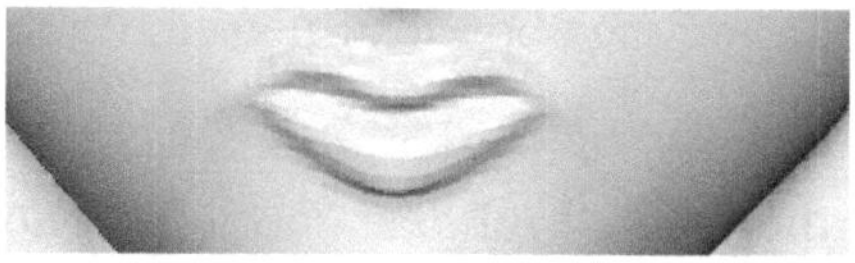

Figure 6-146 *Shape of the lips refined using the* ***Pinch*** *brush*

Figure 6-147 *Depth added to the eyes using the* ***Standard*** *brush*

Figure 6-148 *Depth added to the hair using the* ***Standard*** *brush*

Creating the Accessories for the Mannequin

In this section, you will create the accessories of the mannequin using different brushes.

1. Press and hold the CTRL key; the **MaskPen** brush is activated. Next, with the CTRL key pressed, create a mask on the feet of the body to form the shape of the shoes, refer to Figure 6-149. Make sure you create a mask on the back side of the feet also.

2. Expand the **SubTool** subpalette. In this subpalette, expand the **Extract** area. Next, in this area, choose the **Extract** button. After some time, the shape of the mask is extracted from the surface of the feet, refer to Figure 6-150.

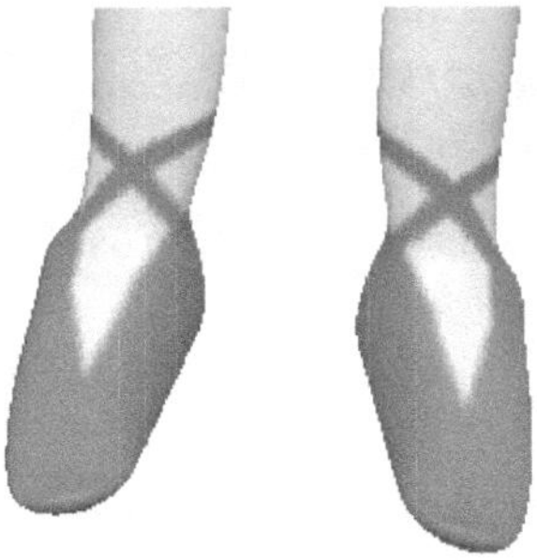

Figure 6-149 *Mask created for the shoes*

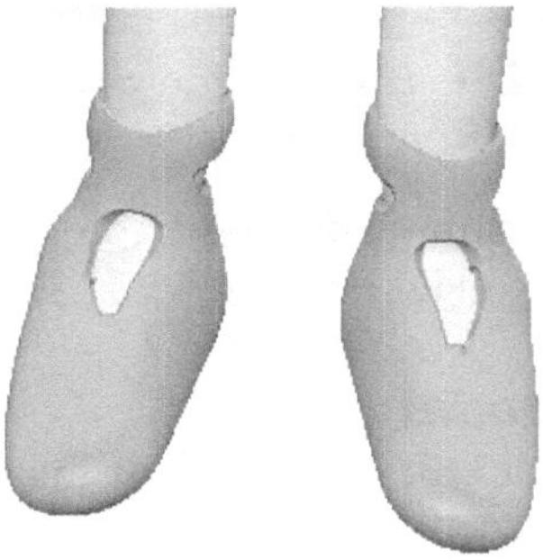

Figure 6-150 *The mask extracted from the surface*

3. Choose the **Accept** button; the extracted shape is displayed in the subtool list as a separate entity.

4. Choose the Current Brush button from the left shelf; a flyout containing different sculpting brushes is displayed. Choose the **InsertHRing** brush from this flyout and create a ring on the ears; a mask is applied on the body. Also, a ring is inserted on the left side as the symmetry is activated in the X-axis by default, refer to Figure 6-151.

5. Choose the Current Brush button from the left shelf; a flyout containing different sculpting brushes is displayed. Choose the **InsertCylndrExt** brush from this flyout and drag the cursor on the left side of the neck; a necklace is created, as shown in Figure 6-152. Next, press and hold the CTRL key and drag the cursor in the canvas area; the mask is removed from the entire body.

Figure 6-151 *Earrings created using the **InsertHRing** brush*

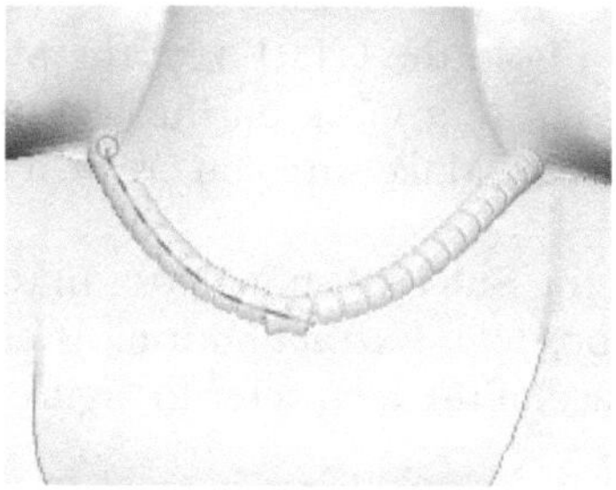

Figure 6-152 *Necklace created using the **InsertCylndrExt** brush*

6. If required, manipulate the shape of the body using the **Move** brush to create the final model, refer to Figures 6-92.

Saving the Model

In this section, you will save the file using the steps given next.

1. Choose the **Save As** button from the **Tool** palette; the **Save ZTool** dialog box is displayed. In this dialog box, browse to the location: *\Documents\ZBrushprojects\c06*.

2. Enter **c06tut3** in the **File name** edit box and then choose the **Save** button.

Tutorial 4

In this tutorial, you will create a bangle using the **NanoMesh** tool. The final output of the model is shown in Figure 6-153. **(Expected time: 40 min)**

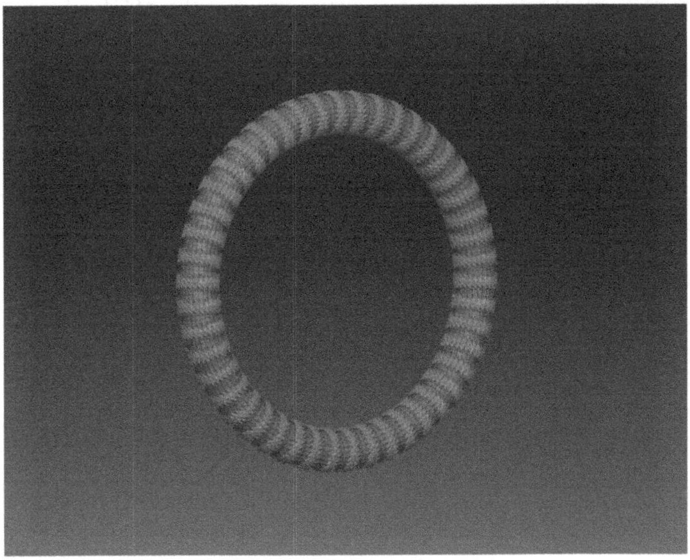

Figure 6-153 *The model of bangle*

The following steps are required to complete this tutorial:

a. Create the bangle.
b. Create design of the bangle.
c. Save the model.

Creating a Bangle

In this section, you will create the bangle.

1. Choose the **Init ZBrush** button from the **Preferences** palette; ZBrush is initialized to its default state.

2. Choose the Current Tool button from the **Tool** palette; a flyout is displayed. Choose the **Ring3D** primitive from this flyout and create it in the canvas, refer to Figure 6-154.

3. Choose the **Edit** button from the top shelf. Next, choose the **PolyF** button from the **Transform** palette; the polygon edges on the sphere are displayed.

4. Press and hold the left mouse button and drag the cursor downward in the canvas area such that the ring is rotated. While dragging the cursor, press the SHIFT key; the ring is snapped at right angle to the canvas, as shown in Figure 6-155.

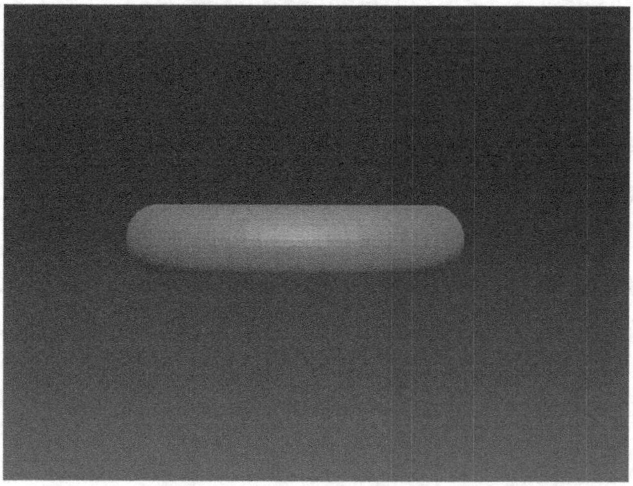

Figure 6-154 *The **Ring3D** created in the canvas*

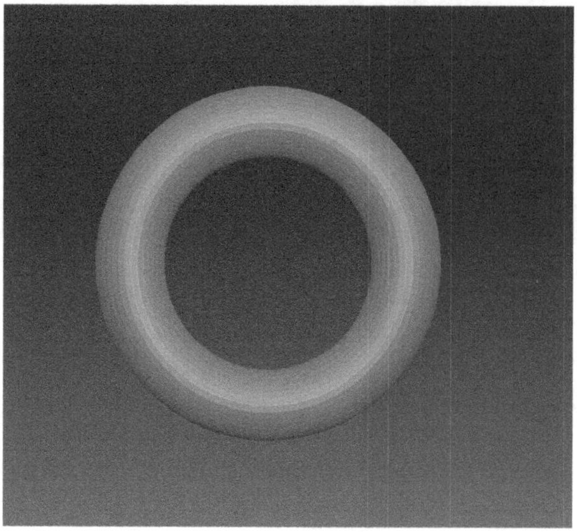

Figure 6-155 *Ring is snapped at right angle to the canvas*

5. Expand the **Initialize** subpalette in the **Tool** palette. In this subpalette, set the value of **SRadius** to **32**. Next, set the value of the **SDivide** slider to **14** and **LDivide** slider to **32**; the shape of sphere changes, as shown in Figure 6-156.

Figure 6-156 *Shape of the ring changed*

6. Choose the **Make PolyMesh3D** button from the **Tool** palette to convert the primitive sphere into polymesh. Next, choose the **PolyF** button from the right shelf; the polygon edges on the sphere disappear.

Creating Design of the Bangle

In this section, you will create design of the bangle.

1. Choose the Current Brush button from the left shelf; a flyout containing different sculpting brushes is displayed. Choose the **ZModeler** brush from this flyout.

2. Hover the cursor on the polygon of the ring and then right-click; a **ZMODELER** window is displayed. Next, choose the **Insert NanoMesh** option from the **POLYGON ACTIONS** area and the **All Polygons** option from the **TARGET** area of the **ZMODELER** window, as shown in Figure 6-157.

3. Press the M key; the Current Tool flyout is displayed. Next, choose the **PolyMesh3D** primitive from the flyout.

4. Hover the cursor on the polygon of the ring, as shown in Figure 6-158 and drag; the instances of **PolyMesh3D** are created, as shown in Figure 6-159.

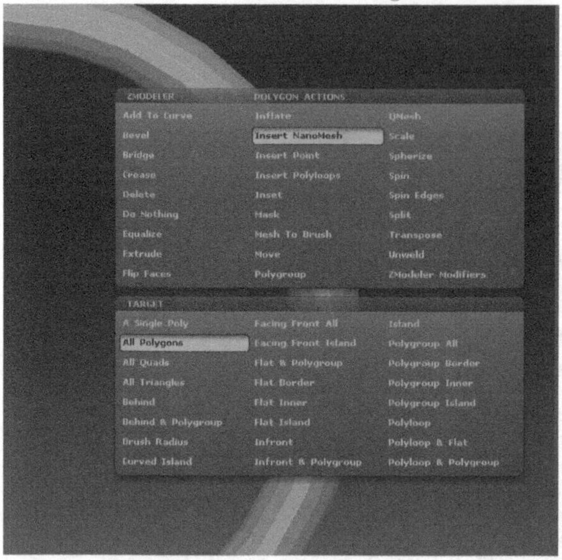

Figure 6-157 *The **Insert NanoMesh** and **All Polygons** options chosen from the **ZMODELER** window*

Figure 6-158 *Hover the cursor on the polygon*

Figure 6-159 *The instances of* ***PolyMesh3D***

5. Expand the **NanoMesh** subpalette in the **Tool** palette. In this subpalette, set the value **2** in the **H Title** slider and the value **2** in the **V Title** slider. The NanoMesh is arranged on the bangle, as shown in Figure 6-160.

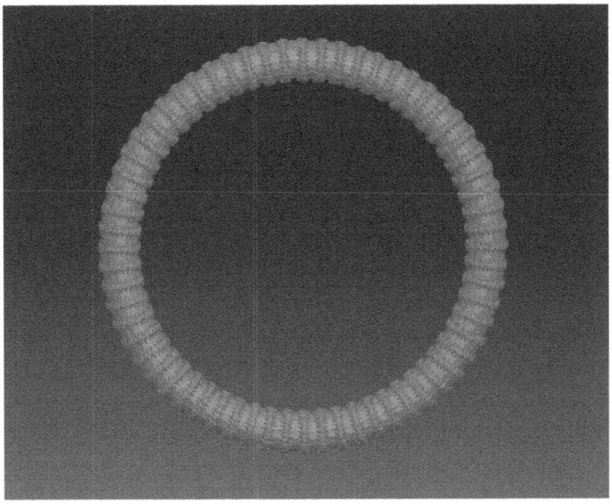

Figure 6-160 *The bangle is created*

Saving the Model

In this section, you will save the file using the steps given next.

1. Choose the **Save As** button from the **Tool** palette; the **Save ZTool** dialog box is displayed. In this dialog box, browse to the location: *\Documents\ZBrushprojects\c06*.

2. Enter **c06tut4** in the **File name** edit box and then choose the **Save** button.

Self-Evaluation Test

Answer the following questions and then compare them to those given at the end of this chapter:

1. Which of the following buttons is used to retain the existing details in the model when it is converted into DynaMesh?

   (a) **DynaMesh** (b) **Group**
   (c) **Add** (d) **Project**

2. Which of the following buttons is used to retain the intersecting geometry between two meshes and delete the remaining geometry?

   (a) **And** (b) **Sub**
   (c) **Project** (d) **Add**

3. Which of the following sliders is used to determine the level to which the ZRemesher follows the guide curves that are created using the **ZRemesherGuides** brush?

   (a) **MaskDensity** (b) **CStiffness**
   (c) **Resolution** (d) **Blur**

4. The __________ button is used to increase the polygon count in a retopologized model to almost double the original value.

5. The __________ slider is used to control the number of polygons that are added to the masked areas of the model on choosing the **ZRemesher** button.

6. The __________ slider is used to control the depth of the hole created on the surface of the DynaMesh using the **Create Shell** button.

7. The **Resolution** slider is used to used to control the number of polygons in a DynaMesh. (T/F)

8. The **ZRemesher** button is used to define the number the polygons that will be present in the retopologized model. (T/F)

9. The **ZRemesher Guides** brush enables you to draw curves on the surface of an object to guide the flow of polygons according to the curves. (T/F)

10. Higher the value of the **MDensity** slider, lower will be number of polygons in the retopologized model. (T/F)

Review Questions

Answer the following questions:

1. Which of the following buttons is used to split the mesh into separate pieces depending upon the number of poly groups in the mesh?

   (a) **Group** (b) **Polish**
   (c) **Project** (d) **Add**

2. The change in the topology of a model is referred to as _________ .

3. The **ZRemesher** button is located in the _________ subpalette .

4. DynaMesh modeling is similar to _________ modeling.

5. The _________ slider is used to define the number of polygons that will be present in the retopologized model.

6. The **Blur** slider is used to control the level of smoothness and blurring in the edges of a primitive when it is converted into DynaMesh. (T/F)

7. On choosing the **Same** button along with the **ZRemesher** button, the topology of the model will not change. (T/F)

8. If the value of the **CStiffness** slider in the **ZRemesher** area is set to **1**, the flow of polygons will exactly match the guide curves. (T/F)

EXERCISE

The output of the model used in the exercise can be accessed by downloading the *c06_ZBrush_2022_exr.zip* file from *www.cadcim.com*. The path of the file is as follows: *Textbooks > Animation and Visual Effects > ZBrush > ZBrush 2022: A Comprehensive Guide.*

Exercise 1

Create the model of a cartoon monkey, as shown in Figure 6-161 using the **DefaultWaxSphere.ZPR** file and the **DynaMesh** tool. **(Expected time: 30 min)**

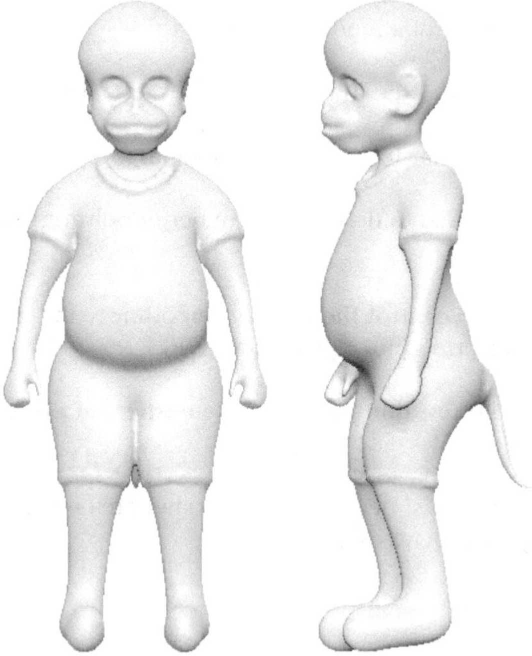

Figure 6-161 *Model of the cartoon monkey*

Answers to Self-Evaluation Test

1. d, **2.** a, **3.** b, **4. Double**, **5. MDensity**, **6. Thickness**, **7.** T, **8.** F, **9.** T, **10.** F

Chapter 7

ShadowBox

Learning Objectives

After completing this chapter, you will be able to:

- *Work with the ShadowBox*
- *Create different models using the ShadowBox*

INTRODUCTION

In this chapter, you will learn to create different models using the ShadowBox tool. This tool is used to create basic shapes and not the highly detailed models. However, the basic models created in ShadowBox can be sculpted later using different brushes.

ShadowBox

The ShadowBox tool consists of three planes and is used to create basic 3D models with low details. The 3D models will be created inside the Shadow Box. To create the basic shape of the model, you need to paint on a desired plane with the profile of the model to be created using the Mask brushes. To create a Shadow Box, you need to create a primitive in the canvas.

Next, you need to convert the primitive object into a polymesh. To do so, choose the **Make PolyMesh3D** button from the **Tool** palette. Next, expand the **Geometry** subpalette in the **Tool** palette. In this subpalette, expand the **ShadowBox** area and then choose the **ShadowBox** button, refer to Figure 7-1; a ShadowBox will be created in the canvas and the shape of the sphere will change. Figure 7-2 shows the ShadowBox created using Sphere D primitive.

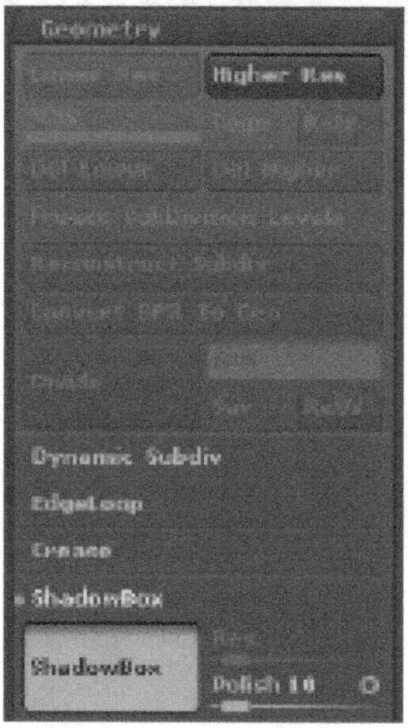

*Figure 7-1 The **ShadowBox** button chosen in the **Geometry** subpalette*

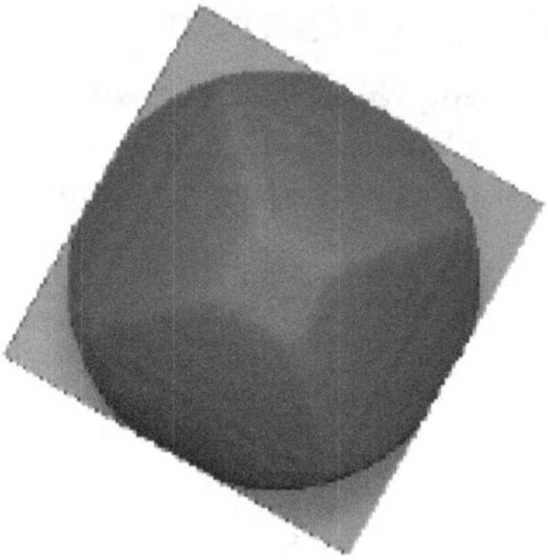

Figure 7-2 ShadowBox displayed in the canvas

On rotating the view of the canvas, you will be able to view the cubic ShadowBox, refer to Figure 7-3. You will notice that the mask is applied on the three planes of the ShadowBox. These masks represent the front, side, and bottom projections of the sphere that are placed inside the ShadowBox, refer to Figure 7-4. Figures 7-5 and 7-6 show different primitives and their corresponding projections displayed in the ShadowBox.

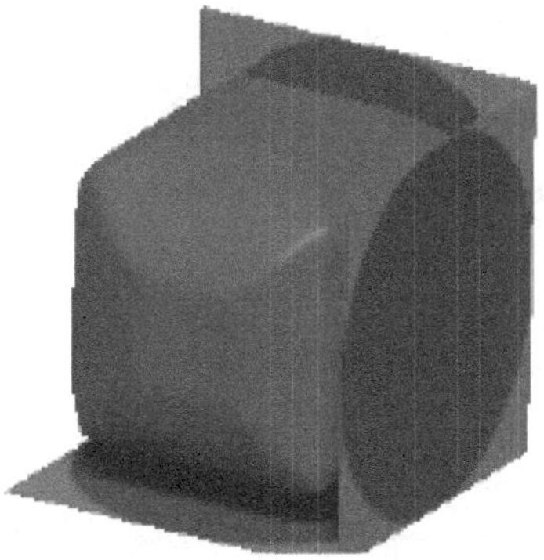

Figure 7-3 *The cubic ShadowBox*

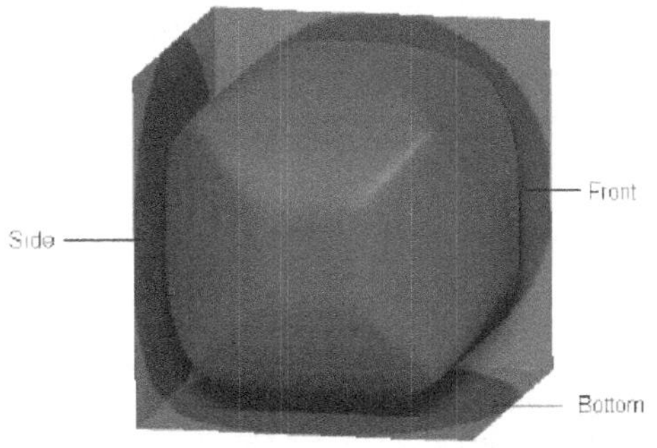

Figure 7-4 *The front, side, and bottom projections of the sphere in the ShadowBox*

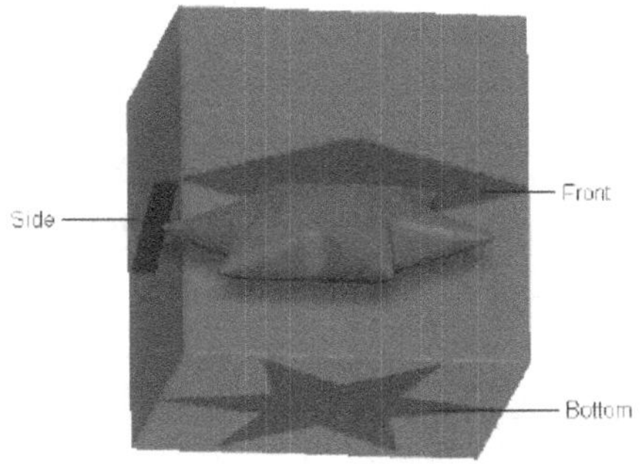

Figure 7-5 *The front, side, and bottom projections of the* ***PolyMesh3D_1*** *primitive*

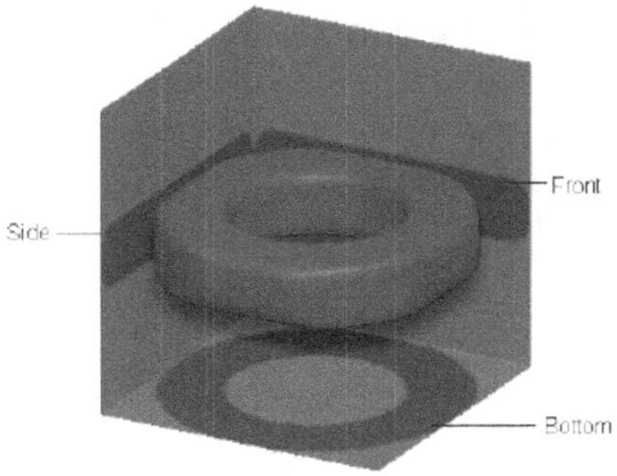

Figure 7-6 *The front, side, and bottom projections of the* ***Ring3D*** *primitive*

Creating 3D Objects Using ShadowBox

You can also create different 3D objects inside the ShadowBox by painting their front, side, and bottom projections in the planes of the ShadowBox using the Mask brushes. However, before painting the projections, you need to create a primitive object in the canvas and then convert it into a polymesh. After creating the polymesh, choose the **ShadowBox** button from the **Geometry** subpalette; the ShadowBox will be displayed. Now, you need to clear the existing object inside the ShadowBox. To do so, press and hold the CTRL key and drag the cursor in the canvas area; the existing projections and the 3D object will be cleared from the ShadowBox, refer to Figure 7-7. After clearing the projections from the ShadowBox, you can create the projections of your own choice. On doing so, a 3D object corresponding to the projections will be displayed in the ShadowBox.

To create the projections, you need to activate the Mask brushes. You can use any of the Mask brushes or simply use the default **MaskPen** brush. To create projections using the **MaskPen** brush, press and hold the CTRL key and drag the cursor on the front plane of the ShadowBox to create a projection of your choice, refer to Figure 7-8; a 3D mesh corresponding to that projection will be created inside the ShadowBox, refer to Figure 7-9.

You will notice that the front view of the 3D mesh will be exactly the same as the projection painted in the front plane. In addition to this, gray lines will be displayed on all the planes of the ShadowBox. These lines represent the bounding box for the mesh and enable you to know the location from where you can create projections on the planes of the ShadowBox. On rotating the canvas, you can view the side and top views of the 3D mesh, refer to Figures 7-10 and 7-11.

Figure 7-7 *The projections and 3D object cleared from the ShadowBox*

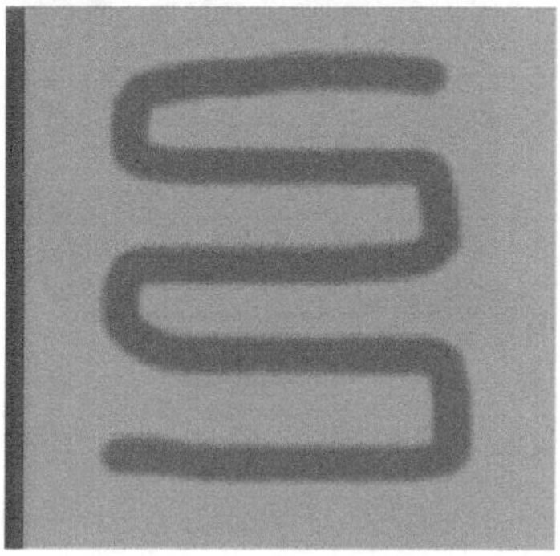

Figure 7-8 *Projection created in the front plane using the **MaskPen** brush*

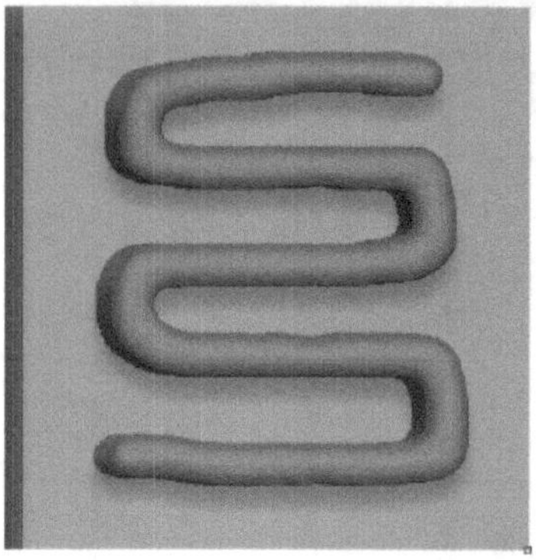

Figure 7-9 *3D mesh created inside the ShadowBox*

Figure 7-10 *Side view of the 3D mesh*

Figure 7-11 *Top view of the 3D mesh*

You can also modify the 3D mesh by painting the corresponding projections in the bounding boxes of the bottom and side planes of the ShadowBox. For instance, you can decrease the depth of the 3D mesh by painting a projection in the side view. To do so, choose the Current Brush button; a flyout containing different brushes will be displayed. From this flyout, choose the **MaskRect** brush; a message box prompting you to press CTRL key to activate this brush will be displayed. Choose the **OK** button to close this message box. Next, rotate the canvas such that you can view the back of the side plane of the ShadowBox. While rotating the canvas, press the SHIFT key; the side plane of the ShadowBox will be snapped to the canvas, refer to Figure 7-12. Next, press and hold the CTRL key and drag the cursor between the bounding box on the side plane to create a rectangular stroke, refer to Figure 7-13. On releasing the left mouse button and rotating the canvas, you will notice that the depth of the 3D mesh will decrease and will exactly match the mask created in the side plane, refer to Figure 7-14.

Figure 7-12 *Side plane of the ShadowBox snapped to the canvas*

Figure 7-13 *Rectangular stroke created in the side plane of the ShadowBox*

Figure 7-14 *Depth of the 3D mesh decreased according to the mask*

You can also modify the top/bottom part of the 3D mesh by painting the corresponding projection in the bottom plane of the ShadowBox. To do so, choose the Current Brush button; a flyout containing different brushes will be displayed. In this flyout, choose the **MaskPen** brush; a message box asking you to press the CTRL key to activate this brush will be displayed. Choose the **OK** button to close this message box. Next, rotate the canvas such that you can view the back side of the bottom plane of the ShadowBox. While rotating the canvas, press the SHIFT key; the bottom plane of the ShadowBox will be snapped to the canvas. Next, press and hold the CTRL key and drag the cursor to create a shape, as shown in Figure 7-15. On releasing the left mouse button and rotating the canvas, you will notice that the top view of the 3D mesh changes and matches the mask created on the bottom plane and it has matched with the mask created in the bottom plane, refer to Figure 7-16.

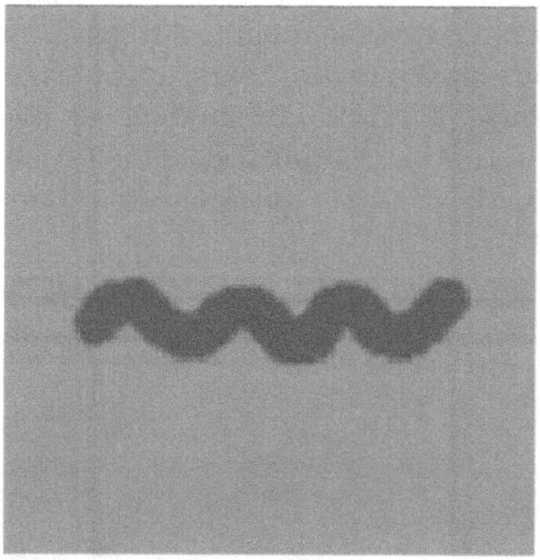

Figure 7-15 *Mask created in the bottom plane of the ShadowBox*

Figure 7-16 *Top view of the 3D mesh modified according to the mask*

Modifying 3D Objects in the ShadowBox

You can modify the shape of the 3D objects in the ShadowBox. To modify the shape of the 3D objects, you need to modify the shape of the mask. When you modify the shape, the corresponding changes are reflected in the 3D object. You can add depth to an existing mesh or delete some areas of the mesh. To modify the shape of an object, create a projection in the front plane of the ShadowBox using the **MaskPen** brush, as discussed earlier, refer to Figure 7-17. After creating the mask, the 3D mesh having the same shape as that of the mask will be created in the ShadowBox, refer to Figure 7-18.

Figure 7-17 *Mask created in the front plane of the ShadowBox*

Figure 7-18 *3D mesh created in the ShadowBox*

You can modify the 3D mesh in the front view by modifying the shape of the mask. To do so, you need to rotate the canvas such that you can view the back side of the front plane of the ShadowBox. While rotating the canvas, press the SHIFT key; the back side of the front plane of the ShadowBox will be snapped to the canvas. Next, press and hold the CTRL key and drag the cursor to modify the shape of the mask, refer to Figure 7-19. Now, rotate the canvas to view the 3D mesh; the modified 3D mesh will be displayed in the ShadowBox, refer to Figure 7-20.

Figure 7-19 *Shape of the mask modified in the back side of the front plane*

Figure 7-20 *Shape of the 3D mesh modified*

You can also delete a particular area from the 3D mesh. To do so, rotate the canvas such that you can view the back side of the front plane of the ShadowBox. While rotating the canvas, press the SHIFT key; the back side of the front plane of the ShadowBox will be snapped to the canvas. Next, press and hold the CTRL+ALT keys and drag the cursor to delete certain areas of the mask, refer to Figure 7-21. Rotate the canvas to view the front plane of the ShadowBox; the modified 3D mesh will be displayed in the ShadowBox, refer to Figure 7-22.

Figure 7-21 *Shape of the mask modified in the back side of the front plane*

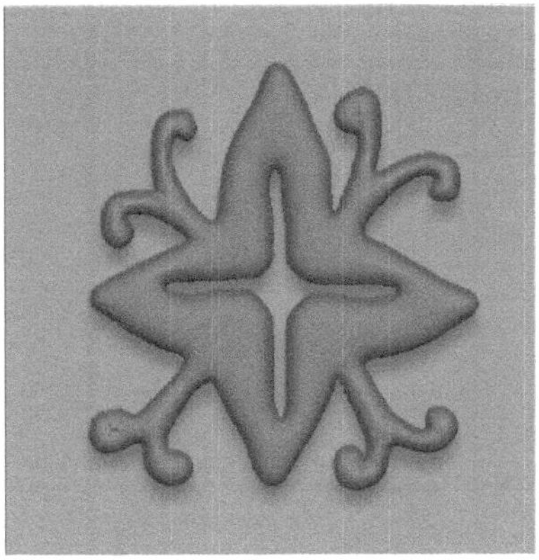

Figure 7-22 *Shape of the 3D object modified*

You can also use different alpha images for creating masks in the ShadowBox. Besides this, you can also use different reference images in the ShadowBox for creating a 3D object. The procedure for using the reference images will be discussed in the later chapters.

Symmetry in the ShadowBox

You can create symmetrical shapes conveniently by activating the symmetry in the ShadowBox. When you activate the symmetry, the mask created on one side will be replicated on the opposite side as well, depending upon the axis chosen. The symmetry can be activated by choosing the **Activate Symmetry** button located in the **Transform** palette. By default, the symmetry will be activated for the X-axis. Create a mask on the back side of the front plane using the **MaskPen** brush, refer to Figure 7-23. Rotate the canvas; the 3D mesh will be displayed in the ShadowBox, refer to Figure 7-24.

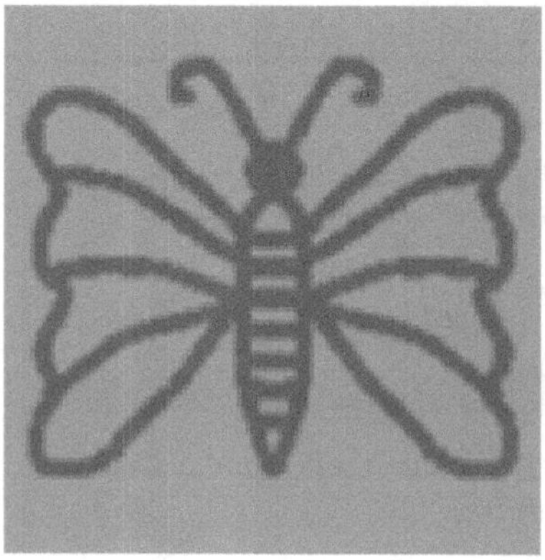

Figure 7-23 *Mask created with the symmetry activated in X-axis*

Figure 7-24 *3D object created in the ShadowBox*

You can also activate radial symmetry to create circular shapes in the ShadowBox. To create a circular shape in the ShadowBox, clear the mesh inside it by pressing and holding the CTRL key and then dragging the cursor in the canvas area. Next, choose the **>Y<** and **(R)** buttons in the **Activate Symmetry** area of the **Transform** palette, refer to Figure 7-25. Set the value of the **RadialCount** slider to **20**, refer to Figure 7-25; the radial symmetry will be activated in the Y-axis, refer to Figure 7-26.

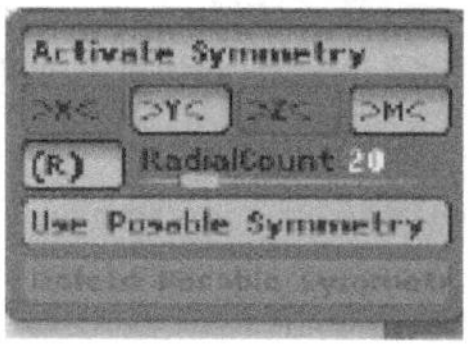

Figure 7-25 *The value of the* ***RadialCount*** *slider set to* ***20***

Figure 7-26 *Radial symmetry activated in the Y-axis*

Press and hold the CTRL key; the **MaskPen** brush will be activated. Decrease the brush size and then drag the cursor on the front plane of the ShadowBox to create a pattern, refer to Figure 7-27; a circular 3D mesh will be created in the ShadowBox, refer to Figure 7-28.

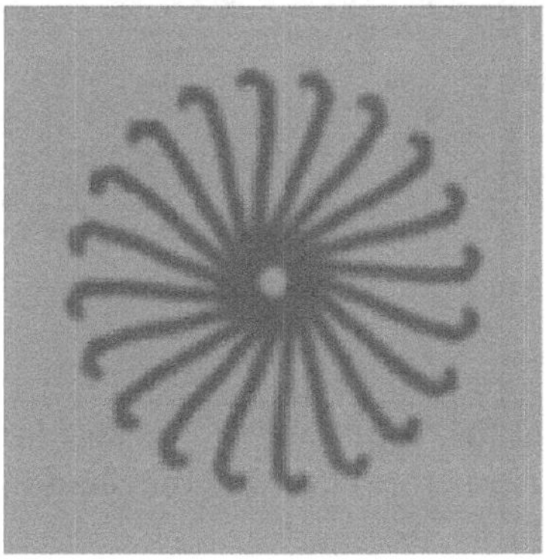

Figure 7-27 *Mask created in the front plane of the ShadowBox*

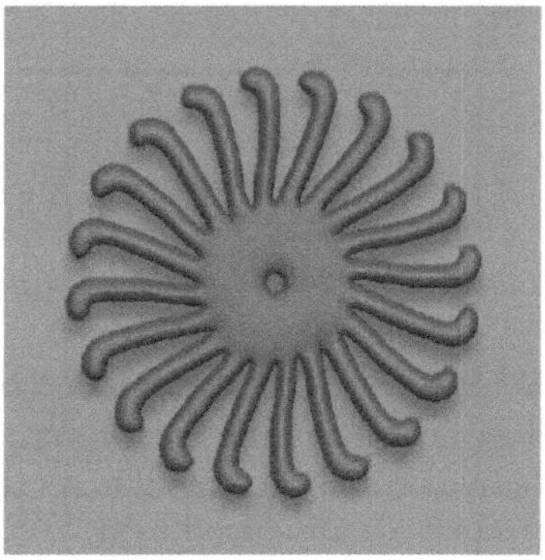

Figure 7-28 *A circular 3D mesh created in the ShadowBox*

You can also modify the shape of the circular 3D mesh. To do so, rotate the canvas to view the back side of the front plane. Next, press and hold the CTRL+ALT keys and then drag the cursor to remove the mask in a radial pattern, refer to Figure 7-29. Rotate the canvas to view the front side of the plane; the shape of the 3D mesh will be modified according to the mask, refer to Figure 7-30.

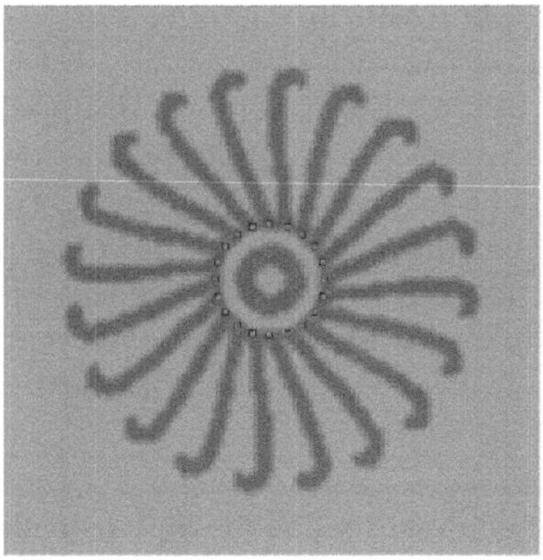

Figure 7-29 *Shape of the mask modified in the back side of the front plane*

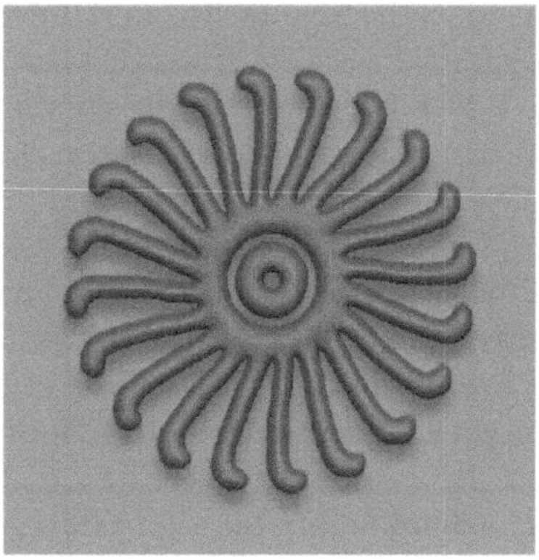

Figure 7-30 *Shape of the 3D object modified*

When a 3D object is created in the ShadowBox, its projections remain hidden behind it. To view the projections, you need to rotate the canvas such that you can view the back sides of the planes. However, you can view the projections in the front side of the ShadowBox by turning on the transparency in the 3D mesh. To do so, choose the **Transp** button in the right shelf and then choose the **Ghost** button located below the **Transp** button; the 3D mesh will become transparent and the mask will be clearly visible in the front plane of the ShadowBox, refer to Figure 7-31. Now, you can modify the 3D mesh without rotating the canvas. For example, in Figure 7-32, the depth of the 3D mesh has been decreased by creating a rectangular mask in the side plane of the ShadowBox.

Figure 7-31 Ghost transparency activated

Figure 7-32 Depth of the object modified

Attributes of the ShadowBox

The ShadowBox area in the **Geometry** subpalette of the **Tool** palette consists of two attributes namely **Res** and **Polish**. You need to set these attributes before choosing the **ShadowBox** button. These attributes are discussed next.

Res

The **Res** slider is used to specify the number of polygons in the planes of the ShadowBox. The default value set in this slider is 128. If the value of this slider is higher, the 3D mesh created in the ShadowBox will have more number of polygons and will be more accurate. To set the number of polygons in the planes of the ShadowBox, create a primitive sphere in the canvas and then convert it into a polymesh. Set the value of the **Res** slider to **16** and then choose the **ShadowBox** button. Next, choose the **PolyF** button from the right shelf; the polygon edges will be displayed on the ShadowBox and the shape of the sphere will also change, refer to Figure 7-33.

Press the CTRL key and drag the cursor in the canvas area; the sphere will disappear from the ShadowBox. Choose the **PolyF** button again to hide the polygon edges in the ShadowBox. Next, choose the Current Brush button from the left shelf; a flyout containing different brushes will be displayed. In this flyout, choose the **MaskCircle** brush; a message box asking you to press CTRL key to activate this brush will be displayed. Choose the **OK** button to close this message box. Next, press and hold the CTRL key and drag the cursor in the front plane to create a circular stroke; a low resolution mask will be created in the front plane and the 3D mesh created will have a very low resolution, refer to Figure 7-34.

Choose the **ShadowBox** button to deactivate it; the ShadowBox will disappear from the canvas and only the 3D mesh will be displayed, refer to Figure 7-35. Set the value of the **Res** slider to **400** and then choose the **ShadowBox** button again; a high resolution mask will be created in the front plane. Also, the 3D mesh created will be of a high resolution, refer to Figure 7-36.

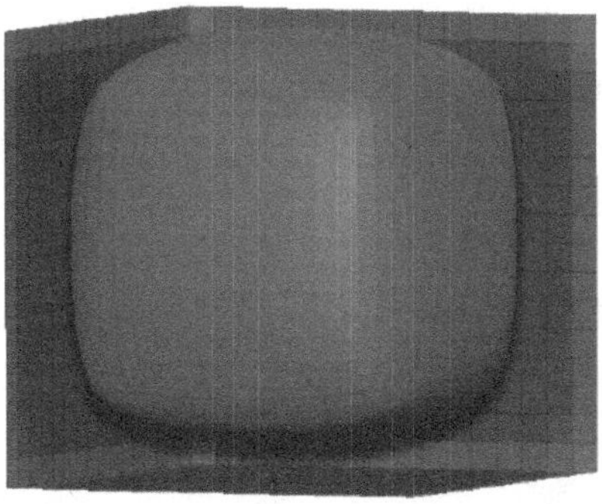

Figure 7-33 *Polygon edges displayed on the ShadowBox*

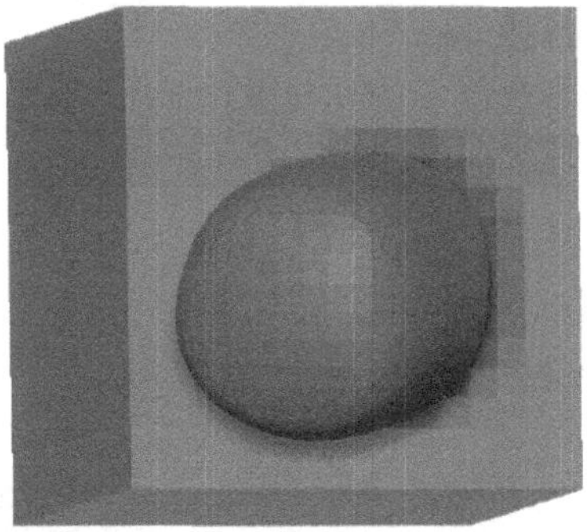

Figure 7-34 *Low resolution 3D mesh created in the ShadowBox*

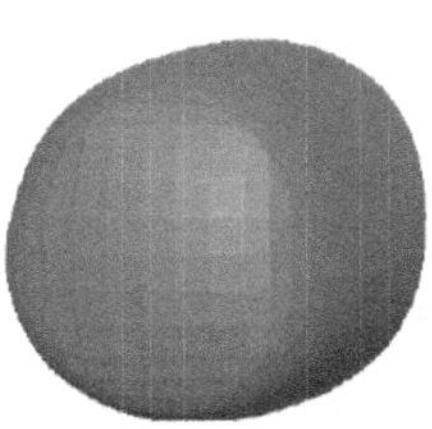

Figure 7-35 *Low resolution 3D object displayed in the canvas*

Figure 7-36 *High resolution 3D mesh created in the ShadowBox*

Polish

The **Polish** slider is used to set the level of smoothness in a 3D mesh. If the value of this slider is set to a higher value, the 3D mesh thus created in the ShadowBox will have smoother edges. However, if the value of this slider is set to a low value, the 3D mesh will have jagged edges. The value of this slider ranges between 0 and 100. Figures 7-37 and 7-38 display the 3D meshes with the value of the **Polish** slider set to **0** and **100**, respectively. In these figures, the mask has been created using the **MaskPen** brush and the value of the **Res** slider has been set to **128**.

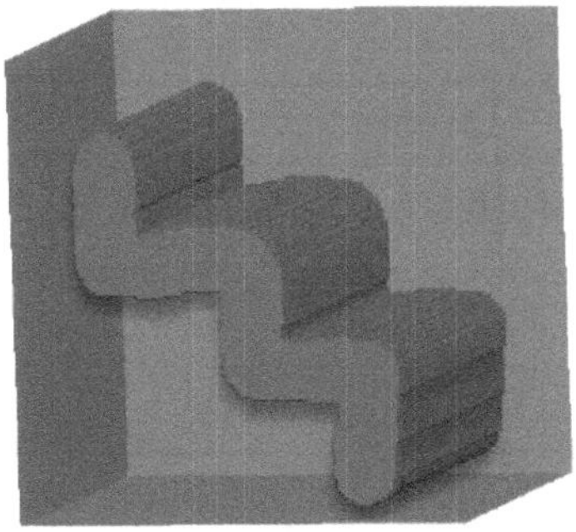

Figure 7-37 *The 3D object created with the value of the* ***Polish*** *slider set to* ***0***

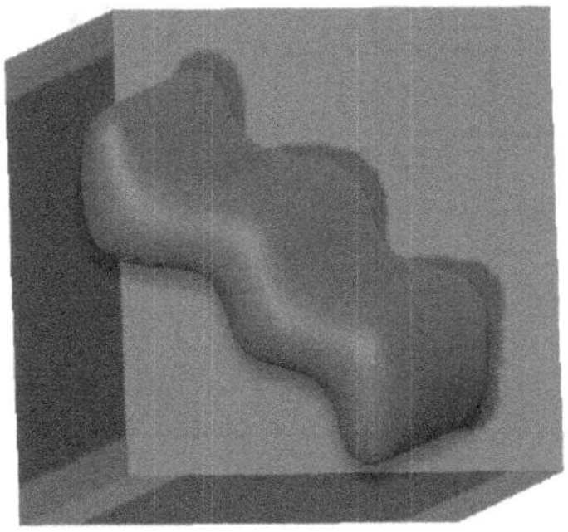

Figure 7-38 *The 3D object created with the value of the* ***Polish*** *slider set to* ***100***

TUTORIALS

Before you start the tutorials of this chapter, navigate to *\Documents\ZBrushprojects* and then create a new folder with the name *c07*.

Tutorial 1

In this tutorial, you will create the model of a key using the ShadowBox. The final output of the model is shown in Figure 7-39. **(Expected time: 20 min)**

Figure 7-39 *The model of a key*

The following steps are required to complete this tutorial:

a. Create the shape of the key in the ShadowBox.
b. Modify the key outside the ShadowBox.
c. Save the model.

Creating the Shape of the Key in the ShadowBox

In this section, you will create the shape of the key using the Mask brushes on the planes of ShadowBox.

1. Choose the **Init ZBrush** button from the **Preferences** palette; the message box is displayed. Choose the **Yes** button from the message box; ZBrush is initialized to its default state.

2. Choose the Current Tool button from the **Tool** palette; a flyout is displayed. Choose the **Sphere3D** primitive from this flyout and create it in the canvas.

3. Choose the **Edit** button from the top shelf.

4. Choose the **Make PolyMesh3D** button from the **Tool** palette to convert the primitive sphere into a polymesh.

5. Expand the **Geometry** subpalette in the **Tool** palette. In this subpalette, set the value of **Res** slider in the **ShadowBox** area to **400**, refer to Figure 7-40.

6. Choose the **ShadowBox** button in the ShadowBox area; a ShadowBox containing a 3D mesh is displayed in the canvas. Rotate the canvas such that you can view the front view of the ShadowBox, refer to Figure 7-41.

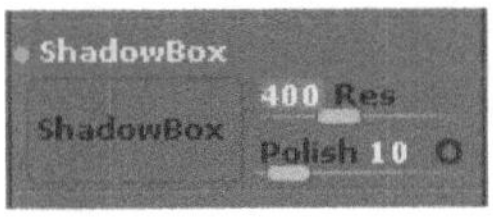

Figure 7-40 *The value of the* ***Res*** *slider set to* ***400***

Figure 7-41 *The front view of the ShadowBox displayed in the canvas*

7. Press and hold the CTRL key and then drag the cursor in the canvas area; the 3D mesh disappears from the ShadowBox. Rotate the canvas such that you can view the back side of the front plane.

8. Choose the Current Brush button from the left shelf; a flyout containing different sculpting brushes is displayed. Choose the **MaskCircle** brush from this flyout; a message box prompting you to press CTRL to use this brush is displayed. Choose the **OK** button to close this message box.

9. Press and hold the CTRL key and choose the Current Stroke button; a flyout is displayed. In this flyout, choose the **Center** button located at the bottom of the flyout, refer to Figure 7-42. Next, release the CTRL key.

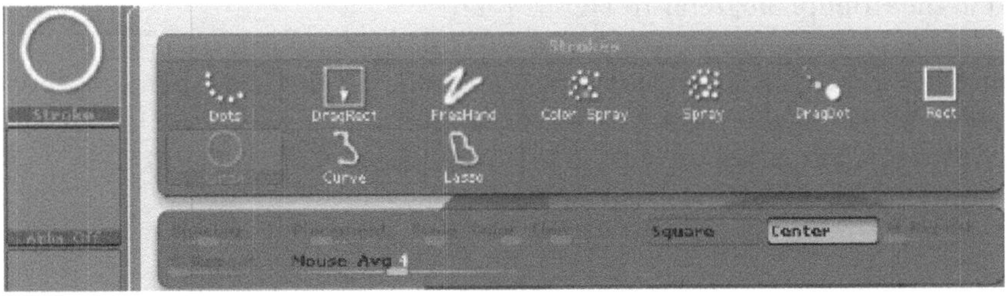

Figure 7-42 *The* ***Center*** *button chosen from the flyout*

10. Press and hold the CTRL key and drag the cursor on the front plane of the ShadowBox to create an elliptical shape on the plane, refer to Figure 7-43. Release the CTRL key; a mask is created in the front plane.

11. Press and hold the CTRL key and choose the Current Stroke button; a flyout is displayed. In this flyout, choose the **Square** button located at the bottom of the flyout. This button enables you to create a perfect circle. Next, release the CTRL key.

12. Press and hold the CTRL key and drag the cursor on the top of the mask created earlier to create a circular stroke, refer to Figure 7-44. Release the CTRL key; another mask is created on the front plane.

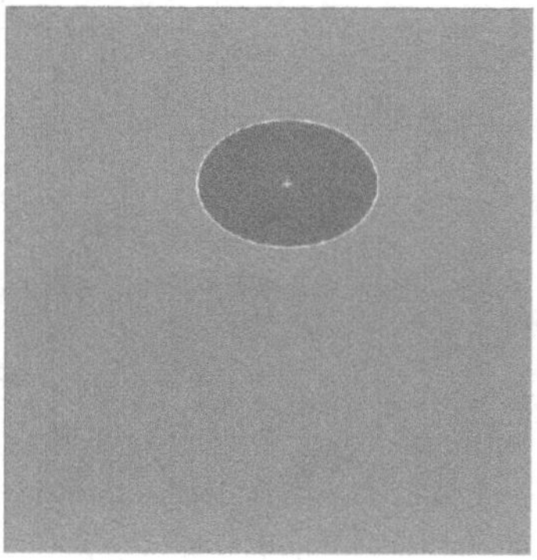

Figure 7-43 *An elliptical stroke created in the backside of the front plane*

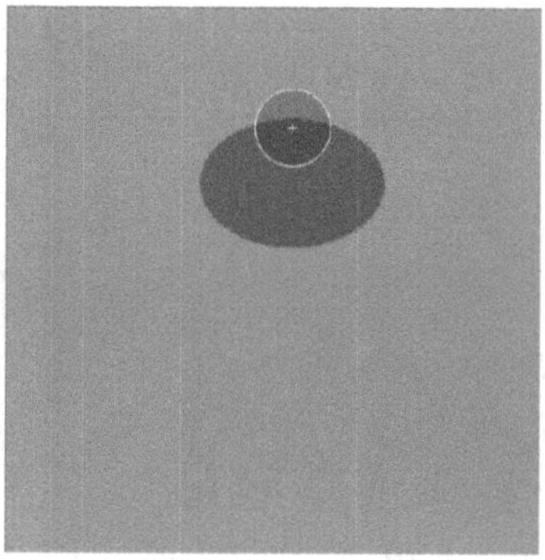

Figure 7-44 *A circular stroke created above the elliptical mask*

13. Press and hold the CTRL+ALT keys and drag the cursor to create a circular stroke at that location, as shown in Figure 7-45. Release the CTRL key; a hole is created in the mask and the 3D object, refer to Figure 7-46.

14. Choose the Current Brush button from the left shelf; a flyout containing different sculpting brushes is displayed. Choose the **MaskRect** brush from this flyout; a message box prompting you to press CTRL to use this brush is displayed. Choose the **OK** button to close this message box.

15. Press and hold the CTRL key and drag the cursor on the front plane of the ShadowBox to create a rectangular stroke below the mask created earlier. Release the CTRL key; a mask is created in the front plane, refer to Figure 7-47.

16. Press and hold the CTRL key and drag the cursor in the front plane to create another rectangular stroke on the right side of the mask created earlier. Release the CTRL key; another rectangular mask is created in the front plane, refer to Figure 7-48.

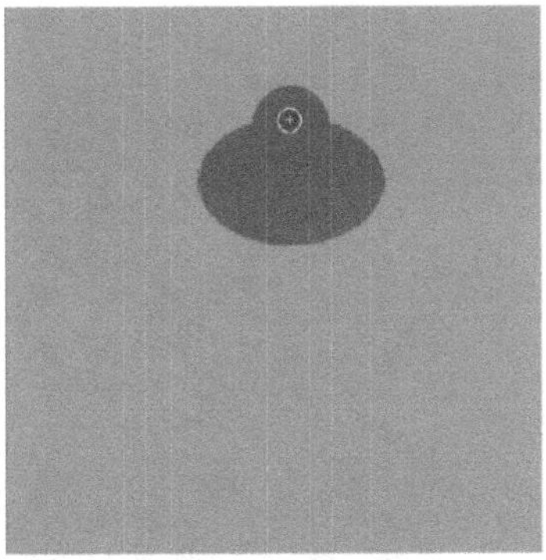

Figure 7-45 *A circular stroke created on the mask with the ALT key pressed*

Figure 7-46 *A hole created in the mask*

Figure 7-47 *A rectangular mask created using the **MaskRect** brush*

Figure 7-48 *A rectangular mask created on the right side of the mask*

17. Press and hold the CTRL+ALT keys and drag the cursor to create another rectangular stroke on the top of the rectangular mask created earlier, refer to Figure 7-49. Release the CTRL+ALT keys; the area where the stroke was created gets deleted and the shape of the mask is modified, refer to Figure 7-50.

18. Press and hold the CTRL key and drag the cursor to create a rectangular stroke below the mask created in Step 15. Release the CTRL key; a mask is created, refer to Figure 7-51.

19. Similarly, create more rectangular strokes to create the bottom part of the key using the **MaskRect** brush, refer to Figure 7-52.

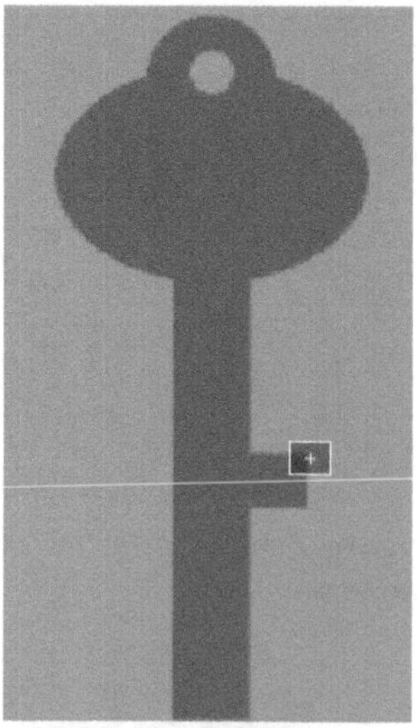

Figure 7-49 *A rectangular stroke created on the mask with the ALT key pressed*

Figure 7-50 *The shape of the mask modified*

Figure 7-51 *Shape of the mask modified using the **MaskRect** brush*

Figure 7-52 *Bottom part of the key created using the **MaskRect** brush*

20. Choose the Current Brush button from the left shelf; a flyout containing different sculpting brushes is displayed. Choose the **MaskCurve** brush from this flyout; a message box prompting you to press CTRL to use this brush is displayed. Choose the **OK** button to close this message box.

21. Press and hold the CTRL+ALT keys and drag the cursor diagonally in the upward direction, as shown in Figure 7-53; the shape of the mask is modified, as shown in Figure 7-54.

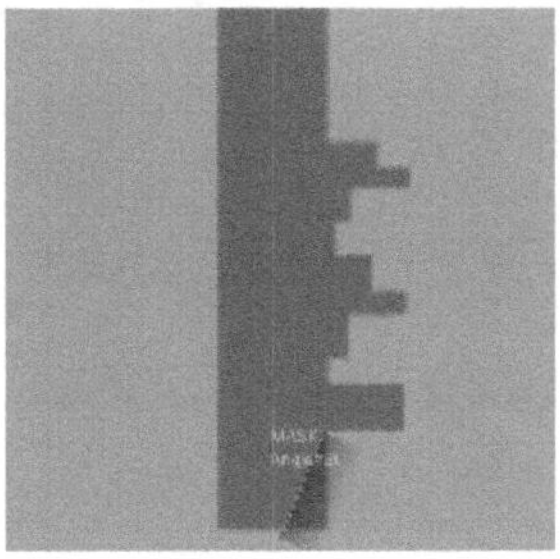

Figure 7-53 *Curved stroke created using the* ***MaskCurve*** *brush*

Figure 7-54 *Shape of the mask modified*

22. Rotate the canvas such that you can view the front view of the ShadowBox; the 3D mesh for the key is displayed in the ShadowBox, refer to Figure 7-55.

23. Rotate the canvas such that you can view the side view of the ShadowBox. On rotating the canvas, you will notice that the depth of the key is too large, refer to Figure 7-56.

Figure 7-55 *A key created in the ShadowBox*

Figure 7-56 *Side view of the key*

24. Rotate the canvas such that you can view the back side view of the side plane of the ShadowBox.

25. Choose the Current Brush button from the left shelf; a flyout containing different sculpting brushes is displayed. Choose the **MaskRect** brush from this flyout; a message box prompting you to press CTRL to use this brush is displayed. Choose the **OK** button to close this message box.

26. Press and hold the CTRL key and drag the cursor on the side plane of the ShadowBox to create a rectangular stroke, as shown in Figure 7-57; a rectangular mask is created. Now, rotate the canvas to view the front side of the ShadowBox. On rotating the canvas, you will notice that the depth of the key is decreased, refer to Figure 7-58.

Figure 7-57 A rectangular stroke created in the side plane

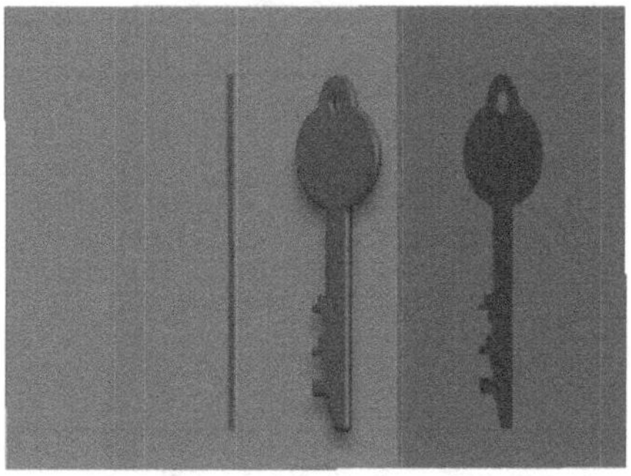

Figure 7-58 The depth of the key decreased

Modifying the Key Outside the ShadowBox

In this section, you will modify the shape of the key outside the ShadowBox.

1. Choose the **Make PolyMesh3D** button from the **Tool** palette, refer to Figure 7-59; the ShadowBox disappears from the canvas and 3D model of the key is displayed, refer to Figure 7-60.

*Figure 7-59 The **Make PolyMesh3D** button chosen*

Figure 7-60 The key displayed in the canvas

2. Choose the Current Brush button from the left shelf; a flyout containing different sculpting brushes is displayed. Choose the **MaskRect** brush from this flyout; a message box prompting you to press CTRL to use this brush is displayed. Choose the **OK** button to close this message box.

3. Press and hold the CTRL key and drag the cursor on the lower part of the key to create a rectangular mask, as shown in Figure 7-61.

4. Rotate the canvas such that you can view the back side view of the key. You will notice that a mask is applied on the backside of the key also. You need to remove the mask.

5. Rotate the canvas such that you can view the side view of the key. Press and hold the CTRL+ALT keys and drag the cursor to create a rectangular stroke to select the back side of the key. Release the CTRL+ALT keys; the mask is removed from the back side of the key, refer to Figure 7-62.

Figure 7-61 *Rectangular stroke created using the* ***MaskRect*** *brush*

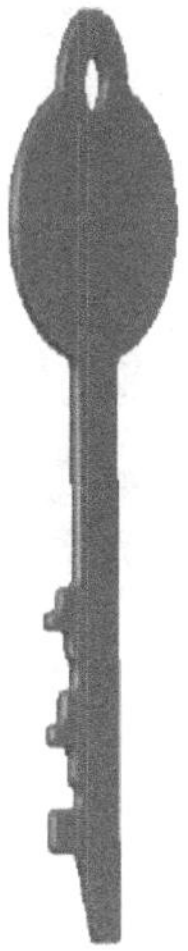

Figure 7-62 *Mask removed from the back side of the key*

6. Press CTRL+I; the mask is inverted, refer to Figure 7-63.

7. Expand the **Deformation** subpalette in the **Tool** palette.

   You need to change the offset of the unmasked area of the key along the Y-axis using the **Offset** slider.

8. Deactivate the x option corresponding to the **Offset** slider by choosing the **x** button located on the right side of the slider. Next, choose the **y** button to activate the y option, refer to Figure 7-64.

9. Drag the **Offset** slider toward left till the unmasked area moves slightly inward. Press and hold the CTRL key and drag the cursor in the empty area of the canvas; the mask is removed. The final model of the key is created, refer to Figure 7-65.

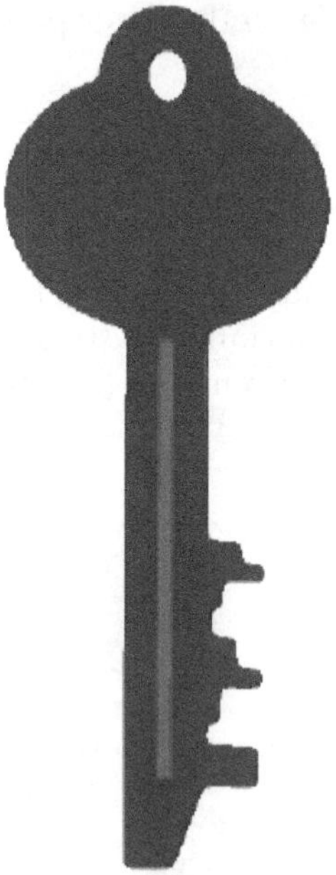

Figure 7-63 *The mask inverted*

Figure 7-64 *The **Offset** slider*

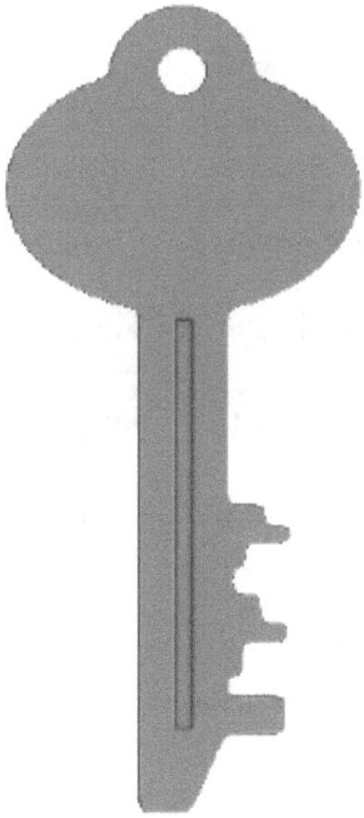

Figure 7-65 *The final model of the key*

Saving the Model

In this section, you will save the file using the steps given next.

1. Choose the **Save As** button from the **Tool** palette; the **Save ZTool** dialog box is displayed. In this dialog box, browse to the location: *\Documents\ZBrushprojects\c07*.

2. Enter **c07tut1** in the **File name** edit box and then choose the **Save** button.

Tutorial 2

In this tutorial, you will create the model of a guitar using the ShadowBox. The final output of the model is shown in Figure 7-66. **(Expected time: 30 min)**

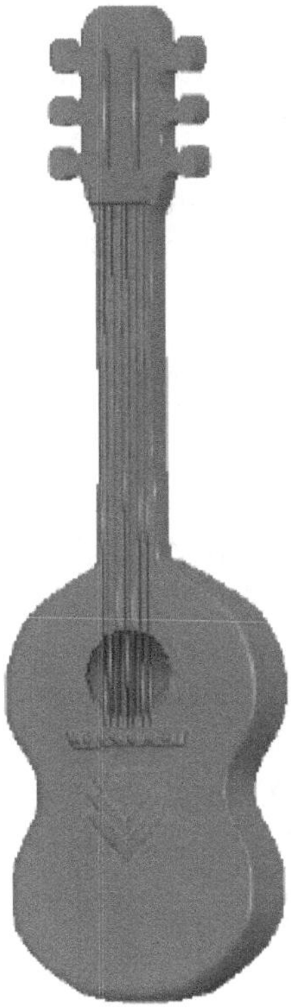

Figure 7-66 *The model of a guitar*

The following steps are required to complete this tutorial:

a. Create the shape of the guitar in the ShadowBox.
b. Modify the guitar outside the ShadowBox.
c. Save the model.

Creating the Shape of the Guitar in the ShadowBox

In this section, you will create the shape of the guitar in the shadow box.

1. Choose the **Init ZBrush** button from the **Preferences** palette; the message box is displayed. Choose the **Yes** button from the message box; ZBrush is initialized to its default state.

2. Choose the Current Tool button from the **Tool** palette; a flyout is displayed. Choose the **Sphere3D** primitive from this flyout and create it in the canvas.

3. Choose the **Edit** button from the top shelf.

4. Choose the **Make PolyMesh3D** button from the **Tool** palette to convert the primitive sphere into a polymesh.

5. Expand the **Geometry** subpalette in the **Tool** palette. In this subpalette, set the value of the **Res** slider in the ShadowBox area to **400**.

6. Choose the **ShadowBox** button in the ShadowBox area; the ShadowBox is displayed in the canvas. Rotate the canvas such that you can view the front side of the ShadowBox, refer to Figure 7-67.

7. Press and hold the CTRL key and then drag the cursor in the canvas area; the 3D mesh disappears from the ShadowBox. Rotate the canvas such that you can view the back side of the front plane.

8. Expand the **Transform** palette. In this palette, choose the **Activate Symmetry** button; the symmetry in the X-axis is activated, refer to Figure 7-68.

Figure 7-67 *The ShadowBox*

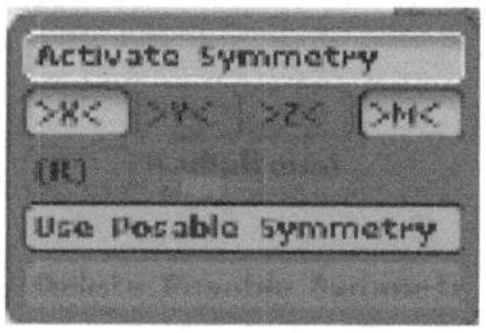

Figure 7-68 *The symmetry activated in the X-axis*

9. Choose the Current Brush button from the left shelf; a flyout containing different sculpting brushes is displayed. Choose the **MaskRect** brush from this flyout; a message box prompting you to press CTRL to use this brush is displayed. Choose the **OK** button to close this message box.

10. Press and hold the CTRL key and drag the cursor on the plane to create a rectangular stroke, as shown in Figure 7-69. As the symmetry is activated in the X-axis, mask is created, as shown in Figure 7-70.

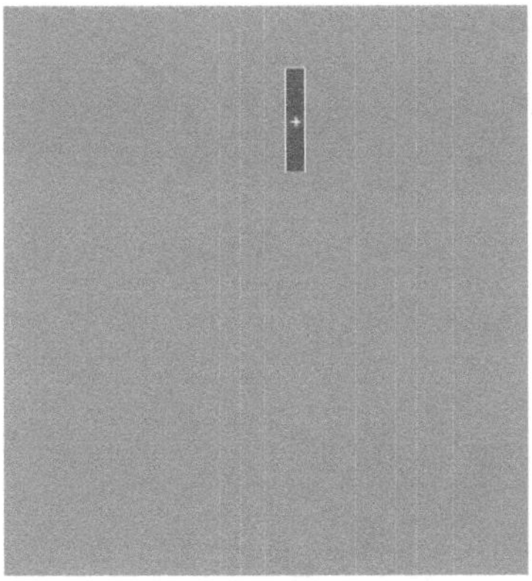

Figure 7-69 *A rectangular stroke created in the front plane*

Figure 7-70 *A mask created in the front plane*

11. Press and hold the CTRL key and drag the cursor below the existing mask. Release the CTRL key; a rectangular mask is created, as shown in Figure 7-71.

12. Choose the Current Brush button from the left shelf; a flyout containing different sculpting brushes is displayed. Choose the **MaskCurve** brush from this flyout; a message box prompting you to press CTRL to use this brush is displayed. Choose the **OK** button to close this message box.

13. Press and hold the CTRL+ALT keys and drag the cursor diagonally in the upward direction to create a curved stroke, as shown in Figure 7-72; the shape of the mask is modified, as shown in Figure 7-73.

14. Similarly, create another curved stroke at the top of the mask, refer to Figure 7-74; the shape of the mask is modified, refer to Figure 7-75.

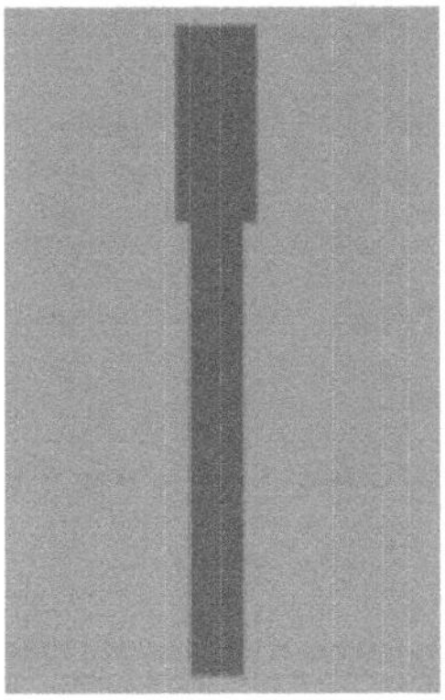

Figure 7-71 *Another rectangular mask created in the front plane*

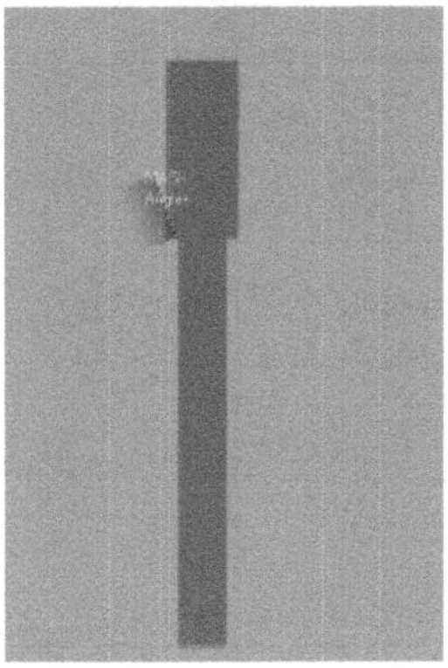

Figure 7-72 *Curved stroke created using the* ***MaskCurve*** *brush*

15. Choose the Current Brush button from the left shelf; a flyout containing different sculpting brushes is displayed. Choose the **MaskRect** brush from this flyout; a message box prompting you to press CTRL to use this brush is displayed. Choose the **OK** button to close this message box.

16. Press and hold the CTRL key and drag the cursor to create a rectangular stroke on the right side of the mask, refer to Figure 7-76. As the symmetry is activated in the X-axis, a mask is created on both the sides, as shown in Figure 7-76.

Figure 7-73 *Shape of the mask modified*

Figure 7-74 *Curved stroke created using the **MaskCurve** brush*

Figure 7-75 *Shape of the mask modified*

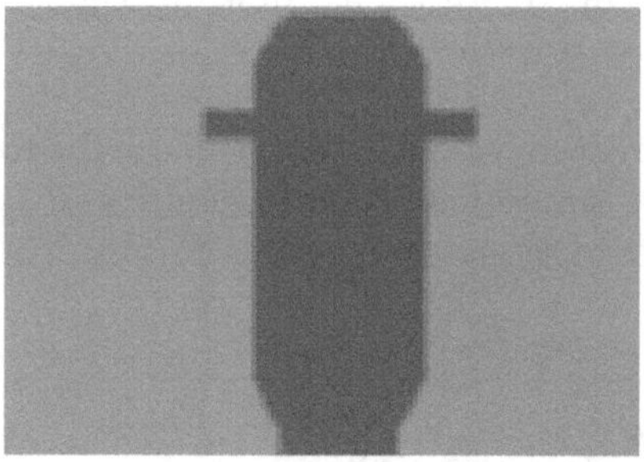

Figure 7-76 *Rectangular mask created*

17. Make sure the **MaskRect** brush is chosen. Create two more rectangular masks below the mask created in Step 16, refer to Figure 7-77.

18. Choose the Current Brush button from the left shelf; a flyout containing different sculpting brushes is displayed. Choose the **MaskCircle** brush from this flyout; a message box prompting you to press CTRL to use this brush will be displayed. Choose the **OK** button to close this message box.

19. Press and hold the CTRL key and drag the cursor to create an elliptical stroke on the right side of the mask, refer to Figure 7-78.

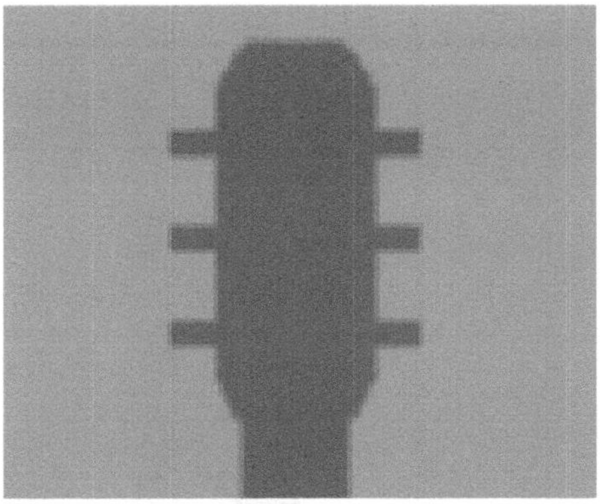

Figure 7-77 Two more rectangular masks created

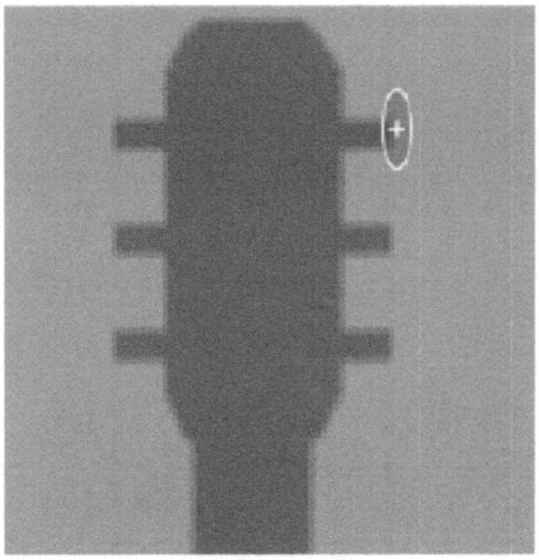

*Figure 7-78 An elliptical stroke created using the **MaskCircle** brush*

20. Make sure the **MaskCircle** brush is chosen. Create two more elliptical masks below the mask created in Step 19, refer to Figure 7-79.

21. Choose the Current Brush button from the left shelf; a flyout containing different sculpting brushes is displayed. Choose the **MaskRect** brush from this flyout; a message box prompting you to press CTRL to use this brush will be displayed. Choose the **OK** button to close this message box.

22. Press and hold the CTRL+ALT keys and drag the cursor to create a rectangular stroke on the right side of the mask, refer to Figure 7-80. As the symmetry is activated in X-axis, the shape is modified on both the sides, as shown in Figure 7-81.

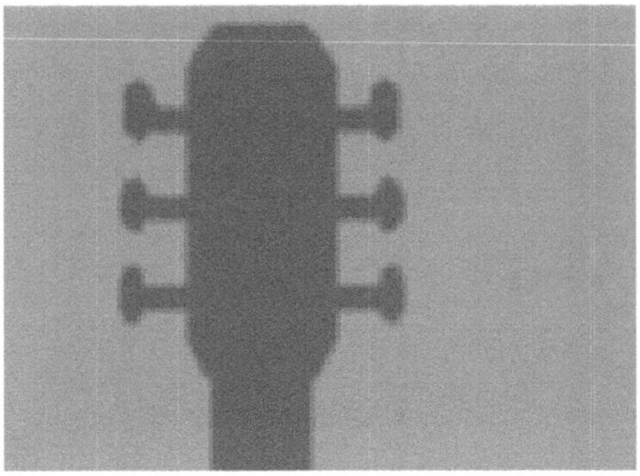

Figure 7-79 Two more elliptical masks created

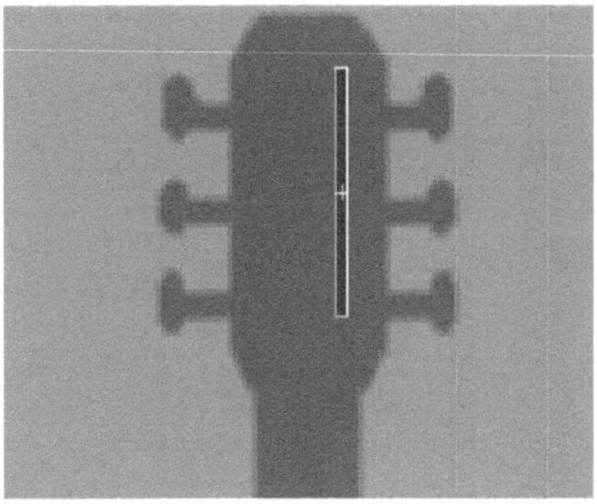

Figure 7-80 A rectangular stroke created with the ALT key pressed

23. Choose the Current Brush button from the left shelf; a flyout containing different sculpting brushes is displayed. Choose the **MaskLasso** brush from this flyout; a message box prompting you to press CTRL to use this brush will be displayed. Choose the **OK** button to close this message box.

24. Press and hold the CTRL key and drag the cursor to create a mask, as shown in Figure 7-82; a mask is created for the guitar, refer to Figure 7-83.

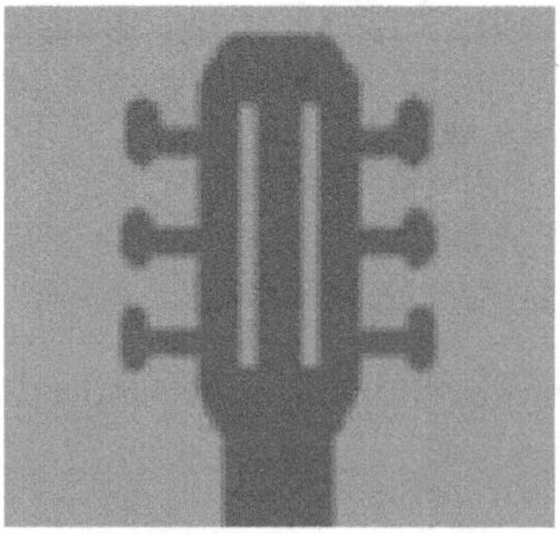

Figure 7-81 Shape of the mask modified

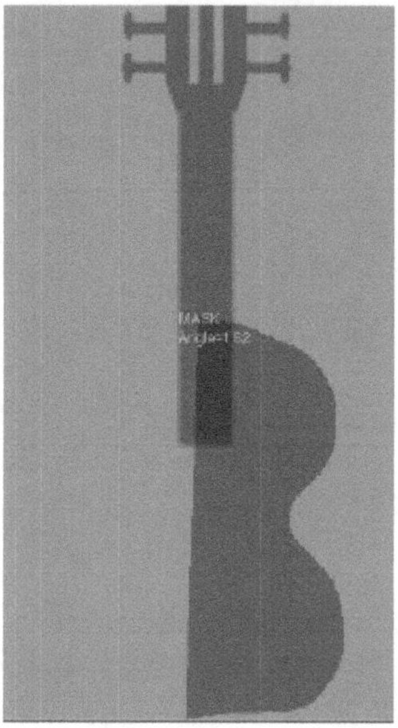

*Figure 7-82 A mask created using the **MaskLasso** brush*

25. Rotate the canvas such that you can view the front view of the ShadowBox. On rotating the canvas, you will notice that the depth of the guitar is too large, refer to Figure 7-84.

Figure 7-83 A mask created for the guitar

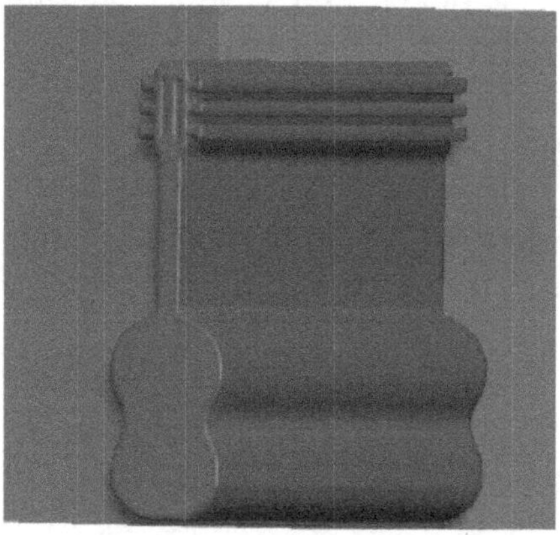

Figure 7-84 A 3D mesh for a guitar created in the ShadowBox

26. Rotate the canvas such that you can view the back side view of the side plane of the ShadowBox.

27. Choose the Current Brush button from the left shelf; a flyout containing different sculpting brushes is displayed. Choose the **MaskRect** brush from this flyout; a message box prompting you to press CTRL to use this brush is displayed. Choose the **OK** button to close this message box.

28. Press and hold the CTRL key and drag the cursor on the side plane of the ShadowBox to create a rectangular stroke, as shown in Figure 7-85.

29. Rotate the canvas to view the front side of the ShadowBox. On rotating the canvas, you will notice that depth of the guitar is decreased, refer to Figure 7-86.

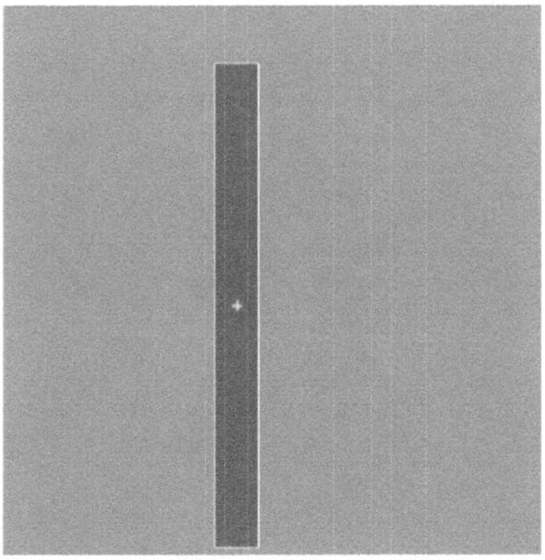

Figure 7-85 *A rectangular stroke created in the side plane*

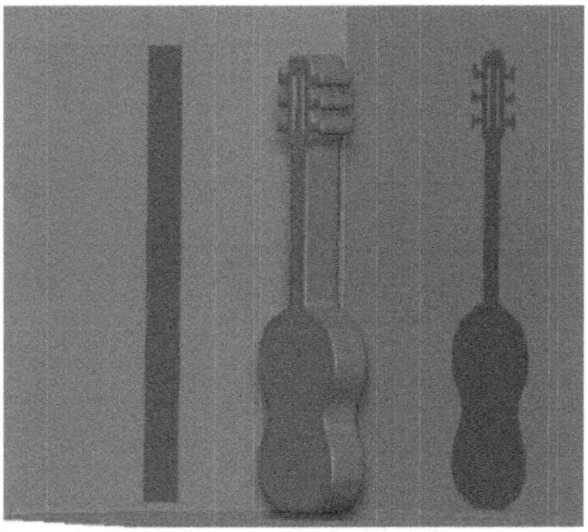

Figure 7-86 *Width of the guitar decreased*

30. Press and hold the CTRL+ALT key and drag the cursor on the top portion of the guitar to create a rectangular stroke, as shown in Figure 7-87; the masked area is deleted and the shape of the guitar is modified, refer to Figure 7-88.

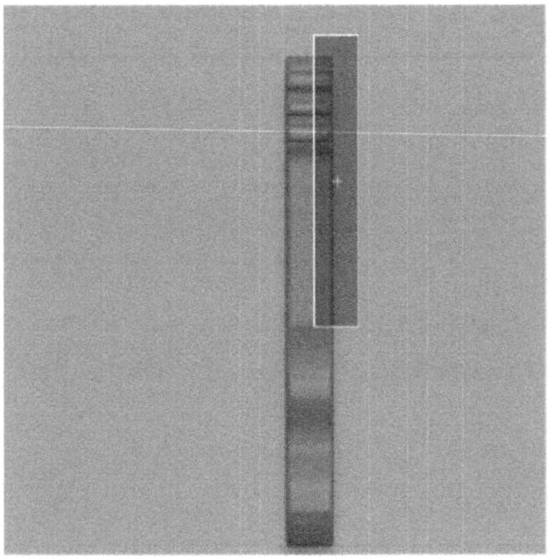

Figure 7-87 *A rectangular stroke created with the ALT key pressed*

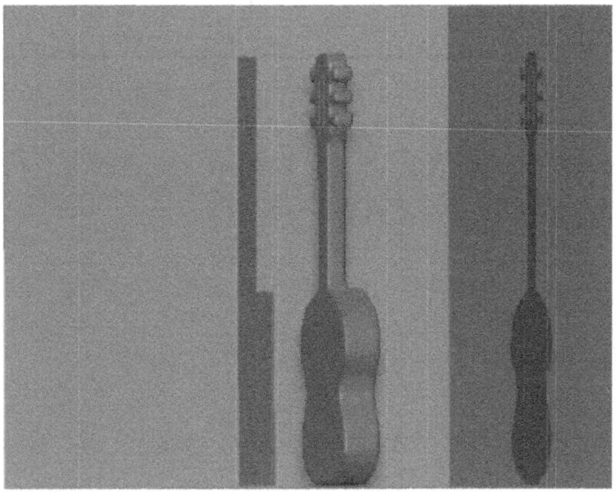

Figure 7-88 *The shape of the guitar modified*

Modifying the Guitar Outside the ShadowBox

In this section, you will modify the shape of the guitar outside the ShadowBox.

1. Choose the **Make PolyMesh3D** button from the **Tool** palette, refer to Figure 7-89; the ShadowBox disappears from the canvas and the 3D model of the guitar is displayed, refer to Figure 7-90.

Figure 7-89 The ***Make PolyMesh3D*** *button chosen*

Figure 7-90 The guitar displayed in the canvas

In Figure 7-90, you will notice that the edges of the guitar are very smooth. You need to remove the smoothness from the model of the guitar.

2. Choose the Current Brush button from the left shelf; a flyout containing different sculpting brushes is displayed. Choose the **ClipRect** brush from this flyout; a message box is displayed prompting you to press CTRL+SHIFT keys to activate this brush. Press and hold the CTRL+SHIFT and drag the cursor on the top portion of the guitar to create a rectangular stroke, as shown in Figure 7-91; the selected area is retained and rest of the area is deleted. In addition, the smoothness from the guitar is removed and the edges become sharp, refer to Figure 7-92.

3. Choose the **InsertCube** brush from the **Brush** tab in the **LightBox** browser. Press and hold the left mouse button and drag the cursor on the body of the guitar; a cube is inserted on the body of the guitar, refer to Figure 7-93.

4. Expand the **Deformation** subpalette in the **Tool** palette.

   You need to change the size of the inserted cube along the X-axis using the **Offset** slider.

5. Deactivate the y and z options corresponding to the **Size** slider by choosing the **y** and **z** buttons located on the right side of the slider. Make sure the **x** button is chosen.

6. Drag the **Size** slider toward right; the size of the inserted cube is increased, refer to Figure 7-94.

Figure 7-91 A rectangular stroke created with the ALT key pressed

Figure 7-92 The smoothness in the model removed

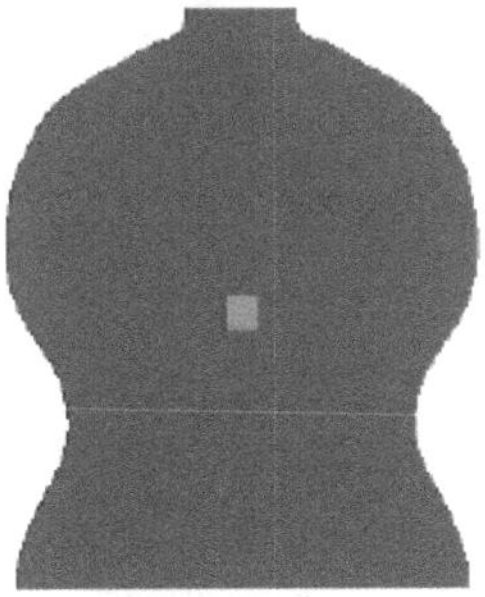

*Figure 7-93 A cube inserted using the **InsertCube** brush*

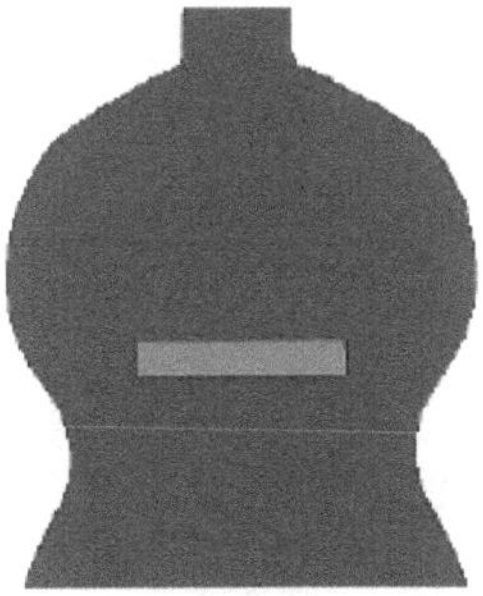

Figure 7-94 Width of the cube increased

7. Choose the Current Brush button from the left shelf; a flyout containing different sculpting brushes is displayed. Choose the **InsertCylinder** brush from this flyout. Press and hold the left mouse button and drag the cursor at the beginning of the cube; a cylinder is inserted on the cube, refer to Figure 7-95.

8. Choose the **Move** button from the top shelf; an action line is displayed. Drag the cursor on the surface of the guitar to increase the length of action line. Hover the cursor on the middle most circle of the action line. Press and hold the CTRL key and drag the cursor toward the right; a duplicate of the cylinder is created, refer to Figure 7-96. Similarly, create five more copies of the cylinder and position them, as shown in Figure 7-97.

9. Press and hold the CTRL key and drag the cursor on the canvas area; the mask is removed from the surface of the guitar, refer to Figure 7-98. Next, choose the **Draw** button from the top shelf.

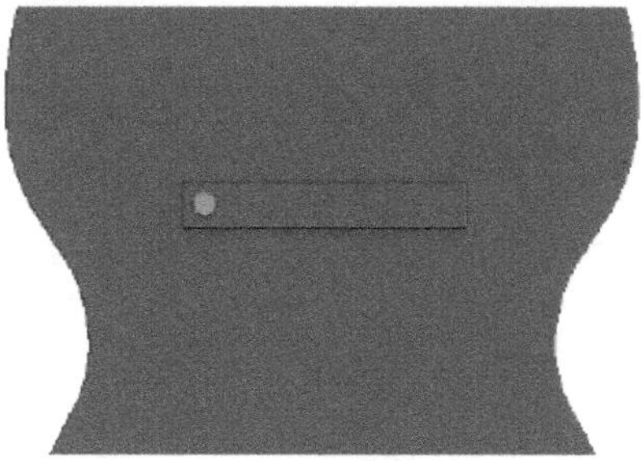

Figure 7-95 A cylinder inserted using the ***InsertCylinder*** brush

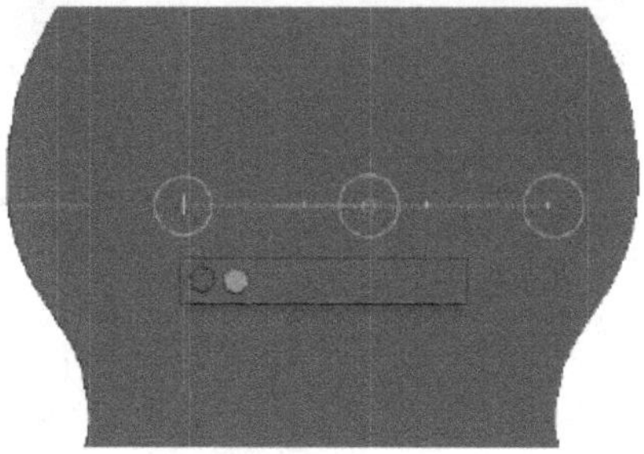

Figure 7-96 A duplicate copy of the cylinder created

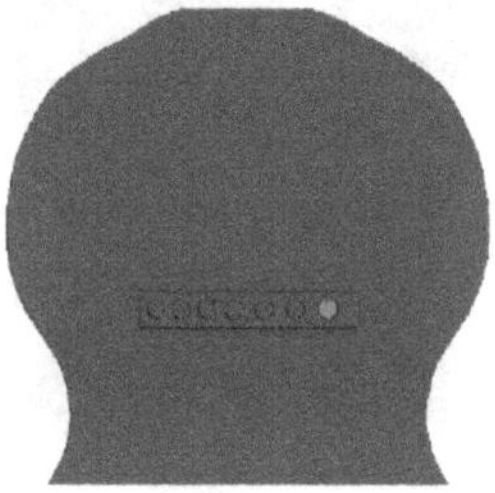

Figure 7-97 More copies of cylinder created

Figure 7-98 The mask removed from the guitar

10. Choose the Current Brush button from the left shelf; a flyout containing different sculpting brushes is displayed. Choose the **MaskCircle** brush from this flyout; a message box prompting you to press CTRL to use this brush is displayed. Choose the **OK** button to close this message box.

11. Press and hold the CTRL key and choose the Current Stroke button; a flyout is displayed. In this flyout, choose the **Square** button located at the bottom of the flyout. Similarly, choose the **Center** button from this flyout. Next, release the CTRL key.

    The **Square** and **Center** buttons will enable you to start the brush stroke from the center of the guitar and create a perfect circle.

12. Press and hold the CTRL key and drag the cursor on the surface of guitar to create a circular stroke, refer to Figure 7-99; a circular mask is applied on the top of the guitar body.

On rotating the view of the canvas, you will notice that the circular mask is applied on the back side of the guitar also.

13. Choose the Current Brush button from the left shelf; a flyout containing different sculpting brushes is displayed. Choose the **MaskRect** brush from this flyout; a message box prompting you to press CTRL to use this brush is displayed. Choose the **OK** button to close this message box.

14. Rotate the canvas such that you can view the side view of the guitar. Press and hold the CTRL+ALT keys and drag the cursor on the back side of the guitar to create a rectangular stroke, refer to Figure 7-100; the mask is removed from the back side of the guitar.

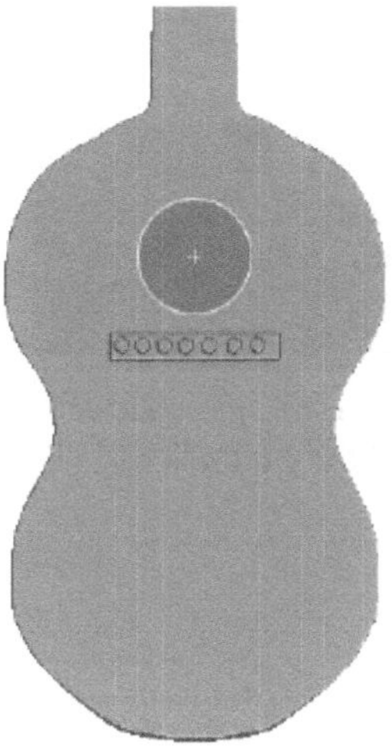

Figure 7-99 *The circular mask created using the* ***MaskCircle*** *brush*

Figure 7-100 *A rectangular stroke created with the CTRL+ALT key pressed*

15. Press CTRL+I; the mask is inverted, refer to Figure 7-101.

16. Expand the **Visibility** subpalette in the **Tool** palette. In this subpalette, choose the **HidePt** button, refer to Figure 7-102; a hole is created in the guitar, refer to Figure 7-103.

    In Figure 7-103, you will notice that you can see through the hole. Now, you will fill the hole.

17. Expand the **Display Properties** subpalette in the **Tool** palette. In this subpalette, choose the **Double** button, refer to Figure 7-104; the hole is filled, refer to Figure 7-105.

Figure 7-101 The mask inverted

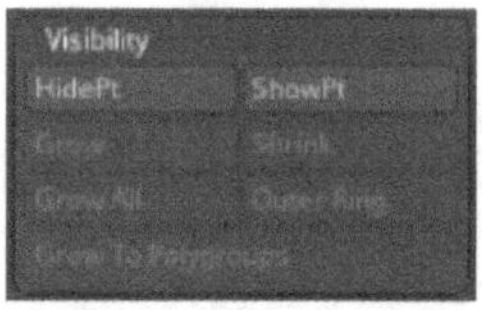

*Figure 7-102 The **HidePt** button chosen in the **Visibility** subpalette*

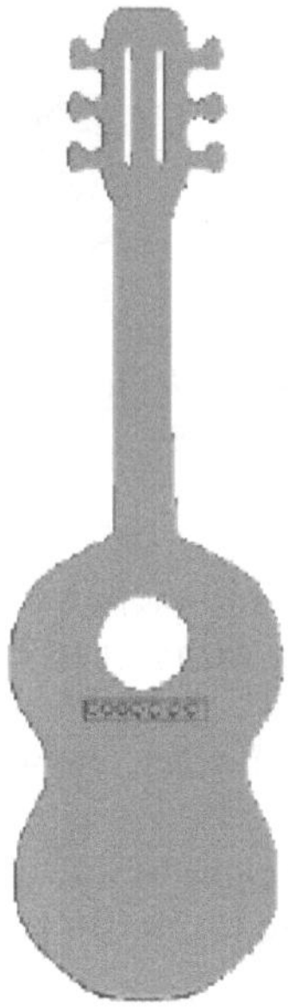

Figure 7-103 A hole created in the guitar

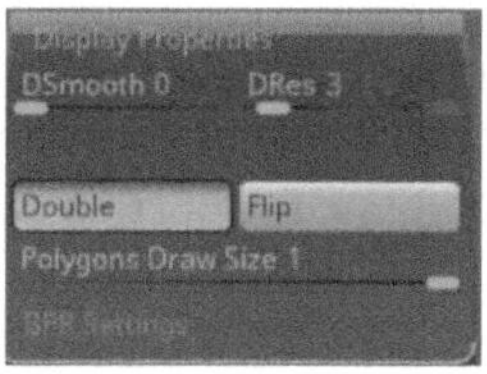

*Figure 7-104 The **Double** button chosen*

18. Choose the Current Brush button from the left shelf; a flyout containing different sculpting brushes is displayed. Choose the **InsertCube** brush from this flyout. Press and hold the left mouse button and drag the cursor on the top of the guitar; a cube is inserted on the top of the guitar, refer to Figure 7-106.

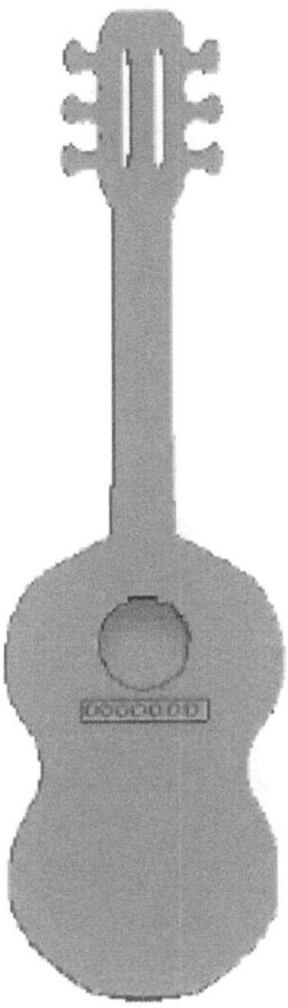

Figure 7-105 The hole in the backside of the guitar filled

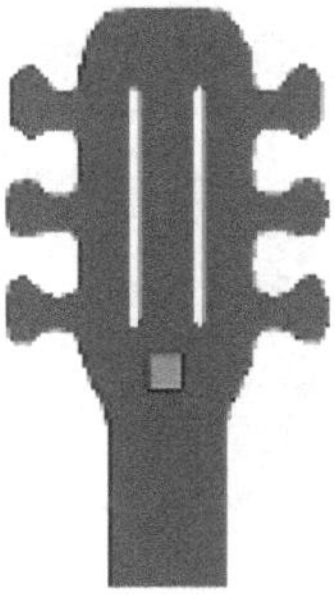

*Figure 7-106 A cube inserted using the **InsertCube** brush*

19. Expand the **Deformation** subpalette in the **Tool** palette

    You need to change the size of the inserted cube along the X-axis using the **Offset** slider.

20. Deactivate y and z options corresponding to the **Size** slider by choosing the **y** and **z** buttons located on the right side of the slider. Make sure the **x** button is chosen.

21. Drag the **Size** slider toward right; the size of the inserted cube increases, refer to Figure 7-107.

22. Press and hold the CTRL key and drag the cursor in the canvas area; the mask is removed from the surface of the guitar, refer to Figure 7-108.

23. Expand the **SubTool** subpalette in the **Tool** palette. In this subpalette, choose the **Append** button, refer to Figure 7-109; a flyout is displayed. Choose the **Cylinder3D** primitive in this flyout; the cylinder is created in the canvas and it overlaps the guitar, refer to Figure 7-110. A thumbnail for the cylinder is displayed in the subtool list.

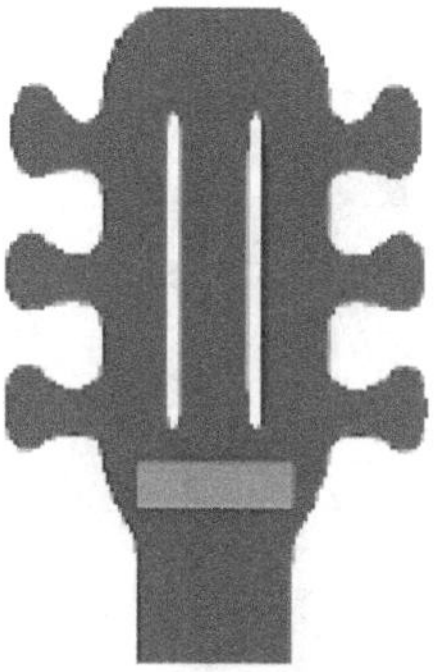

Figure 7-107 *Width of the cube increased*

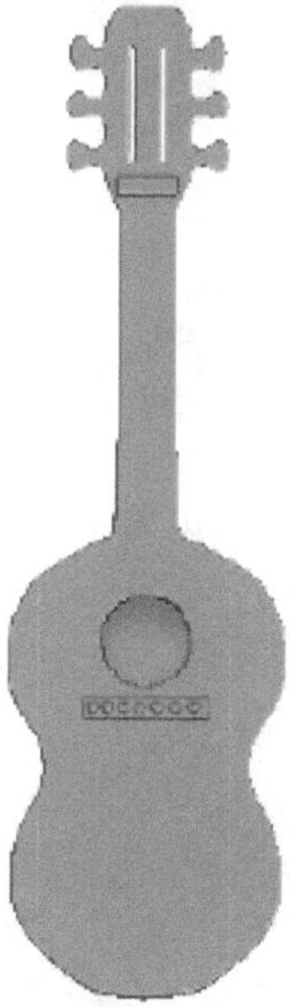

Figure 7-108 *The mask removed from the guitar*

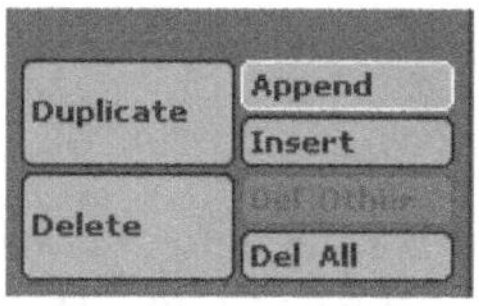

Figure 7-109 *The* ***Append*** *button chosen*

Figure 7-110 *A cylinder created in the canvas*

24. Make sure that you select the thumbnail for the cylinder from the subtool list. Expand the **Deformation** subpalette in the **Tool** palette.

    You need to decrease the size of the cylinder along the X and Y axes using the **Size** slider.

25. Activate the x and y options corresponding to the **Size** slider by choosing the **x** and **y** buttons located on the right side of the slider. Make sure the **z** button is not chosen.

26. Drag the **Size** slider toward left; the size of the cylinder decreases. Continue dragging the slider till the size of the cylinder becomes equal to the size of a guitar string, refer to Figure 7-111.

    You need to decrease the height of the cylinder using the **Size** slider.

27. In the **Deformation** subpalette, deactivate the x and y options corresponding to the **Size** slider by choosing the **x** and **y** buttons located on the right side of the slider. Next, choose the **z** button.

28. Drag the **Size** slider toward the left; the height of the cylinder decreases. Next, choose the **Move** button from the top shelf and position the cylinder such that it fits between the two cubes in the guitar, refer to Figure 7-112.

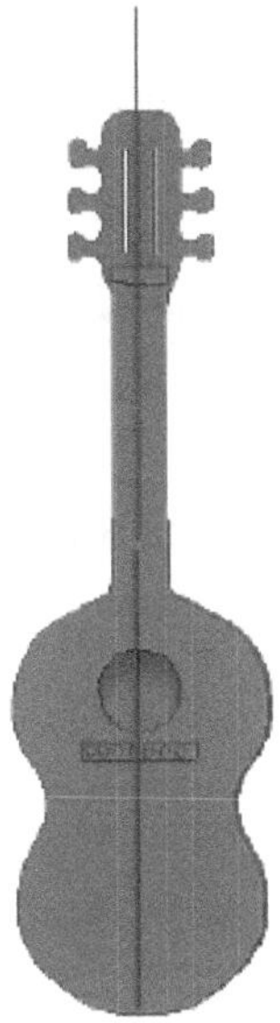

Figure 7-111 *The size of the cylinder decreased along the X and Y axes*

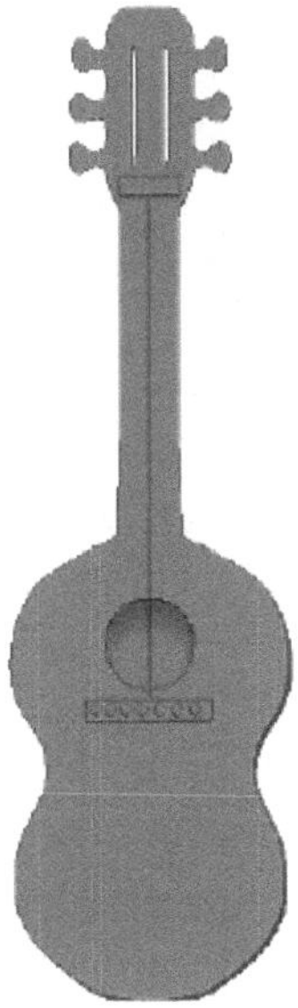

Figure 7-112 *The height of the cylinder decreased*

29. Rotate the canvas such that you can view the side view of the guitar, refer to Figure 7-113.

30. Choose the **Move** button from the top shelf; an action line is displayed. Drag the cursor on the surface of the guitar to increase the length of action line. Hover the cursor on the middle most circle of the action line and move the cylinder toward right such that it fits between the two cubes of the guitar. In Figure 7-113, the two cubes have been encircled.

31. Rotate the canvas such that you can view the front view of the guitar.

32. Make sure the **Move** button is chosen in the top shelf. Again, increase the length of the action line. Hover the cursor on the inner middle circle of the action line. Press and hold the CTRL key and drag the cursor toward right; a duplicate copy of the cylinder is created, refer to Figure 7-114. Similarly, create five more copies of the cylinder and position them, as shown in Figure 7-115.

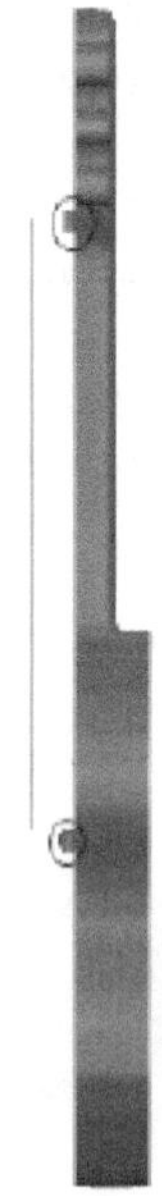

Figure 7-113 The side view of the guitar

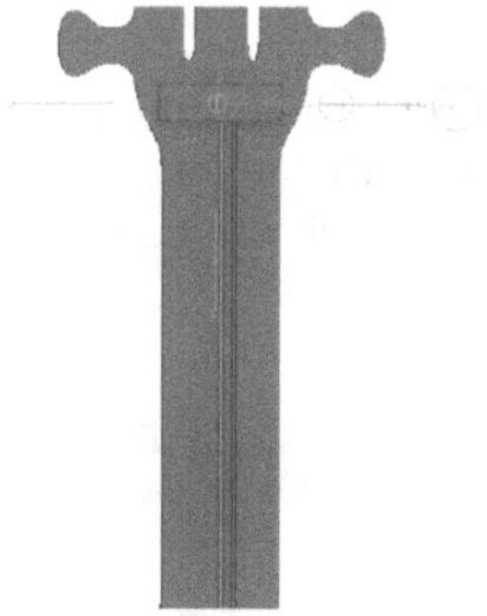

Figure 7-114 Duplicate copy of the cylinder created

33. Press and hold the CTRL key and drag the cursor in the canvas area; the mask is removed from the strings of the guitar.

34. In the **SubTool** subpalette, select the thumbnail for the guitar; the mask is removed from the guitar, refer to Figure 7-116.

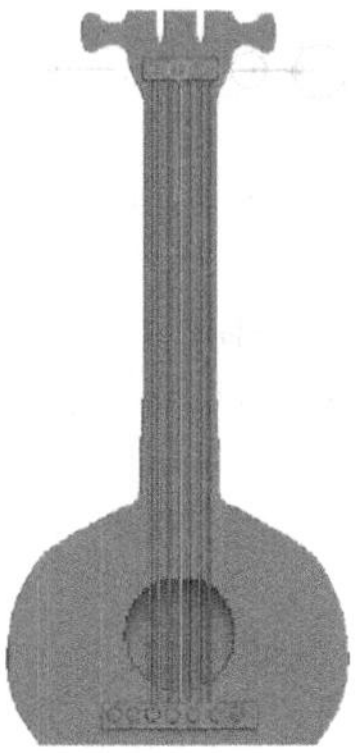

Figure 7-115 More copies of the cylinder created

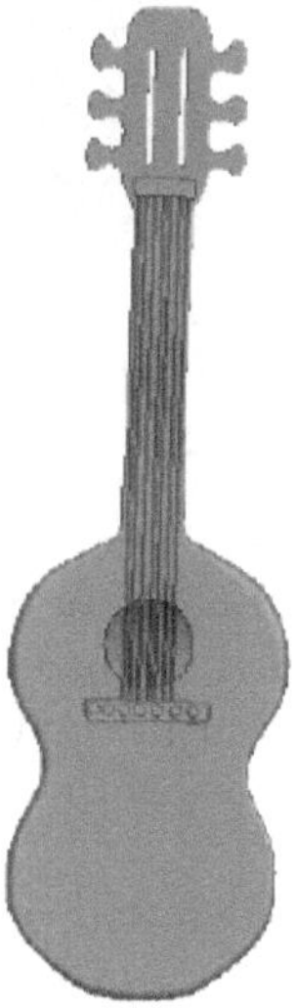

Figure 7-116 Mask removed from the guitar

35. Choose the Current Brush button from the left shelf; a flyout containing different sculpting brushes is displayed. Choose the **Move** brush from this flyout. Next, using the **Move** brush, reduce the size of the lower part of the guitar, as required, refer to Figure 7-117.

36. Choose the Current Brush button from the left shelf; a flyout containing different sculpting brushes is displayed. Choose the **Standard** brush from this flyout.

37. Choose the Current Stroke button from the left shelf; a flyout containing different types of strokes is displayed. Choose the **DragRect** stroke from this flyout.

38. Choose the Current Alpha button from the left shelf; a flyout containing different alpha images is displayed. Choose the **Alpha 29** alpha image from this flyout.

39. Press and hold the left mouse button and drag the cursor on the surface of the guitar to create a pattern, as shown in Figure 7-118.

Figure 7-117 *Shape of the guitar refined using the* ***Move*** *brush*

Figure 7-118 *A pattern created using the* ***Alpha 29*** *alpha image*

Saving the Model

In this section, you will save the file using the steps given next.

1. Choose the **Save As** button from the **Tool** palette; the **Save ZTool** dialog box is displayed. In this dialog box, browse to the location: *\Documents\ZBrushprojects\c07*.

2. Enter **c07tut2** in the **File name** edit box and then choose the **Save** button.

Self-Evaluation Test

Answer the following questions and then compare them to those given at the end of this chapter:

1. In which of the following subpalettes is the **ShadowBox** button located?

   (a) **SubTool** (b) **Geometry HD**
   (c) **Geometry** (d) **Masking**

2. Which of the following combinations of keys is used to invert a mask?

   (a) CTRL+SHIFT+I (b) CTRL+I
   (c) CTRL+ALT (d) CTRL+M

3. The __________ slider in the **ShadowBox** area is used to set the number of polygons in the ShadowBox.

4. The value of the **Polish** slider ranges between 0 and __________ .

5. To activate the transparency in the 3D mesh inside the ShadowBox, choose the **Transp** button in the right shelf and then choose the __________ button.

6. You do not need to convert a primitive object into a polymesh for using the ShadowBox tool. (T/F)

7. You can clear the ShadowBox by pressing and holding the ALT key and then dragging the cursor in the canvas area. (T/F)

8. You can add masks on the planes of the ShadowBox by pressing the CTRL+ALT keys. (T/F)

9. You can use different reference images in the ShadowBox for creating 3D objects. (T/F)

Review Questions

Answer the following questions:

1. Which of the following keys is used to remove the mask from specific areas?

   (a) CTRL+I (b) CTRL+SHIFT
   (c) CTRL+SHIFT+I (d) CTRL+ALT

2. Which of the following brushes are used to create projections in the planes of the ShadowBox?

   (a) Clip brushes (b) Pen brushes
   (c) Clay brushes (d) Mask brushes

3. The __________ slider in the **ShadowBox** area is used to set the level of smoothness in a 3D object.

4. The __________ brush is used to create elliptical mask in the planes of the ShadowBox.

5. If the value of the **Polish** slider is higher, the 3D object created in the ShadowBox will have __________ edges.

6. You can view the projections in the front view of the ShadowBox by turning on the transparency in the 3D mesh. (T/F)

7. The **ShadowBox** area in the **Geometry** subpalette of the **Tool** palette consists of three attributes. (T/F)

8. You cannot activate radial symmetry in the ShadowBox. (T/F)

EXERCISES

The output of the models used in the following exercises can be accessed by downloading the *c07_ZBrush_2022_exr.zip* file from *www.cadcim.com*. The path of the file is as follows: *Textbooks > Animation and Visual Effects > ZBrush > ZBrush 2022: A Comprehensive Guide*.

Exercise 1

Create the model of a chair using the ShadowBox and Mask brushes, as shown in Figure 7-119. **(Expected time: 20 min)**

Figure 7-119 *Model of a chair*

Exercise 2

Create the model of a hut using the ShadowBox and the Mask brushes, as shown in Figure 7-120.
(Expected time: 30 min)

Figure 7-120 Model of a hut

Answers to Self-Evaluation Test

1. c, **2.** b, **3. Res**, **4.** 100, **5. Ghost**, **6.** F, **7.** F, **8.** F, **9.** T

Chapter 8

Materials in ZBrush

Learning Objectives

After completing this chapter, you will be able to:

- *Understand the working of the MatCap materials*
- *Understand the working of the Standard materials*
- *Work with the Material palette*
- *Assign different materials to the objects*

INTRODUCTION

In this chapter, you will learn to assign various materials to 3D meshes created in ZBrush. A material is applied to an object to give it a realistic look. ZBrush comes with a library of materials that can either be accessed through the **Material** palette or the left shelf.

MATERIALS IN ZBrush

ZBrush has an extensive library of materials. To access these materials, choose the Current Material button from the left shelf; a flyout containing different types of materials will be displayed, refer to Figure 8-1. This flyout consists of three areas namely **Quick Pick**, **MatCap Materials**, and **Standard Materials**. The **Quick Pick** area stores a library of materials that have been used recently. The **MatCap Materials** and **Standard Materials** areas are discussed next.

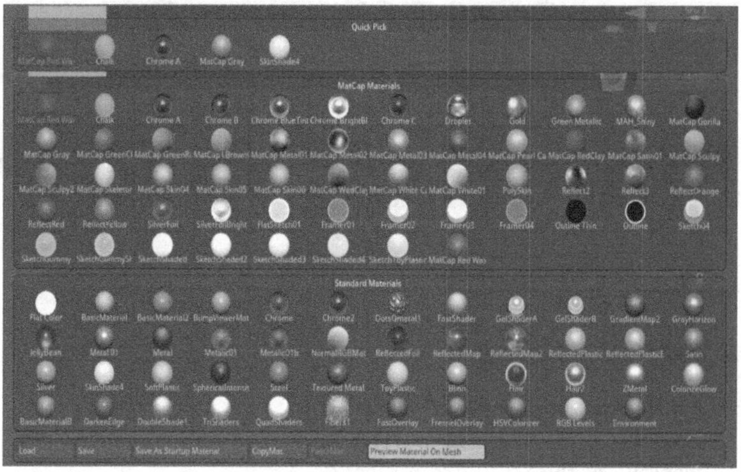

Figure 8-1 *The flyout displayed on choosing the Current Material button*

MatCap Materials

The term MatCap stands for Material Capture. This area consists of a library of MatCap materials. The MatCap materials have inbuilt lights assigned to them. If you use a light in a scene, the MapCap materials will not respond to the light, as they already have a light baked into them. There are about 49 types of MatCap materials in ZBrush. These materials are used to give an appearance of metal, skin, chalk, and so on to an object. Figures 8-2 through 8-7 show the different types of MatCap materials applied to a sphere.

To apply a MatCap material to an object, select the desired material from the **MatCap Materials** area; the chosen material will be applied to the object. By default, the **MapCap Red Wax** material is applied to all the objects created in ZBrush.

You can also change the color of the material by choosing the desired color from the Current Color swatch located below the Current Material button.

Figure 8-2 The ***Chrome BrightBlue Tint*** *material applied to the sphere*

Figure 8-3 The ***MatCap Pearl Cavity*** *material applied to the sphere*

Figure 8-4 The ***MatCap Skin06*** *material applied to the sphere*

Figure 8-5 The ***ReflectOrange*** *material applied to the sphere*

Figure 8-6 The ***FlatSketch01*** *material applied to the sphere*

Figure 8-7 The ***SketchToyPlastic*** *material applied to the sphere*

You can view the preview of a material on an object before applying it to that object. To do so, select the object and then hover the cursor on a material slot; the preview of the object with that material will be displayed, refer to Figure 8-8.

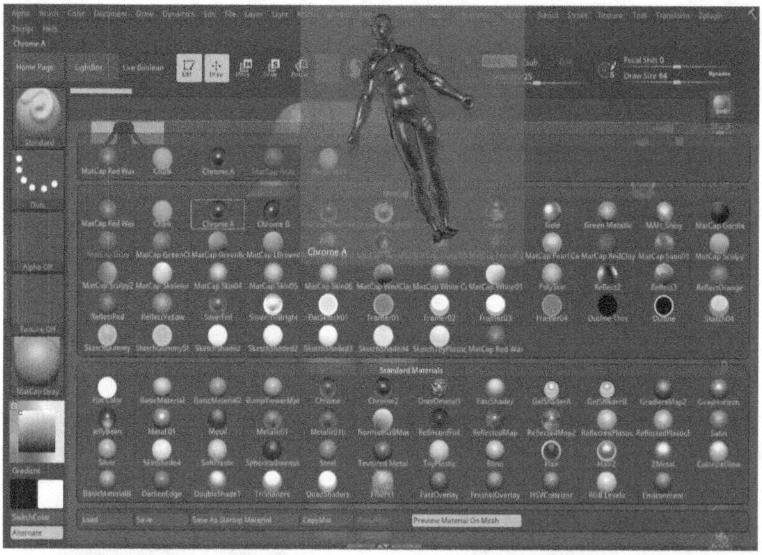

Figure 8-8 *The preview of the object with a material*

Standard Materials

The Standard materials do not contain any in-built baked light. If you use a light in a scene, the Standard materials will respond to the light depending on its intensity, position, and so on of the light. There are about 43 types of Standard materials in ZBrush. Figures 8-9 through 8-12 show different types of Standard materials applied to a sphere.

Figure 8-9 *The* ***GelShaderA*** *material applied to the sphere*

Figure 8-10 *The* ***GradientMap2*** *material applied to the sphere*

Figure 8-11 *The* ***NormalRGBMat*** *material applied to the sphere*

Figure 8-12 *The* ***ReflectedMap*** *material applied to the sphere*

MATERIAL PALETTE

The **Material** palette is located at the top of the interface. This palette contains options that are used to modify the properties of a material. When you choose this palette, it expands and the subpalettes containing different settings for modifying materials are displayed, refer to Figure 8-13. Besides the subpalettes, this palette also contains different buttons and sliders. These buttons, sliders, and subpalettes are discussed next.

Figure 8-13 *The* ***Material*** *palette*

> **Note**
>
> *The materials can also be accessed from the left tray. To open the left tray, click on the arrow on the left side of the left shelf.*

Load

The **Load** button is used to import a downloaded material into ZBrush. You can download additional materials from *https://pixologic.com/zbrush/downloadcenter/library/*. This site has a library of different categories of materials, refer to Figure 8-14.

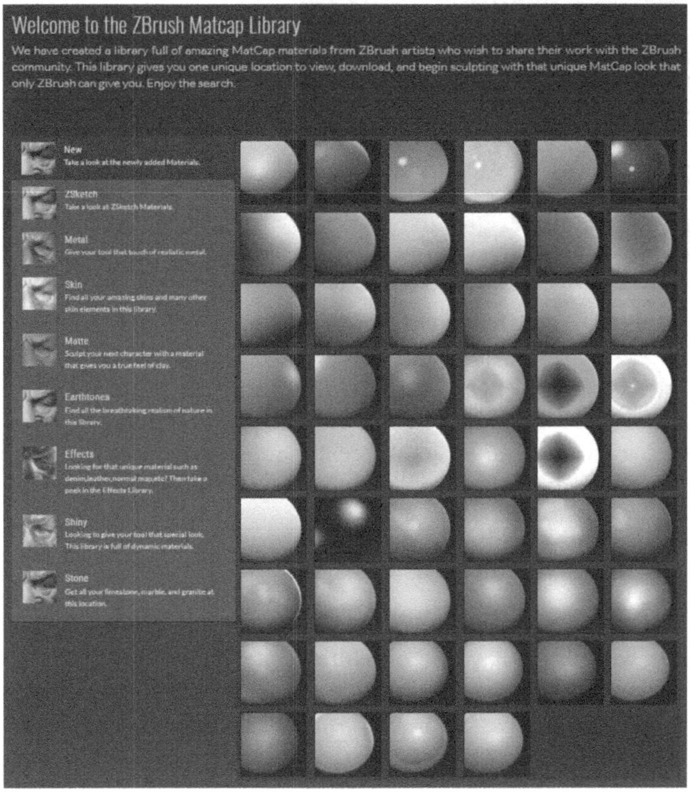

Figure 8-14 *The* ***MatCap*** *library*

To download a material from this site, choose the desired category under the **MatCap Library** tab. For instance, to download different materials for the skin, click on the **Skin** category from the library, refer to Figure 8-15; different skin materials will be displayed, refer to Figure 8-16. Choose the desired material; a preview of that material on a character will be displayed. Next, click on the **Download Now** link located on the right side of the preview to download the material, refer to Figure 8-17.

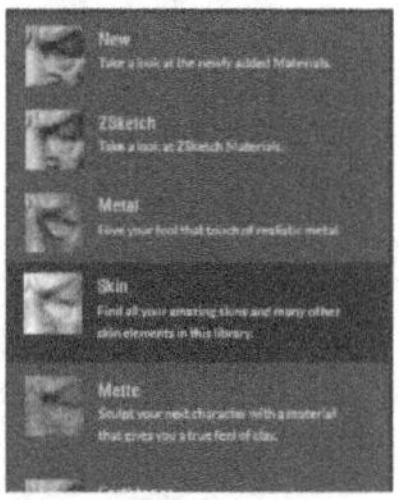

Figure 8-15 *Different categories*

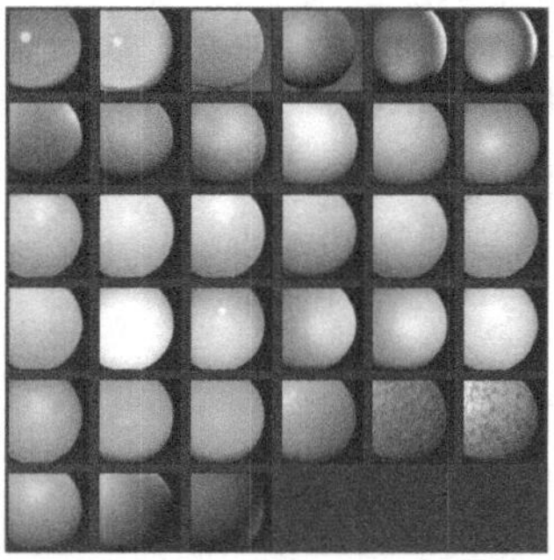

Figure 8-16 *The different skin materials*

The material will be downloaded as a zip file. You need to extract the material from the zip file. The material will be extracted with *.ZMT* extension, refer to Figure 8-18.

Figure 8-17 *The* ***Download Now*** *link*

Figure 8-18 *The material file extracted from the zip file*

Now, you need to switch back to ZBrush. In ZBrush, choose the **Material** palette. In this palette, choose the **Load** button; the **Load Material** dialog box will be displayed, refer to Figure 8-19. Browse to the downloaded file and select it. Next, choose the **Open** button in the dialog box; the default **MapCap Red Wax** material will be replaced by the new downloaded material, refer to Figure 8-20.

Save

The **Save** button is used to save a material into the disk. On choosing this button, the **Save Material** dialog box will be displayed. You can specify the location where you want to save a material. It is recommended to save the material at the location *C:\Program Files\Pixologic\ZBrush 2022\ZMaterials.* On doing so, the material will be displayed under the **Material** tab of the **LightBox** browser.

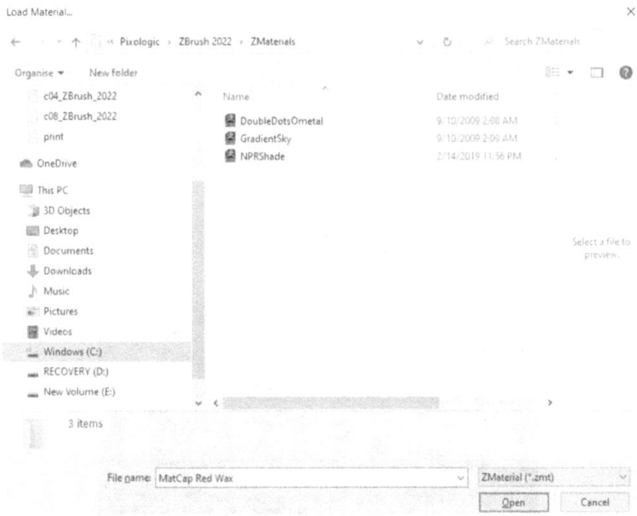

*Figure 8-19 The **Load Material** dialog box*

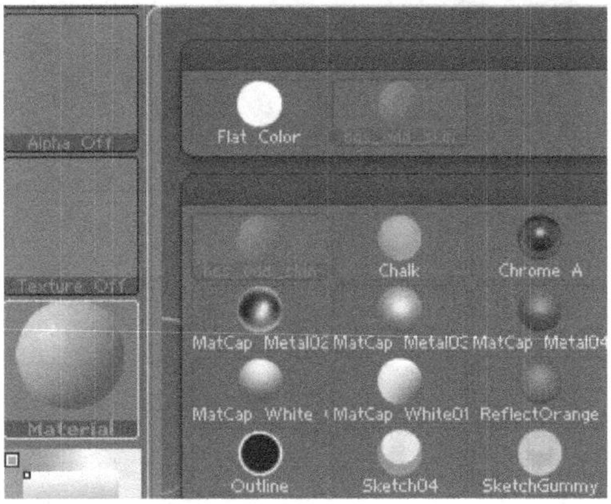

Figure 8-20 The default material replaced by the downloaded material

LightBox Materials

This button is used to display the materials present in the **LightBox** browser, refer to Figure 8-21.

Save As Startup Material

This button is used to save a material as a default material from the list of materials displayed in the Current Material window. When you change the selected material as a default material, a message box will be displayed informing you about successfully changing and restoring material.

Item Info

This slider is located just below the **Save As Startup Material** button. This slider is used to scroll through different types of materials in ZBrush. You can select a material from the material slots displayed below this slider, refer to Figure 8-22.

Show Used
The **Show Used** button is used to display the materials that have been used in a scene.

CopyMat
This button is located just below the **Show Used** button. The **CopyMat** button is used to copy a material from a slot.

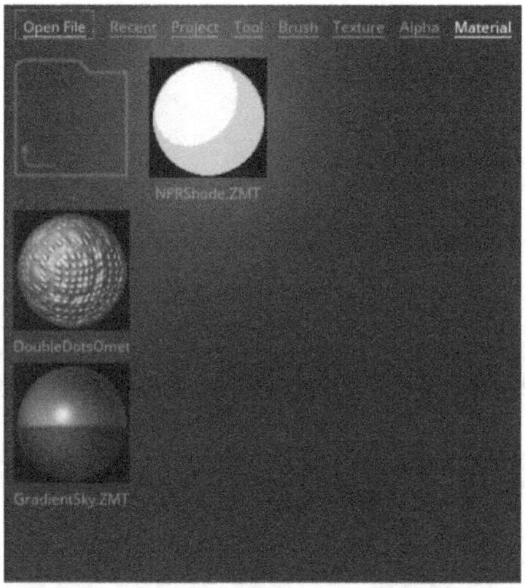

*Figure 8-21 The materials in the **LightBox** browser*

PasteMat
This button is located next to the **CopyMat** button. The **PasteMat** button is used to paste the copied material into another slot.

Wax Modifiers
The **Wax Modifiers** subpalette contains different options that are used to give an appearance of wax to a selected material and make it translucent. Before setting the options in this subpalette, you need to choose the **WaxPreview** button from the **Render Properties** subpalette of the **Render** palette, refer to Figure 8-23. This button will enable you to preview the effect of wax material in the canvas while sculpting an object. The **Render** palette will be discussed in detail in later chapters.

The different options in the **Wax Modifiers** subpalette are discussed next.

Strength
The **Strength** slider is used to set the intensity of the wax effect on a material. If the value of this slider is higher, the wax effect will be more prominent, refer to Figure 8-24. Choose the **Render** palette. In this palette, expand the **Render Properties** subpalette and then choose the **WaxPreview** button. Next, in the **Wax Modifiers** subpalette of the **Material** palette, set the value of **Strength** slider to **100**; a wax effect will be applied to the model, refer to Figure 8-25.

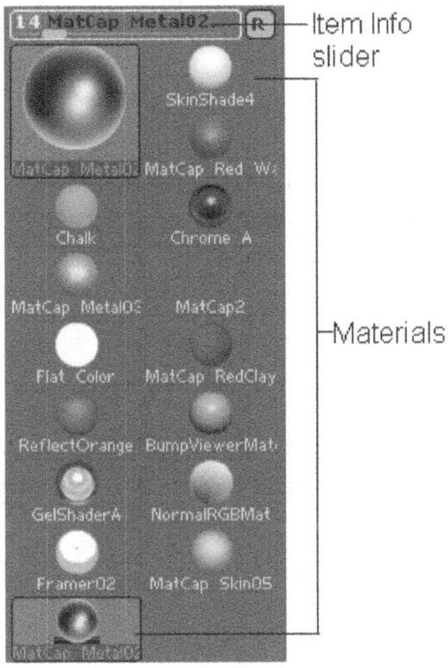

*Figure 8-22 The **Item Info** slider*

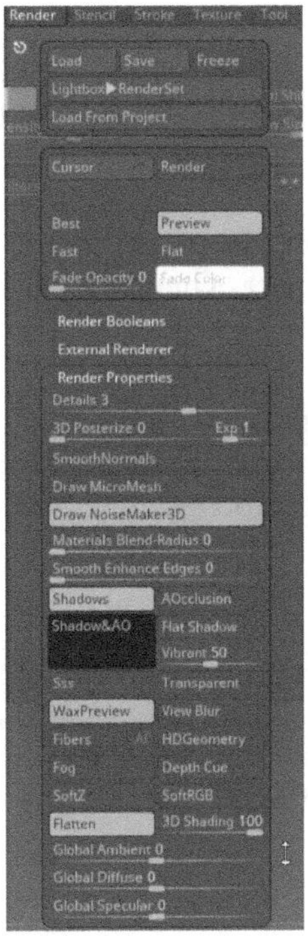

*Figure 8-23 The **WaxPreview** button chosen*

Spec

The **Spec** slider is used to set the impact of wax material on the specularity of a material. This slider will not have any effect on the MatCap materials. However, the effect of this slider is visible in the Standard materials.

Fresnel

The **Fresnel** slider is used to determine whether the wax effect will be prominent on the areas of an object facing the camera or on the areas that are not facing the camera.

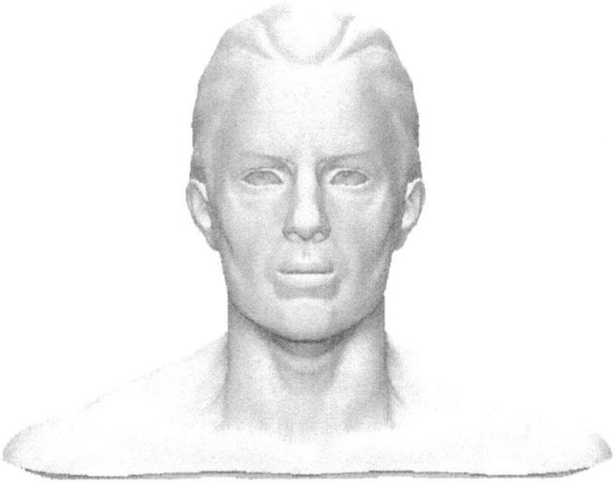

Figure 8-24 The material applied to the model

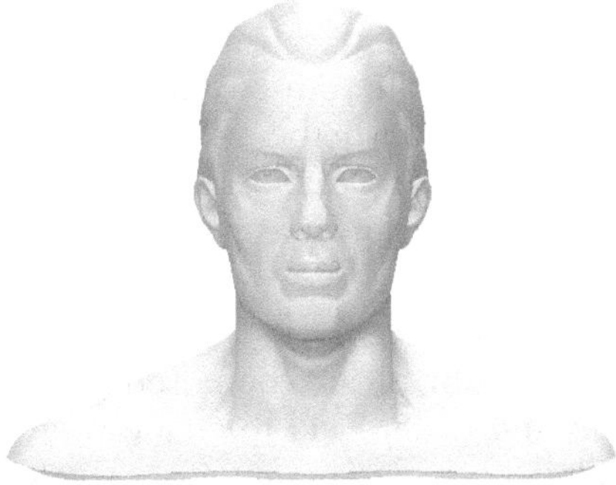

*Figure 8-25 Wax effect at **Strength** value **100***

Exponent

The **Exponent** slider is used along with the **Fresnel** slider. This slider is used to specify the speed at which the wax effect is applied to an object, when the object is rotated in the canvas.

Radius

The **Radius** slider is used to specify the distance up to which the wax effect will spread on the surface of an object. The effect of this slider is visible when a scene is rendered using the **BPR** renderer.

Temperature

The **Temperature** slider is used to add blue or red tint to the wax material when it is rendered using the **BPR** button located in the right shelf. The **BPR** button is used to produce high quality realistic renders on the canvas. The blue tint represents cold wax while the red tint represents the hot wax.

If the value of the **Temperature** slider is set to **-100**, a blue tint will be applied to the wax material when it is rendered by choosing the **BPR** button, refer to Figure 8-26. However, if the value of this slider is set to **100**, a red tint will be applied to the wax material when it is rendered by choosing the **BPR** button, refer to Figure 8-27.

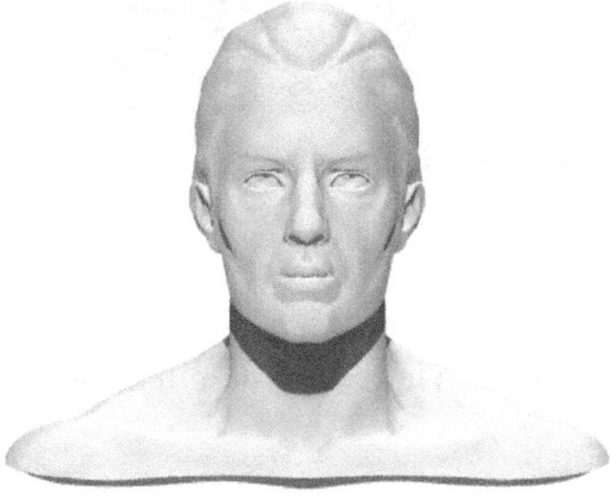

Figure 8-26 *Blue tint at **Temperature** value **-100***

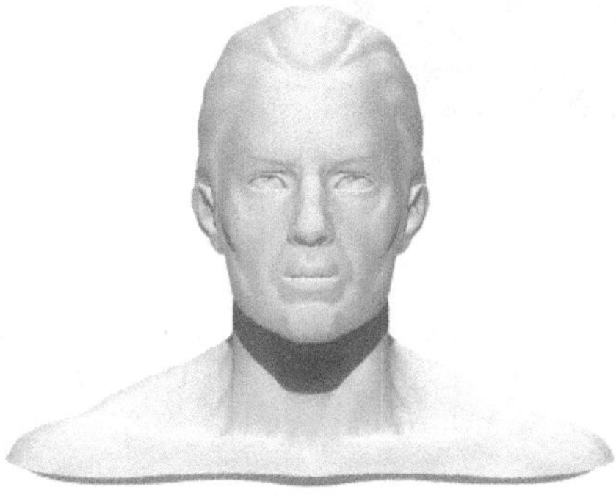

Figure 8-27 *Red tint at **Temperature** value **100***

Modifiers

The **Modifiers** subpalette consists of different options that are used to set the attributes of a material. You can create your own materials using these options. The options displayed in this subpalette depend on whether a MatCap material is chosen or a Standard material is chosen, refer to Figures 8-28 and 8-29. Some of the options in the **Modifiers** subpalette for the MatCap materials are discussed next.

CopySH and PasteSH

The materials in ZBrush are composed of different shaders. These shaders give different effects to materials and enable you to create your own materials. Some materials contain only one shader while others contain up to four shaders. The shaders are represented by the **S1**, **S2**, **S3**, and **S4** buttons located in the **Modifiers** subpalette, refer to Figure 8-28.

The **CopySH** button is used to copy the shader of one material to another material. The **PasteSH** button is used to paste the shader of one material into another material.

To understand the working of these buttons, create a sphere in the canvas and then choose the **Edit** button from the top shelf. Next, assign the material **Chrome BrightBlue Tint** to it. Choose the **CopySH** button in the **Modifiers** subpalette of the **Material** palette. Next, assign the material **MatCap Skeleton** to the sphere. Now, choose the **PasteSH** button in the **Modifiers** subpalette; the newly assigned **MatCap Skeleton** material will be replaced by the **Chrome BrightBlue Tint** material.

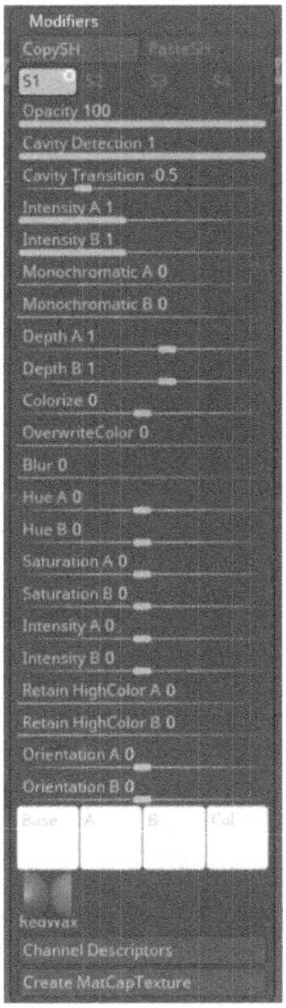

*Figure 8-28 Partial view of the **Modifiers** subpalette for MatCap materials*

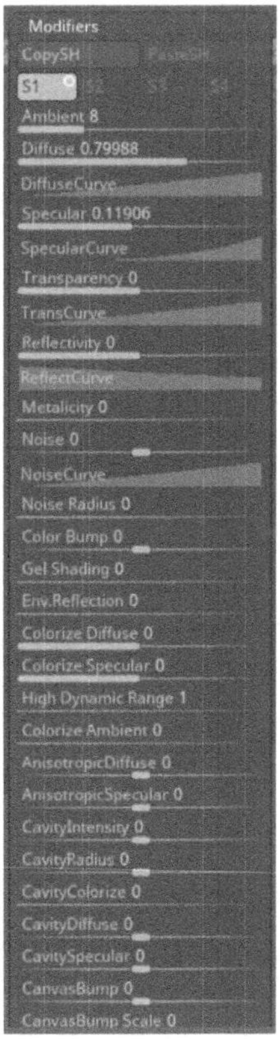

*Figure 8-29 Partial view of the **Modifiers** subpalette for Standard materials*

Opacity

The **Opacity** slider is used to control the visibility of a shader in a material. To view the actual effect of a shader in the material, the value of this slider should be set to **100**.

Cavity Detection

The **Cavity Detection** slider is used to enable the material to distinguish between the raised surfaces and the cavities in an object. If the value of this slider is higher, the material will identify the cavities and raised surfaces on an object and apply the different effects accordingly.

Cavity Transition

The **Cavity Transition** slider is used to control the degree of smoothness of the cavities in the object.

Intensity A

The **Intensity A** slider is used to specify the amount of brightness in the raised surfaces of the object if the object contains cavities, refer to Figure 8-30. In this Figure, you will notice that the raised surfaces will be very bright as the value of **Intensity A** slider has been set to **5** and the **MatCap Red Wax** material has been applied to the model.

Intensity B

The **Intensity B** slider is used to specify the amount of brightness in the cavities of an object, refer to Figure 8-31. In this figure, you will notice that the cavities in the object will be very bright as the value of the **Intensity B** slider has been set to **5**.

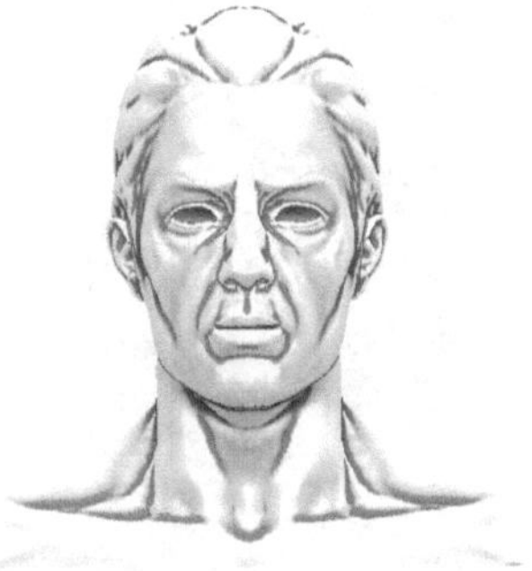

Figure 8-30 *Brightness displayed in the raised surfaces of an object*

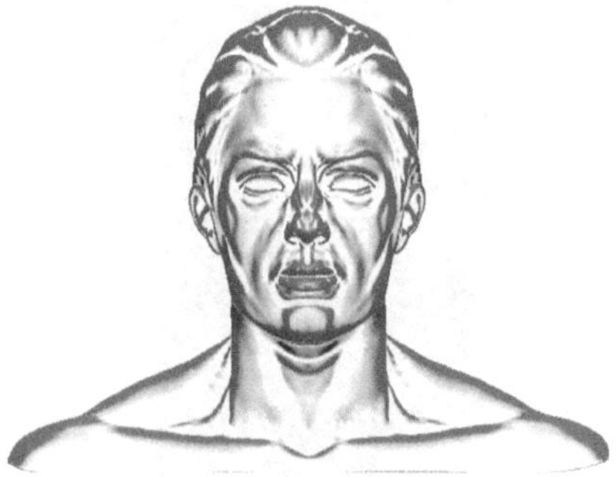

Figure 8-31 *Brightness displayed in the cavities of an object*

Monochromatic A

The **Monochromatic A** slider is used to change the color of the raised surfaces to gray, refer to Figure 8-32. In this figure, the value of the **Monochromatic A** slider has been set to **1**.

Monochromatic B

The **Monochromatic B** slider is used to change the color of the cavities to gray, refer to Figure 8-33. In this figure, the value of the **Monochromatic B** slider has been set to **1**.

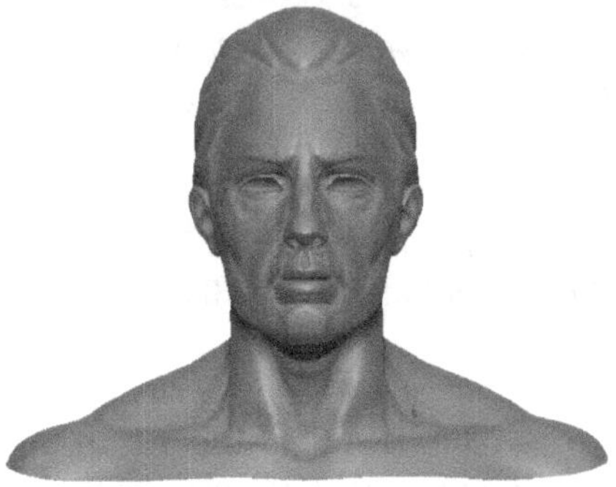

Figure 8-32 *Color of the raised surfaces converted to gray*

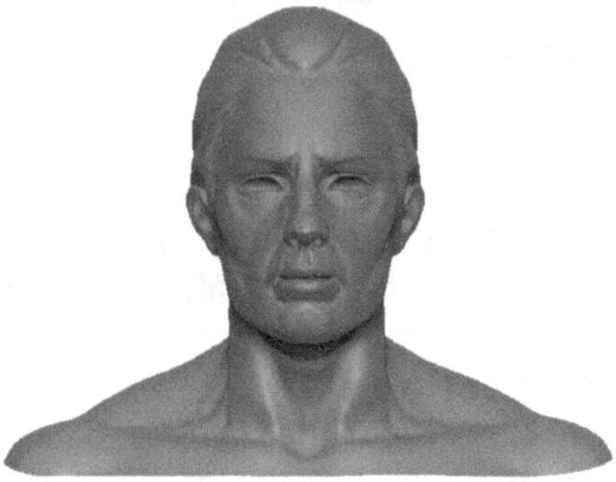

Figure 8-33 *Color of the cavities converted to gray*

Depth A

The **Depth A** slider is used to determine whether a raised surface of an object will appear more raised, less raised, or recessed on rendering.

Depth B

The **Depth B** slider is used to determine whether the cavities in an object will appear more recessed, less recessed, or raised on rendering.

Colorize

The **Colorize** slider is used along with the **Col** picker located at the bottom of the **Modifiers** subpalette, refer to Figure 8-34. On clicking on the **Col** picker, a color swatch is displayed. You can choose a color from this swatch, refer to Figure 8-35.

The **Colorize** slider is used to determine whether the chosen color from the **Col** picker will be filled on the surface of an object facing the canvas or on the surface facing away from the canvas. If the value of this slider is set to **-1**, the surface facing the canvas will be filled with the color and if the value of this slider is set to **1**, the surface facing away from the canvas will be filled with the color, refer to Figures 8-36 and 8-37.

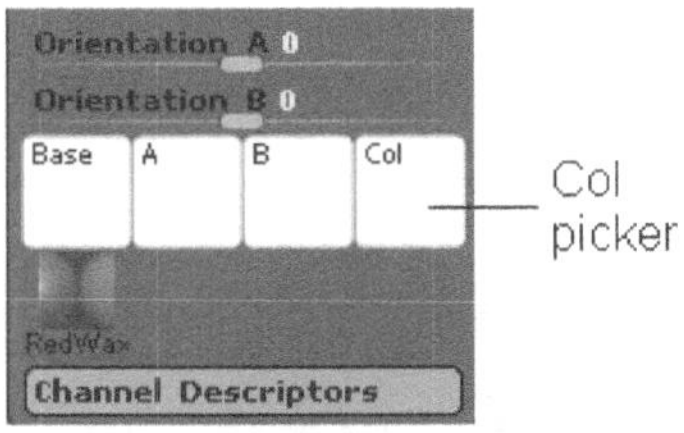

*Figure 8-34 The **Col** picker in the **Modifiers** subpalette*

Figure 8-35 Choosing a color from the color swatch

Figure 8-36 The surface facing the canvas filled with color

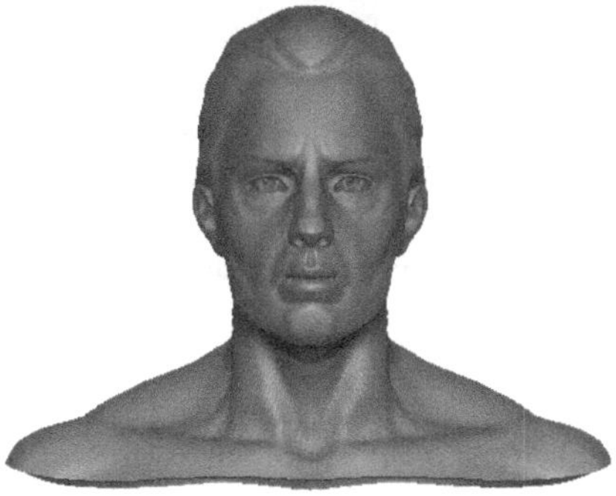

Figure 8-37 The surface facing away from the canvas filled with color

OverwriteColor

The **OverwriteColor** slider is used to blend the color of the material with the color chosen from the color picker of the **Current Color** button located in the left shelf. To understand the working of this slider, assign the **ReflectYellow** material to the model, refer to Figure 8-38. Next, choose the red color from the color picker, refer to Figure 8-39; red color will be applied to the model, refer to Figure 8-40.

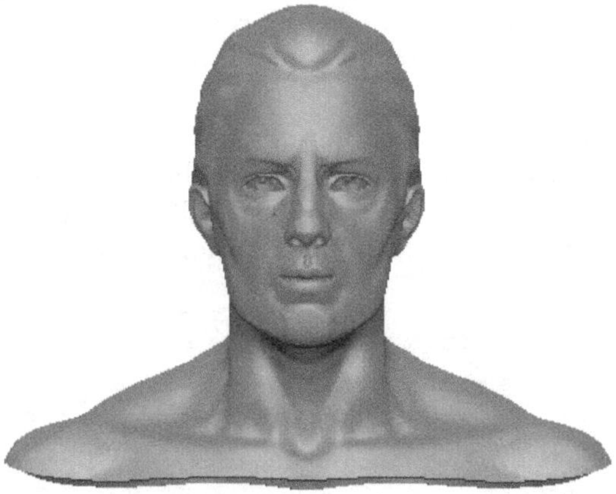

Figure 8-38 The ReflectYellow material assigned to the model

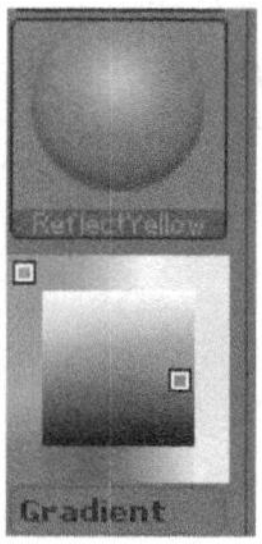

Figure 8-39 Red color chosen from the color picker

In the **Modifiers** subpalette of the **Material** palette, drag the **OverwriteColor** slider toward the right; the yellow and red color in the model will blend together to create a new color, refer to Figure 8-41.

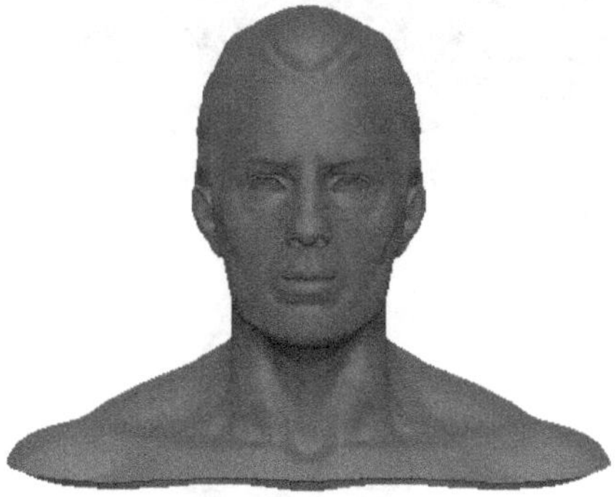

Figure 8-40 Red color applied to the model

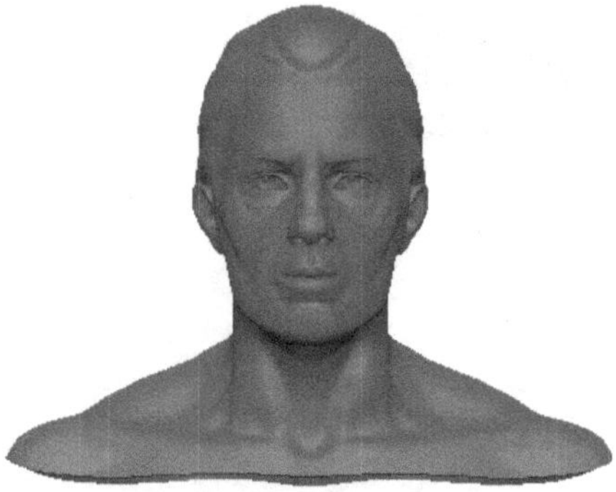

Figure 8-41 Red and yellow colors blended together

Blur

The **Blur** slider is used to blur the effect of the texture that has been applied to a material. The texture can be applied on a material with the help of the **Material Texture** button located at the bottom of the **Modifiers** subpalette, refer to Figure 8-42. To understand this concept, choose the **Material Texture** button; a flyout containing different textures will be displayed, refer to Figure 8-43. Choose the **Texture 23** texture from this flyout; the texture will be applied to the model, refer to Figure 8-44.

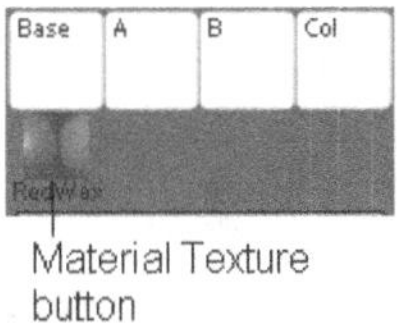

*Figure 8-42 The **Material Texture** button*

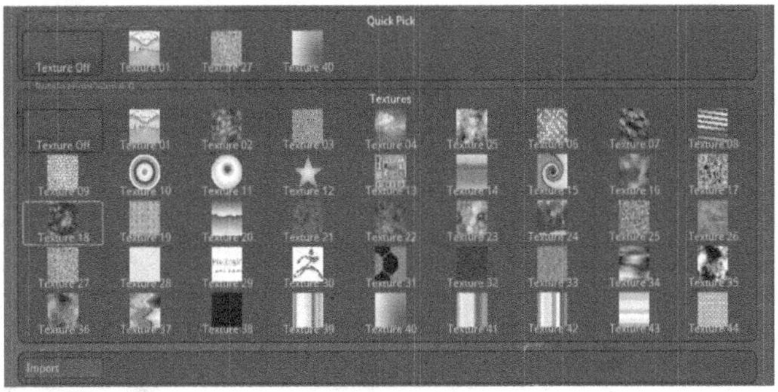

*Figure 8-43 The flyout displayed on choosing the **Material Texture** button*

In the **Modifiers** subpalette of the **Material** palette, drag the **Blur** slider toward the right; the texture applied on the model will be blurred, refer to Figure 8-45.

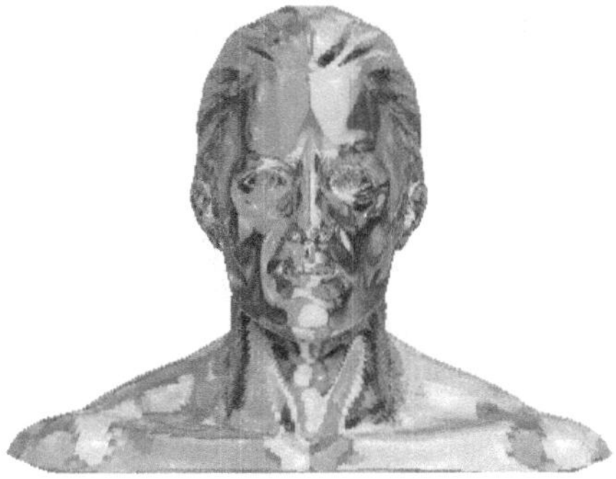

Figure 8-44 The texture applied to the model

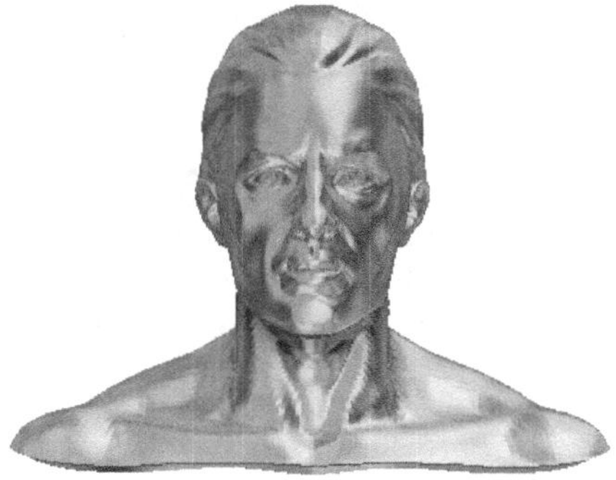

*Figure 8-45 The texture blurred using the **Blur** slider*

Hue A

The **Hue A** slider is used to change the color of the raised surfaces of an object. On setting different values using this slider, different colors will be applied to the raised surfaces of a model. For instance, if the value of this slider is set to **0.1**, yellow color will be applied to the raised surfaces of a model, refer to Figure 8-46.

Hue B

The **Hue B** slider is used to change the color of the cavities in an object. On setting different values using this slider, different colors will be applied to the cavities. For instance, if the value of this slider is set to **0.5**, blue color will be applied to the cavities in a model, refer to Figure 8-47.

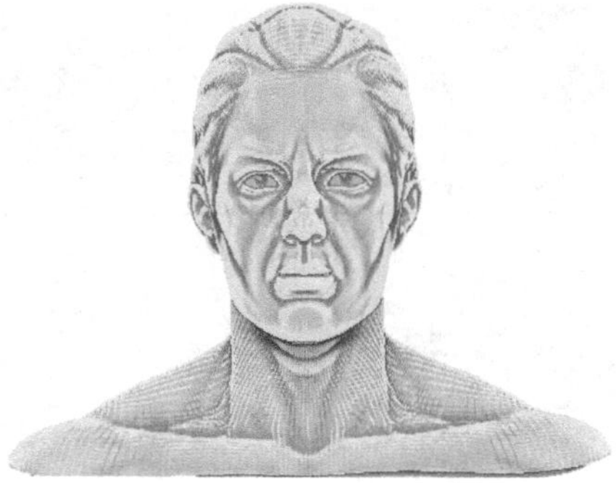

Figure 8-46 Yellow color applied to the raised surfaces of the model

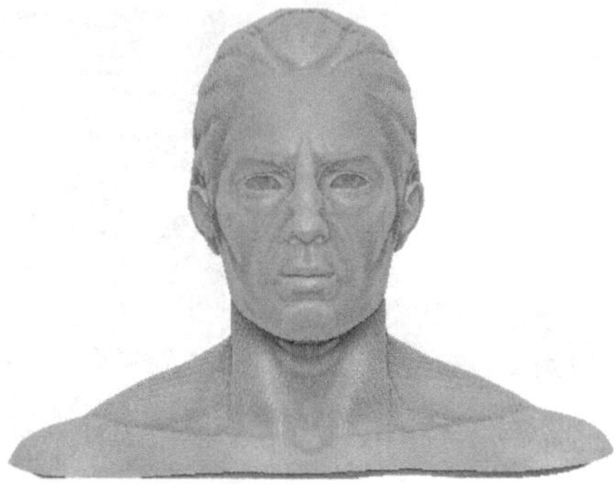

Figure 8-47 Blue color applied to the cavities of the model

Saturation A and Saturation B

The **Saturation A** and **Saturation B** sliders are used to change the saturation of the raised surfaces and the cavities of an object, respectively. If the value of both these sliders is set to **-1**, the color of the model is desaturated, refer to Figure 8-48.

Intensity A and Intensity B

The **Intensity A** and **Intensity B** sliders are used to change the intensity of the colors in the raised surfaces and the cavities of an object, respectively. If the value of both these sliders is set to **1**, the intensity of the color in both raised areas and cavities will be very high, refer to Figure 8-49. In this figure, the **MapCap Red Wax** material has been applied to the model.

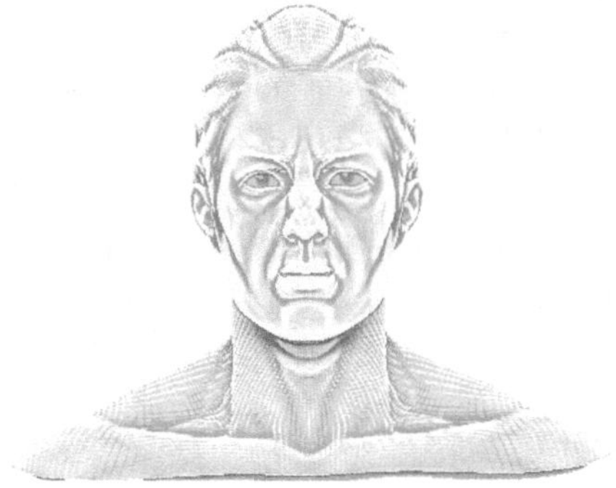

Figure 8-48 The color of the model desaturated

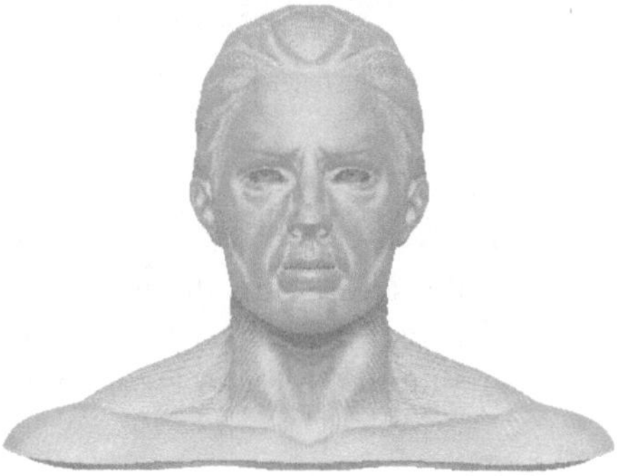

Figure 8-49 The intensity of the color increased

Retain HighColor A

This slider is used to retain the bright color of the A channel and change the darker shade of the original shade into new shade.

Retain HighColor B

This slider is used to retain the bright color of the B channel and change the darker shade of the original shade into new shade.

Orientation A and Orientation B

The **Orientation A** and **Orientation B** sliders are used to control the light orientation of the material.

The most commonly used options in the **Modifiers** subpalette for the Standard materials are discussed next.

Ambient

The **Ambient** slider is used to control the amount of ambient light in a material. To understand the working of this slider, assign the **BasicMaterial** material to the model, refer to Figure 8-50. Next, expand the **Modifiers** subpalette of the **Material** palette. In this subpalette, set the value of the **Ambient** slider to **100**; ambient light will be applied to the material and the model will appear to be illuminated, refer to Figure 8-51.

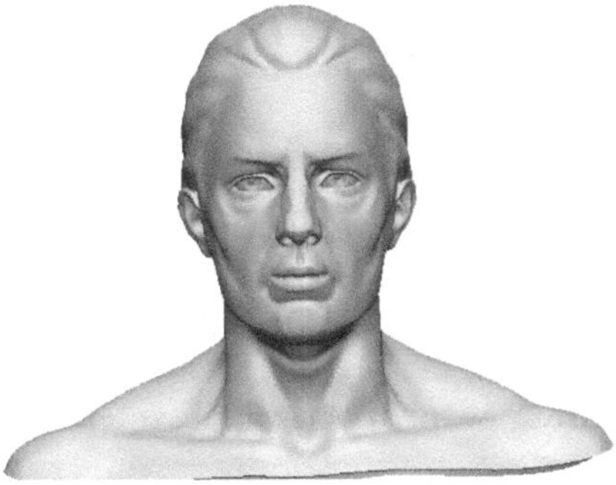

***Figure 8-50** The **BasicMaterial** material applied to the model*

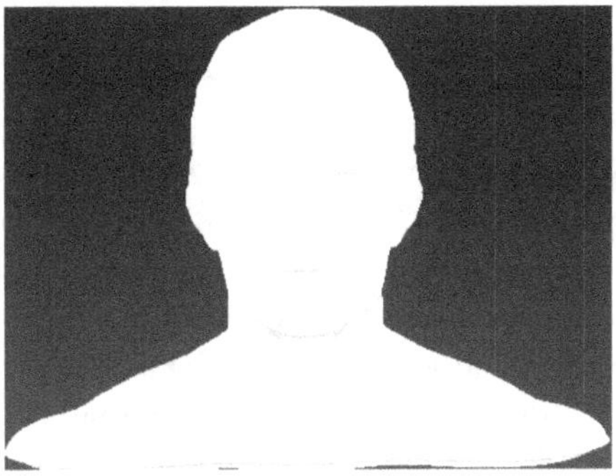

***Figure 8-51** Ambient light applied to the material*

Diffuse

The **Diffuse** slider is used to adjust the intensity of the color in a material. To understand the working of this slider, assign the **BasicMaterial** material to the model and then apply red color to it using the **Current Color** swatch. Next, set the value of the **Diffuse** slider to **0**; the red color will disappear, refer to Figure 8-52. Next, set the value of this slider to **100**; the intensity of the red color in the material will increase, refer to Figure 8-53.

***Figure 8-52** Disappearance of red color from the model*

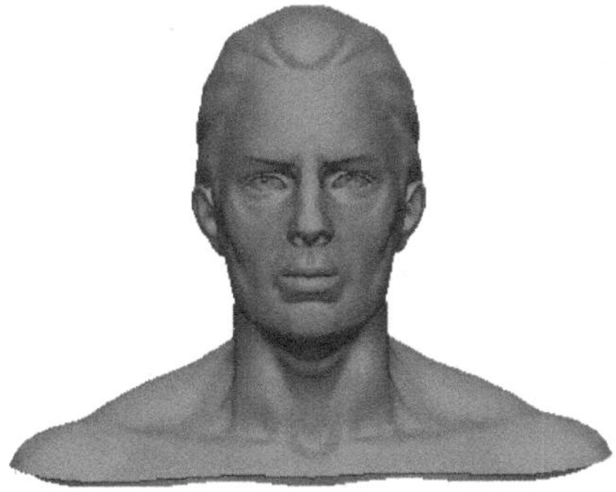

***Figure 8-53** Intensity of the red color increased*

Specular

The **Specular** slider is used to adjust the amount of specularity in a material, refer to Figure 8-54. In this figure, the value of the **Specular** slider has been set to **100**.

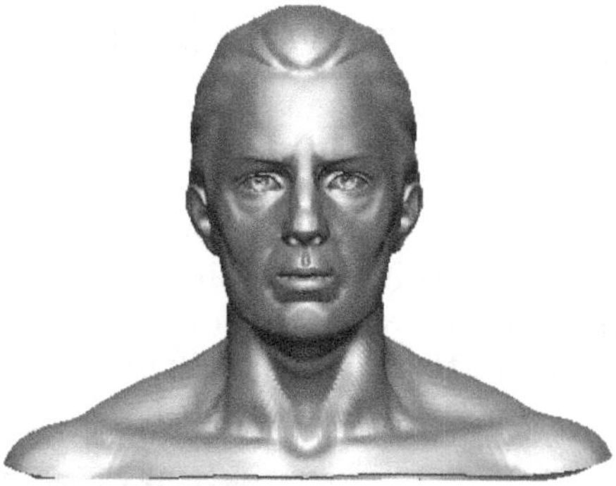

Figure 8-54 Specularity applied to the material

Transparency

The **Transparency** slider is used to adjust the amount of transparency in a material. This slider works only when the objects have been created in different layers. To understand the working of this slider, choose the Current Tool button from the **Tool** palette; a flyout will be displayed. In this flyout, choose the **Plane3D** primitive and create it in the canvas. Choose the **Edit** button from the top shelf. Next, assign the material **GradientMap2** to the plane, refer to Figure 8-55.

*Figure 8-55 The **GradientMap2** material applied to the plane*

Choose the **Layer** palette. In this palette, choose the **Create** button; a new layer will be created in this palette, refer to Figure 8-56. Choose the newly created layer from this palette. Next, choose the Current Tool button from the **Tool** palette; a flyout will be displayed. In this flyout, choose the **Cylinder3D** primitive and create it on the plane. Choose the **Move** button from the top shelf; a gyro is displayed. Move the cylinder upward using the gyro, refer to Figure 8-57. Choose the **Edit** button from the top shelf. Next, choose the **M** button from the top shelf and make sure the **Zadd** button is not chosen, refer to Figure 8-58.

Choose the Current Material button from the left shelf; a flyout will be displayed. In this flyout, choose the **BasicMaterial2** material; the material will be applied to the cylinder. Choose the **Render** palette. In this palette, choose the **Flatten** button in the **Render Properties** area to deactivate it, refer to Figure 8-59. Deactivating this button ensures that the transparency is visible in the canvas area. Now, set the value of the **Transparency** slider to **-71**; the cylinder will become transparent, refer to Figure 8-60.

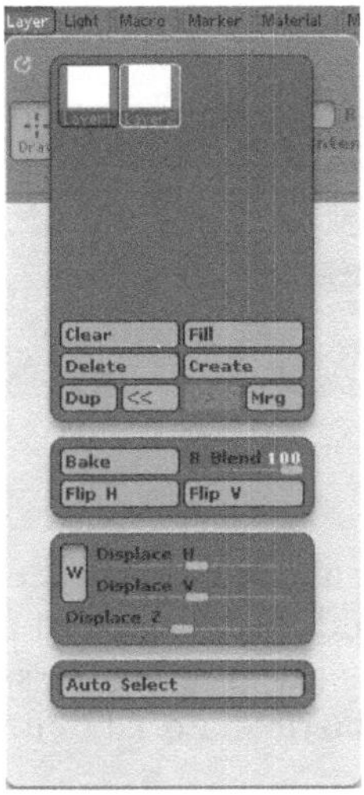

Figure 8-56 A new layer created in the **Layer** palette

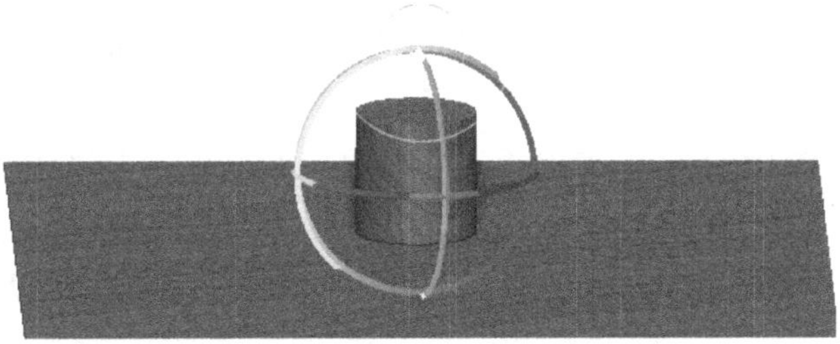

Figure 8-57 The cylinder moved up using the gyro

Figure 8-58 The **M** button chosen in the top shelf

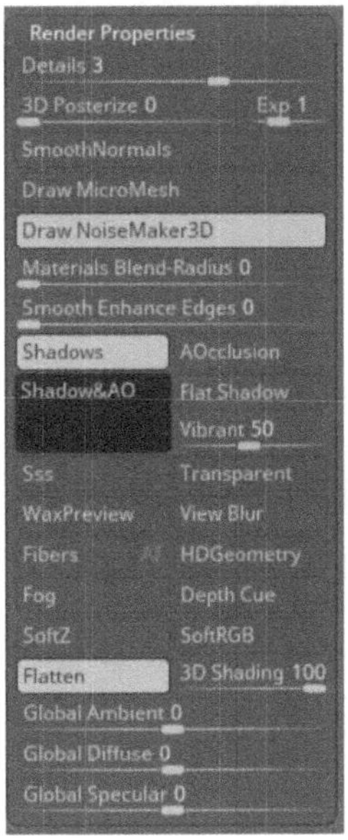

Figure 8-59 The **Flatten** button chosen in the **Render** palette

Note

The method explained above for transparency can be used for illustration purposes only. After working on the layers, the scene is converted into a 2D illustration and can be saved as a 2D image.

Figure 8-60 *Transparency displayed in the cylinder*

Reflectivity

The **Reflectivity** slider is used to adjust the amount of reflectivity in a material. You need to select a texture which has to be reflected by the material. To understand the working of this slider, create a sphere in the canvas. Make sure you press the **Edit** button after creating the sphere and subdivide the sphere to make it smoother. Next, assign the **ToyPlastic** material to it.

Expand the **Modifiers** subpalette of the **Material** palette. In this subpalette, choose the **Material Texture 1** button, refer to Figure 8-61; a flyout containing different textures will be displayed. In this flyout, choose the **Texture 42** texture. Next, set the value of the **Reflectivity** slider to **50**; the texture will reflect from the surface of the model, refer to Figure 8-62.

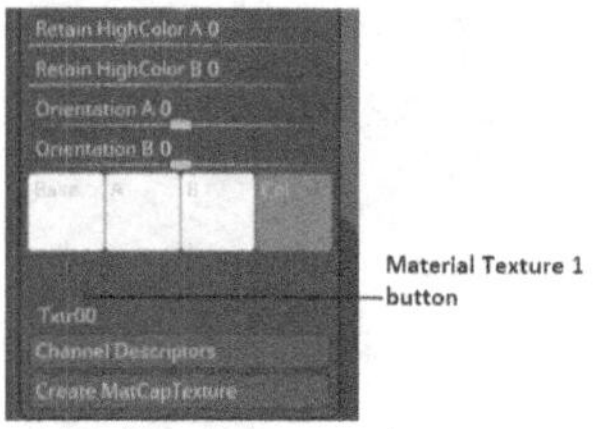

Figure 8-61 *The* ***Material Texture 1*** *button chosen*

Figure 8-62 *The texture reflected from the surface of the model*

Metalicity

The **Metalicity** slider is used to give a metallic appearance to a material by blending the color of the material with the color of light that has been applied in the scene.

Noise

The **Noise** slider is used to give a granular appearance to a material, refer to Figure 8-63. In this figure, the value of the **Noise** slider has been set to **0.4**.

Note

*The **Diffuse**, **Specular**, **Transparency**, **Reflectivity**, and **Noise** sliders have graph curves associated with them. The graph curves are located below these sliders. You can modify these attributes by manipulating these graph curves.*

Noise Radius

The **Noise Radius** slider is used to specify the size of the grains created on the surface of the material using the **Noise** slider, refer to Figure 8-64. In this figure, the value of the **Noise** slider has been set to **0.5** and the value of the **Noise Radius** slider has been set to **75**.

Figure 8-63 *The value of the **Noise** slider set to **0.4***

Figure 8-64 *The value of the **Noise Radius** slider set to **75***

Color Bump

The **Color Bump** slider is used to give a bumpy appearance to the noise or texture that has been applied to a material, refer to Figures 8-65 and 8-66. In Figure 8-65, the value of the **Noise** slider has been set to **0.4** and the value of the **Color Bump** slider has been set to **20**. In Figure 8-66, the texture **Texture 06** has been applied to the material and the value of the **Color Bump** slider has been set to **20**. To make the texture visible, the value of the **Reflectivity** slider has been set to **100**.

Figure 8-65 *Bumpiness displayed in the noise applied to the material*

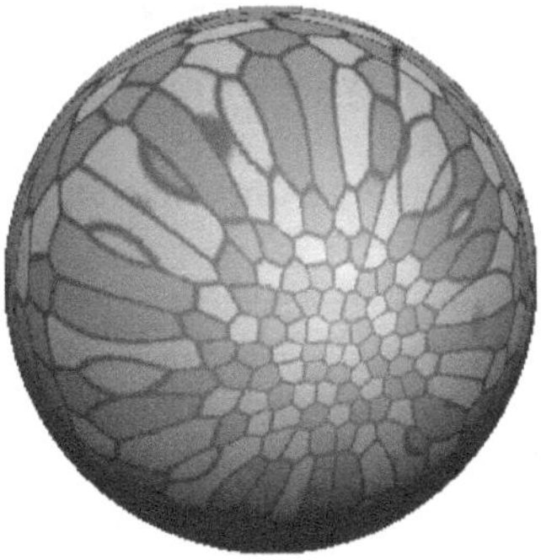

Figure 8-66 *Bumpiness displayed in the texture*

Gel Shading

The **Gel Shading** slider is used to make a material translucent giving it an appearance of gel, refer to Figure 8-67. In this figure, the **BasicMaterial2** material has been applied to the sphere and the value of the **Gel Shading** slider has been set to **3**.

Figure 8-67 *Gel shading applied to the sphere*

Env.Reflection

The **Env.Reflection** slider is used to adjust the intensity of the environmental reflection in material. The environment can be chosen from the **Render** palette and the reflection will be only visible if the **Best** button in the **Render** palette is chosen. To select an environment, choose the **Render** palette. In this palette, choose the **Txtr** button located in the **Environment** subpalette, refer to Figure 8-68. Next, choose the **Environment Texture** button located below the **Txtr** button, refer to Figure 8-68; a flyout containing different textures will be displayed. In this flyout, choose the **Texture 01** texture.

Set the value of the **Env.Reflection** slider in the **Material** palette to **60**. Next, choose the **Render** palette. In this palette, choose the **Best** button; the object will be rendered and the material will contain the environmental reflections, refer to Figure 8-69.

APPLYING DIFFERENT MATERIALS TO AN OBJECT

You can apply different types of materials to the same object or apply different materials to different subtools contained in an object. To understand how to apply different materials to the same object, create a sphere and subdivide it. By default, the **MatCap Red Wax** material will be applied to the sphere.

Choose the **M** button in the top shelf. If you do not want to add depth to sphere, make sure the **Zadd** button in the top shelf is not chosen. Next, choose the **Color** palette. In this palette, choose the **FillObject** button, refer to Figure 8-70. Choose the Current Material button in the left shelf; a flyout containing different materials will be displayed. In this flyout, choose the **Chrome A** material in the **MatCap Materials** area. Next, paint the material on the surface of the sphere. Choose different types of materials one by one and continue painting on the surface of the sphere, refer to Figure 8-71.

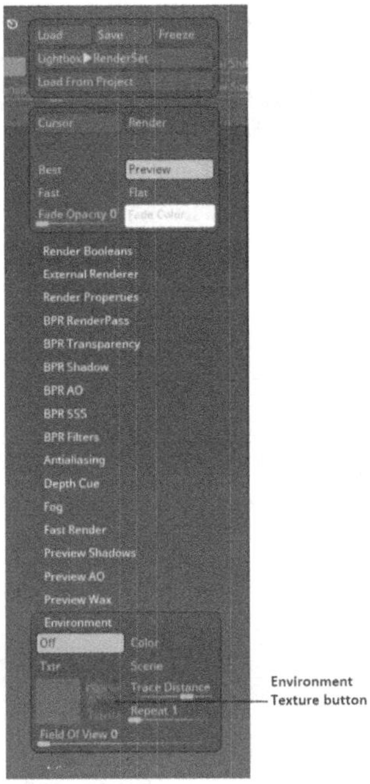

Figure 8-68 *The* ***Render*** *palette*

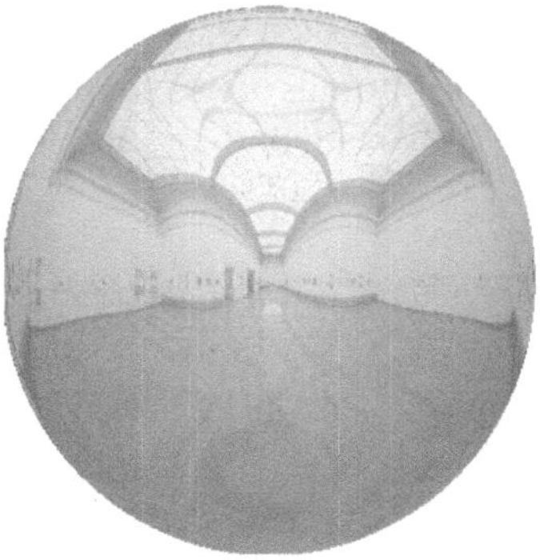

Figure 8-69 *The environmental reflection displayed on rendering*

Figure 8-70 *The* ***FillObject*** *button in the* ***Color*** *palette*

Figure 8-71 *Different materials painted on the surface of the sphere*

For applying different materials to different subtools, load the file *DemoSoldier.ZTL* from the **LightBox** Browser. This file consists of different subtools which can be selected from the **SubTool** subpalette of the **Tool** palette. In this subpalette, select the **DemoSoldier_1** subtool. Next, choose the **Mrgb** button from the top shelf. Choosing this button enables you to apply both color and material to an object. Choose the desired color and material and then choose the **FillObject** button in the **Color** palette. You will notice that the chosen material will be applied to all the subtools. You need to select each subtool individually and then apply different materials to them by choosing the **FillObject** button in the **Color** palette.

TUTORIALS

Before you start the tutorials of this chapter, you need to download the *c08_ZBrush_2022_tut.zip* file from *www.cadcim.com*. The path of the file is as follows: *Textbooks > Animation and Visual Effects > Pixologic ZBrush 2022> Pixologic ZBrush 2022: A Comprehensive Guide*

Navigate to *\Documents\ZBrushprojects* and then create a new folder with the name *c08*. Next, extract the contents of the zip file in this folder.

Tutorial 1

In this tutorial, you will create the model of an eyeball using different colors. The final output of the model is shown in Figure 8-72. **(Expected time: 20 min)**

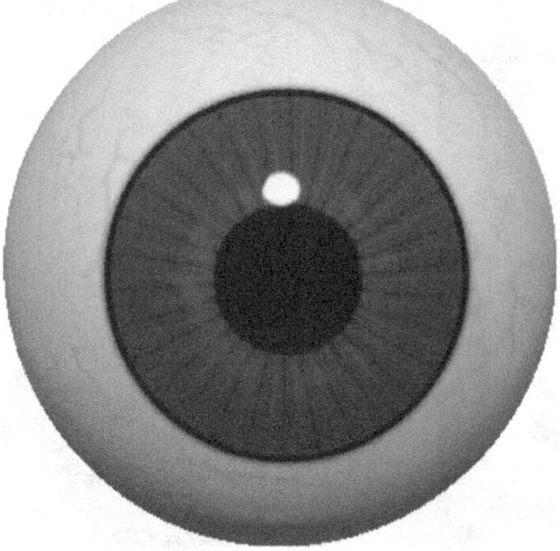

Figure 8-72 *The model of an eyeball*

The following steps are required to complete this tutorial:

a. Create the iris and pupil of the eyeball.
b. Add details to the eyeball.
c. Save the model.

Creating the Iris and Pupil of the Eyeball

In this section, you will create the iris and pupil of the eyeball using different colors.

1. Choose the **Init ZBrush** button from the **Preferences** palette; the message box is displayed. Choose the **Yes** button from the message box; ZBrush is initialized to its default state.

2. Choose the **DynaWaxSphere128.ZPR** file from the **Project** tab of the **LightBox** browser by double-clicking on it; the sphere is created in the canvas.

3. Choose the Current Material button from the left shelf; a flyout containing different materials is displayed. In this flyout, choose the **ToyPlastic** material from the **Standard Materials** area; the material is applied to the sphere. You will notice that the material is gray in color.

4. Choose the white color from the Current Color swatch located below the Current Material button; the white color is applied to the sphere, refer to Figure 8-73.

5. Choose the **Transform** palette. In this palette, make sure the **Activate Symmetry** button is chosen. Next, choose the **(R)** button; the **RadialCount** slider is activated. By default, the **>X<** button is chosen. To deactivate this button, choose it again. Next, choose the **>Z<** button; the radial symmetry in Z-axis is activated. Set the value of the **RadialCount** slider to **82**, refer to Figure 8-74.

Figure 8-73 *The white color applied to the sphere*

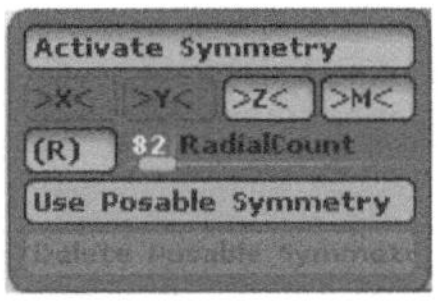

Figure 8-74 *The value of the **RadialCount** slider set to **82***

6. In the **Geometry** subpalette, click on the **Divide** button four times; the value of the **SDiv** slider becomes equal to **5** and the sphere becomes smoother.

7. Choose the **Mrgb** button from the top shelf and then choose the **Zadd** button to deactivate it. Next, choose the **Color** palette. In this palette, choose the **FillObject** button, refer to Figure 8-75.

8. In the **Color** palette, set the values of the **R**, **G**, and **B** sliders to **72**, **46**, and **28**, respectively, as shown in Figure 8-76.

*Figure 8-75 The **FillObject** button chosen in the **Color** palette*

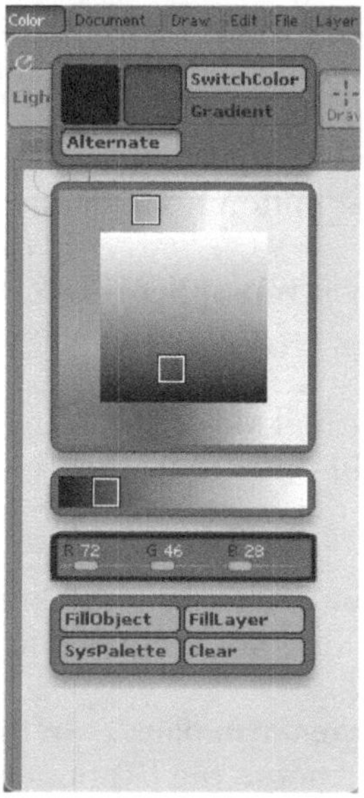

***Figure 8-76** Setting the values of **R**, **G**, and **B** sliders*

9. Hover the cursor on the surface of the sphere, refer to Figure 8-77. Next, drag the cursor inward to create the iris for the eyeball, refer to Figure 8-78.

***Figure 8-77** The cursor hovered on the surface of the sphere*

***Figure 8-78** The iris created for the eyeball*

10. Choose the **Color** palette. In this palette, set the values of the **R**, **G**, and **B** sliders to **5**, **5**, and **5**, respectively. Set the value of the **Draw Size** slider in the top shelf to **3** and hover the cursor at the circumference of the iris, refer to Figure 8-79.

11. Drag the cursor in a circular stroke to create an outline for the iris, refer to Figure 8-80.

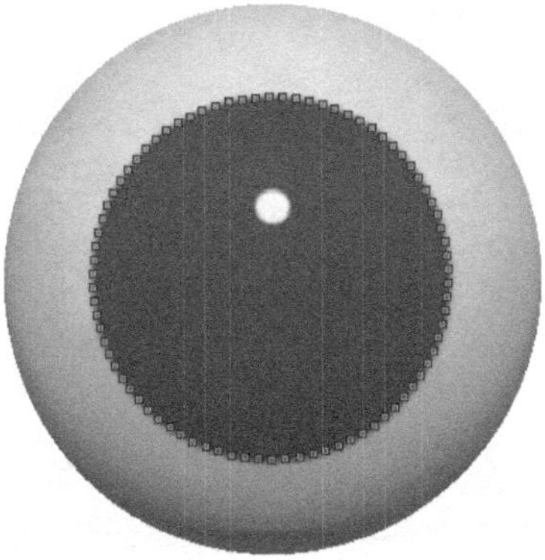

Figure 8-79 The cursor hovered on the circumference of the iris

Figure 8-80 An outline created for the iris

12. Set the value of the **Draw Size** slider in the top shelf to **64.** Hover the cursor at the center of the circle and drag the cursor outward to create a pupil, refer to Figure 8-81.

Adding Details to the Eyeball

In this section, you will add details to the eyeball.

1. Choose the **Transform** palette. In this palette, set the value of the **RadialCount** slider to **30**.

2. Set the value of the **Rgb Intensity** slider in the top shelf to **20** to decrease the intensity of the black color, refer to Figure 8-82. Next, set the value of the **Draw Size** slider to **7**.

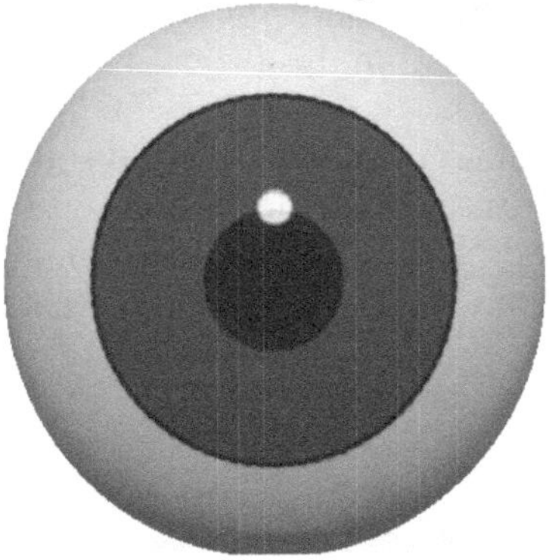

Figure 8-81 Pupil created for the eyeball

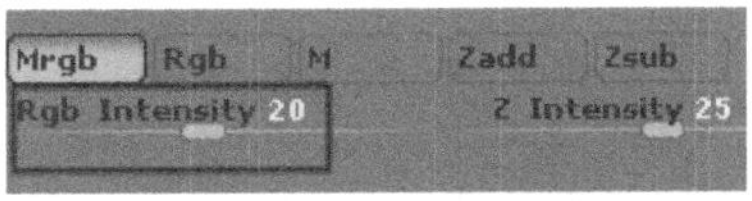

*Figure 8-82 The value of the **Rgb Intensity** slider set to **20***

3. Hover the cursor at the circumference of the pupil. Next, drag the cursor outward till it reaches the outline of the iris; thin lines are created on the surface of the iris, refer to Figure 8-83.

4. Choose the **Color** palette. In this palette, set the values of the **R**, **G**, and **B** sliders to **224**, **216**, and **216**, respectively. Next, set the value of the **Rgb Intensity** slider in the top shelf to **3**. Create more thin lines adjacent to the black lines created in Step 3, refer to Figure 8-84.

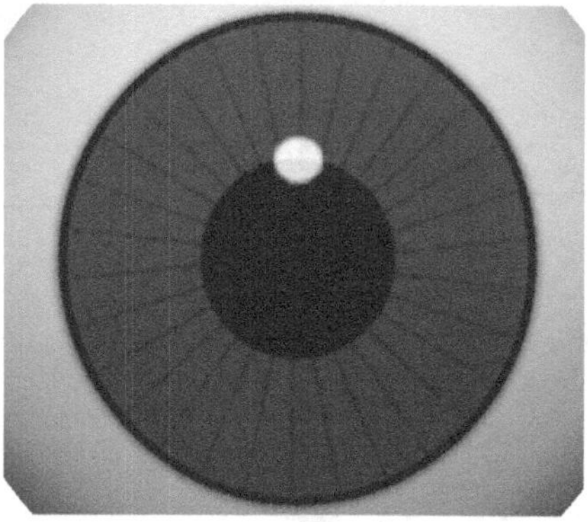

Figure 8-83 *Thin lines created on the surface of the iris*

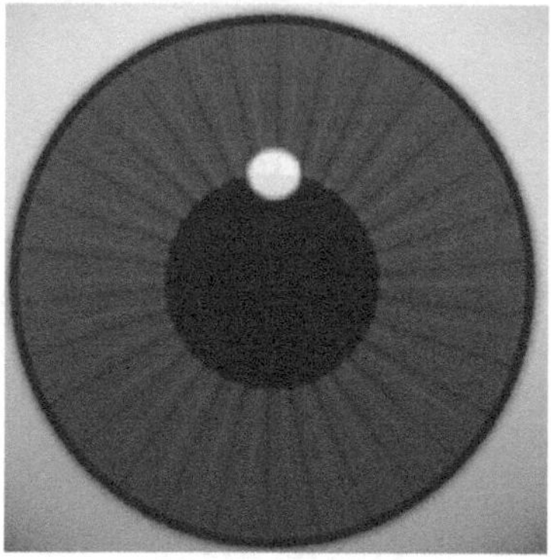

Figure 8-84 *More lines created on the surface of the iris*

5. Choose the **Transform** palette. In this palette, choose the **Activate Symmetry** button to deactivate symmetry.

6. Choose the **Color** palette. In this palette, set the values of the **R**, **G**, and **B** sliders to **101**, **103**, and **37**, respectively. Set the value of the **Draw Size** slider in the top shelf to **25**. Next, drag the cursor in the area outside the pupil to add more detail to the iris, refer to Figure 8-85.

7. Choose the Current Stroke button from the left shelf; a flyout containing different types of strokes is displayed. Choose the **DragRect** stroke from this flyout.

8. Choose the Current Alpha button from the left shelf; a flyout containing different alpha images is displayed. Choose the **Alpha 22** alpha image from this flyout.

9. Choose the **Color** palette. In this palette, set the values of the **R**, **G**, and **B** sliders to **160**, **85**, and **80**, respectively. Set the value of the **Rgb Intensity** slider in the top shelf to **20**. Next, drag the cursor to the white portion of the eyeball to create a pattern, as shown in Figure 8-86. Similarly, create more such patterns on the white area of the eyeball, refer to Figure 8-87.

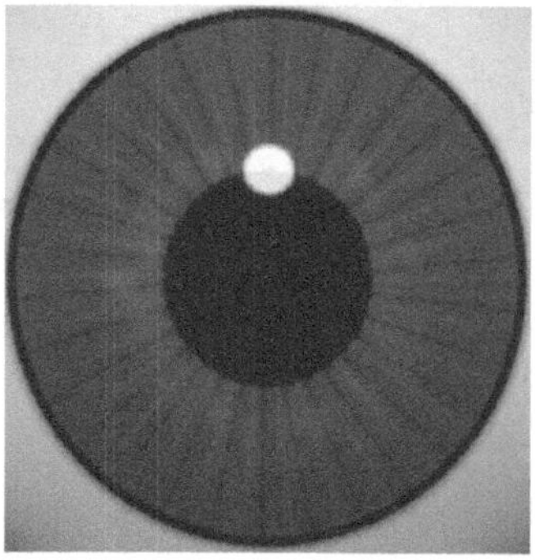

Figure 8-85 *Detail added to the iris*

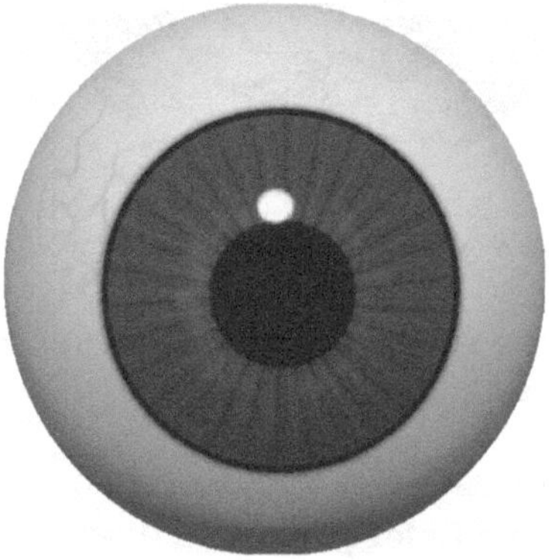

Figure 8-86 *A pattern created on the white area of the eyeball*

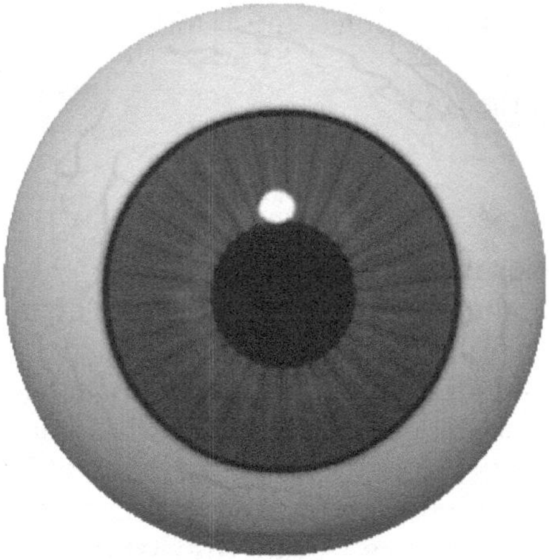

Figure 8-87 More patterns created on the white area of the eyeball

Saving the Model

In this section, you will save the file using the steps given next.

1. Choose the **Save As** button from the **Tool** palette; the **Save ZTool** dialog box is displayed. In this dialog box, browse to the location *\Documents\ZBrushprojects\c08*.

2. Enter **c08tut1** in the **File name** edit box and then choose the **Save** button.

Tutorial 2

In this tutorial, you will create the model of a ring using different materials. The final output of the model is shown in Figure 8-88. **(Expected time: 30 min)**

Figure 8-88 The model of the ring

The following steps are required to complete this tutorial:

a. Create the basic shape of the ring.
b. Add details to the ring.
c. Save the model.

Creating the Basic Shape of the Ring

In this section, you will create the basic shape of the ring using the **Ring3D** primitive.

1. Choose the **Init ZBrush** button from the **Preferences** palette; the message box is displayed. Choose the **Yes** button from the message box; ZBrush is initialized to its default state.

2. Choose the Current Tool button from the **Tool** palette; a flyout is displayed. Choose the **Ring3D** primitive from this flyout and create **Ring3D** in the canvas. Next, choose the **Edit** button from the top shelf to switch to the edit mode.

3. Expand the **Initialize** subpalette in the **Tool** palette. In this subpalette, set the value of the **SRadius** slider to **14**, refer to Figure 8-89; the shape of the ring changes, refer to Figure 8-90.

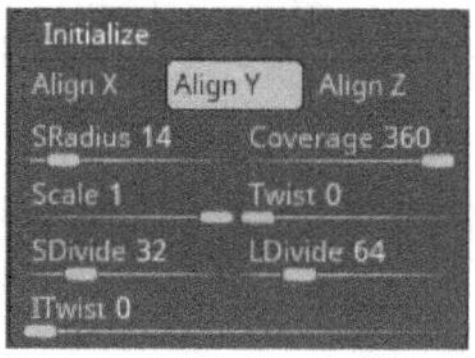

*Figure 8-89 The value of the **SRadius** slider set to **14***

Figure 8-90 The shape of the ring changed

4. Choose the **Make PolyMesh3D** button from the **Tool** palette to convert the primitive into a polymesh.

5. Set the value of the **SDiv** slider in the **Geometry** subpalette to **5** by choosing the **Divide** button four times.

6. Choose the Current Brush button from the left shelf; a flyout containing different sculpting brushes is displayed. Choose the **MaskRect** brush from this flyout; a message box is displayed prompting you to press CTRL to use this brush. Choose the **OK** button to close this message box.

7. Rotate the canvas such that you can view the side view of the ring, refer to Figure 8-91.

8. Press and hold the CTRL key and drag the cursor on the surface of the ring to create a rectangular stroke, as shown in Figure 8-91; a mask is created on the surface of the ring.

9. Press CTRL+I; the mask is inverted. Next, expand the **Deformation** subpalette in the **Tool** palette.

   Next, you will decrease the size of the unmasked area along the Y-axis using the **Size** slider.

10. Deactivate the **x** and **z** options corresponding to the **Size** slider by choosing the **x** and **z** buttons located on the right side of the slider.

11. Set the value of the **Size** slider to **-5**; the unmasked area is pushed in. Next, press and hold the CTRL key and then drag the cursor in the canvas area; the mask is removed from the ring, refer to Figure 8-92.

    Now, you need to download a material from the MatCap library of the Pixologic website *https://pixologic.com/zbrush/downloadcenter/library/*. The process of downloading materials has already been discussed.

Figure 8-91 *A rectangular stroke created on the surface of the ring*

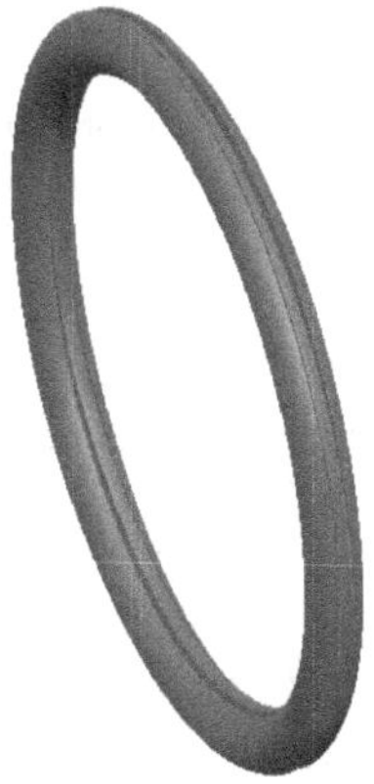

Figure 8-92 *The mask removed from the ring*

12. Download the **Gold 1** material from the **METAL** category of the **MatCap** library and extract the material from the zip file.

13. Choose the **Material** palette. In this palette, choose the **Load** button; the **Load Material** dialog box is displayed. In this dialog box, browse to the location where you have saved the material. Select the *sl_gold_1.ZMT* file and then choose the **Open** button in the **Load Material** dialog box; the gold material is applied to the ring, refer to Figure 8-93.

14. Choose the **Material** palette. In this palette, expand the **Modifiers** subpalette. In this subpalette, set the value of the **Intensity A** slider to **5**, refer to Figure 8-94; the ring becomes brighter.

Figure 8-93 The gold material applied to the ring

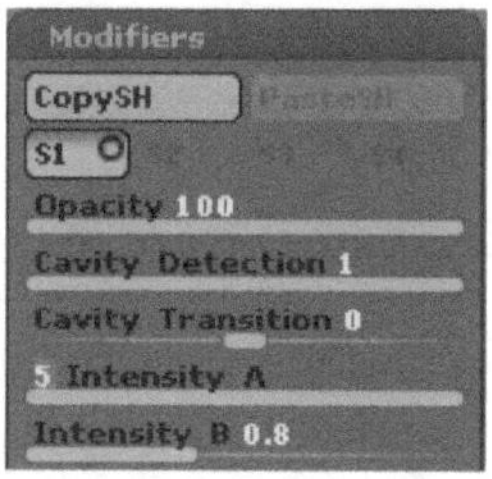

Figure 8-94 *The value of the **Intensity A** slider set to **5***

Adding Details to the Ring

In this section, you will add details to the ring using Insert brushes and different materials.

1. Choose the **Mrgb** button from the top shelf and make sure the **Zadd** button is chosen. Next, choose the **Color** palette. In this palette, choose the **FillObject** button.

2. Choose the Current Material button from the left shelf; a flyout containing different materials is displayed. In this flyout, choose the **ReflectedMap2** material from the **Standard Materials** area.

3. Choose the **Material** palette. In this palette, expand the **Modifiers** subpalette. In this subpalette, set the value of the **Ambient** and **Specular** sliders to **100** and the value of the **Diffuse** slider to **50**, refer to Figure 8-95.

4. Choose the **Transform** palette. In this palette, choose the **Activate Symmetry** button. Next, choose the **(R)** button; the **RadialCount** slider is activated. By default, the **>X<** button is chosen. To deactivate this button, choose it again. Next, choose the **>Z<** button; the radial symmetry in Z-axis is activated. Set the value of the **RadialCount** slider to **100**.

   Next, you will create diamonds in the ring using the **InsertHSphere** brush. Before using this brush, you have to make sure the geometry has not been subdivided.

5. Expand the **Geometry** subpalette in the **Tool** palette. In this subpalette, choose the **Del Lower** button, refer to Figure 8-96.

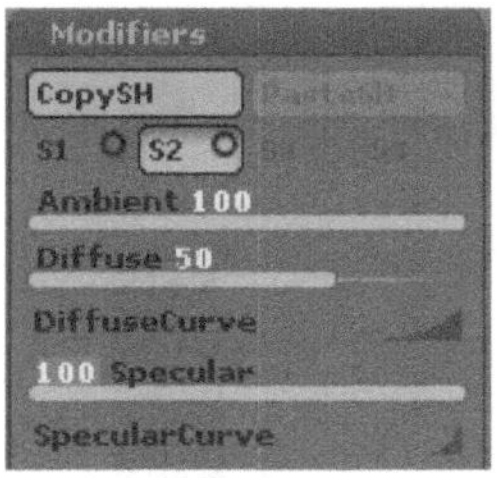

Figure 8-95 *The values of the **Ambient** and **Specular** sliders set to **100***

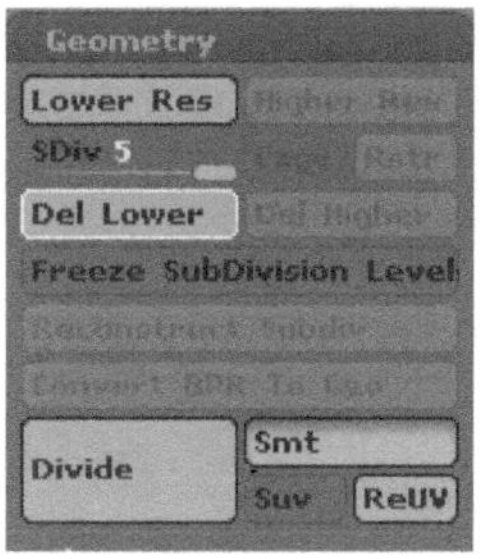

Figure 8-96 *The **Del Lower** button chosen in the **Geometry** subpalette*

6. Choose the **InsertHSphere** brush from the **Brush** tab of the **LightBox** browser. Next, drag the cursor on the recessed area of the ring; small diamonds are created in the recessed area of the ring, refer to Figure 8-97.

7. Choose the **Mrgb** button in the top shelf. Choose the **Color** palette again. In this palette, choose the **FillObject** button. Remove the mask from the ring by pressing and holding the CTRL key and then dragging the cursor in the canvas area.

8. Rotate the view of the canvas such that the ring is snapped horizontally to the canvas, refer to Figure 8-98.

Figure 8-97 *Diamonds created in the recessed area of the ring*

Figure 8-98 *Ring snapped horizontally with the canvas*

9. Choose the Current Material button from the left shelf; a flyout containing different materials is displayed. In this flyout, choose the **sl_gold_1** material.

10. Choose the **Transform** palette. In this palette, choose the **Activate Symmetry** button to deactivate symmetry.

11. Choose the Current Brush button from the left shelf; a flyout containing different sculpting brushes is displayed. Choose the **IMM SteamGears** brush from this flyout. Next, drag the cursor to the center of the ring; a golden mesh is inserted in the ring, refer to Figure 8-99.

12. Rotate the view of the canvas and then position the newly created mesh using the action line of the **Rotate** button, refer to Figure 8-100.

Figure 8-99 *A golden mesh inserted in the ring*

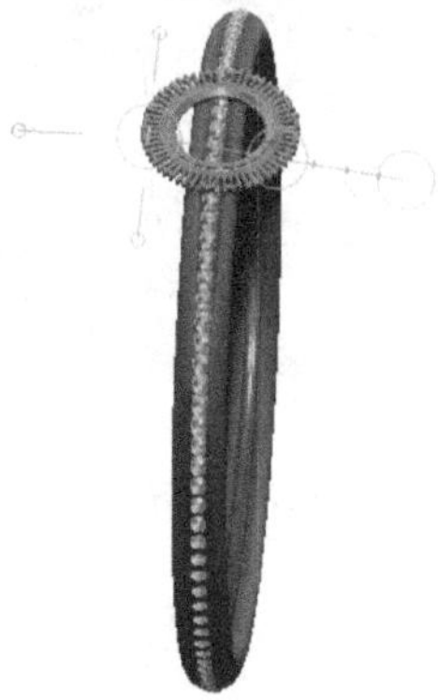

Figure 8-100 *The golden mesh adjusted using the action line*

13. Increase the size of the mesh along the Z-axis using the **Size** slider of the **Deformation** subpalette, refer to Figure 8-101.

14. Make sure the **Draw** button is chosen in the top shelf. Make sure the **Mrgb** and **Zadd** buttons are chosen in the top shelf. Next, choose the **Color** palette. In this palette, choose the **FillObject** button.

15. Choose the Current Material button from the left shelf; a flyout containing different materials is displayed. In this flyout, choose the **ReflectedMap2** material.

16. Choose the **Color** palette. In this palette, set the values of the **R**, **G**, and **B** sliders to **155**, **5**, and **5**, respectively.

17. Choose the **InsertHSphere** brush from **Insert-IMM** in the **Brush** tab of the **LightBox** browser. Next, drag the cursor inside the mesh created; a red colored stone is created.

18. Increase the size of the mesh along the Z-axis using the **Size** slider of the **Deformation** subpalette such that it fits inside the golden mesh, refer to Figure 8-102. Remove the mask from the ring by pressing and holding the CTRL key and then dragging the cursor in the canvas area.

Figure 8-101 *The size of the golden mesh increased along the Z-axis*

Figure 8-102 *The red stone fitted inside the golden mesh*

You can also create a ring box and place the ring inside it.

19. Expand the **SubTool** subpalette of the **Tool** palette. In this subpalette, choose the **Append** button; a flyout is displayed. In this flyout, choose the **Cube3D** primitive; a cube is created in the canvas.

20. Choose the thumbnail for the cube from the list of subtools. Set the value of **SDiv** slider in the **Geometry** subpalette to **5** by choosing the **Divide** button four times; the cube becomes smoother.

21. Modify the shape of the cube using the modeling techniques discussed in the previous chapters to create a ring box. Next, assign a red colored plastic material to it, refer to Figure 8-103.

Figure 8-103 *The ring placed inside the ring box*

Saving the Model

In this section, you will save the file using the steps given next.

1. Choose the **Save As** button from the **Tool** palette; the **Save ZTool** dialog box is displayed. In this dialog box, browse to the location: *\Documents\ZBrushprojects\c08*.

2. Enter **c08tut2** in the **File name** edit box and then choose the **Save** button.

Tutorial 3

In this tutorial, you will assign different materials to different subtools in a scene. The final output of the model is shown in Figure 8-104. **(Expected time: 30 min)**

The following steps are required to complete this tutorial:

a. Open the file.
b. Apply different materials to different subtools.
c. Save the model.

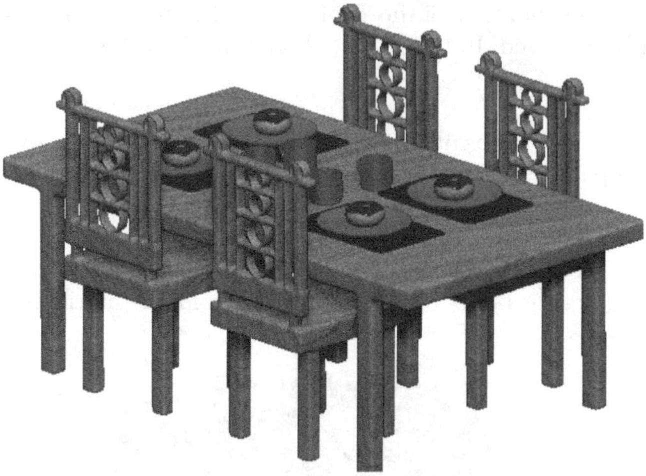

Figure 8-104 *The final output of the scene*

Opening the File

In this section, you will open the file.

1. Choose the **Init ZBrush** button from the **Preferences** palette; the message box is displayed. Choose the **Yes** button from the message box; ZBrush is initialized to its default state.

2. Choose the **Tool** palette. In this palette, choose the **Load Tool** button; the **Load ZTool** dialog box is displayed. In this dialog box, browse to*\Documents\ZBrushprojects\c08* and select the *c08tut3start.ZTL* file in it. Next, choose the **Open** button in this dialog box.

3. Press and hold the left mouse button and drag the cursor in the canvas area; the scene is displayed in the canvas, refer to Figure 8-105. Next, choose the **Edit** from the top shelf to switch to the edit mode. Rotate the view of the canvas, refer to Figure 8-106.

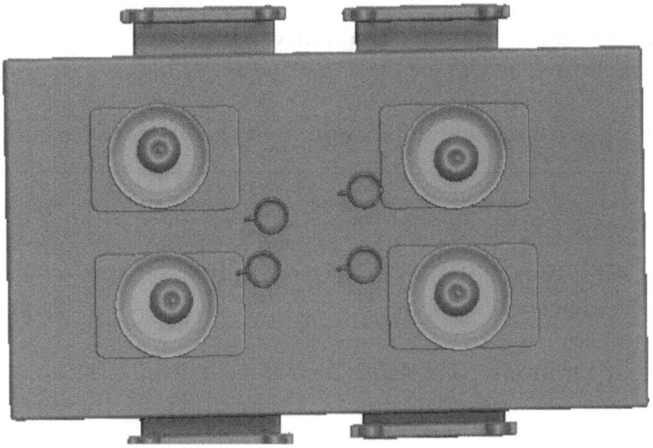

Figure 8-105 *The scene displayed in the canvas*

Figure 8-106 The view of the canvas rotated

Applying Different Materials to Different Subtools

In this section, you will apply different materials to different subtools in the scene.

1. Expand the **SubTool** subpalette in the **Tool** palette. In this subpalette, choose the first subtool from the list of subtools, refer to Figure 8-107.

2. Choose the eye icon located on the right side of all the subtools except the first subtool, refer to Figure 8-108; the visibility of all the subtools is turned off and only the plates are visible in the canvas, refer to Figure 8-109.

Note

*You can also use visibilty sets in the **Subtool** subpalette for storing visibility of subtools.*

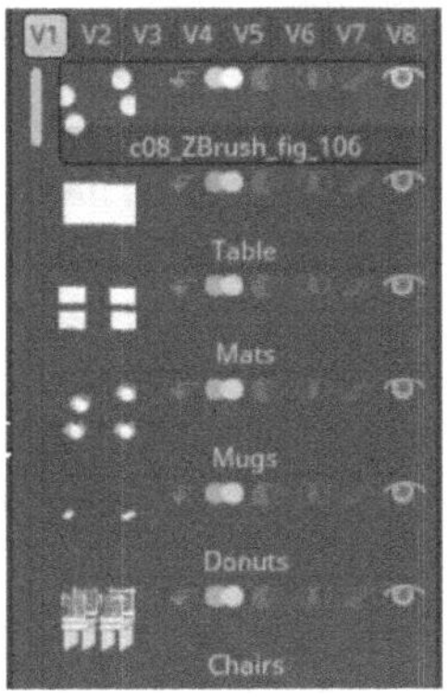

Figure 8-107 The first subtool chosen from the list

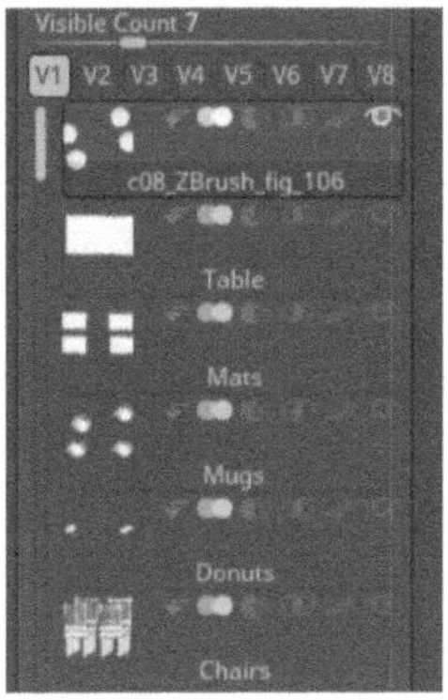

Figure 8-108 Visibility of other subtools turned off

Figure 8-109 The plates displayed in the canvas

3. Choose the **Mrgb** button from the top shelf and make sure the **Zadd** button is not chosen. Next, choose the **Color** palette. In this palette, choose the **FillObject** button, refer to Figure 8-110.

4. Choose the Current Material button from the left shelf; a flyout containing different materials is displayed. In this flyout, choose the **ToyPlastic** material from the **Standard Materials** area.

5. Choose the **Color** palette. In this palette, set the values of the **R**, **G**, and **B** sliders to **169**, **3**, and **3**, respectively, refer to Figure 8-111. Next, in this palette, choose the **FillObject** button; the material is applied to the plates and the color of the plates changes to red, refer to Figure 8-112.

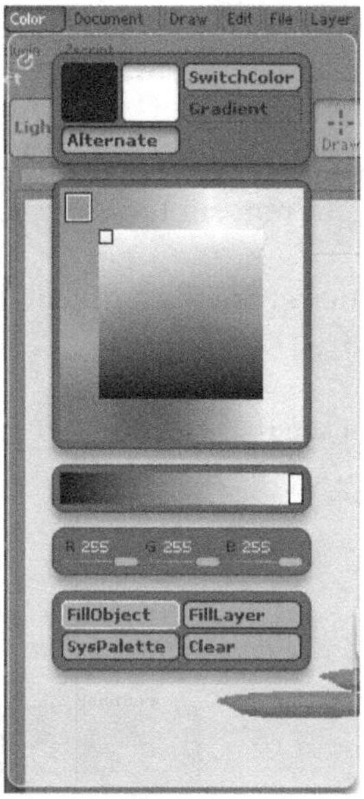

***Figure 8-110** The **FillObject** button chosen*

***Figure 8-111** The values of the **R**, **G**, and **B** sliders set*

***Figure 8-112** The material applied to the plates*

6. Choose the second subtool in the list; the table is displayed. You will notice that the red plastic material is applied to the table.

7. Choose the Current Material button from the left shelf; a flyout containing different materials is displayed. In this flyout, choose the **GradientMap2** material from the **Standard Materials** area; the material is applied to the table, refer to Figure 8-113.

Figure 8-113 *The* ***GradientMap2*** *material applied to the table*

Next, you will remove the specularity from the material applied to the table.

8. Choose the **Material** palette. In this palette, expand the **Modifiers** subpalette. In this subpalette, set the value of the **Diffuse** and **Specular** sliders to **97** and **0**, respectively, refer to Figure 8-114; the specularity in the table is removed.

9. Choose the **Color** palette. In this palette, choose the **FillObject** button.

10. Choose the eye icon on the right side of the third subtool and then choose the third subtool in the list; the mats are displayed. You will notice that the **GradientMap2** material is applied to the mats, refer to Figure 8-115.

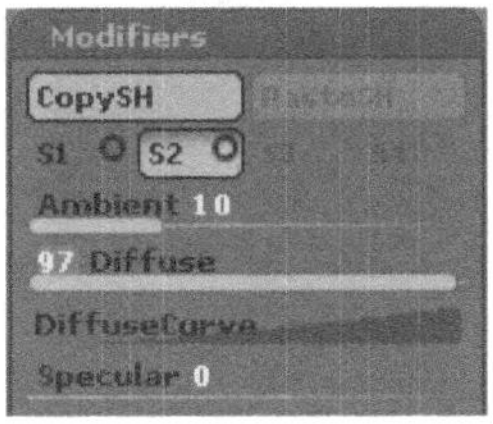

Figure 8-114 *The values of the* ***Diffuse*** *and* ***Specular*** *sliders set*

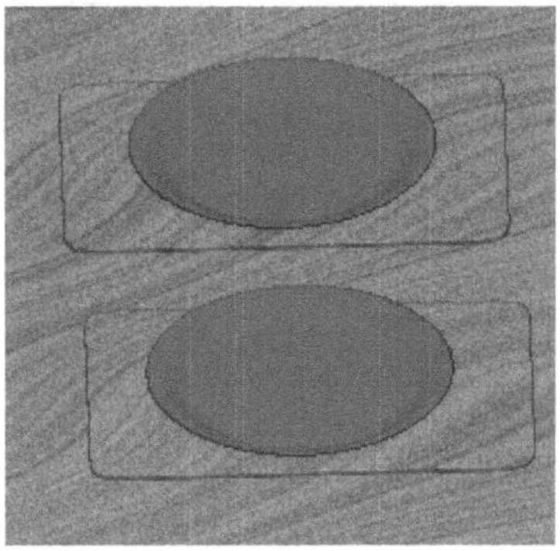

Figure 8-115 *The* ***GradientMap2*** *material applied to the mats*

11. Choose the Current Material button from the left shelf; a flyout containing different materials is displayed. In this flyout, choose the **SoftPlastic** material from the **Standard Materials** area.

12. Choose the **Color** palette. In this palette, set the values of the **R**, **G**, and **B** sliders to **19**, **11**, and **11**, respectively; the material is applied to the mats, refer to Figure 8-116. Next, choose the **Color** palette. In this palette, choose the **FillObject** button.

Figure 8-116 *The* ***SoftPlastic*** *material applied to the mats*

13. Choose the eye icon on the right side of the fourth subtool and then choose the fourth subtool in the list; the mugs are displayed. You will notice that the **SoftPlastic** material is applied to the mugs.

14. Choose the Current Material button from the left shelf; a flyout containing different materials is displayed. In this flyout, choose the **Metalic01** material.

15. Choose the **Color** palette. In this palette, set the values of the **R**, **G**, and **B** sliders to **219**, **11**, and **11**, respectively; the material is applied to the mugs, refer to Figure 8-117. In this palette, choose the **FillObject** button.

Figure 8-117 *The* ***Metalic01*** *material applied to the mugs*

16. Choose the fifth subtool in the list and then turn off the visibility of other subtools; the donuts are displayed. Turn off the visibility of all other subtools. You will notice that the **Metalic01** material is applied to the donuts, refer to Figure 8-118.

17. Make sure the **Mrgb** button is chosen in the top shelf. Choose the Current Material button from the left shelf; a flyout containing different materials is displayed. In this flyout, choose the **BasicMaterial** material from the **Standard Materials** area.

18. Choose the **Color** palette. In this palette, set the values of the **R**, **G**, and **B** sliders to **212**, **110**, and **68**, respectively; the material is applied to the donuts, refer to Figure 8-119. In this palette, choose the **FillObject** button.

Figure 8-118 The ***Metalic01*** *material applied to the donut*

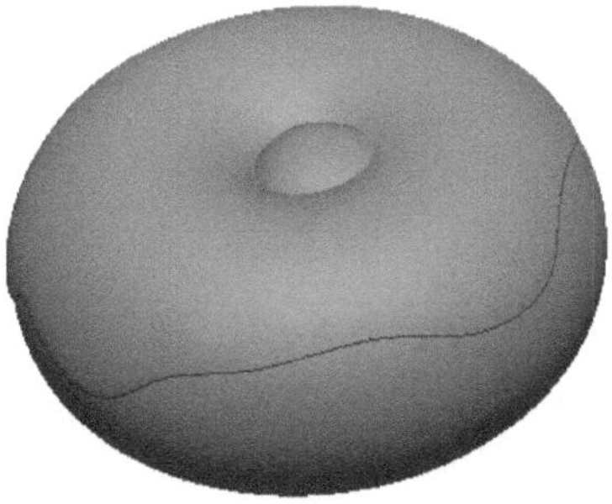

Figure 8-119 The ***BasicMaterial*** *material applied to the donut*

19. Choose the **Material** palette. In this palette, expand the **Modifiers** subpalette, if not already expanded. In this subpalette, set the value of the **Noise** slider to **0.1152**, refer to Figure 8-120; a noise is applied to the donut.

20. Choose the Current Material button from the left shelf; a flyout containing different materials is displayed. In this flyout, choose the **ToyPlastic** material.

21. Choose the **Color** palette. In this palette, set the values of the **R**, **G**, and **B** sliders to **22**, **8**, and **8**, respectively. Next, decrease the brush size as required and then drag the cursor on the extruded part of the donut to create a chocolate layer on the donut, as shown in Figure 8-121. Similarly, create a chocolate layer on all the donuts, refer to Figure 8-122.

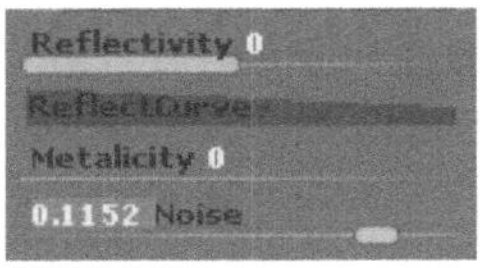

Figure 8-120 The value of the ***Noise*** *slider set to* ***0.1152***

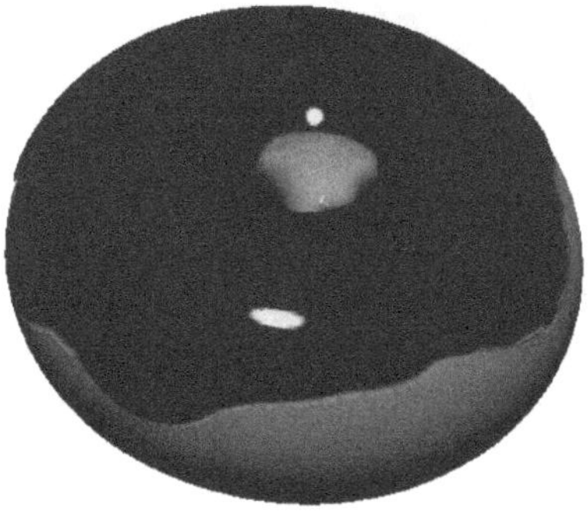

Figure 8-121 A chocolate layer created on the extruded part of the donut

22. Choose the Current Material button from the left shelf; a flyout containing different materials is displayed. In this flyout, choose the **JellyBean** material from the **Standard Materials** area.

23. Choose the **Color** palette. In this palette, set the values of the **R**, **G**, and **B** sliders to **171**, **9**, and **9**, respectively.

Figure 8-122 The chocolate layer created on all the donuts

24. Choose the **Material** palette. In this palette, expand the **Modifiers** subpalette. In this subpalette, set the value of the **Ambient** slider to **100**, refer to Figure 8-123.

25. Drag the cursor on the middle part of the donut to create jelly on the surface of the donut, refer to Figure 8-124. Similarly, create jelly on all the donuts. Turn on the visibility of all the subtools, refer to Figure 8-125.

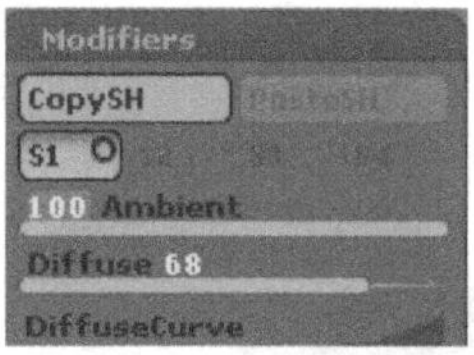

Figure 8-123** The value of the **Ambient** slider set to **100

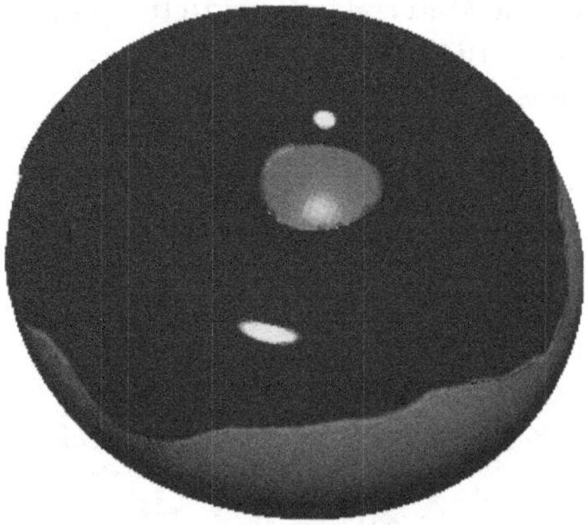

***Figure 8-124** The **JellyBean** material painted on the middle part of the donut*

26. Choose the sixth subtool from the list of subtools. Next, choose the Current Material button from the left shelf; a flyout containing different materials is displayed. In this flyout, choose the **GradientMap2** material from the **Standard Materials** area; the material is applied to the chairs, refer to Figure 8-126. Next, choose the **Color** palette. In this palette, choose the **FillObject** button.

Figure 8-125 *The visibility of all the subtools turned on*

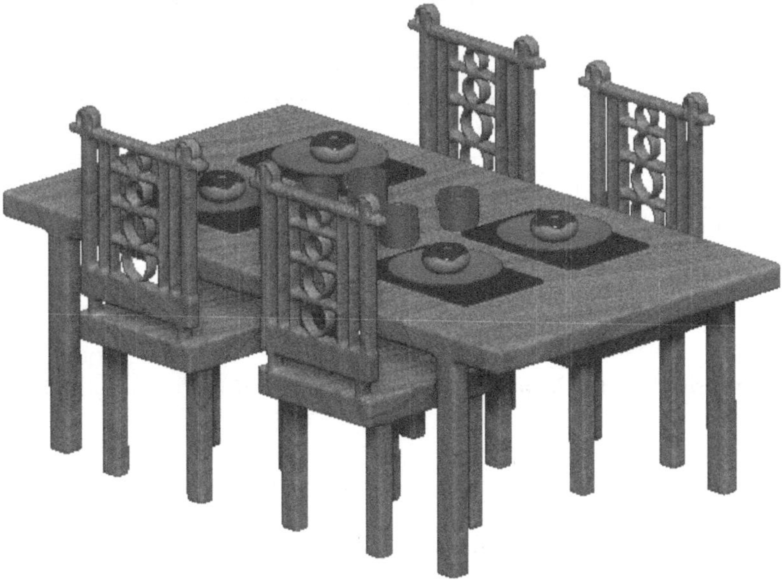

Figure 8-126 *The* ***GradientMap2*** *material applied to the chairs*

Saving the Model

In this section, you will save the file using the steps given next.

1. Choose the **Save As** button from the **Tool** palette; the **Save ZTool** dialog box is displayed. In this dialog box, browse to the location: *\Documents\ZBrushprojects\c08*.

2. Enter **c08tut3** in the **File name** edit box and then choose the **Save** button.

Self-Evaluation Test

Answer the following questions and then compare them to those given at the end of this chapter:

1. Which of the following sliders in the **Modifiers** subpalette is used to control the visibility of a shader in a material?

   (a) **Opacity** (b) **Depth A**
   (c) **Depth B** (d) **Hue A**

2. Which of the following sliders in the **Modifiers** subpalette is used to change the color of the raised surfaces of a MatCap material to gray?

   (a) **Monochromatic B** (b) **Monochromatic A**
   (c) **OverwriteColor** (d) **Colorize**

3. The __________ button in the **Material** palette is used to import a downloaded material into ZBrush.

4. The __________ slider in the **Material** palette is used to scroll through different types of materials in ZBrush.

5. The __________ slider in the **Wax Modifiers** subpalette is used to set the intensity of the wax effect on a material.

6. The _________ slider in the **Modifiers** subpalette is used to enable the MatCap material to distinguish between the raised surfaces and cavities in the object.

7. The **Metalicity** slider in the **Modifiers** subpalette is used to give a granular appearance to a Standard material. (T/F)

8. The materials in ZBrush are composed of different shaders. (T/F)

9. The options displayed in the **Modifiers** subpalette depend on whether a MatCap material is chosen or a Standard material is chosen. (T/F)

Review Questions

Answer the following questions:

1. Which of the following sliders in the **Modifiers** subpalette is used to blend the color of the material with the color of light applied in the scene?

   (a) **Color Bump** (b) **Reflectivity**
   (c) **Blur** (d) **Metalicity**

2. Which of the following sliders in the **Modifiers** subpalette is used to add blue or red tint to the wax material when it is rendered using the **BPR** button located in the right shelf?

   (a) **Temperature** (b) **Fresnel**
   (c) **Exponent** (d) **Spec**

3. The __________ slider in the **Modifiers** subpalette is used to control the degree of smoothness of the cavities in the object.

4. The __________ button in the **Modifiers** subpalette is used to copy the shader of one material onto another material.

5. The term MatCap stands for __________.

6. The **Spec** slider in the **Wax Modifiers** subpalette does not have any effect on the MatCap materials. (T/F)

7. If the value of the **Saturation A** and **Saturation B** sliders is set to **-1**, the color of the model will become gray. (T/F)

8. The **Exponent** slider in the **Wax Modifiers** subpalette is used to specify the distance up to which the wax effect will spread on the surface of an object. (T/F)

EXERCISES

The output of the models used in the following exercises can be accessed by downloading the *c08_ZBrush_2022_exr.zip* file from *www.cadcim.com*. The path of the file is as follows: *Textbooks > Animation and Visual Effects > ZBrush > ZBrush 2022: A Comprehensive Guide*.

Exercise 1

Create the model of a cake using the radial symmetry and apply different materials to it, as shown in Figure 8-127. **(Expected time: 20 min)**

Figure 8-127 *Model of a cake*

Exercise 2

Create the model of a hut and apply different materials to it, as shown in Figure 8-128.

(Expected time: 30 min)

Figure 8-128 *Model of a hut*

Exercise 3

Load the *Julie.ZTL* file from the **Tool** tab of the **LightBox** browser and apply different materials to it, as shown in Figure 8-129. **(Expected time: 20 min)**

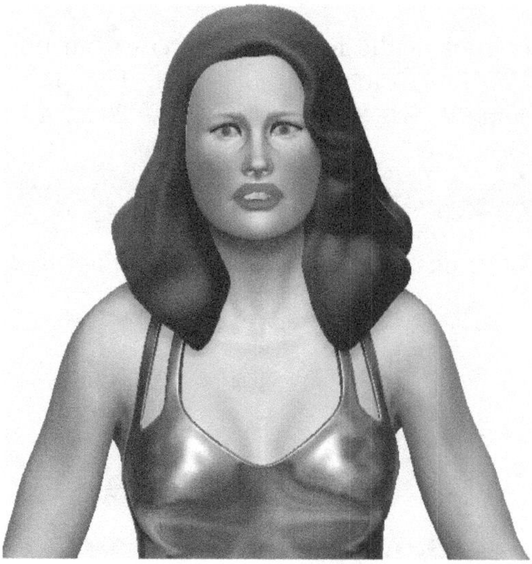

Figure 8-129 *The final output*

Answers to Self-Evaluation Test

1. a, **2.** b, **3. Load**, **4. Item Info**, **5. Strength**, **6. Cavity Detection**, **7.** F, **8.** T, **9.** T

Chapter 9

Texturing in ZBrush

Learning Objectives

After completing this chapter, you will be able to:

- *Work with the Texture palette*
- *Work with the Spotlight tool*
- *Apply textures on different objects*

INTRODUCTION

In this chapter, you will learn to assign various textures to 3D meshes created in ZBrush. These textures give a realistic look to the objects. ZBrush consists of a library of textures that can either be accessed from the Current Texture button located in the left shelf or the **LightBox** browser.

TEXTURES IN ZBrush

ZBrush consists of an extensive library of textures. To access these textures, choose the Current Texture button from the left shelf; a flyout containing different types of textures will be displayed, refer to Figure 9-1. This flyout consists of two areas namely **Quick Pick** and **Textures**. The **Quick Pick** area consists of the recently chosen textures and the **Textures** area consists of all the textures available in ZBrush. Besides this, there are some additional textures in ZBrush that can be accessed from the **Texture** tab of the **LightBox** browser, refer to Figure 9-2.

***Figure 9-1** The flyout displayed on choosing the Current Texture button*

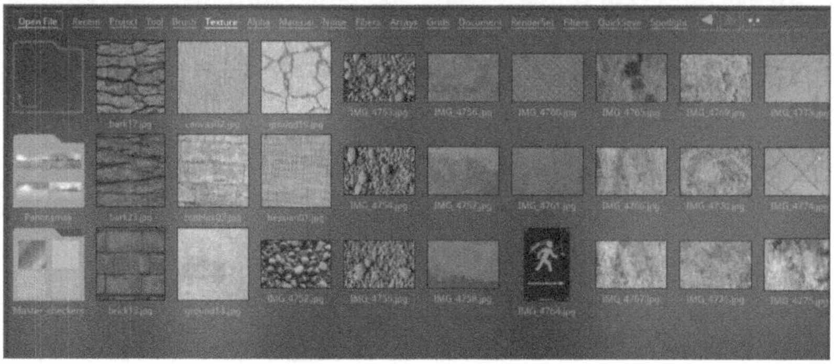

***Figure 9-2** The textures displayed in the **Texture** tab of the **LightBox** browser*

The flyout displayed on choosing the Current Texture button consists of different buttons located at its bottom. These buttons are discussed next.

Import

The **Import** button is used to import a new texture file to ZBrush. On choosing this button, the **Import Image** dialog box will be displayed. You can download additional textures from the Pixologic site by visiting the following URL: *https://pixologic.com/zbrush/downloadcenter/texture/*. This site has different categories of textures displayed under the **Texture Library** tab, refer to Figure 9-3. To download a texture from this site, choose the desired category under the **Texture Library** tab. For instance, to download different brick textures, choose the **BRICK** category from the library; different textures of bricks will be displayed, refer to Figure 9-4.

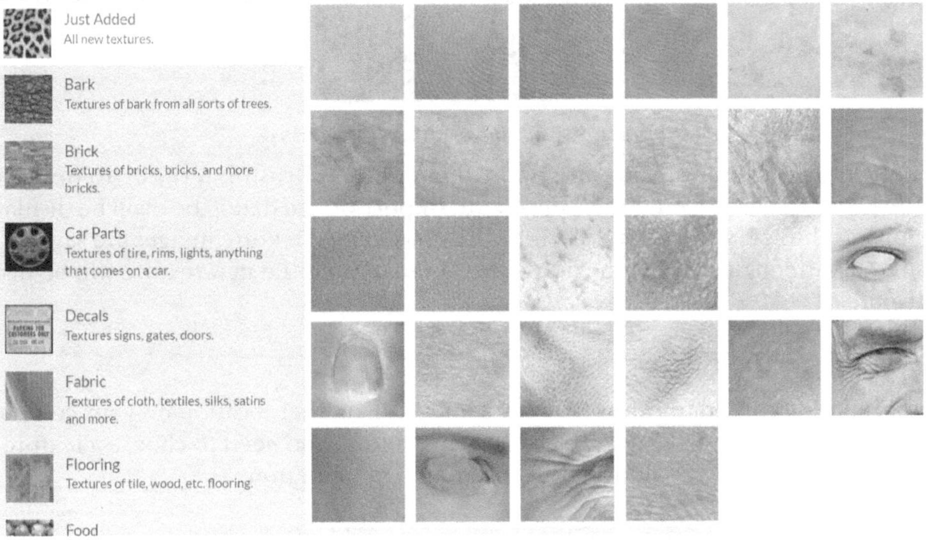

Figure 9-3 *The textures in the* ***Texture Library*** *tab*

Figure 9-4 *Different brick textures displayed*

Select the desired texture; a preview of that texture will be displayed, refer to Figure 9-5. Next, choose the **DOWNLOAD Now** button located below the preview, refer to Figure 9-5. The material will be downloaded as a zip file. Next, you need to extract the material from the zip file.

Figure 9-5 *Preview of the brick texture*

After extracting the textures, you can import them to the ZBrush interface. To do so, choose the **Import** button. On choosing this button, the **Import Image** dialog box will be displayed. In this dialog box, browse to the location where the downloaded texture images are saved. Choose the desired texture image and then choose the **Open** button; the new texture will be displayed in the flyout.

Export

The **Export** button is used to export a texture image to another location on your computer. By default, this button is not activated. To activate this button, you need to choose a texture image from the flyout displayed on choosing the Current Texture button.

You can export the texture image as a *.psd* file. You can modify the exported texture in Photoshop and then import it again to ZBrush.

Clone

The **Clone** button is used to create a copy of a chosen texture image.

MakeAlpha

The **MakeAlpha** button is used to convert a texture into a gray scale alpha image. To do so, choose the Current Texture button; a flyout containing different texture images will be displayed. In this flyout, choose the **Texture 01** texture image. Next, choose the **MakeAlpha** button; the texture will be displayed as a gray scale alpha image in the Current Alpha button.

FillLayer

The **FillLayer** button is used to fill the canvas in a particular layer with a color, material, or a texture. On choosing this button, the objects in a layer will be deleted. To fill the canvas in a particular layer with a color, choose the Current Texture button; a flyout containing different textures will be displayed. From this flyout, choose the **Texture 01** texture image. Now, choose the Current Material button; a flyout containing different materials will be displayed. In this flyout, choose the **ReflectRed** material from the **MatCap Materials** area; the object in the canvas will be filled with the material. Choose the Current Texture button again; a flyout will be displayed. In this flyout, choose the **FillLayer** button, refer to Figure 9-6.

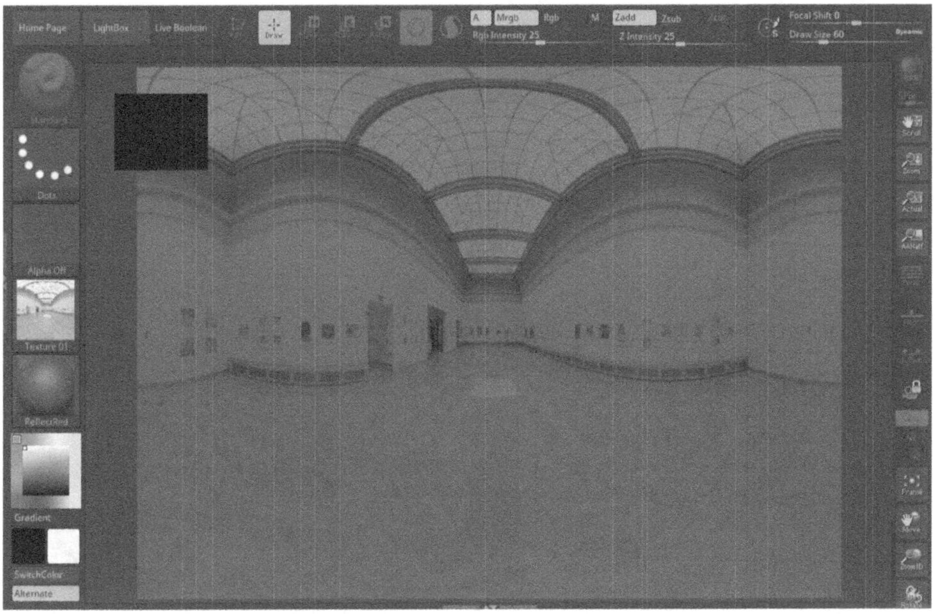

Figure 9-6 The canvas filled with the texture and the material

Cd

The term Cd stands for Clear Depth. The **Cd** button is used to determine whether the canvas will be filled with the selected texture or not. If this button is not chosen, then the canvas will not be filled with a texture on choosing the **FillLayer** button.

CropAndFill

The **CropAndFill** button is used to crop a document according to the dimensions of the selected texture and fills it with that texture. For example, to crop a document and fill it with **Texture 10**, choose the Current Texture button; a flyout will be displayed. In this flyout, choose the **Texture 10** texture image. Next, choose the **CropAndFill** button, refer to Figure 9-7.

Before choosing this button, make sure the **Cd** button is chosen. If the **Cd** button is not chosen before choosing the **CropAndFill** button, the document will be cropped according to the dimensions of the selected texture, but it will not be filled with the texture.

GrabDoc

The **GrabDoc** button is used to capture the canvas and add this capture as a texture in the flyout displayed on choosing the Current Texture button. To add the capture as a texture, choose the Current Texture button; a flyout will be displayed. In this flyout, choose the **GrabDoc** button; a new texture image with the name **ZGrab01** will be displayed in the **Quick Pick** area, refer to Figure 9-8.

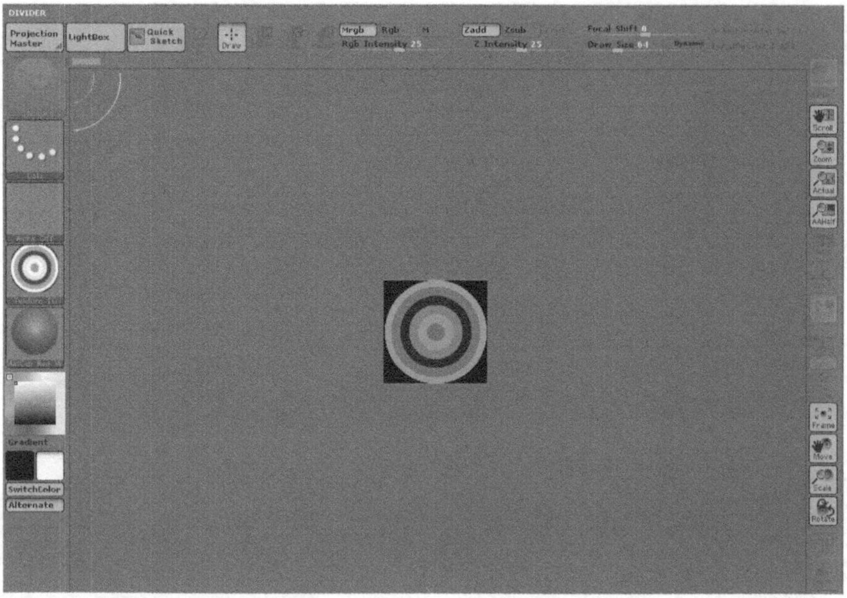

Figure 9-7 The document cropped and filled with ***Texture 10***

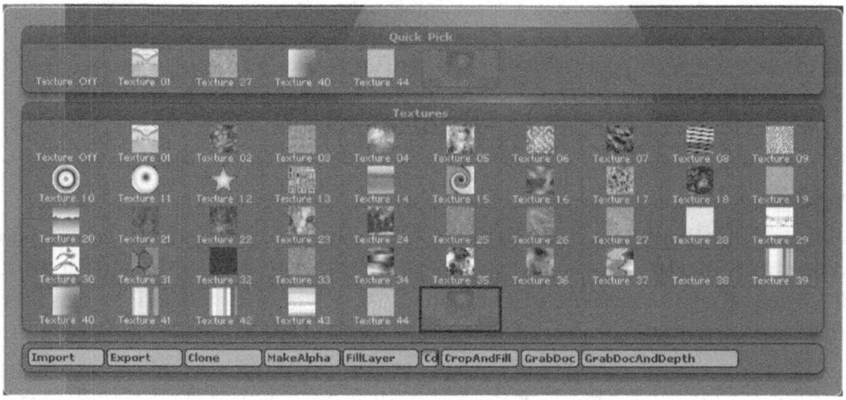

Figure 9-8 A new texture image with the name ***ZGrab01*** *displayed in the flyout*

GrabDocAndDepth

The **GrabDocAndDepth** button is used to capture the canvas and add this capture as a texture in the flyout displayed on choosing the Current Texture button. These textures can then be exported in the *.png* format containing transparency or can also be exported as alpha images containing depth.

Texture Palette

The **Texture** palette consists of different options that enable you to open and modify texture images. The **Texture** palette is located at the top of the interface. On choosing this palette, it will be expanded and different buttons and sliders will be displayed, refer to Figure 9-9. Most commonly used buttons and sliders are discussed next.

Load Spotlight

The **Load Spotlight** button is used to load a saved Spotlight file that has been manipulated using the Spotlight tool. To load the Spotlight, choose the **Load Spotlight** button from the **Texture** palette; the **Load Spotlight** dialog box will be displayed. In this dialog box, browse to the location where you have saved the Spotlight file. Select the file and then choose the **Open** button.

The Spotlight tool enables you to manipulate a 2D image as per your requirement without using any image editing software applications. Besides this, the **Spotlight** tool is also used for texturing a 3D model. This tool will be discussed in detail later in this chapter.

Save Spotlight

The **Save Spotlight** button is used to save the 2D image that has been manipulated using the **Spotlight** tool as a Spotlight file. This file can be loaded later into ZBrush by choosing the **Load Spotlight** button.

Lightbox Spotlights

The **Lightbox Spotlights** button is used to load the Spotlight files that are available in the **LightBox** browser.

Import and Export

The **Import** and **Export** buttons are used to import or export a texture image. These buttons have been discussed earlier in this chapter.

*Figure 9-9 The **Texture** palette*

Tip: *You can drop the **Texture** palette in the left or right tray for convenient access. For example, to drop the **Texture** palette in the right tray, expand the **Texture** palette. In this palette, hover the cursor on the arrow displayed at the top left corner of the palette; the shape of the cursor will change. Next, drag the cursor to the right tray and drop the palette in it.*

Lightbox Texture

The **Lightbox Texture** button is used to display the texture images present in the **LightBox** browser, refer to Figure 9-10.

Item Info

The **Item Info** slider is located just below the **Lightbox Texture** button. This slider is used to scroll through different types of texture images available in ZBrush. You can choose a texture from the texture slots displayed below this slider.

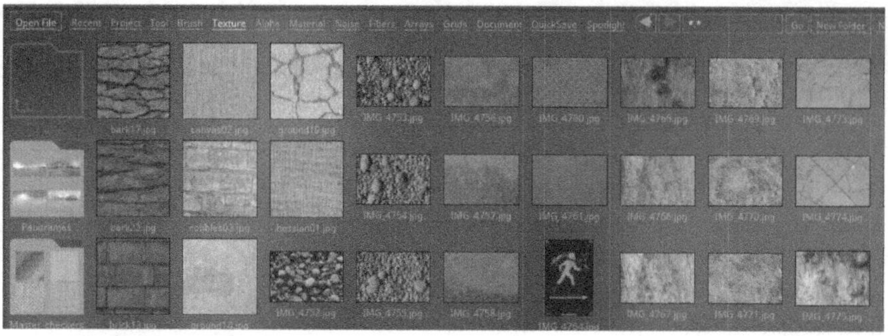

*Figure 9-10 The texture images displayed in the **LightBox** browser*

The **R** button located beside the **Item Info** slider is used to restore the **Texture** palette to its default state when a large number of textures are loaded into ZBrush due to which the size of palette is increased.

Note

*To view all the textures available in the **LightBox** browser, hover the cursor in the browser and press and hold the left mouse button and drag the cursor toward left.*

Current Texture

The Current Texture button is used to display the currently chosen texture. On choosing this button, a flyout consisting of different types of textures will be displayed, as shown in Figure 9-11. On choosing a texture from this flyout, the Current Texture button will display the chosen texture.

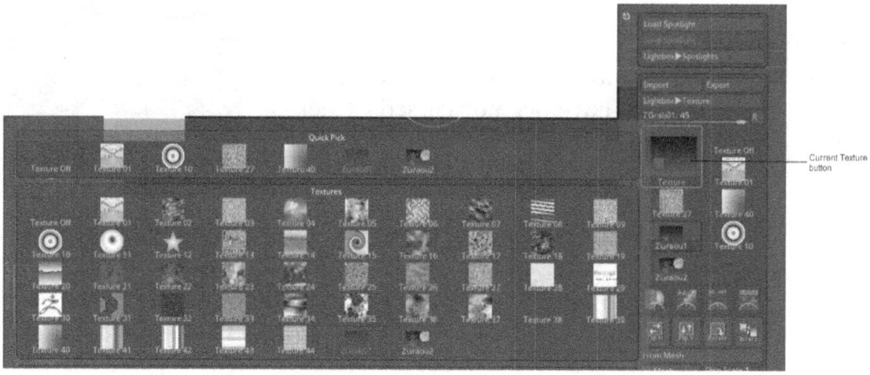

Figure 9-11 The flyout displayed on choosing the Current Texture button

Transparent Texture

The **Transparent Texture** button is located below the texture slots. This button is used to make the black areas of the texture transparent. To activate this button, choose a texture image using the Current Texture button in the **Texture** palette.

Antialiased Texture

The **Antialiased Texture** button is used to remove the jagged edges in low resolution texture images.

Turn On Spotlight

The **Turn On Spotlight** button is used to turn the Spotlight on or off.

Add To Spotlight

The **Add to Spotlight** button is used to add a selected texture file to the Spotlight tool.

Flip Horizontally

The **Flip Horizontally** button is used to flip a texture image horizontally. To do so, expand the **Texture** palette. In this palette, choose the Current Texture button; a flyout will be displayed. From this flyout, choose the **Texture 15** texture image; the texture image will be displayed in this button, refer to Figure 9-12. Next, choose the **Flip Horizontally** button, refer to Figure 9-13.

Figure 9-12 The texture image displayed

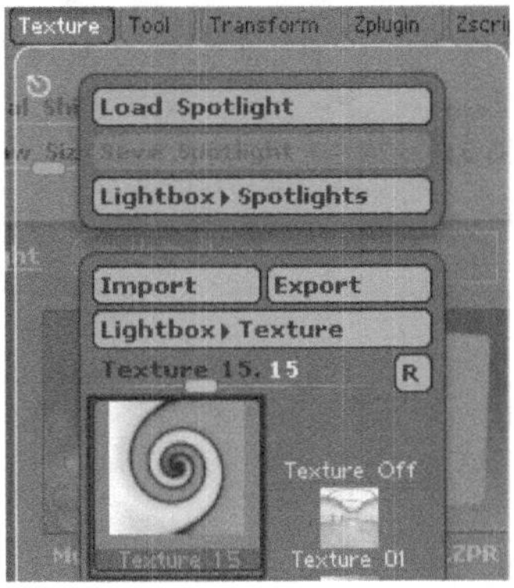

Figure 9-13 The texture image flipped horizontally

Flip Vertically

The **Flip Vertically** button is used to flip a texture image vertically.

Rotate

The **Rotate** button is used to rotate a texture image clockwise at 90 degrees.

Invert

The **Invert** button is used to invert the colors in the selected texture. To invert the colors in a selected texture, expand the **Texture** palette. From this palette, choose the Current Texture button; a flyout will be displayed. In this flyout, choose the **Texture 30** texture image; the texture image will be displayed in this button, refer to Figure 9-14. Next, choose the **Invert** button, refer to Figure 9-15.

Grad

The **Grad** button is used to apply gradient to a texture image. Before choosing this button, you need to select the primary and secondary colors for the gradient. To select a primary color for the gradient, choose the **Main** button, located on the right side of the **Grad** button; a color swatch will be displayed. Select the desired color from this swatch. Next, select the secondary color by choosing the **Sec** button located on the left side of the **Main** button.

After selecting the primary and secondary colors, choose the **Grad** button; the gradient will be applied to the texture image.

Figure 9-14 The texture image displayed

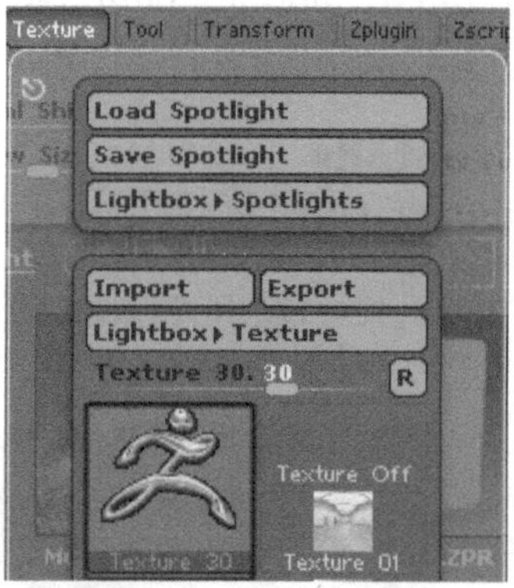

Figure 9-15 The colors in the texture image inverted

Clear

The **Clear** button is used to remove the texture image and replace it with the selected primary color using the **Main** button.

Adjust Colors

The **Adjust Colors** button is used to make color adjustments based on hue, intensity, contrast, gamma, and so on.

Width and Height

The **Width** and **Height** sliders are used to adjust the width and height of the currently chosen texture image.

Clone

The **Clone** button is used to create a duplicate copy of a chosen texture image.

New

The **New** button is used to create a new blank slot for a texture image. The newly created slot will be filled with the primary color that has been selected using the Main Color swatch located in the left shelf. Before creating a new texture slot, you can specify its width and height using the **Width** and **Height** sliders.

MakeAlpha

The **MakeAlpha** button is used to add the selected texture to the **Alpha** palette. In this palette, a texture image is converted to a grayscale image.

Remove

The **Remove** button is used to delete a currently chosen texture image from the **Texture** palette.

Image Plane

The **Image Plane** subpalette consists of different buttons and sliders that are used to import an image, refer to Figure 9-16. This image is used as a reference image for texturing or modeling. These buttons and sliders are discussed next.

***Figure 9-16** The **Image Plane** subpalette*

Load Image

The **Load Image** button is used to load the image that you want to use as a reference either for modeling or texturing. To use a reference image for modeling or texturing, you need to import it to ZBrush.

To import an image to ZBrush, expand the **Texture** palette. In this palette, choose the **Import** button; the **Import Image** dialog box will be displayed. In this dialog box, browse to the location where you have saved the reference image. Select the reference image and then choose the **Open** button, refer to Figure 9-17. Note that in this figure, a reference image has been selected from the default textures available in ZBrush. These textures can also be loaded from the **LightBox** browser by double clicking on them.

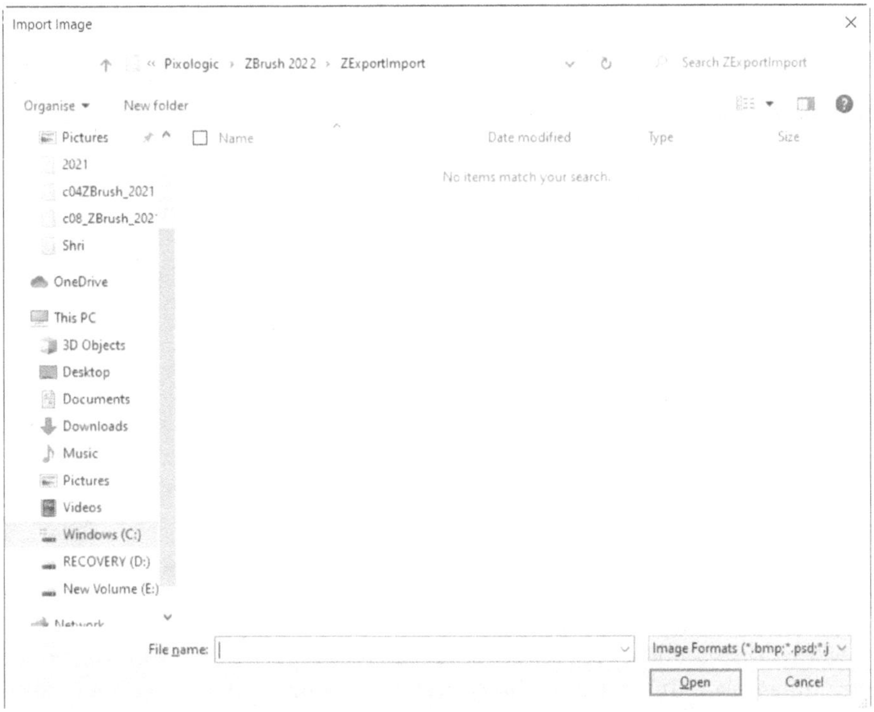

***Figure 9-17** The **Import Image** dialog box*

In the **Texture** palette, choose the Current Texture button; a flyout will be displayed. In this flyout, choose the reference image that you have imported; the image will be displayed in the Current Texture button. Choose the **Load Image** button; the reference image will be displayed in the canvas, refer to Figure 9-18.

Figure 9-18 The reference image displayed in the canvas

Image Size

The **Image Size** slider is used to specify the size of the reference image before loading it to the canvas.

Reference Views

The **Reference Views** area consists of different options that enable you to store the front, side, top, and bottom views of a reference image. To understand the working of the option, make sure a sphere is created in the canvas. Next, choose the **Edit** button from the top shelf to get the object in the edit mode. If you want to model the object in the canvas using the reference images, you need to import the different views of the reference image. To do so, expand the **Texture** palette. In this palette, expand the **Image Plane** subpalette and the **Reference Views** area.

Figure 9-19 The ***Load Image*** *button chosen*

Choose the **Front** button in the **Reference Views** menu; the front side of the sphere will be displayed in the canvas. Next, choose the **Load Image** button, refer to Figure 9-19; the **Please select an image file** dialog box will be displayed. In this dialog box, browse to the location where you have saved the front view of the reference image. Select the reference image and then choose the **Open** button; the front view of the reference image will be displayed behind the sphere, refer to Figure 9-20. You will notice that the reference image is stationary and the sphere can be manipulated without disturbing the reference image.

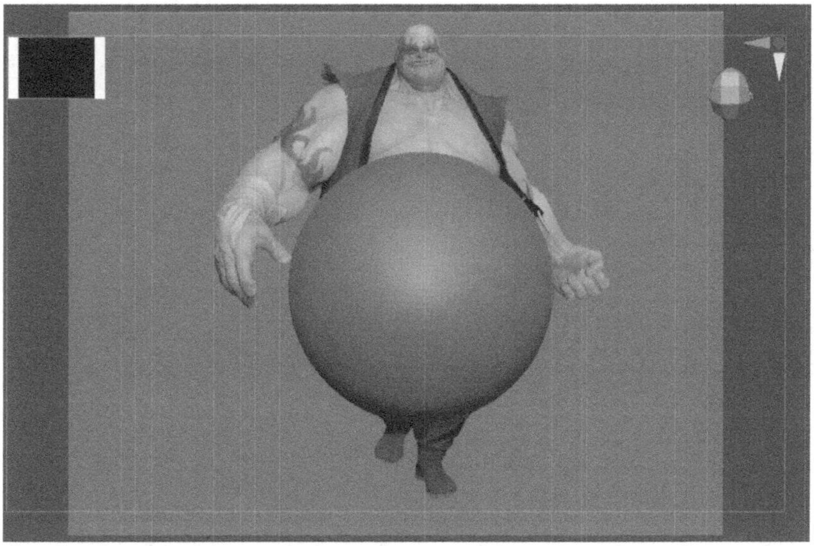

Figure 9-20 *The front view of the reference image displayed behind the sphere*

After loading the front view of the reference image, you need to store this view so that it can be used later. To do so, choose the **Store View** button located at the bottom of the **Reference Views** area.

Next, you will load the back view of the reference image. To do so, choose the **Back** button; the back side of the sphere will be displayed and the front view of the reference image will disappear from the canvas. Choose the **Load Image** button; the **Please select an image file** dialog box will be displayed. In this dialog box, browse to the location where you have saved the back side view of the reference image. Select the reference image and then choose the **Open** button; the back side view of the reference image will be displayed behind the sphere, refer to Figure 9-21. Next, choose the **Store View** button located at the bottom of the **Reference Views** area. Similarly, you can import the right, left, top, and bottom views of the reference images by choosing the **Right**, **Left**, **Top**, and **Bottom** buttons, respectively. Make sure you store all the views by choosing the **Store View** button.

You can cycle between different views by choosing the **<<** and **>>** buttons located at the bottom right corner of the **Reference Views** area. After loading all the reference images you can start modeling or texturing the 3D object.

You can also make the sphere transparent to view the reference image in the background. In the **Reference Views** area, drag the **Model Opacity** slider toward left; the sphere will become transparent and the view of the reference image will not be obstructed by the sphere, refer to Figure 9-22.

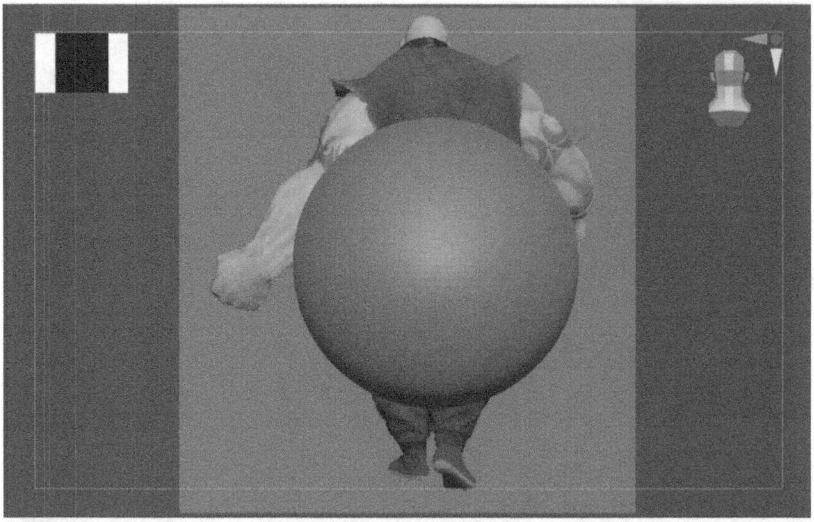

Figure 9-21 *The back view of the sphere and the reference image displayed in the canvas*

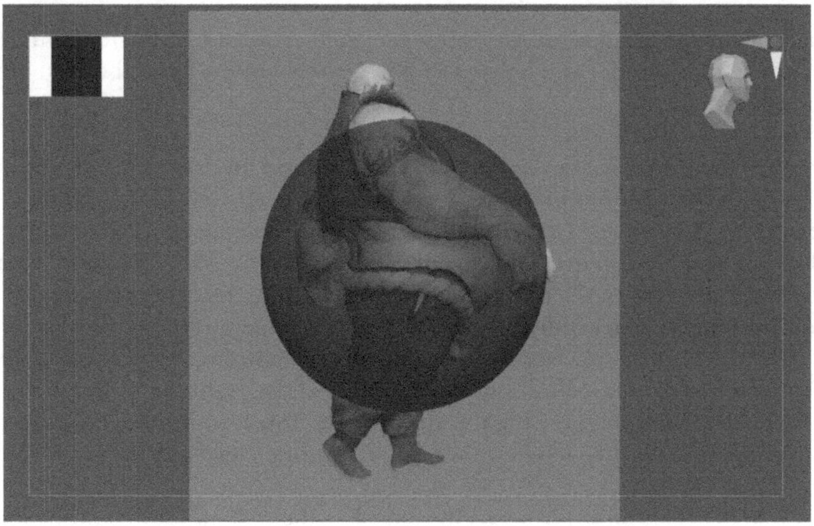

Figure 9-22 *The transparency in the sphere displayed*

Note

The different reference images used in the previous topic have been created using the ***Kotelnikoff Earthquake.ZPR*** *file available in the* ***Project*** *tab of the* ***LightBox*** *browser. After loading this model into the canvas, it was rotated in the canvas to display its different views and then a jpeg image of each view was created by choosing the* ***Export*** *button in the* ***Document*** *palette. In addition to this, the background color of the canvas was changed to white while creating the jpeg images of the views.*

ZProject

The **ZProject** brush is mainly used for texturing. By using the **ZProject** brush, you can transfer the texture from the reference image into a 3D model. The **ZProject** brush uses the Z axis of the canvas to transfer the texturing details from the reference image into a 3D model. To transfer the texture from the reference image into a 3D model, make sure a sphere is selected in the canvas and then choose the **Edit** button from the top shelf. Next, convert the sphere into a polymesh by choosing the **Make PolyMesh3D** button in the **Tool** palette.

To view the texture on the sphere clearly, you need to subdivide the geometry. To do so, expand the **Geometry** subpalette in the **Tool** palette. From this subpalette, set the value of the **SDiv** slider to **5** by clicking on the **Divide** button four times. Next, choose the Current Material button; a flyout will be displayed. From this flyout, choose the **SkinShade4** material; the material will be applied to the sphere, refer to Figure 9-23. Expand the **Texture** palette. In this palette, choose the Current Texture button; a flyout will be displayed. In this flyout, choose the **Texture 42** texture image; the texture image will be displayed in the Current Texture button, refer to Figure 9-24.

Figure 9-23 The material applied to the sphere

Figure 9-24 The texture image displayed in the Current Texture button

Next, expand the **Image Plane** subpalette. In this subpalette, choose the **Load Image** button; the texture image will be displayed behind the sphere, refer to Figure 9-25. Choose the Current Brush button; a flyout containing different types of brushes will be displayed. In this flyout, choose the **ZProject** brush. Choose the **Zsub** button in the top shelf to deactivate it and make sure the **Rgb** button is chosen. Next, press and hold the left mouse button and drag the cursor on the sphere; the texture will be projected from the background texture image to the sphere, refer to Figure 9-26.

Before loading the texture image, you can also specify the image size as required by using the **Image Size** slider located in the **Image Plane** subpalette. To remove the image from the canvas, press CTRL+N.

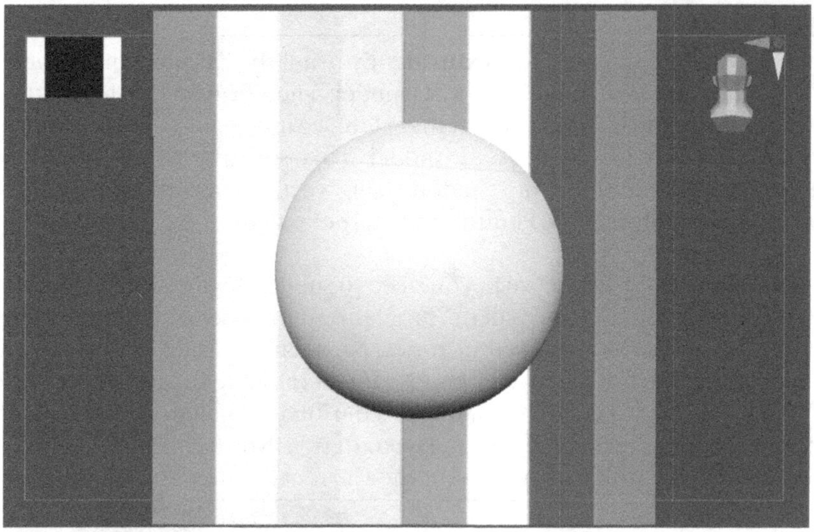

Figure 9-25 *The texture image displayed behind the sphere*

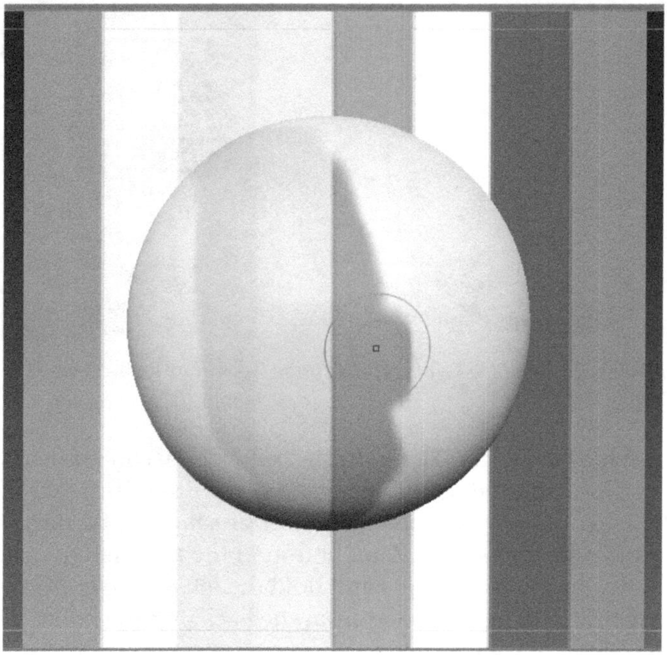

Figure 9-26 *The texture projected from the texture image onto the sphere*

Spotlight

The Spotlight tool is used to modify an existing texture image or project the details from an image into a 3D model. This tool consists of different options that enable you to manipulate an existing texture image as per your requirement and then apply that texture to a 3D model.

The Spotlight tool can be invoked from the **Texture** palette. To load the Spotlight tool, you need to select a texture image first. You can either import a new texture image or use the existing default textures in ZBrush. To load the Spotlight, expand the **Texture** palette. In this palette, choose the Current Texture button; a flyout will be displayed. In this flyout, choose the **Texture 01** texture image; the texture image will be displayed in the Current Texture button. You can also import a new texture image using the **Import** button.

Choose the **Add To Spotlight** button in the **Texture** palette, refer to Figure 9-27; the texture image will be displayed in the canvas. Besides the texture image, a ring containing different icons will be displayed on the texture image, refer to Figure 9-28. The different icons in the ring enable you to manipulate the image as required, refer to Figure 9-29. The icons used for manipulating an image are discussed next.

Figure 9-27 *The **Add To Spotlight** button chosen*

Figure 9-28 *The texture image and the ring displayed in the canvas*

Note

On hovering the cursor on the individual icons of the ring, their names are displayed inside the ring.

The icons that are used for texturing will be discussed later in this chapter.

Rotate

The **Rotate** icon is used to rotate the image in the Spotlight. To rotate the image, hover the cursor on this icon and then drag it in a clockwise or anti-clockwise direction.

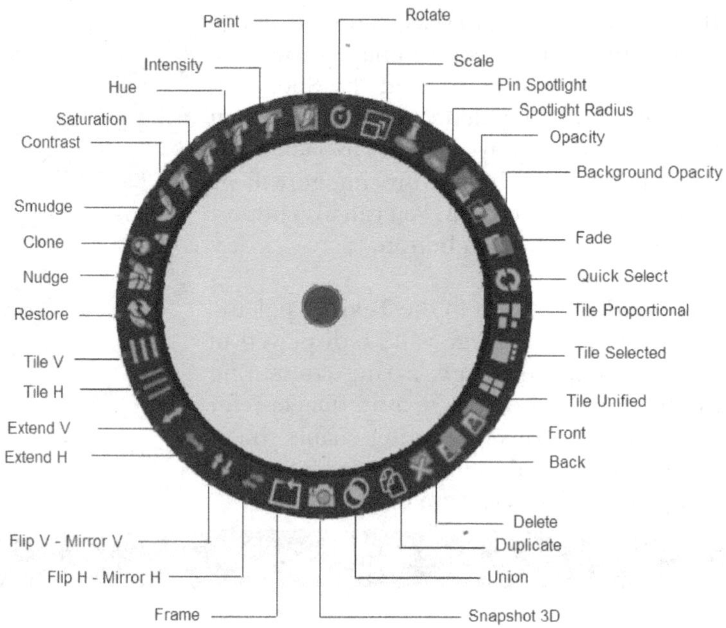

Figure 9-29 *The different icons in the ring*

Scale

The **Scale** icon is used to scale the image in the Spotlight. To scale the image, hover the cursor on this icon and then drag it in the clockwise or anti-clockwise direction.

Opacity

The **Opacity** icon is used to increase or decrease the transparency of the image in the Spotlight. To increase the transparency of the image, hover the cursor on this icon and drag it in the anti-clockwise direction.

Background Opacity

The **Background Opacity** icon is used to change the opacity of the background image in the spotlight interface.

Fade

The **Fade** icon is used to control the influence of the selected image in a stack of images. To fade an image, click on this icon and drag it in both the clockwise and the anti-clockwise directions.

Quick Select

The **Quick Select** icon is used to replace the selected texture or alpha in the spotlight interface with the next selected texture. The replaced texture will have the same location, scale, and orientation as that of the selected texture.

Tile Proportional

The **Tile Proportional** icon is used to reset the scaled texture images in the Spotlight to their default size such that their proportions are maintained.

You can also add multiple texture images into the Spotlight. To do so, choose different images using the Current Texture button in the **Texture** palette one by one and then add them to the Spotlight by choosing the **Add To Spotlight** button in the **Texture** palette; all the chosen images will be displayed in the canvas, refer to Figure 9-30. After adding all the images to the Spotlight, choose the **Tile Proportional** icon; all the images will be stacked together proportionately, refer to Figure 9-31.

Figure 9-30 *The chosen images displayed in the canvas*

Tile Selected

The **Tile Selected** icon is used to display only the selected texture image in its full size. You can select a texture image by clicking on it. After selecting the image, you need to choose the **Tile Selected** icon.

Tile Unified

The **Tile Unified** icon is used to used to stack all the images in the Spotlight on the left side of the canvas and to make their sizes same. To do so, add multiple images to the Spotlight and then choose this icon.

Front

The **Front** icon is used to move the selected image from the multiple overlapping images to the front. This can be done by selecting an image from the overlapping images and then choosing the **Front** icon.

Figure 9-31 The images stacked together proportionately

Back

The **Back** icon is used to move the selected image to the back if multiple number of images overlap each other.

Delete

The **Delete** icon is used to delete the selected image from the Spotlight. This can be done by selecting an image from the multiple images and then choosing the **Delete** icon.

Duplicate

The **Duplicate** icon is used to create a copy of the selected image in the spotlight interface.

Union

The **Union** icon is used to perform boolean operations between alphas or images in the spotlight interface. These boolean operations allow you to create more complex images out of simple images. The type of boolean operation performed on the alphas or images depends on the keys used along with this icon.

Snapshot 3D

The **Snapshot 3D** icon is used to convert the selected alpha to a 3D model as a new subtool or as an addition to an existing subtool, depending on the key pressed while using the icon. For example, if you press the SHIFT key, the subtool created will be added to the current subtool.

Frame

When you select an alpha and then click and drag on the **Frame** icon, the outline of the selected alpha is displayed in the spotlight interface. When you select an image, outlines will be created around the white pixels in the image. If you press the SHIFT key and click and drag on this icon, these outlines will shrink if you pull inward and will expand if you pull outward in the selected image.

Flip H - Mirror H

The **Flip H - Mirror H** icon is used to flip an image horizontally, refer to Figure 9-32. If a number of images are added to the Spotlight and none of them is selected, then on choosing this icon, all images will be flipped horizontally. If you press the SHIFT key or the ALT key, the mirror operation will be performed on the selected image.

Figure 9-32 *The image flipped horizontally*

Flip V - Mirror V

The **Flip V - Mirror V** icon is used to flip the selected image vertically, refer to Figure 9-33. If a number of images are added to the Spotlight and none of them is selected, then on choosing this icon, all the images in the Spotlight will be flipped vertically. If you press the SHIFT key or the ALT key, the mirror operation will be performed on the selected image.

Figure 9-33 *The image flipped vertically*

Extend H

The **Extend H** icon is used to grow or shrink the alpha or texture image along the vertical axis, refer to Figure 9-34. When you click on this icon, the pixels located at the center of the spotlight dial get duplicated. The green vertical axis specifies the position of the extension or shrinkage of the image horizontally. If you press the SHIFT key and click on this icon, the extension or shrinkage of the image will take place from the center of the texture or alpha, regardless of the position of the spotlight dial.

Figure 9-34 *The image extended horizontally*

Extend V

The **Extend V** icon is used to grow or shrink the alpha or texture image along the horizontal axis, refer to Figure 9-35. When you click on this icon, the pixels located at the center of the spotlight dial get duplicated. The red horizontal axis specifies the position of the extension or shrinkage of the image vertically. If you press the SHIFT key and click on this icon, the extension or shrinkage of the image will take place from the center of the texture or alpha, regardless of the position of the spotlight dial.

Tile H

The **Tile H** icon is used to tile the selected image horizontally. To tile an image horizontally, hover the cursor on this icon and drag it in the clockwise direction, refer to Figure 9-36.

Tile V

The **Tile V** icon is used to tile a selected image vertically. To tile an image vertically, hover the cursor on this icon and drag it in the clockwise direction. If you hold the SHIFT key while dragging the cursor, the image will be tiled both horizontally and vertically, refer to Figure 9-37.

Figure 9-35 *The image extended vertically*

Figure 9-36 *The image tiled horizontally*

Figure 9-37 *The image tiled horizontally and vertically*

Clone

The **Clone** icon is used to select a particular region of an image and paste it at different locations either in the same image or in some different image added to the Spotlight. To clone the image, add the **Texture 01** and **Texture 29** texture images to the Spotlight, refer to Figure 9-38. Next, select the **Texture 01** image and drag it upward. Scale up this image using the **Scale** icon. Scale down the **Texture 29** texture image and place it on the **Texture 01** image, refer to Figure 9-39.

***Figure 9-38** **Texture 01** and **Texture 29** images added to the Spotlight*

***Figure 9-39** Texture images scaled and moved*

You will copy the **Texture 29** image and paste it at different places in the **Texture 01** image. To do so, select the **Texture 01** image first (target image). Next, choose the **Clone** icon; a bar will be displayed on this icon. Hover the cursor at the center of the ring; an orange colored circle will be displayed. Drag this circle to move the ring and position it such that the entire **Texture 29** image (source image) is covered, refer to Figure 9-40. On moving the cursor, the preview of the selected texture will be displayed. Click at different places in the **Texture 01** image; the **Texture 29** image will be pasted at those locations, refer to Figure 9-40.

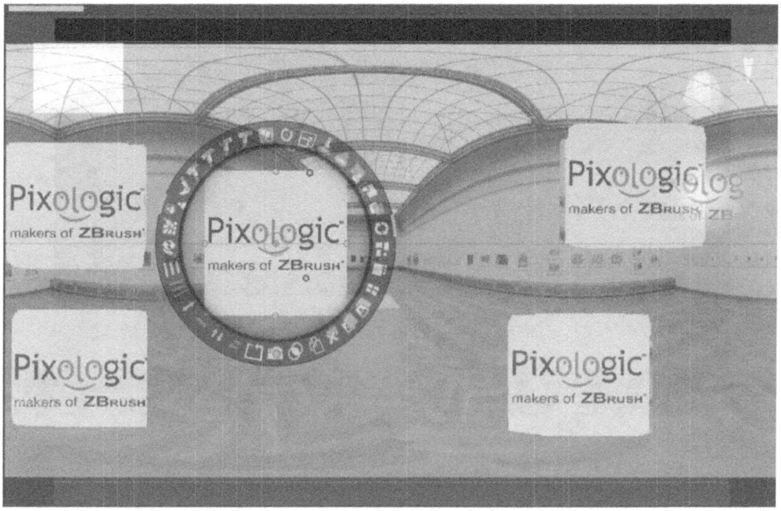

Figure 9-40 *Texture pasted at different locations*

In Figure 9-40, you will notice that the intensity of the texture is low. Before pasting the texture on the image, increase its intensity by dragging the **Rgb Intensity** slider located at the top shelf toward right.

Smudge

The **Smudge** icon is used to blur the selected areas of an image or an entire image. The amount of the blur depends upon the value of the **Rgb** slider in the top shelf. Higher the value of the slider, higher will be the amount of blur applied to the image.

To blur only the selected areas of an image, select the image and then choose this icon. Next, adjust the brush size and the **Rgb Intensity** slider as per your requirement. Now, drag the cursor on the selected areas; the selected areas will be blurred, refer to Figure 9-41.

To blur an entire image, hover the cursor on the **Smudge** icon and drag it in the clockwise direction, refer to Figure 9-42.

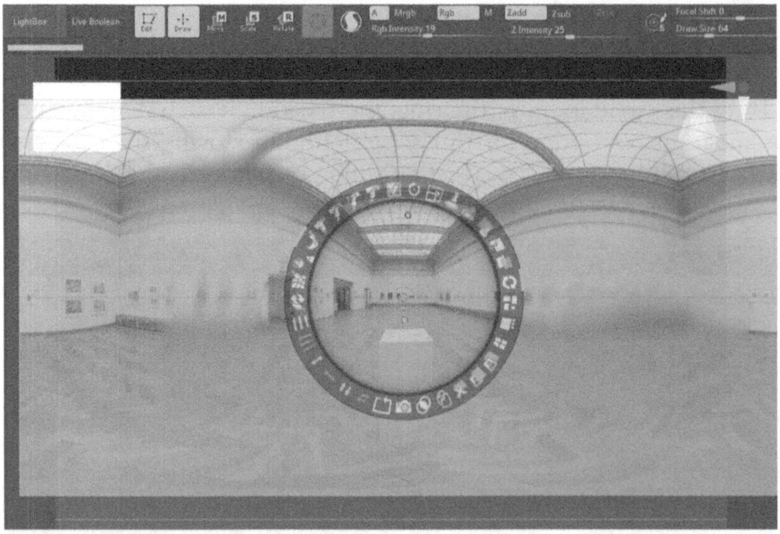

Figure 9-41 *Blur applied on the selected areas of the image*

Figure 9-42 *Blur applied on the entire image*

Contrast

The **Contrast** icon is used to adjust the value of contrast in an image. You can adjust the contrast either in the selected areas of an image or an entire image. The value of the contrast depends upon the value of the **Rgb Intensity** slider in the top shelf. Higher the value of the slider, higher will be the value of the contrast applied to the image.

To apply contrast only for the selected areas of an image, select the image and then choose this icon. Next, adjust the brush size and the **Rgb Intensity** slider, as required. Now, drag the cursor on the selected areas of the image; contrast will be applied on the selected areas, refer to Figure 9-43.

To apply contrast on an entire image, hover the cursor on the **Contrast** icon and drag it in the clockwise direction, refer to Figure 9-44.

Figure 9-43 *Contrast applied on the selected areas of the image*

Figure 9-44 *Contrast applied on the entire image*

Saturation

The **Saturation** icon is used to adjust the value of saturation in an image. You can adjust the saturation either of the selected areas of an image or of the entire image. The value of the saturation depends upon the value of the **Rgb** slider in the top shelf. Higher the value of the slider, higher will be the value of saturation. The higher value of saturation will make the colors of the image darker and the lower value of saturation will make the colors lighter or gray scale.

To adjust saturation only for the selected areas of an image, select the image and then choose this icon. Next, adjust the brush size and the **Rgb Intensity** slider as per your requirement. Now, drag the cursor on the selected areas of the image; the saturation will increase for those areas, refer to Figure 9-45.

To decrease saturation of an entire image, hover the cursor on the **Saturation** icon and drag it in the anti-clockwise direction, refer to Figure 9-46.

Figure 9-45 *The saturation increased in the selected areas of the image*

Figure 9-46 *The saturation decreased in the entire image*

Hue

The **Hue** icon is used to change the color of an image. You can change the color either in the selected areas of an image or an entire image.

To change the color of only the selected areas of an image, select the image and then choose this icon. Next, choose any color from the color swatch in the left shelf. Adjust the brush size and the **Rgb Intensity** slider as required. Now, drag the cursor on the selected areas of the image; the color of the selected areas will change.

To change the color of an entire image, hover the cursor on the **Hue** icon and drag it in the clockwise direction; different colors will be applied to the image as you drag the cursor.

Intensity

The **Intensity** icon is used to adjust the brightness in an image. You can adjust the brightness either of the selected areas of an image or an entire image. The value of the brightness depends upon the value of the **Rgb Intensity** slider in the top shelf. Higher the value of the slider, higher will be the value of the brightness applied in the image.

To increase brightness of only some selected areas of an image, select the image and then choose this icon. Next, adjust the brush size and the **Rgb Intensity** slider as required. Now, drag the cursor on the selected areas of the image; brightness of those areas will be increased.

To increase brightness in an entire image, hover the cursor on the **Intensity** icon and drag it in the clockwise direction, refer to Figure 9-47.

Figure 9-47 *Brightness increased in the entire image*

Paint

The **Paint** icon is used to paint different colors on an image, fill the specific areas of an image with the selected color, or fill an entire image with the selected color. The strength of the color depends upon the **Rgb Intensity** slider in the top shelf. Higher the value of this slider, higher will be the strength of the color.

To paint the specific areas of an image, select the image and then choose this icon. Next, choose any color from the color swatch in the left shelf. Adjust the brush size and the **Rgb Intensity** slider as required. Now, drag the cursor on the selected areas of the image; the color will be painted on those areas, refer to Figure 9-48.

To fill a selected color in a specific area of an image, press and hold the CTRL key and drag the cursor on the areas where you want to fill the color, refer to Figure 9-49. In this figure, the color of the ceiling in the picture is changed to cyan by clicking and dragging the cursor in the ceiling area. Similarly, the color of the walls and the white box is also changed. If you continue dragging on the entire image, it will be filled with the selected color.

Figure 9-48 Different colors painted on the image

Figure 9-49 Colors filled in the specific areas of the image

Restore

The **Restore** icon is used to reset an image to its default state after different effects have been applied to it. For instance, when you blur an image using the **Smudge** icon, you can restore it back by choosing this icon and then dragging it in the clockwise direction.

Texturing with Spotlight

Spotlight also enables you to apply textures to the 3D objects. You need to place the texture image and the 3D object in the canvas to project the texture from the image to the 3D object. To project the texture to the 3D object, create a sphere in the canvas and then choose the **Edit** button. Convert the sphere into a polymesh and then subdivide it to make it smoother.

Next, assign the **SkinShade4** material from the **Standard Materials** to the sphere. Now, expand the **Texture** palette. In this palette, choose the Current Texture button; a flyout will be displayed. In this flyout, choose the **Texture 30** texture image; the texture image will be displayed in the Current Texture button.

Choose the **Add To Spotlight** button in the **Texture** palette; the texture image will be added to the Spotlight and the sphere will be placed behind it, refer to Figure 9-50.

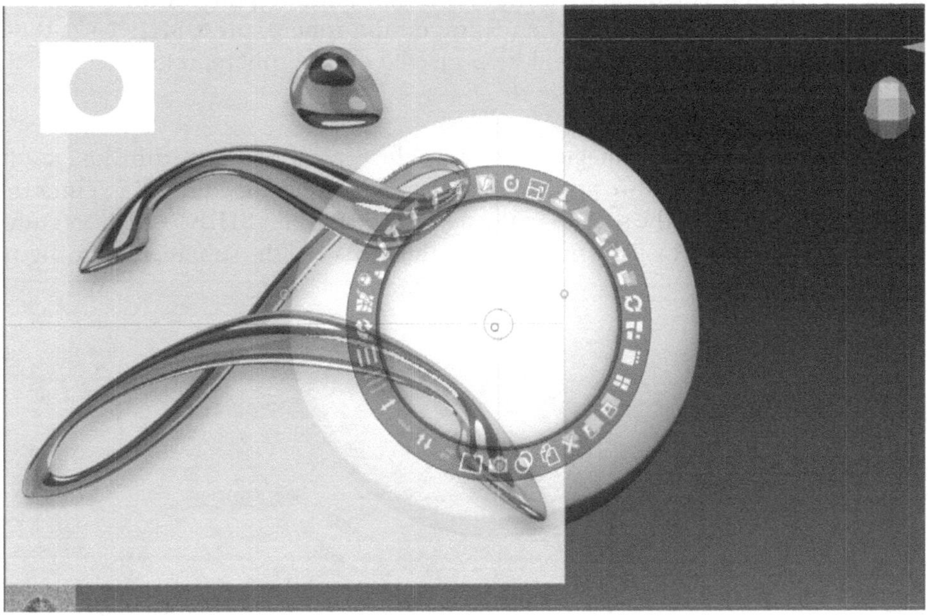

Figure 9-50 *The texture image added to the Spotlight*

Drag the texture image such that it covers the sphere. Choose the **Scale** icon in the Spotlight ring and scale down the image by dragging the cursor in the anti-clockwise direction, refer to Figure 9-51.

Figure 9-51 *The texture image scaled down*

To enable texturing, you need to activate the paint mode. To do so, press Z; the ring will disappear from the canvas. Next, choose the **Rgb** button from the top shelf and make sure the **Zadd** button is not activated. Drag the cursor on the texture and start painting; the texture will be projected on the surface of the sphere. To view the texture on the sphere, press SHIFT+Z; the texture image will disappear and the texture will be projected on the sphere, refer to Figure 9-52. To view the image, press SHIFT+Z again.

Next, add the **Texture 29** texture image to the Spotlight. Scale down the texture image and move it such that it lies below the texture applied on the sphere previously. Press Z to enter the paint mode and drag the cursor on the surface of the texture (text). Press SHIFT+Z; the texture image will disappear and the texture will be projected on the surface of the sphere, refer to Figure 9-53.

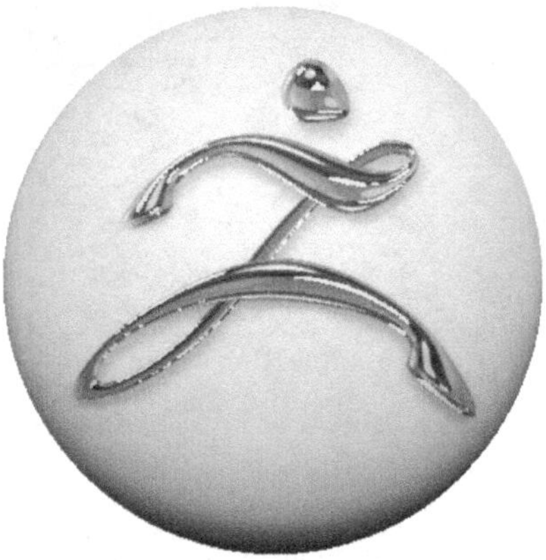

Figure 9-52 *The **Texture 30** texture image projected on the sphere*

Figure 9-53 *The **Texture 29** texture image projected on the sphere*

Some of the icons present in the Spotlight ring are used for texturing. These icons are discussed next.

Pin Spotlight

The **Pin Spotlight** icon is used to repeat a selected texture on the surface of a 3D object when the Spotlight is used for texturing a 3D object. To repeat a selected texture on the surface of a 3D object, make sure the **Rgb** button is chosen and the **Zadd** button is not activated in the top shelf. Expand the **Texture** palette and choose the **LightBox Texture** button; different textures will be displayed in the **LightBox** browser. Hover the cursor on the **LightBox** browser and drag it toward left to view all the textures available in the browser. Choose the **IMG_4779.jpg** texture image, refer to Figure 9-54, and double-click on it; this image will be displayed in the Current Texture button in the **Texture** palette.

Choose the **Add To Spotlight** button from the **Texture** palette; the image with ring will be displayed in the canvas. Scale and move the image on the 3D object using ring, as shown in Figure 9-55. Choose the **Pin Spotlight** icon in the ring and then press Z; the ring will disappear. Drag the cursor on the center of the texture. Next, drag the cursor at different places on the sphere; the face of the lion will be projected at those places, refer to Figure 9-56. Press SHIFT+Z; the image will disappear and the same texture will be repeated on the surface of the sphere.

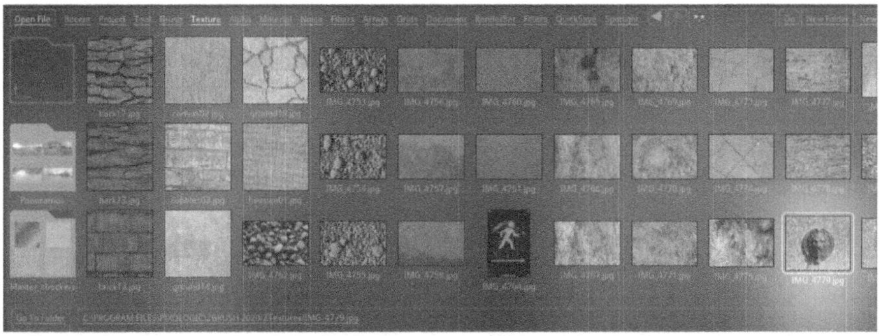

***Figure 9-54** The **IMG_4779.jpg** texture image chosen from the browser*

***Figure 9-55** The texture image scaled and positioned*

***Figure 9-56** The selected texture repeated on the surface of the sphere*

Spotlight Radius

The **Spotlight Radius** icon is used to preview the texture image in the form of a transparent circular frame when the Spotlight is used for texturing a 3D object. To increase the radius of the preview image, hover the cursor on the **Spotlight Radius** icon in the ring, and drag it in the clockwise direction. Next, press Z; a circular preview of the texture image will be displayed, refer to Figure 9-57.

***Figure 9-57** The circular preview of the texture image displayed in the canvas*

Fade

The **Fade** icon is used to determine whether the texture applied on the 3D object will be dimmed or not. To fade the texture, hover the cursor on this icon and then drag it in the anti-clockwise direction. Press Z to project the texture on the 3D object. You will notice that the applied texture will be faded.

Nudge

The **Nudge** icon is used to move the portions of the texture image such that you can match the image with the 3D model in the background.

POLYPAINTING

The polypainting technique allows you to paint colors directly on to the 3D objects using different sculpting brushes. To paint colors directly on to the 3D object, apply the **SkinShade4** material to 3D object.

In the **Tool** palette, expand the **Polypaint** subpalette. In this subpalette, choose the **Colorize** button, refer to Figure 9-58. Next, choose the desired colors from the Current Color swatch and then by using different brushes and alphas, start painting on the surface of the sphere, refer to Figure 9-59. If you want to add depth along with the color, make sure the **Zadd** button is chosen in the top shelf.

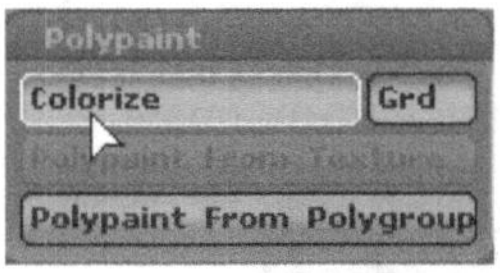

Figure 9-58 The ***Colorize*** *button chosen*

Figure 9-59 Different colors painted on the surface of the sphere

TUTORIALS

Before you start the tutorials of this chapter, you need to download the *c09_ZBrush_2022_tut.zip* file from *www.cadcim.com*. The path of the file is as follows: *Textbooks > Animation and Visual Effects > Pixologic ZBrush 2022 > Pixologic ZBrush 2022: A Comprehensive Guide.*

Next, you need to browse to the *Documents/ZBrushprojects* folder and create a new folder with the name *c09*. Next, extract the contents of the zip file in this folder.

Tutorial 1

In this tutorial, you will apply different colors and textures on the surface of the hut. The final output of the model is shown in Figure 9-60. **(Expected time: 20 min)**

The following steps are required to complete this tutorial:

a. Apply wooden texture on the walls of the hut.
b. Apply textures on the door, windows, and roof of the hut.
c. Apply textures on the remaining parts of the hut.
d. Save the model.

Figure 9-60 *The textured model of the hut*

Applying Wooden Texture on the Walls of the Hut

In this section, you will apply a wooden texture on the walls of the hut using Spotlight.

1. Choose the **Init ZBrush** button from the **Preferences** palette; the message box is displayed. Choose the **Yes** button from the message box; ZBrush is initialized to its default state.

2. Choose the **Tool** palette. In this palette, choose the **Load Tool** button; the **Load ZTool** dialog box is displayed. In this dialog box, browse to *\Documents\ZBrushprojects\c09* and select the **c09tut1start.ZTL** file in it. Next, choose the **Open** button in this dialog box.

3. Press and hold the left mouse button and drag the cursor in the canvas area; the scene is displayed in the canvas. Next, choose the **Edit** button from the top shelf to switch to the edit mode. Rotate the view of the canvas, refer to Figure 9-61.

4. Choose the Current Material button from the left shelf; a flyout containing different materials is displayed. In this flyout, choose the **RGB Levels** material from the **Standard Materials**; the material is applied to the hut.

5. Choose the Current Brush button from the left shelf; a flyout containing different sculpting brushes is displayed. Choose the **MaskRect** brush from this flyout; a message box prompting you to press CTRL to use this brush is displayed. Choose the **OK** button to close this message box.

6. Press and hold the CTRL key and drag the cursor on the door and window of the hut to create a rectangular mask, refer to Figure 9-62.

7. Choose the Current Brush button from the left shelf; a flyout containing different sculpting brushes is displayed. Choose the **MaskCircle** brush from this flyout; a dialog box prompting you to press CTRL to use this brush is displayed. Choose the **OK** button to close this dialog box.

Figure 9-61 *The untextured model of the hut*

8. Press and hold the CTRL key and choose the Current Stroke button; a flyout is displayed. In this flyout, choose the **Square** button located at the bottom of the flyout. Similarly, choose the **Center** button. Next, release the CTRL key.

9. Press and hold the CTRL key and drag the cursor on the surface of hut to create two circular masks on the ventilators of the hut, refer to Figure 9-62.

   As the symmetry in X-axis is activated in this model by default, the mask will be created on the right side also. Remove the mask on the right hand side by pressing CTRL+ALT and then drag the mouse.

10. Choose the Current Brush button from the left shelf; a flyout containing different sculpting brushes is displayed. Choose the **MaskCurve** brush from this flyout; a message box prompting

you to press CTRL to use this brush is displayed. Choose the **OK** button to close this dialog box.

11. Press and hold the CTRL key and drag the cursor in an upward direction to create a stroke, as shown in Figure 9-63; a mask is applied on the roof of the hut. Similarly, create a mask on the top portion of the hut, refer to Figure 9-64.

Figure 9-62 *Masks created on the door, windows, and ventilators of the hut*

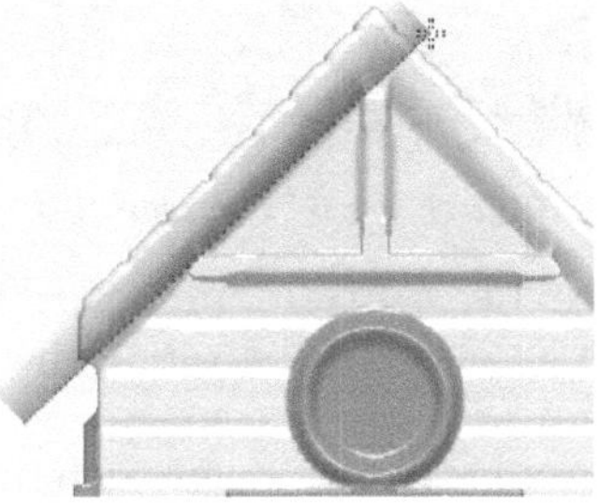

Figure 9-63 *Mask created on the roof of the hut using the **MaskCurve** brush*

12. Expand the **Texture** palette. In this palette, choose the **LightBox Texture** button, refer to Figure 9-65; different textures are displayed in the **LightBox** browser.

Figure 9-64 *Mask created on the top area of the hut*

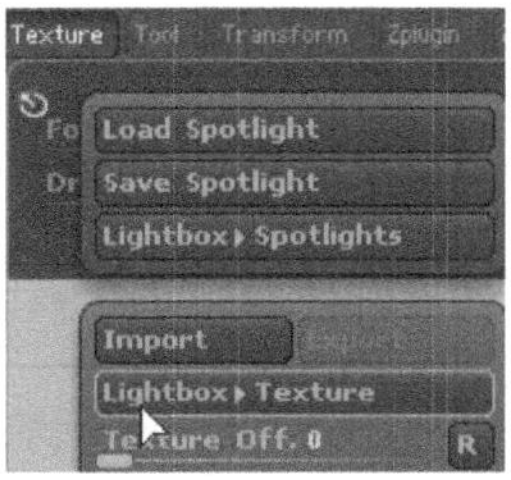

Figure 9-65 *The **LightBox Texture** button chosen*

13. Hover the cursor on the **LightBox** browser and drag it toward left to view all the textures available in the browser. Choose the **wood08.jpg** texture image, refer to Figure 9-66, and double-click on it; the image is displayed in the Current Texture button in the **Texture** palette.

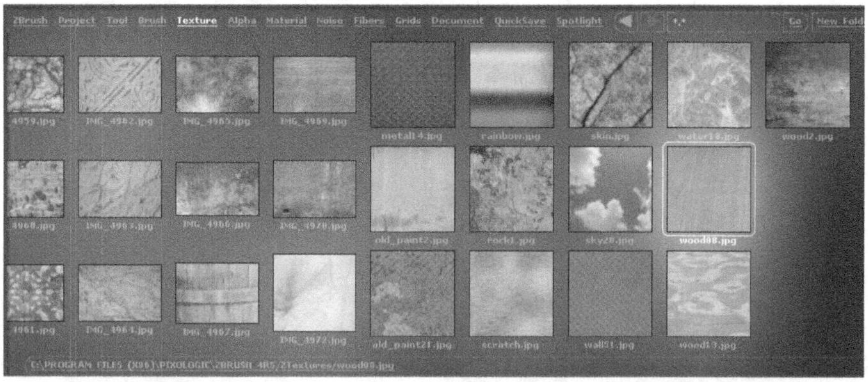

Figure 9-66 *The **wood08.jpg** texture image chosen from the **LightBox** browser*

14. Choose the **Add To Spotlight** button in the **Texture** palette; the image is added to the Spotlight and is displayed in the canvas.

15. Move and scale the image such that it covers the hut. In the Spotlight ring, hover the cursor over the **Rotate** icon and drag it in the clockwise direction; the image is rotated, refer to Figure 9-67.

    The image should be rotated in such a way that the pattern on the image is displayed horizontally.

16. Press Z; the ring disappears from the canvas. Next, choose the **Rgb** button from the top shelf and make sure the **Zadd** button is not chosen. Drag the cursor on the texture on the image; the texture is projected on the surface of the hut.

17. Rotate the view of the canvas such that you can view the side and back views of the hut and project the texture on all the views of the hut. To view the texture on the hut, press SHIFT+Z; the texture image disappears and the texture is projected on the unmasked areas of the hut, refer to Figure 9-68.

18. Press CTRL+I; the mask is inverted. Next, create a mask on the door using the **MaskRect** brush, refer to Figure 9-69.

19. Press Z again; the image is displayed in the canvas. Rotate the image, as shown in Figure 9-69, using the **Rotate** icon of the Spotlight ring. Press Z; the ring disappears. Next, drag the cursor on the door frame; the texture is projected on the door frame. Next, press SHIFT+Z to view the texture on the hut.

20. Remove the mask from the hut by pressing and holding the CTRL key and dragging the cursor in the canvas area, refer to Figure 9-70.

Figure 9-67 The texture image rotated in the canvas

Figure 9-68 The texture projected on the unmasked areas of the hut

Figure 9-69 The texture image rotated in the canvas

Figure 9-70 The mask removed from the surface of the hut

Applying Textures on the Door, Windows, and Roof of the Hut

In this section, you will apply textures on the door, windows, and roof of the hut using the Spotlight.

1. Create a mask on the door of the hut using the **MaskRect** brush. Next, press CTRL+I; the mask is inverted.

2. Choose the **IMG_4850.jpg** texture image from the **LightBox** browser and then double-click on it; the image is displayed in the Current Texture button of the **Texture** palette.

3. Choose the **Add To Spotlight** button from the **Texture** palette; the image is displayed in the canvas. Scale and move the image, as shown in Figure 9-71.

4. Press Z; the ring disappears. Next, drag the cursor on the door of the hut; the texture is projected on its surface. Press SHIFT+Z to hide the texture image and then remove the mask from the surface of the hut, refer to Figure 9-72.

Figure 9-71 *The texture image moved and rotated in the canvas*

Figure 9-72 *The mask removed from the surface of the hut*

5. Expand the **Color** palette. In this palette, set the values of the **R**, **G**, and **B** sliders to **100**, **32**, and **15**, respectively, as shown in Figure 9-73.

6. Choose the Current Brush button from the left shelf; a flyout containing different brushes is displayed. In this flyout, choose the **MaskCircle** brush; a message box prompting you to press CTRL to use this brush is displayed. Choose the **OK** button to close this message box.

7. Press and hold the CTRL key and choose the Current Stroke button; a flyout is displayed. In this flyout, choose the **Square** button located at the bottom of the flyout. Similarly, choose the **Center** button. Next, release the CTRL key.

8. Press and hold the CTRL key and drag the cursor on the circular ventilators of the hut. Remove the mask from the inner part of the ventilator by pressing CTRL+ALT, refer to Figure 9-74. Make sure the mask is removed from the backside of the hut.

9. Press CTRL+I; the mask is inverted. Make sure the **Rgb** button is chosen in the top shelf. Drag the cursor on the surface of the frame of the ventilator to apply paint on it, refer to Figure 9-75. Remove the mask from the hut by pressing and holding the CTRL key and dragging the cursor in the canvas area.

10. Apply mask on the entire hut and then remove masks from the window frame and the ventilator frame on the left side of the hut. Next, drag the cursor on the unmasked areas of the hut to paint them, refer to Figure 9-76.

11. Press and hold the CTRL key and then drag the cursor in the canvas area; mask is removed from the hut, refer to Figure 9-77.

***Figure 9-73** The values of the **R**, **G**, and **B** sliders set*

***Figure 9-74** Mask removed from the inner part of the ventilator*

***Figure 9-75** The frame of the ventilator painted*

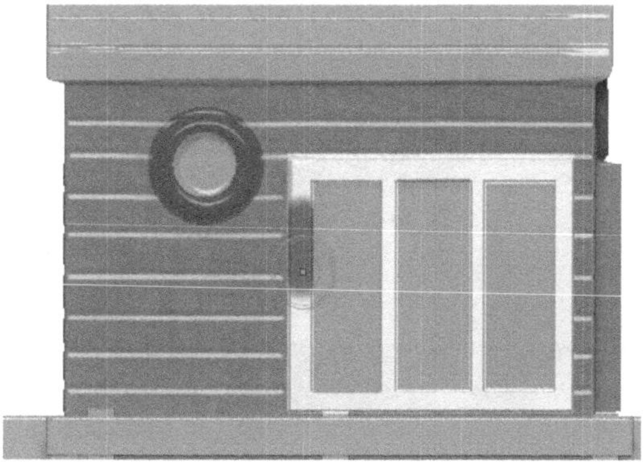

***Figure 9-76** The frame of the window painted*

12. Create a mask on the window panes and the inner area of the ventilator, refer to Figure 9-78. Next, press CTRL+I to invert the mask.

13. Choose the **IMG_4801.jpg** texture image from the **LightBox** browser and then double-click on it; the image is displayed in the Current Texture button of the **Texture** palette.

14. Choose the **Add To Spotlight** button from the **Texture** palette; the image is displayed in the canvas, refer to Figure 9-79.

15. Scale up the texture image such that the glass window area in the texture image covers the window area of the hut.

Figure 9-77 *Mask removed from the hut*

Figure 9-78 *The mask applied on the window panes and the inner area of the ventilators*

16. Press Z; the ring disappears. Next, drag the cursor on the window panes of the hut; the texture is projected on its surface. Press SHIFT+Z to hide the texture image; the texture is displayed on the window panes, refer to Figure 9-80.

Figure 9-79 *The texture image displayed in the canvas*

Figure 9-80 *The texture projected on the window panes of the hut*

17. Choose the **IMG_4790.jpg** texture image from the **LightBox** browser and then double-click on it; the image is displayed in the Current Texture button of the **Texture** palette.

18. Choose the **Add To Spotlight** button from the **Texture** palette; the image is displayed in the canvas, refer to Figure 9-81.

19. Scale down the texture image such that it covers the ventilator of the hut.

20. Press Z; the ring disappears. Next, drag the cursor on the inner area of the ventilators; texture is projected on their surface. Press SHIFT+Z to hide the texture image; the texture is displayed on the ventilators, refer to Figure 9-82.

21. Create a mask on the roof of the hut using the **MaskCurve** brush and then create a mask on the window frame at the top of the hut using the **MaskRect** brush. Next, press CTRL+I; the mask gets inverted, refer to Figure 9-83.

Figure 9-81 *The texture image displayed in the canvas*

Figure 9-82 *The texture displayed on the ventilators*

22. Make sure the **Rgb** button is chosen in the top shelf. Drag the cursor on the top area of the hut to apply paint on it, as shown in Figure 9-84.

Figure 9-83 *The inverted mask*

Figure 9-84 *Paint applied on the top area of the hut*

23. Press CTRL+I to invert the mask. Expand the **Color** palette. In this palette, set the values of the **R**, **G**, and **B** sliders to **14**, **9**, and **9**, respectively. Drag the cursor on the top window of hut to apply paint on it, as shown in Figure 9-85.

Applying Textures on the Remaining Parts of the Hut

In this section, you will apply textures on the remaining parts of the hut.

1. Press SHIFT+Z; the Spotlight ring is displayed in the canvas. Next, select the **wood08.jpg** texture image from the canvas and move it such that it covers the staircase area of the hut, refer to Figure 9-86.

2. Press Z; the ring disappears. Next, drag the cursor on the staircase area of the hut; the texture is projected on the staircase. Press SHIFT+Z to hide the texture image; the texture is displayed on the staircase, refer to Figure 9-87.

3. Choose the **brick13.jpg** texture image from the **LightBox** browser and then double-click on it; the image is displayed in the Current Texture button of the **Texture** palette.

4. Choose the **Add To Spotlight** button from the **Texture** palette; the image is displayed in the canvas. Move the image to the base of the hut and scale it down, as shown in Figure 9-88.

Figure 9-85 *The color painted on the top windows*

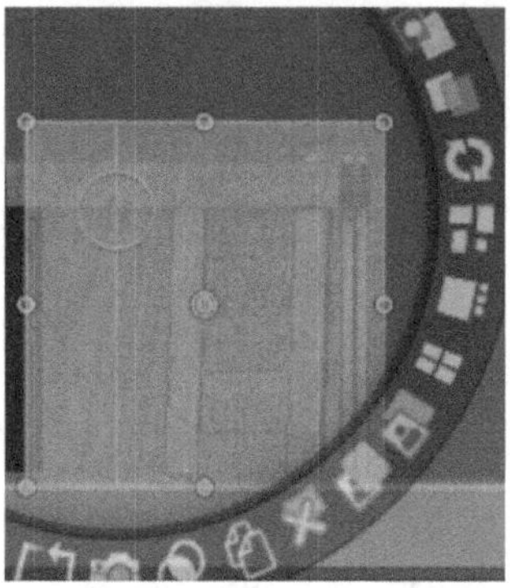

Figure 9-86 *The texture image placed on the staircase area*

5. Choose the **Pin Spotlight** icon in the Spotlight ring; a bar is displayed on the icon, refer to Figure 9-88.

Figure 9-87 *The texture projected on the staircase area*

Figure 9-88 *The texture image moved and scaled down*

6. Press Z and drag the cursor on the texture image. Next, drag the cursor on the surface of the base; the texture is cloned on the front side of the base, refer to Figure 9-89.

7. Rotate the view of the canvas and continue dragging the cursor on all the sides of the base to project the brick texture on it, refer to Figure 9-90. Now, press SHIFT+Z to hide the texture image.

8. Choose the **IMG_4819.jpg** texture image from the **LightBox** browser and then double-click on it; the image is displayed in the Current Texture button of the **Texture** palette.

9. Choose the **Add To Spotlight** button from the **Texture** palette; the image is displayed in the canvas.

10. Rotate the view of the canvas such that the top view of the hut is visible. Move the texture image such that it covers the floor of the base. Create a mask on the surface of the hut.

Press Z and project the texture on the surface of the floor. Next, press SHIFT+Z to hide the texture image. Remove the mask from the hut; the texture is displayed on the floor, refer to Figure 9-91.

Figure 9-89 *The texture projected on the front side of the base*

Figure 9-90 *The texture projected on all the sides of the base*

11. Create a mask on the top of the ground, refer to Figure 9-92.

Figure 9-91 *The texture projected on the floor of the base*

Figure 9-92 *A mask created on the top of the ground*

12. Expand the **FiberMesh** subpalette in the **Tool** palette. In this subpalette, choose the **LightBox Fibers** button; different types of fibers are displayed in the **LightBox** browser. Choose the **Fibers78.ZFP** file from the browser and double-click on it; the fibers are displayed on the ground.

13. Expand the **Modifiers** area in the **FiberMesh** subpalette. In this area, set the value of the **MaxFibers** slider to **209.4099** and then set the value of the **Length** slider to **93.042**, refer to Figure 9-93. Next, choose the **Accept** button; grass is displayed on the ground, refer to Figure 9-94.

Saving the Model

In this section, you will save the file using the steps given next.

1. Choose the **Save As** button from the **Tool** palette; the **Save ZTool** dialog box is displayed. In this dialog box, browse to the location: *\Documents\ZBrushprojects\c09*.

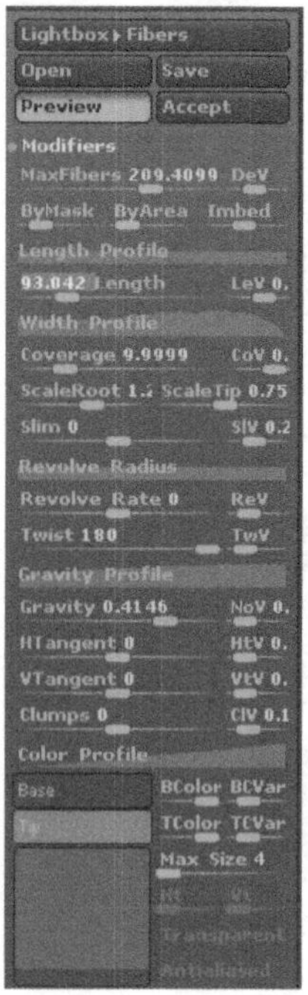

Figure 9-93 The values of the sliders set

Figure 9-94 The grass displayed on the ground

2. Enter **c09tut1** in the **File name** edit box and then choose the **Save** button.

Tutorial 2

In this tutorial, you will apply a texture on a face using the Spotlight tool. The final output of the model is shown in Figure 9-95. **(Expected time: 20 min)**

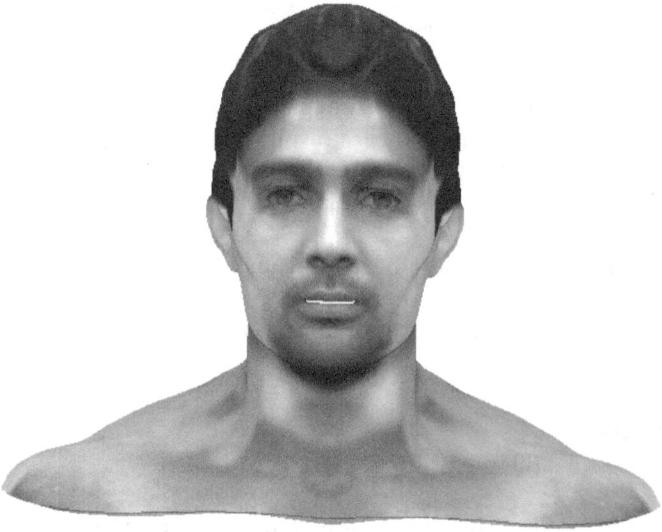

Figure 9-95 The textured face

The following steps are required to complete this tutorial:

a. Project texture on the face.
b. Set the properties of the material.
c. Save the model.

Projecting Texture on the Face

In this section, you will project the texture on the *DemoHead.ZTL* model.

1. Choose the **Init ZBrush** button from the **Preferences** palette; a message box is displayed. Choose the **Yes** button from the message box; ZBrush is initialized to its default state.

2. Choose the **DemoHead.ZTL** file from the **Tool** tab of the **LightBox** browser by double-clicking on it. Next, drag the cursor in the canvas area; the *DemoHead.ZTL* is displayed in the canvas.

3. Choose the **Edit** button in the top shelf to switch to the edit mode.

4. Expand the **Geometry** subpalette in the **Tool** palette. In this subpalette, click on the **Divide** button twice; the value in the **SDiv** slider becomes equal to **5**.

5. Choose the Current Material button from the left shelf; a flyout is displayed. In this flyout, choose the **SkinShade4** material; the material is assigned to the model, refer to Figure 9-96.

6. Expand the **Texture** palette. In this palette, choose the **Import** button; the **Import Image** dialog box is displayed. In this dialog box, browse to *\Documents\ZBrushprojects\c09*. Select the **face.jpg** file from the dialog box and then choose the **Open** button; the texture is loaded into the **Texture** palette.

7. In the **Texture** palette, choose the Current Texture button; a flyout is displayed. In this flyout, choose the **face** texture image; the image is displayed in the Current Texture button.

8. In the **Texture** palette, choose the **Add To Spotlight** button; the image is added to the Spotlight and is displayed in the canvas, refer to Figure 9-97.

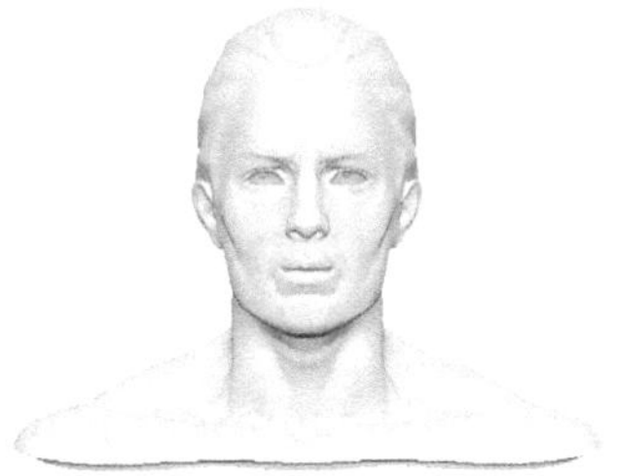

Figure 9-96 *The* ***SkinShade4*** *material applied to the model*

Figure 9-97 *A texture image displayed in the canvas*

9. In the Spotlight ring, hover the cursor on the **Opacity** icon and drag it in the anti clockwise direction; the image becomes transparent, refer to Figure 9-98.

10. Press Z; the Spotlight ring disappears. Make sure the **Rgb** button in the top shelf is chosen and the **Zadd** button is not chosen. Next, drag the cursor on the texture image, refer to Figure 9-99.

Figure 9-98 *The transparency in the image increased*

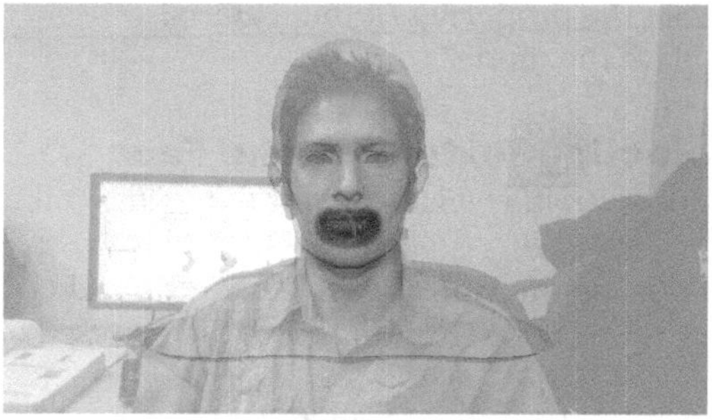

Figure 9-99 *The cursor dragged on the surface of the image*

You will notice that the texture image does not exactly match with the model. You need to match the image with the model.

11. Press Z again; the Spotlight ring is displayed. Choose the **Nudge** icon in the Spotlight ring. Next, adjust the brush size as required and move different areas of the image such that the image matches exactly with the model, refer to Figure 9-100.

12. Press Z and then drag the cursor on the surface of image to project the texture on the model, refer to Figure 9-101.

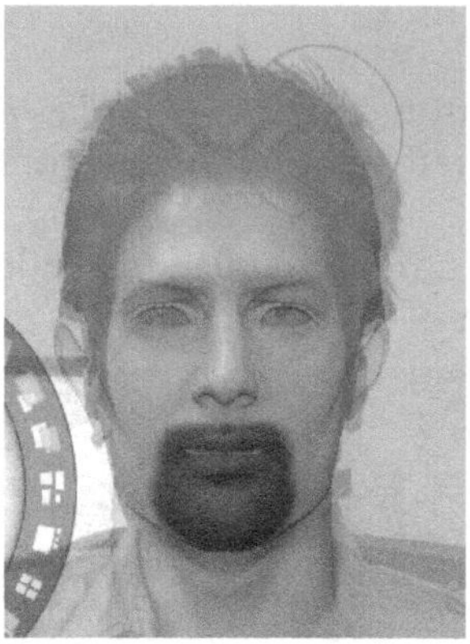

Figure 9-100 *The image manipulated using the **Nudge** icon*

Figure 9-101 *The cursor dragged on the face area of the texture image*

13. Press SHIFT+Z; the texture image disappears and the projected texture is displayed on the surface of the model, refer to Figure 9-102.

14. Rotate the view of the canvas such that you can view the side view of the model. Press SHIFT+Z; the texture image is displayed. Increase the size of the texture image and project the texture on the neck area of the model, refer to Figure 9-103.

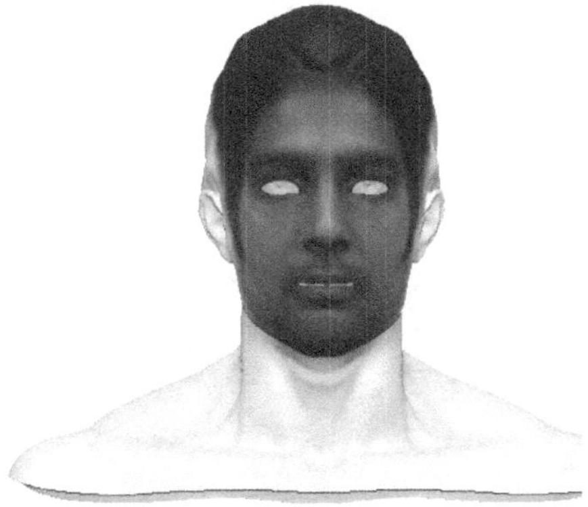

Figure 9-102 The projected texture displayed on the face of the model

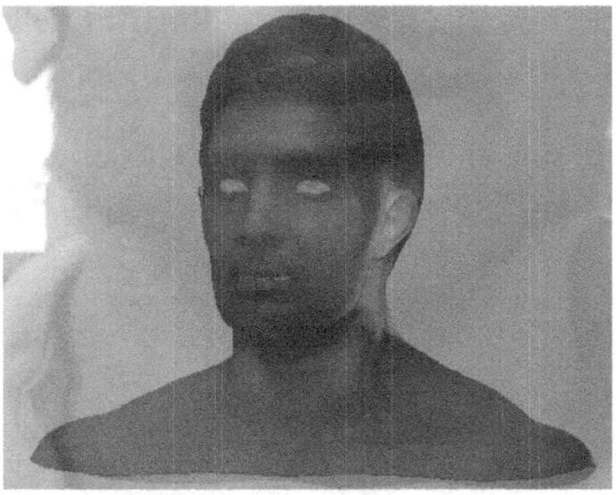

Figure 9-103 The texture projected on the neck of the model

You will notice that the texture is not projected on the eyes and teeth of the model as separate subtools are available for eyes and teeth.

15. Expand the **SubTool** subpalette in the **Tool** palette. In this subpalette, select the **eyes** subtool from the list of subtools, refer to Figure 9-104.

16. Expand the **Geometry** subpalette in the **Tool** palette. In this subpalette, click the **Divide** button four times; the value in the **SDiv** slider becomes equal to **6**, refer to Figure 9-105.

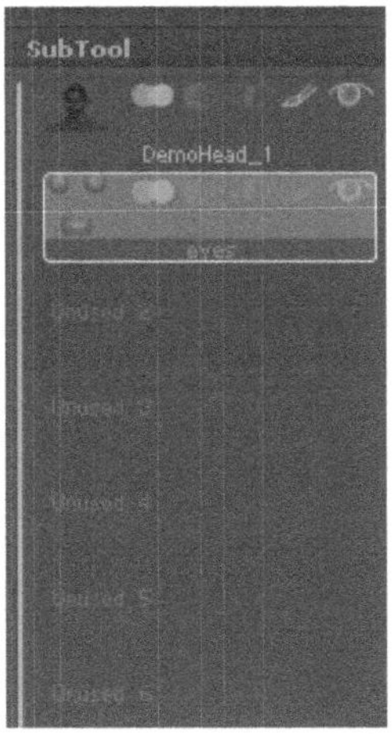

*Figure 9-104 The **eyes** subtool chosen from the list*

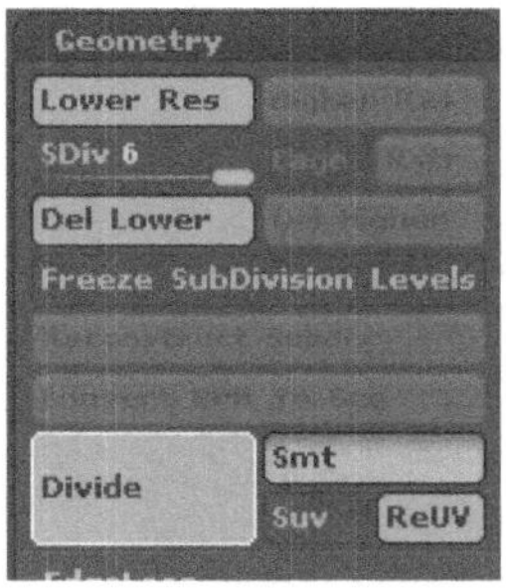

*Figure 9-105 The value of the **SDiv** slider set to **6***

17. Press X to activate the symmetry in the X-axis. Move the texture image such that the eyes in the image lie exactly on top of the eyes of the model, refer to Figure 9-106.

18. Press Z and then drag the cursor on the surface of the eyes in the image to project the texture on the model.

19. Press SHIFT+Z; the texture image disappears. Next, choose the Current Brush button from the left shelf; a flyout containing different sculpting brushes is displayed. Choose the **Move** brush from this flyout.

20. Make sure the **Zadd** button is chosen in the top shelf. Move the teeth of the model inward using the **Move** brush, refer to Figure 9-107.

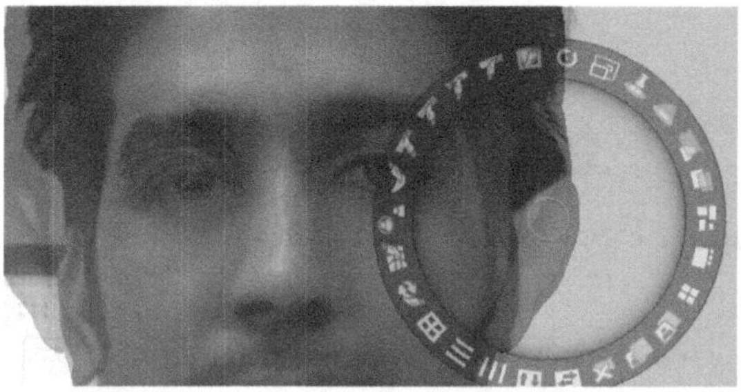

Figure 9-106 *The texture image moved to match the model*

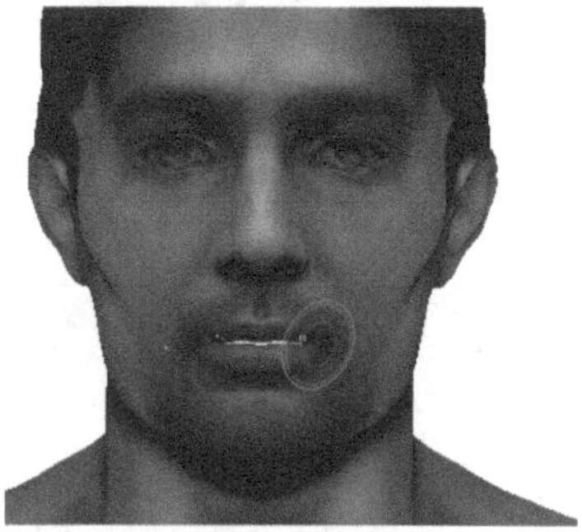

Figure 9-107 *Teeth of the model moved inward using the **Move** brush*

Setting the Properties of the Material

In this section, you will set properties of the material applied to the model.

1. Expand the **Material** palette. In this palette, expand the **Modifiers** subpalette.

2. In the **Modifiers** subpalette, set the values in the **Ambient** and **Diffuse** sliders to **100**, refer to Figure 9-108; the texture on the model is displayed more clearly, refer to Figure 9-109.

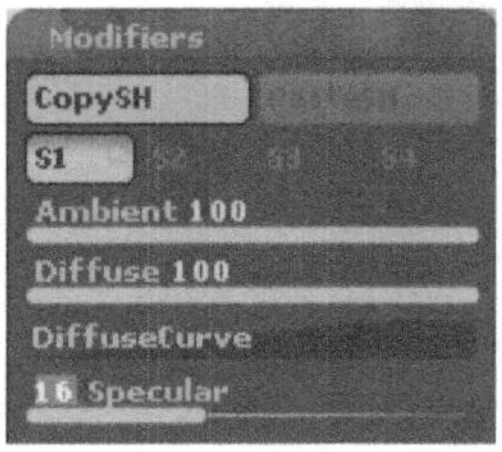

Figure 9-108 *The values of the **Ambient** and **Diffuse** sliders set*

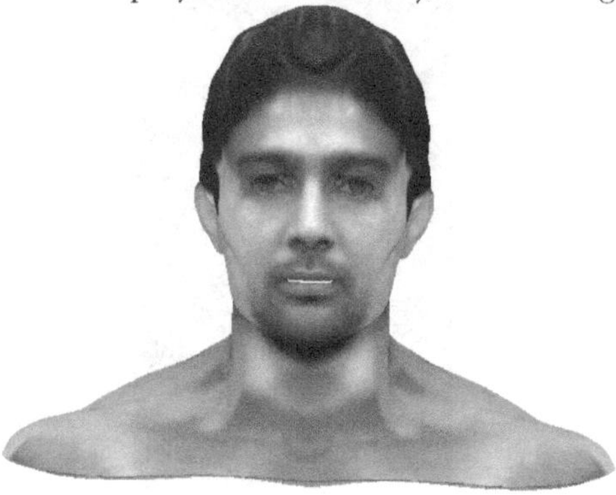

Figure 9-109 *The texture on the model displayed clearly*

Saving the Model

In this section, you will save the file using the steps given next.

1. Choose the **Save As** button from the **Tool** palette; the **Save ZTool** dialog box is displayed. In this dialog box, browse to the location: *\Documents\ZBrushprojects\c09*.

2. Enter **c09tut2** in the **File name** edit box and then choose the **Save** button.

Self-Evaluation Test

Answer the following questions and then compare them to those given at the end of this chapter:

1. Which of the following icons in the Spotlight ring is used to blur the selected areas of an image or an entire image?

   (a) **Nudge** (b) **Smudge**
   (c) **Hue** (d) **Paint**

2. Which of the following buttons in the **Texture** palette is used to determine whether the canvas will be filled with a selected texture or not?

   (a) **GrabDoc** (b) **Clone**
   (c) **Cd** (d) **Grad**

3. The __________ button in the **Texture** palette is used to convert a texture into a gray scale alpha image.

4. The __________ button in the **Texture** palette is used to display the texture images present in the **LightBox** browser.

5. The __________ icon in the Spotlight ring is used to stack all the images in the Spotlight on the left hand side of the canvas and to make sizes of the images same.

6. The __________ icon in the Spotlight ring is used to reset an image to its default state after different effects have been applied on it.

7. The **ZProject** brush uses the X-axis of the canvas to transfer the texturing details from the reference image to the 3D model. (T/F)

8. To display grid on the surface of a texture image, hover the cursor on the **Grid** icon of the Spotlight ring and drag it in the anti-clockwise direction. (T/F)

9. When the Spotlight is used for texturing a 3D object, the **Nudge** icon in the Spotlight ring is used to preview the texture image in the form of a transparent circular frame. (T/F)

Review Questions

Answer the following questions:

1. In which of the following palettes is the **Polypaint** subpalette located?

   (a) **Texture** (b) **Material**
   (c) **Color** (d) **Tool**

2. The _________ icon in the Spotlight ring is used to paint an image with different or a selected color or fill specific areas of an image with selected color.

3. The __________ icon in the Spotlight ring is used to change the color of an image.

4. The __________ slider in the **Texture** palette is used to specify the size of the reference image before loading it into the canvas.

5. You can adjust the contrast either in the selected areas of an image or an entire image using the **Brightness** icon in the Spotlight ring. (T/F)

6. The **Invert** button in the **Texture** palette is used to flip a texture image vertically. (T/F)

7. The **FillLayer** button is used to fill the canvas in a particular layer with color, material, or texture. (T/F)

EXERCISE

The output of the model used in this exercise can be accessed by downloading the *c09_ZBrush_2022_exr.zip* file from *www.cadcim.com*. The path of the file is as follows: *Textbooks > Animation and Visual Effects > ZBrush > ZBrush 2022: A Comprehensive Guide*.

Exercise 1

Download the file *c09_ZBrush_2022_exr.zip* from *www.cadcim.com*. Extract the contents of the zipped file and open *c09_exr1_start.ztl* from it, refer to Figure 9-110. Next, assign different textures to the scene using the LightBox textures, refer to Figure 9-111.

(Expected time: 20 min)

Figure 9-110 *Model of the hut without textures*

Figure 9-111 *Textured model of the hut*

Answers to Self-Evaluation Test

1. b, **2.** c, **3. MakeAlpha**, **4. LightBox Texture**, **5. Tile Unified**, **6. Restore**, **7.** F, **8.** T, **9.** F

This page is intentionally left blank

Chapter 10

UV Master

Learning Objectives

After completing this chapter, you will be able to:

- *Work with the UV Master subpalette*
- *Unwrap different 3D models*

INTRODUCTION

In this chapter, you will work with the UV Master plugin. The UV Master plugin is used to unwrap the UVs in a 3D object by creating seams on its surface. Unwrapping a 3D object enables you to apply textures on the surface of that object accurately.

UV MASTER

The **UV Master** tool can be accessed through the **ZPlugin** palette, refer to Figure 10-1. This plugin gets automatically installed when you install ZBrush. On choosing the **ZPlugin** palette, it gets expanded and different subpalettes are displayed. The **UV Master** subpalette consists of different buttons and sliders that are used to control the way unwrapping is done in a 3D object, refer to Figure 10-2. The different buttons and sliders in the **UV Master** subpalette are discussed next.

Figure 10-1 The ***ZPlugin*** *palette*

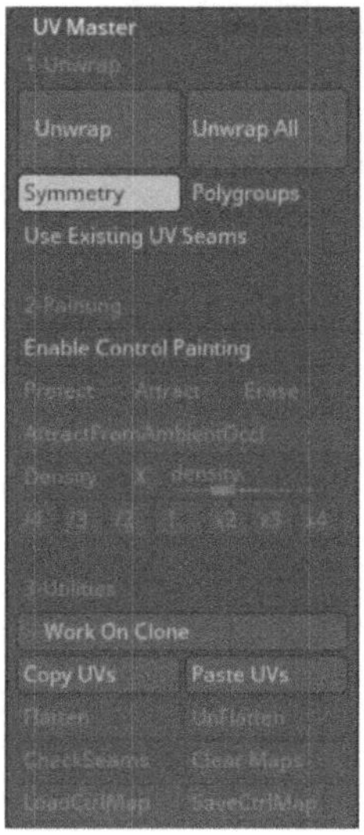

Figure 10-2 The ***UV Master*** *subpalette*

Unwrap

The **Unwrap** button is used to unwrap a model and apply UV mapping to it. To unwrap a model in the canvas, make sure the **Edit** button is chosen. Next, convert the model into a polymesh by choosing the **Make PolyMesh3D** button from the **Tool** palette.

Expand the **Texture Map** subpalette in the **Tool** palette. In this subpalette, choose the **Texture Map** button; a flyout containing different texture images will be displayed. In this flyout, choose the **Texture 03** texture image; the texture image will be displayed in the **Texture Map** button and the checker texture will be applied to the model, refer to Figures 10-3 and 10-4.

You will notice that the texture applied to the model is stretched. To rectify this, you need to unwrap the model using the **Unwrap** button located in the **UV Master** subpalette. In order to access the **UV Master** subpalette easily, you need to dock the **ZPlugin** palette in the right tray or the left tray. To do so, expand the **ZPlugin** palette. In this palette, hover the cursor on the arrow located at the top left corner of the palette; the shape of cursor will change, refer to Figure 10-5. Next, drag the cursor toward the right tray; the **ZPlugin** palette will be docked on the right tray and can be easily accessed.

In the **ZPlugin** palette, expand the **UV Master** subpalette. Next, choose the **Unwrap** button in this subpalette; the ring will be unwrapped and the stretching in the texture will be rectified, refer to Figure 10-6.

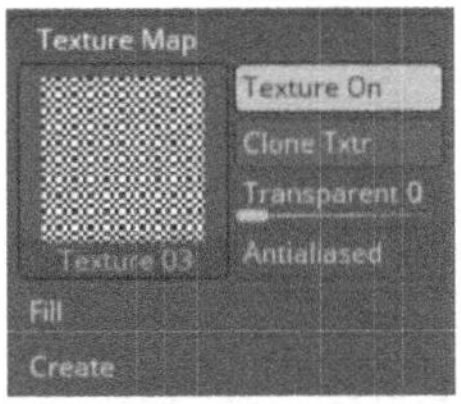

***Figure 10-3** The **Texture Map** subpalette*

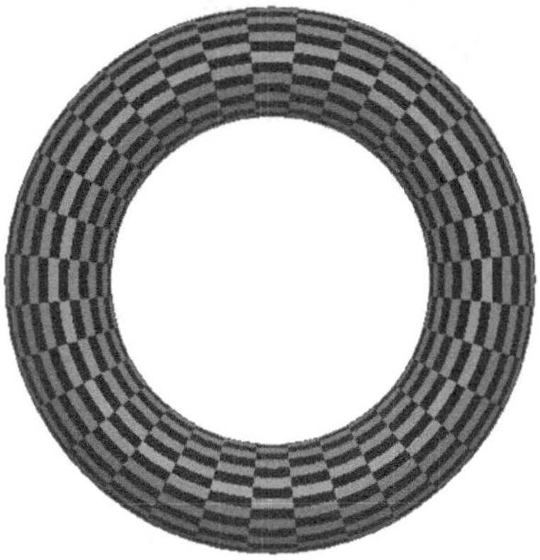

***Figure 10-4** The checker texture applied to the model*

Note
Before unwrapping an object, make sure the object is at its lowest subdivision level.

Unwrap All

The **Unwrap All** button is used to unwrap all the subtools from the canvas and apply UV mapping to them. It is used when a model is composed of different subtools. If you want to unwrap only a specific subtool, then you need to select that subtool from the **SubTool** subpalette and then choose the **Unwrap** button.

Symmetry

The **Symmetry** button is used to unwrap a model symmetrically. To unwrap a model symmetrically, load the model from the **Tool** tab of the **LightBox** browser into the canvas and choose the **Edit** button from the top shelf, refer to Figure 10-7.

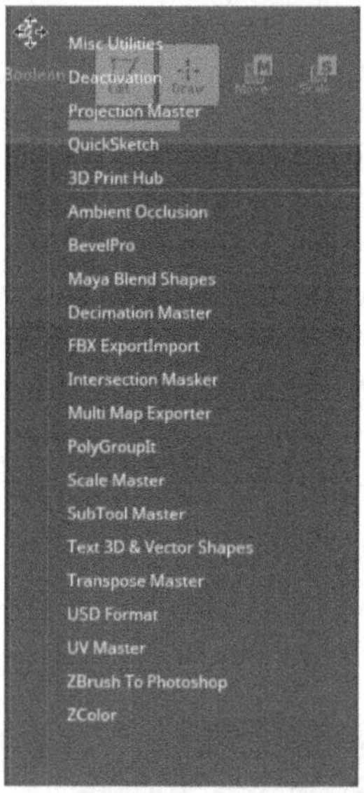

Figure 10-5 The shape of the cursor changed

Figure 10-6 The stretching in the texture rectified

Make sure the **Symmetry** button is chosen in the **UV Master** subpalette. Next, choose the **Unwrap** button; the model will be unwrapped. To view the flattened image of the model in the canvas, choose the **Flatten** button from the **UV Master** subpalette, refer to Figures 10-8 and 10-9. The flattened image of the 3D model is also referred to as UV island.

Figure 10-7 The model loaded into the canvas

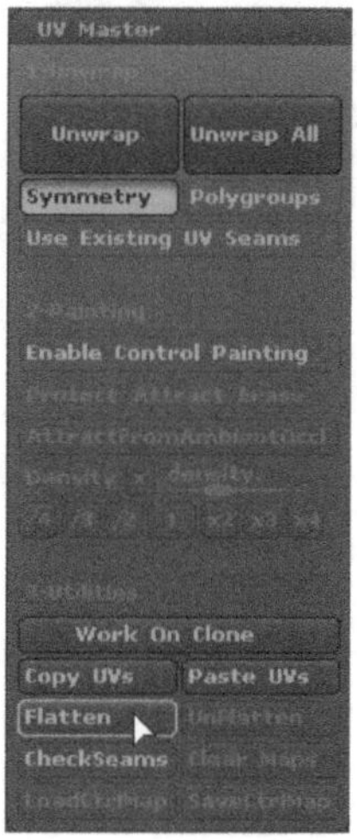

*Figure 10-8 The **Flatten** button chosen*

In Figure 10-9, you will notice that the model is unwrapped symmetrically. Now, you need to switch back to the 3D model. To do so, choose the **UnFlatten** button located beside the **Flatten** button. Next, choose the **Symmetry** button to deactivate it and then choose the **Unwrap** button. Choose the **Flatten** button again from the **UV Master** subpalette; the unsymmetrical flattened image of the model will be displayed in the canvas, refer to Figure 10-10.

Polygroups

The **Polygroups** button is used to create separate UV islands for a model if it is composed of different polygroups. To create separate UV islands for a model, load a model into the canvas. Choose the **Edit** button from the top shelf and then choose the **PolyF** button from the right shelf; the polygon edges will be displayed on the surface of the model. Next, press and hold CTRL+SHIFT; the **SelectRect** brush will be activated. Drag the cursor on the upper part of the model to create a rectangular marquee selection, refer to Figure 10-11; only the selected area will be displayed in the canvas and the rest of the area will disappear.

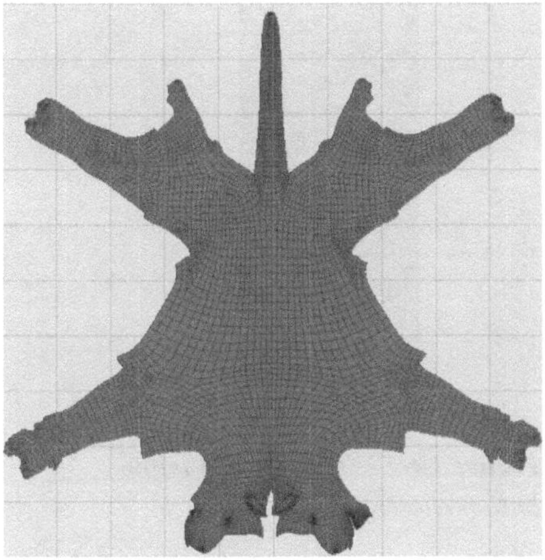

Figure 10-9 *The model flattened with the* ***Symmetry*** *button chosen*

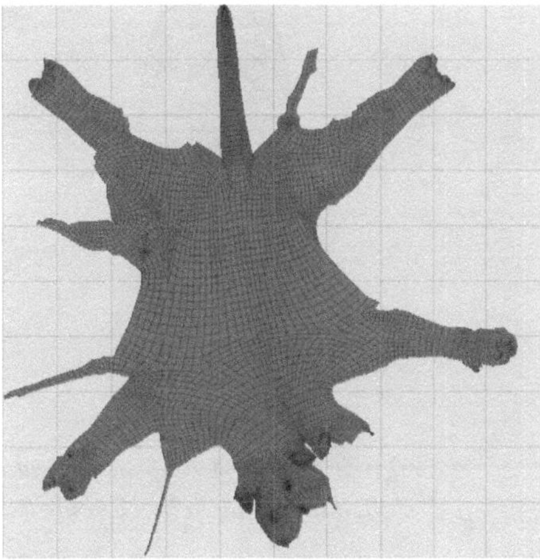

Figure 10-10 *The model flattened without the* ***Symmetry*** *button chosen*

In the **Tool** palette, expand the **Polygroups** subpalette. In this subpalette, choose the **GroupVisible** button, refer to Figure 10-12; the color of the selected area will change. Press and hold CTRL+SHIFT again and click in the open area of the canvas; the entire model will be displayed again. Similarly, different polygroups on the surface of the model will be displayed, refer to Figure 10-13. In the **UV Master** subpalette of the **ZPlugin** palette, choose the **Polygroups** button first and then choose the **Unwrap** button. Now, choose the **Flatten** button; the separate UV islands will be created for each polygroup, refer to Figure 10-14.

Use Existing UV Seams

The **Use Existing UV Seams** button is used to unwrap an imported model based on its existing seams. To view the seams in the model, you need to choose the **CheckSeams** button in the **UV Master** subpalette. The seams in the model determine the way unwrapping will be done.

Enable Control Painting

The **Enable Control Painting** button is used to activate different buttons that enable you to guide the **UV Master** in creating seams in a model and unwrapping it. These buttons enable you to manually control the way in which the unwrapping will be done.

Protect

The **Protect** button is used to paint the areas of the model where you do not want the seams to be created. The **Protect** button is not activated by default. To activate this button, you need to choose the **Enable Control Painting** button. The different positions of seams can produce different results in the unwrapped model.

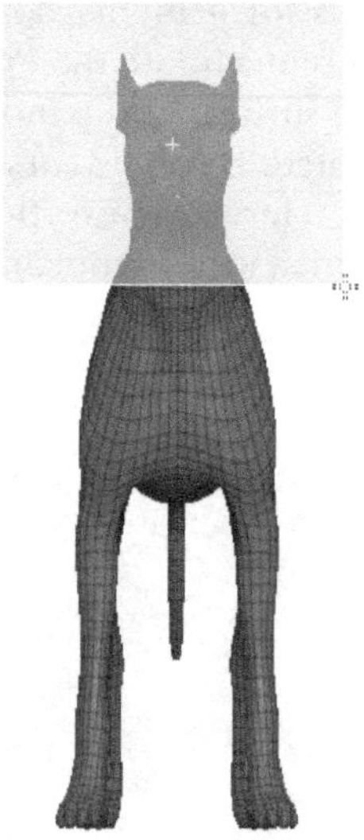

*Figure 10-11 A portion of model selected using the **SelectRect** brush*

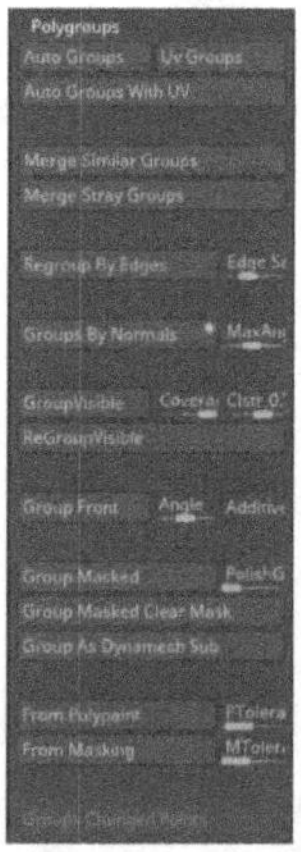

*Figure 10-12 The **GroupVisible** button chosen*

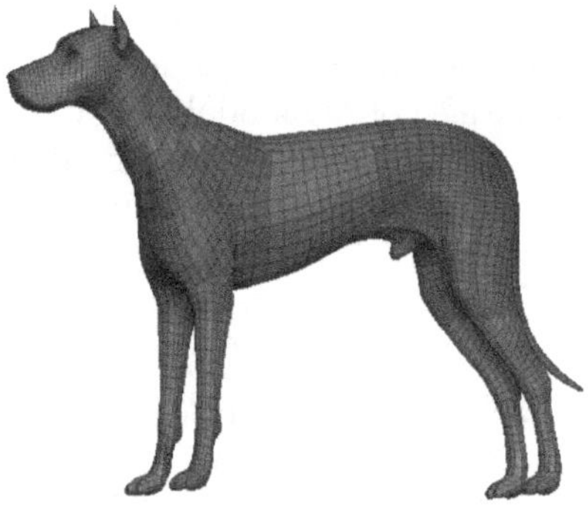

Figure 10-13 Different polygroups created in the model

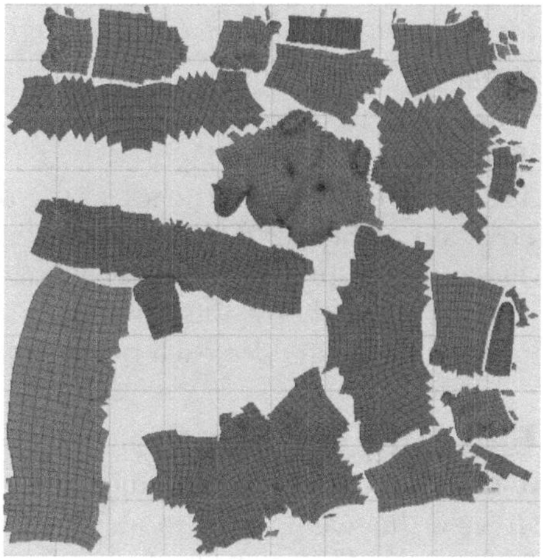

Figure 10-14 Separate UV islands created for different polygroups

To check the seams in the *Dog.ZTL* model, first choose the **Unwrap** button and then view the seams in the model by choosing the **CheckSeams** button, refer to Figure 10-15. Next, choose the **Enable Control Painting** button in the **UV Master** subpalette; the **Protect** button will be activated. Choose the **Protect** button and drag the cursor on the front area of the model; the area will turn red in color, refer to Figure 10-16. After painting the front area of the model, choose the **Unwrap** button again; the model will be unwrapped and the seams will disappear from the painted area of the model, refer to Figure 10-17.

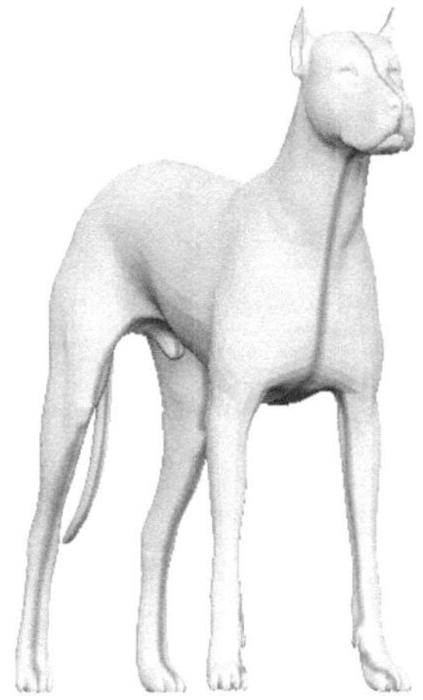

Figure 10-15 *The seams in the model displayed*

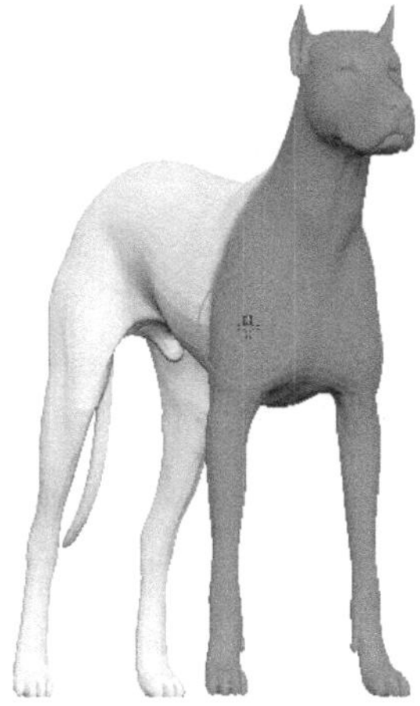

Figure 10-16 *The front area of the model protected*

Attract

The **Attract** button is used to paint the areas of the model where you want the seams to be created. This button is activated only when you choose the **Enable Control Painting** button. To understand the working of this button, choose the **Attract** button and drag the cursor on the front area of the model; the area will turn blue, refer to Figure 10-18. After painting the front area of the model, choose the **Unwrap** button; the model will be unwrapped and the seams will be displayed in the painted area of the model, refer to Figure 10-19.

Figure 10-17 *The seam removed from the painted area*

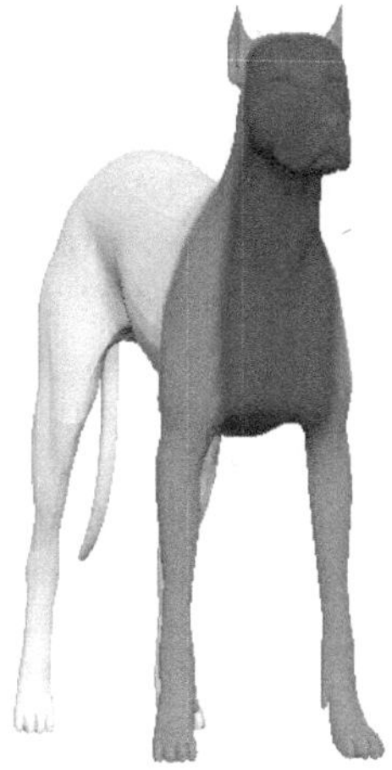

Figure 10-18 *The front area of the model painted blue*

Erase

The **Erase** button is used to erase the areas of the model that have been painted using the **Protect** or **Attract** button, refer to Figure 10-20.

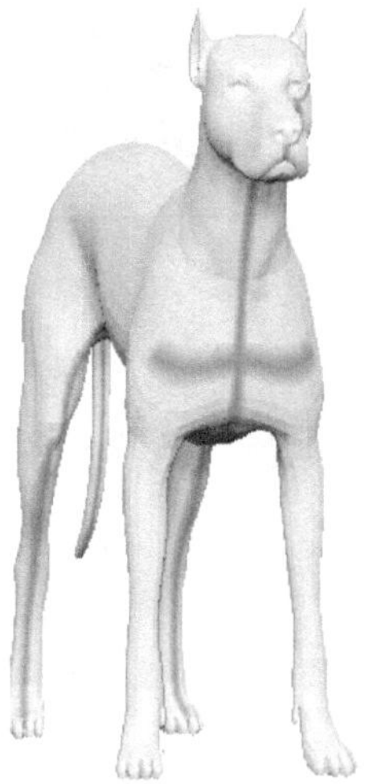

Figure 10-19 *A seam created in the painted area*

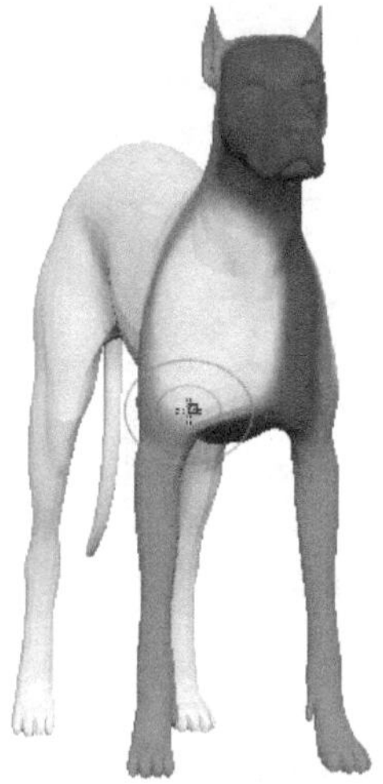

Figure 10-20 *A painted area erased using the **Erase** button*

AttractFromAmbientOccl

The **AttractFromAmbientOccl** button is used to automatically paint the hidden areas of the model. The painted areas are the areas that are less visible in the model, refer to Figure 10-21. In this figure, you will notice that the inner parts of the model are painted blue. By default, this button is not activated. To activate this button, choose the **Enable Control Painting** button.

Density

The **Density** button is used to increase or decrease the size of the UVs when the model is unwrapped. If the size of the UVs is more, the resolution of the texture will also increase. You can increase the size of the UVs at high detail areas of the model such as face. To increase or decrease the size of the UVs, unwrap the model of the *Dog.ZTL* file by choosing the **Unwrap** button. Next, choose the **Flatten** button; the flattened image of the unwrapped model will be displayed, refer to Figure 10-22.

In this figure, you will notice that the size of the UVs in the face area of the model is small. To increase the size of the UVs, you need to use the **Density** button. Choose the **UnFlatten** button and then choose the **Enable Control Painting** button. Next, choose the **Density** button, refer to Figure 10-23. After choosing the **Density** button, set the value of the **density** slider to **4**. Then, start painting on the face area of the model, refer to Figure 10-24. After painting on the face area of the model, choose the **Unwrap** button again and then choose the **Flatten** button; the size of the UVs will increase in the painted area, refer to Figure 10-25.

The size of the UVs can be controlled by using the **Density** slider. Higher the size of this slider, higher will be size of the UVs.

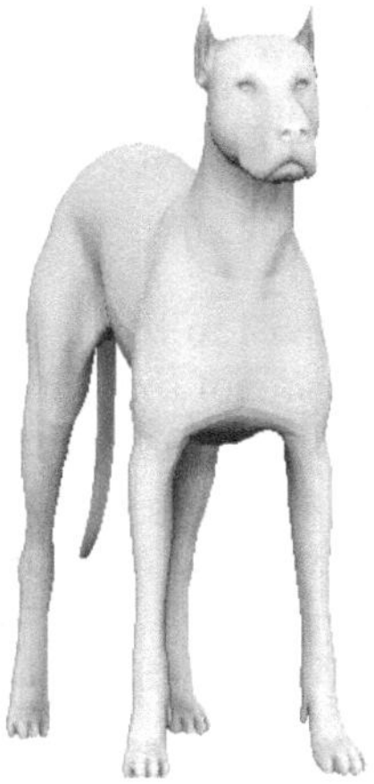

Figure 10-21 *An attraction area painted automatically*

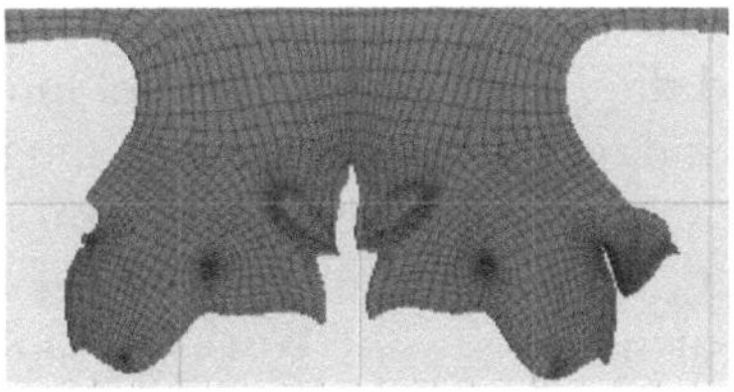

Figure 10-22 *The flattened image of the model*

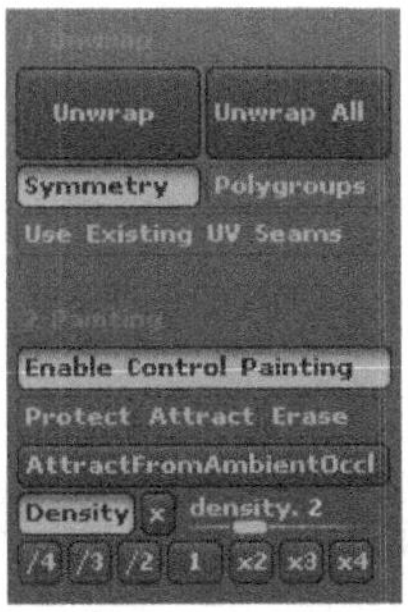

Figure 10-23 *The* **Density** *button chosen*

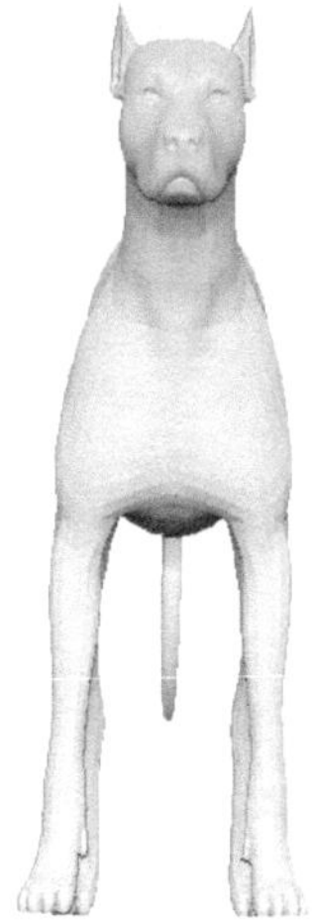

Figure 10-24 *The face of the model painted*

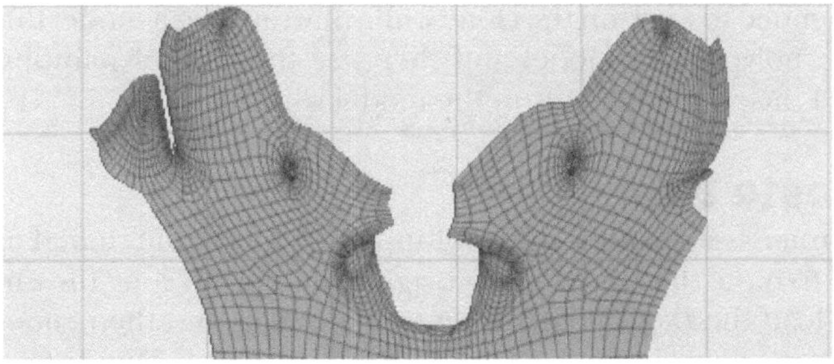

Figure 10-25 *The size of the UVs increased in the painted area*

Work On Clone

The **Work On Clone** button is used to create a copy of the model and perform unwrapping operations on it. The results of the unwrap can be later transferred from the cloned model to the original model.

A model can be unwrapped only if it is at its lowest subdivision level. If you want to unwrap a model at higher subdivision level, you need to create a clone of that model. The cloned model will be at its lowest subdivision level. To create a copy of the model and perform unwrapping operations, load the *DemoHead.ZTL* model into the canvas from the **Tool** tab of the **LightBox** browser. After loading the model and switching to edit mode, choose the **Unwrap** button from the **UV Master** subpalette; a message box prompting you to switch to lowest subdivision level will be displayed, refer to Figure 10-26. Instead of choosing the **Del Lower** button from the **Geometry** subpalette, choose the **Work On Clone** button; a cloned model of the *DemoHead.ZTL* model will be displayed, refer to Figure 10-27.

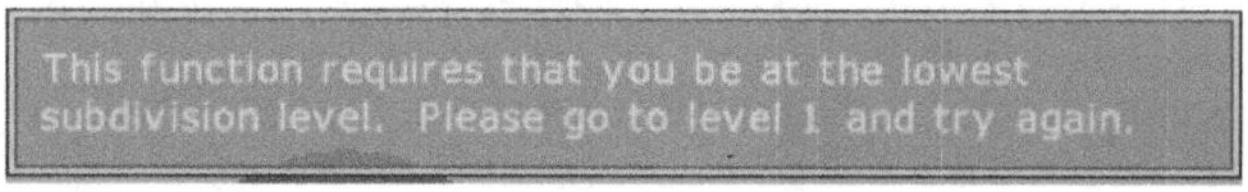

Figure 10-26 *The message box displayed on choosing the **Unwrap** button*

Next, choose the Current Tool button from the **Tool** palette; a flyout will be displayed. In this flyout, the cloned model with the term **CL** prefixed to it will be displayed, refer to Figure 10-28.

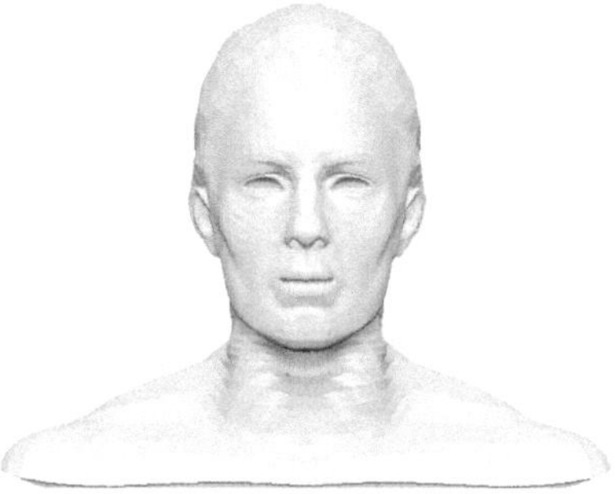

Figure 10-27 *The cloned model at its lowest subdivision level*

Figure 10-28 *The cloned model displayed in the flyout*

It is highly recommended to work on the clone while unwrapping a model that has been painted. If you work on the polypainted model and then use the control painting for protecting or attracting seams, all the painted details in the model will be lost.

Copy UVs, Paste UVs

The **Copy UVs** button is used to copy the unwrapped UVs from the cloned model and the **Paste UVs** button is used to paste the UVs into the original model. To copy the unwrapped UVs from the cloned model, load the *Dog.ZTL* model into the canvas and then choose the **Edit** button. Next, in the **Geometry** subpalette of the **Tool** palette, click on the **Divide** button twice; the value of the **SDiv** slider becomes equal to **3** and the model becomes smoother.

In the **UV Master** subpalette, choose the **Work on Clone** button; a clone of the model will be created in the canvas. Next, choose the **Unwrap** button; the model will be unwrapped. After unwrapping the model, choose the **Copy UVs** button. Then, choose the Current Tool button in the **Tool** palette; a flyout will be displayed. In this flyout, choose the original model of the dog; it will be displayed in the canvas. Next, in the **UV Master** subpalette, choose the **Paste UVs** button; the UVs will be pasted into the original model.

Flatten, Unflatten

The **Flatten** button is used to flatten a 3D model and display the UV islands on a plane after unwrapping the model. This button enables you to view the result of unwrapping. The flattened images can vary depending on the position of the seams in a model. The **UnFlatten** button is used to restore the flattened 2D image of the model back to the 3D representation.

Check Seams

The **Check Seams** button is used to view the seams in a 3D model. These seams will determine the way in which the unwrapping of the model will be done.

Clear Maps

The **Clear Maps** button is used to delete all the painting that has been done on a model using the **Protect**, **Attract**, and **Density** buttons.

LoadCtrlMap and SaveCtrlMap

The **SaveCtrlMap** button is used to save the control painting done in a model and the **LoadCtrlMap** button is used to save control painting. To save the control painting done in a model, load the *Dog.ZTL* model into the canvas and then choose the **Edit** button. In the **UV Master** subpalette of the ZPlugin palette, choose the **Unwrap** button and then choose the **Check Seams** button; the default seams will be displayed.

Now, choose the **Enable Control Painting** button and then choose the **Protect** button. Next, start painting on the front portion of the model. Choose the **Unwrap** button again and then choose the **Check Seams** button; the seams will be erased from the painted area. Next, choose the **SaveCtrlMap** button; the **Save As** dialog box will be displayed. In this dialog box, choose the **Save** button; the control map file will be saved with the *.CMp* extension.

Restart ZBrush and load the *Dog.ZTL* model in the canvas. In the **UV Master** subpalette of the **ZPlugin** palette, choose the **Enable Control Painting** button. Next, choose the **LoadCtrlMap** button; the **Open** dialog box will be displayed. In this dialog box, select the previously saved control map file and then choose the **Open** button.

Now, choose the **Unwrap** button and then choose the **Check Seams** button; the seams in the model will be same as that in the previously painted model.

TUTORIALS

Before you start the tutorials of this chapter, navigate to *\Documents\ZBrushprojects* and then create a new folder with the name *c10*.

Tutorial 1

In this tutorial, you will unwrap the model of the *DemoHead.ZTL* file present in the **LightBox** browser, refer to Figure 10-29. **(Expected time: 20 min)**

Figure 10-29 *The unwrapped model of the head*

The following steps are required to complete this tutorial:

a. Unwrap the model.
b. Adjust the seams in the model by control painting.
c. Save the unwrapped model.

Unwrapping the Model

In this section, you will unwrap the model using the default position of the seams.

1. Choose the **Init ZBrush** button from the **Preferences** palette; the message box is displayed. Choose the **Yes** button from the message box; ZBrush is initialized to its default state.

2. Choose the **DemoHead.ZTL** file from the **Tool** tab of the **LightBox** browser by double-clicking on it. Next, drag the cursor in the canvas area; the *DemoHead.ZTL* is displayed in the canvas.

3. Choose the **Edit** button in the top shelf to switch to the edit mode.

4. Expand the **Texture Map** subpalette in the **Tool** palette. In this subpalette, choose the **Texture Map** button; a flyout containing different texture images is displayed. In this flyout, choose the **Texture 03** texture image; a message box prompting you to apply UV mapping to the model is displayed, refer to Figure 10-30. Choose the **OK** button to close this message box.

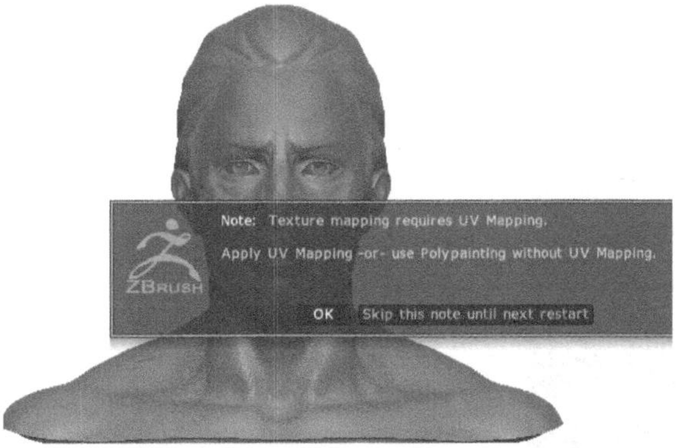

Figure 10-30 The message box displayed on choosing the texture image

5. Dock the **ZPlugin** palette in the right tray. In this palette, expand the **UV Master** subpalette. In this subpalette, choose the **Work On Clone** button; a clone of the model at its lowest subdivision level is displayed in the canvas, refer to Figure 10-31.

6. Choose the **Unwrap** button in the **UV Master** subpalette; the model is unwrapped and the **Texture 03** texture image is applied to it, refer to Figure 10-32. In this figure, you will notice that the checker pattern is distorted at the middle of the face.

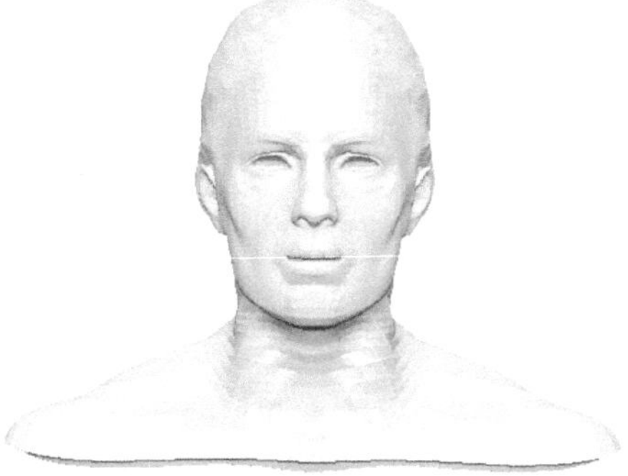

Figure 10-31 The cloned model displayed in the canvas

Figure 10-32 The texture image applied to the model

Adjusting the Seams in the Model by Control Painting

In this section, you will manually adjust the seams in the model using the **Protect** and **Attract** buttons.

1. In the **Texture Map** subpalette, choose the **Texture On** button to deactivate it, refer to Figure 10-33; the texture is removed from the model.

2. In the **UV Master** subpalette, choose the **CheckSeams** button; the seams are displayed on the model, refer to Figure 10-34.

Figure 10-33 *The* ***Texture On*** *button chosen*

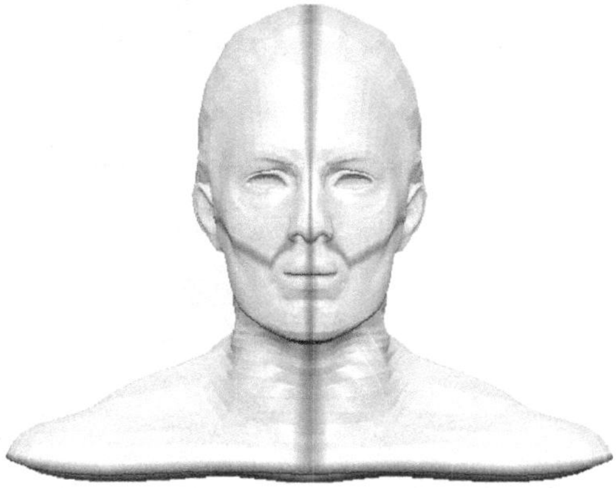

Figure 10-34 *The seams displayed on the model*

3. In the **UV Master** subpalette, choose the **Flatten** button; the flattened 2D image of the model is displayed, refer to Figure 10-35. In this figure, you will notice that the unwrapped image is not properly displayed.

4. Choose the **UnFlatten** button to display the 3D model again.

5. Choose the **Enable Control Painting** button in the **UV Master** subpalette. Next, choose the **Protect** button and then start painting on the front side of the face to remove seams from it, refer to Figure 10-36.

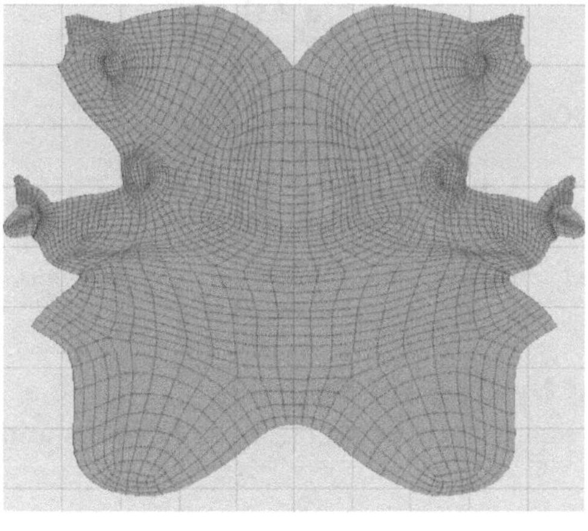

Figure 10-35 *The flattened image of the model*

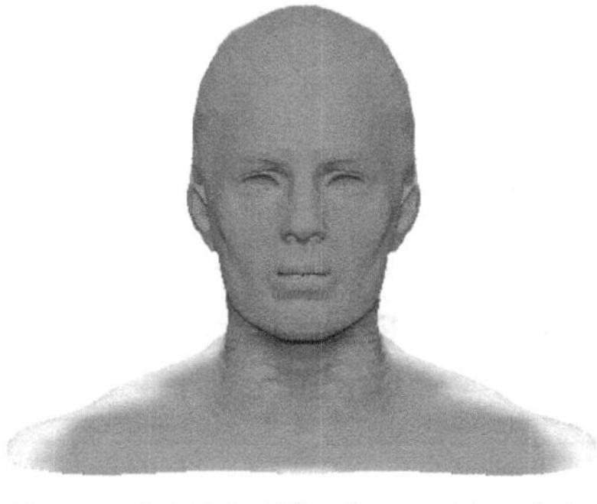

Figure 10-36 *The front side of the model painted using the* ***Protect*** *button*

6. In the **UV Master** subpalette, choose the **Attract** button and paint on the back side of the model to display the seams on it, refer to Figure 10-37.

7. Choose the **Unwrap** button; the seam is displayed on the model, as shown in Figure 10-38.

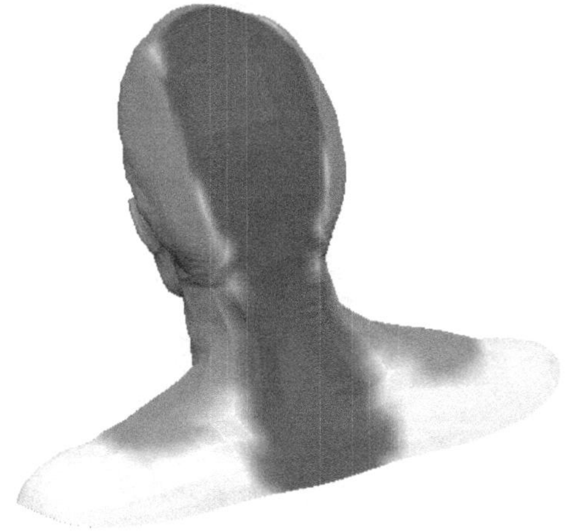

*Figure 10-37 The back side of the model painted using the **Attract** button*

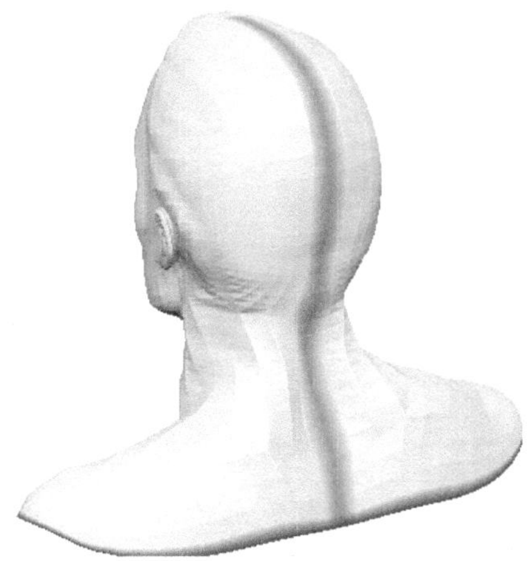

*Figure 10-38 The seam displayed after choosing the **Unwrap** button*

8. Choose the **Flatten** button; the flattened image of the model is displayed, refer to Figure 10-39. In this figure, you will notice that the size of UVs on the face area is too small. Choose the **UnFlatten** button to switch back to the 3D model.

   Next, you will increase the size of the UVs on the face so that the texture is applied properly.

9. Choose the **Density** button in the **UV Master** subpalette. Next, set the value in the **density** slider to **4**, refer to Figure 10-40.

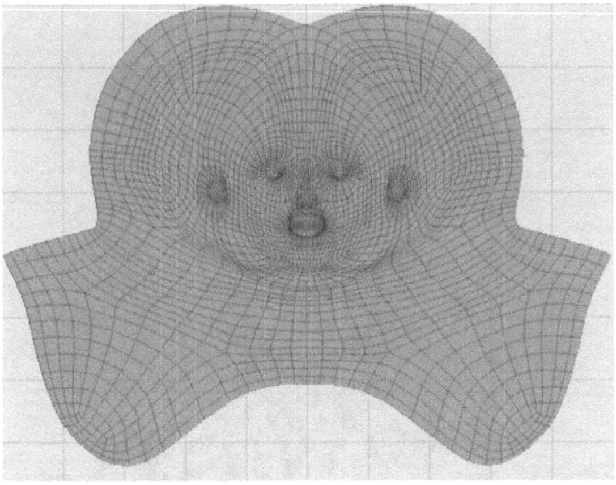

Figure 10-39 The flattened image of the model displayed

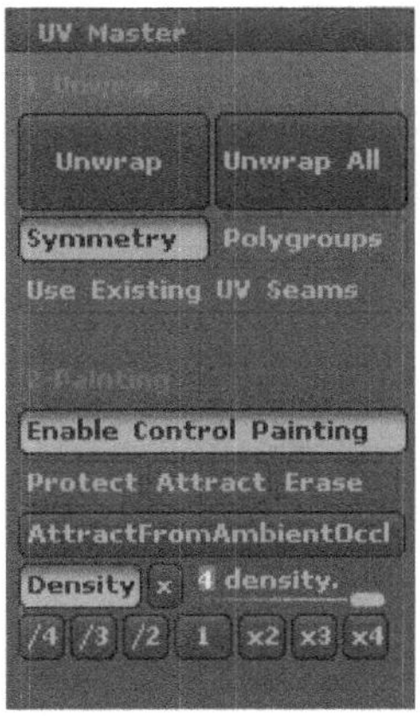

*Figure 10-40 The value of the **density** slider set to **4***

10. With the **Density** button chosen, start painting on the face area of the model, refer to Figure 10-41.

11. Choose the **Unwrap** button in the **UV Master** subpalette. Next, choose the **Flatten** button; the flattened image of the model is displayed, as shown in Figure 10-42.

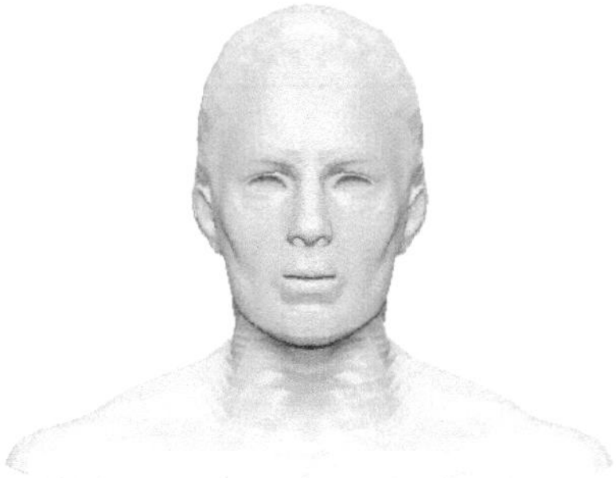

Figure 10-41 *The model with face area painted*

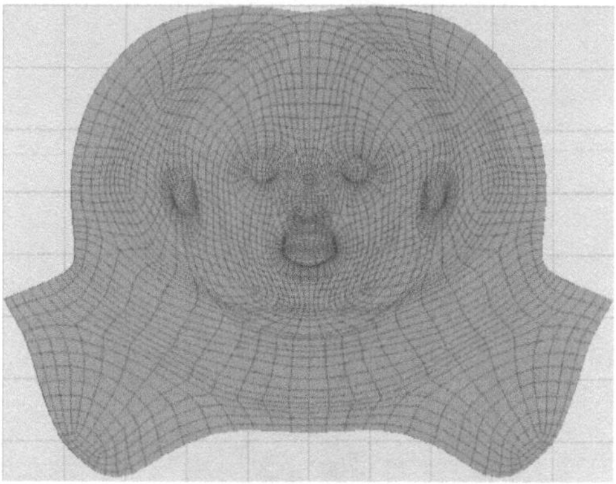

Figure 10-42 *The flattened image of the unwrapped model*

12. Choose the **UnFlatten** button to switch back to the 3D model. Next, choose the **Copy UVs** button, refer to Figure 10-43.

13. Choose the Current Tool button in the **Tool** palette; a flyout is displayed. In this flyout, choose the original *DemoHead* model; the model is displayed in the canvas.

14. Choose the **Paste UVs** button in the **UV Master** subpalette; the UVs are pasted on the original model, refer to Figure 10-44.

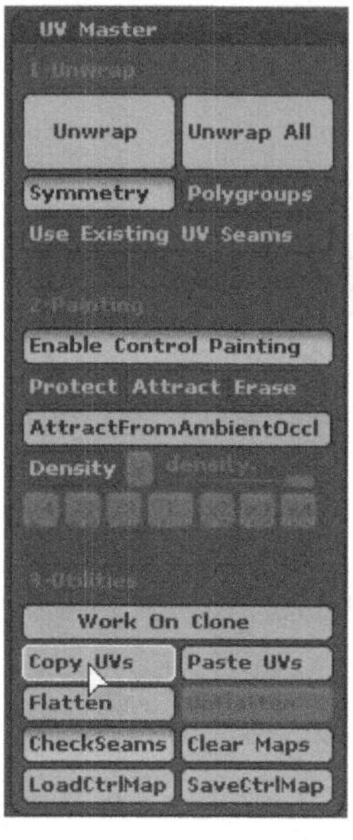

Figure 10-43 *The* ***Copy UVs*** *button chosen*

Figure 10-44 *The UVs pasted on the original model*

Saving the Model

In this section, you will save the file using the steps given next.

1. Choose the **Save As** button from the **Tool** palette; the **Save ZTool** dialog box is displayed. In this dialog box, browse to the location: *\Documents\ZBrushprojects\c10*.

2. Enter **c10tut1** in the **File name** edit box and then choose the **Save** button.

Tutorial 2

In this tutorial, you will create a texture map and apply it to the *Dog.ZTL* model. The final output of the model is shown in Figure 10-45. **(Expected time: 20 min)**

Figure 10-45 *Texture map applied to the model*

The following steps are required to complete this tutorial:

a. Unwrap the model.
b. Paint on the flattened image.
c. Create a texture map and apply it to the model.
d. Save the model.

Unwrapping the Model

In this section, you will unwrap the model using the default settings of the **UV Master** subpalette.

1. Choose the **Init ZBrush** button from the **Preferences** palette; the message box is displayed. Choose the **Yes** button from the message box; ZBrush is initialized to its default state.

2. Choose the *Dog.ZTL* file from the **Tool** tab of the **LightBox** browser by double-clicking on it. Next, drag the cursor in the canvas area; the *Dog.ZTL* is displayed in the canvas, refer to Figure 10-46.

3. Choose the **Edit** button in the top shelf to switch to the edit mode.

4. Dock the **ZPlugin** palette in the right tray. In this palette, expand the **UV Master** subpalette. In this subpalette, choose the **Unwrap** button.

5. Choose the **CheckSeams** button in the **UV Master** subpalette; the seams are displayed on the model, refer to Figure 10-47.

Figure 10-46 *The Dog.ZTL model displayed in the canvas*

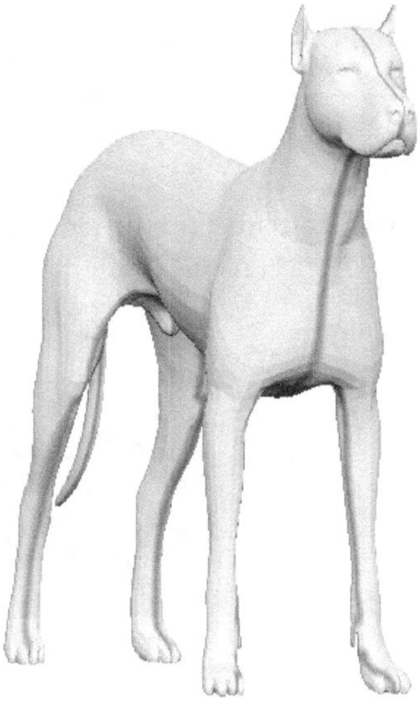

Figure 10-47 *The seams displayed on the model*

6. Choose the **Flatten** button in the **UV Master** subpalette; the flattened image of the model is displayed, as shown in Figure 10-48. For painting on the image, you need to increase its subdivisions level. To do so, press CTRL+D thrice; the flattened image is modified, as shown in Figure 10-49.

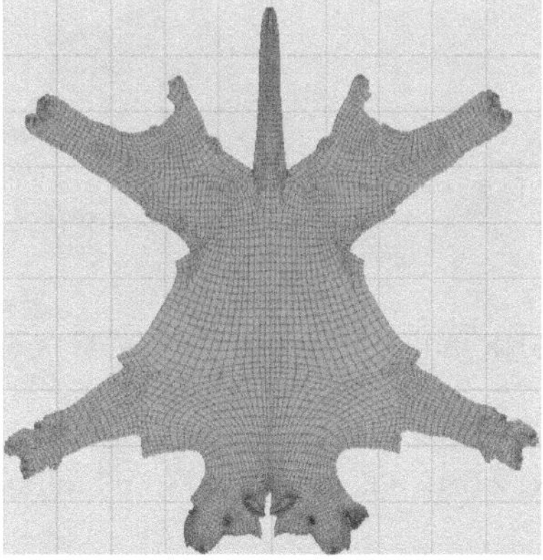

Figure 10-48 *The flattened image of the model*

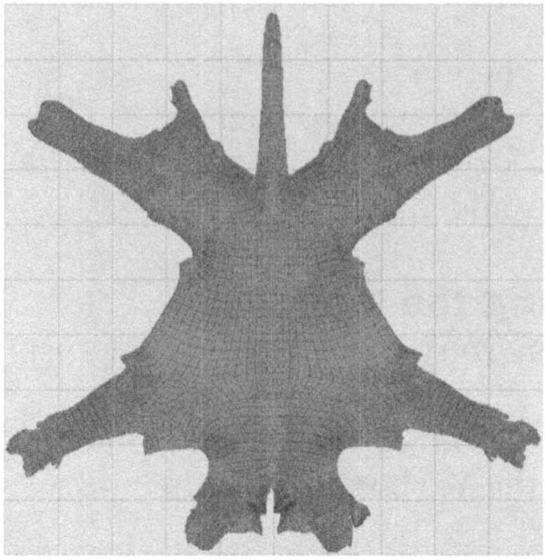

Figure 10-49 *The modified flattened image after pressing CTRL+D thrice*

Painting on the Flattened Image

In this section, you will paint on the surface of the flattened image.

1. Choose the Current Material button from the left shelf; a flyout is displayed. In this flyout, choose the **SkinShade4** material from the **Standard Materials** area; the material is applied on the flattened image.

2. To view the material, choose the **PolyF** button in the right shelf; the flattened image is displayed, as shown in Figure 10-50.

3. Expand the **Color** palette. In this palette, choose the **FillObject** button to fill the image with white color.

4. Choose the **PolyF** button again to display the polygon edges on the flattened image.

5. Make sure the **Rgb** button is chosen and the **Zadd** button is not chosen in the top shelf. Choose the black color from the **Current Color** swatch. Next, paint on the surface of the image to create the patterns, as shown in Figure 10-51.

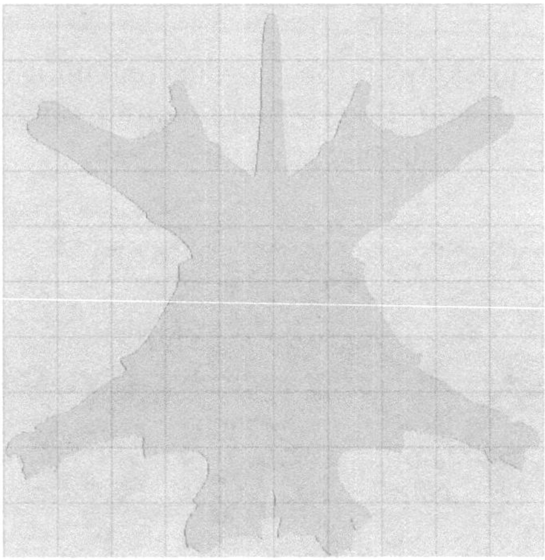

Figure 10-50 *The **SkinShade 4** material applied to the image*

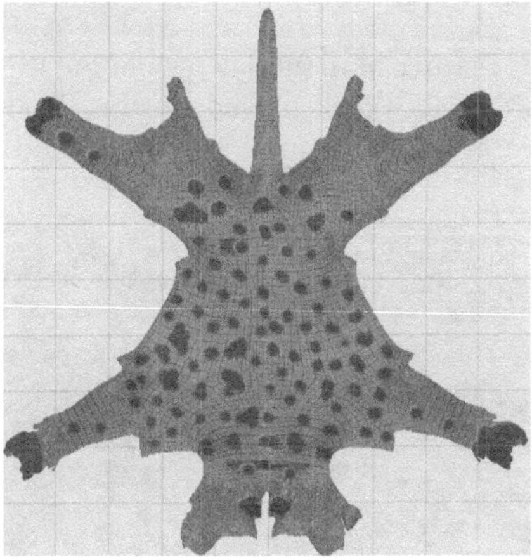

Figure 10-51 *A pattern created on the surface of the image*

Creating a Texture Map and Applying it to the Model

In this section, you will create a texture map from the flattened image and then apply it to the model.

1. Expand the **Texture Map** subpalette in the **Tool** palette. In this subpalette, choose the **Create** option; it expands. Next, choose the **New From Polypaint** button, refer to Figure 10-52; the flattened image is displayed in the **Texture Map** button, refer to Figure 10-53.

2. In the **Texture Map** subpalette, choose the **Clone Txtr** button, refer to Figure 10-53; the flattened image is cloned and is added to the **Texture** palette.

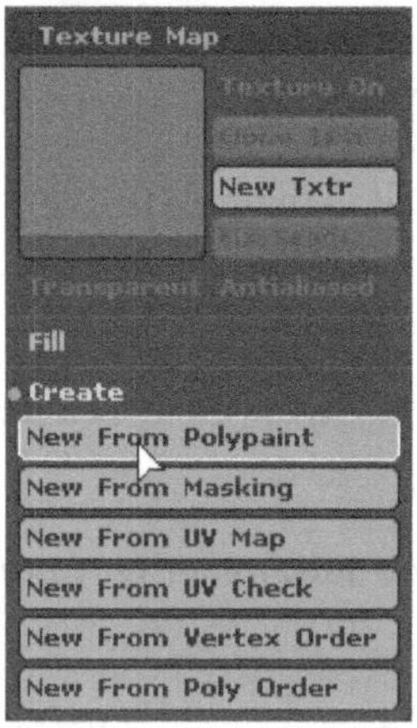

*Figure 10-52 The **New From Polypaint** button chosen*

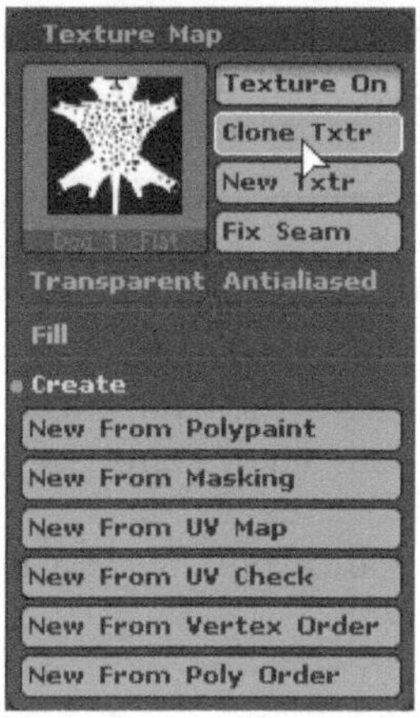

*Figure 10-53 The **Clone Txtr** button chosen*

3. In the **UV Master** subpalette, choose the **UnFlatten** button; the 3D model of the dog is displayed in the canvas.

4. In the **Texture Map** subpalette, choose the **Texture Map** button; a flyout containing different texture images is displayed. In this flyout, choose the **Dog_1_Flat** texture image, refer to Figure 10-54; the texture map is applied to the model, refer to Figure 10-45.

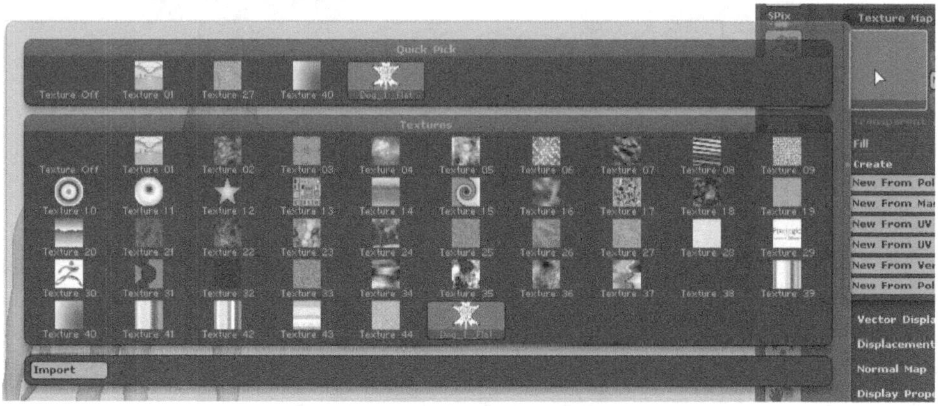

Figure 10-54 The texture image chosen from the flyout

Saving the Model

In this section, you will save the file using the steps given next.

1. Choose the **Save As** button from the **Tool** palette; the **Save ZTool** dialog box is displayed. In this dialog box, browse to the location: *\Documents\ZBrushprojects\c10*.

2. Enter **c10tut2** in the **File name** edit box and then choose the **Save** button.

Self-Evaluation Test

Answer the following questions and then compare them to those given at the end of this chapter:

1. In which of the following palettes is the **UV Master** subpalette located?

   (a) **Texture** (b) **Zplugin**
   (c) **Document** (d) **Stroke**

2. In which of the following palettes is the **Texture Map** subpalette located?

   (a) **Texture** (b) **Stroke**
   (c) **Zplugin** (d) **Tool**

3. The __________ button in the **UV Master** subpalette is used to unwrap all the subtools in the canvas and apply UV mapping to them.

4. To view the seams in a model, you need to choose the __________ button in the **UV Master** subpalette.

5. The __________ button in the **UV Master** subpalette is used to unwrap a model symmetrically.

6. The **Protect** button in the **UV Master** subpalette is used to paint the areas of the model where you do not want the seams to be created. (T/F)

7. The seams in a model determine the way in which the model unwraps. (T/F)

8. The **Density** button in the **UV Master** subpalette is used to create separate UV islands for a model if the model comprises of different polygroups. (T/F)

Review Questions

Answer the following questions:

1. Which of the following buttons is used to automatically paint the seam attracting areas of the model?

   (a) **AttractFromAmbientOccl** (b) **Attract**
   (c) **Check Seams** (d) **Enable Control Painting**

2. After unwrapping a 3D model, the __________ button in the **UV Master** subpalette is used to flatten the model and display the UV islands on a plane.

3. The __________ button in the **UV Master** subpalette is used to increase or decrease the size of the UVs while unwrapping the model.

4. The __________ button in the **UV Master** subpalette is used to copy the unwrapped UVs from the cloned model to the original model.

5. If the size of the UVs is large, the resolution of the texture will be low. (T/F)

6. To activate the **Protect** button, you need to choose the **Enable Control Painting** button in the **UV Master** subpalette. (T/F)

7. The results of the unwrap cannot be transferred from the cloned model to the original model. (T/F)

EXERCISE

The output of the model used in this exercise can be accessed by downloading the *c10_ZBrush_2022_exr.zip* from *www.cadcim.com*. The path of the file is as follows: *Textbooks > Animation and Visual Effects > Pixologic ZBrush 2022 > Pixologic ZBrush 2022: A Comprehensive Guide.*

Exercise 1

Load the *DemoHead.ZTL* file from the **Tool** tab of the **LightBox** browser and then unwrap it. Next, create a texture map and apply it to the model, as shown in Figure 10-55.

(Expected time: 20 min)

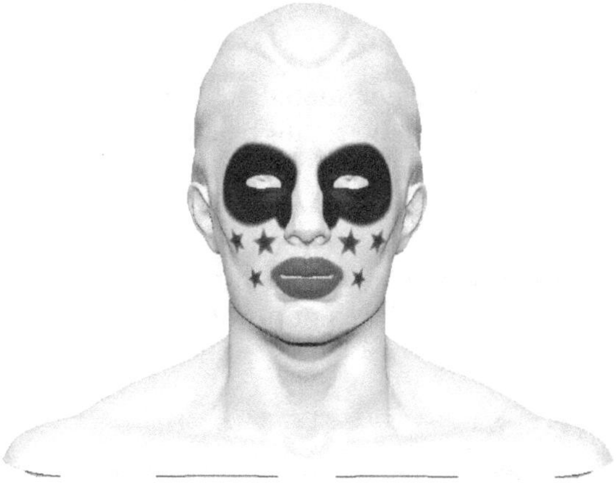

Figure 10-55 *The final output*

Answers to Self-Evaluation Test

1. b, **2.** d, **3. Unwrap All**, **4. Check Seams**, **5. Symmetry**, **6.** T, **7.** T, **8.** F

Chapter 11

Lighting

Learning Objectives

After completing this chapter, you will be able to:

- *Work with the Light palette*
- *Understand the different types of lights in ZBrush*
- *Light up a scene using the three point lighting setup*

INTRODUCTION

In this chapter, you will work with different lights in ZBrush. Lighting is used to illuminate a scene. The **Light** palette in ZBrush is used to add lights to a scene and then to manipulate them using different settings.

Light PALETTE

The **Light** palette has different settings and subpalettes that are used to manipulate the lights to produce the desired outputs, refer to Figure 11-1. Before applying the lights to a scene, you have to make sure that MatCap materials are not applied to the objects in a scene. The MatCap materials do not respond to the lights in a scene as they already have lights baked into them. Therefore, you need to apply the Standard materials to the objects in a scene before adding lights. The different settings and subpalettes in the **Light** palette are discussed next.

Load and Save

The **Save** button is used to save the different settings of a light. The **Load** button is used to load the saved light settings into a different scene. To load the saved light settings into a different scene, create different objects in the canvas, refer to Figure 11-2. Next, apply the **BasicMaterial** material to them.

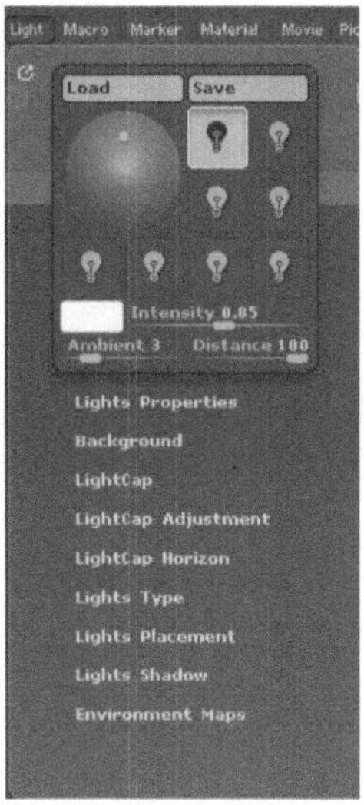

Figure 11-1 *The* ***Light*** *palette*

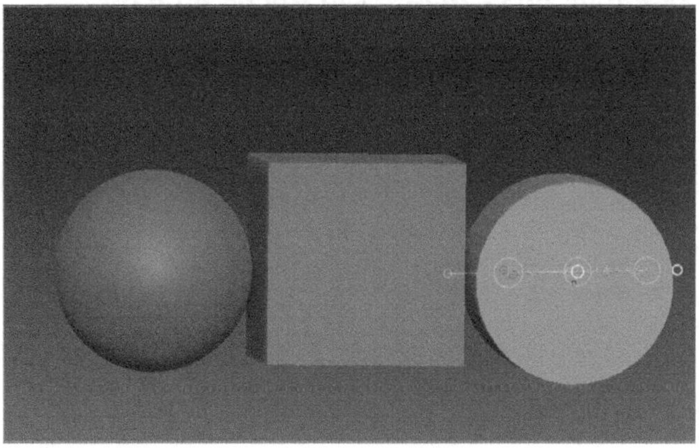

Figure 11-2 *Different objects created in the canvas*

Expand the **Light** palette. In this palette, change the color of the light to yellow by choosing the Light Color swatch, refer to Figure 11-3. Set the value of the **Intensity** and **Ambient** sliders to **6.6183** and **44**, respectively; the light settings will be applied to the scene, refer to Figure 11-4. These settings will be discussed in detail later in this chapter.

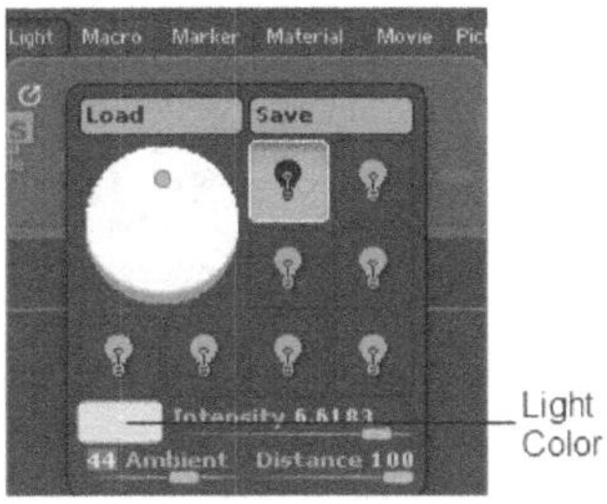

*Figure 11-3 Different settings in the **Light** palette*

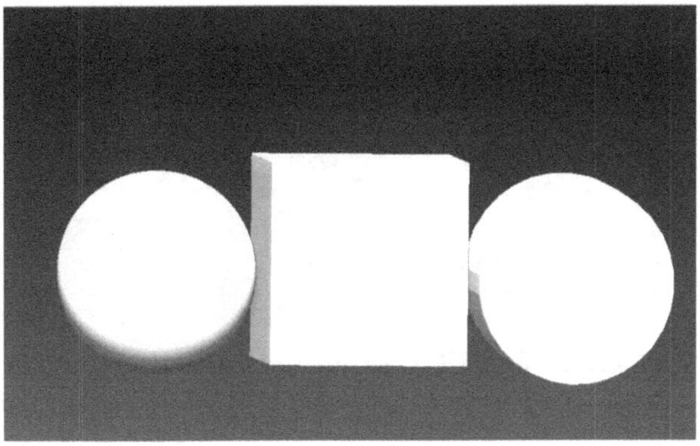

Figure 11-4 Light settings applied to the scene

Choose the **Save** button in the **Light** palette; the **Save Lights** dialog box will be displayed. In this dialog box, choose the **Save** button; the light settings will be saved with the name **ZLights.zli**, refer to Figure 11-5.

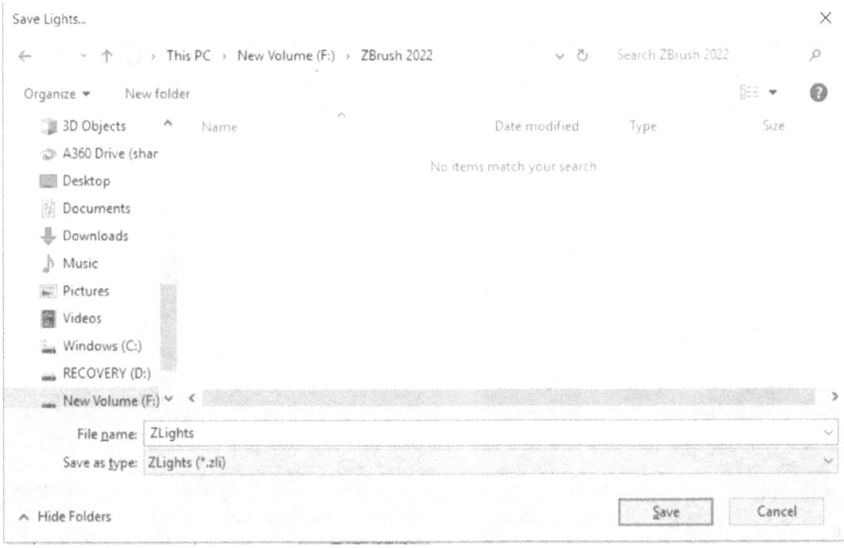

*Figure 11-5 The **Save Lights** dialog box*

Choose the **Init ZBrush** button from the **Preferences** palette; ZBrush is initialized to its default state. Next, create an object in the canvas and assign the **BasicMaterial** material to it, refer to Figure 11-6. Expand the **Light** palette. In this palette, choose the **Load** button; the **Load Lights** dialog box will be displayed. In this dialog box, choose the **Open** button; the light settings applied to the previous scene will be applied to the new scene also, refer to Figure 11-7.

*Figure 11-6 The **BasicMaterial** material applied to the object*

Figure 11-7 The light settings applied in the new scene

To save the scene with lights, you need to save the scene using the **File** palette. To do so, expand the **File** palette. In this palette, choose the **Save As** button; the **Save Project** dialog box will be displayed. In this dialog box, enter the desired name in the **File Name** text box and then choose the **Save** button. If you save the scene using the **Save As** button in the **Tool** palette, only the 3D scene will be saved and the lighting information will be lost.

Light Placement

The **Light Placement** window is used to change the position of the light in a scene. The orange dot in this window represents the position of the light. On moving this orange dot, the position of the light in the scene changes correspondingly and is reflected in the canvas area, refer to Figures 11-8 and 11-9.

*Figure 11-8 The position of light in the **Light Placement** window*

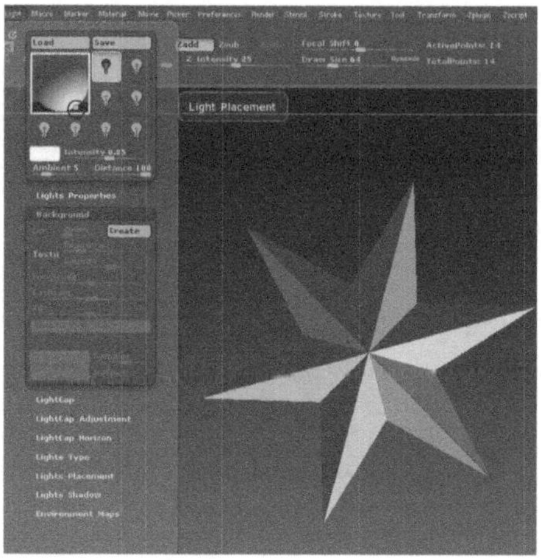

*Figure 11-9 The position of light changed in the **Light Placement** window*

Light Switches

The Light Switches are used to switch on or switch off the lights in a scene. There are eight light switches in the **Light** palette, refer to Figure 11-10. By default, only one light switch is switched on. To switch on the other lights, you need to select the light switch and then click on the bulb icon. The light that is switched on will be highlighted in the palette.

Each light has different intensity. You can change the intensity, ambient value, and the color of each light by selecting it and then setting the values as required. Figure 11-11 displays a scene with all the lights turned on.

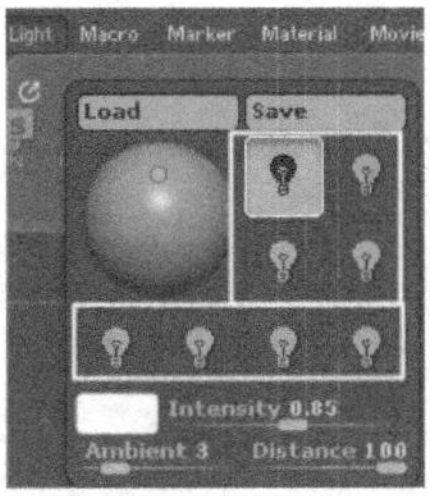

*Figure 11-10 The light switches in the **Light** palette*

Figure 11-11 The scene illuminated by switching on all the lights

Light Color

The Light Color swatch is used to change and display the color of the selected light. If you set different colors for each light, all the colors will be blended together in the scene.

Intensity

The **Intensity** slider is used to increase or decrease the brightness of a scene. The greater the value of this slider, the higher will be the brightness in the scene. Figures 11-12 and 11-13 display a scene with the value of the **Intensity** slider set to **0** and **10**, respectively.

*Figure 11-12 The scene with the value of the **Intensity** slider set to **0***

*Figure 11-13 The scene with the value of the **Intensity** slider set to **10***

Ambient

The **Ambient** slider is used to set the value of brightness in an object even if no light is present in the scene. To understand the working of this slider, turn off all the lights in the **Light** palette, refer to Figure 11-14. Next, set the value of the **Ambient** slider to **100**; the objects in the scene will be lit up without any source of light, refer to Figure 11-15.

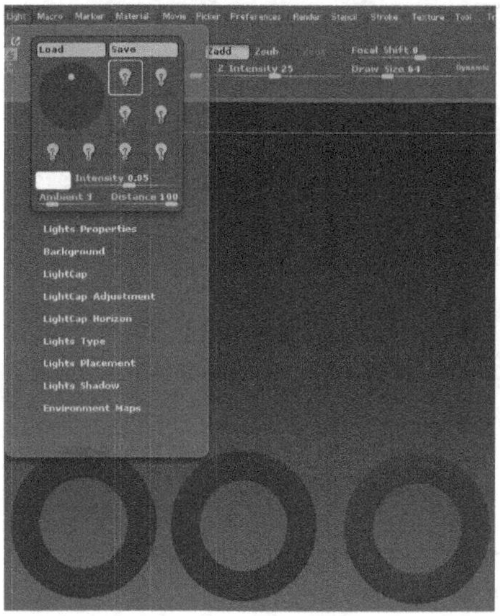

Figure 11-14 *All the lights turned off*

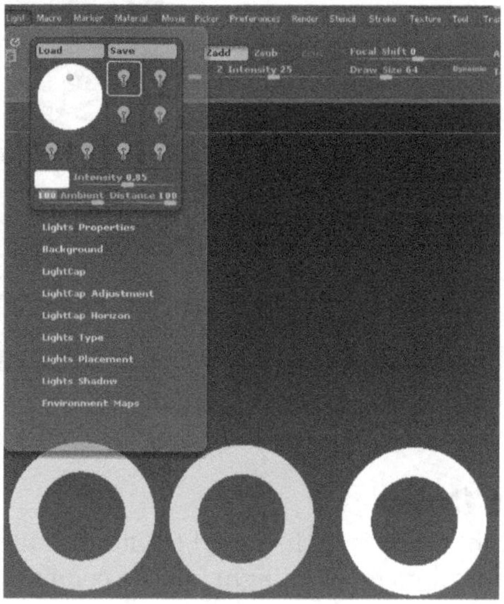

Figure 11-15 *The value of the **Ambient** slider set to **100***

Distance

The **Distance** slider is used to adjust the distance of lights from the objects in a scene. By default, the value of this slider is set to 100 which means that the light is at an infinite distance from the objects in the scene.

Lights Properties

The **Lights Properties** subpalette consists of different attributes that are used to control the shadows, the Subsurface scattering, and the intensity of the light in the scene. These attributes are discussed next.

Shadow

The **Shadow** button is used to determine whether the shadows will be cast in the scene or not. These shadows can be viewed when the scene is rendered using the **Best-Preview Render** button.

Sss

The term **Sss** stands for Subsurface scattering. Subsurface scattering is used to produce realistic renders for the materials such as skin, wax, and so on by scattering the light that penetrates into them. The **Sss** button is used to produce the realistic Sss renders. To view the results of Subsurface scattering, you need to choose the **Sss** button in the **Render Properties** subpalette of the **Render** palette. Next, you need to render the scene using the **Best-Preview Render** button. The **Render** palette will be discussed in detail later in this chapter.

Intensity Curve

The **Intensity Curve** button is used to manually control the brightness in the scene using a graph curve. To view the graph curve, click on the **Intensity Curve** button; it will expand, refer to Figure 11-16. You will notice that different buttons and sliders are located below the graph curve. These buttons and sliders are used to manipulate the graph curve as required.

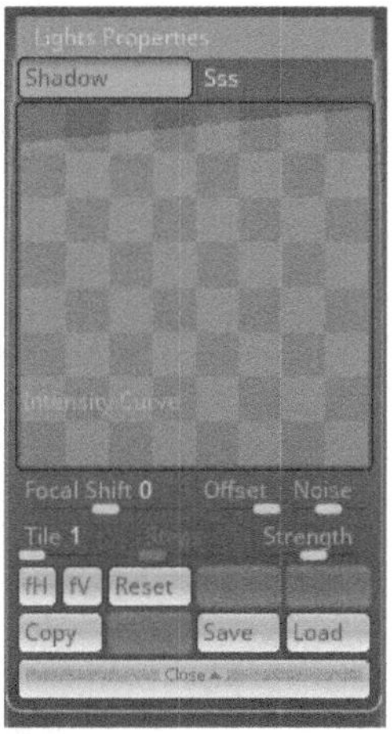

Figure 11-16 *The graph curve*

Background

The **Background** subpalette consists of different attributes that are used to create and manipulate a background image in the scene. This subpalette consists of different buttons and sliders and they are discussed next.

On

The **On** button is used to toggle the visibility of the background image. By default, this button is not activated. To activate this button, you need to load a background image using the **Environment Texture** button located below the **On** button.

On choosing the **Environment Texture** button, a flyout consisting of different texture images will be displayed, refer to Figure 11-17. Choose the desired texture image from the flyout; the image will be displayed as a background image, refer to Figure 11-18.

Figure 11-17 *The flyout displayed on choosing the* ***Environment Texture*** *button*

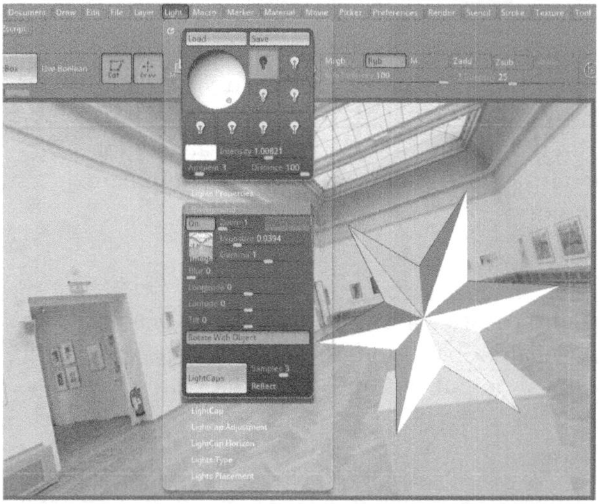

Figure 11-18 The chosen texture image displayed in the background

Zoom

The **Zoom** slider is used to adjust the zoom level of the texture image as required, refer to Figure 11-19. However, you cannot change the zoom level of the 3D Scene using this slider.

Figure 11-19 The background image zoomed in

Create

The **Create** button is used to create a colored background in the canvas. The color of the background depends upon the color that is selected in the **Back** button of the **Document** palette.

Exposure

The **Exposure** slider is used to specify an exposure value in the HDRI (High Dynamic Range Image) background image as it contains multiple exposure ranges.

Gamma

The **Gamma** slider is used to control the gamma value in the mid tones of the HDRI (High Dynamic Range Image) background image.

Blur

The **Blur** slider is used to control the blurriness of the HDRI (High Dynamic Range Image) background image.

Longitude

The **Longitude** slider is used to rotate the background image horizontally. This slider is useful in manipulating the panoramic images.

Latitude

The **Latitude** slider is used to rotate the background image vertically. This slider is useful in manipulating the panoramic background images.

Tilt

The **Tilt** slider is used to tilt the panoramic background image as required.

Rotate With Object

The **Rotate With Object** button is used to rotate the background image with the 3D object in the scene. If this button is not chosen, the background image will remain stationary on rotating the 3D object.

LightCaps

The **LightCaps** button is used to change the lighting in the 3D object according to the background image. To understand the working of this button, load different background images in the canvas using the **Environment Texture** button and then choose the **LightCaps** button; the lighting in the 3D object will change according to the background images, refer to Figures 11-20 and 11-21.

Figure 11-20 *The lighting in the sphere changed according to the* ***Texture 01*** *image*

Samples

The **Samples** slider is used to specify the number of lights in the scene when the lighting is changed using the **LightCaps** button. If the value of this slider is set to **0**, only one light will be created in the scene on choosing the **LightCaps** button, refer to Figure 11-22. If the value of this slider is set to **5**, 32 lights will be created in the scene on choosing the **LightCaps** button, refer to Figure 11-23.

***Figure 11-21** The lighting in the sphere changed according to the **Texture 24** image*

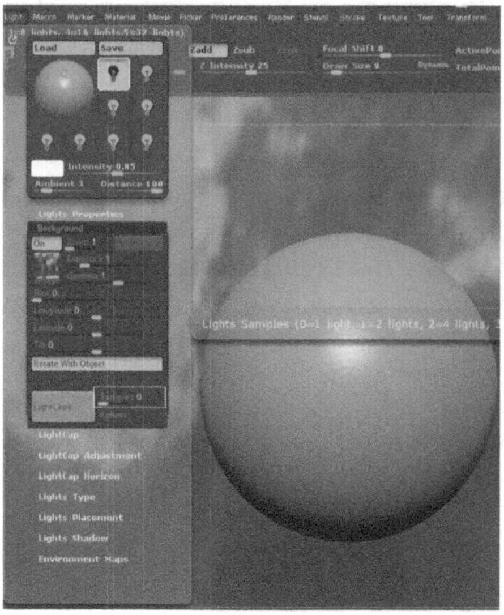

Figure 11-22** The object when the value of the **Samples** slider is set to **0

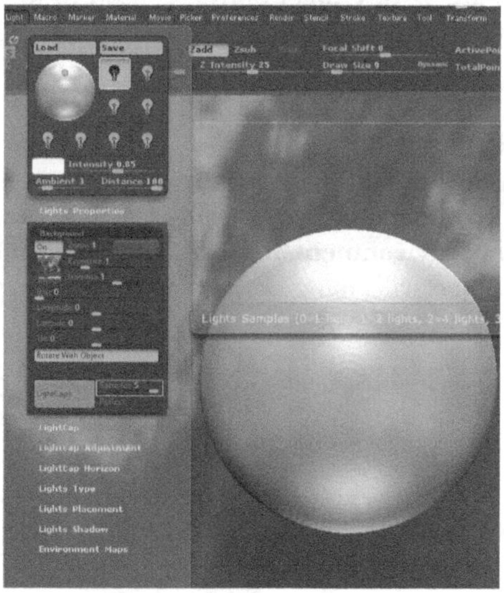

Figure 11-23** The object when the value of the **Samples** slider is set to **5

Reflect

The **Reflect** button is used to create reflections in the 3D object based on the background image. To understand the working of this button, choose the **Texture 06** texture image using the **Environment Texture** button. Next, choose the **Reflect** button and then choose the **LightCaps** button; the background image will be reflected in the 3D object, refer to Figure 11-24.

LightCap

The **LightCap** subpalette consists of attributes that are used to create a light capture using different lights and adjust different settings that can be saved and then loaded into some other scene. This subpalette consists of different buttons and sliders, refer to Figure 11-25. These buttons and sliders are discussed next.

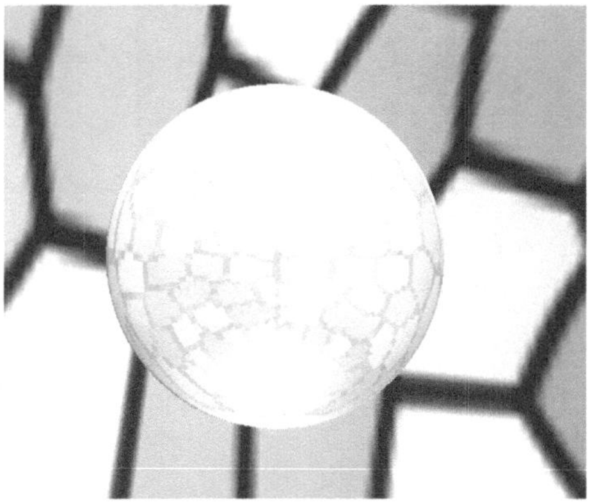

Figure 11-24 *The texture reflected in the sphere*

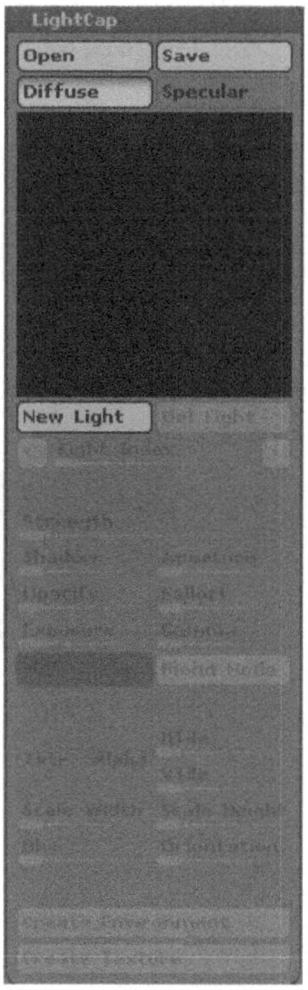

Figure 11-25 *The* ***LightCap*** *subpalette*

Open

The **Open** button is used to load a saved light capture into a scene. On choosing this button, the **Load LightCap file** dialog box will be displayed. In this dialog box, you can select the saved light captures and then load them into a scene.

Save

The **Save** button is used to save the current light capture so that it can be loaded later on.

Diffuse and Specular

The **Diffuse** and **Specular** buttons are used to independently control the diffuse lighting and specular reflections of a light capture. You can choose only one of these buttons at a time.

LightCap Preview

The **LightCap Preview** window is used to display the preview of the light capture. You can manipulate the position of the lights in the light capture by moving their corresponding red dots in the window.

New Light

The **New Light** button is used to add a light to the light capture. By default, the newly added light is positioned at the center of the **LightCap Preview** window. To create a light in the light capture, choose this button; the light will be added at the center of the **LightCap Preview** window, refer to Figure 11-26. You can add a number of lights in the light capture and change their positions in the window by moving their corresponding dots in the window, refer to Figure 11-27. In this figure, the red dot represents the currently selected light and the gray dots represent the unselected lights.

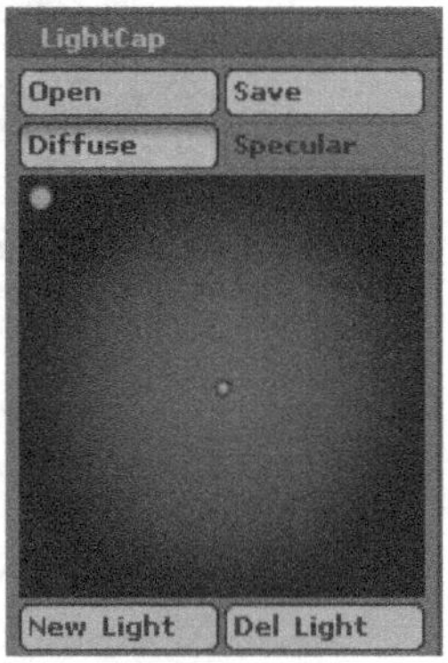

Figure 11-26 *The light added in the **LightCap Preview** window*

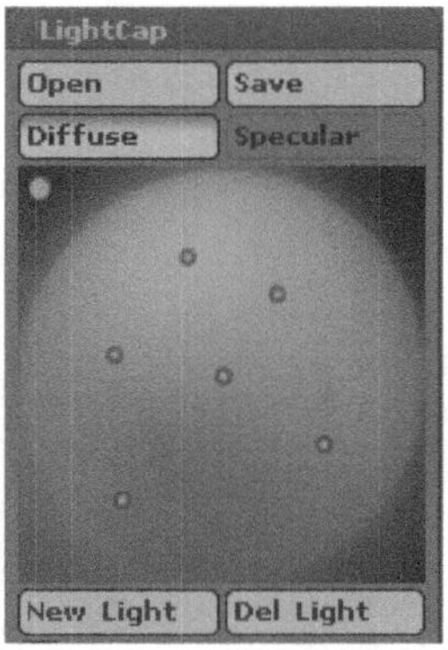

Figure 11-27 *More lights added and moved in the window*

Del Light

The **Del Light** button is used to delete lights from the light capture. The effect of deleted lights will be visible in the **LightCap Preview** window.

Light Index

The **Light Index** slider is used to scroll through different lights that have been added to the **LightCap Preview** window. On creating a new light in the light capture, the value of this slider is increased by 1. Similarly, on deleting a light from the light capture, the value of this slider is decreased by 1. If the value of this slider is set to 1, it means that there is only one light in the light capture.

Strength

The **Strength** slider is used to control the intensity of the light in the **LightCap Preview** window. The higher the value of this slider, the more will be the intensity of the light, refer to Figures 11-28 and 11-29.

Shadow

The **Shadow** slider is used to adjust the strength of the shadows that will be cast in the light capture.

Aperture

The **Aperture** slider is used to control the spread of the light in an object. The higher the value of this slider, the bigger will be the spread of light on the object, refer to Figures 11-30 and 11-31.

*Figure 11-28 The **Strength** slider set to **0.2611***

*Figure 11-29 The **Strength** slider set to **20***

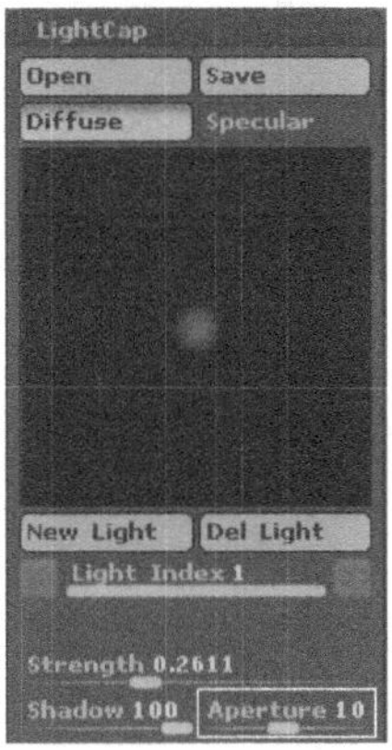

*Figure 11-30 The **Aperture** slider set to **10***

*Figure 11-31 The **Aperture** slider set to **120***

Opacity

The **Opacity** slider is used to adjust the opacity of a selected light in the light capture.

Falloff

The **Falloff** slider is used to specify the distance up to which the light spreads on an object.

Exposure

The **Exposure** slider is used to increase the amount of light that falls on an object.

Gamma

The **Gamma** slider is used to affect the contrast in the color of the light.

Color

The **Color** swatch is used to select the color that will be applied to the light, refer to Figure 11-32.

Blend Mode

The **Blend Mode** button is used to access different blending modes that determine how the currently selected light will blend with other lights. On choosing this button, a flyout consisting of different blending modes will be displayed, as shown in Figure 11-33. You can choose the required blending mode from this flyout and the output will be displayed in the **LightCap Preview** window.

Figure 11-32 The color of the light changed to red

*Figure 11-33 The flyout displayed on choosing the **Blend Mode** button*

Txtr

The **Txtr** button is used to select the texture image that will be projected on the light capture. On choosing this button, a flyout consisting of different texture images is displayed. You can choose the required texture image from this flyout and the output will be visible in the **LightCap Preview** window, refer to Figure 11-34.

Alpha

The **Alpha** button is used to select the shape of the light in the light capture. On choosing this button, a flyout consisting of different alpha images is displayed. You can choose the required alpha image to specify the shape of the light and the output will be visible in the **LightCap Preview** window, refer to Figure 11-35.

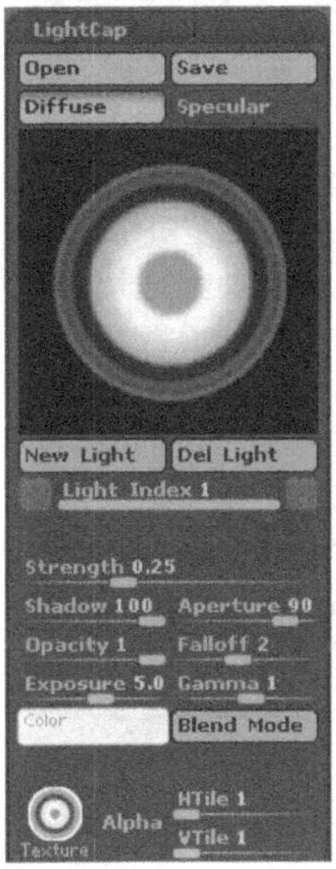

Figure 11-34 The texture image projected on the light

Figure 11-35 The shape of the light changed

HTile and VTile

The **HTile** and **VTile** sliders are used to tile the applied texture or alpha images along the horizontal and vertical axes, respectively, refer to Figure 11-36.

Scale Width and Scale Height

The **Scale Width** and **Scale Height** sliders are used to scale the applied texture or alpha images along the horizontal and vertical axes, respectively, refer to Figure 11-37.

Blur

The **Blur** slider is used to apply blur effect to the texture image that has been selected using the **Txtr** button.

Orientation

The **Orientation** slider is used to change the position and angle of the texture or alpha image that has been applied to a light.

Create Environment and Create Texture

The **Create Environment** button is used to convert the LightCap into a background texture. The background texture is automatically loaded as background in the **Background** subpalette.

The **Create Texture** button is used to create a texture of the lights that have been added to the LightCap system. This texture will be available in the **Texture** palette for use with any **MatCap** material.

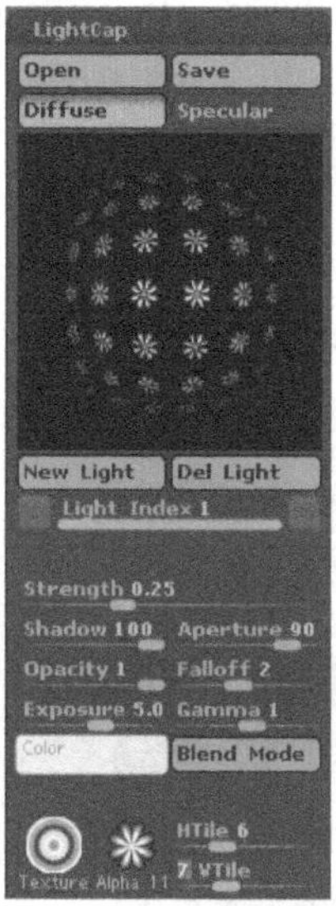

*Figure 11-36 The tiling displayed in the **LightCap Preview** window*

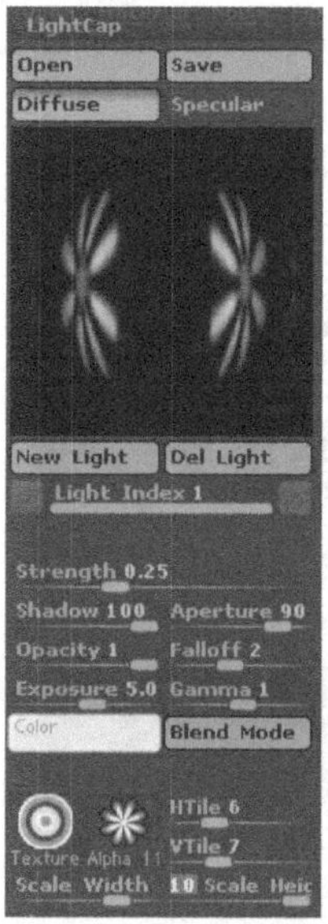

*Figure 11-37 Displaying the scaled texture in the **LightCap Preview** window*

LightCap Adjustment

The **LightCap Adjustment** subpalette is used to globally adjust the settings of the entire light capture and not of the single lights in the light capture. The different settings in the **LightCap** subpalette enable you to manipulate each light in the light capture individually by selecting a particular light and applying the settings to it. By default, the different settings in the **LightCap Adjustment** subpalette are deactivated. These settings are activated only if a light capture is created using the **LightCap** subpalette. The different settings in the **LightCap Adjustment** subpalette are discussed next.

Exposure

The **Exposure** slider is used to globally adjust the amount of light in a light capture once it has been created.

Gamma

The **Gamma** slider is used to globally adjust the gamma values of the light capture.

Hue

The **Hue** slider is used to change the global color tint of the light capture.

Saturation

The **Saturation** slider is used to control the amount of the color in the entire light capture. If the value of this slider is low, the light capture will turn grayscale.

Intensity
The **Intensity** slider is used to adjust the global intensity of the light capture.

Retain Highlights
The **Retain Highlights** slider is used to specify whether the specular highlights will be visible in the light capture or not.

Use Material Curves
If this button is chosen, you can change the diffuse and specular curve information by using the Standard Material Shaders.

LightCap Horizon
The **LightCap Horizon** subpalette consists of attributes that are used to adjust the position of the entire light capture. This subpalette consists of different settings that are discussed next.

Longitude
The **Longitude** slider is used to rotate the entire light capture along a horizontal axis.

Latitude
The **Latitude** slider is used to rotate the entire light capture along the vertical axis.

Horizon Opacity
The **Horizon Opacity** slider is used to adjust the opacity of the horizon line that is created in the light capture. To understand the working of this slider, create a sphere in the canvas and assign any Standard material to it. Next, expand the **LightCap** subpalette in the **Light** palette and create a light capture by clicking on the **New Light** button thrice; the light capture will be applied to the scene, refer to Figure 11-38.

Expand the **LightCap Horizon** subpalette. In this subpalette, move the **Horizon Opacity** slider toward right; a horizon line will be displayed in the scene, refer to Figure 11-39. On moving this slider toward left, the opacity of the horizon line will decrease.

C1, C2, C3, and C4
The **C1**, **C2**, **C3**, and **C4** color swatches are used to select the colors that will be applied to the light capture starting from top to bottom of the horizon line, refer to Figure 11-40.

The **O1**, **O2**, **O3**, and **O4** sliders located next to the **C1**, **C2**, **C3**, and **C4** color swatches, respectively, are used to increase or decrease the fall off of the colors.

Rate Top and Rate Bot
The **Rate Top** slider is used to specify the offset of the color at the top of the horizon line. The **Rate Bot** slider is used to specify the offset of the color at the bottom of the horizon line, refer to Figure 11-41.

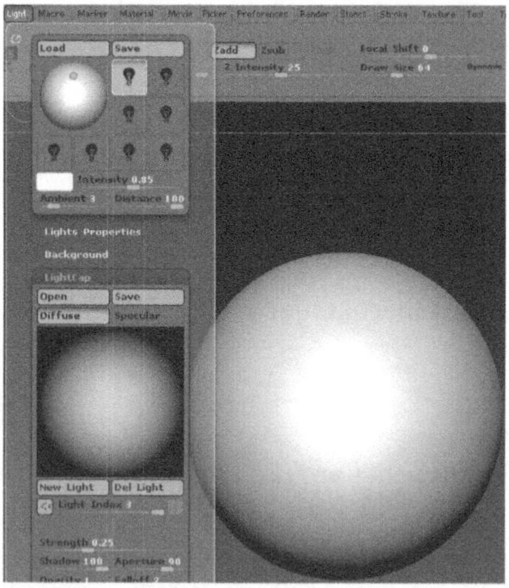

Figure 11-38 The light capture applied to the scene

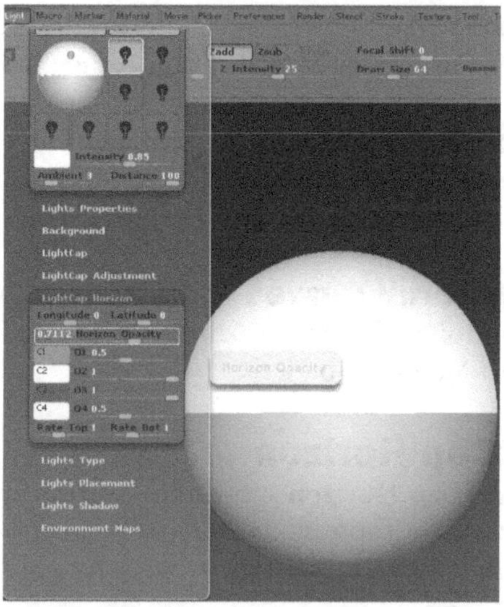

Figure 11-39 The opacity of the horizon line increased

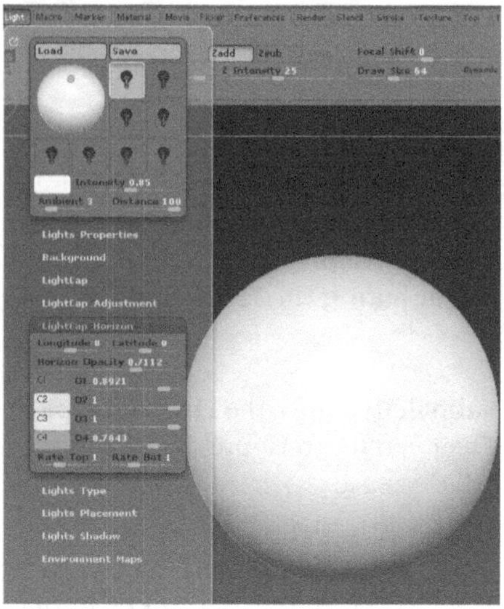

Figure 11-40 Four different colors applied to the light capture

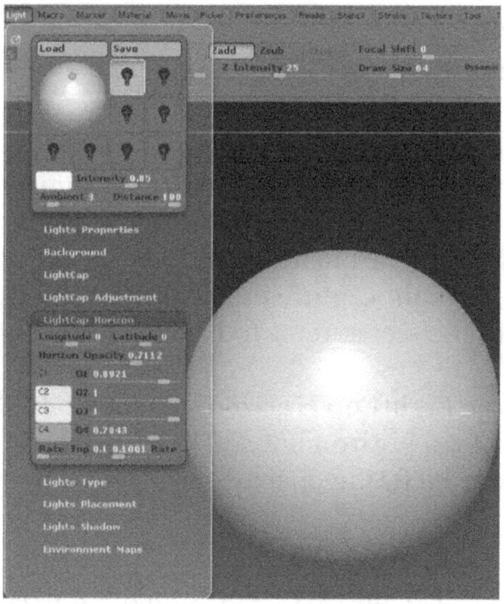

Figure 11-41 The offset of the top and bottom colors increased

Lights Type

The options in the **Lights Type** subpalette are used to select the light that will be applied to the scene. There are five types of lights available in this subpalette. These lights are discussed next.

Sun

The **Sun** button is used to produce the sun light effect. In this light, the emitted rays are parallel to each other.

Point

The **Point** button is used to produce the effect of light emitted from a single source of light. In this light, the light rays are cast in all directions.

Spot

The **Spot** button is used to focus the light on a particular object. In this light, the light rays are projected in the shape of a cone.

Glow

The **Glow** button is used to illuminate the objects equally without depending on the direction of the light.

Radial

The **Radial** button is used to illuminate those areas of the object that face away from the light source.

Lights Placement

The **Lights Placement** subpalette is used to change the position of the light in a scene. However, the settings in this subpalette do not work for the **Sun** light. This subpalette consists of a picker button **P**, refer to Figure 11-42. This picker button is also known as Local Light Position Selector button. The picker button enables you to pick the position of the point light, spot light, or glow light from the canvas. On picking the position of required light from the canvas, the value of the **X Pos**, **Y Pos**, and **Z Pos** sliders will change according to the picked position of the light. To pick the position of the light from the canvas, choose the required light from the **Lights Type** subpalette. Make sure you do not select the **Sun** light.

Next, click on the **P** button in the **Lights Placement** subpalette and then drag the cursor on the canvas; the shape of the cursor will change and the values in the **X Pos**, **Y Pos**, and **Z Pos** sliders will also change, refer to Figure 11-43. The **Radius** slider is used to specify the radius of the selected light.

Lights Shadow

The **Lights Shadow** subpalette is used to control the shadows that are cast by the selected light. This subpalette consists of different settings that are discussed next.

Intensity

The **Intensity** slider is used to control the strength of the shadow that is cast by a selected light.

Shadow Curve

The **Shadow Curve** graph is used to control the way the shadows fade in a scene. The fading of the shadows is visible only when the scene is rendered using the **BPR** renderer.

Length

The **Length** slider is used to specify the length of the shadow that is cast by the selected light.

ZMode

The **ZMode** button is used to match the shape of the shadow with the shape of the object in the canvas. If the part of the object is not visible in the canvas, the **ZMode** button creates the shadow of the complete object including the part of the object that is not visible in the canvas.

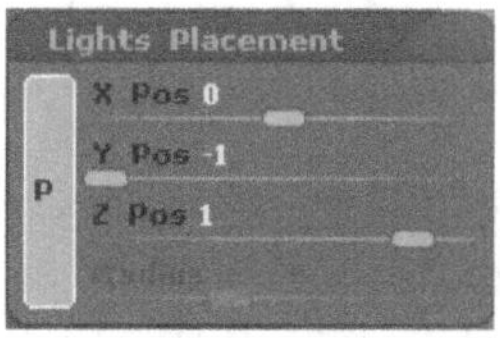

Figure 11-42 The ***Lights Placement*** *subpalette*

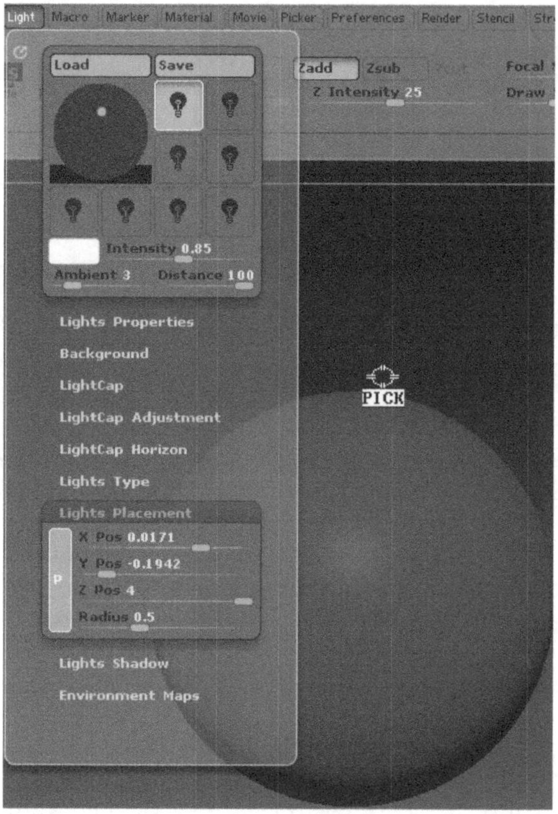

Figure 11-43 The values of the ***X Pos, Y Pos,*** *and* ***Z Pos*** *sliders updated*

Uni

The **Uni** slider is used to reduce the noise in the shadow cast by a light. The higher the value of this slider, the lesser will be the noise in the shadows.

Blur

The **Blur** slider is used to blur the shadows cast by the selected light. The higher the value of this slider, the greater will be the amount of blur in the shadows.

Rays

The **Rays** slider is used to increase the accuracy of the shadows. However, this slider increases the render time. The higher the value of this slider, the greater will be the accuracy of the shadows cast by the selected light.

Aperture

The **Aperture** slider is used to specify whether the shadows cast by the light will have sharp edges or blurred edges. The higher the value of this slider, the more blurred will be the images in the edges of the shadows.

Environment Maps

The **Environment Maps** subpalette is used to control the global illumination of the environment in a scene. This subpalette allows you to specify different settings that are discussed next.

Gdm

The term Gdm stands for Global Diffuse Map. The **Gdm** button is used to select the image that will be used in diffuse shading of the environment in the scene. On choosing this button, a flyout consisting of different texture images will be displayed. You need to choose the texture image of your choice and the colors in the texture image will be used for the diffuse shading of the environment in the scene.

Gsm

The term Gsm stands for Global Specular Map. The **Gsm** button is used to select the image that will be used in the specular lighting of the environment in the scene. On choosing this button, a flyout consisting of different texture images will be displayed. You need to choose the texture image of your choice. This texture image will be used for the specular lighting of the environment in the scene.

Gdi

The term Gdi stands for Global Diffuse Intensity. The **Gdi** slider is used to adjust the strength of diffuse shading in the environment.

Gsi

The term Gsi stands for Global Specular Intensity. The **Gsi** slider is used to adjust the strength of specular lighting in the environment.

TUTORIAL

Before you start the tutorial of this chapter, navigate to *\Documents\ZBrushprojects* and then create a new folder with the name *c11*.

Tutorial 1

In this tutorial, you will apply three point lighting to a model. The final output of the lighting is shown in Figure 11-44. **(Expected time: 20 min)**

The following steps are required to complete this tutorial:

a. Create the key light.
b. Create the fill light.
c. Create the back light and render the scene.
d. Save the scene.

Creating the Key Light

In this section, you will create a key light. The key light is the main source of illumination in the scene.

1. Choose the **Init ZBrush** button from the **Preferences** palette; the message box is displayed. Choose the **Yes** button from the message box; ZBrush is initialized to its default state.

2. Choose the **Ryan_Kingslien_Anatomy_Model.ZTL** file from the **Tool** tab of the **LightBox** browser by double-clicking on it. Next, drag the cursor in the canvas area; the model is displayed in the canvas.

3. Choose the **Edit** button in the top shelf to switch to the edit mode.

4. Choose the Current Material button from the left shelf; a flyout consisting of different types of materials is displayed. In this flyout, choose the **FastShader** material; the material is applied to the model, refer to Figure 11-45.

   In order to access the **Light** palette easily, you need to dock the **Light** palette in the right or left tray.

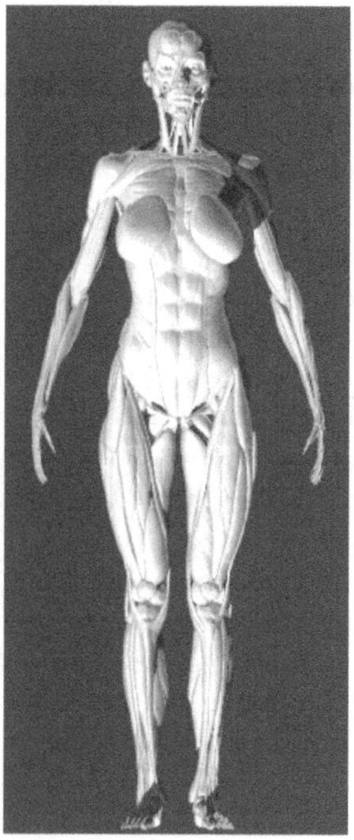

Figure 11-44 *The output after applying lights*

5. Expand the **Light** palette and hover the cursor on the arrow located at the top left corner of the palette; the shape of cursor changes, refer to Figure 11-46. Next, drag the cursor toward the right tray; the **Light** palette is docked in the right tray and can be easily accessed.

6. In the **Light** palette, make sure the first light switch is turned on, refer to Figure 11-46.

7. Select the orange dot on the **Light Placement** window and drag it to the location, as shown in Figure 11-47.

8. Set the **Intensity** slider to **1**, refer to Figure 11-47.

9. In the **Light** palette, expand the **Light Properties** subpalette and choose the **Shadow** button, if not already chosen, refer to Figure 11-48.

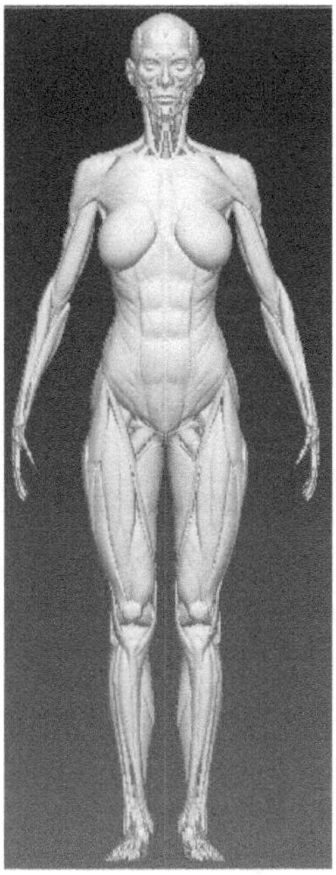

Figure 11-45 *The **FastShader** material applied to the model*

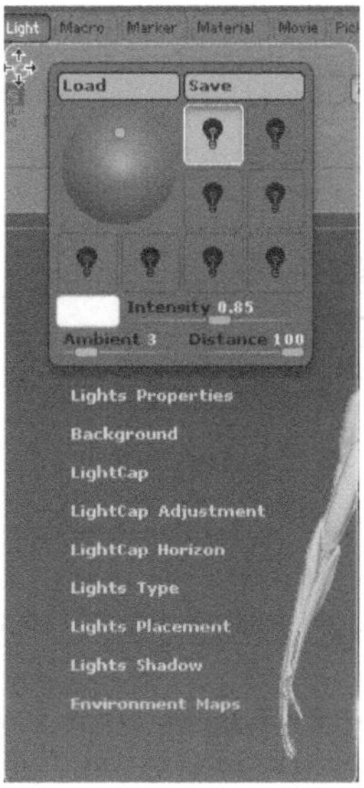

Figure 11-46 *The **Light** palette*

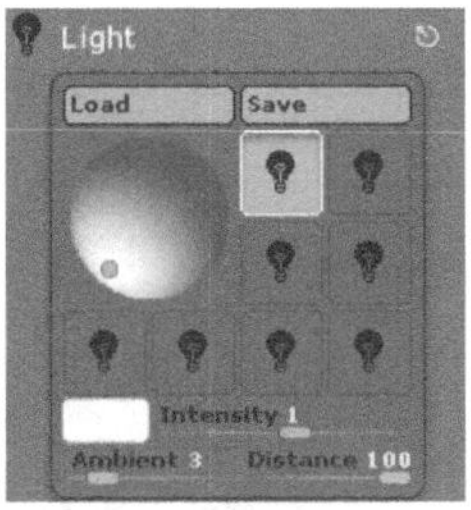

Figure 11-47 *The key light positioned in the **Light Placement** window*

Figure 11-48 *The **Shadow** button chosen*

10. Expand the **Lights Type** subpalette in the **Light** palette. In this subpalette, choose the **Sun** button to activate the sunlight, if not already chosen, refer to Figure 11-49; the key light is created.

Creating the Fill Light

In this section, you will create a fill light. The fill light is used to fill the shadows generated by the key light to make the object more visible.

1. Double-click on the second light switch to activate the second light. Make sure the light switch turns orange when you click on it.

2. Select the orange dot on the **Light Placement** window and drag it to the position, as shown in Figure 11-50.

3. Choose the Light Color swatch located below the light switches and choose light red shade from the color picker. Next, set the value of the **Intensity** slider to **0.5**, refer to Figure 11-50.

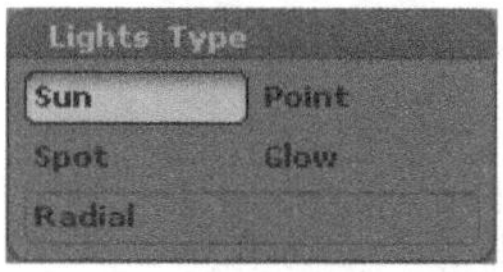

Figure 11-49 *The* ***Sun*** *button chosen*

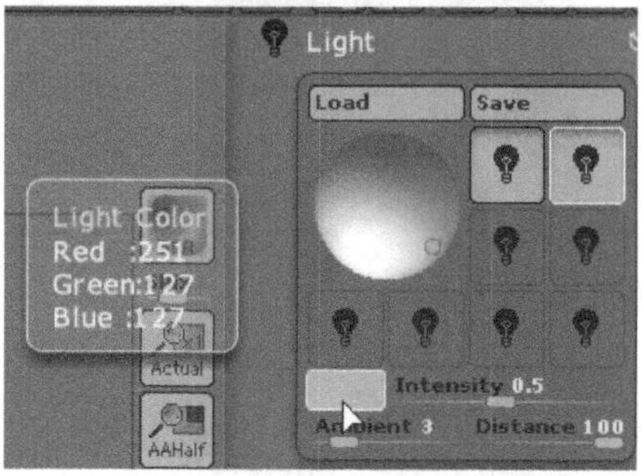

Figure 11-50 *The fill light positioned in the* ***Light Placement*** *window with its color changed*

4. Expand the **Lights Type** subpalette in the **Light** palette. In this subpalette, choose the **Spot** button to activate the spot light, refer to Figure 11-51; the fill light is created.

Creating the Back Light and Rendering the Scene

In this section, you will create a back light. The back light is used to separate the object in the scene from the background.

1. Double-click on the third light switch to activate the third light. Make sure the light switch turns orange.

2. Select the orange dot on the **Light Placement** window and drag it to the position, as shown in Figure 11-52.

3. Set the value of the **Intensity** slider to **0.3**, refer to Figure 11-52.

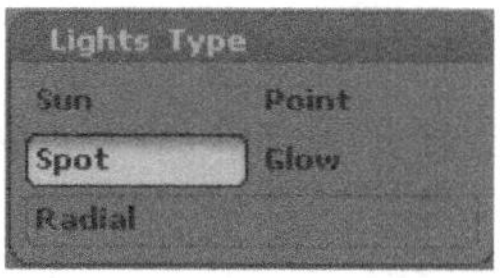

Figure 11-51 *The* ***Spot*** *button chosen*

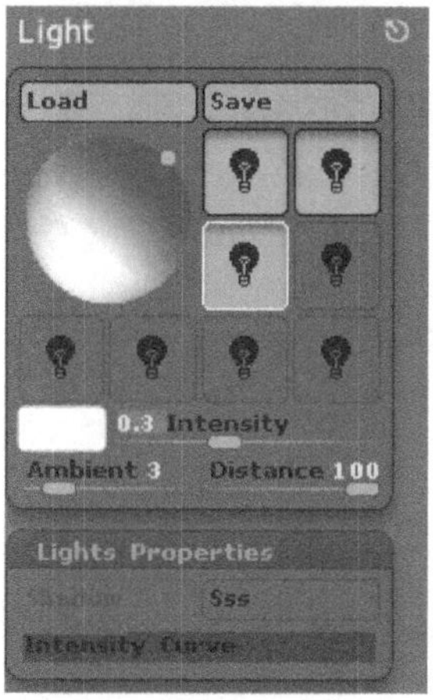

Figure 11-52 *The back light positioned in the* ***Light Placement*** *window*

4. Expand the **Lights Type** subpalette in the **Light** palette. In this subpalette, choose the **Spot** button to activate the spot light; the back light is created.

5. Expand the **Background** subpalette in the **Light** palette. In this subpalette, choose the **Create** button to create the panoramic background, refer to Figure 11-53.

6. Choose the **BPR** button in the right shelf; the model is rendered, as shown in Figure 11-54.

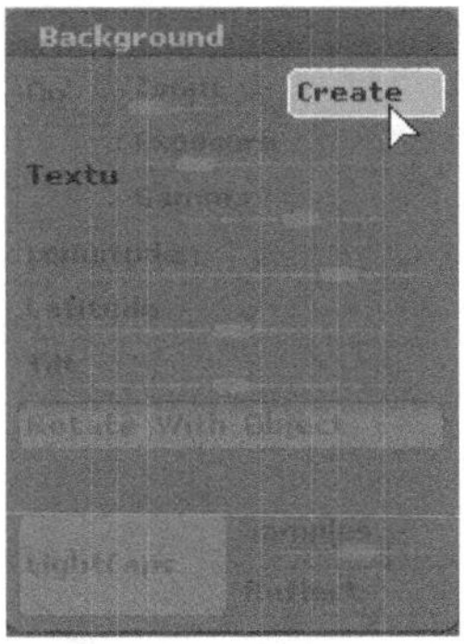

*Figure 11-53 The **Create** button chosen in the **Background** subpalette*

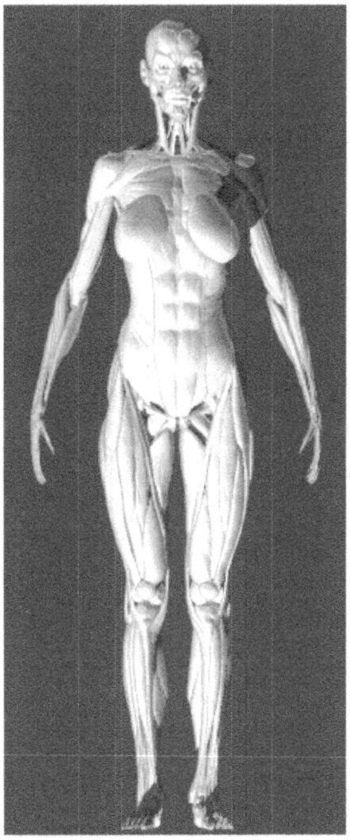

*Figure 11-54 The model rendered using the **BPR** renderer*

Saving the File

In this section, you will save the file using the steps given next.

1. Choose the **Save As** button from the **File** palette; the **Save Project** dialog box is displayed. In this dialog box, browse to the location: *\Documents\ZBrushprojects\c11*.

2. Enter **c11tut1** in the **File name** edit box and then choose the **Save** button.

Self-Evaluation Test

Answer the following questions and then compare them to those given at the end of this chapter:

1. Which of the following types of lights is used to illuminate the areas of the object that face away from the light source?

   (a) **Radial** (b) **Sun**
   (c) **Glow** (d) **Point**

2. Which of the following sliders in the **Lights Shadow** subpalette is used to reduce the noise in the shadow cast by a light?

   (a) **Aperture** (b) **Uni**
   (c) **Blur** (d) **Rays**

3. The term Sss stands for __________.

4. The __________ subpalette in the **Light** palette is used to change the position of the light in a scene.

5. The __________ subpalette in the **Light** palette is used to control the shadows that are cast by the selected light.

6. The term Gsi stands for __________.

7. The **Latitude** slider in the **LightCap Horizon** subpalette of the **Light** palette is used to rotate the entire light capture along the horizontal axis. (T/F)

8. There are four light switches in the **Light** palette. (T/F)

9. The **LightCap Adjustment** subpalette in the **Light** palette is used to adjust the settings of the entire light capture globally and not just the single light in the light capture. (T/F)

Review Questions

Answer the following questions:

1. In which of the following subpalettes of the **Light** palette is the **LightCap Preview** window located?

   (a) **LightCap Adjustment** (b) **LightCap Horizon**
   (c) **Lights Placement** (d) **LightCap**

2. The __________ slider in the **LightCap Horizon** subpalette is used to adjust the opacity of the horizon line that is created in the light capture.

3. The __________ slider in the **LightCap** subpalette is used to scroll between different lights that have been added to the **LightCap Preview** window.

4. The __________ subpalette in the **Light** palette is used to create and manipulate a background image in the scene.

5. The **Background** subpalette in the **Light** palette is used to control the global illumination of the environment in a scene. (T/F)

6. The **Hue** slider in the **LightCap Adjustment** subpalette is used to change the global color tint of the light capture. (T/F)

7. The Standard materials do not respond to the lights in a scene as they already have lights baked into them. (T/F)

EXERCISE

The output of the model used in this exercise can be accessed by downloading the *c11_ZBrush_2022_exr.zip* from *www.cadcim.com*. The path of the file is as follows : *Textbooks > Animation and Visual Effects > Pixologic ZBrush 2022 > Pixologic ZBrush 2022: A Comprehensive Guide.*

Exercise 1

Load the *DemoHead.ZTL* file from the **Tool** tab of the **LightBox** browser and then light it up using the three point lighting set up, as shown in Figure 11-55. **(Expected time: 20 min)**

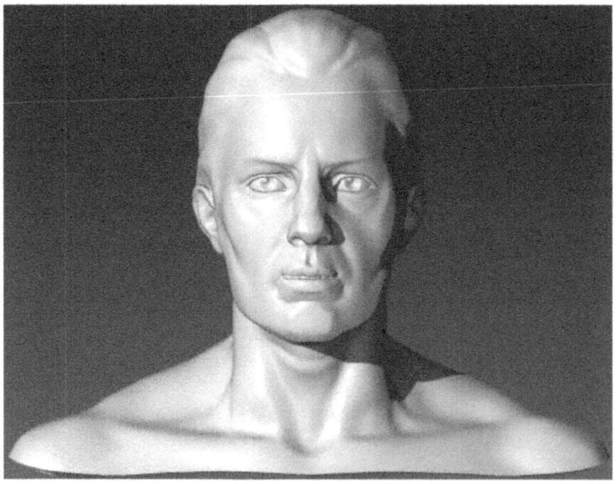

Figure 11-55 *The final output*

Answers to Self-Evaluation Test

1. a, **2.** b, **3.** Subsurface scattering, **4. Lights Placement**, **5. Lights Shadow**, **6.** Global Specular Intensity, **7.** F, **8.** F, **9.** T

Chapter 12

Rendering

Learning Objectives

After completing this chapter, you will be able to:

- *Work with the Render palette*
- *Generate render passes for compositing*

INTRODUCTION

In this chapter, you will work with different render settings in ZBrush. Rendering is a process of generating a 2D image for a 3D or 2.5D scene created in ZBrush. Rendering helps in visualizing the lighting effects, materials, and other settings that have been applied to a scene. ZBrush provides several ways to render both 2D and 3D scenes.

KeyShot Renderer

KeyShot is a rendering software developed by the company Luxion. KeyShot allows you to create your own lights as well as materials in order to have full control over rendering. In order to render ZBrush models using the KeyShot renderers, you need to install KeyShot in your system. Also, you need to make sure that ZBrush to KeyShort Bridge is working. In ZBrush, all rendering options are available in the **Render** palette. These options enable you to control the different render settings in a scene. The **Render** palette is discussed next.

Render PALETTE

The **Render** palette consists of different buttons and subpalettes that are used to generate a 2D image for a 3D or 2.5D scene created in ZBrush. The **Render** palette consists of four types of rendering modes, namely, **Best**, **Preview**, **Fast**, and **Flat**. These rendering modes enable you to render both 3D and 2.5D scenes. In addition to this, there is another rendering mode namely **BPR** (Best Preview Render). This type of rendering works only for 3D scenes in the edit mode. The 2.5D scenes cannot be rendered in this mode. The different options and the subpalettes in the **Render** palette are discussed next.

Cursor

The **Cursor** button is used to render only the selected part of a scene. To render the selected part of a scene, create a scene in the canvas. Next, expand the **Render** palette. In this palette, press and hold the **Cursor** button and drag the cursor to the area that you want to render, refer to Figure 12-1; the selected area will be rendered, refer to Figure 12-2.

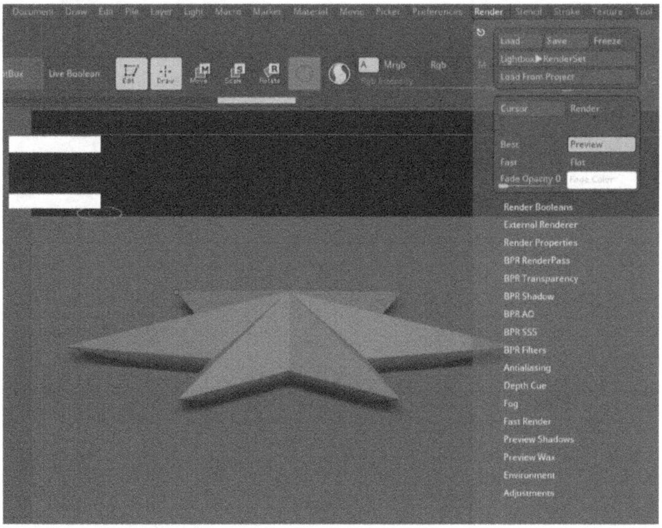

__Figure 12-1__ The area to be rendered selected using the __Cursor__ button

Figure 12-2 The selected area of the scene rendered

Render

The **Render** button is used to render the entire scene in the canvas using any of the selected rendering modes.

Best

The **Best** button is used to render both 3D and 2.5D scenes in the best preview mode. On rendering a scene using this button, the different attributes such as shadows, reflections, anti-aliasing, and so on are added to the final rendered images. These attributes can be modified as required using different options in the **Render** palette. To understand the process of rendering both the 3D and 2.5D scenes in the best preview mode, choose the **Load Tool** button from the **Tool** palette; the **Load ZTool** dialog box will be displayed. In this dialog box, browse to *\Documents\ZBrushprojects* and select the *Kotelnikoff.ZPR* file in it. Next, append a plane below it using the **SubTool** subpalette of the **Tool** palette, refer to Figure 12-3. Expand the **Render** palette. In this palette, choose the **Best** button; the scene will be rendered, as shown in Figure 12-4.

Preview

The **Preview** button is used to render both the 3D and 2.5D scenes in the preview mode. In this rendering mode, the rendered image remains same as that of the scene in the canvas with no additional attributes applied on it.

Fast

The **Fast** button is used to render both the 3D and 2.5D scenes in the fast preview mode. In this rendering mode, the different material attributes that have been applied to the scene are not displayed in the final rendered image, refer to Figure 12-5. Moreover, this mode enables you to generate the render image quickly.

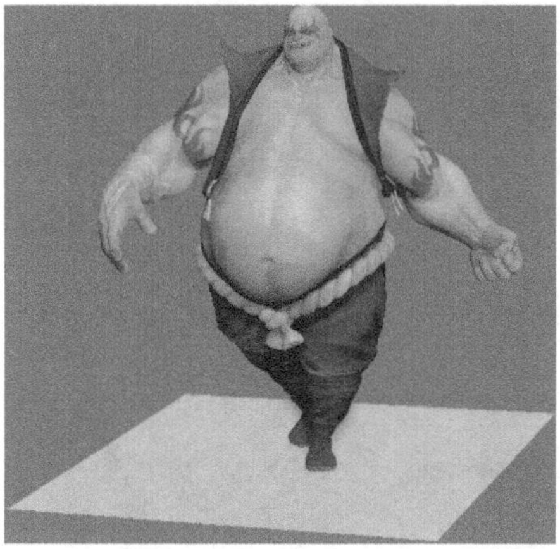

Figure 12-3 The plane placed below the model

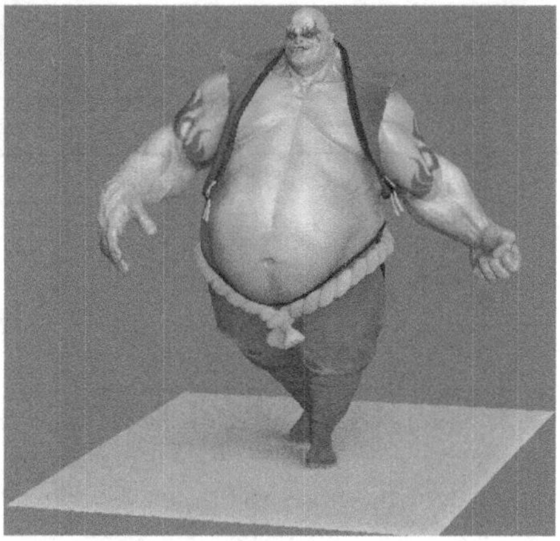

*Figure 12-4 The scene rendered using the **Best** button*

Flat

The **Flat** button is used to render both the 3D and 2.5D scenes in the flat preview mode. In the flat preview mode, the different colors and materials applied to the scene are not displayed in the rendered image and the image appears flat, refer to Figure 12-6.

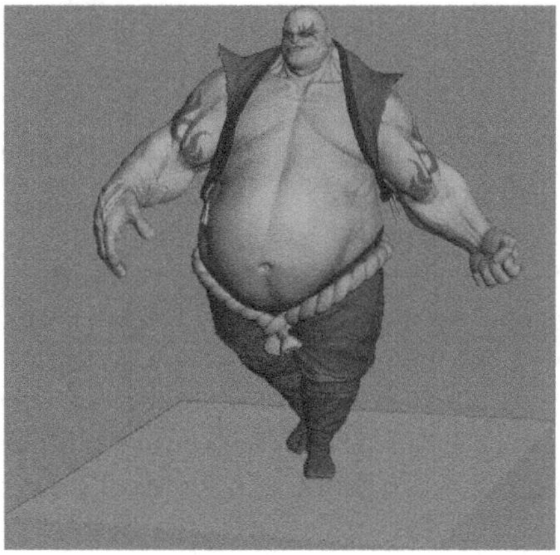

*Figure 12-5 The scene rendered using the **Fast** button*

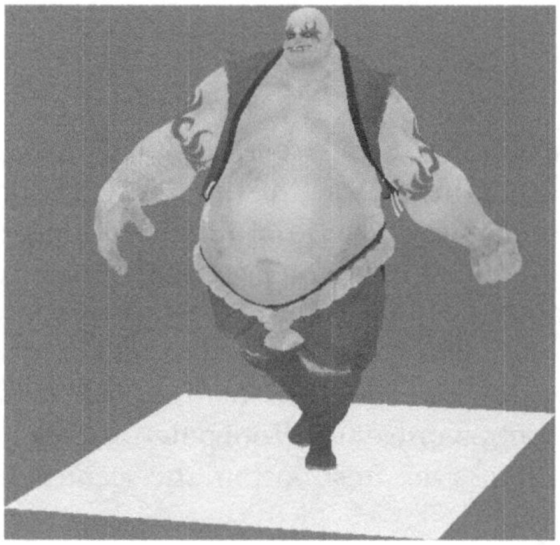

*Figure 12-6 The scene rendered using the **Flat** button*

Render Booleans

The **Render Booleans** subpalette consists of different buttons and sliders that are used to check topology issues and errors during boolean operation.

External Renderer

The **External Renderer** subpalette consists of different buttons and sliders that are used to adjust different attributes in the keyshot rendered image. These buttons and sliders are discussed next.

KeyShot

The **KeyShot** button is used to enable the bridge between ZBrush and KeyShot. When the **KeyShot** button is chosen, ZBrush will automatically render the model to the KeyShot renderer. If disabled, ZBrush will use its own BPR renderer.

Max Faces

You can split the current model into smaller parts by using the **Max Faces** slider. The higher the value specified using this slider, the larger parts will be sent to KeyShot for rendering. This may lead to slowing down of the rendering process.

Auto Merge

The **Auto Merge** slider is used to weld all the parts to rebuild the models as they were originally in ZBrush. As ZBrush can send large amounts of data to KeyShot, the information usually needs to be split into smaller chunks to speed up the bridging process.

Group by Materials

You can create a separate group for each ZBrush material by using the **Group by Materials** slider. These groups are simply defined by the materials in ZBrush. After the model is sent to KeyShot, you need to drag the material from the KeyShot library onto any part of the model. On doing so, the selected material will be applied to the different parts of the model. When the **Group by Materials** option is disabled, each model will become independent and dragging a material from the KeyShot library onto the model will affect only the respective model.

Send Document Color

Using this slider, you can instruct KeyShot to set its own document background color to match the ZBrush document.

Render Properties

The **Render Properties** subpalette consists of different buttons and sliders that are used to adjust different attributes in the rendered image. Most commonly used buttons and sliders are discussed next.

Details

The **Details** slider is used to improve the quality of the render when a light capture is created from the background image in the scene. It also helps in creating highly dynamic range environment map,s thus increasing the quality of the render.

3D Posterize

The **3D Posterize** slider is used to generate a cartooned render of a scene. On increasing the value of this slider, the level of posterization or cartoon effect in a scene will increase, refer to Figure 12-7.

Exp

The **Exp** slider is used to adjust the amount of roll off that will be received by the 3D posterization.

SmoothNormals

The **SmoothNormals** button is used to smoothen the hard edges on the surface of an object when it is rendered using the **BPR** renderer. Before choosing this button, you need to make sure that the **BPR Smooth Normals Render Mode** button in the **Display Properties** subpalette of the **Tool** palette is chosen, refer to Figure 12-8.

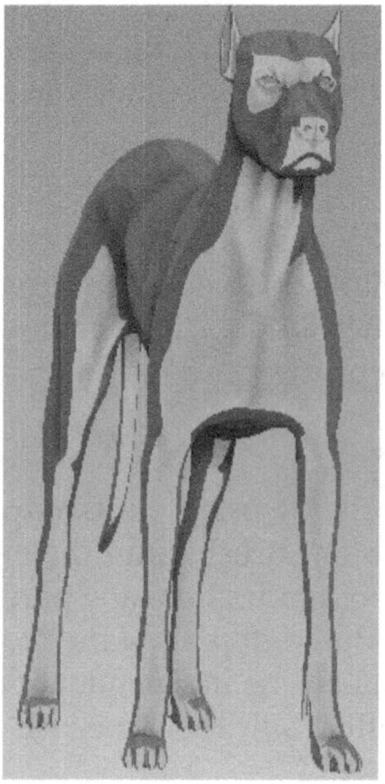

Figure 12-7 The cartoon effect applied to a model

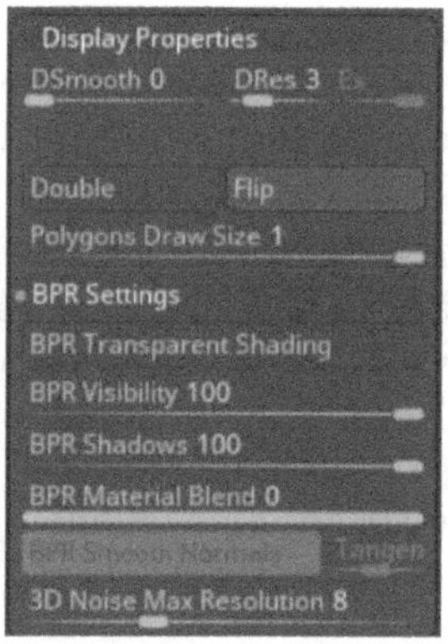

Figure 12-8 *The* ***BPR Smooth Normals Render Mode*** *button chosen*

Draw Micromesh

The **Draw Micromesh** button is used to replace the polygons of an object or the fibers of a fibermesh with a new geometry when the object is rendered using the **BPR** renderer. To replace the polygons of an object, create a sphere in the canvas, refer to Figure 12-9. After choosing the **Edit** button from the top shelf, convert the sphere into a polymesh.

Figure 12-9 *A sphere created in the canvas*

Expand the **Geometry** subpalette in the **Tool** palette. In this subpalette, expand the **Modify Topology** area. Next, choose the **Micro Mesh** button from this area; a flyout will be displayed, refer to Figure 12-10. In this flyout, choose the **PolyMesh3D** primitive or any other primitive of your choice; a message box prompting you to choose the **Draw Micromesh** button in the **Render** palette will be displayed, refer to Figure 12-11.

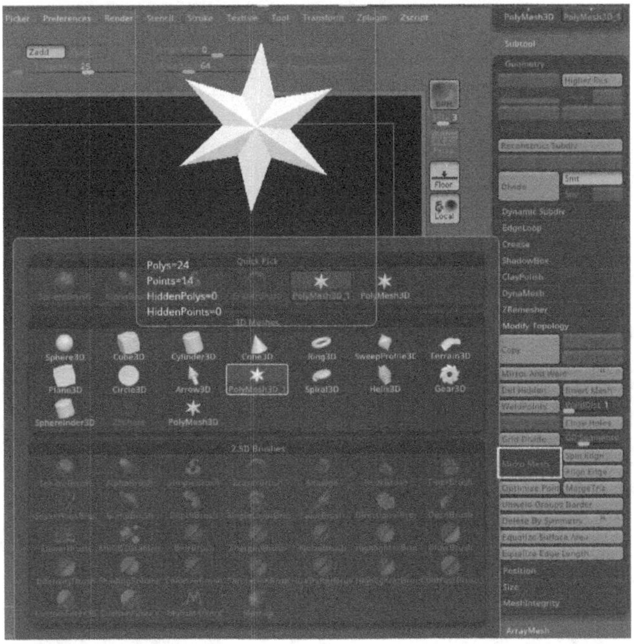

***Figure 12-10** A flyout displayed on choosing the **Micro Mesh** button*

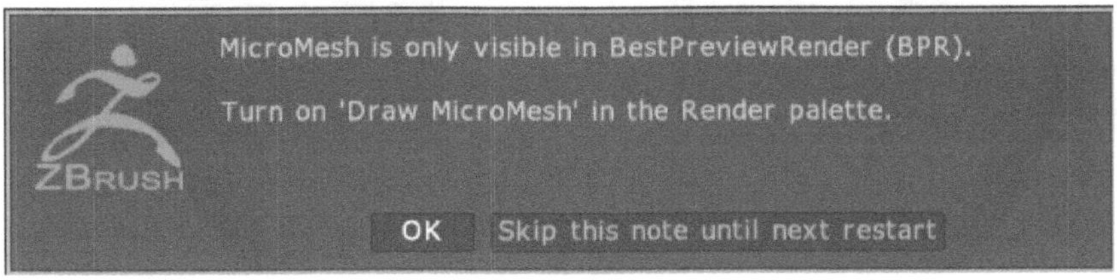

***Figure 12-11** The message box displayed on choosing the primitive*

Choose the **OK** button to close this message box. Next, expand the **Render** palette. In this palette, expand the **Render Properties** subpalette. Next, choose the **Draw Micromesh** button in this subpalette. Now, choose the **BPR** button from the right shelf; the sphere will be rendered and the polygons in the sphere will be replaced by the **PolyMesh3D** (stars), refer to Figure 12-12.

Materials Blend-Radius

The **Materials Blend-Radius** slider is used to blend different materials in an object when rendered using the **BPR** renderer. To blend the different materials in an object, paint two different materials on the surface of a sphere, as discussed in Chapter 8. In the **Render Properties** subpalette, make sure the value of the **Materials Blend-Radius** slider is **1**. Next, render the scene using the **BPR** renderer; the rendered sphere will be displayed, refer to Figure 12-13. Next, set the value of the **Materials Blend-Radius** slider to **50**; both the materials will be blended, refer to Figure 12-14.

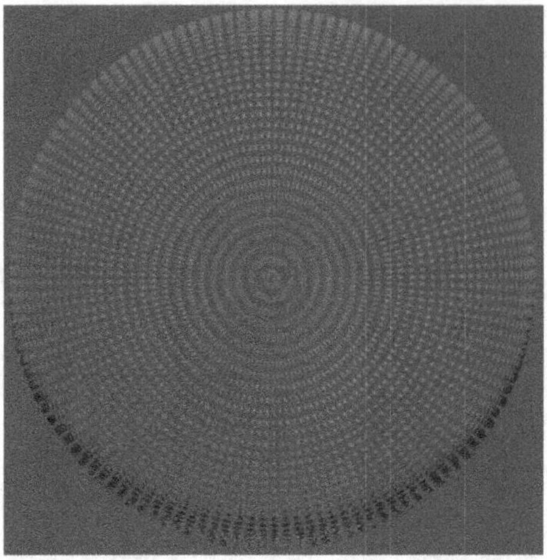

Figure 12-12 *The polygons of the sphere replaced by stars on rendering*

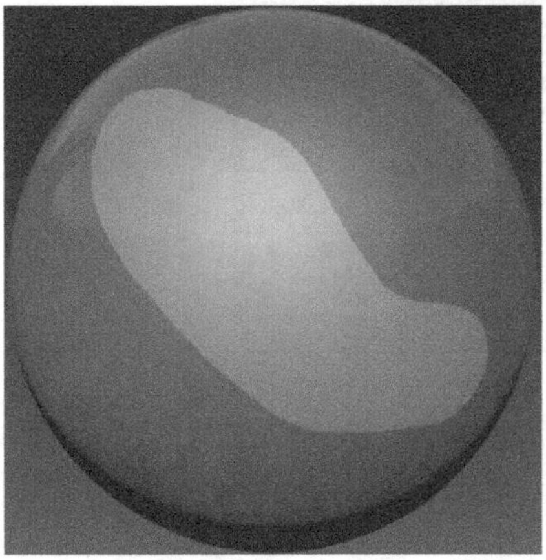

Figure 12-13 *Rendered sphere with the value of the **Materials Blend-Radius** slider set to **0***

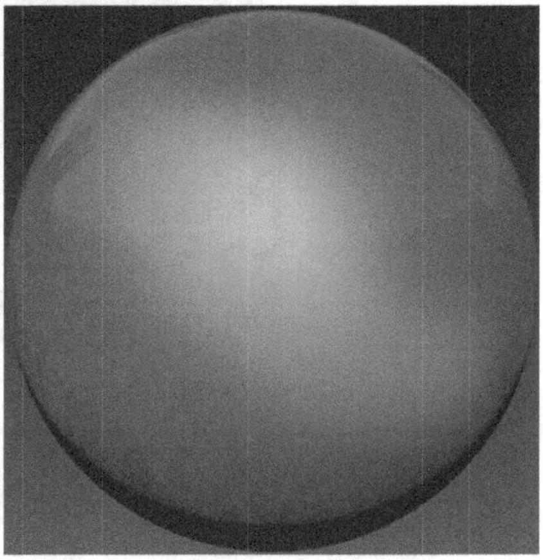

Figure 12-14 *Rendered sphere with the value of the **Materials Blend-Radius** slider set to **50***

Shadows

The **Shadows** button is used to display the shadows when the scene is rendered using the **BPR** renderer. If this button is not chosen, the shadows will not be displayed in the rendered image.

Vibrant

The **Vibrant** slider is used to globally control the saturation of shadows and ambient occlusion when a scene is rendered.

AOcclusion

The **AOcclusion** button is used to enable ambient occlusion when a scene is rendered using the **BPR** renderer.

Flat Shadow

The **Flat Shadow** button is used to provide flat type of shadows when a scene is rendered using the **BPR** renderer. These flat shadows are monochromatic and provide a non-photorealistic rendering style to your models.

Sss

The **Sss** button is used to enable the Subsurface scattering when a scene is rendered using the **BPR** renderer. On choosing this button, the light absorption in some materials such as skin and plastic will be visible in the rendered image. Before choosing this button, you need to make sure the **Sss** button in the **Light Properties** subpalette of the **Tool** palette has been chosen.

Transparent

The **Transparent** button is used to enable transparency in the objects while rendering using the **BPR** renderer. To enable transparency in the objects, create a cube in the canvas. Next, append a sphere in it. On rendering the scene, you will notice that the sphere will not be visible in the rendered image, refer to Figure 12-15. In the **Render** palette, choose the **Transparent** button, refer to Figure 12-16.

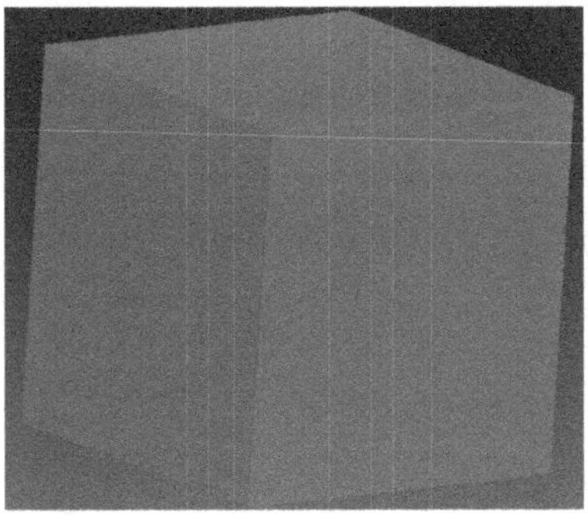

Figure 12-15 *The rendered scene in the canvas*

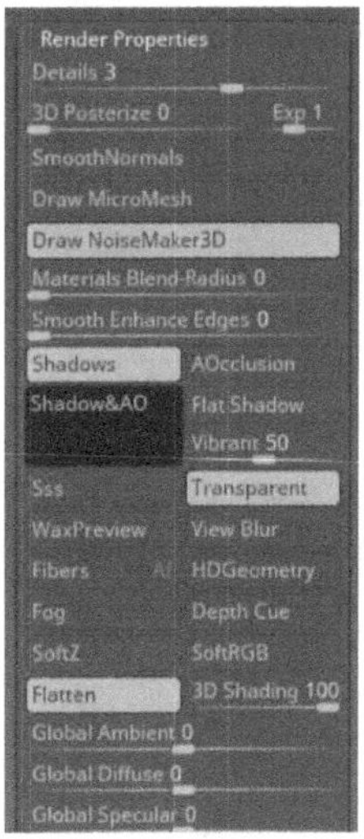

Figure 12-16 *The **Transparent** button chosen*

Expand the **Display Properties** subpalette in the **Tool** palette and then expand **BPR Setting** in the **Tool** palette. Next, choose the **BPR Transparent Shading** button in this subpalette, refer to Figure 12-17. Now, choose the **BPR** button from the right shelf; the scene will be rendered and the transparency in the cube will be displayed in the rendered image, refer to Figure 12-18.

WaxPreview

The **WaxPreview** button is used to give a wax like appearance to the material in the scene.

View Blur

The **View Blur** button is used to apply a blur effect to a scene. To apply a blur effect to a scene in the canvas, choose the **View Blur** button from the **Render Properties** subpalette and then expand the **BPR RenderPass** subpalette. In this subpalette, set the value of the **VBlur Radius** to **10**, refer to Figure 12-19. On doing so, the blur effect will be applied to the model, refer to Figure 12-20.

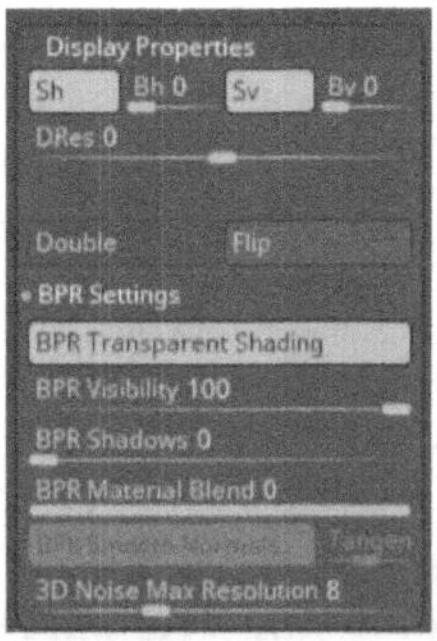

Figure 12-17 The ***Display Properties*** *subpalette*

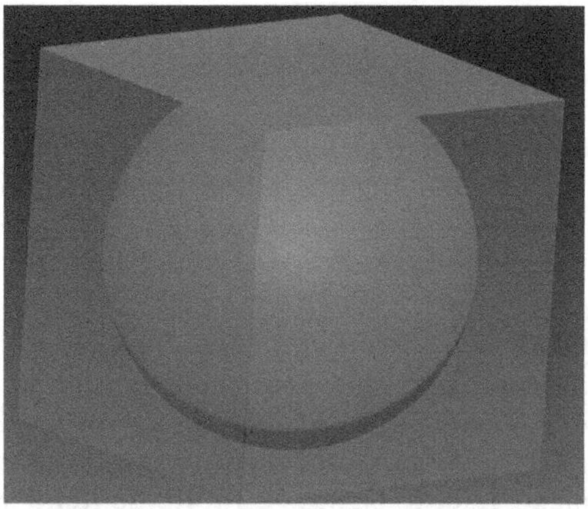

Figure 12-18 The transparency in the cube displayed on rendering

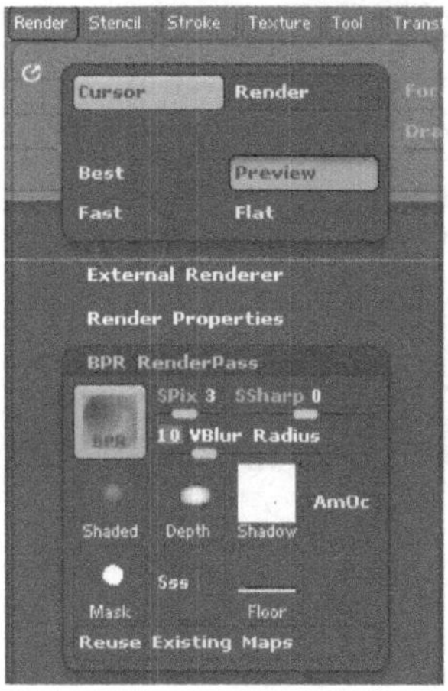

Figure 12-19 The value of the ***VBlur Radius*** *slider set to* ***10***

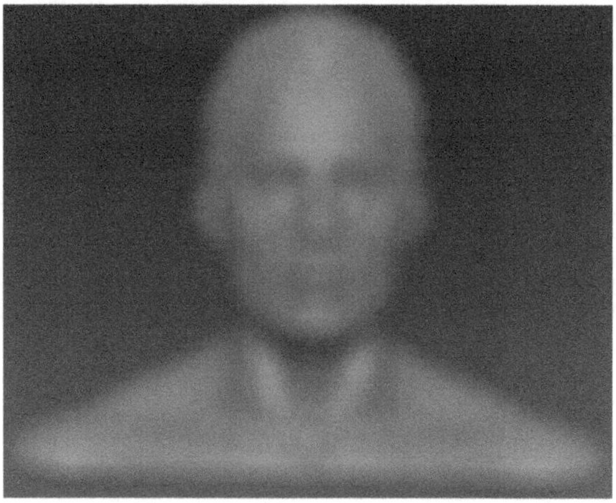

Figure 12-20 The blur effect applied to the model

Fibers

The **Fibers** button is used to render the fibers in the scene, thus giving them a realistic appearance.

Af

The term **Af** stands for Antialiase fibers. By default, this button is deactivated. To activate this button, you need to choose the **Fibers** button. This button is used to smoothen the fibers when rendered using the **BPR** button.

HDGeometry

The **HDGeometry** button is used to render the subtools having high resolution at once when rendered using the **BPR** button.

Fog
The **Fog** button is used to apply the fog effect in a scene.

Depth Cue
The **Depth Cue** button is used to soften or sharpen focus on different depths in the canvas, depending on the settings that have been made in the **Depth Cue** subpalette located in the **Render** palette. The **Depth Cue** subpalette will be discussed in detail later in this chapter.

SoftZ
The **SoftZ** button is used to smoothen the stray pixels in the canvas when the scene is rendered using the **Best** renderer.

SoftRGB
The **SoftRGB** button is used to apply anti-aliasing in a scene while rendering.

Flatten
The **Flatten** button is used to smoothen different layers in a scene while rendering.

3D Shading
The **3D Shading** slider is used to reduce the effect of depth shading in a scene when it is rendered using the **Preview** button.

Global Ambient
The **Global Ambient** slider is used to control the overall amount of ambient in a scene when it is rendered using the **BPR** button.

Global Diffuse
The **Global Diffuse** slider is used to control the overall amount of diffuse in a scene when it is rendered using the **BPR** button.

Global Specular
The **Global Specular** slider is used to control the overall amount of specularity in a scene when it is rendered using the **BPR** button.

BPR RenderPass
The **BPR RenderPass** subpalette consists of different buttons and sliders that are used to generate render passes of a scene for compositing, refer to Figure 12-21. These buttons and sliders are discussed next.

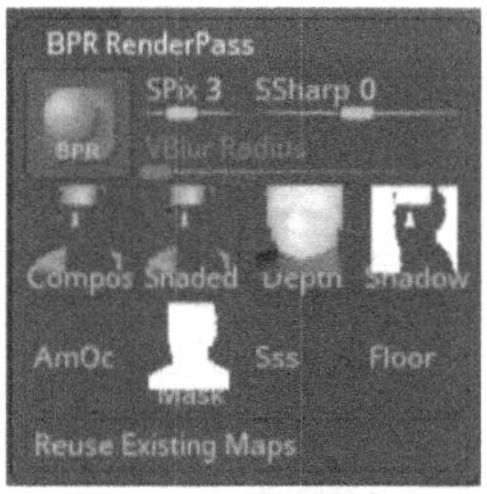

***Figure 12-21** The **BPR RenderPass** subpalette*

BPR
The **BPR** button is used to render a scene using the **BPR** button. The scenes rendered using this button will contain all the details such as shadows, ambient occlusion, transparency, fog, and so on. This button renders only 3D scenes.

SPix

The **SPix** slider is used to control the amount of anti aliasing in a scene. Higher the value of this slider, higher will be quality of the rendered image.

SSharp

The **SSharp** slider is used to control the sharpness of the anti-aliasing.

VBlur Radius

The **VBlur Radius** slider is used to increase or decrease the amount of blur in a rendered scene. Before using this slider, you need to choose the **View Blur** button in the **Render Properties** subpalette.

Shaded

The **Shaded** button is used to generate a shaded render pass for a scene. To generate a shaded render pass of a scene, refer to Figure 12-22, expand the **Render** palette. In this palette, expand the **BPR RenderPass** subpalette. Choose the **BPR** button in this subpalette; the scene will be rendered and the different slots for the render passes will be filled with the corresponding passes, refer to Figure 12-23.

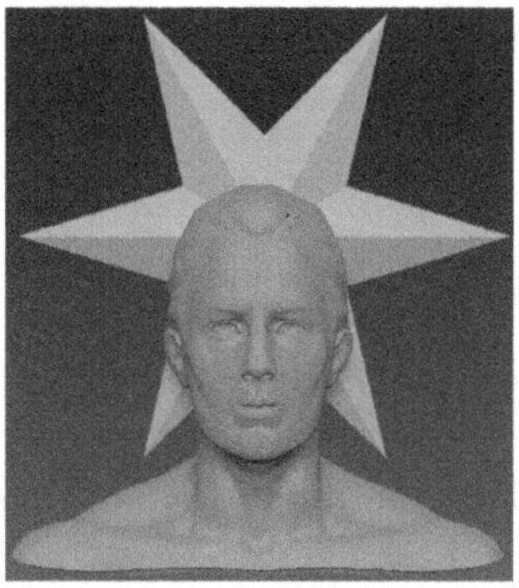

Figure 12-22 *The scene rendered using the* ***BPR*** *renderer*

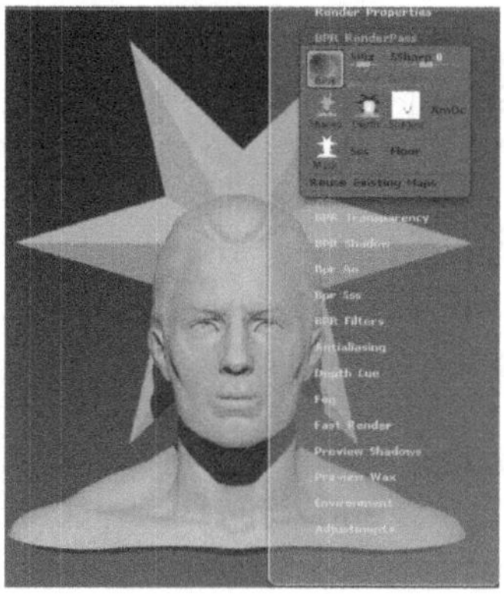

Figure 12-23 *The different slots in the* ***BPR RenderPass*** *subpalette filled up*

The **Shaded** render pass will have a black background and there will be no anti aliasing. This will give better results while compositing. You can export this render pass in *.PSD, .JPG, .png, .BMP*, and *.TIF* formats. To do so, choose the **Shaded** button; the **Export Image** dialog box will be displayed, refer to Figure 12-24. In this dialog box, save the render pass with a desired name and format. This pass can then be imported into Photoshop for compositing.

Depth

The **Depth** button is used to generate a depth pass which can be exported and then composited.

Shadow

The **Shadow** button is used to generate a shadow pass. Before choosing this button, you need to choose the **Shadow** button in the **Render Properties** subpalette.

AmOc
The **AmOc** button is used to generate an ambient occlusion pass. Before choosing this button, you need to choose the **AOcclusion** button in the **Render Properties** subpalette.

Mask
The **Mask** button is used to create a mask pass.

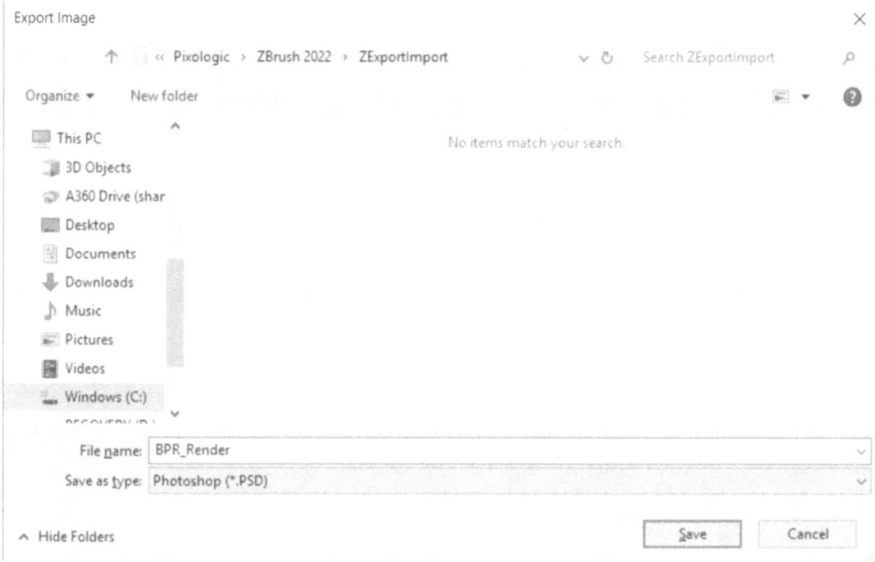

*Figure 12-24 The **Export Image** dialog box*

Sss
The **Sss** button is used to generate a sub surface scattering pass.

Floor
The **Floor** button is used to generate a floor depth map pass.

Reuse Existing Maps
The **Reuse Existing Maps** button is used to reuse the existing maps for another scene when they are rendered using the BPR renderer.

BPR Transparency
The **BPR Transparency** subpalette consists of different sliders that enable you to add transparency in a scene, refer to Figure 12-25. By default, these sliders are not activated. To activate these sliders, you need to choose the **Transparent** button in the **Render Properties** subpalette. To view the transparency in the rendered image, you need to choose the **BPR Transparent Shading** button in the **Display Properties** subpalette of the **Tool** palette. The different sliders in the **BPR Transparency** subpalette are discussed next.

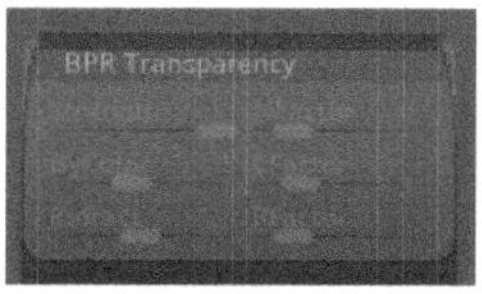

*Figure 12-25 The **BPR Transparency** subpalette*

Strength

The **Strength** slider is used to control the amount of transparency in an object.

NFactor

The **NFactor** slider is used to specify whether the areas of an object facing the canvas will be transparent or opaque. If the value of this slider is set to **0**, the entire object will be transparent and if the value of this slider is set to **1**, only the areas facing the canvas will be transparent.

ByColor

The **ByColor** slider is used to control the transparency in the object according to the intensity of the color in an object. Higher the value of this slider, more will be the transparency in the object.

CFactor

The **CFactor** slider is used to control the color variation in an object. If the value of this slider is set to **0**, there will be no distinction in the colors of an object on rendering. If the value of this slider is set to **4**, the black areas in the object will be completely transparent and the white areas will be completely opaque.

Refract

The **Refract** slider is used to control the amount of refraction in an object. Higher the value of this slider, more will be the amount of refraction.

RFactor

The **RFactor** slider is used to control the refraction factor in an object. Higher the value of this slider, more will be the refraction. If the value of this slider is set to **250**, it will produce an effect similar to a magnifying glass.

BPR Shadow

The **BPR Shadow** subpalette consists of different options that are used to control the settings of the shadows that are generated on rendering a scene using the **BPR** renderer, refer to Figure 12-26. These options are discussed next.

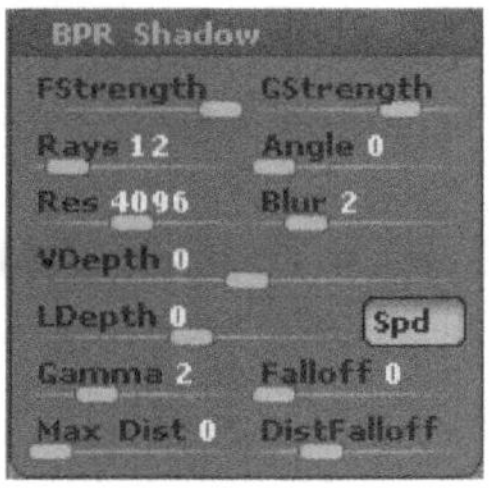

***Figure 12-26** The **BPR Shadow** subpalette*

FStrength

The **FStrength** slider is used to control the intensity of the shadows that are cast on the floor when the scene is rendered using the **BPR** renderer. To view the shadows on the floor grid, you need to choose the **Floor** button in the right shelf.

GStrength

The **GStrength** slider is used to control the overall shadows of an object. Higher the value of this slider, higher will be the intensity of the shadows.

Rays
The **Rays** slider is used to adjust the softness of the shadows. Higher the value of this slider, more will be the softness in the shadows.

Angle
The **Angle** slider is used to set the focus of the shadows in the scene.

Res
The **Res** slider is used to set the resolution of the shadows in pixels. Higher the value of this slider, more will be the resolution of the shadows.

Blur
The **Blur** slider is used to adjust the amount of blur in the shadows. Higher the value of this slider, more will be the amount of blur in the shadows.

VDepth
The **VDepth** slider is used to set the offset of the view depth. The value of this slider ranges from **-100** to **100**. If you set a negative value in this slider, the intensity of the light and shadows will increase.

LDepth
The **LDepth** slider is used to set the offset of the light depth. The value of this slider ranges from **-100** to **100**. If you set a negative value in this slider, the intensity of the light and shadows will increase.

Spd
The **Spd** button is used to increase the accuracy of the shadows in a scene. If this button is not chosen, the render time will decrease but the accuracy in the shadows will also be decreased.

Gamma
The **Gamma** slider is used to adjust the gradient in the shadow contrast.

Falloff
The **Falloff** slider is used to adjust the falloff in the shadows generated using the **BPR** renderer.

Max Dist
The **Max Dist** slider is used to control the length of the shadows. Higher the value of this slider, longer will be the shadows.

DistFalloff
The **DistFalloff** slider is used to control the speed of fading of the shadows. If the value of this slider is higher, the shadows will fade quickly.

Bpr Ao

The **Bpr Ao** subpalette consists of different options that are used to control the settings in the ambient occlusion generated on rendering a scene using the **BPR** renderer, refer to Figure 12-27. By default, all the options in this subpalette are not activated. To activate these options, you need to choose the **AOcclusion** button in the **Render Properties** subpalette. The different options in the **BPR Ao** subpalette are discussed next.

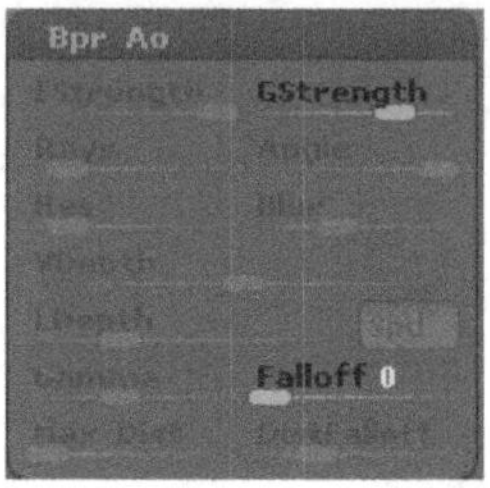

*Figure 12-27 The **Bpr Ao** subpalette*

FStrength

The **FStrength** slider is used to control the strength of the ambient occlusion on the floor. To view the effect of ambient occlusion on the floor, you need to choose the **Floor** button in the right shelf.

GStrength

The **GStrength** slider is used to control the overall ambient occlusion in a scene.

Rays

The **Rays** slider is used to set the number of rays that will be used in ambient occlusion calculation.

Angle

The **Angle** slider is used to set the focus of the ambient occlusion in the scene.

Res

The **Res** slider is used to set the resolution of the ambient occlusion in pixels.

Blur

The **Blur** slider is used to adjust the radius of blur in the ambient occlusion.

VDepth

The **VDepth** slider is used to set the offset of the view depth. The value of this slider ranges from **-100** to **100**.

LDepth

The **LDepth** slider is used to set the offset of the light depth. The value of this slider ranges from **-100** to **100**.

Spd

The **Spd** button is used to increase the accuracy of the ambient occlusion in a scene. If this button is not chosen, the render time will decrease but the accuracy in ambient occlusion will also be decrease.

Gamma

The **Gamma** slider is used to adjust the brightness in the ambient occlusion.

Falloff

The **Falloff** slider is used to adjust the falloff in the ambient occlusion generated using the **BPR** renderer.

Max Dist

The **Max Dist** slider is used to specify the distance up to which the ambient occlusion will stretch.

DistFalloff

The **DistFalloff** slider is used to control the speed of fading in the ambient occlusion. The higher the value of this slider, the more quickly the ambient occlusion will fade.

Bpr Sss

The **Bpr Sss** subpalette consists of different options that are used to control the settings in the sub surface scattering generated on rendering a scene using the **BPR** renderer, refer to Figure 12-28. By default, the different options in this subpalette are not activated. To activate these options, you need to choose the **Sss** button in the **Render Properties** subpalette. The different options in the **BPR Sss** subpalette are discussed next.

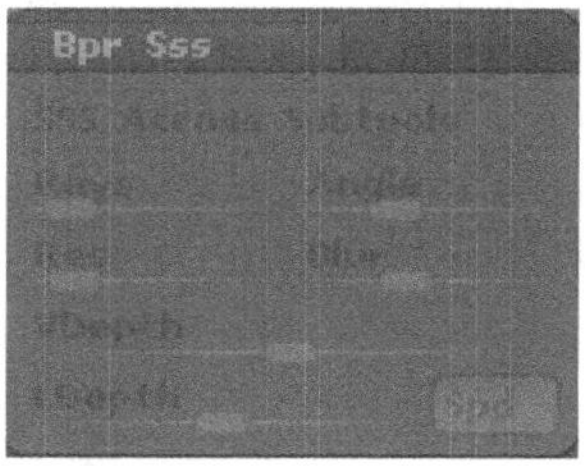

Figure 12-28 *The **Bpr Sss** subpalette*

SSS Across Subtools

The **SSS Across Subtools** button is used to calculate the Subsurface scattering for all the subtools in the scene. If this button is not chosen, the subsurface scattering will be calculated for each subtool individually.

Rays

The **Rays** slider is used to set the number of rays that will be used in calculating the sub surface scattering.

Angle

The **Angle** slider is used to set the focus of the Subsurface scattering in the scene.

Res

The **Res** slider is used to set the resolution of the Subsurface scattering in pixels.

Blur

The **Blur** slider is used to adjust the radius of blur in the Subsurface scattering.

VDepth

The **VDepth** slider is used to set the offset of the view depth. The value of this slider ranges from **-100** to **100**.

LDepth

The **LDepth** slider is used to set the offset of the light depth. The value of this slider ranges from **-100** to **100**.

Spd

The **Spd** button is used to increase the accuracy of the Subsurface scattering in a scene. If this button is not chosen, the render time will decrease but the accuracy in Subsurface scattering will also decrease.

BPR Filters

The **BPR Filters** subpalette consists of different options that are used to apply different filters or effects to the scenes after being rendered using the **BPR** renderer, refer to Figure 12-29. This subpalette consists of different buttons labeled from **F1** to **F12**, refer to Figure 12-29. These buttons represent the filter numbers that are applied to a BPR render image. By default, these filters are not activated.

To activate the filters, you need to click on the black/grey dot located at the top right corner of the button. On clicking on the black/grey dot, it will be replaced by a circle and the filter will be activated. Besides this, the different buttons and sliders located below the slots will also be activated. For instance, if you choose the **F1** button, different parameters for applying noise filter will be displayed, refer to Figure 12-30.

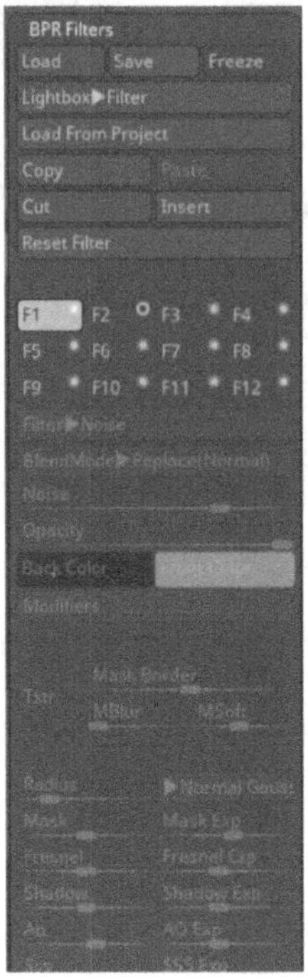

*Figure 12-29 The partial view of **BPR Filters** subpalette*

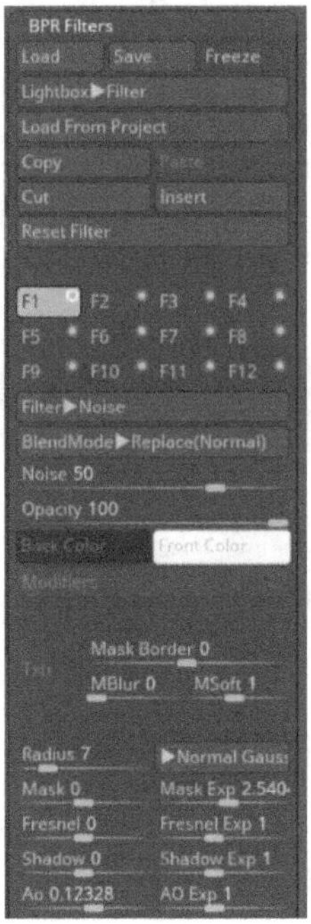

Figure 12-30 Different parameters for applying noise filter

On choosing the **F2** button, different parameters for applying blur filter will be displayed. Similarly, **F3** represents the sharpen filter, **F4** represents the orton filter, **F5** represents the glow filter, **F6** represents the fade filter, **F7** represents the colorize filter, **F8** represents the red filter, **F9** represents the green filter, **F10** represents the blue filter, **F11** represents the saturation filter, and **F12** represents the hue filter.

Before using these filters, you need to make sure the scene has been rendered using the BPR renderer. Figures 12-31 through 12-42 display different filters applied to a BPR render.

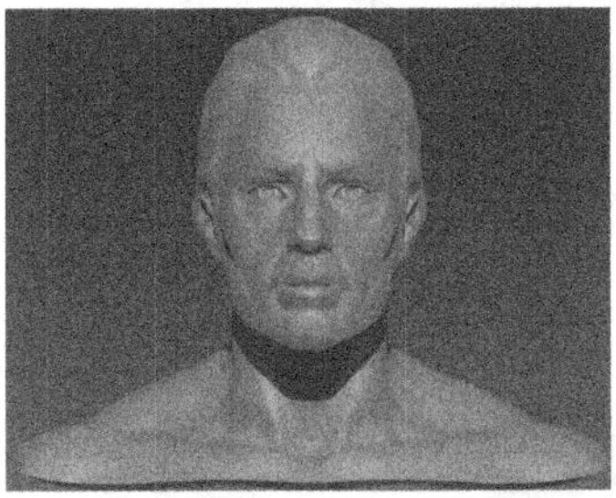

Figure 12-31 *The noise filter applied to the rendered image*

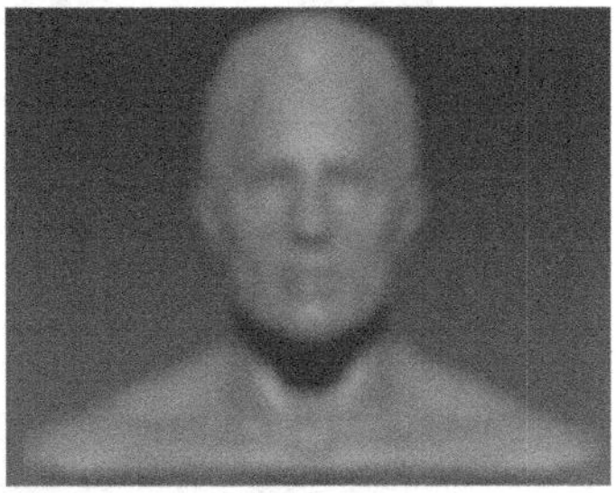

Figure 12-32 *The blur filter applied to the rendered image*

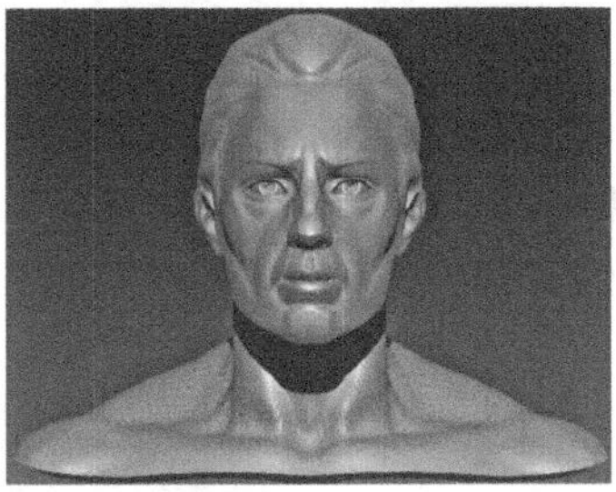

Figure 12-33 *The sharpen filter applied to the rendered image*

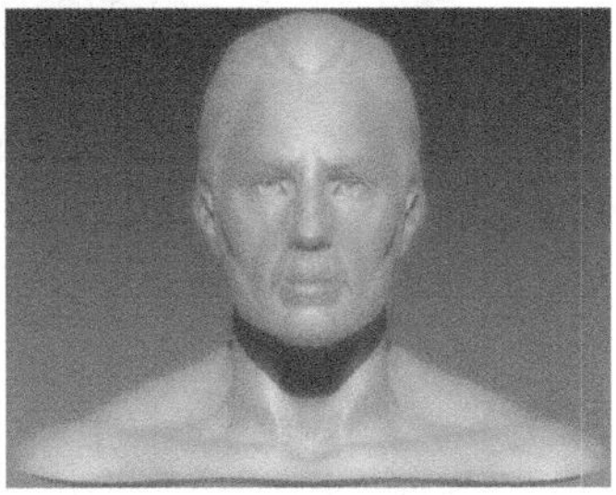

Figure 12-34 *The orton filter applied to the rendered image*

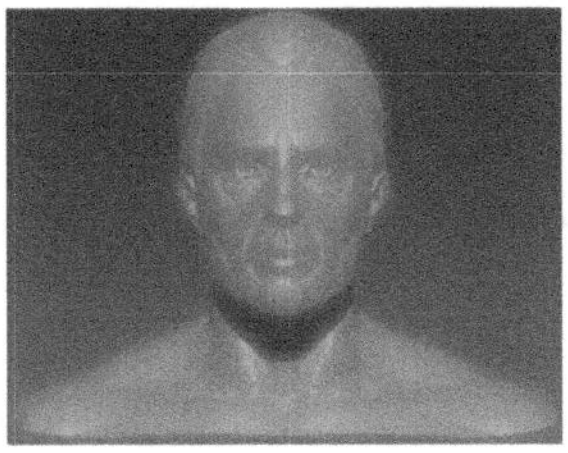

Figure 12-35 *The glow filter applied to the rendered image*

Figure 12-36 *The fade filter applied to the rendered image*

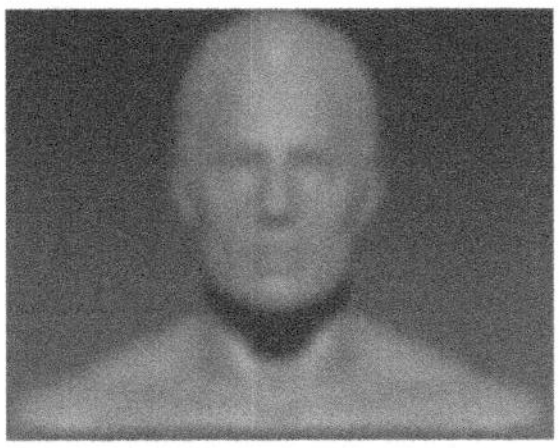

Figure 12-37 *The colorize filter applied to the rendered image*

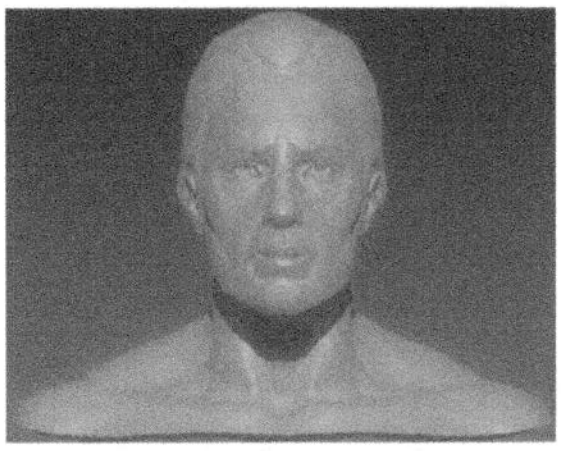

Figure 12-38 *The red filter applied to the rendered image*

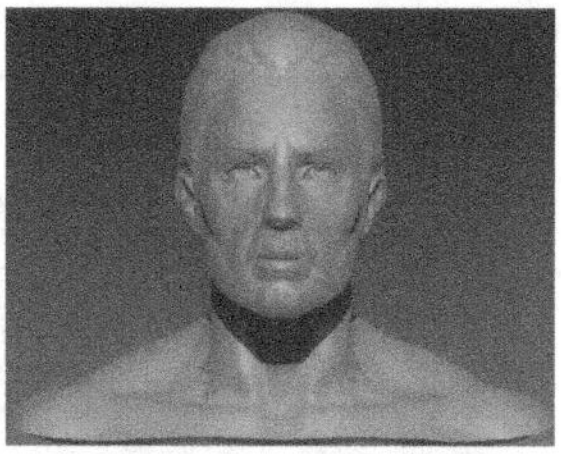

Figure 12-39 *The green filter applied to the rendered image*

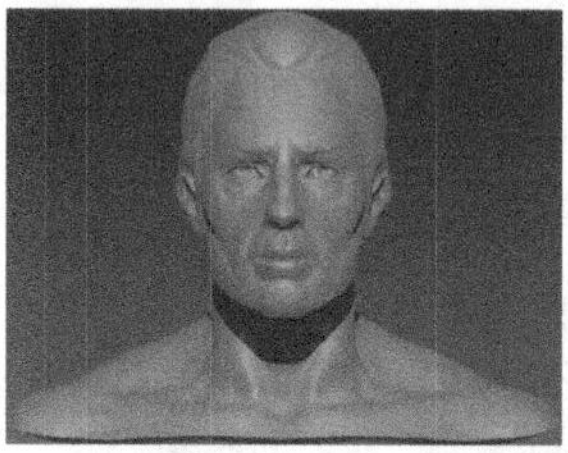

Figure 12-40 *The blue filter applied to the rendered image*

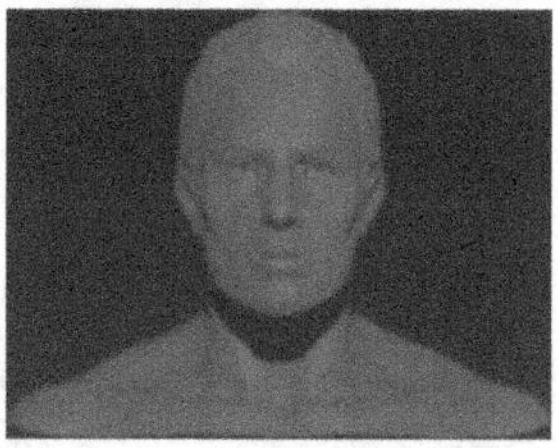

Figure 12-41 *The saturation filter applied to the rendered image*

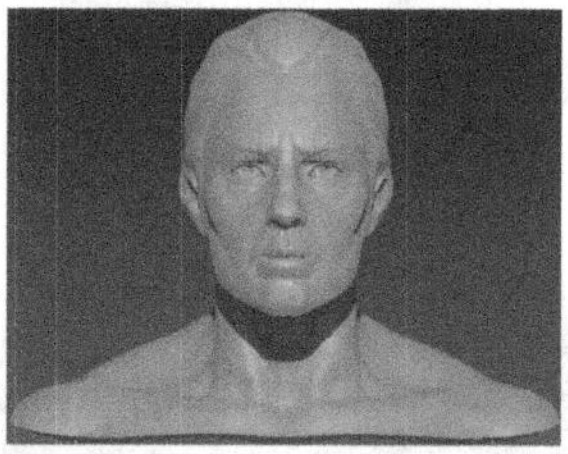

Figure 12-42 *The hue filter applied to the rendered image*

Antialiasing

The **Antialiasing** subpalette consists of different sliders that are used to control the quality of antialiasing in the rendered image, refer to Figure 12-43. These sliders are discussed next.

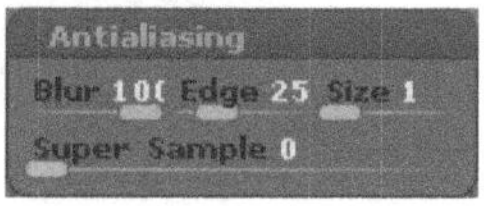

Figure 12-43 *The* ***Antialiasing*** *subpalette*

Blur

The **Blur** slider is used to specify the amount of softness in the antialiasing effect. Higher the value of this slider, more will be the amount of smoothness in the edges of the rendered image.

Edge

The **Edge** slider is used to control the antialiasing of the edges. If the value of this slider is set to **0**, only the sharp edges will be antialiased. If the value of this slider is set to **100**, all the edges will be antialiased.

Size

The **Size** slider is used to determine the influence of antialiasing on the areas surrounding the edges. Higher the value of this slider, more will be the influence of the antialiasing on the surrounding areas.

Super Sample

The **Super Sample** slider is used only with the **Best** renderer. It is used to increase the accuracy of the antialiasing. Higher the value of this slider, more will be the accuracy in the antialiasing. However, higher values extend the rendering process.

Depth Cue

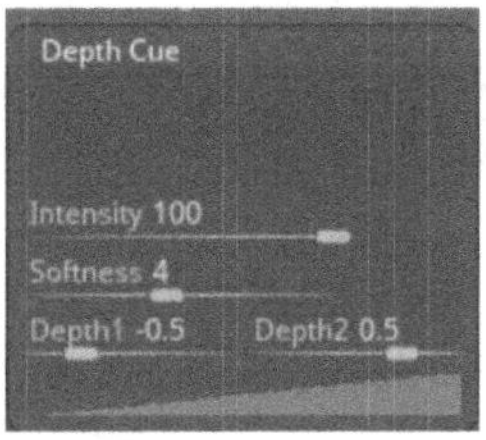

***Figure 12-44** The **Depth Cue** subpalette*

The **Depth Cue** subpalette consists of different options that are used to blur different parts of a scene based on their position along the Z-axis, refer to Figure 12-44. These options work only with the **Best** renderer. Before working with this subpalette, you need to choose the **Depth Cue** button in the **Render Properties** subpalette. The different options in this subpalette are discussed next.

Depth Cue Alpha

The **Depth Cue Alpha** button is used to select the alpha image that will be used to map the depth cue effect. On choosing this button, a flyout containing different texture images will be displayed, refer to Figure 12-45.

***Figure 12-45** The flyout displayed on choosing the **Depth Cue Alpha** button*

Intensity

The **Intensity** slider is used to specify the strength of the depth cue effect.

Softness

The **Softness** slider is used to specify the amount of blurring that occurs in the areas that face away from the canvas.

Depth1

The **Depth1** slider is used to specify the depth along the Z-axis where the blurring does not occur.

Depth2

The **Depth2** slider is used to specify the depth along the Z-axis where the maximum blur occurs.

Fog

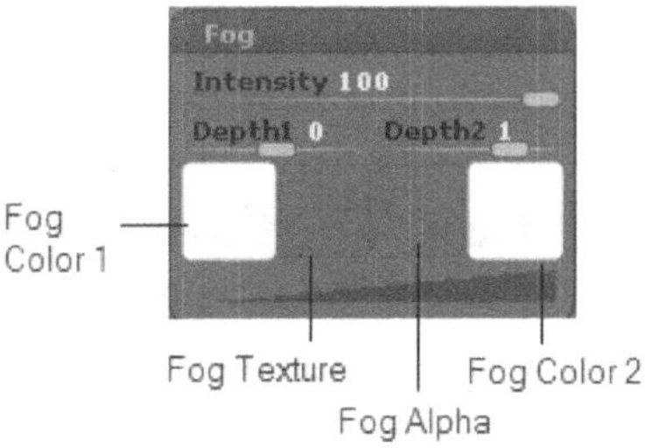

***Figure 12-46** The **Fog** subpalette*

The **Fog** subpalette consists of different options that are used to apply fog effect to a scene, refer to Figure 12-46. Before working with this subpalette, you need to choose the **Fog** button in the **Render Properties** subpalette. The different options in this subpalette are discussed next.

Intensity
The **Intensity** slider is used to specify the strength of the fog effect in a scene.

Depth1
The **Depth1** slider is used to specify the depth along the Z-axis where the fog effect is not displayed in the scene.

Depth2
The **Depth2** slider is used to specify the depth along the Z-axis where the maximum fog effect is displayed in the scene.

Fog Color 1
The **Fog Color 1** swatch is used to select the color of the fog effect at the position that is nearer to the canvas along the Z-axis.

Fog Texture
The **Fog Texture** button is used to select the texture that will be applied to the fog. On choosing this button, a flyout containing different texture images will be displayed.

Fog Alpha
The **Fog Alpha** button is used to select the texture that will be used in the mapping of the fog effect. On choosing this button, a flyout containing different alpha images will be displayed.

Fog Color 2
The **Fog Color 2** swatch is used to select the color of the fog effect at the position that is farther from the canvas along the Z-axis.

Fast Render
The **Fast Render** subpalette is used to control the properties of the **Fast** renderer. This subpalette consists of two sliders that are discussed next.

Ambient
The **Ambient** slider is used to specify the amount of ambient light applied to a scene when it is rendered using the **Fast** renderer.

Diffuse
The **Diffuse** slider is used to specify the amount of diffuse shading applied to a scene when it is rendered using the **Fast** renderer.

Preview Shadows
The **Preview Shadows** subpalette consists of different options that are used to adjust the shadows in a scene in a normal preview mode, refer to Figure 12-47. The settings of this subpalette will be reflected in the shadows in the canvas in real time without rendering the scene. The different options in this subpalette are discussed next.

ObjShadow

The **ObjShadow** slider is used to control the intensity of the shadows in the canvas in real time.

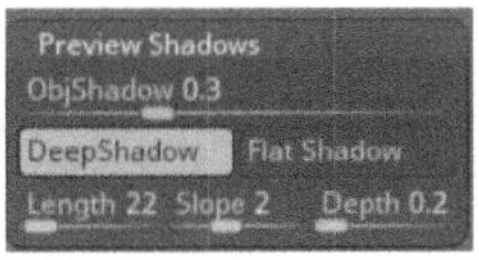

*Figure 12-47 The **Preview Shadows** subpalette*

DeepShadow

The **DeepShadow** button is used to increase the intensity of preview shadows. If this button is not chosen, the preview shadows will not be very sharp.

Flat Shadow

The **Flat Shadow** button is used to display a flat shadow in the real-time renderer while sculpting and also at the time of final rendering.

Length

The **Length** slider is used to control the length and softness of the preview shadows.

Slope

The **Slope** slider is used to control the angle of the preview shadows cast by the objects in a scene.

Depth

The **Depth** slider is used to deepen and enlarge the preview shadows.

Preview Wax

The **Preview Wax** subpalette consists of different options that are used to give a wax like appearance to the materials in real time without rendering the scene, refer to Figure 12-48. Before using the options available in this subpalette, you need to choose the **WaxPreview** button in the **Render Properties** subpalette. You also need to make sure that the **Strength** slider in the **Wax Modifiers** subpalette of the **Material** palette has been set to a value greater than **0**, refer to Figure 12-49. The different options in this subpalette are discussed next.

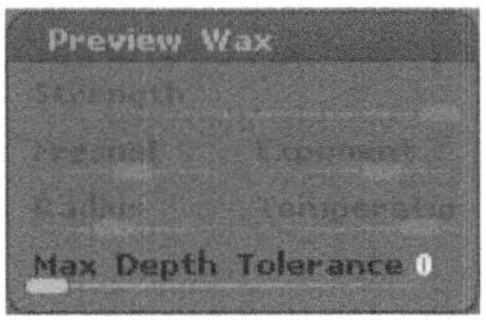

*Figure 12-48 The **Preview Wax** subpalette*

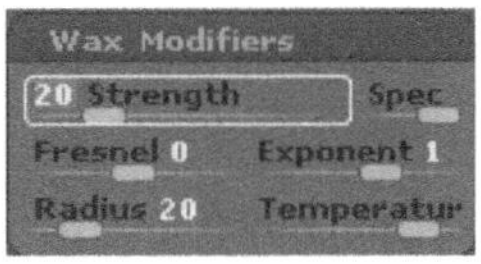

*Figure 12-49 The value of the **Strength** slider set to **20***

Strength

The **Strength** slider is used to control the strength of the wax material that is applied to an object.

Fresnel

The **Fresnel** slider is used to specify whether the wax effect will be applied to the surfaces of an object facing the canvas or to the surfaces facing away from the canvas.

Exponent
The **Exponent** slider is used along with the **Fresnel** slider. This slider is used to specify the speed at which the wax effect is applied to an object when the object is rotated in the canvas.

Radius
The **Radius** slider is used to specify the distance up to which the wax effect will spread on the surface of an object.

Temperature
The **Temperature** slider is used to add blue or red tint to the wax material in the canvas. The blue tint represents cold wax while the red tint represents the hot wax.

Max Depth Tolerance
The **Max Depth Tolerance** slider is used to interpret the distance between different areas of an object to apply realistic wax effect to it.

Environment
The **Environment** subpalette consists of different options that are used to control the environmental reflections, refer to Figure 12-50. These options work only when a scene is rendered using the **Best** renderer and are discussed next.

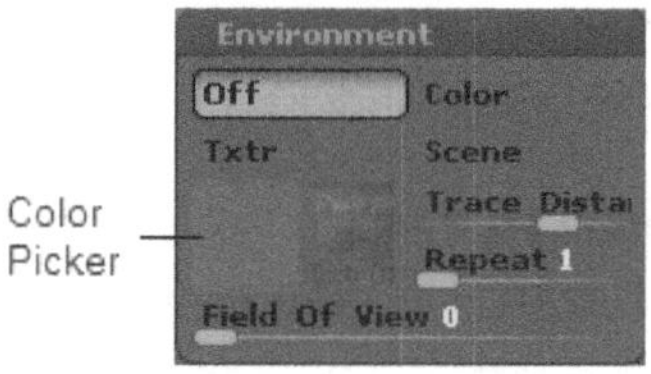

***Figure 12-50** The **Environment** subpalette*

Off
The **Off** button is used to disable the reflection of the environment in a scene.

Color
The **Color** button is used to apply a color that will be reflected by the materials in the objects. On choosing this button, the **Off** button gets deactivated and the color picker button gets activated, refer to Figure 12-50. You can select the desired color from the color picker and that color will be reflected by the materials.

Txtr
The **Txtr** button is used to apply a texture that will be reflected by the materials in the objects. On choosing this button, the **Off** button gets deactivated and the **Environment Texture** button located next to the color picker button gets activated, refer to Figure 12-50. On choosing the **Environment Texture** button, a flyout containing different texture images will be displayed. You can select the desired texture from the flyout and that texture will be reflected by the materials.

Scene
The **Scene** button is used to apply the reflections to the materials in a scene such that the entire canvas is reflected by the objects in the scene.

Trace Distance
The **Trace Distance** slider is used to specify the distance that will be used in calculating the environmental reflections.

Repeat

The **Repeat** slider is used along with the **Scene** button. As discussed earlier, the **Scene** button grabs the entire canvas and uses it as a reflection map. The **Repeat** slider is used to specify the number of times the reflections will be applied before creating the reflection map.

Field Of View

The **Field of View** slider is used to specify whether the fitted texture image will be reflected by the objects or only a part of it will be reflected.

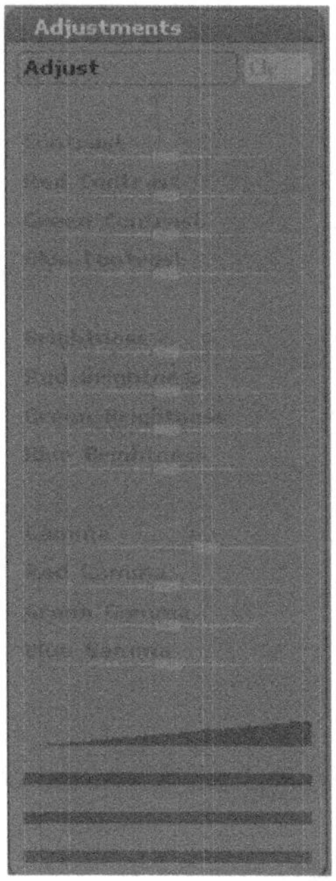

*Figure 12-51 The **Adjustments** subpalette*

Adjustments

The **Adjustments** subpalette consists of different options that are used to apply various color correction settings to the rendered image, refer to Figure 12-51. The commonly used options are discussed next.

Adjust

The **Adjust** button is used to enable different sliders in the **Adjustments** subpalette that will be used in color correcting a rendered image.

Clr

The **Clr** button is used to clear all the settings that have been applied to a rendered image.

Contrast

The **Contrast** slider is used to adjust the amount of overall contrast in a rendered image. The **Red Contrast**, **Green Contrast**, and **Blue Contrast** sliders are used to adjust the contrast levels in red, green, and blue colors in a rendered image, respectively.

Brightness

The **Brightness** slider is used to adjust the amount of overall brightness in a rendered image. The **Red Brightness**, **Green Brightness**, and **Blue Brightness** sliders are used to adjust the brightness in red, green, and blue colors in a rendered image, respectively.

Gamma

The **Gamma** slider is used to adjust the amount of overall gamma levels in a rendered image. The **Red Gamma**, **Green Gamma**, and **Blue Gamma** sliders are used to adjust the gamma levels in red, green, and blue colors in a rendered image, respectively.

ZPlugin PALETTE

The **Zplugin** palette consists of different subpalettes such as **Maya Blend** subpalette, **Zbrush to Photoshop** subpalette, and so on. These subpalettes are used as additional utilities that can extend ZBrush core functionalities. Using the options in the **Maya Blend Shapes** subpalette, you can export 3D models in various formats like obj, fbx, and so on to Maya software. Similarly, you can send the BPR render passes to Photoshop CC directly using the options in the **ZBrush to Photoshop** subpalette.

TUTORIALS

Before you start the tutorials of this chapter, navigate to *\Documents\ZBrushprojects* and then create a new folder with the name *c12*.

Tutorial 1

In this tutorial, you will set up a scene and then create render passes of the scene.

(Expected time: 20 min)

The following steps are required to complete this tutorial:

a. Set up a scene.
b. Generate different render passes.
c. Save the scene.

Setting up the Scene

In this section, you will set up a scene.

1. Choose the **Init ZBrush** button from the **Preferences** palette; ZBrush is initialized to its default state.

2. Choose the **DemoHead.ZTL** file from the **Tool** tab of the **LightBox** browser by double-clicking on it. Next, choose the **LightBox** button to close the **LightBox** browser. Now, drag the cursor in the canvas area; the model is displayed in the canvas.

3. Choose the **Edit** button in the top shelf to switch to the edit mode.

4. Expand the **Geometry** subpalette in the **Tool** palette. In this subpalette, click twice on the **Divide** button; the value of **SDiv** slider becomes equal to **5**.

5. Expand the **SubTool** subpalette in the **Tool** palette. In this subpalette, choose the **Append** button; a flyout is displayed. In this flyout, choose the **Plane3D** primitive, refer to Figure 12-52. On doing so, the plane is displayed in the canvas, as shown in Figure 12-53.

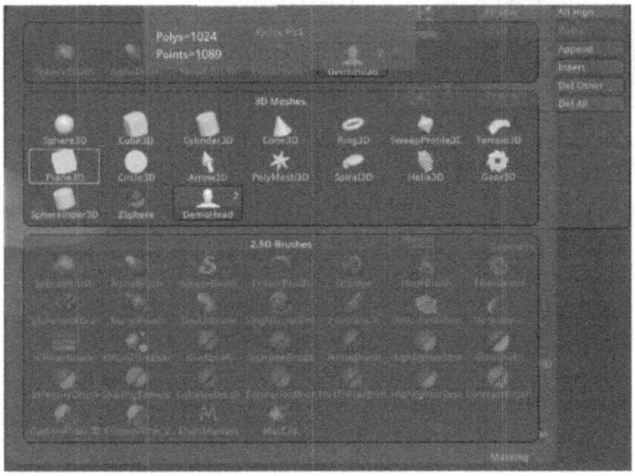

*Figure 12-52 The **Plane3D** primitive chosen from the flyout*

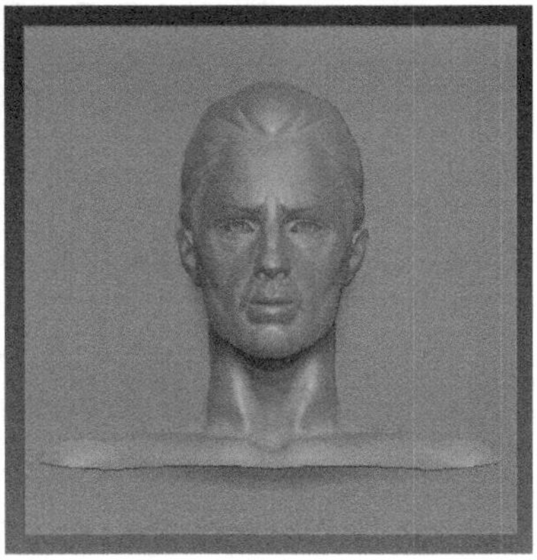

Figure 12-53 The plane displayed in the canvas

6. Make sure the plane is selected in the SubTool list in the **SubTool** subpalette of the **Tool** palette. Expand the **Deformation** subpalette in the **Tool** palette.

   You need to rotate the plane along the X-axis using the **Rotate** slider in the **Deformation** subpalette.

7. Deactivate the **y** and **z** buttons corresponding to the **Rotate** slider and activate the **x** button. Next, set the value of the **Rotate** slider to **90**, refer to Figure 12-54; the plane rotates in the canvas, however, it is not visible in the canvas.

8. Expand the **Display Properties** subpalette in the **Tool** palette. In this subpalette, make sure the **Double** button is chosen, refer to Figure 12-55; the rotated plane is visible in the canvas.

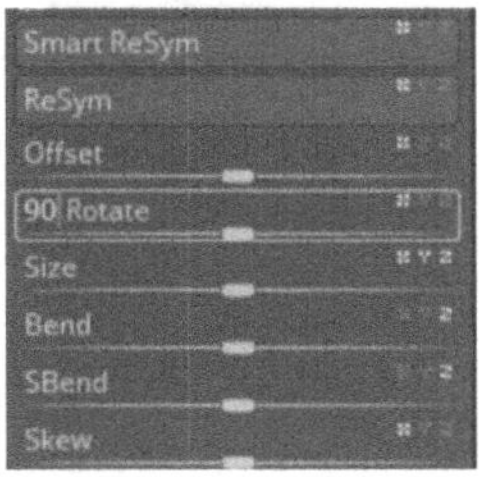

*Figure 12-54 The value of the **Rotate** slider set to **90***

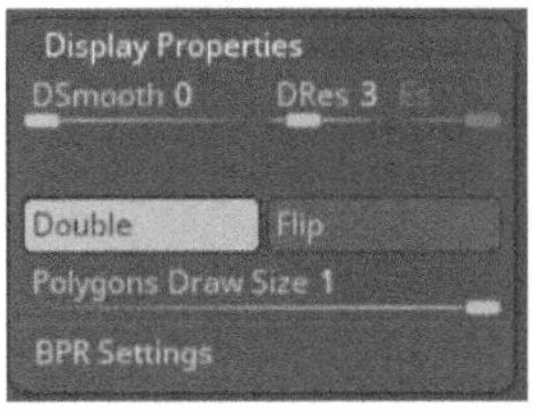

*Figure 12-55 The **Double** button chosen*

9. Increase the size of the plane using the **Size** slider in the **Deformation** subpalette. Next, move the plane below the model using the **Move** tool, refer to Figure 12-56. Now, the scene is set.

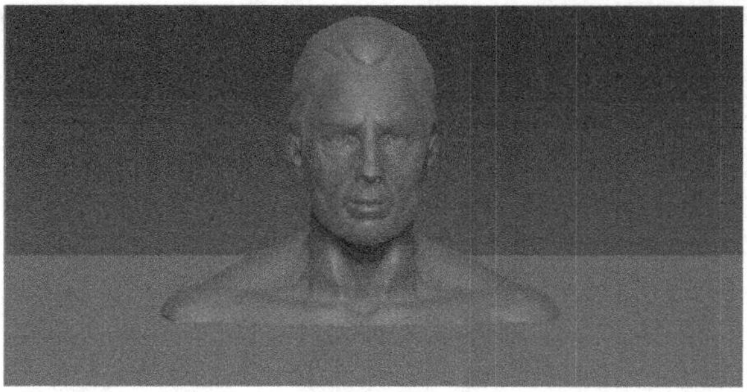

Figure 12-56 The plane placed below the model

Generating Different Render Passes

In this section, you will generate different render passes of the scene using the **BPR** renderer.

1. Expand the **Light** palette. In this palette, make sure the first light switch is turned on.

2. Select the orange dot on the **Light Placement** window and drag it to the position shown in Figure 12-57.

3. Expand the **Render Properties** subpalette in the **Render** palette. In this subpalette, choose the **AOcclusion** button, refer to Figure 12-58.

*Figure 12-57 The light positioned in the **Light Placement** window*

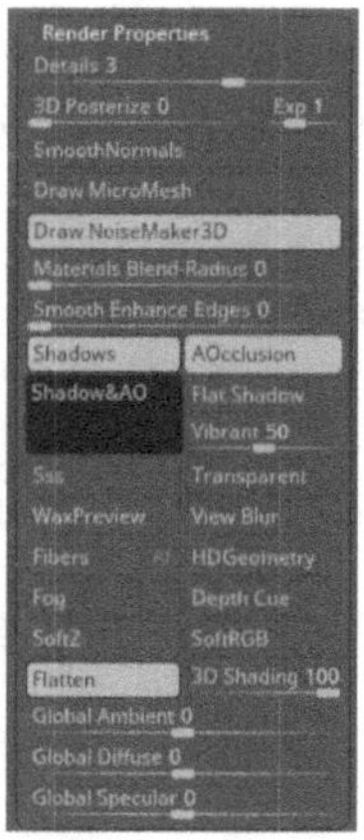

*Figure 12-58 The **AOcclusion** button chosen*

4. Expand the **BPR RenderPass** subpalette in the **Render** palette. In this subpalette, choose the **BPR** button; the scene is rendered and different render passes are generated, refer to Figure 12-59.

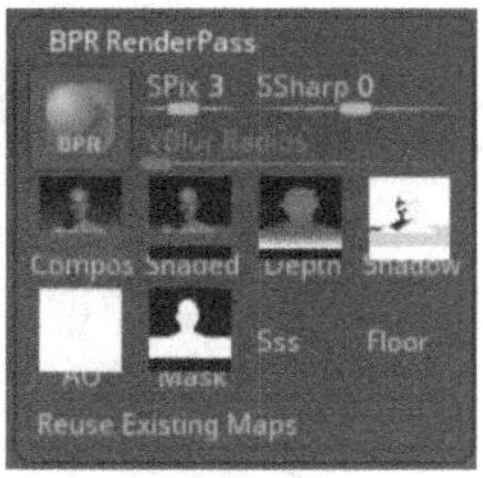

Figure 12-59 *The render passes generated*

5. Click on the **Shaded** render pass; the **Export Image** dialog box is displayed, refer to Figure 12-60. In this dialog box, browse to the desired location and create a new folder in that location. Save the **Shaded** render pass in that folder in the .BMP format. Similarly, save the rest of the render passes in the folder.

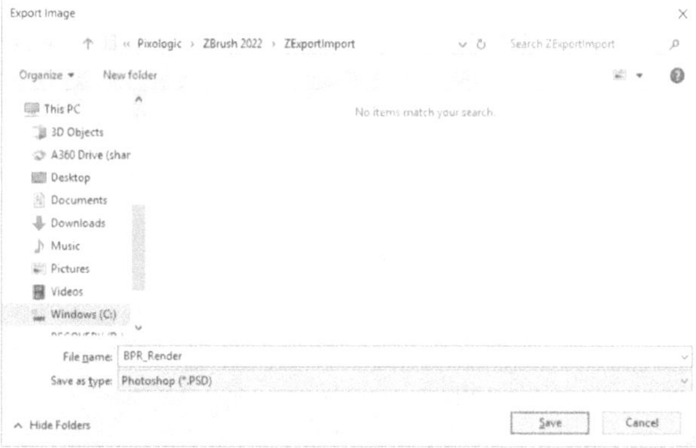

Figure 12-60 *The **Export Image** dialog box*

6. Expand the **Light** palette. In this palette, select the orange dot on the **Light Placement** window and drag it to the position shown in Figure 12-61.

7. Expand the **BPR RenderPass** subpalette in the **Render** palette. In this subpalette, choose the **BPR** button; the scene is rendered and different render passes are generated again.

8. Click on the **Shaded** render pass, refer to Figure 12-62; the **Export Image** dialog box is displayed. In this dialog box, save the **Shaded** render pass in the .BMP format and name it as specular, refer to Figure 12-63.

After generating all the render passes, you can composite these passes in different compositing software applications such as Adobe Photoshop, Nuke, Fusion, and so on.

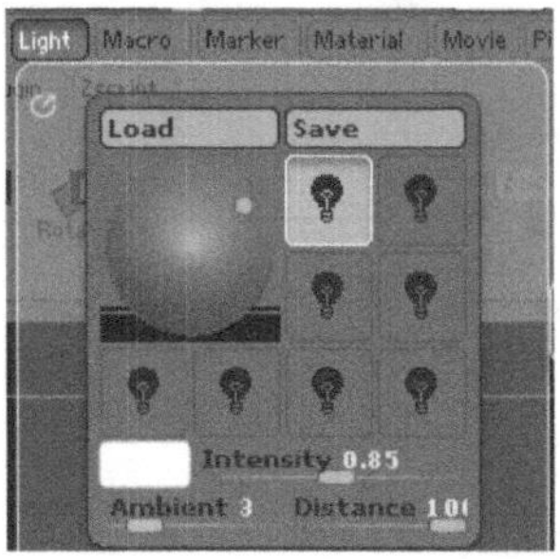

Figure 12-61 The light positioned in the ***Light Placement*** *window*

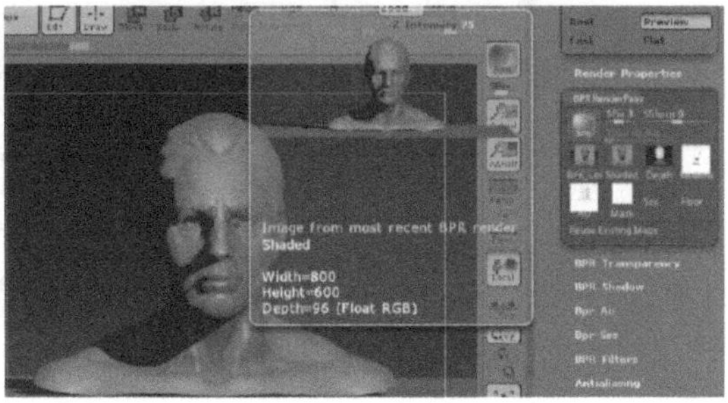

Figure 12-62 The ***Shaded*** *render pass selected*

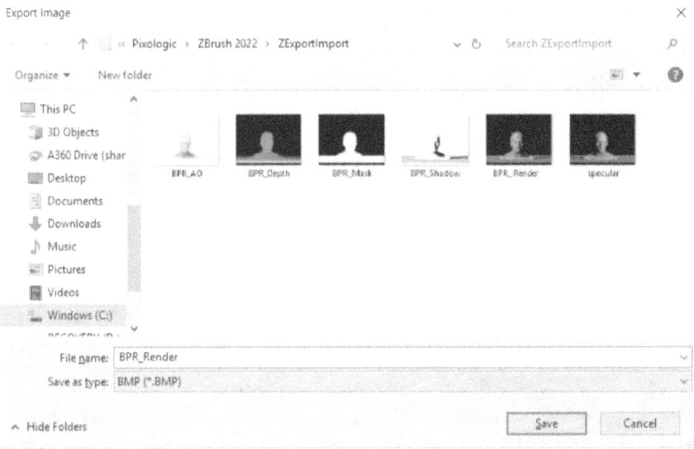

Figure 12-63 The render passes saved in the .BMP format

Saving the Scene

In this section, you will save the file using the steps given next.

1. Choose the **Save As** button from the **Tool** palette; the **Save ZTool** dialog box is displayed. In this dialog box, browse to the location: *\Documents\ZBrushprojects\c12.*

2. Enter **c12tut1** in the **File name** edit box and then choose the **Save** button.

Tutorial 2

In this tutorial, you will set up a scene and then create a KeyShot render of the scene.

(Expected time: 15 min)

The following steps are required to complete this tutorial:

a. Set up the scene.
b. Create the KeyShot render of the scene.
c. Save the scene.

Setting up the Scene

In this section, you will set up a scene.

1. Choose the **Init ZBrush** button from the **Preferences** palette; ZBrush is initialized to its default state.

2. Choose the **Load Tool** button from the **Tool** palette; the **Load ZTool** dialog box is displayed. In this dialog box, browse to*\Documents\ZBrushprojects\c12* and select the **c12tut2start.ZTL** file from it. Next, choose the **Open** button from this dialog box; the model is displayed in the canvas, as shown in Figure 12-64.

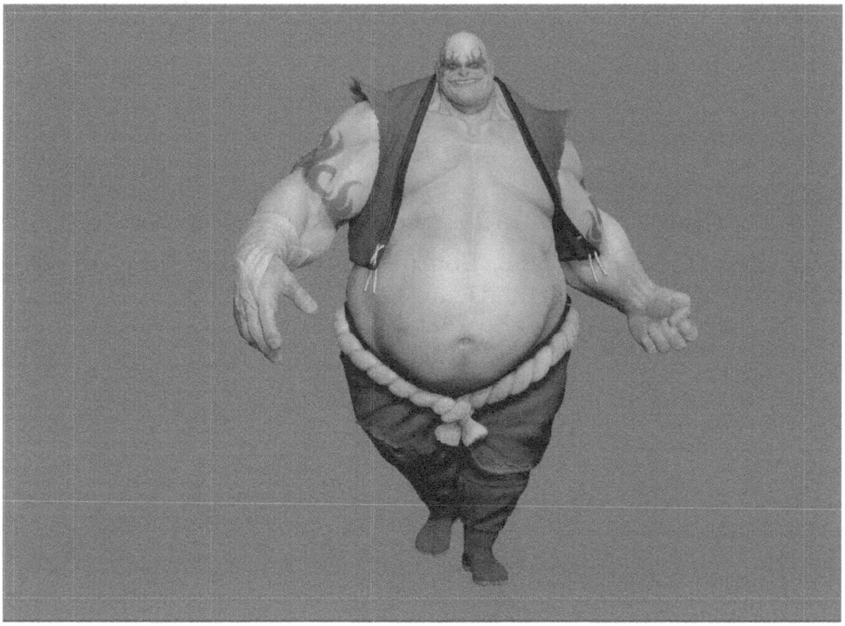

***Figure 12-64** The **Kotelnikoff Earthquake** model displayed in the canvas*

Creating the KeyShot Render of the Scene

In this section, you will create the keyshot render of the scene.

1. Run the KeyShot version available in your system.

2. Expand the **External Renderer** subpalette in the **Render** palette. In this subpalette, choose the **Keyshot** button and press SHIFT+R; the scene is rendered using the KeyShot renderer.

3. Switch to KeyShot renderer and check the render of the model, as shown in Figure 12-65.

Figure 12-65 The rendered model in the KeyShot renderer

4. In KeyShot, choose the **Tumble** button from the Ribbon, as shown in Figure 12-66 and rotate the camera to set the model, refer to Figure 12-67.

*Figure 12-66 Choosing the **Tumble Camera** button from the Ribbon*

Note

*1. If the **Library** window is not open, then choose **Window> Library >Material** from the menubar.*

2. Depending on the keyshort version, the names of materials may change.

***Figure 12-67** Model rotated using the **Tumble Camera** button*

5. Choose the **Materials** tab from the **Library** window in the KeyShot renderer, refer to Figure 12-68. Next, expand the **Metal** node and then select and drag the **Anodized Light Blue** material on to the dress of the model; this material is applied on the dress of the model, as shown in Figure 12-69.

6. From the **Materials** tab of the **Library** window, drag the **Anodized Rough Black** material on to the shoes of the model; the selected material is applied on the shoes of the model.

7. From the **Materials** tab of the **Library** window, drag the **Anodized Brushed Yellow** material on to the rope of the model; the selected material is applied on the rope of the model.

8. Choose the **Colors** tab from the **Library** window and then drag the **Sunburst** material to the body of the model; the material is applied to the body of the model. Figure 12-70 shows the materials applied to the model.

9. Choose the **Backplates** tab from the **Library** window and then drag the **Doch-Design_Dirt-Lot.jpg** material on to the canvas; the material is applied to the environment, refer to Figure 12-71.

10. Choose the **Render** menu from the menu bar; a flyout is displayed. Next, choose the **Render** option from the flyout; the

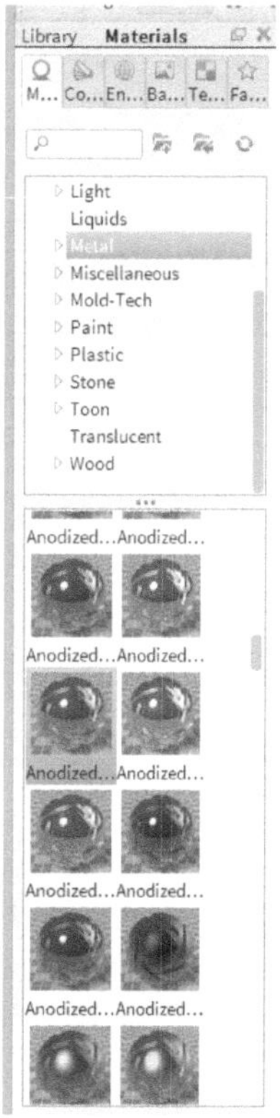

Figure 12-68** The **Metal** node in the **Library

Render dialog box is displayed. Now, enter the name **scene** in the **Name** text box, as shown in Figure 12-72. Now, choose the **Render** button; the rendering window is displayed with rendered model, as shown in Figure 12-73.

Figure 12-69 *The **Anodized Light Blue** material applied to the dress*

Figure 12-70 *The **Sunburst** material applied to the model*

*Figure 12-71 The **Doch-Design_Dirt-Lot** material applied*

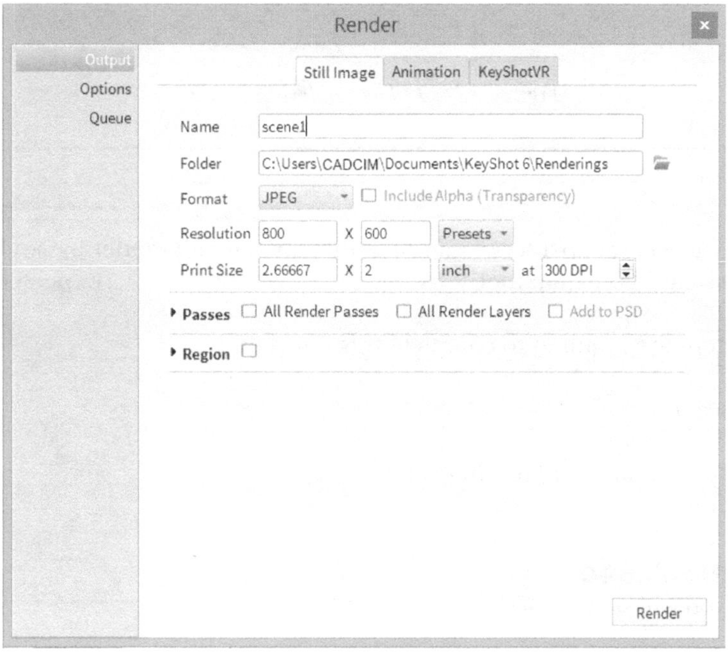

*Figure 12-72 The **Render** dialog box*

Figure 12-73 *The rendering window*

Tutorial 3

In this tutorial, you will set up a scene and then directly send all render passes for compositing using the **ZBrush To Photoshop** tool. **(Expected time: 15 min)**

The following steps are required to complete this tutorial:

a. Set up the scene.
b. Set the light in the scene.
c Render the passes and send to Photoshop.
d. Save the scene.

Setting up the Scene

In this section, you will set up a scene.

1. Choose the **Init ZBrush** button from the **Preferences** palette; ZBrush is initialized to its default state.

2. Choose the **LightBox** button; the **LightBox** browser is displayed. In this browser, make sure the **Project** tab is chosen. Next, double click on the **DemoProjects** preset; various presets are displayed. Now, choose the **QuichHeavyLoadMechanical** preset; the model is displayed in the canvas. You can align the CamView to front, refer to Figure 12-74.

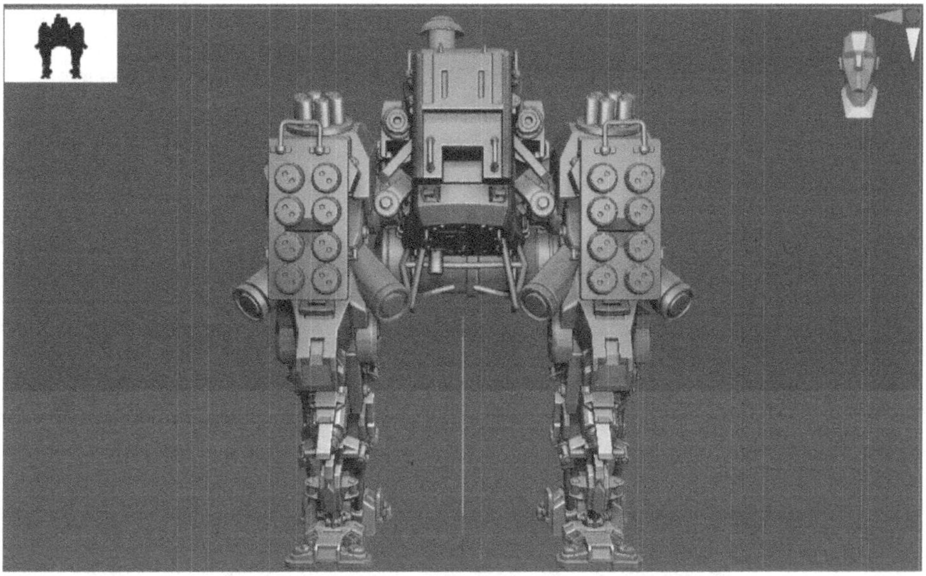

Figure 12-74 *The model displayed in the canvas*

Setting the Light in the Scene

In this section, you will set the light in the scene.

1. Expand the **Light** palette and hover the cursor on the arrow located at the top left corner of the palette; the shape of cursor changes. Next, drag the cursor toward the right tray; the **Light** palette is docked in the right tray and can be easily accessed.

2. In the **Light** palette, make sure the first light switch is turned on. Select the orange dot on the **Light Placement** window and drag it to the location, as shown in Figure 12-75.

3. Set the **Intensity** slider to **1**. Next, set **Ambient** and **Distance** sliders to **3** and **48**, as shown in Figure 12-75.

4. In the **Light** palette, expand the **Light Properties** subpalette and choose the **Shadow** button, if not already chosen, refer to Figure 12-75.

5. Expand the **Lights Type** subpalette in the **Light** palette. In this subpalette, make sure the **Sun** button is chosen to activate the sunlight, if not already chosen, as shown in Figure 12-76.

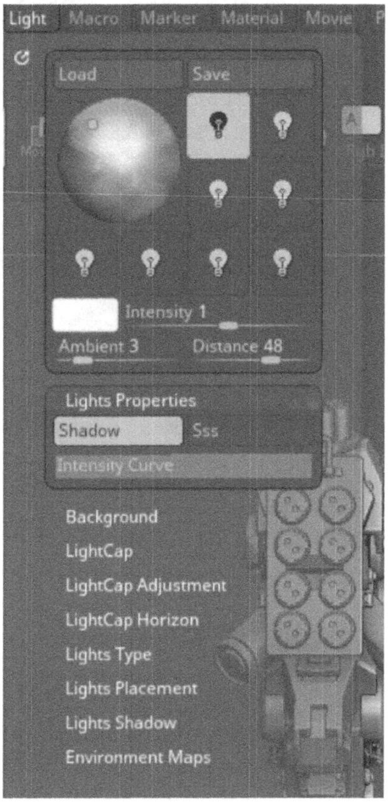

Figure 12-75 *The attributes set in the* ***Light*** *palette*

6. Choose the **BPR** button in the right shelf, refer to Figure 12-77; the model is rendered, as shown in Figure 12-78.

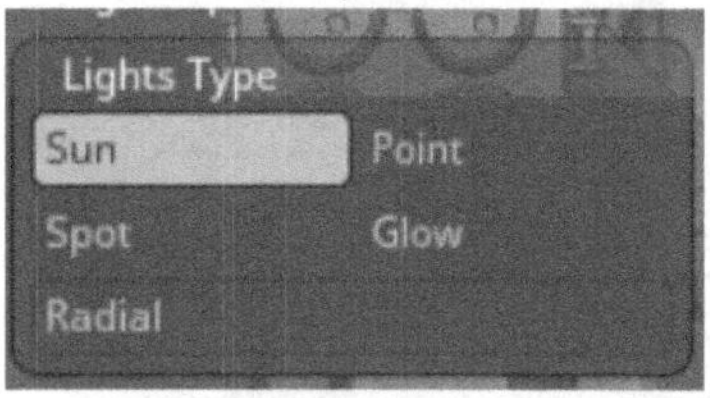

***Figure 12-76** The **Sun** button chosen*

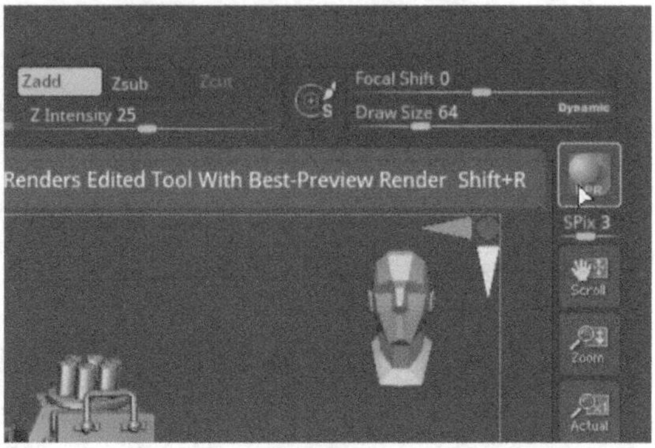

***Figure 12-77** The **BPR** button*

***Figure 12-78** The model rendered using the **BPR** renderer*

Rendering the Passes and Sending to Photoshop

In this section, you will send the render passes of the model to Photoshop.

1. Expand the **ZPlugin** palette and then expand the **ZBrush to Photoshop** subpalette. In this subpalette, notice that a list of render passes buttons is displayed, refer to Figure 12-79.

2. In the **ZBrush to Photoshop** subpalette, choose the **R** button; the **Select Photoshop CC Application** dialog box is displayed. In this dialog box, navigate to the Photoshop executable file in the C drive and choose the **Open** button; the message "**Photoshop CC application Location stored**" is displayed, as shown in Figure 12-80. Next, choose the render passes you

want to send to Photoshop, refer to Figure 12-81 and then choose the **Sent To Photoshop CC** button; ZBrush now renders the selected passes. This process takes some time. Different passes are shown in Figures 12-82 to 12-84.

3. After the rendering process is completed, Photoshop CC is launched and all the passes are imported as layers. You can now work with color adjustment options and filters in Photoshop and modify the passes to beautify your final image, refer to Figure 12-85.

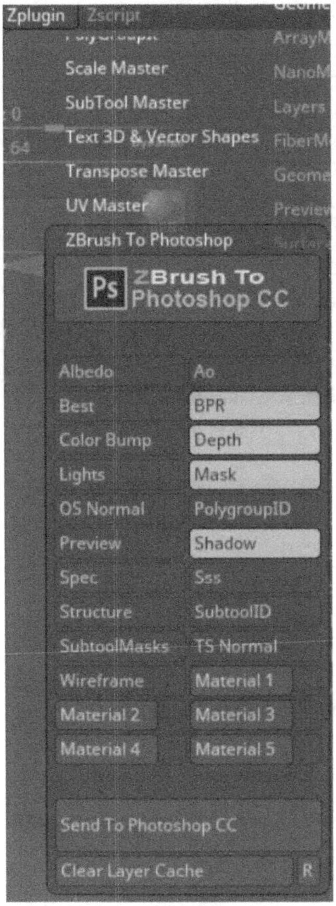

Figure 12-79 *The* ***ZBrush To Photoshop*** *subpalette*

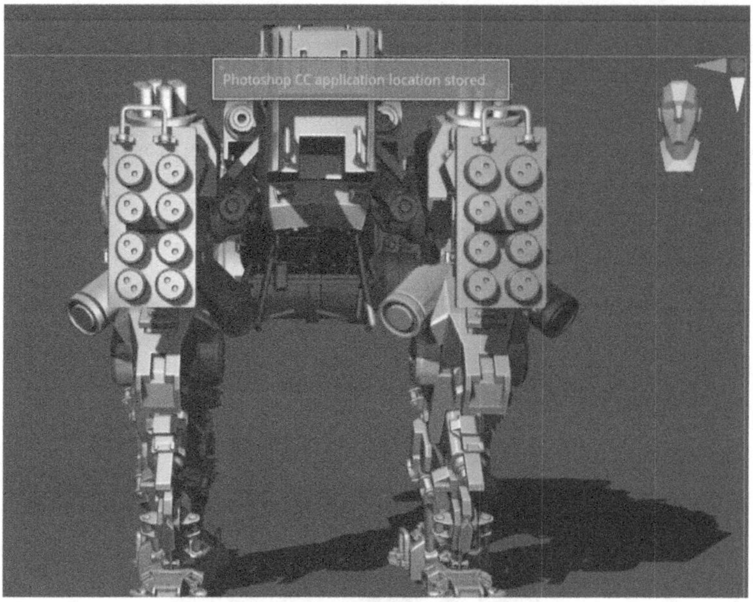

Figure 12-80 The message displayed

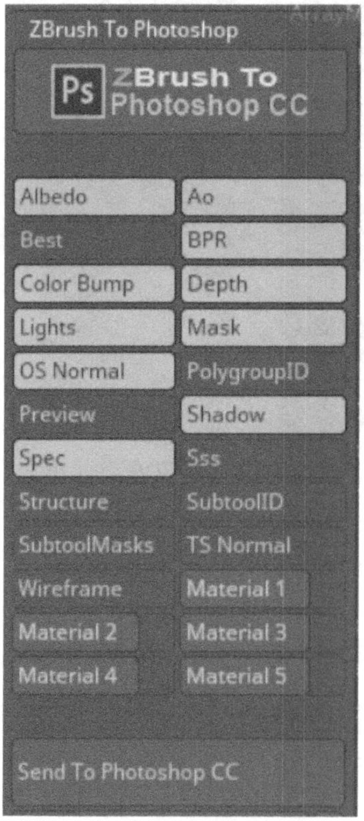

Figure 12-81 Some of the buttons chosen

Saving the Scene

In this section, you will save the file using the steps given next.

1. Choose the **Save As** button from the **Tool** palette; the **Save ZTool** dialog box is displayed. In this dialog box, browse to the location: *\Documents\ZBrushprojects\c12*.

2. Enter **c12tut3** in the **File name** edit box and then choose the **Save** button.

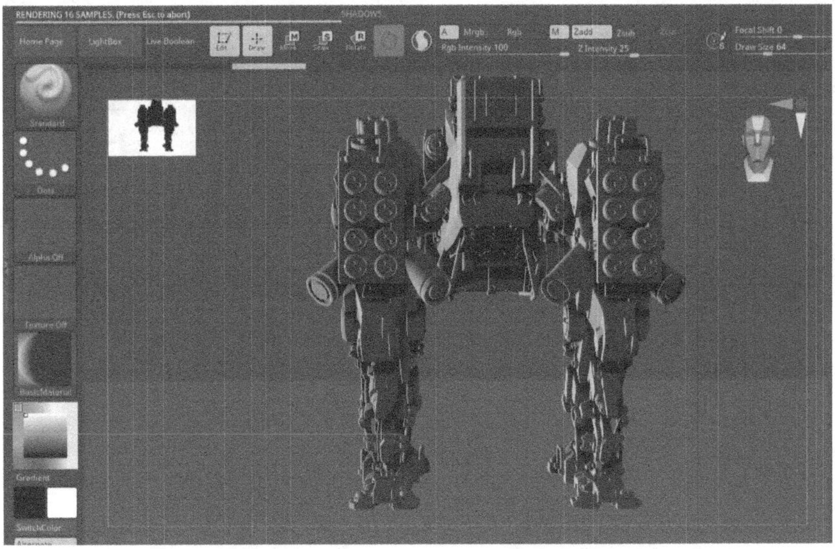

Figure 12-82 The process of rendering

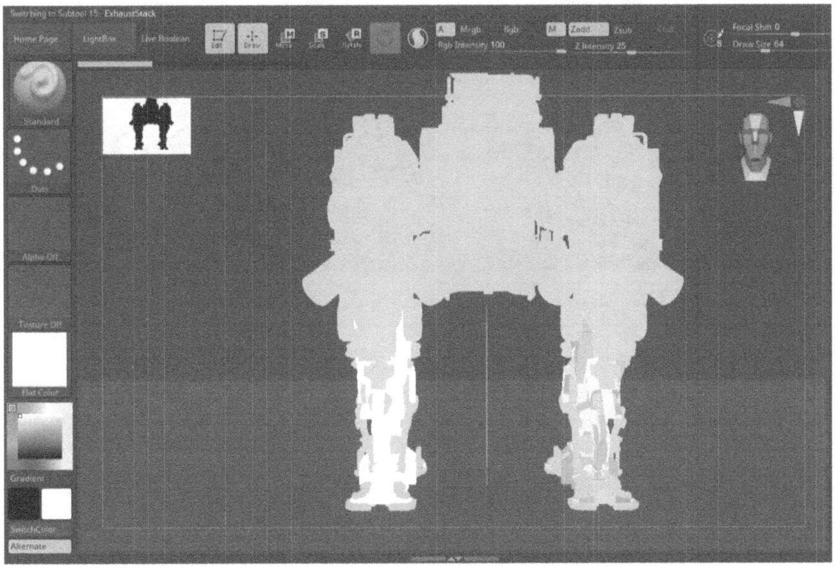

Figure 12-83 The process of rendering with different render passes

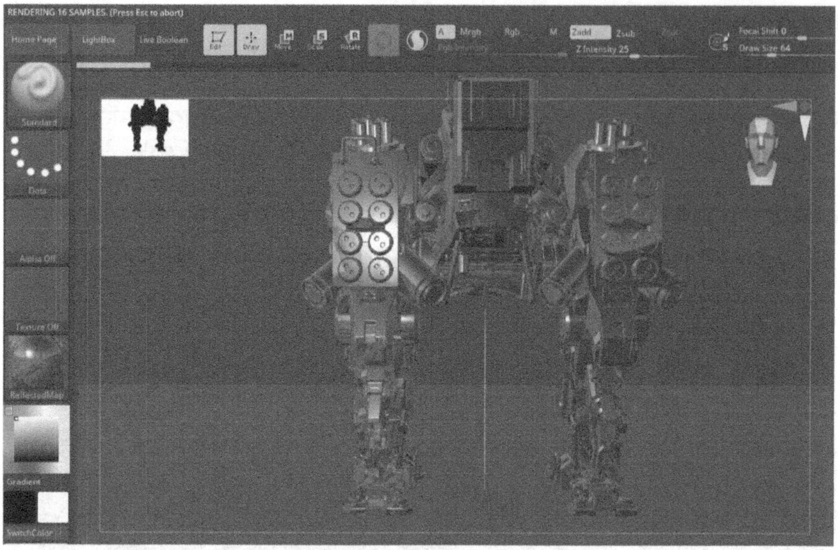

Figure 12-84 *The process of rendering with different render passes*

Figure 12-85 *Compositing render passes in a scene using Photoshop*

Self-Evaluation Test

Answer the following questions and then compare them to those given at the end of this chapter:

1. Which of the following sliders in the **Render Properties** subpalette is used to globally control the saturation of shadows and ambient occlusion when a scene is rendered?

   (a) **Exp** (b) **Global Ambient**
   (c) **Vibrant** (d) **Details**

2. Which of the following buttons in the **Render Properties** subpalette is used to smoothen the stray pixels in the canvas when the scene is rendered using the **Best** renderer?

   (a) **SoftRGB** (b) **SmoothNormals**
   (c) **Depth Cue** (d) **SoftZ**

3. Which of the following sliders in the **Bpr Ao** subpalette is used to control the strength of the ambient occlusion on the floor when a scene is rendered using the **BPR** renderer?

   (a) **FStrength** (b) **VDepth**
   (c) **LDepth** (d) **GStrength**

4. The term AF stands for __________.

5. The __________ slider in the **BPR Shadow** subpalette is used to adjust the gradient in the shadow contrast.

6. The __________ subpalette consists of different options that are used to control the settings in the Subsurface scattering generated on rendering a scene using the **BPR** renderer.

7. The __________ subpalette consists of different options that are used to blur different parts of a scene based on their position along the Z-axis.

8. The **SPix** slider in the **BPR RenderPass** subpalette is used to increase or decrease the amount of blur in a rendered scene. (T/F)

9. The **BPR** renderer works only for 3D scenes in edit mode. (T/F)

10. The **Cursor** button in the **Render** palette is used to render only a selected part of a scene. (T/F)

Review Questions

Answer the following questions:

1. Which of the following sliders in the **Bpr Sss** subpalette is used to set the focus of the Subsurface scattering in the scene?

   (a) **Res** (b) **Rays**
   (c) **Blur** (d) **Angle**

2. The __________ subpalette consists of different options that are used to apply various color correction settings to the rendered image.

3. The __________ slider in the **Environment** subpalette is used to specify whether the fitted texture image will be reflected by the objects or only a part of it will be reflected.

4. The __________ slider in the **Preview Wax** subpalette is used to specify whether the wax effect will be applied to the surfaces of an object facing the canvas or to the surfaces facing away from the canvas.

5. The **DistFalloff** slider in the **Bpr Ao** subpalette is used to control the speed of fading in the ambient occlusion. (T/F)

6. The **HDGeometry** button in the **Render Properties** subpalette is used to replace the polygons of an object or the fibers of a fibermesh with a new geometry when the object is rendered using the **BPR** renderer. (T/F)

7. The **Flat** button in the **Render** palette is used to render both the 3D and 2.5D scenes in the fast preview mode. (T/F)

EXERCISE

The output of the model used in this exercise can be accessed by downloading the *c12_ZBrush_2022_exr.zip* from *www.cadcim.com*. The path of the file is as follows: *Textbooks > Animation and Visual Effects > Pixologic ZBrush 2022 > Pixologic ZBrush 2022: A Comprehensive Guide.*

Exercise 1

Load the *DemoHead.ZTL* file from the **Tool** tab of the **LightBox** browser and then append a sphere to it. Next, apply transparency settings to the sphere, as shown in Figure 12-86.

(Expected time: 20 min)

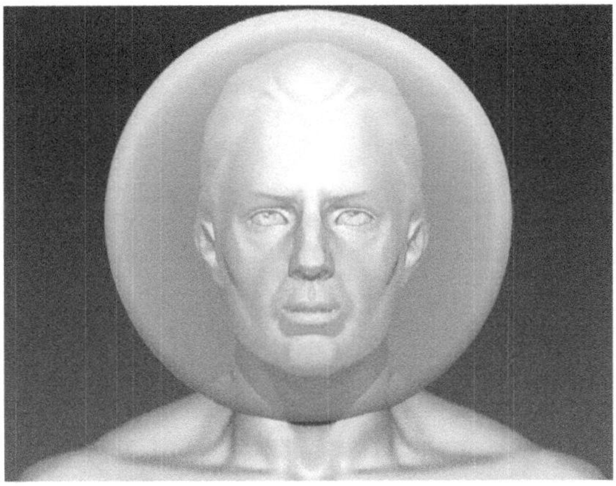

Figure 12-86 *The final output*

Answers to Self-Evaluation Test

1. c, **2.** d, **3.** a, **4.** Antialiase Fibers, **5. Gamma**, **6. Bpr Sss**, **7. Depth Cue**, **8.** F, **9.** T, **10.** T

Chapter 13

Dynamics

Learning Objectives

After completing this chapter, you will be able to:

- *Understand the Dynamics System*
- *Create the FiberMesh Dynamics simulation*
- *Create Cloth Dynamics Simulation*

INTRODUCTION TO DYNAMICS

In ZBrush 2022, Dynamics system is introduced for simulation. Using the Dynamics system, you can contract, expand, or inflate any surface. As a result, you can create realistic cloth simulation, fiber mesh simulation, and so on. In this chapter, you will understand Dynamics simulation in detail.

Dynamics PALETTE

The **Dynamics** palette is located below the title bar. Figure 13-1 shows the **Dynamics** Palette. This palette consists of different buttons and sliders that are used for simulation and are discussed next.

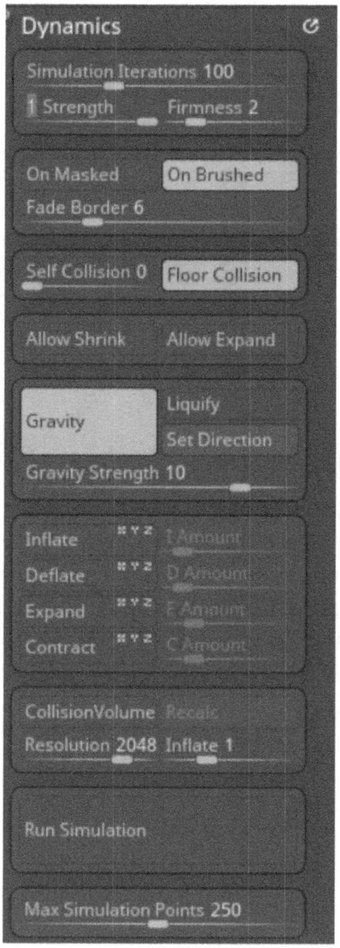

*Figure 13-1 The **Dynamics** Palette*

Simulation Iterations

This slider is used to determine the number of simulation cycles carried out for each movement. You can keep higher value in this slider to get more accurate results, but simulation also slows down. Contrarily, if you keep lower value in this slider, there will be effect of more stretching on simulating surface because of less simulation time.

Strength

As the name suggests, this slider specifies the strength of the simulating surface. If the value in this slider is higher, then there will be less stretching effect on the simulating surface and vice versa. Figures 13-2 and 13-3 show cloth simulation with strength value **0.5** and **1**, respectively.

Firmness

The value in this slider affects the wrinkles and folds on the simulating surface. Higher value results in less folds and wrinkles on the simulating surface and vice versa. This slider is useful in cloth simulation. Figures 13-4 and 13-5 show cloth simulation with firmness value **1** and **4**, respectively.

On Masked

If you choose this button, there will be simulation on the masked portion of the simulating surface. But as a result, the unmasked area will also move.

On Brushed

This button is chosen by default. As a result, simulation will affect the area of the simulating surface where brushes are applied. If you deactivate this button, then simulation will affect the whole mesh of the simulating surface.

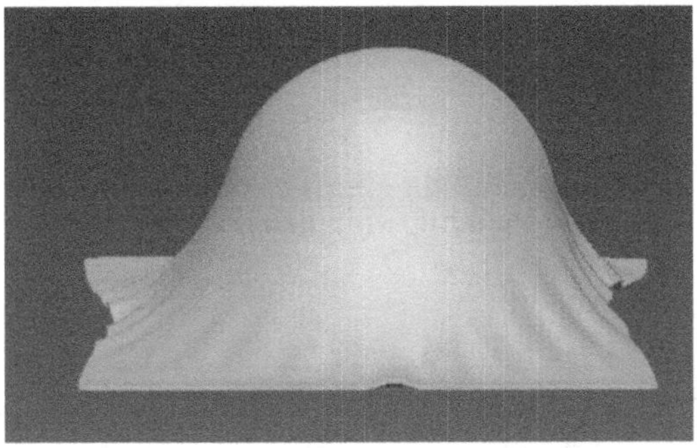

Figure 13-2 Cloth simulation with ***Strength = 0.5***

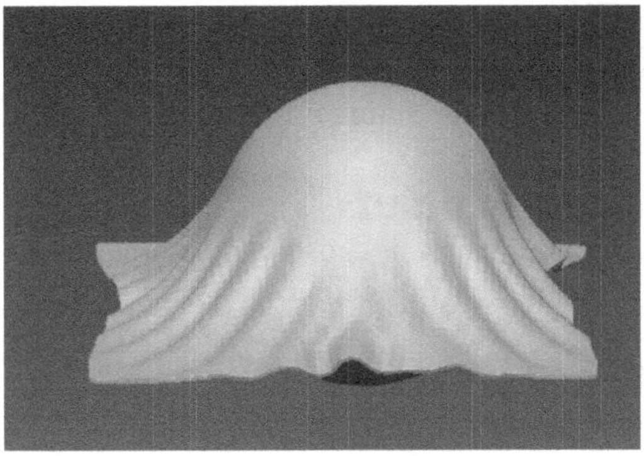

Figure 13-3 Cloth simulation with ***Strength = 1***

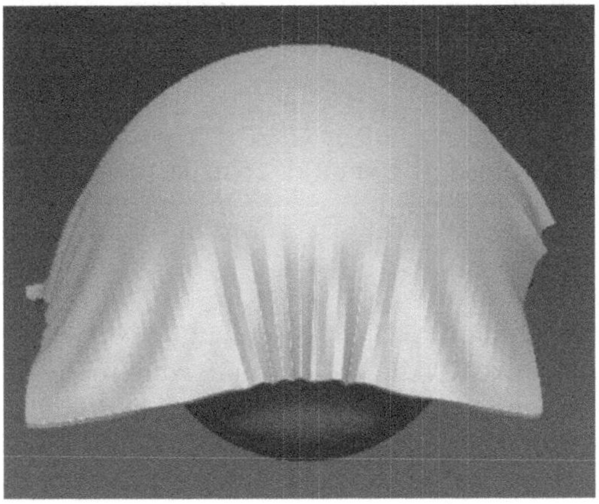

Figure 13-4 Cloth simulation with ***Firmness = 1***

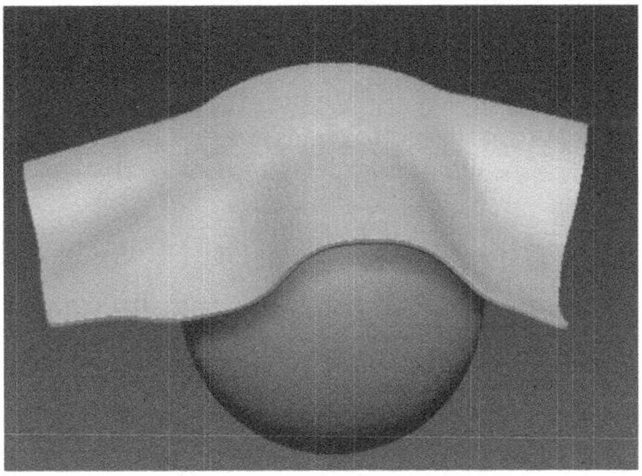

Figure 13-5 Cloth simulation with ***Firmness = 4***

Fade Border

This slider is used to fade the simulation effect when the **On Brushed** button is chosen. If the value is higher, the fading will be more whereas if the value is 0, fading will be turned off.

Self Collision

The value in this slider determines the amount of collision of the object with itself. If the value is higher, simulation detects self collision with greater accuracy and vice versa. Maximum value for this slider is 4.

Floor Collision

This button turns ON or OFF collision of the simulating object with the floor grid. Note that to turn on the floor grid, you can choose the **Floor Grid** button from the right shelf.

Note

To adjust the floor height, you need to change the value in the **Elv** slider in the **Draw** palette.

Allow Shrink

When this button is chosen, the simulating surface area will shrink to match the surfaces underneath the simulating surface.

Allow Expand

When this button is chosen, the simulating surface area will expand similar to the effect of using the **Cloth Pull** brush on the object.

Gravity

This button is used to apply gravity equally to all parts of the mesh of the selected object. The effect of gravity also depends on the dynamic thickness of the object. To modify dynamic thickness of the object, you need to first choose the **Dynamic** button from the **Dynamic Subdivision** area in the **Geometry** subpalette of the **Tool** palette. Next, change the value in the **Thickness** slider in this area to modify dynamic thickness.

Liquify

This button is used to change the dynamics algorithm from cloth to liquid. To make this happen, you need to make some variations in the mesh.

Set Direction

This button is used to set the gravity direction for the simulating object. By default, this direction is set from top to bottom in the ZBrush window. To set the new direction, you need to rotate the model and then choose the **Set Direction** button to save that angle of direction. On doing so, gravity will set in that direction even if the object is rotated later in the canvas.

Gravity Strength

The value in this slider is used to specify the strength of the gravity applied to a simulating object. If the value in both sliders, **Gravity Strength** and **Simulation Iterations**, is higher, the simulating object will be stretched. So, you need to keep a balance of these parameters to get a desired simulating effect.

Inflate, Inflate Amount

When you choose the **Inflate** button, the simulating surface will expand at the time of simulation. Note that this inflation will be in the facing direction of the polygons of the simulating surface. Also, the value in the **Inflate Amount** slider that is located next to the **Inflate** button determines the simulation speed. Additionally, you can restrict the inflation to any of the specific axes by turning ON the **X**, **Y**, or **Z** button.

Deflate, Deflate Amount

When you choose the **Deflate** button, the simulating surface will shrink at the time of simulation. Note that this deflation will be opposite to the facing direction of the polygons of the simulating surface. Also, the value in the **Deflate Amount** slider that is located next to the **Deflate** button determines the simulation speed. Additionally, you can restrict the deflation to any of the specific axes by turning ON the **X**, **Y**, or **Z** button.

Expand, Expand Amount

As the name suggests, the **Expand** button is used to grow the simulating surface area with ripples. Simulating surface points move away from each other in all the directions. The **Expand Amount** slider specifies the speed at which the simulating surface will grow when the **Expand** button is activated.

Contract Amount

As the name suggests, the **Contract** button is used to shrink the simulating surface area. Simulating surface points move toward each other from all the directions. The **Contract Amount** slider specifies the speed at which the simulating surface will shrink when the **Contract** button is activated.

CollisionVolume

When you click this button, collision volume of the simulating surface with the nearby colliding surface is calculated. But, when this button is not activated, the simulating surface will not react to any other object in the scene.

Recalc

This button is used to reflect scene changes such as turning ON/OFF the visibility of subtool(s), deleting the subtool(s) and so on in the simulation process.

Resolution

The value in this slider is used to control the smoothness of the collision volume. The value in this slider should be higher to get the good simulation results.

Inflate

The value in this slider specifies the inflated collision volume amount of the simulating surface. If this value is higher, the simulating surface will be a bit above the colliding surface. If you want the simulating surface to stick to the colliding surface, you need to reduce the value in this slider.

Run Simulation

This button is used to run the simulation. You need to press SPACEBAR to stop the simulation. After that you can make the desired changes and then choose this button again to continue the simulation. To start the simulation from the start, you need to press the ESC key and then choose this button again.

Max Simulation Points

The value in this slider specifies maximum simulation points. If maximum simulation points of the simulating surface are higher than this value, the simulation process will not be carried out. To get good simulation results, you also need to tweak values in the **Simulation Iterations** and **Gravity Strength** sliders along with this slider.

TUTORIALS

Before you start the tutorials of this chapter, navigate to *\Documents\ZBrushprojects* and then create a new folder with the name *c13*.

Tutorial 1

In this tutorial, you will create hair on the head of a model using Fiber Mesh and simulate the same using the Dynamics system. **(Expected time: 35 min)**

The following steps are required to complete this tutorial:

a. Create hair.
b. Simulate hair.
c. Save the scene.

Creating Hair

In this section, you will create hair on the head of a model using Fiber Mesh.

1. Choose the **Init ZBrush** button from the **Preferences** palette; the message box is displayed. Choose the **Yes** button from the message box; ZBrush is initialized to its default state.

2. Choose **DemoHeadFema** from the **Project** tab of the **LightBox** browser by double-clicking on it. Next, drag the cursor in the canvas area; the model is displayed in the canvas. Also, make sure the **Edit** button is chosen in the top shelf.

3. Choose the Current Brush button from the left shelf; a flyout containing different sculpting brushes is displayed. Choose the **MaskLasso** brush from this flyout; a message box is displayed. Choose **OK** in this message box.

4. Press and hold the CTRL key and draw a mask on the head of the model, as shown in Figure 13-6.

Note

*To change the background in ZBrush viewport, choose **Back** from the **Documents** palette.*

5. In the **Tools** palette, expand the **FiberMesh** subpalette. In this subpalette, choose the **Preview** button; the parameters in this subpalette are activated. Also, fibers are generated on the masked part of the head, refer to Figure 13-7.

6. In the **FiberMesh** subpalette, expand the **Modifiers** area located below the **Preview** button. Next, enter **5** in the **MaxFibers** edit box and **750** in the **Length** edit box. Also, change the width profile, as shown in Figure 13-8; fibers are modified, as shown in Figure 13-9.

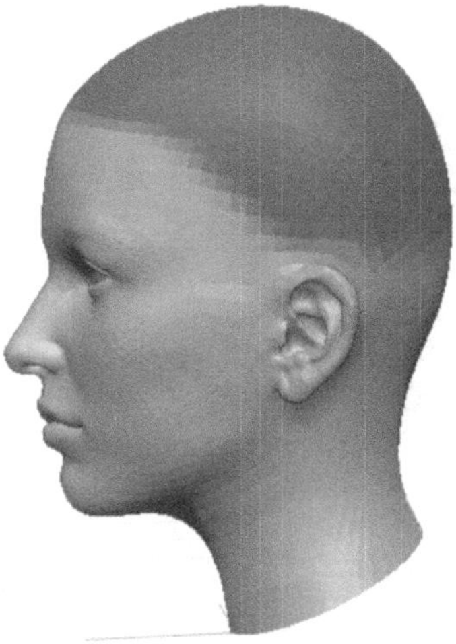

Figure 13-6 *mask created on the head of a model*

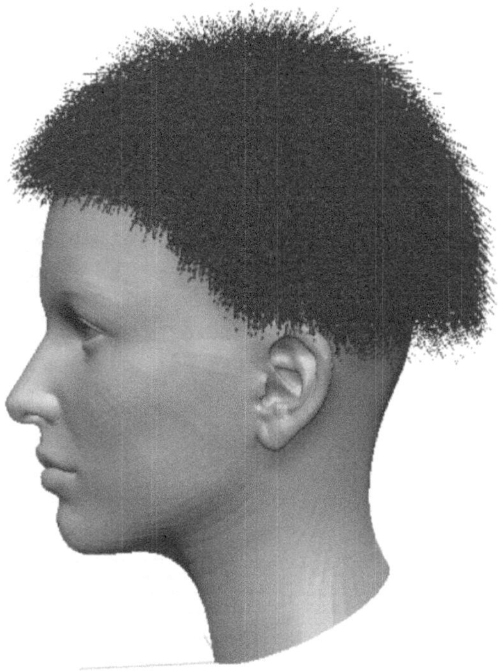

Figure 13-7 *Fibers generated on the head of a model*

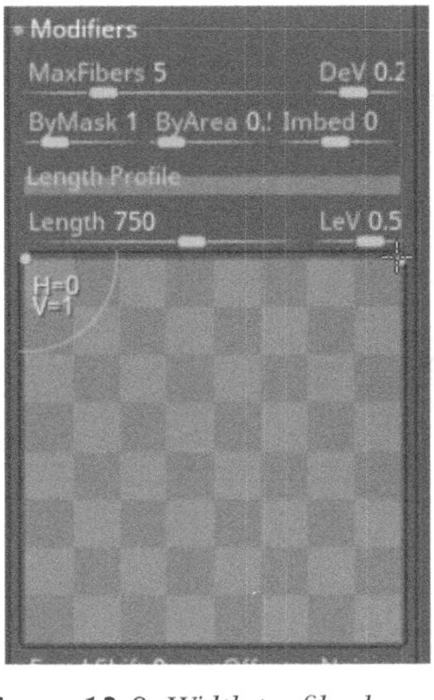

Figure 13-8 *Width profile changed*

Figure 13-9 *Fibers modified on the head of a model*

7. Enter **1500** in the **Coverage** slider and then enter **1** in the **ScaleTip** and **ScaleRoot** sliders. Next, Enter **0** in the **Twist** slider and enter **1** in the **Gravity** slider. Fibers are modified again, as shown in Figure 13-10.

Figure 13-10 *Fibers modified again*

8. Enter **10** in the **Segments** slider. You will notice that the fiber tilts down toward the ground. refer to Figure 13-11.

Figure 13-11 *Fibers tilted down*

9. Choose **Accept**; a message box is displayed. Choose **No** in this message box.

10. Next, activate the **GroomHairToss** brush and modify the hair style of the model as desired, refer to Figure 13-12.

Figure 13-12 Hairstyle modified

Simulating Hair

In this section, you will simulate hair using Dynamics system.

1. Choose the **Dynamics** palette to expand it. Next, pin this palette at the left of interface by clicking on the upper left most icon on this palette, refer to Figure 13-13.

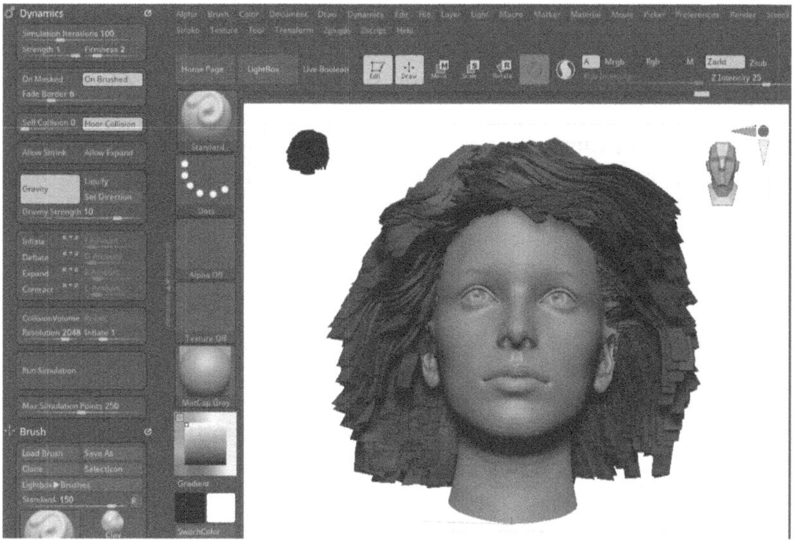

Figure 13-13 The ***Dynamics*** *palette pinned at the left of the interface*

2. Choose the **Run Simulation** button from the **Dynamics** palette. You will notice that hair falls off on the floor. Now, choose the **Run Simulation** button again to stop the simulation. Next, press CTRL+ Z to undo the simulation.

3. Enter **5** in the **Simulation Iterations** slider of the **Dynamics** palette.

4. Click on the **Masking** subpalette from the **Tools** palette. Next, choose the **Mask by Fibers** button from the **Masking** subpalette. Next, choose the **FiberMaskProfile** button; the fiber mask profile is displayed. Change this profile, as shown in Figure 13-14. Next, choose the **FiberMask** button located above the fiber mask profile.

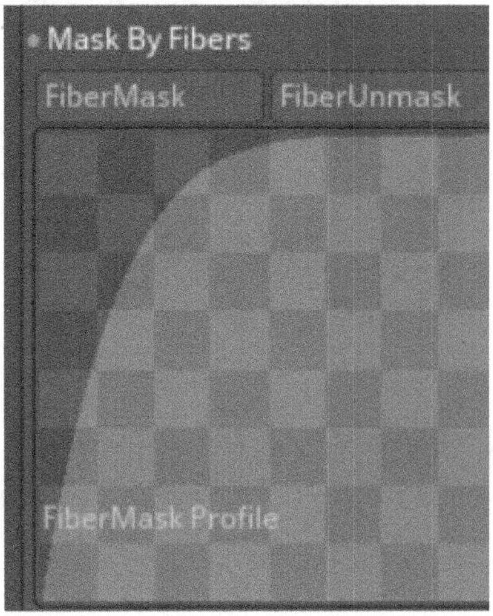

Figure 13-14 *FiberMask Profile changed*

5. Choose the **Run Simulation** button from the **Dynamics** palette. You will notice that now the roots of the hair are stuck to the head at the time of simulation. Next, choose the **Run Simulation** button again to stop the simulation. Next, press CTRL+ Z to undo the simulation.

6. Choose the **CollisionVolume** button from the **Dynamics** palette and then choose the **Run Simulation** button from the **Dynamics** palette. You will notice that hair collides with the head. Now, choose the **Run Simulation** button again to stop the simulation. Next, press CTRL+ Z to undo the simulation.

7. Enter **1** in the **Self Collision** slider and then choose the **Run Simulation** button from the **Dynamics** palette.

8. Expand the **Geometry** subpalette in the **Tools** palette. Next, expand the **Dynamic SubDiv** subpalette and **then** choose the **Dynamic SubDiv** button in this subpalette.

9. Choose the **Dynamic** button; hair turns into dynamic geometry. Enter **0.04** in the **Thickness** slider of the **Dynamic Subdivision** subpalette. Activate cloth brushes like **ClothWind** and **ClothInflate** brushes one by one and change the hairstyle of the model as desired, refer to Figure 13-15.

10. Enter **0.5** in the **Inflate** slider located next to the **Resolution** slider to keep hair closer to the head of the model. Also, enter **4** in the **Firmness** slider. Next, repeat the simulation process again as discussed earlier. Figure 13-16 shows simulating hair of the model.

Figure 13-15 *Modified hairstyle of the model*

Figure 13-16 *Simulating hair of the model*

Saving the Model

In this section, you will save the file using the steps given next.

1. Choose the **Save As** button from the **Tool** palette; the **Save ZTool** dialog box is displayed. In this dialog box, browse to the location: *\Documents\ZBrushprojects\c13*.

2. Enter **c13tut1** in the **File name** edit box and then choose the **Save** button.

Tutorial 2

In this tutorial, you will create the model of mattress, bedsheet, and pillow and then simulate a bedsheet and pillow using the Dynamics system, as shown in Figure 13-17.

(Expected time: 35 min)

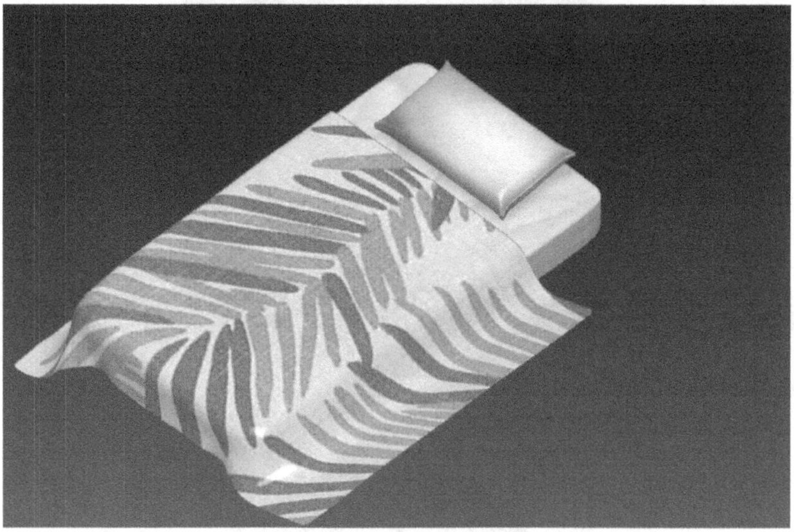

Figure 13-17 The mattress, bedsheet, and pillow model

The following steps are required to complete this tutorial:

a. Create mattress.
b. Simulate bedsheet.
c. Simulate pillow.
d. Apply texture on mattress, bedsheet, and pillow.
e. Save the scene.

Creating Mattress

In this section, you will create a mattress.

1. Choose the **Init ZBrush** button from the **Preferences** palette; a message box is displayed. Choose the **Yes** button from the message box; ZBrush is initialized to its default state.

2. Choose the Current Tool button from the **Tool** palette; a flyout is displayed. Choose the **Cube3D** primitive from this flyout, refer to Figure 13-18.

3. Press and hold the left mouse button and drag the cursor on the canvas; a cube is created in the canvas, as shown in Figure 13-19.

4. Choose the **Edit** button from the top shelf. Next, choose the **Make PolyMesh3D** button from

the **Tool** palette to convert the cube into a polymesh. Select the thumbnail for the newly created **Cube3D_1** from the subtool list. Rename it to **Mattress**.

***Figure 13-18 Cube3D** chosen from the flyout*

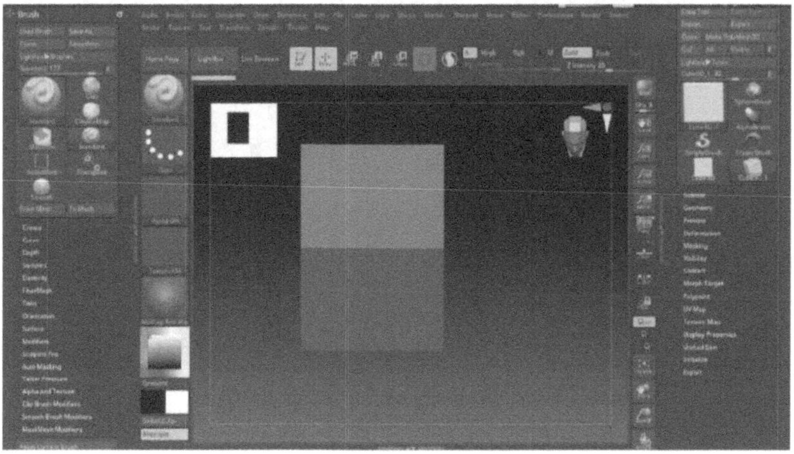

***Figure 13-19** The **Cube3D_1** created in the canvas*

5. In the **Tool** palette, expand the **Geometry** subpalette. In this subpalette, expand the **Dynamic Subdiv** area and choose the **Dynamic** button; the parameters in this subpalette are activated. Also, *Mattress* is smoothened and bevelled. refer to Figure 13-20. Activate the **Scale** tool and scale *Mattress*, as shown in Figure13-21.

Figure 13-20 The Mattress bevelled and smoothened

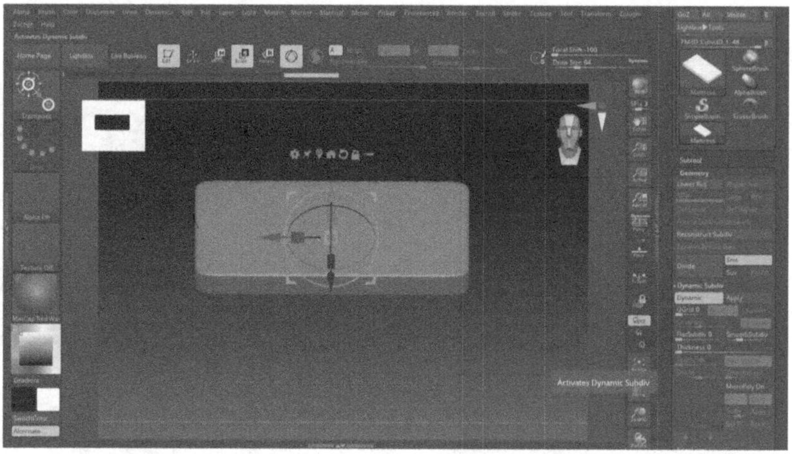

Figure 13-21 Mattress scaled using the ***Scale*** *tool*

Simulating Bedsheet

In this section, you will create a bedsheet and simulate it.

1. Expand the **Subtool** subpalette. In this subpalette, choose the **Append** button and add **Terrain 3D**, refer to Figure 13-22.

2. Select the thumbnail for the newly created **Terrain3D1** from the subtool list. Rename it to *Bedsheet*. Activate the **Rotate** tool and rotate it. Now, activate the **Scale** tool and scale it, as shown in Figure 13-23. Activate the **Move** tool and move *Bedsheet* upward and align it with *Mattress*.

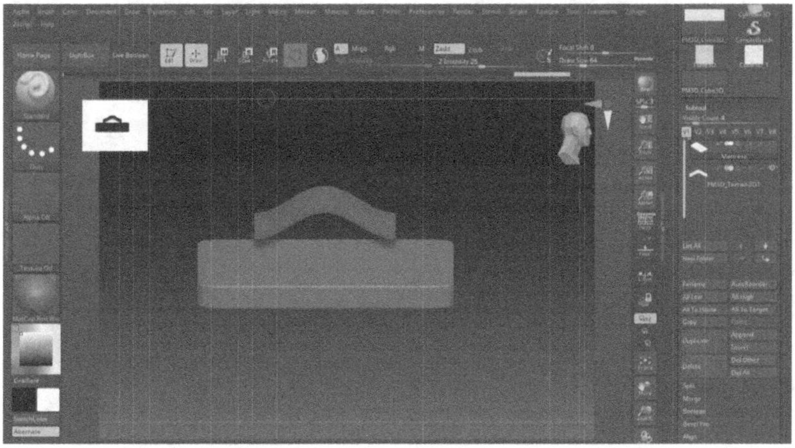

Figure 13-22 *The **Terrain 3D1** added in canvas*

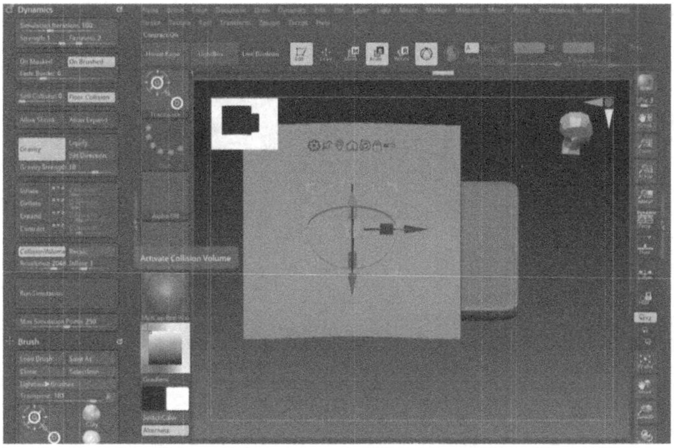

Figure 13-23 *Scaled bedsheet*

3. Choose the **Dynamics** subpalette to expand it. Next, pin this palette at the left of interface by clicking on the upper left most icon on this palette. Make sure the **Gravity** button is chosen. Now, choose the **CollisionVolume** button and then choose the **Run Simulation** button. Now, choose the **Run Simulation** button again so that simulation stops at the point where bedsheet completely falls on the mattress. You will notice the simulation of bedsheet falling on Mattress, as shown in Figure 13-24.

4. Expand the **Geometry** subpalette. In this subpalette, choose the **Divide** button to smoothen *Bedsheet*, as shown in Figure 13-25.

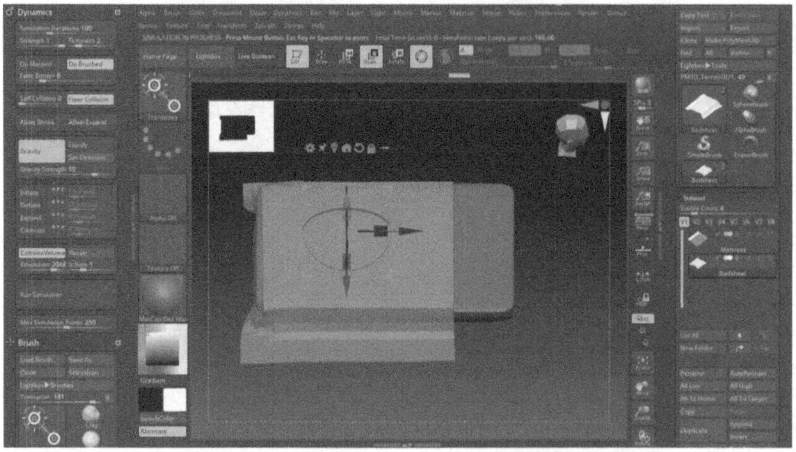

Figure 13-24 *Simulation of Bedsheet falling on Mattress*

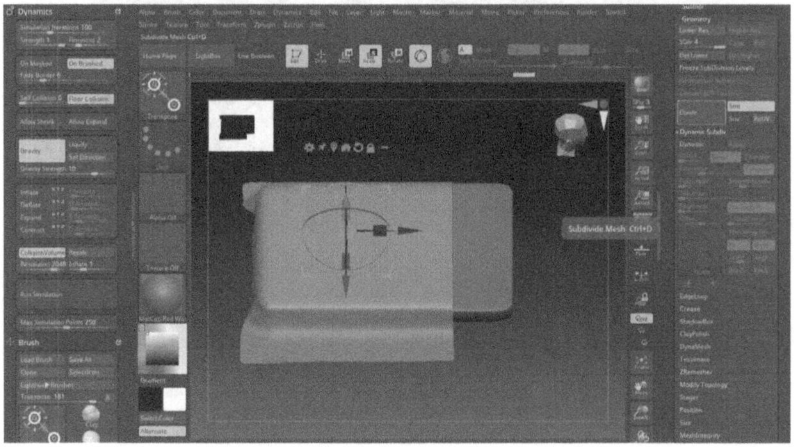

Figure 13-25 *The smoothened bedsheet*

Simulating Pillow

In this section, you will create a pillow and simulate it.

1. Choose the **Append** button in the **SubTool** subpalette; a flyout is displayed. Choose **Plane3D** from this flyout; a plane is created in the canvas. Select the thumbnail for the newly created plane from the subtool list. Rename it to **Pillow**.

2. Expand the **Deformation** subpalette in the **Tool** palette. Decrease the size of *Pillow* along the Z-axis by choosing the **z** button and moving the **Size** slider toward left. Similarly, increase the size of pillow along the X and Y axes and then align it, refer to Figure 13-26.

3. Expand the **Dynamic Subdiv** subpalette in the **Geometry** palette. Choose the **Dynamic** button and set the value **0.00204** in the **Thickness** slider, refer to Figure 13-27. Now, choose the **Apply** button located next to the **Dynamic** button.

4. Choose the **Inflate** button from the **Dynamics** palette. Make sure the **On Brushed** and **FloorCollision** button are chosen. Next, choose the **Run Simulation** button from the **Dynamics** palette, refer to Figure 13-28. You will notice that the air is filled inside the pillow, as shown in Figure 13-28. Now, choose the **Run Simulation** button again to stop the simulation. Align the pillow using the **Move** and **Rotate** tools and set it on the mattress, refer to Figure 13-29.

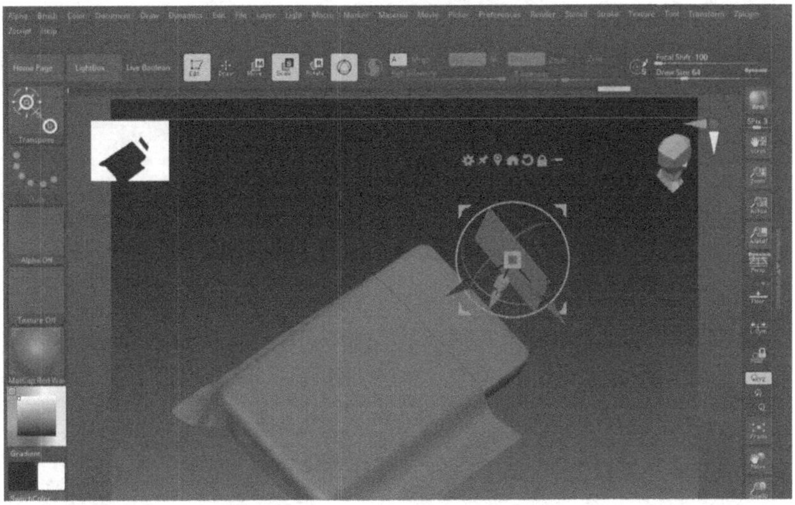

Figure 13-26 *Aligning pillow*

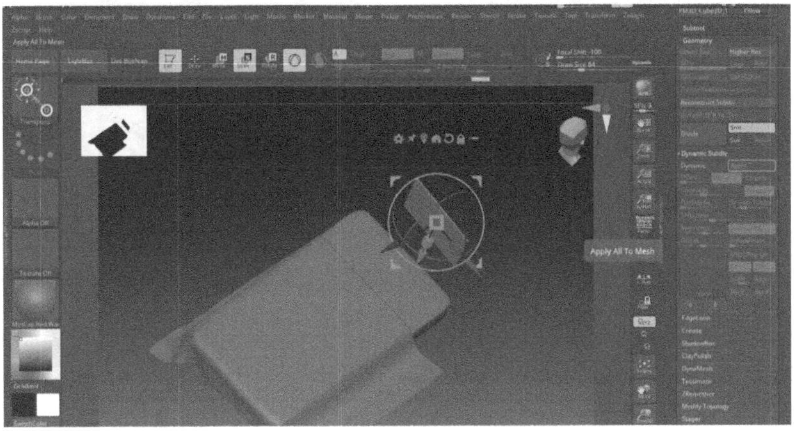

Figure 13-27 *Increasing the thickness of pillow*

Applying Texture to the Mattress, Bedsheet, and Pillow

In this section, you will apply a wooden texture to the mattress, bedsheet, and pillow.

1. Choose the Current Material button from the left shelf; a flyout containing different materials is displayed. In this flyout, choose the **RGB Levels** material from the **Standard Materials**; the material is applied to the *Mattress*, *Bedsheet*, and *Pillow*, as shown in Figure 13-30.

Figure 13-28 *Simulating Pillow*

Figure 13-29 *Setting Pillow on Mattress*

2. Expand the **SubTool** subpalette in the **Tool** palette. In this subpalette, choose the **Mattress** subtool from the list of subtools.

3. Expand the **Texture Map** subpalette in the **Tool** palette and choose the **Texture Map** button from it; a flyout is displayed, as shown in Figure 13-31. Next, choose the **Import** button; the **Import Image** dialog box is displayed. Navigate to the *Documents\ZBrushProjects\C13* and select the **mattress.jpg** file and then choose the **Open** button; the mattress texture is applied to *Mattress*. Click on the eye icon of the *Bedsheet* subtool in the **SubTool** subpalette; the bedsheet is hidden in the canvas area and you can see the texture on the mattress, refer to Figure 13-32. Again, click on the eye icon of the *Bedsheet* subtool in the **SubTool** subpalette; the bedsheet is displayed in the canvas.

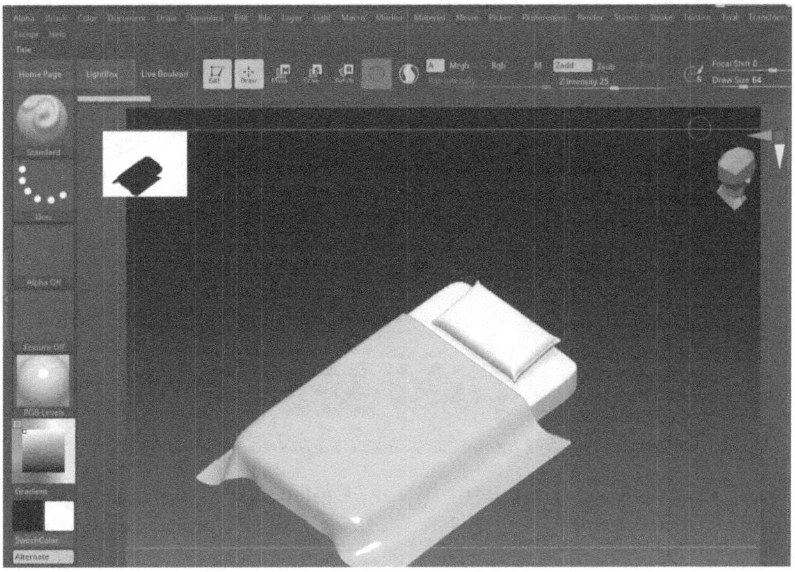

Figure 13-30 *The* ***RGB*** *material applied to the Mattress, Bedsheet, and Pillow*

4. Expand the **SubTool** subpalette in the **Tool** palette. In this subpalette, choose the **Bedsheet** subtool from the list of subtools.

Figure 13-31 *The flyout displayed*

Figure 13-32 *The mattress texture applied to the Mattress*

5. Expand the **Texture Map** subpalette in the **Tool** palette and choose the **Texture Map** button from it; a flyout is displayed. Next, choose the **Import** button; the **Import Image** dialog box is displayed. Navigate to the *Documents\ZBrushProjects\C13* and select the **bedsheet.jpg** file, and then choose the **Open** button; the bedsheet texture is applied to *Bedsheet*, as shown in Figure 13-33.

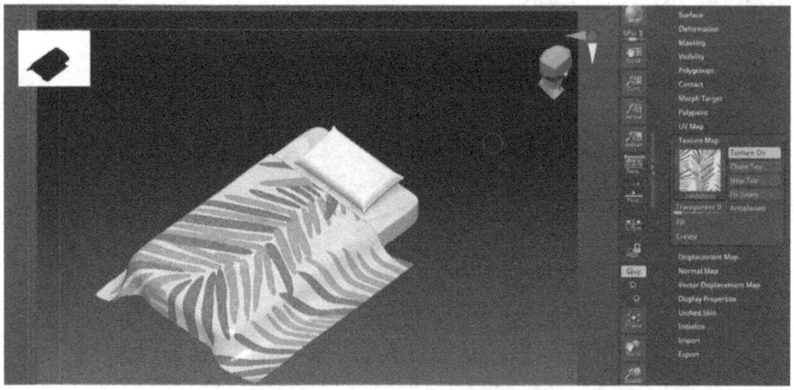

Figure 13-33 *The bedsheet texture applied to the Bedsheet*

6. Expand the **SubTool** subpalette in the **Tool** palette. In this subpalette, choose the **Pillow** subtool from the list of subtools.

7. Expand the **Texture Map** subpalette in the **Tool** palette and choose the **Texture Map** button from it; a flyout is displayed. Next, choose the **Import** button; the **Import Image** dialog box is displayed. Navigate to the *Documents\ZbRushProjects\C13* and select the **pillow.jpg** file and then choose the **Open** button; the pillow texture is applied to *Pillow*, as shown in Figure 13-34.

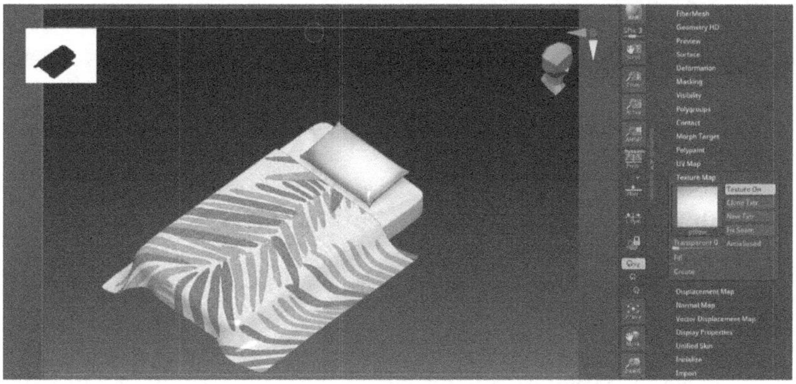

***Figure 13-34** The pillow texture applied to the Pillow*

Saving the Scene

In this section, you will save the file using the steps given next.

1. Choose the **Save As** button from the **Tool** palette; the **Save ZTool** dialog box is displayed. In this dialog box, browse to the location: *\Documents\ZBrushprojects\c13*.

2. Enter **c13tut2** in the **File name** edit box and then choose the **Save** button.

Self-Evaluation Test

Answer the following questions and then compare them to those given at the end of this chapter:

1. Which of the followings slider affects the wrinkles and folds on the simulating surface?

   (a) **Strength** (b) **Firmness**
   (c) **Simulation Iterations** (d) **Gravity Strength**

2. Which of the following sliders controls the amount above which the simulation will be disabled?

   (a) **Strength** (b) **Simulation Iterations**
   (c) **Resolution** (d) **Max Simulation Points**

3. The __________ button is used to shrink the simulating surface at the time of simulation.

4. The __________ slider specifies the speed at which the simulating surface will grow when the **Expand** button is activated.

5. The value in the **Resolution** slider should be higher to get the good simulation results. (T/F)

Review Questions

Answer the following questions:

1. Which of the following sliders is used to control the smoothness of the collision Volume?

   (a) **Resolution** (b) **Max Simulation Points**
   (c) **Strength** (d) **Firmness**

2. The __________ slider specifies the speed at which the simulating surface will shrink when the **Contrast** button is activated.

3. The __________ slider is used to fade the simulation effect when the **On Brushed** button is chosen.

4. When you choose the __________ button, the simulating surface will expand at the time of simulation and inflation will be in the __________ direction of the polygons of the simulating surface.

5. You need to press SPACEBAR or click anywhere else on the screen to stop the simulation. (T/F)

EXERCISE

The output of the model used in this exercise can be accessed by downloading the *c13_ZBrush_2022_exr.zip* from *www.cadcim.com*. The path of the file is as follows: *Textbooks > Animation and Visual Effects > Pixologic ZBrush 2022 > Pixologic ZBrush 2022: A Comprehensive Guide.*

Exercise 1

In this exercise, you will create a simulation of a cloth falling on a log of wood, refer to Figure 13-35. **(Expected time: 30 min)**

Figure 13-35 *Cloth simulation*

Answers to Self-Evaluation Test

1. b, **2.** d, **3.** **Contract**, **4.** **Expand Amount**, **5.** T

Project 1

Cartoon Character Model with a Background Scene - I

PROJECT DESCRIPTION

This project guides you through the process of creating a cartoon character and a background scene, refer to Figure P1-1. The procedure used in this project can be applied to any character modeling project. You will also add a ground and a tree on the side of this character, as shown in Figure P1-1.

Figure P1-1 *The model of a cartoon character with a background scene*

Before you start the project, you need to download the *p01_ZBrush_2022_tut.zip* file from *www.cadcim.com*. The path of the file is as follows: *Textbooks > Animation and Visual Effects > Pixologic ZBrush 2022 > Pixologic ZBrush 2022: A Comprehensive Guide*

Navigate to *\Documents\ZBrushprojects* and then create a new folder with the name *p01*. Next, extract the contents of the zip file in this folder.

Creating the Body of the Cartoon Character Using ZSpheres

In this section, you will create the basic body of the character using ZSpheres.

1. Choose the **Init ZBrush** button from the **Preferences** palette; ZBrush is initialized to its default state.

2. Choose the Current Tool button from the **Tool** palette; a flyout is displayed. In this flyout, choose the **ZSphere** primitive and create it on the canvas, as shown in Figure P1-2. Next, choose the **Edit** button from the top shelf.

3. Activate the symmetry in the X-axis by pressing the X key.

4. Hover the cursor on the right side of the ZSphere and create a ZSphere for the shoulders of the body, refer to Figure P1-3. As the symmetry is activated in the X axis, a ZSphere is created on the left side also.

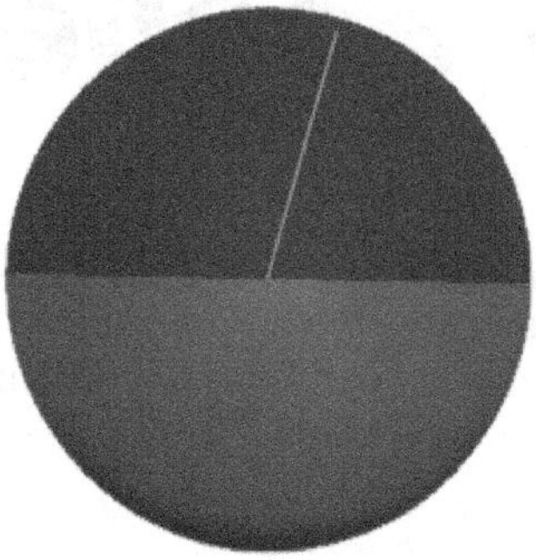

Figure P1-2 *A ZSphere created in the canvas*

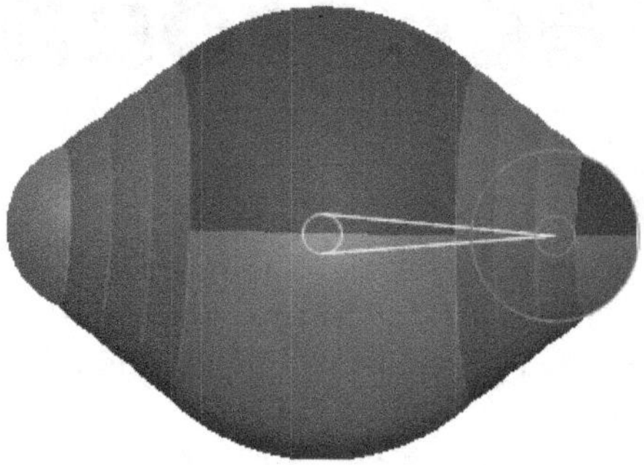

Figure P1-3 *A ZSphere created for the shoulders*

5. Hover the cursor on the ZSphere created for the shoulders of the body and create another ZSphere on it.

6. Choose the **Move** button from the top shelf. Move the newly created ZSphere downward, refer to Figure P1-4. Next, choose the **Draw** button from the top shelf.

7. Hover the cursor on the ZSphere created in Step 5 and create a new ZSphere on it.

8. Choose the **Move** button from the top shelf. Next, move the newly created ZSphere downward, refer to Figure P1-5. Next, choose the **Draw** button from the top shelf.

9. Hover the cursor at the centre of the bottom portion of the middle most ZSphere; a green circle is displayed.

10. Create a ZSphere at the position where the green circle is displayed. Hover the cursor on the newly created ZSphere and create another ZSphere on it. Choose the **Move** button from the top shelf. Next, move the newly created ZSphere downward to create a torso, refer to Figure P1-6. Now, choose the **Draw** button from the top shelf.

11. Hover the cursor on the right side of the ZSphere created in Step 10. Next, create a ZSphere for the hips of the body, refer to Figure P1-7. As the symmetry is activated in the X axis, a ZSphere is created on the left side also.

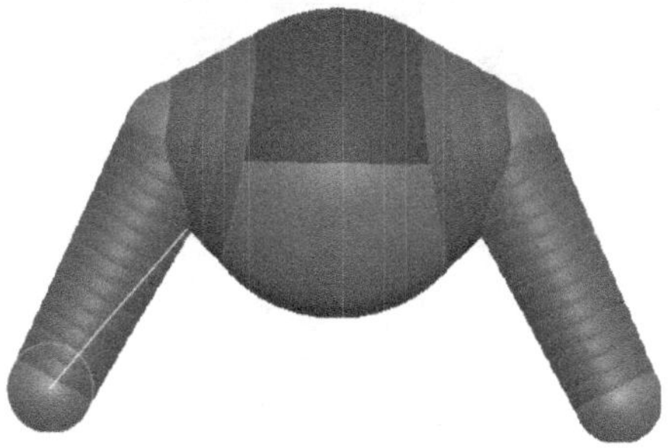

Figure P1-4 *A ZSphere created for elbow and moved downward*

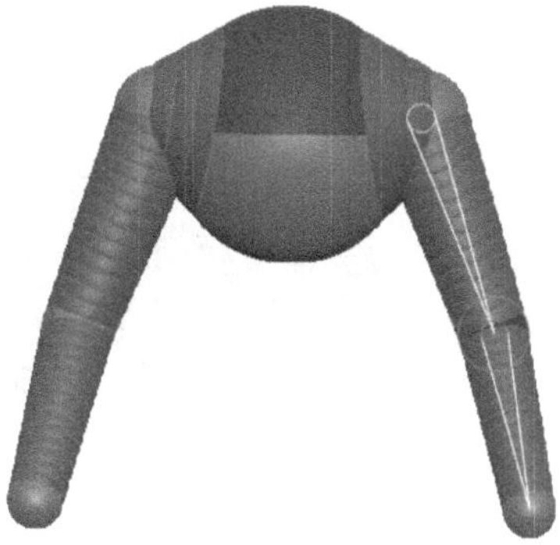

Figure P1-5 *A ZSphere created and moved outward*

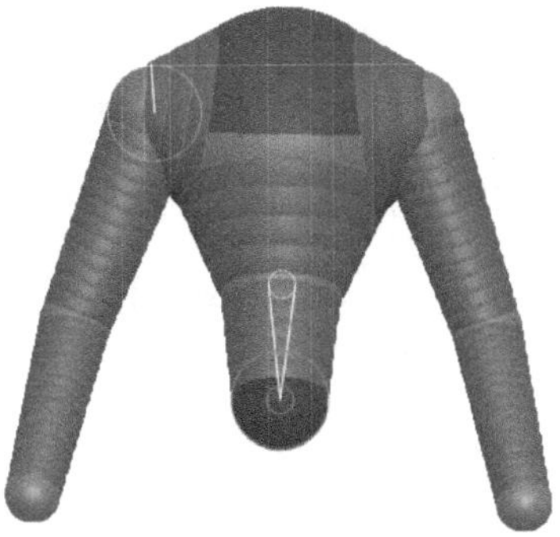

Figure P1-6 *The torso created*

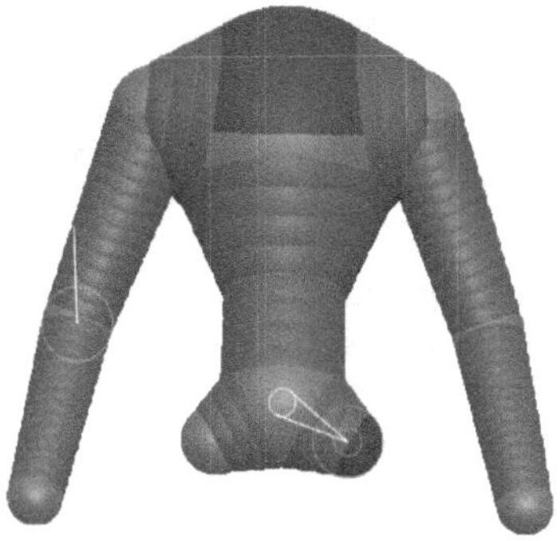

Figure P1-7 *A ZSphere created for the hips*

12. Hover the cursor at the bottom of the ZSphere created for the hips. Next, create a ZSphere for the knees of the body.

13. Choose the **Move** button from the top shelf. Next, move the newly created ZSphere downward, refer to Figure P1-8. Next, choose the **Draw** button from the top shelf.

14. Create another ZSphere at the bottom of the knees and move it downward using the **Move** button in the top shelf, refer to Figure P1-9. Next, choose the **Draw** button from the top shelf.

15. Hover the cursor at the centre of the top portion of the ZSphere created in Step 2; a green circle is displayed.

16. Create a ZSphere for the neck at the position where the green circle is displayed, refer to Figure P1-10.

17. Hover the cursor on the newly created ZSphere and create another ZSphere on it. Choose the **Move** button from the top shelf. Next, move the newly created ZSphere upward to create the head, refer to Figure P1-11.

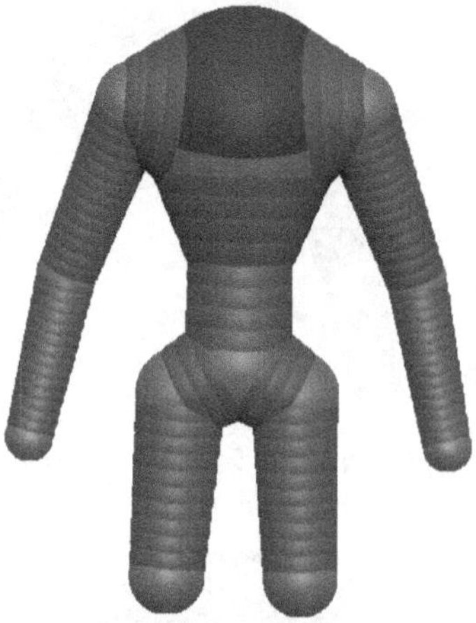

Figure P1-8 *A ZSphere created for the knees and moved downward*

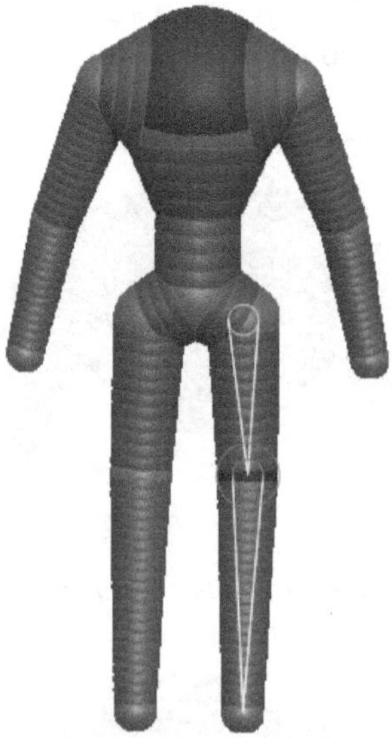

Figure P1-9 *A ZSphere created for the legs and moved downward*

18. Make sure the **Draw** button is chosen in the top shelf. Next, insert four editable ZSpheres on two linked ZSpheres, refer to Figure P1-12.

19. Hover the cursor at the lower most ZSphere and create a new sphere at its front side. Next, choose the **Move** button from the top shelf and move the newly created ZSphere toward front, refer to Figure P1-13.

20. Make sure the **Draw** button is chosen in the top shelf. Next, insert an editable ZSphere at the middle of the feet. Choose the **Scale** button and scale up the middle ZSphere and scale down the front ZSphere, refer to Figure P1-14. Next, choose the **Draw** button from the top shelf.

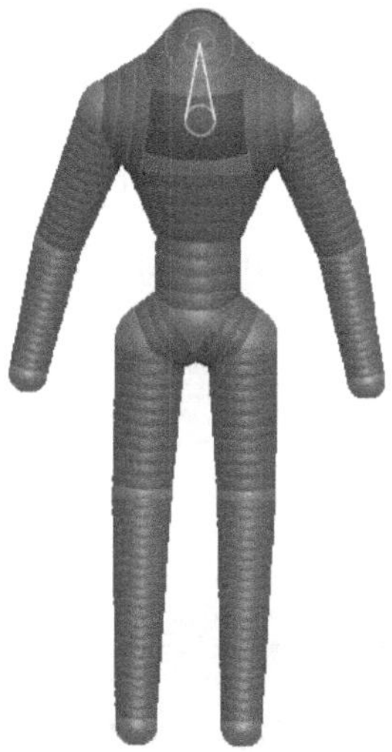

Figure P1-10 A ZSphere created for the neck

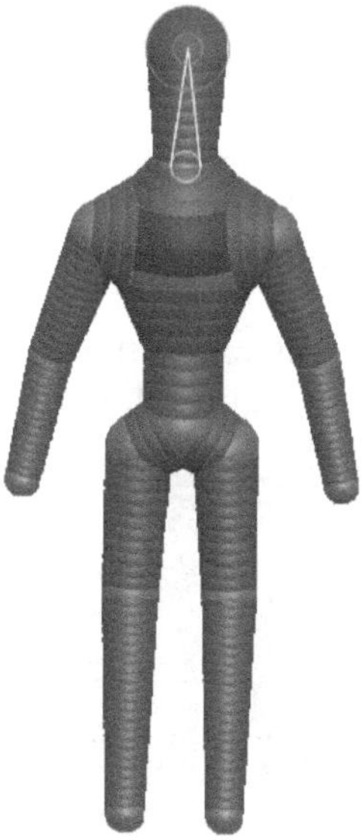

Figure P1-11 A ZSphere created for the head and moved upward

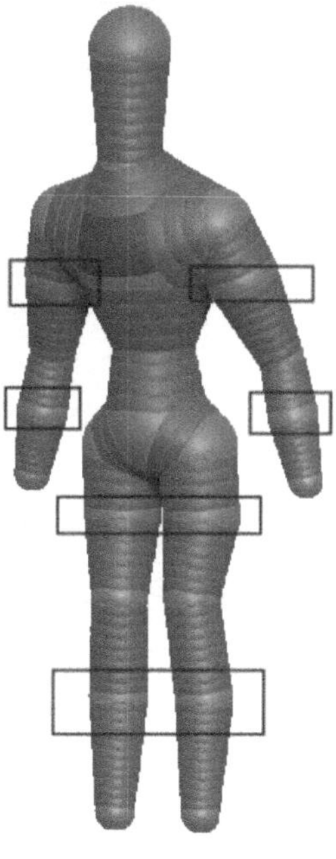

Figure P1-12 More ZSpheres added to refine the shape

Figure P1-13 A ZSphere created for the feet and moved outward

21. Create a new ZSphere for the hand and move it downward, as shown in Figure P1-15.

22. Choose the **Move** button from the top shelf and select the ZSphere created for the hand. You will notice that its color changes. Hover the cursor at the area that divides the red and maroon tones of the ZSphere. Next, choose the **Draw** button, and create a ZSphere for the knuckle of thumb and move it slightly outward, as shown in Figure P1-16.

23. Create four more ZSpheres for the knuckles of the rest of the fingers and move them slightly outward, as shown in Figure P1-17.

Figure P1-14 *The shape of the feet refined*

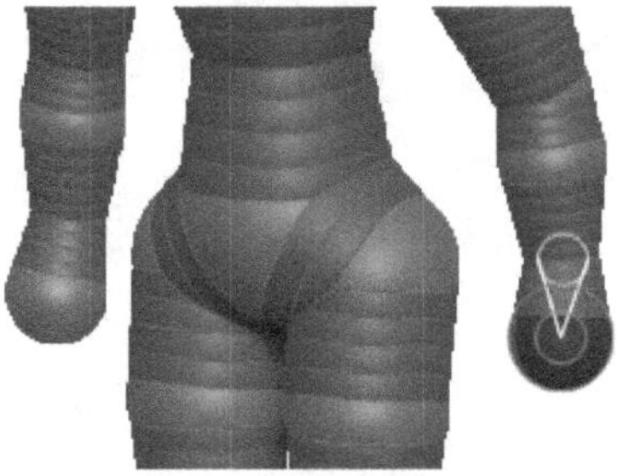

Figure P1-15 *A ZSphere created for the hand*

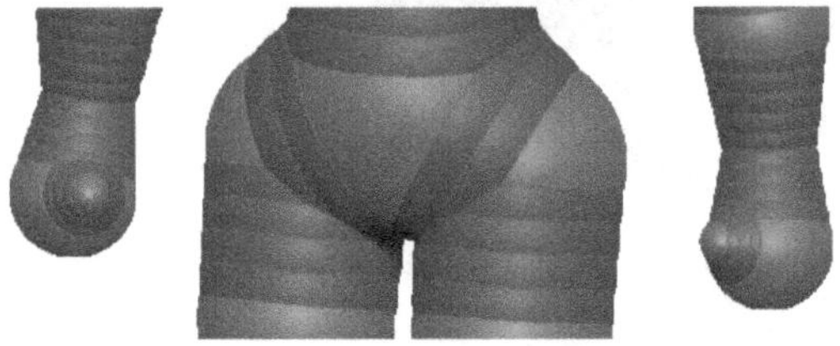

Figure P1-16 *A ZSphere created for the knuckle*

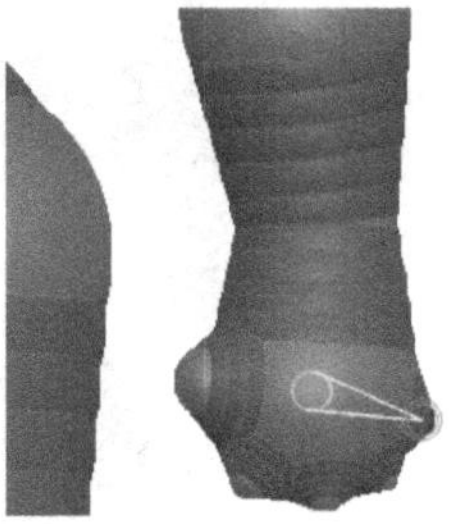

Figure P1-17 *The knuckles created*

24. Create new ZSpheres for the thumb and the index finger, and move them outward, refer to Figures P1-18 and P1-19.

25. Similarly, create the middle finger, ring finger, and little finger. Next, adjust the fingers created by scaling and moving the ZSpheres in them, refer to Figure P1-20.

26. Expand the **Adaptive Skin** subpalette in the **Tool** palette. In this subpalette, choose the **Make Adaptive Skin** button; a thumbnail for the new skinned mesh with the name **Skin_ZSphere_1** is displayed in the **Tool** palette. Next, double-click on this thumbnail; the skinned mesh is displayed in the canvas, refer to Figure P1-21.

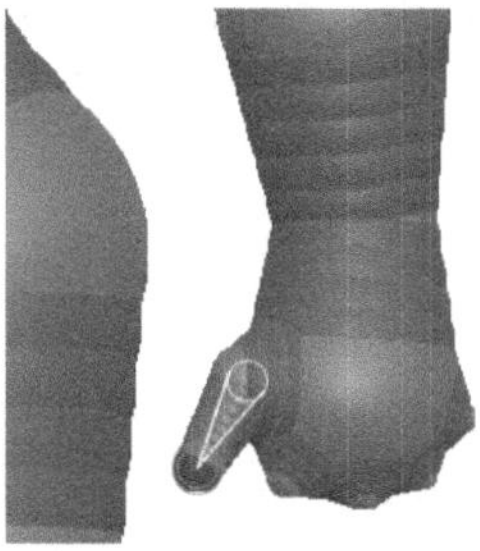

Figure P1-18 *A ZSphere created for the thumb and moved outward*

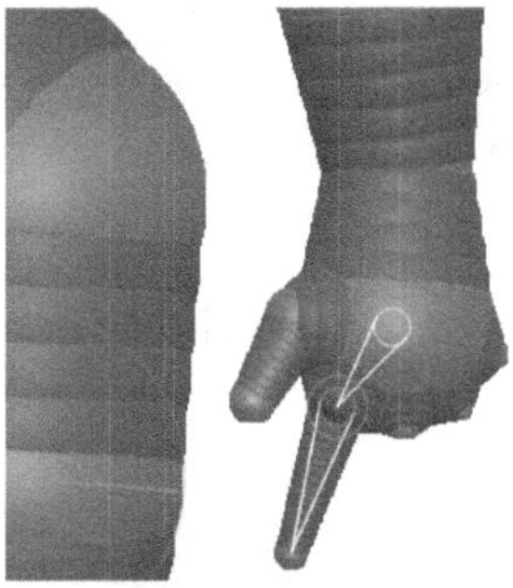

Figure P1-19 *The index finger created*

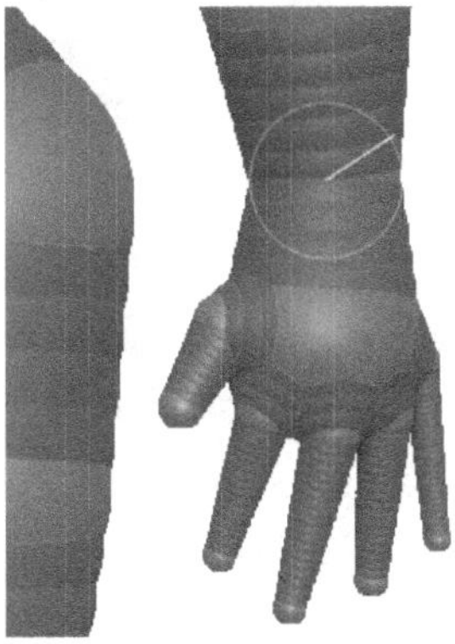

Figure P1-20 *All the fingers created*

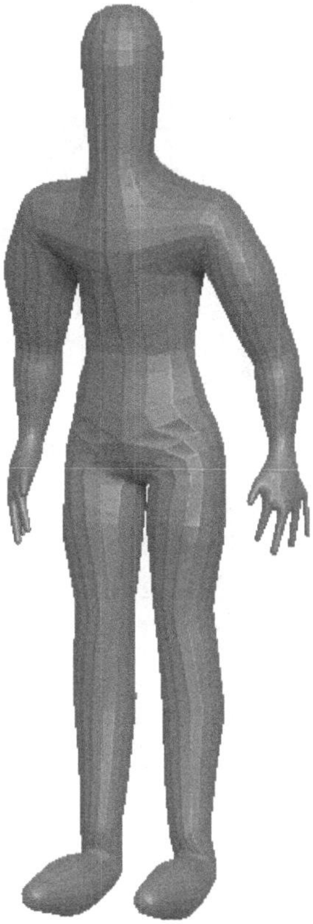

Figure P1-21 *The adaptive skin mesh*

Refining the Body and the Facial Features of the Cartoon Character

In this section, you will refine the body and the facial features of the cartoon character using different brushes.

1. Make sure the symmetry in the X-axis is activated.

2. Choose the Current Brush button from the left shelf; a flyout containing different sculpting brushes is displayed. Choose the **Move** brush from this flyout and using the **Move** brush create the shape of the head, refer to Figure P1-22. You need to adjust the brush size as required.

3. Make sure the **Move** brush is chosen. Next, using this brush refine the shape of the feet, refer to Figure P1-23.

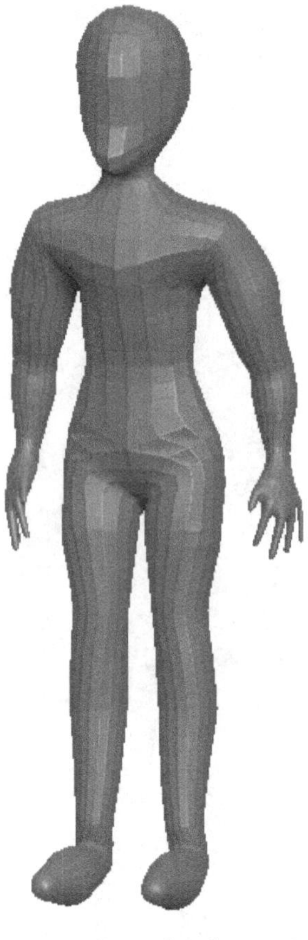

Figure P1-22 *The shape of the head created using the **Move** brush*

Figure P1-23 *The shape of the feet refined using the **Move** brush*

4. Rotate the view of the canvas such that you can view the side view of the body. Refine the shape of the body in the side view using the **Move** brush, refer to Figure P1-24. Expand the **Geometry** subpalette in the **Tool** palette and choose the **Divide** button.

5. Choose the Current Brush button from the left shelf; a flyout containing different sculpting brushes is displayed. Choose the **Standard** brush from this flyout. Next, choose the **Zsub** button from the top shelf. Press and hold the left mouse button and drag the cursor to create eye sockets, refer to Figure P1-25.

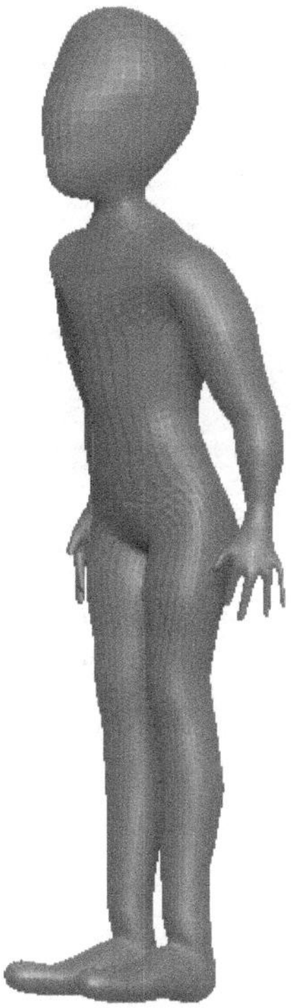

Figure P1-24 *The shape of the body refined in the side view*

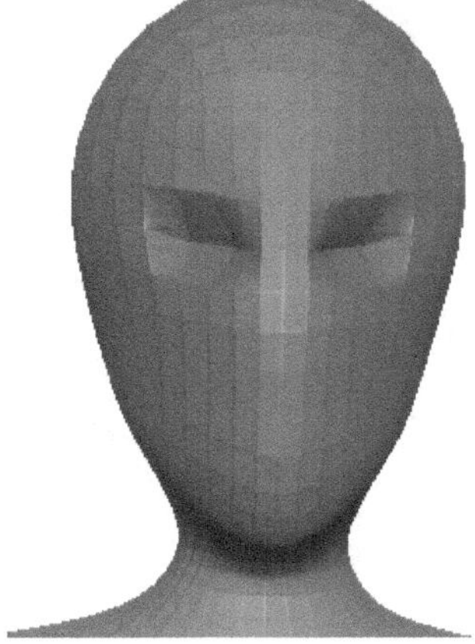

Figure P1-25 *The eye socket created using the **Standard** brush*

6. Make sure the **Standard** brush is chosen. Next, choose the **Zadd** button from the top shelf. Adjust the brush size as required and then create depth for the nose, refer to Figure P1-26.

7. Rotate the view of the canvas such that you can view the side view of the body.

8. Choose the Current Brush button from the left shelf; a flyout containing different sculpting brushes is displayed. Choose the **Move** brush from this flyout.

9. Refine the shape of the nose in the side view using the **Move** brush, refer to Figure P1-27.

10. Expand the **Geometry** subpalette in the **Tool** palette. In this subpalette, choose the **Divide** button; the geometry is subdivided.

11. Choose the **Current Brush** button from the left shelf; a flyout containing different sculpting brushes is displayed. Choose the **Standard** brush from this flyout. Next, choose the **Zsub** button from the top shelf. Press and hold the left mouse button and drag the cursor to create the shape of the mouth, refer to Figure P1-28.

Figure P1-26 The depth of the nose created using the ***Standard*** *brush*

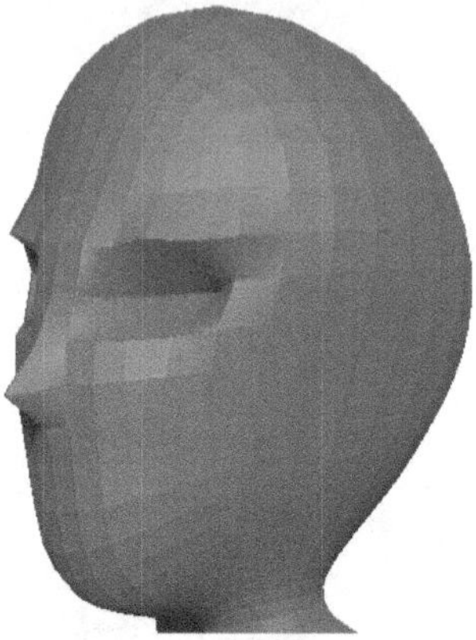

Figure P1-27 The shape of the nose refined using the ***Move*** *brush*

12. Choose the Current Brush button from the left shelf; a flyout containing different sculpting brushes is displayed. Choose the **Move** brush from this flyout. Next, using the **Move** brush, refine the shape of the eyes, nose, and mouth, refer to Figure P1-29. While refining the shape, you need to adjust the brush size as required.

Figure P1-28 The shape of the mouth created using the ***Standard*** *brush*

Figure P1-29 The shape of the eyes, nose, and mouth refined using the ***Move*** *brush*

13. Choose the Current Brush button from the left shelf; a flyout containing different sculpting brushes is displayed. Choose the **ClayBuildup** brush from this flyout. Next, using the **ClayBuildup** brush, create depth at the jaw line, refer to Figure P1-30.

14. Press and hold the SHIFT key; the **Smooth** brush is activated. With the SHIFT key pressed, set the value of the **Z Intensity** slider to **15**. Next, drag the cursor on the jaw line; the jaw line is smoothened, refer to Figure P1-31.

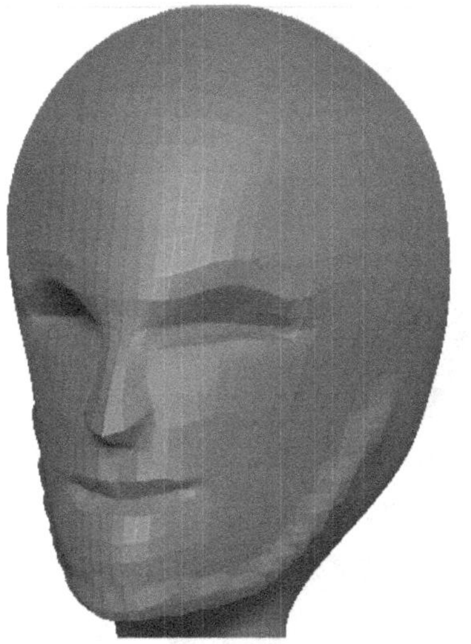

***Figure P1-30** The shape of the jaw line created using the **ClayBuildup** brush*

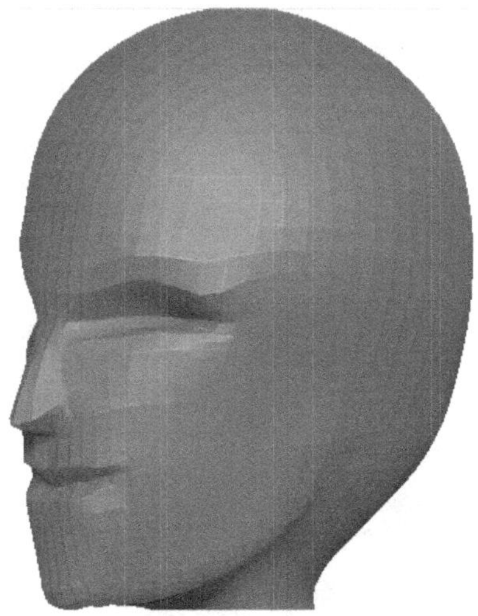

***Figure P1-31** The shape of the jaw line smoothened using the **Smooth** brush*

15. Choose the Current Brush button from the left shelf; a flyout containing different sculpting brushes is displayed. Choose the **Standard** brush from this flyout.

16. Make sure the **Zadd** button is chosen in the top shelf. Next, create the shape of the ear using the **Standard** brush, refer to Figure P1-32.

17. Expand the **Geometry** subpalette in the **Tool** palette. In this subpalette, click on the **Divide** button; the geometry is subdivided again.

18. Choose the Current Brush button from the left shelf; a flyout containing different sculpting brushes is displayed. Choose the **Move** brush from this flyout. Next, using the **Move** brush, refine the shape of the eyes, refer to Figure P1-33.

19. Expand the **Geometry** subpalette in the **Tool** palette. In this subpalette, choose the **Divide** button; the geometry is subdivided again.

20. Choose the Current Brush button from the left shelf; a flyout containing different sculpting brushes is displayed. Choose the **Standard** brush from this flyout.

21. Make sure the **Zadd** button is chosen in the top shelf. Next, create the shape of the lips using the **Standard** brush, refer to Figure P1-34.

22. Choose the Current Brush button from the left shelf; a flyout containing different sculpting brushes is displayed. Choose the **Pinch** brush from this flyout. Drag the cursor at the ends of the lips to refine their shape, refer to Figure P1-34.

23. Choose the Current Brush button from the left shelf; a flyout containing different sculpting brushes is displayed. Choose the **Move** brush from this flyout. Next, refine the shape of the lips using the **Move** brush, refer to Figure P1-35.

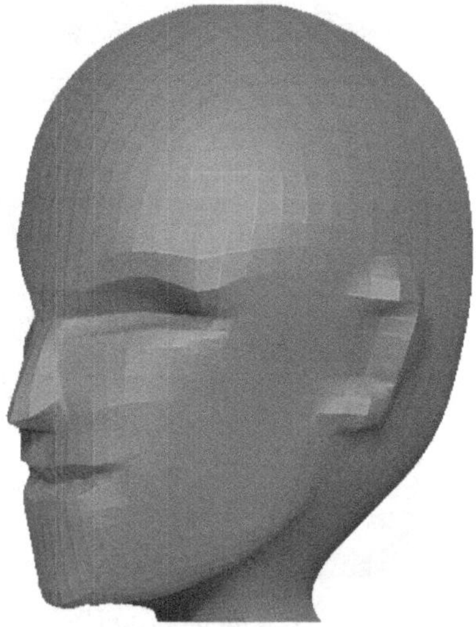

*Figure P1-32 The shape of the ear created using the **Standard** brush*

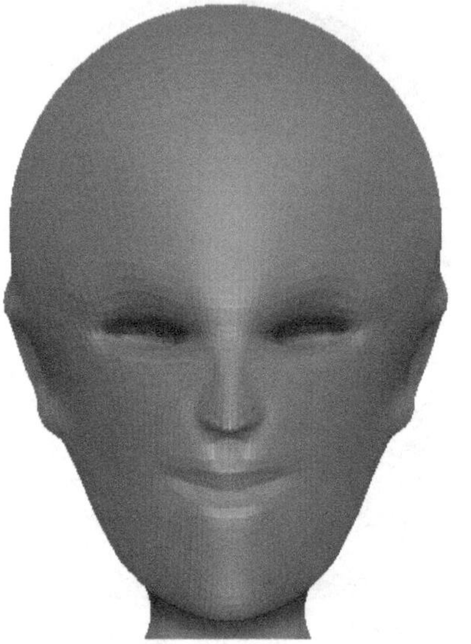

*Figure P1-33 The shape of the eyes refined using the **Move** brush*

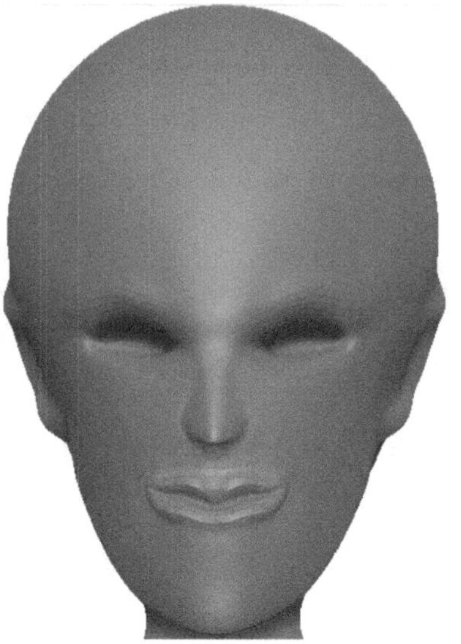

*Figure P1-34 The shape of the lips created using the **Standard** brush and the **Pinch** brush*

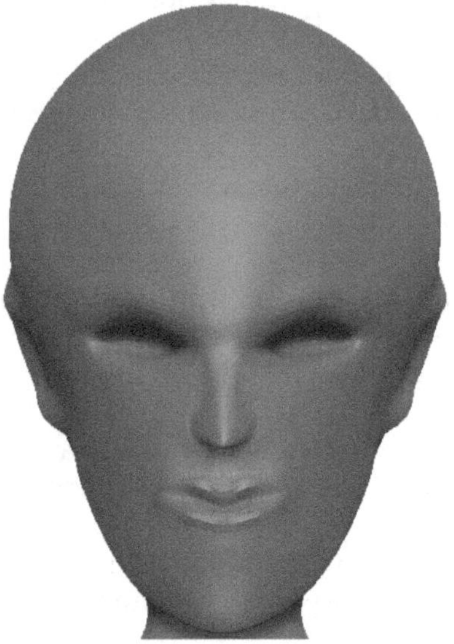

*Figure P1-35 The shape of the lips refined using the **Move** brush*

24. Subdivide the geometry one more time by clicking on the **Divide** button in the **Geometry** subpalette. Choose the Current Brush button from the left shelf; a flyout containing different sculpting brushes is displayed. Choose the **Dam_Standard** brush from this flyout. Next, decrease the brush size and create partition in the lips using the **Dam_Standard** brush, refer to Figure P1-36.

25. Make sure the **Dam_Standard** brush is chosen. Next, create a partition for the eyelids, refer to Figure P1-37.

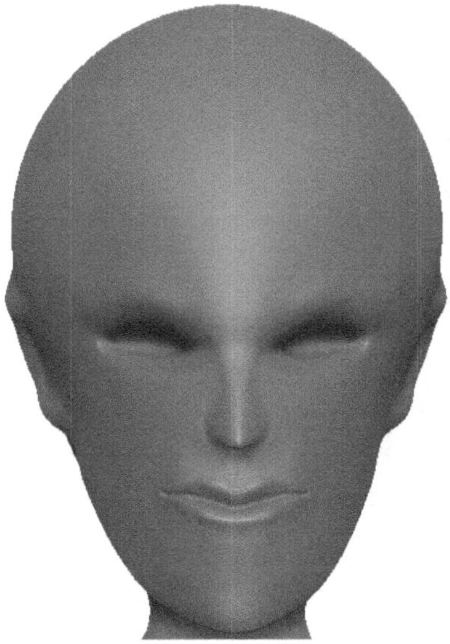

Figure P1-36 *The shape of the lips refined using the **Dam_Standard** brush*

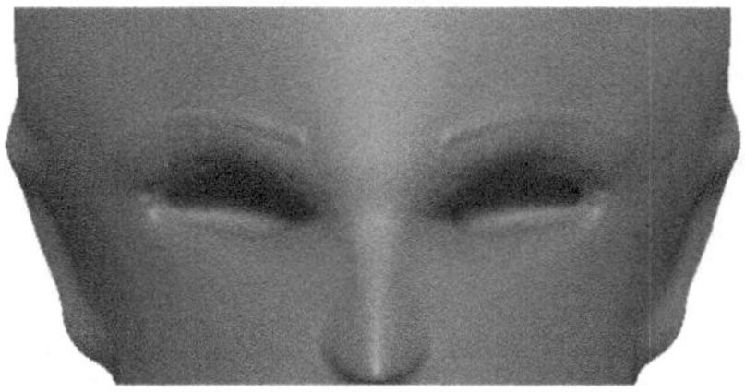

Figure P1-37 *The eyebrows and eyelids created*

26. Choose the Current Brush button from the left shelf; a flyout containing different sculpting brushes is displayed. Choose the **Standard** brush from this flyout. Next, decrease the brush size and create depth for the eye brows, refer to Figure P1-37.

27. Expand the **SubTool** subpalette in the **Tool** palette. In this subpalette, choose the **Append** button; a flyout is displayed. Choose the **Sphere3D** primitive from this flyout; a sphere overlapping with the body is created in the canvas. The thumbnail for the sphere is displayed in the **SubTool** list. Select the thumbnail of the sphere in the list.

28. Expand the **Geometry** subpalette. In this subpalette, click on the **Divide** button thrice; the sphere becomes smoother, refer to Figure P1-38.

29. Expand the **Deformation** subpalette in the **Tool** palette. In this subpalette, move the **Size** slider toward left so that the size of the sphere decreases, refer to Figure P1-39.

30. Choose the **Move** button from the top shelf; an action line is displayed. Move the sphere inside the right eye socket using the action line, refer to Figure P1-39.

31. In the **SubTool** subpalette, make sure the thumbnail for the sphere is selected. Next, choose the **Duplicate** button in this subpalette; a duplicate copy of the sphere is created but it overlaps with the existing sphere.

32. Choose the **Move** button from the top shelf; an action line is displayed. Move the sphere inside the left eye socket using the action line, refer to Figure P1-40.

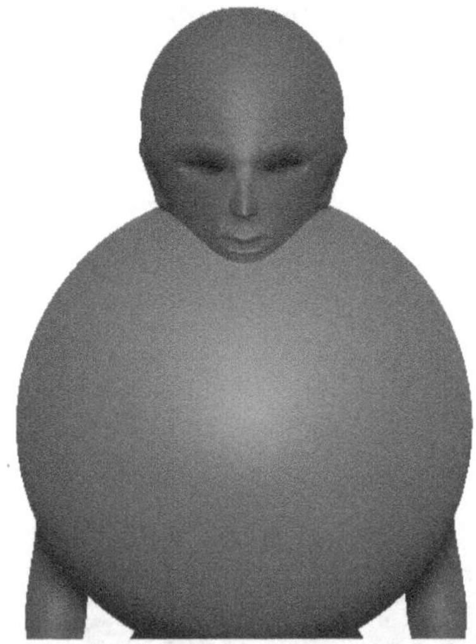

Figure P1-38 A sphere smoothened

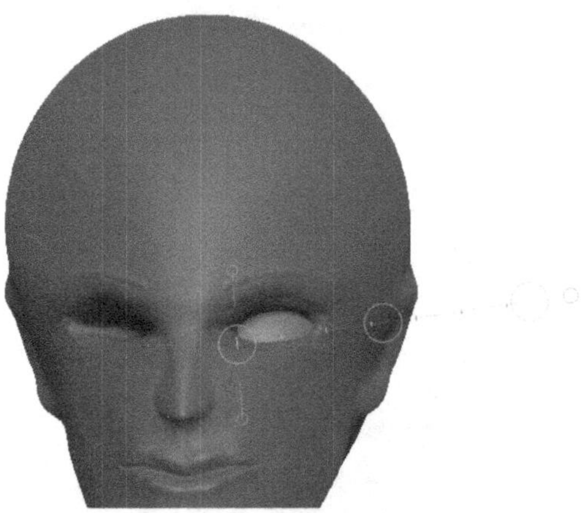

Figure P1-39 The sphere scaled down and moved inside the eye socket

33. In the **SubTool** subpalette, select the thumbnail for the body. Rotate the view of the canvas such that you can view the side view of the body.

34. Make sure the **Standard** brush is chosen. Next, refine the shape of the ear, refer to Figure P1-41.

35. Choose the Current Brush button from the left shelf; a flyout containing different sculpting brushes is displayed. Choose the **Move** brush from this flyout. Next, refine the shape of the ear using the **Move** brush, refer to Figure P1-41.

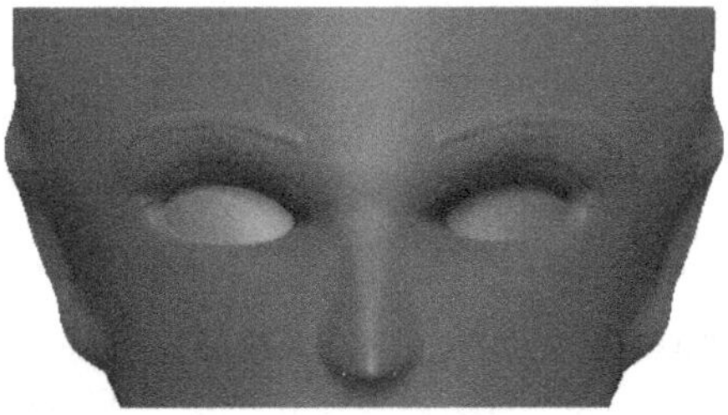

Figure P1-40 The duplicate copy of the eye ball created and moved to the left eye socket

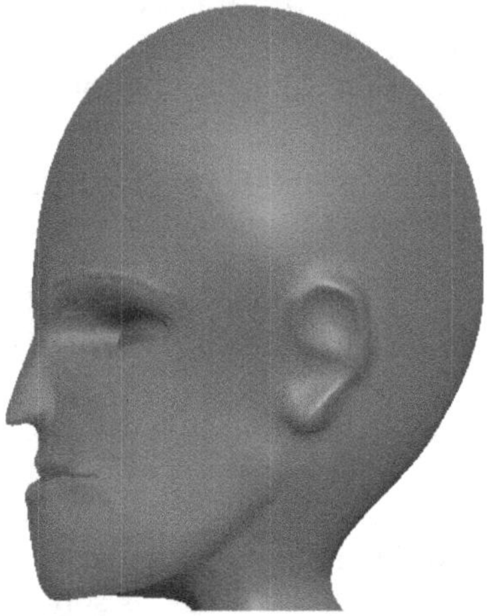

*Figure P1-41 The shape of the ear refined using the **Standard** and **Move** brushes*

36. Make sure the **Move** brush is selected. Next, in the side view, refine the shape of the face, refer to Figure P1-42.

Creating the Hair and Clothes of the Cartoon Character

In this section, you will create the hair and clothes of the cartoon character.

1. Press and hold the CTRL key; the **MaskPen** brush is activated. Next, with the CTRL key pressed, create a mask on the head for the hair. Make sure you create mask on the back side of the head also.

2. Expand the **FiberMesh** subpalette in the **Tool** palette. In this subpalette, choose the **Preview** button. On choosing this button, a fibrous mesh is displayed on the masked area of the head.

3. Expand the **Modifiers** area in the **FiberMesh** subpalette. Click on the **MaxFibers** slider to display the **MaxFibers** edit box. Next, enter the value **200** in the **MaxFibers** edit box.

4. Choose the **Tip** button; a color swatch is displayed. Select black color from this swatch. Next, click on the **Coverage** slider; the **Coverage** edit box is displayed. Enter **20** in this edit box.

5. Similarly, enter **4** in the **ScaleRoot** slider, **2** in the **ScaleTip** slider, and **1** in the **Cov** slider.

6. Enter the value **20** in the **Length** edit box; the length of the fibers decreases, refer to Figure P1-43. Next, choose the **Accept** button in the **FiberMesh** subpalette; a message box is displayed prompting to activate the fast preview mode. In this message box, choose the **Yes** button.

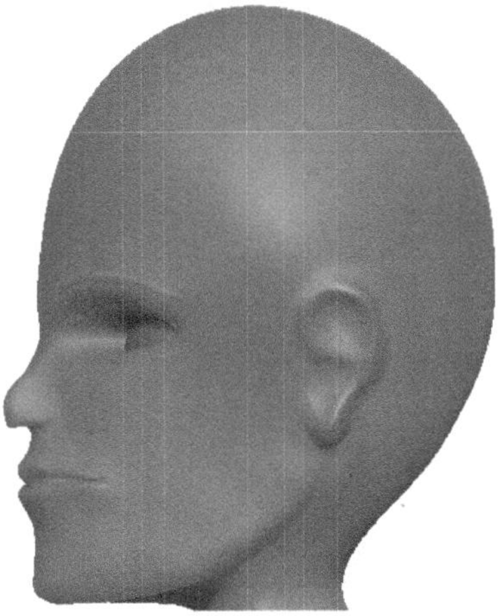

Figure P1-42 *The facial features refined in the side view using the **Move** brush*

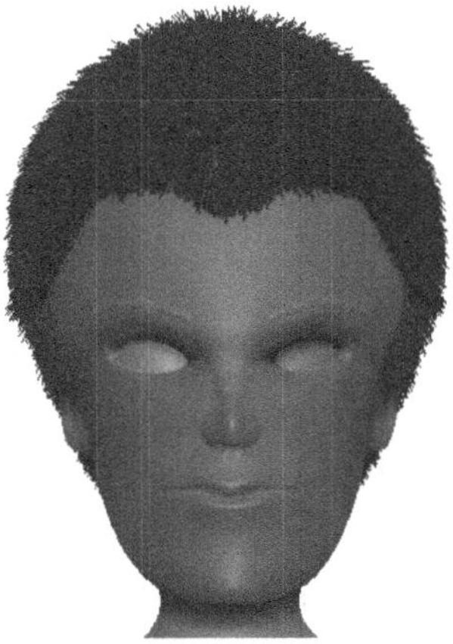

Figure P1-43 *The length of the fibers decreased*

7. After creating the hair, press and hold the CTRL key and then drag the cursor on the open area of the canvas; the mask is removed from the head of the body.

8. Press and hold the CTRL key; the **MaskPen** brush is activated. Next, with the CTRL key pressed, create a mask on the upper part of the body to form the shape of a shirt. Make sure you create mask on the back side also.

9. Expand the **SubTool** subpalette. In this subpalette, expand the **Extract** area. Next, in this area, choose the **Extract** button. After some time, the shape of the mask is extracted from the surface of the body and a shirt is created, refer to Figure P1-44. Next, choose the **Accept** button in the **SubTool** subpalette. Press and hold the CTRL key and then drag the cursor on the open area of the canvas; the mask is removed.

10. Press and hold the CTRL key; the **MaskPen** brush is activated. Next, with the CTRL key pressed, create a mask on the lower part of the body to form the shape of pants. Make sure you create mask on the back side also.

11. Expand the **SubTool** subpalette. In this subpalette, expand the **Extract** area. Next, in this area, set the value of the **Thick** slider to **0.01** and then choose the **Extract** button. After some time, the shape of the mask is extracted from the surface of the body and pants are created, refer to Figure P1-44. Next, choose the **Accept** button in the **SubTool** subpalette. Press and hold the CTRL key and then drag the cursor on the open area of the canvas; the mask is removed.

12. In the **SubTool** subpalette, select the thumbnail for the pants. Next, modify the shape of the pants using the **Move** brush, refer to Figure P1-45.

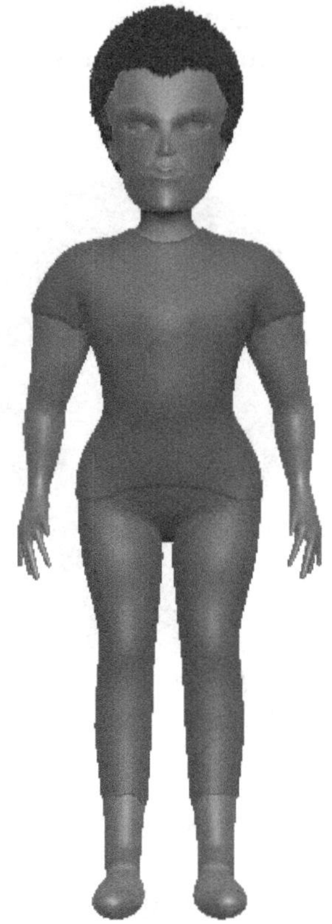

Figure P1-44 *The clothes created using the **Extract** button*

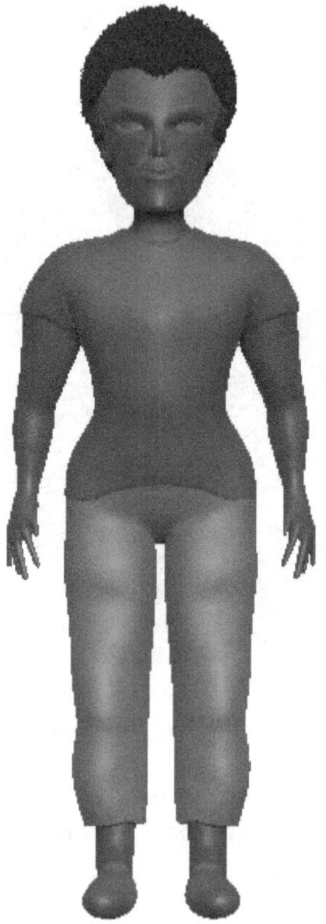

Figure P1-45 *The shape of the pants refined using the **Move** brush*

13. In the **SubTool** subpalette, select the thumbnail for the body. Press and hold the CTRL key; the **MaskPen** brush is activated. Next, with the CTRL key pressed, create a mask on the feet of the body to form the shape of shoes, refer to Figure P1-46. Make sure you create mask on the back side also.

14. Expand the **SubTool** subpalette. In this subpalette, expand the **Extract** area. Next, in this area, choose the **Extract** button. After some time, the shape of the mask is extracted from the surface of the body and shoes are created, refer to Figure P1-47. Next, choose the **Accept** button in the **SubTool** subpalette. Press and hold the CTRL key and then drag the cursor on the open area of the canvas; the mask is removed.

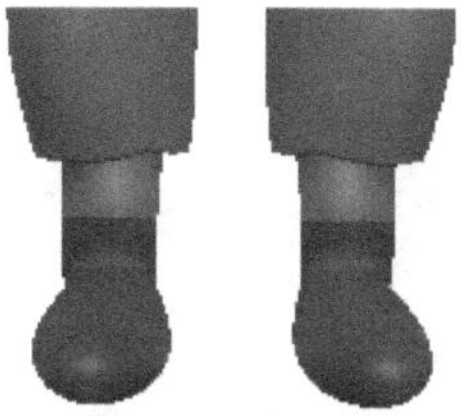

Figure P1-46 *The mask created for the shoes*

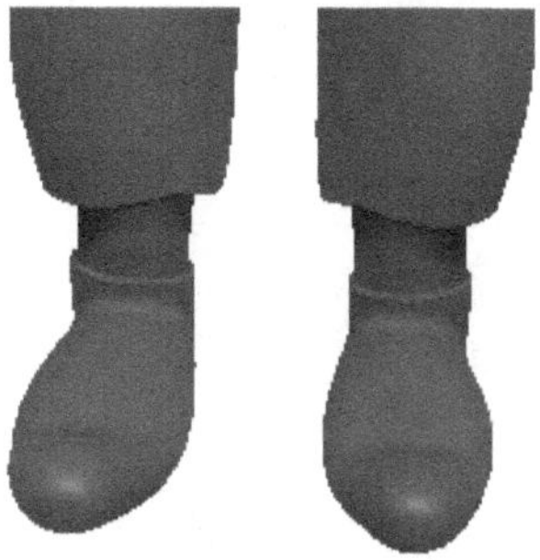

Figure P1-47 *The shoes created using the* ***Extract*** *button*

Applying Materials and Colors to the Cartoon Character

In this section, you will apply materials and colors to the cartoon character.

1. Make sure the thumbnail for the body is selected in the list of subtools in the **SubTool** subpalette and the **Mrgb** button is chosen in the top shelf.

2. Choose the Current Material button from the left shelf; a flyout containing different materials is displayed. In this flyout, choose the **MatCap Skin06** material; the material is applied to the body and all other subtools.

3. Choose the **Color** palette. In this palette, choose the **FillObject** button; the skin material is displayed on the body, refer to Figure P1-48.

4. In the **SubTool** subpalette, select the thumbnail for the shirt of the character. Next, choose the **Color** palette. In this palette, set the values of the **R**, **G**, and **B** sliders to **248**, **25**, and **25**, respectively; red color is applied to all the subtools except the body. In the **Color** palette, choose the **FillObject** button.

5. In the **SubTool** subpalette, select the thumbnail for the pants of the character. Next, choose the **Color** palette. In this palette, set the values of the **R**, **G**, and **B** sliders to **1**, **22**, and **95**, respectively; blue color is applied to all the subtools except the body and the shirt. In the **Color** palette, choose the **FillObject** button.

6. In the **SubTool** subpalette, select the thumbnail for the shoes of the character. Next, choose the **Color** palette. In this palette, set the values of the **R**, **G**, and **B** sliders to **103**,

37, and **37**, respectively; brown color is applied to the shoes, refer to Figure P1-49. In the **Color** palette, choose the **FillObject** button.

7. In the **SubTool** subpalette, select the thumbnail for the eyeball of the character. Choose the Current Material button from the left shelf; a flyout containing different materials is displayed. In this flyout, choose the **ToyPlastic** material; the plastic material is applied to the eyeballs, shoes, and hair.

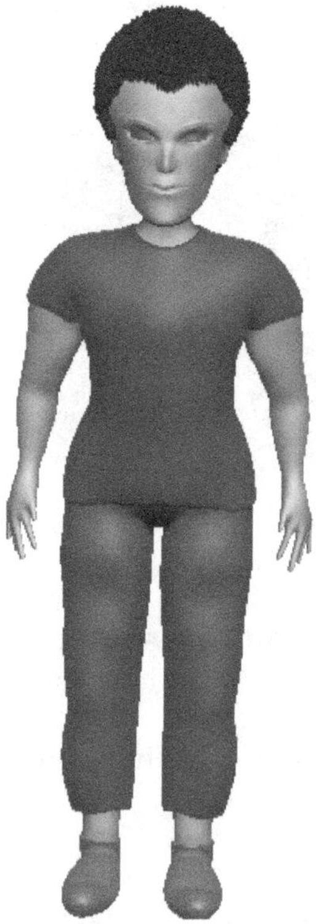

Figure P1-48 *The* ***MatCap Skin06*** *material applied to the body*

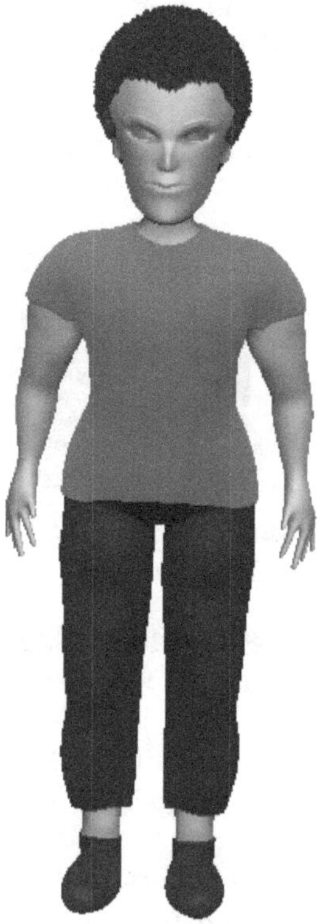

Figure P1-49 *The colors applied to the clothes and the shoes*

8. Choose the **Color** palette. In this palette, set the values of the **R**, **G**, and **B** sliders to **255**; white color is applied to the eyeballs. In the **Color** palette, choose the **FillObject** button.

9. In the **Color** palette, set the values of the **R**, **G**, and **B** sliders to **82**, **58**, and **58**; brown color is applied to the eyeball that is not selected in the list of subtools.

10. Make sure the **Zadd** and **Mrgb** buttons in the top shelf are not chosen. Next, choose the Current Stroke button from the left shelf; a flyout containing different types of strokes is displayed. Choose the **DragRect** stroke from this flyout.

11. Choose the Current Alpha button from the left shelf; a flyout containing different alpha images is displayed. Choose the **Alpha 48** alpha image from this flyout.

12. Drag the cursor on the surface of the eyeball to create a brown circular stroke.

13. In the **Color** palette, set the values of the **R**, **G**, and **B** sliders to **0**. Drag the cursor at the center of the brown circular stroke created in Step 12, refer to Figure P1-50.

14. In the **SubTool** subpalette, select the thumbnail for the second eyeball and then repeat the Steps 7 to 13 to create the texture for another eyeball, refer to Figure P1-50.

15. In the **SubTool** subpalette, select the thumbnail for the body of the character. Next, choose the Current Material button from the left shelf; a flyout containing different materials is displayed. In this flyout, choose the **MatCap Skin06** material.

16. Choose the Current Stroke button from the left shelf; a flyout containing different types of strokes is displayed. Choose the **FreeHand** stroke from this flyout.

17. Choose the Current Alpha button from the left shelf; a flyout containing different alpha images is displayed. Choose **Alpha Off** from this flyout.

18. In the **Color** palette, set the values of the **R**, **G**, and **B** sliders to **191**, **109**, and **109**, respectively. Next, set the value of the **Rgb Intensity** slider in the top shelf to **10**.

19. Make sure the **Zadd** button in the top shelf is not chosen. Drag the cursor on the surface of the lips; light red color is applied to the lips, refer to Figure P1-51.

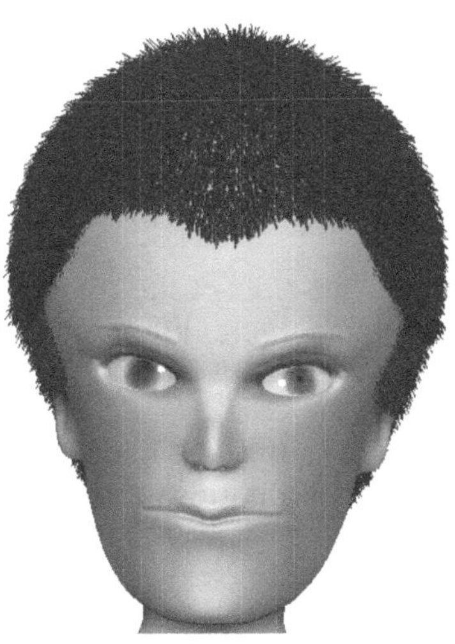

Figure P1-50 *The texture for the eyes created*

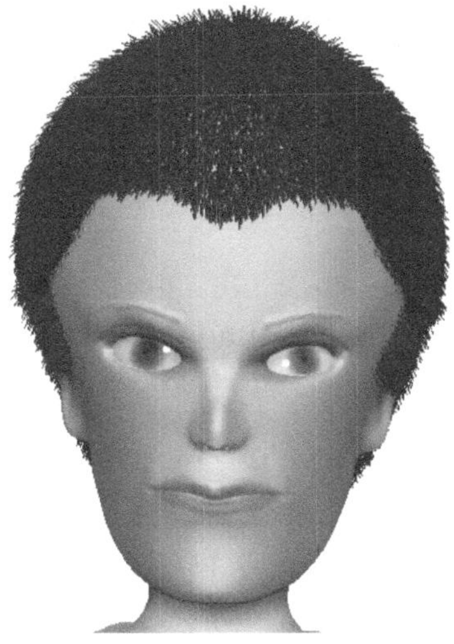

Figure P1-51 *The lips painted*

20. Press and hold the CTRL key; the **MaskPen** brush is activated. Next, with the CTRL key pressed, create a mask on the eyebrows of the character, refer to Figure P1-52.

21. Expand the **FiberMesh** subpalette in the **Tool** palette. In this subpalette, choose the **Preview** button. On choosing this button, a fibrous mesh is displayed on the masked area.

22. Expand the **Modifiers** area in the **FiberMesh** subpalette. Click on the **MaxFibers** slider to display the **MaxFibers** edit box. Next, enter the value **100** in the **MaxFibers** edit box.

23. Enter the value **15** in the **Length** edit box; the length of the fibers decreases, refer to Figure P1-53. Next, choose the **Accept** button in the **FiberMesh** subpalette; a message box is displayed prompting to activate the fast preview mode. In this message box, choose the **Yes** button.

Figure P1-52 *The mask created for the eyebrows*

Figure P1-53 *The eyebrows created using the FiberMesh*

24. After creating the hair, press and hold the CTRL key and then drag the cursor on the open area of the canvas; the mask is removed from the eyebrows.

25. In the **SubTool** subpalette, select the thumbnail for the shirt of the character. Choose the Current Stroke button from the left shelf; a flyout containing different types of strokes is displayed. Choose the **DragRect** stroke from this flyout.

26. Choose the Current Alpha button from the left shelf; a flyout containing different alpha images is displayed. Choose the **Alpha 17** alpha image from this flyout.

27. Make sure the **Zadd** button is not chosen in the top shelf. Next, drag the cursor on the surface of the shirt to create a pattern, refer to Figure P1-54.

Figure P1-54 A pattern created on the shirt

Merging Parts of the Character

In this section, you will merge all the parts of the cartoon character using the buttons in the **Merge** area of the **SubTool** subpalette.

1. Expand the **SubTool** subpalette in the **Tool** palette. Next, select the thumbnail for the body. Next, expand the **Merge** area in the **SubTool** subpalette. Now, choose the **Merge Down** button; a message box is displayed, as shown in Figure P1-55. Choose the **Always OK (skip this note until next restart)** button in the message box; the part of the character located just below the body of the character is merged into its body.

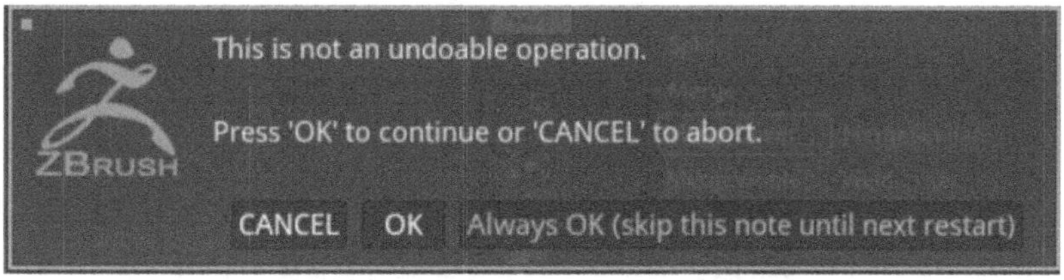

Figure P1-55 The message box displayed

2. Make sure the thumbnail for the body is selected. Next, choose the **Merge Down** button 6 times; all the parts of the character are merged into it.

3. Rotate and align the merged character, refer to Figure P1-56. Rename the merged character as **character**.

Creating Ground

In this section, you will create a ground using the **Plane 3D** primitive.

1. In the **SubTool** subpalette, choose the **Append** button; a flyout is displayed. Choose the **Plane 3D** primitive from this flyout; a plane is created in the canvas. Also, the thumbnail for the plane is displayed in the **SubTool** list. Make sure that you select the thumbnail for the plane in the list. Next, rename it to **ground**.

2. Align *ground* at the bottom of the character using the **Move**, **Scale**, and **Rotate** tools, refer to Figure P1-56. Also, scale and position the character, as shown in Figure P1-56.

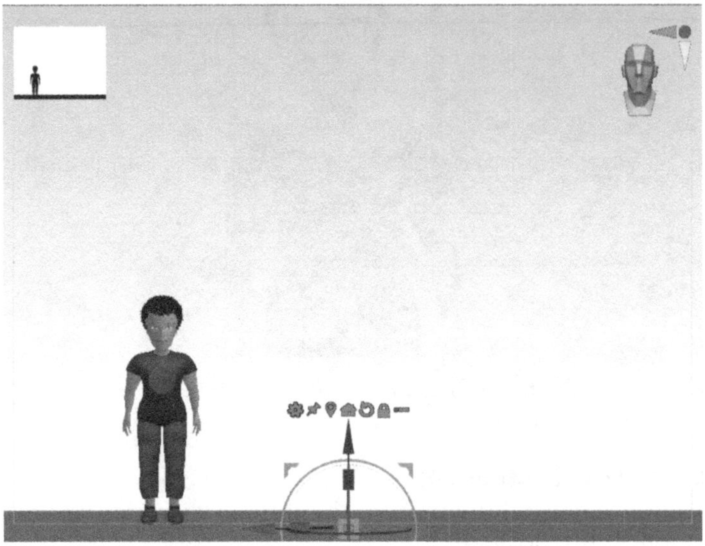

Figure P1-56 *The ground and character scaled and aligned*

3. Make sure *ground* is selected. Next, choose the Current Material button; a flyout is displayed. In this flyout, choose the **MatCap Gray** material; the **MatCap Gray** material is applied to the ground.

4. Expand the **Texture** palette. In this palette, choose the **Lightbox Texture** button, refer to Figure P1-57; different textures are displayed in the **LightBox** browser.

Figure P1-57 *The* ***Lightbox Texture*** *button chosen*

5. Hover the cursor on the **LightBox** browser and drag it toward left to view all the textures available in the browser. Choose the **IMG_4789.jpg** texture image and double-click on it; the image is displayed in the Current Texture button of the **Texture** palette.

6. In the **Tool** palette, expand the **Texture Map** subpalette. Next, choose the **Texture Map** button; a flyout containing different texture images will be displayed. In this flyout, choose

Image and make sure the **Texture On** button is chosen; you will notice that the texture is applied to the ground, as shown in Figure P1-58.

Figure P1-58 *Texture applied to the ground*

Creating a Tree Bark

In this section, you will create a tree bark at the left of the cartoon character using FiberMesh.

1. In the **SubTool** subpalette, choose the **Append** button; a flyout is displayed. Choose the **Plane 3D** primitive from this flyout; a plane is created in the canvas. The thumbnail for the plane is displayed in the **SubTool** list. Now, select the thumbnail for the plane in the list.

2. Align the plane using the **Move**, **Rotate**, and **Scale** tools, as shown in Figure P1-59.

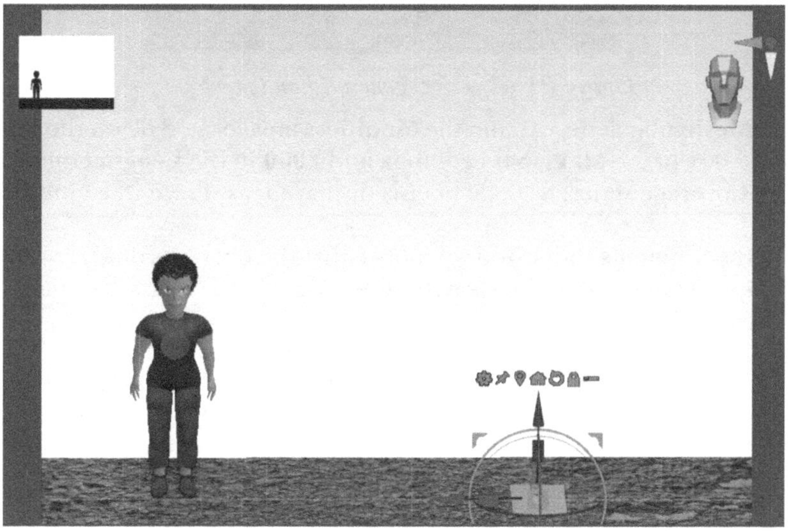

Figure P1-59 *Plane aligned*

3. Choose the **Draw** button and then choose the Current Brush button; a flyout is displayed. Next, choose the **MaskPen** brush; a message box is displayed. Choose **OK** in this message box. Next, press and hold the CTRL key and apply the strokes at the center of the plane, as shown in Figure P1-60.

Figure P1-60 *Strokes applied to the plane*

4. In the **Tools** palette, expand the **FiberMesh** subpalette. In this subpalette, choose the **Preview** button; the parameters in this subpalette are activated. Also, fibers are generated on the part of the plane where the strokes are applied, as shown in Figure P1-61.

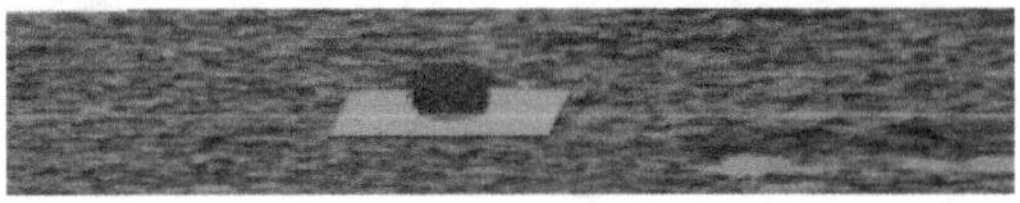

Figure P1-61 *Fibers generated on the plane*

5. In the **FiberMesh** subpalette, expand the **Modifiers** area located below the **Preview** button. Next, enter **0.001** in the **MaxFibers** edit box and **2000** in the **Length** edit box. Also, enter **5000** in the **Coverage** slider; a single fiber is displayed, as shown in Figure P1-62.

6. Enter **10** in the **Segments** slider. You will notice that the fiber tilts down toward the ground. To make it upright, enter **0** in the **Gravity** slider; the fiber is set to the upright position, as shown in Figure P1-63.

7. Enter **6** in the **Profile** slider; a message box is displayed. Choose **Skip this note until next restart** in this message box. Also, enter **-0.55** in the **Gravity** slider to make the fiber straight, refer to Figure P1-64.

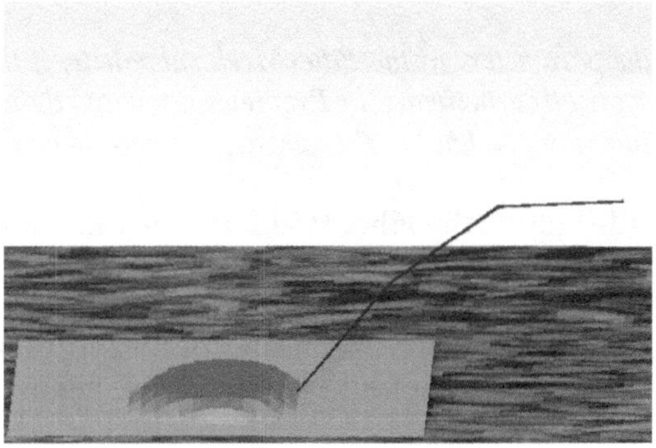

Figure P1-62 *Single fiber displayed*

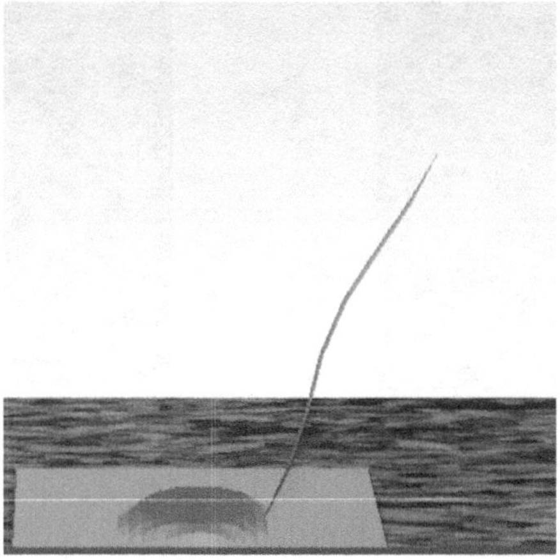

Figure P1-63 *Fiber set to upright position*

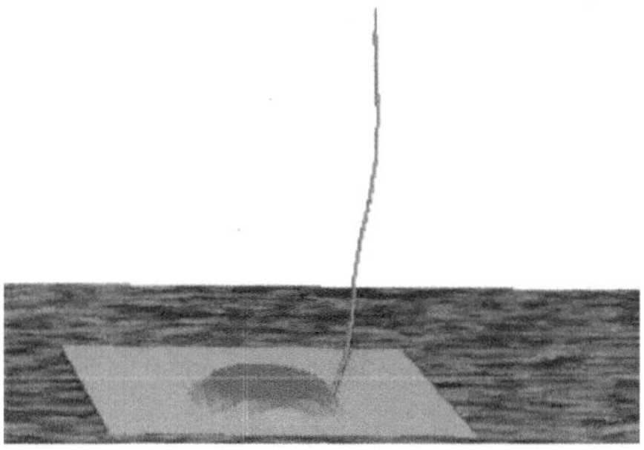

Figure P1-64 *The fiber straightened*

Note

*When you tweak the parameters in the **FiberMesh** subpalette, if the PC remains idle for some time, ZBrush automatically deactivates the **Preview** button and the current fiber becomes invisible from the canvas. To restore the fiber in the canvas, you need to activate the **Preview** button.*

8. Choose the **Width Profile** button; the **Fiber Width Profile** window is displayed with a straight width profile curve, as shown in Figure P1-65.

9. Create two more points on the curve by clicking on it and then move all the points to change the width profile curve, as shown in Figure P1-66. Figure P1-67 shows the changes in the fiber.

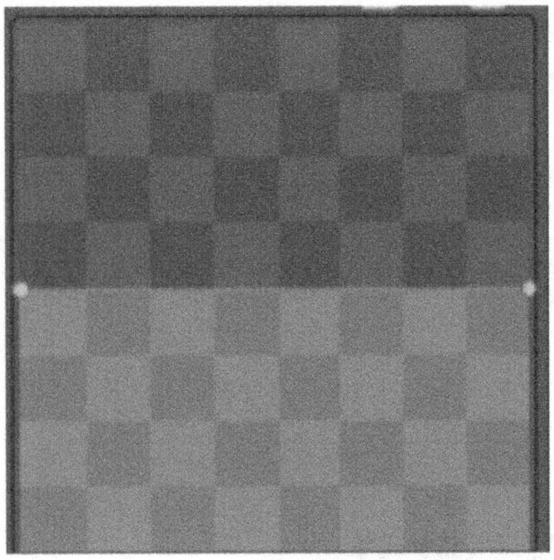

Figure P1-65 *The width profile curve displayed*

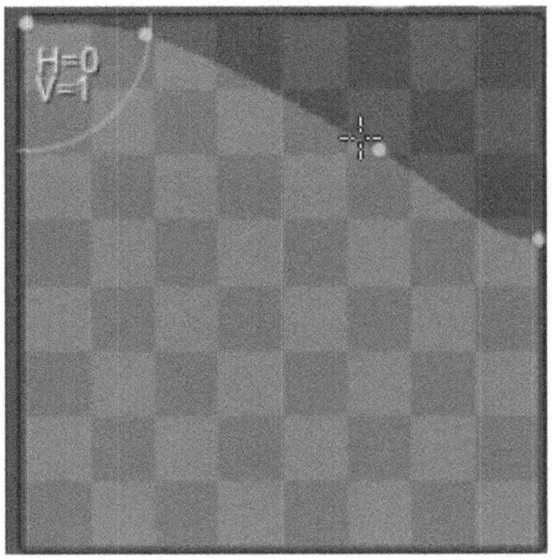

Figure P1-66 *The width profile curve changed*

Note that the change in the position of the left most point on the width profile curve changes the width at the extreme bottom part of the fiber whereas the change in the position of the right most point changes the width at the extreme top part of the fiber.

10. Click on the **Length Profile** button; the **Fiber Length Profile** window is displayed with a length profile curve. Change the length profile curve, as shown in Figure P1-68. Also, enter **-0.8** in the **Gravity** slider to make the fiber straight.

11. Enter **2** in the **Twist** slider and **1** in the **Revolve Rate** slider. Also, choose the **Revolve Radius** button; the **Fiber Revolve Radius** window is displayed with a revolve radius profile curve. Next, change this curve as per your requirement, refer to Figure P1-69. Also, enter **15** in the **Segments** spinner and then choose the **Accept** button. Figure P1-70 shows the fiber that resembles a tree bark.

The **Accept** button is used to save all the modified attributes of the fiber mesh. Also, the fiber mesh is added as a subtool in the **Subtool** subpalette. Rename it as **bark**.

Figure P1-67 *The fiber changed*

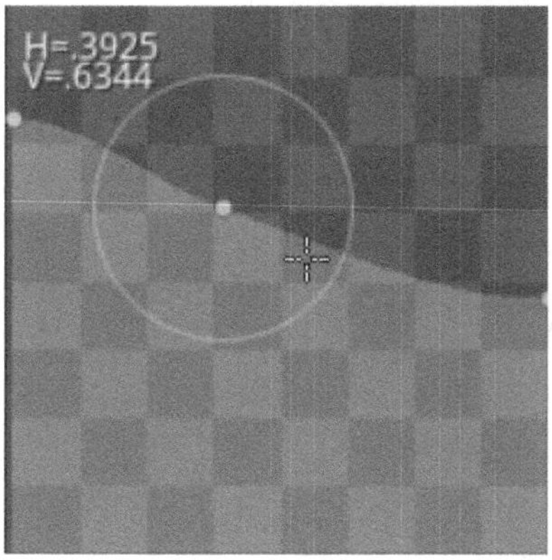

Figure P1-68 *Changed length profile curve*

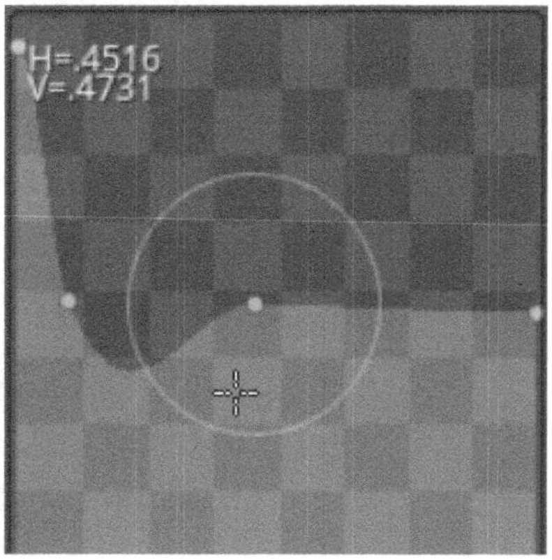

Figure P1-69 *Changed revolve radius profile curve*

Creating Branches of the Tree

1. Choose the **Draw** button and then choose the Current Brush button; a flyout is displayed. Next, choose the **MaskLasso** brush from this flyout; a message box is displayed. Choose **OK** in this message box. Now, press CTRL and apply the mask on the top half part of the fiber, as shown in Figure P1-71.

2. Choose the **Preview** button; you will notice that one branch is created on the masked part of the fiber. In the **Modifiers** area, enter **1000** in the **Length** slider; length of the branch is reduced. Next, enter **11** in the **Segments** slider.

Figure P1-70 *Fiber resembling a tree bark*

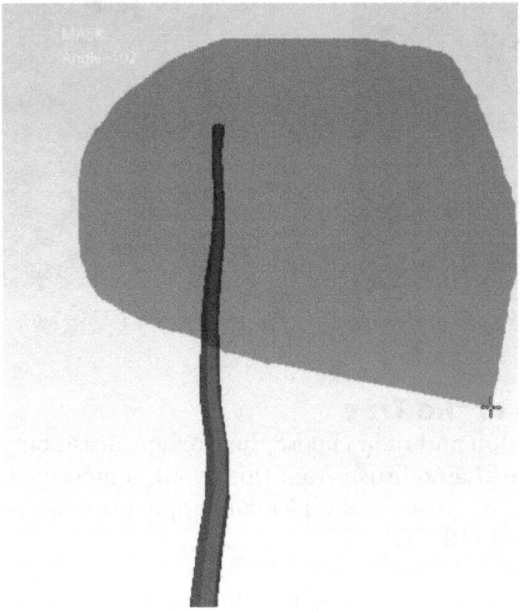

Figure P1-71 *Mask applied on the fiber*

3. To increase the number of branches, enter **0.03** in the **Maxfibers** slider. Next, enter **1250** in the **Length** slider to further increase the length of the branches. Now, tweak the **Revolve Radius** curve and finalize the curve shape of branches as per your requirement.

Note
*You can also tweak other parameters in the **Modifiers** area to change the shape of the branches.*

4. Enter **-0.6** in the **Gravity** slider. Next, choose the **Accept** button; branches are displayed, refer to Figure P1-72. Also, the fiber mesh is added as a subtool in the **Subtool** subpalette. Rename it as **branches**.

Figure P1-72 *Branches displayed*

5. To add the sub branches to these branches, repeat the procedure discussed above and create sub branches, as shown in Figure P1-73. Rename the created subtool as **subbranches**.

Creating Leaves of the Tree

1. Select sub branches from the **SubTool** subpalette. Next, choose the **Preview** button.

2. In the **Modifiers** area, enter **0** in both the **Gravity** slider and the **Revolve Rate** slider. Next, make sure **2500** is displayed in the **Coverage** slider.

3. Enter **1** in the **Profile** slider and **2** in the **Segments** slider. Also, enter **1** in the **ScaleRoot** and **ScaleTip** sliders.

4. Enter **150** in the **Length** slider. Next, choose the **Width Profile** button and then choose the **Reset** button located below the **Width Profile** window. Now, change the width profile curve, as shown in Figure P1-74.

5. Enter **1.5** in the **MaxFibers** slider; the number of planes are increased. Also, enter **-0.5** in the **Gravity** slider.

Figure P1-73 Sub branches displayed

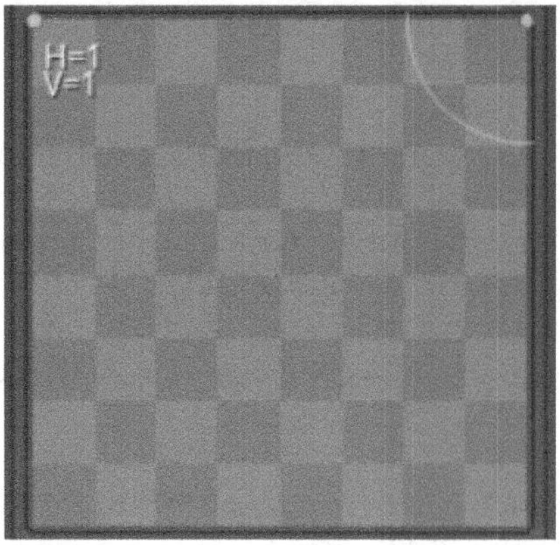

Figure P1-74 Width profile curve changed

Next, you need to apply a leaf texture to these planes.

6. Click on the **Fiber Texture** window located below the **Tip** button; a window is displayed. Choose the **Import** button from this window; the **Import Image** dialog box is displayed.

7. Navigate to *\Documents\ZBrushprojects\p01* and select the *Leaf texture.jpg* file and choose **Open** in this dialog box; a message box is displayed. Choose the **No** button in it. You will notice that the leaf texture is applied to the planes.

   Next, you will increase the transparency to remove black color from the texture.

8. Choose the **Antialised** button located at the right side of the **Fiber Texture** window and then enter **21** in the **Transparency** slider; the tree is displayed with leaves, as shown in Figure P1-75. Now, choose the **Accept** button.

Figure P1-75 *Tree displayed along with leaves*

9. Select **Plane3D_Plane3D1_1** from the **SubTool** subpalette. Next, choose the **Delete** button; a message box is displayed. Choose the **OK** button in it; the plane is deleted from the scene.

10. Select **bark** from the Subtool list. Next, expand the **Merge** area and choose the **Merge Down** button; bark and branches are merged together as the **bark** subtool.

11. Select **bark** from the Subtool list again. Next, choose the **Merge Down** button; **bark** and **subbranches** are merged together as the **bark** subtool.

12. Rename **bark** as **tree**.

    Next, you will apply material to **tree**.

13. Select **tree** from the **SubTool** subpalette. Next, choose the Current Material button; a flyout is displayed. Choose **MatCap Sculpy** from this flyout; the **MatCap Sculpy** material is applied to **tree**, as shown in Figure P1-76.

14. Select **character** from the **SubTool** subpalette. Next, scale and align it, refer to Figure P1-77.

15. Render the scene by pressing SHIFT+R, refer to Figure P1-1.

Figure P1-76 *Material applied to the tree bark and branches*

Figure P1-77 *Character scaled and aligned*

Project 2

Cartoon Character Model with a Background Scene - II

PROJECT DESCRIPTION

This project guides you through the process of creating a sculpture. Later, you will merge this sculpture with the scene created in Project 1. You will also add a background image to the scene, as shown in Figure P2-1.

Figure P2-1 *The model of a cartoon character with a background scene*

Before you start the project, you need to download the *p02_ZBrush_2022_tut.zip* file from *www.cadcim.com*. The path of the file is as follows: *Textbooks > Animation and Visual Effects > Pixologic ZBrush 2022 > Pixologic ZBrush 2022: A Comprehensive Guide*

Navigate to *\Documents\ZBrushprojects* and then create a new folder with the name *p02*. Next, extract the contents of the zip file in this folder.

Creating Body of the Sculpture

In this section, you will create body of the sculpture using the subtraction boolean process.

1. Choose the **Init ZBrush** button from the **Preferences** palette; ZBrush is initialized to its default state.

2. Choose the Current Tool button from the **Tool** palette; a flyout is displayed. In this flyout, choose the **Sphere3D** primitive and create it on the canvas. Next, choose the **Edit** button from the top shelf.

3. Choose the **Make PolyMesh3D** button from the **Tool** palette; the Sphere3D object is converted into a polymesh.

4. Expand the **Geometry** subpalette of the **Tool** palette. Next, expand the **Dynamesh** area and choose the **Dynamesh** button.

5. In the **Geometry** subpalette, set the value of the **SDiv** slider to **4** by clicking on the **Divide** button thrice.

6. Choose the **Scale** button from the top shelf. Next, scale the Sphere3D object 1.5 times along the Y axis; the Sphere3D object is modified, as shown in Figure P2-2.

7. In the **Subtool** subpalette, make sure the **PM3D_Sphere3D_1** is selected. Next, choose the **Duplicate** button; duplicate of **PM3D_Sphere3D_1** is created and the **PM3D_Sphere3D_2** subtool is added.

8. In the **Subtool** subpalette, select **PM3D_Sphere3D_2**. Next, scale it down uniformly till the scale value reaches **0.9**, refer to Figure P2-3.

9. Move **PM3D_Sphere3D_2** along the Z axis about 0.35 points, refer to Figure P2-4.

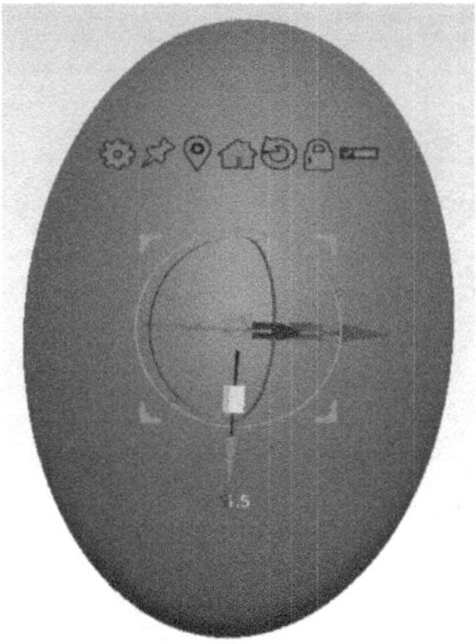

Figure P2-2 *The modified Sphere3D object*

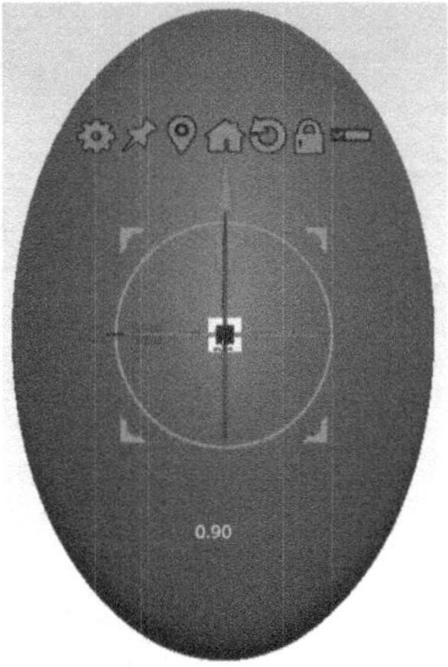

Figure P2-3 *The* ***PM3D_Sphere3D_2*** *subtool scaled down*

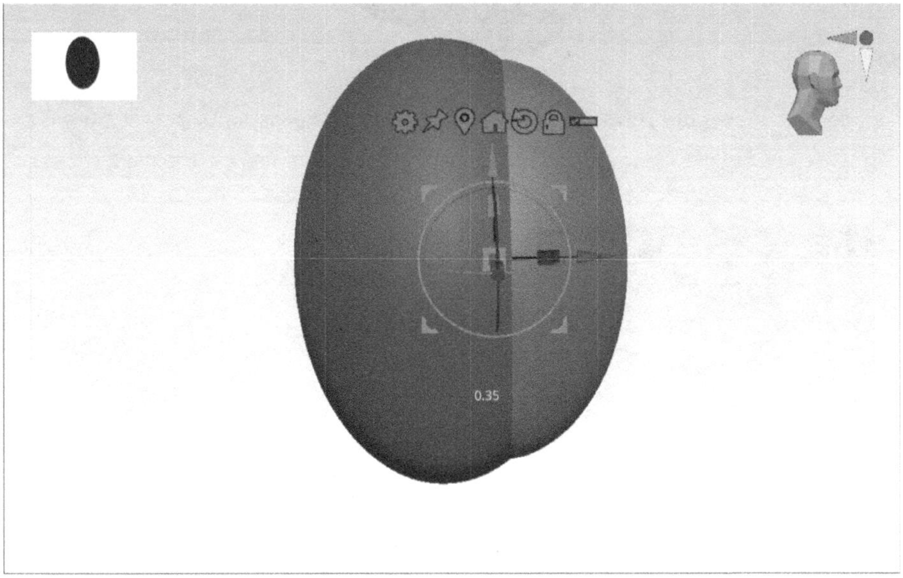

Figure P2-4 *The* ***PM3D_Sphere3D_2*** *subtool moved*

10. Select **PM3D_Sphere3D_1** and scale it down along Z axis till the scale value reaches 0.7, as shown in Figure P2-5.

    Next, you will use the subtraction boolean operation on these spheres.

11. Choose the **Live Boolean** button from the top shelf. Next, make sure **PM3D_Sphere3D_1** is selected. In the **Subtool** subpalette, choose the arrow button that is located next to **PM3D_Sphere3D_1**, refer to Figure P2-6; the arrow button size is modified, as shown in Figure P2-7.

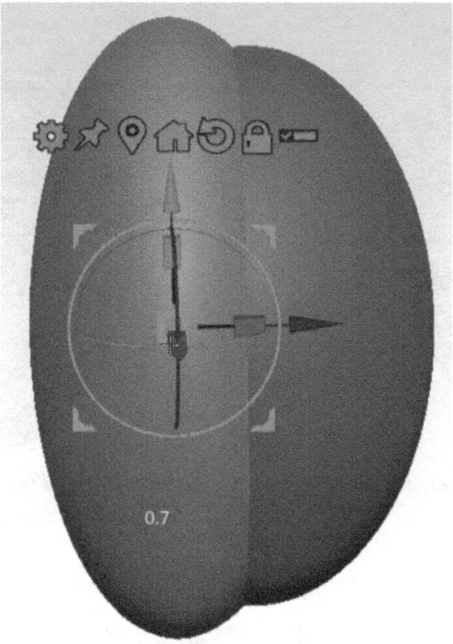

Figure P2-5 *The **PM3D_Sphere3D_1** subtool scaled down*

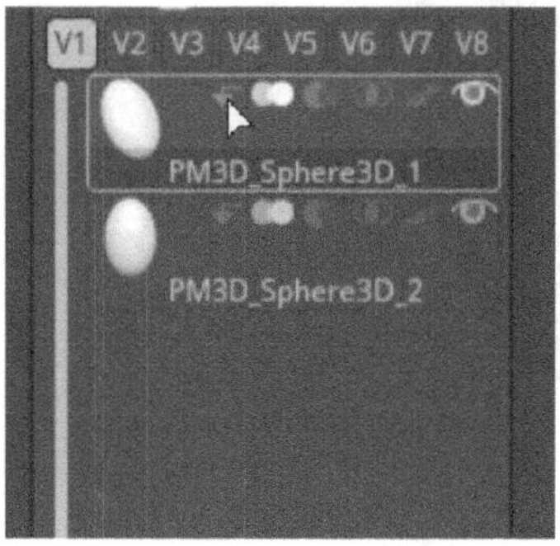

Figure P2-6 *Choosing the arrow button*

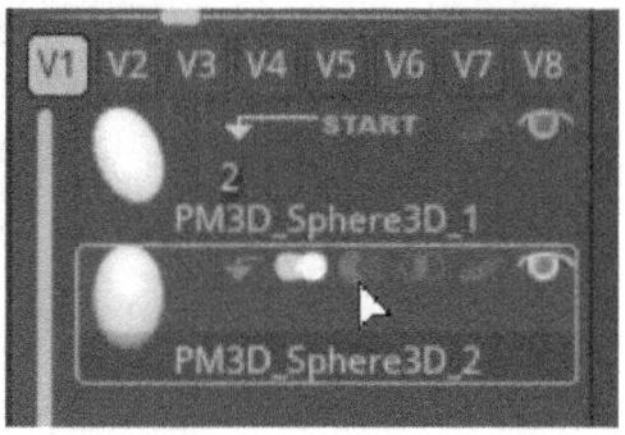

Figure P2-7 *Choosing the subtraction boolean operator button*

12. Select **PM3D_Sphere3D_2** and then select the subtraction boolean operator button from the **Subtool** subpalette. Next, click on the eye icon of **PM3D_Sphere3D_1** to make it visible. Also, rotate it; the **PM3D_Sphere3D_2** is subtracted from **PM3D_Sphere3D_1**, as shown in Figure P2-8.

13. Choose the **Boolean** button from the **Subtool** subpalette; the **Boolean** area is displayed, as shown in Figure P2-9. Next, choose the **Make Boolean Mesh** button from the **Boolean** area; the **UMesh_PM3D_Sphere3D_1** tool is added to the **Tool** palette, as shown in Figure P2-9.

Figure P2-8 PM3D_Sphere3D_2 *subtracted from* ***PM3D_Sphere3D_1***

14. In the **Tool** palette, click on **UMesh_PM3D_Sphere3D_1**; the **UMesh_PM3D_Sphere3D_1** subtool is added and existing subtools are removed from the subtool list; refer to Figure P2-10.

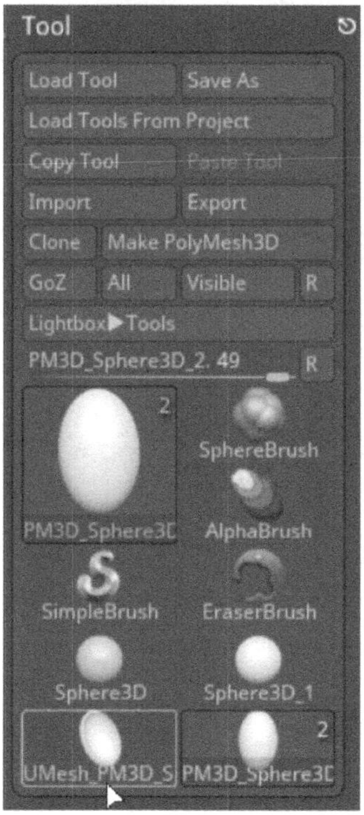

Figure P2-9 *The* ***UMesh_PM3D_Sphere3D_1*** *tool added to the* ***Tool*** *palette*

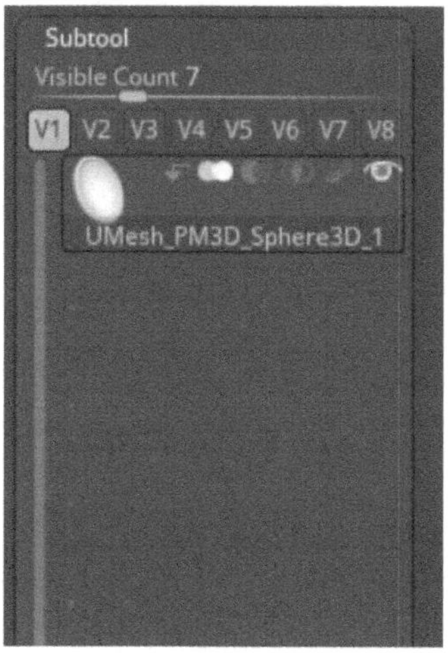

Figure P2-10 *The* ***UMesh_PM3D_Sphere3D_1*** *subtool added*

15. Rename **UMesh_PM3D_Sphere3D_1** with the name *body* using the **Rename** button in the **Subtool** subpalette.

Appending Body with DemoGreyHound

In this section, first you will save the body of the sculpture as a tool and then you will append it to **DemoGreyHound**.

1. Choose **Save As** from the **Tool** palette; the **Save ZTool** dialog box is displayed. In this dialog box, navigate to *\Documents\ZBrushprojects\p02.* Make sure **body** is displayed in the **File name** dialog box and then choose **Save**; the **body** tool is saved at the specified location.

2. Choose the **Init ZBrush** button from the **Preferences** palette; ZBrush is initialized to its default state.

3. Choose the **LightBox** button from the top shelf; the **LightBox** browser is displayed. Double-click on the **DemoProjects** folder from the **Project** tab and then choose the **DemoGreyHound.ZPR** file by double-clicking on it; **DemoGreyHound** is displayed on the canvas along with the message shown in Figure P2-11. Click anywhere on the canvas; the message box disappears.

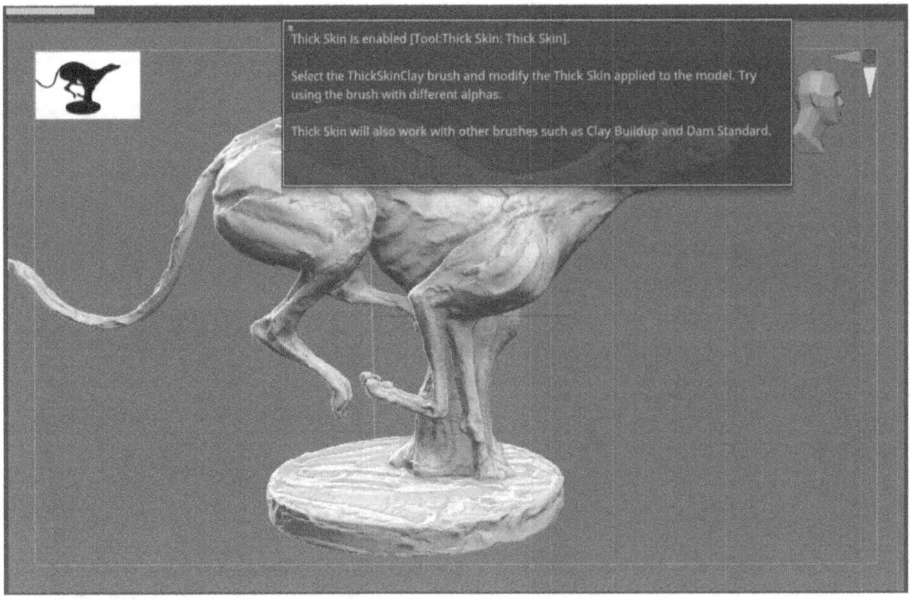

Figure P2-11 *The* ***DemoGreyHound*** *subtool displayed*

4. Expand the **ZPlugin** palette and then the **SubTool Master** subpalette. Next, choose the **MultiAppend** button from the **SubTool Master** subpalette, as shown in Figure P2-12; the **Please select 3D Files to Append** dialog box is displayed.

Figure P2-12 Choosing the ***MultiAppend*** *button from the* ***SubTool Master*** *subpalette*

5. In the **Please select 3D Files to Append** dialog box, navigate to *\Documents\ZBrushprojects\p02* and select *body.ztl,* refer to Figure P2-13. Next, choose the **Open** button; the **body** subtool is displayed in the canvas and added to the subtool list in the **Subtool** subpalette, refer to Figure P2-14.

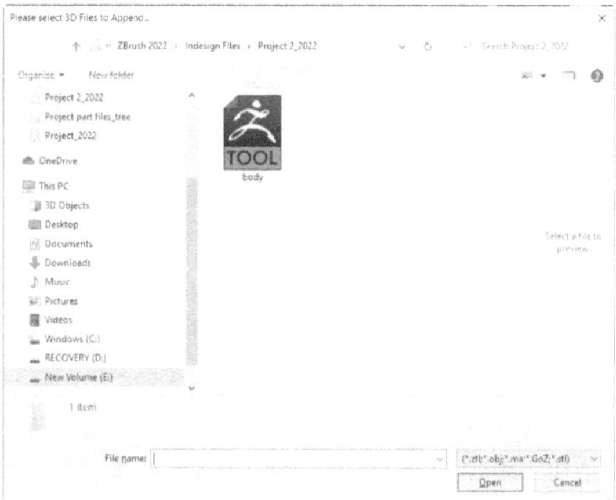

Figure P2-13 The ***Please Select 3D Files to Append*** *dialog box*

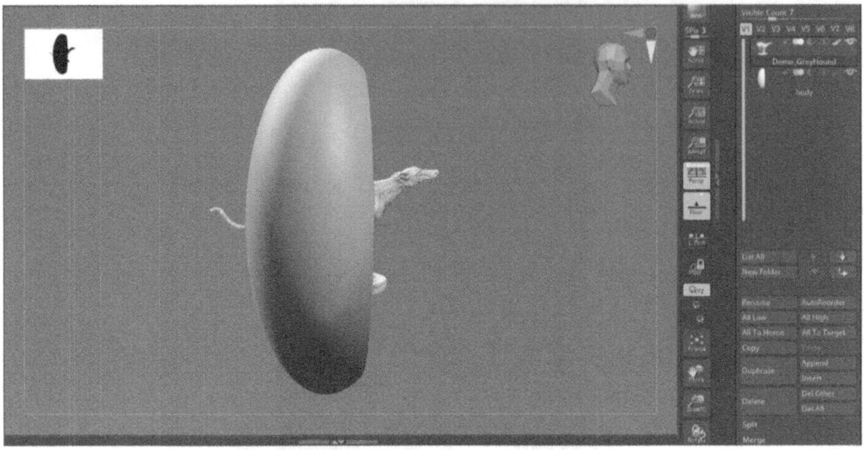

*Figure P2-14 The **body** subtool added*

Projecting DemoGreyHound on the Sculpture

In this section, you will project **DemoGreyHound** on **body** using the Project BasRelief feature.

1. Align **DemoGreyHound** with **body** using the **Move**, **Rotate**, and **Scale** tools, as shown in Figure P2-15.

*Figure P2-15 The **DemoGreyHound** subtool aligned*

2. Expand the **ProjectBasRelief** area and choose the **Project BasRelief** button from the **Subtool** subpalette. Next, choose the **Project BasRelief** button from this area; **DemoGreyHound** is projected on **body**, refer to Figure P2-16.

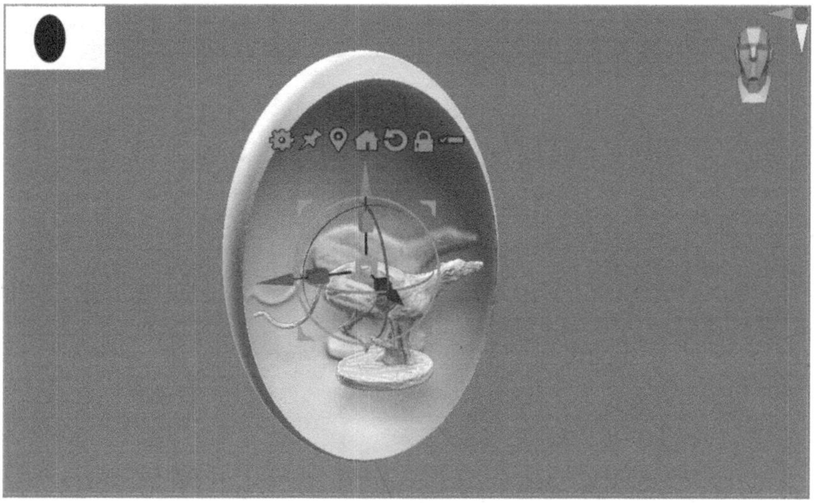

Figure P2-16 *Projected* ***DemoGreyHound***

3. Select **DemoGreyHound** from the subtool list and choose the **Delete** button from the **Subtool** subpalette; a message box is displayed that warns you about the undoable operation. Choose the **OK** button in this message box; the **DemoGreyHound** subtool is deleted.

Creating Base of the Sculpture

In this section, you will create base of the sculpture using the **Cylinder3D** tool.

1. Choose the **Append** button from the **Subtool** subpalette; a flyout is displayed. Choose the **Cylinder3D** primitive from this flyout; a cylinder is created in the canvas. Also, the thumbnail for the cylinder is displayed in the subtool list. Make sure that you select the thumbnail for the cylinder in the list. Next, rename it to **base1**.

2. Expand the **Geometry** subpalette and choose **Divide** three times to smoothen **base1**. Using the **Scale** and the **Move** tool, scale and align **base1**, as shown in Figure P2-17.

3. Similarly, append one more **Cylinder3D** primitive and rename it as **base2**. Next, smoothen it using the **Divide** button in the **Geometry** subpalette. Also, scale and align **base2**, as shown in Figure P2-18.

Figure P2-17 ***base1*** *scaled and aligned*

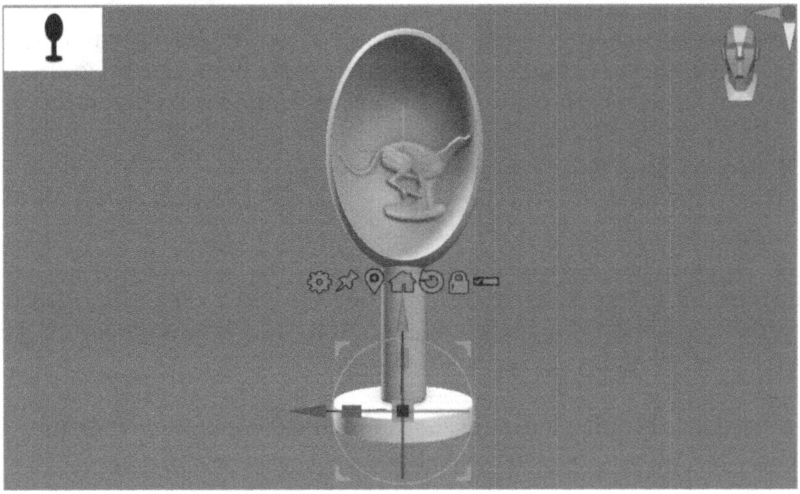

Figure P2-18 ***base2*** *scaled and aligned*

Merging Subtools of the Sculpture

In this section, you will merge all the three subtools of the sculpture to create a single subtool.

1. Select **body** from the subtool list in the **Subtool** subpalette. Next, expand the **Merge** area in the **Subtool** subpalette and then choose the **Merge** button.

2. Choose the **Merge Down** button from the **Merge** area; a message box is displayed. Next, choose the **OK** button from it; **body** and **base1** are merged as the **body** subtool.

3. Choose the **Merge Down** button again; a message box is displayed. Next, choose the **OK** button from it; **body** and **base2** are merged as the **body** subtool.

4. Choose the **Rename** button from the **Subtool** subpalette; the **Please enter subtool title** text box is displayed. Enter **sculpture** in this edit box; the **body** subtool is renamed as **sculpture**.

Applying Texture to the Sculpture

In this section, you will apply texture to sculpture using the **Texture Map** subpalette.

1. Expand the **Texture Map** subpalette in the **Tool** palette. Next, choose the **Texture Map** button from this subpalette, refer to Figure P2-19; a flyout containing different texture images will be displayed. In this flyout, choose the **Import** button; the **Import Image** dialog box is displayed.

2. In this dialog box, navigate to *\Documents\ZBrushprojects\p02* and select the *sculpture texture.jpg* file and choose **Open**; a message box is displayed informing about UV mapping required for texture mapping. Choose the **OK** button in this message box; the thumbnail of the image is displayed on the **Texture Map** button, as shown in Figure P2-20.

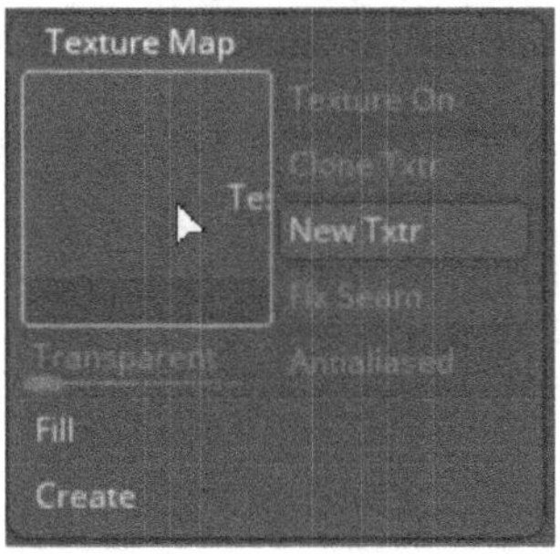

Figure P2-19 *Choosing the **Texture Map** button*

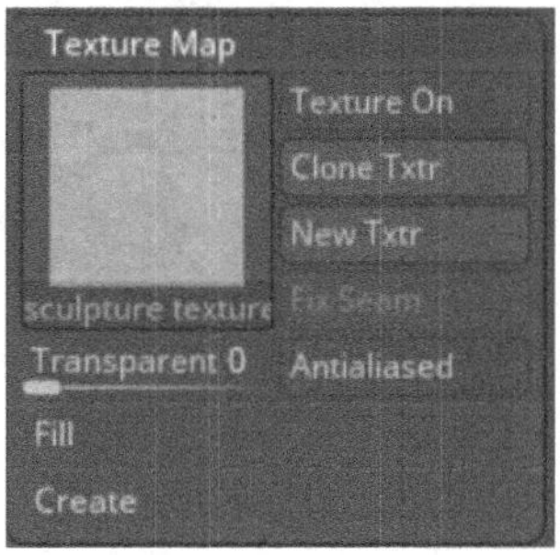

Figure P2-20 *Thumbnail of the image displayed*

3. Expand the **ZPlugin** palette. Next, expand the **UV Master** subpalette and then choose the **Unwrap** button from this subpalette; unwrapping process starts that will take some time. Notice the text message above the top shelf, refer to Figure P2-21. Once the unwrapping is completed, the texture is applied on sculpture and message written above the top shelf is updated that the current subtool is unwrapped, as shown in Figure P2-22.

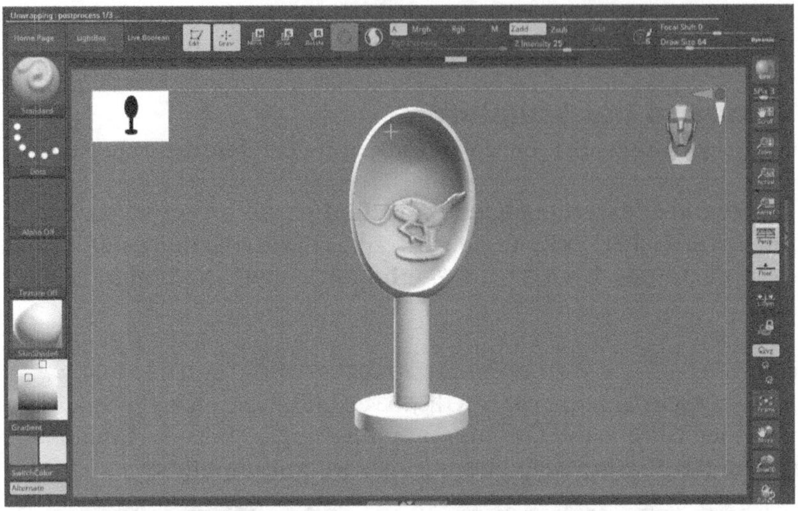

Figure P2-21 Unwrapping process going on

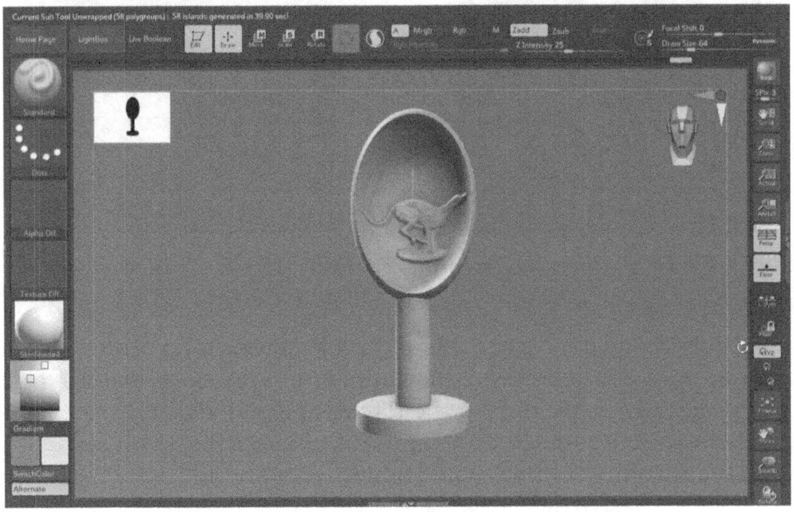

Figure P2-22 Texture displayed on sculpture

Merging Sculpture with the Scene

In this section, you will first save sculpture as a tool and then merge it with the final file created in Project 1.

1. Choose **Save As** from the **Tool** Palette; the **Save ZTool** dialog box is displayed. In this dialog box, navigate to *Documents\ZBrushprojects\p02* and enter **sculpture** in the **File name** edit box and choose **Save**; the **sculpture** tool is saved at the specified location.

2. Choose the **Init ZBrush** button from the **Preferences** palette; ZBrush is initialized to its default state.

3. Expand the **File** palette. Next, choose **Open** from this palette; the **Load Project** dialog box is displayed.

4. In the **Load Project** dialog box, navigate to *Documents\ZBrushprojects\p02* and select the **scene.ZPR** file and then choose the **Open** button; the scene with a character standing near a tree is displayed in the canvas, refer to Figure P2-23.

Figure P2-23 *The scene displayed*

5. Expand the **Zplugin** palette. Next, expand the **SubTool Master** subpalette and then choose the **MultiAppend** button from this subpalette; the **Please select 3D Files to Append** dialog box is displayed.

6. In the **Please select 3D Files to Append** dialog box, navigate to *Documents\ZBrushprojects\p02,* select the **sculpture.ztl** file, and then choose the **Open** button; the **sculpture** subtool is displayed once in the scene but then it becomes invisible.

7. Click on the eye icon of the **sculpture** subtool to make sure it is visible, refer to Figure P2-24.

8. Select the **sculpture** subtool. Next, activate the **Scale** tool from the top shelf and then scale and align it in the scene, as shown in Figure P2-25.

Adding Background to the Scene

In this section, you will add an image that will act as a background for the scene.

1. Expand the **Light** palette. Next, expand the **Background** subpalette and then choose the **Texture** button from this subpalette; a flyout is displayed. In this flyout, choose the **Import** button; the **Import Image** dialog box is displayed.

*Figure P2-24 The **sculpture** subtool displayed*

*Figure P2-25 The **sculpture** subtool scaled and aligned*

2. In the **Import Image** dialog box, navigate to *Documents\ZBrushprojects\p02*, select the **bg_image.jpg** file, and then choose the **Open** button; the background image is added to the scene, as shown in Figure P2-26.

   You can change values of other parameters such as **Longitude**, **Latitude**, **Tilt**, and so on in the **Background** subpalette to adjust the background image in the scene.

Figure P2-26 *The background image added*

This page is intentionally left blank

Index

D

E

F

G

T

U

V

W

X

Z

Other Publications by CADCIM Technologies

The following is the list of some of the publications by CADCIM Technologies. Please visit *www.cadcim.com* for the complete listing.

ZBrush Textbooks

- Pixologic ZBrush 2021: A Comprehensive Guide, 7th Edition
- Pixologic ZBrush 2020: A Comprehensive Guide, 6th Edition
- Pixologic ZBrush 2018: A Comprehensive Guide, 5th Edition
- Pixologic ZBrush 4R8: A Comprehensive Guide, 4th Edition
- Pixologic ZBrush 4R7: A Comprehensive Guide, 3rd Edition

Autodesk Maya Textbooks

- Autodesk Maya 2022: A Comprehensive Guide, 13th Edition
- Autodesk Maya 2020: A Comprehensive Guide, 12th Edition
- Autodesk Maya 2019: A Comprehensive Guide, 11th Edition
- Autodesk Maya 2018: A Comprehensive Guide, 10th Edition
- Autodesk Maya 2017: A Comprehensive Guide, 9th Edition
- Autodesk Maya 2016: A Comprehensive Guide, 8th Edition
- Autodesk Maya 2015: A Comprehensive Guide, 7th Edition

Autodesk 3ds Max Textbooks

- Autodesk 3ds Max 2022 for Beginners: A Tutorial Approach, 22nd Edition
- Autodesk 3ds Max 2021 for Beginners: A Tutorial Approach, 21st Edition
- Autodesk 3ds Max 2020 for Beginners: A Tutorial Approach, 20th Edition
- Autodesk 3ds Max 2019 for Beginners: A Tutorial Approach, 19th Edition
- Autodesk 3ds Max 2018 for Beginners: A Tutorial Approach, 18th Edition
- Autodesk 3ds Max 2017 for Beginners: A Tutorial Approach, 17th Edition
- Autodesk 3ds Max 2016 for Beginners: A Tutorial Approach, 16th Edition
- Autodesk 3ds Max 2022: A Comprehensive Guide, 22nd Edition
- Autodesk 3ds Max 2021: A Comprehensive Guide, 21st Edition
- Autodesk 3ds Max 2020: A Comprehensive Guide, 20th Edition
- Autodesk 3ds Max 2019: A Comprehensive Guide, 19th Edition
- Autodesk 3ds Max 2018: A Comprehensive Guide, 18th Edition
- Autodesk 3ds Max 2017: A Comprehensive Guide, 17th Edition
- Autodesk 3ds Max 2016: A Comprehensive Guide, 16th Edition

Autodesk 3ds Max Design Textbooks

- Autodesk 3ds Max Design 2015: A Tutorial Approach, 15th Edition
- Autodesk 3ds Max Design 2014: A Tutorial Approach
- Autodesk 3ds Max Design 2013: A Tutorial Approach
- Autodesk 3ds Max Design 2012: A Tutorial Approach

CINEMA 4D Textbooks
- MAXON CINEMA 4D S24: A Tutorial Approach, 8th Edition
- MAXON CINEMA 4D Studio R20: A Tutorial Approach, 7th Edition
- MAXON CINEMA 4D Studio R19: A Tutorial Approach, 6th Edition
- MAXON CINEMA 4D Studio R18: A Tutorial Approach, 5th Edition
- MAXON CINEMA 4D Studio R17: A Tutorial Approach, 4th Edition
- MAXON CINEMA 4D Studio R16: A Tutorial Approach, 3rd Edition

Blender Textbook
- Blender 2.79 for Digital Artists

Digital Modeling Textbook
- Exploring Digital Modeling Using 3ds Max and Maya 2015

Fusion Textbooks
- Blackmagic Design Fusion 7 Studio: A Tutorial Approach, 3rd Edition
- The eyeon Fusion 6.3: A Tutorial Approach

Flash Textbooks
- Adobe Flash Professional CC 2015: A Tutorial Approach, 3rd Edition
- Adobe Flash Professional CC: A Tutorial Approach
- Adobe Flash Professional CS6: A Tutorial Approach

Premiere Textbooks
- Adobe Premiere Pro CC: A Tutorial Approach
- Adobe Premiere Pro CS6: A Tutorial Approach
- Adobe Premiere Pro CS5.5: A Tutorial Approach

Nuke Textbook
- The Foundry NukeX 7 for Compositors

Computer Programming Textbooks
- Introducing PHP7/MySQL
- Introduction to C++ Programming, 2nd Edition
- Learning Oracle 12c - A PL/SQL Approach
- Learning ASP.NET AJAX
- Introduction to Java Programming, 2nd Edition
- Learning Visual Basic.NET 2008

AutoCAD Electrical Textbooks
- AutoCAD Electrical 2022 for Engineers and Designers
- AutoCAD Electrical 2021 for Engineers and Designers
- AutoCAD Electrical 2019 for Engineers and Designers
- AutoCAD Electrical 2018 for Electrical Control Designers, 9th Edition

AutoCAD Textbooks

- AutoCAD 2022 for Engineers and Designers - Basic and Intermediate
- AutoCAD 2021 for Engineers and Designers - Basic and Intermediate
- AutoCAD 2021(3D and Advanced) for Engineers and Designers
- AutoCAD 2020 for Engineers and Designers - Basic and Intermediate
- AutoCAD 2019: A Problem-Solving Approach, Basic and Intermediate, 25th Edition
- AutoCAD 2020 Workbook

Autodesk Inventor Textbooks

- Autodesk Inventor Professional 2022 for Engineers and Designers
- Autodesk Inventor Professional 2020 for Engineers and Designers
- Autodesk Inventor Professional 2019 for Designers, 19th Edition
- Inventor 2020 Workbook

Autodesk Fusion 360

Autodesk Fusion 360: A Tutorial Approach
Autodesk Fusion 360: A Learner's Guide, 2nd Edition

AutoCAD MEP Textbooks

- AutoCAD MEP 2020 for Engineers and Designers
- AutoCAD MEP 2018 for Designers, 4th Edition

AutoCAD Plant 3D Textbook

- AutoCAD Plant 3D 2018 for Designers, 4th Edition

Solid Edge Textbooks

- Solid Edge 2021 for Engineers and Designers
- Solid Edge 2019 for Engineers and Designers
- Solid Edge ST 10 for Designers, 15th Edition

SOLIDWORKS Textbooks

- SOLIDWORKS 2021 for Engineers and Designers
- SOLIDWORKS 2020 for Engineers and Designers
- SOLIDWORKS 2019 for Engineers and Designers
- SOLIDWORKS 2018 for Designers, 16th Edition

SOLIDWORKS Simulation Textbooks

- SOLIDWORKS Simulation 2018: A Tutorial Approach
- SOLIDWORKS Simulation 2016: A Tutorial Approach

Creo Parametric Textbooks

- Creo Parametric 6.0 for Engineers and Designers
- Creo Parametric 5.0 for Designers, 5th Edition
- Creo Parametric 6.0 Workbook

CATIA Textbooks
- CATIA V5-6R2019 for Engineers and Designers
- CATIA V5-6R2018 for Engineers and Designers

Autodesk Revit Architecture Textbooks
- Exploring Autodesk Revit 2021 for Architects and Building Designers
- Exploring Autodesk Revit 2020 for Architects and Building Designers
- Exploring Autodesk Revit 2019 for Architecture, 15th Edition

AutoCAD Map 3D Textbooks
- Exploring AutoCAD Map 3D 2018, 8th Edition
- Exploring AutoCAD Map 3D 2017, 7th Edition

Autodesk Navisworks Textbooks
- Exploring Autodesk Navisworks 2019 for BIM
- Exploring Autodesk Navisworks 2017, 4th Edition

Oracle Primavera Textbooks
- Exploring Oracle Primavera P6 Professional 18 for Planners and Engineers
- Exploring Oracle Primavera P6 R8.4

AutoCAD Raster Design Textbook
- Exploring AutoCAD Raster Design 2017

AutoCAD Civil 3D Textbooks
- Exploring AutoCAD Civil 3D 2020 for Engineers and Designers
- Exploring AutoCAD Civil 3D 2019 for Engineers and Designers
- Exploring AutoCAD Civil 3D 2018, 8th Edition

Coming Soon from CADCIM Technologies
- Flow Simulation using SOLIDWORKS 2021
- Finite Element Analysis Using ANSYS Workbench 2021

Online Training Program Offered by CADCIM Technologies
CADCIM Technologies provides effective and affordable online training programon various software packages including computer programming languages, Computer Aided Design, Manufacturing and Engineering (CAD/CAM/CAE), animation, architecture, and GIS. The training will be delivered 'live' via Internet at any time, any place, and at any pace to individuals as well as the students of colleges, universities, and CAD/CAM/CAE training centers. For more information, please visit the following link: ***www.cadcim.com***

Made in United States
Cleveland, OH
10 June 2025

17626846R00359